BRITISH CRUISERS
OF THE
Victorian
Era

BRITISH CRUISERS
OF THE
Victorian Era

NORMAN FRIEDMAN

Ship plans by A D Baker III,
with additional drawings by Paul Webb

To absent friends:
Antony Preston, David Lyon, and David Topliss

Frontispiece: HMS *Boadicea* as refitted and rearmed in 1888. A closed embrasure for an aft-firing gun is visible above her false sailing-ship style quarter lights. The charthouse is barely visible just forward of the foot of the mizzen mast.

(National Maritime Museum G10330)

Copyright © Norman Friedman 2012
Plans © A D Baker III 2012
(except those on pages 172 and 261 © Paul Webb 2012)

First published in Great Britain in 2012 by
Seaforth Publishing
An imprint of Pen & Sword Books Ltd
47 Church Street, Barnsley
S Yorkshire S70 2AS

www.seaforthpublishing.com
Email info@seaforthpublishing.com

British Library Cataloguing in Publication Data
A CIP data record for this book is available from the British Library

ISBN 978 1 84832 099 4

All rights reserved. No part of this publication may be reproduced or transmitted in any form or by any means, electronic or mechanical, including photocopying, recording, or any information storage and retrieval system, without prior permission in writing of both the copyright owner and the above publisher.

The right of Norman Friedman to be identified as the author of this work has been asserted in accordance with the Copyright, Designs and Patents Act 1988

Typeset and designed by Roger Daniels
Printed and bound in China by 1010 Printing International Ltd

Contents

Acknowledgements   6
Illustrator's Notes   6

INTRODUCTION   8
1. STEAM, SAIL AND WOODEN HULLS   52
2. IRON HULLS   80
3. THE FIRST ARMOURED CRUISERS   100
4. FAST STEEL CRUISERS   116
5. THE TORPEDO AND SMALL CRUISERS   174
6. BIG CRUISERS TO PROTECT COMMERCE   218
7. THE FAST WING OF THE BATTLE FLEET   238
   Appendix: Vickers Designs   268
8. EPILOGUE: FISHER'S REVOLUTION   274

Bibliography   292
Notes   294
Data List (specifications)   330
List of Ships   337
Abbreviations   347
Index   348

Acknowledgements

My wife Rhea made this book possible. She helped me think through some of the key issues concerning dramatic changes in British exposure to trade warfare, which are vital to its thesis. As the scope of this book expanded to embrace the whole Victorian era (and a few years afterwards), I had to go back to various archives again and again, and Rhea encouraged me to do so. I could not have written this book without Rhea's loving support and encouragement.

Any project like this book benefits enormously from the help friends can provide. This one particularly benefited as its time scope grew from the late Victorian era (beginning with HMS *Iris* and *Mercury*). Anyone who has worked in the documents of this period will recognize that the extent and quality of documentation declines dramatically for the period before about 1870. For example, no policy documents explain the dramatic cut in cruiser construction in 1863-64. None of the Covers for the big iron frigates appear to have survived (it is as though Edward Reed decamped with all of his design documentation when he stepped down as DNC). I am therefore particularly grateful to those who helped with what documentation has survived. Dr Stephen S Roberts generously provided British material he had collected many years ago for his thesis on French naval development. Professor John Beeler, who is collecting and publishing the Milne papers, provided some key letters. Professor Andrew Lambert, who has specialized in the Victorian Royal Navy, generously provided several papers, one of them unpublished. Chris Wright, editor of *Warship International*, provided his thesis on the Royal Navy of this period, which greatly helped clarify the policy context. I benefited enormously from a lengthy conversation with Colin Jones and with John Houghton, and the latter generously provided a copy of his book on world navies of the early Victorian period.

For both the early and the later eras, I am grateful to Jeremy Michell and to Andrew Choong of the Brass Foundry outstation of the National Maritime Museum for their enormous help with plans and photos. I am also grateful to Bob Todd, photo curator at the Brass Foundry. For photos held by the US Navy, I would like to thank my friend Charles Haberlein, curator emeritus at the Naval Historical and Heritage Command, and his assistants Ed Finney and Robert Hanshew (who is Mr Haberlein's successor). I would like to thank the photo library staff of the US Naval Institute. I am grateful to the State Library of Victoria (Australia), which has made available the superb photography of Allan C Green which it holds. I am also grateful to the staff of the Public Record Office (now called the National Archives) at Kew and to Jennie Wraight, Admiralty Librarian at the Royal Navy Historical Branch in Portsmouth. I would like to thank Dr David Stevens of the Royal Australian Navy Historical Branch and Dr Josef Strazcek, formerly his assistant and an avid photo collector. Both supplied very useful photographs. Stephen McLaughlin very generously provided material on Vickers designs. I can only regret that no comparable record of Armstrong designs seems to have survived. That is particularly unfortunate because Armstrong built the great bulk of the export cruisers of the period covered by this book. I was fortunate to be permitted to use the Vickers collection at Cambridge University Library.

My good friend A D Baker III is listed as illustrator, but he is much more than that. As he painstakingly created drawings of British cruisers, he pointed out their many quirks and the relationships which he could see in the source drawings and photographs. Often they were not evident in other documentation. Mr Baker also kindly provided some of the photographs in this book. Both Mr Baker and I much appreciate the advice and assistance we received from our friend Alan Raven in the course of this project. I would like to thank Paul Webb for the drawings he contributed. I would like to thank Professor Jon Sumida not only for his assistance with this project, but for illuminating, many years ago, the economics of the Royal Navy – which for me explained a lot of what is described in this book.

As grateful as I am for the assistance I received, I am of course responsible for the contents of this book, including any errors.

NORMAN FRIEDMAN

Illustrator's Notes
The drawings in this book by myself and by Paul A Webb are based directly on official Admiralty 'as fitted' plans. Copies of the original plans, usually amounting to several sheets for each ship, can be ordered from the National Maritime Museum in Greenwich, England. The NMM's historic Brass Foundry building at the old Woolwich Arsenal houses one of the world's most extensive collections of ship plans, dating back many centuries into the age of pure sail propulsion. It also has an extensive collection of ship photographs. The expert staff at the Brass Foundry, in particular Andrew Choong Han Lin, has been extremely helpful in selecting and crisply duplicating the plan sets needed for this volume.

Many of the older original plans are now fading and, in some cases, have suffered damage over the past century and more. For some ships, only the basic hull and superstructure sheets have survived. For others, only preliminary plans remain. The actual ships experienced many changes before completion. Usually only one set of plans for one ship of a class survives. Thus the dates of depiction listed for each drawing depended heavily on what was available. 'As fitted' drawings are unusual in showing details not only of the exterior of a ship but also many details of the interior, all on the same sheet. For the period covered by this volume, deck plans often show details of equipment like voice pipes and fire mains that are actually below the deck depicted. Elevations usually do not show the masts beyond a few feet above the decks (in many cases the funnels are also truncated). For most of the ships in this book, rigging and/or sail plans survive, but where they did not, the masting and rigging was deduced from that of the closest contemporary classes and from photographs.

Thus the availability of high-quality photography is vital to producing plans as accurate as possible. For the first volume in this series, there was ample aerial photography, but aerial views of Victorian era ships are, understandably, extremely rare. Thus details of equipment and deckhouses behind the characteristic midships bulwarks of the ships of that time are dependent on the surviving plans, a few on-board views, and photographs of contemporary ship models. The interpretation of period warship photographs is further complicated by the paint scheme used. A black-hulled ship shows few details of her sides unless the sun is at a particularly fortunate angle.

The British-designed cruisers discussed in this book were much more cluttered in appearance than are modern warships. The necessity to provide sturdy masts, first to support sails and the portable rigging for coaling, and then to carry as high as possible the antennas for primitive radio ('wireless telegraphy') required extensive supporting rigging. I have left in the footropes ('ratlines') on the mast support shrouds to help convey the complexity of the rigging and to suggest the amount of effort by the crew needed to maintain it, although regrettably this sometimes obscures some detail of the structures behind the rigging.

The vast profusion of ships' boats (which came in a great many different sizes and forms) also cluttered the ships' appearance. Most of the drawings for the book show the boats in both their at-sea stowage and in their 'swung-out' harbour positions. Due to a lack of reference material, plan view details of the innards of the boats are only shown in the rare instances where the 'as fitted' plans provided them. In the plan views, the outlines for boats stowed inboard are usually shown as dotted lines so that the details of their stowage racks and deck fittings below them could be depicted. In some of the elevation views, the boat profiles are shown as dotted lines for the same reason. One reason for the large number of boats, most of them oar propelled, was that life jackets only came into use late in the period covered by this volume. Carley-type liferafts only began to proliferate during the First World War.

To provide ventilation for the ships' engineering and accommodation spaces, the ships carried numerous cowl ventilators in a great variety of sizes and shapes. Adding to the clutter were exhaust pipes for individual coal-fired heating stoves in the berthing areas and portable supports for the vast amounts of canvas awning that was rigged when in port to keep the ships' interiors as cool as possible. Many of these features fouled the trainable armament and had to be taken down and stowed below or on topside deck racks before the ships could go into action. Most of the elevation and plan drawings also show the portable accommodation ladders, those aft for the officers and those amidships, where fitted, for the enlisted crew; these too had to be stowed on racks amidships when the ships cleared for sea. One feature not shown on the later cruisers was the wire netting that could be rigged amidships to provide some degree of protection for gun crews from splinters caused by shell-fire hits. Another defensive feature found on later, larger Royal Navy cruisers was the complex network of booms to support anti-torpedo netting, and the shelving along the ships' sides that was used to stow the rolled-up netting when the ships were underway.

All of the ships and powered craft in this book, even the tiny 2nd Class Torpedo Boats, were fuelled by coal, hence the numerous small concentric circles drawn on decks amidships that depict the scuttles leading to coal bunkers. Replenishing coal supplies, in addition to being a time-consuming and filthy task, also required rigging temporary lines to support gear, such as the ubiquitous 'Temperley Transporter' patent booms that rolled fore and aft along heavy cables slung between the masts. Numerous portable derricks and booms for coaling, bringing aboard stores, lifting out and retrieving ship's boats, and mooring boats alongside, also added further complexity, as did the clutter of anchor-handling equipment and chains.

Well into the 1890s, carved decorations were considered vital to a Royal Navy warship's portrayal of the power and might of the United Kingdom. Unfortunately, the elaborate bow and stern scrolling and, in some cases, figureheads, were only rarely shown on 'as fitted' plans. Where photos and drawings permitted, I have attempted to show some of the decorations, but for many ships that had them, the available photographs were inadequate. Also missing from the official plans were any suggestions of the equally elaborate striping on the sides of the ships, and no attempt has been made to replicate the paintwork on the drawings. In any case, as the photo illustrations show, such decorative features began to be removed from major RN warships during refits even prior to the universal replacement of black, white, and buff paint schemes with drab greys under Admiral Fisher.

The quality of the drafting on the original plans was almost invariably superb (with the exception of the earlier rigging and sail plans, which look hurried and rather sketchy). Considering that the draftsmen of the day were using ruling pens and large numbers of French curves and ships' curves for their work and had to do all the lettering by hand, it is remarkable how handsome and decorative their final drawings appeared. Paul A Webb's two drawings for the book were done using CAD, but the remainder employed Rapidograph ruling pens, numerous circle and oval templates, a set of ships' curves hand-made by a distant relative just about a century ago – and several magnifying glasses and an ever-busy electric eraser.

Dr Friedman photocopied hundreds of period photo prints and also took numerous photos of ship models during his visits to archives in the United Kingdom and the USA; these were of immense help in interpreting the original drawings. Many friends contributed material from their own collections, including Robin Bursell in the UK, Christopher C Wright (editor of the quarterly *Warship International*), Charles Haberlein, and Rick E Davis in the USA, and Darius Lipinski in Canada, all providing invaluable help. Sufer Printing in Williamsburg, Virginia, made numerous reductions of drawings for the book, and Capture All Ltd, of Falkirk, Scotland, did the precise high-definition laser scanning to reduce the finished drawings to fit the book's pages without loss of detail. The majority of the drawings were rendered in $\frac{1}{16}$th of an inch to the foot scale.

Finally, I would like to add my deepest and heartfelt thanks to my wife, Anne, who patiently endured for a year and a half my several thousand hours hunched over the drafting table in our office. Without her constant support and encouragement, the work could not have been accomplished.

A D Baker III

INTRODUCTION

It used to be said of the Royal Navy that its battleships brought it command of the sea, but that its cruisers – the ships described in this book – exercised that control. Cruisers were expected to protect British trade in wartime and to run enemy commerce off the sea. In peacetime they and their lesser cousins, sloops, guaranteed what is now called 'good order at sea', dealing with pirates and other maritime criminals. They also provided a good deal of the power exerted by local British colonial governments and by British political officers in quasi-colonies. Historians often emphasize the accelerating rate at which technology changed. What is much less appreciated is how radically the British strategic situation changed between the defeat of Napoleon in 1815 and the beginning of the twentieth century, which is about when the last of the ships described in this book were designed.

The Changing Strategic Environment
Geography and context remained remarkably constant from the early eighteenth century down to the defeat of Napoleon in 1815, France always being the main enemy. France presented two different principal threats: direct invasion across the Channel and trade warfare prosecuted mainly by waves of privateers operating out of French ports.
French colonies abroad could also support trade warfare, as in the Indian Ocean campaign during the Napoleonic Wars. French fleets could also attack valuable British colonies, as Villeneuve threatened to do in the Caribbean during the run-up to Trafalgar. Such threats were generally intended to force the British to relax their blockade of French or allied ports.

The most valuable British overseas asset (not yet a colony) was India, from which the British had only recently, at the time of the Napoleonic Wars, largely ejected the French. Throughout the nineteenth century, the two poles of British policy were the need to maintain security in Europe and the need to maintain access to, and control of, India (and hence of valuable possessions and connections further east).

India was too large to attack by sea. The route from Britain to India was another story. The quickest route was by sea to Egypt through the Mediterranean, overland to the Red Sea, and thence by sea to India. This route made the Mediterranean a vital British interest, even before the Suez Canal made the route far more efficient. Thus the closest Napoleon came to threatening British control of India was his campaign in Egypt, which was intended to distract the British from intervening against France in Europe.

In the aftermath of Napoleon's defeat, the world changed. The British gained bases in the Mediterranean (Malta and, more temporarily, the Ionian Islands) which gave them a permanent naval presence there; previously they only had Gibraltar, near the French end of that sea. The sea/land/sea route to India became more important, as the British consolidated their rule and began to use India as a base for operations further east. British interest in the Mediterranean, and therefore in the Ottoman Empire, which (at least nominally) controlled the eastern end of the sea, including Syria (meaning present-day Syria, Lebanon, and Israel) increased. For decades the Russian Empire had been moving south towards and beyond the Black Sea at the expense of the Ottoman Empire. It became a staple

What did the Victorian Royal Navy consider a cruiser? At the upper end of the scale were battleship-size ships like HMS *Powerful*, seen here steaming at 18kts, probably as newly completed. She wears the classic Victorian livery of black hull, white superstructure (and gun mountings), and buff funnels. Ships assigned to hotter climates had white hulls. The cruiser classification appeared, perhaps for the first time, in the 1 January 1878 edition of *Classification of the Armoured and Unarmoured Ships and Vessels Constituting the Fighting and Sea-Going Divisions of the British Navy*. It divided unarmoured cruisers into three classes, the first of which were frigates (new and old) and the *Bacchante*s. The second class were the big new corvettes. The third were smaller corvettes. The official 1880 armament list included not only unarmoured ships described as cruisers, but also armoured cruisers. As might be expected, the latter included the five belted cruisers, but also the ironclads *Warrior* and *Black Prince* as well as *Achilles* and *Repulse* and the smaller *Hector*, *Valiant*, *Defence*, and *Resistance*. The 1886 list split armoured cruisers into two classes, the first including the new *Orlando*s and the five earlier belted cruisers – and the big but obsolescent ironclads. This classification may reflect an abortive project to re-engine the big ironclads to make them into large fast cruisers. It is more difficult to understand inclusion of the smaller ironclads (the 1886 list omitted *Resistance*), which in 1886 were second-class armoured cruisers. The ironclad cruiser categories had been dropped by 1888 in favour of a distinction between first-, second-, and third-class cruisers (whether or not protected). Earlier lists, at least as late as 1875, distinguished armoured ships from unarmoured ships retained for sea service, the latter including the old screw frigates.

of British policy to maintain the Ottoman Empire despite its increasingly decrepit state, both to maintain a balance of power in Europe and to keep the Russians from direct access to the Mediterranean, hence to the sea route to India. By 1840 the Admiralty considered the Mediterranean second in importance only to the Channel.

The French were the principal threat to the route to India via the Mediterranean. In 1830 they established themselves on its southern shore in Algeria. At its eastern end they became involved in Syria and Egypt in 1840. They also became involved in Italian politics leading to the consolidation of that country. The British could see these steps as moves towards French domination of the Mediterranean. By 1840 the largest active British fleet was in the Mediterranean, not the Channel.

The Spanish colonies in South America became independent countries which could, for the first time, trade openly with Britain. The United States began to expand, and it too was an enormous market. The combination of finance provided by the City of London, the British-based industrial revolution, and British shipping created an explosive increase in British ocean trade. In the past, colonies producing particular materials or goods (such as spices or sugar) had been key to national prosperity. Now colonies, except for India and connections further east, became less important economically, particularly after slavery (which had made Caribbean sugar production lucrative) was abolished in the British Empire. Trade itself coupled with manufacturing became much more important. As the centre of the industrial revolution, Britain had goods the world increasingly wanted. The British Government increasingly saw free trade as key to national prosperity.

The British Government adopted free trade policies, abandoning protective tariffs. Perhaps the most important case was the Corn Law, protecting British farmers, abolished in 1846. In addition, in 1849 the British Government abandoned the Navigation Acts, which had limited shipping between Britain and her colonies to British ships. The latter had been tolerated as a way of maintaining a large merchant fleet. British policy had been to keep a large fleet of ships in reserve, expecting to activate the ships in an emergency largely with crews of merchant seamen. In effect, abandoning the Navigation Acts favoured British shipbuilders and engine-makers, because in the 1840s and 1850s Britain absolutely dominated world shipbuilding in the new primary material, iron, and also the engine-building industry. The effect of abolishing the Corn Laws was gradually to move British food production offshore, an early example of what is now called globalization. Those who voted to abolish the Corn Laws expected that corn (wheat) would be imported mainly from Russia (Poland, which Russia controlled, was then the main productive region), but with the collapse of shipping costs, it turned out that Britain was fed mainly from North America and, to a lesser degree, Australasia.

This development changed the meaning of wartime trade protection. During and before the Napoleonic Wars, British merchant ships mainly carried manufactured goods and the raw materials to make them, such as cloth and cotton. Sinking or seizing the ships would certainly affect the British economy, but it could not destroy Britain, which was largely self-sufficient in food. Once Britain relied heavily on foreign sources of food, cutting British seaborne trade threatened starvation: the

imported food had to reach Britain by sea. Furthermore, the new industries relied heavily on raw materials brought by sea from abroad. Cutting that traffic could destroy the ability to produce the weapons needed to defend the British Isles. The Victorian Royal Navy found it difficult to arouse public interest in so abstract an issue as trade defence. Too many in the United Kingdom equated defence simply to defence (by army and militia) against invasion.

During the same period, Russia became the greatest wheat-exporting country in Europe. Before about the 1850s grain pro-

Further down the scale were second-class cruisers like HMS *Minerva*. By the late 1890s they were by far the most numerous British cruisers. *Minerva* was placed in Chatham Reserve upon completion, then used for boiler trials in 1899-1903 as part of the Cruiser Training Squadron. She was later assigned to Devonport (1903-4), and then attached to the Mediterranean Fleet battle squadron in 1904-12 (during which she underwent a 1908 refit). She was then assigned to the new Third (reserve) Fleet's 11th Cruiser Squadron, serving as temporary depot ship for the 6th Destroyer Flotilla in 1912-13. On the outbreak of war the 11th Cruiser Squadron was mobilized for the West Coast of Ireland patrol (*Minerva* captured an Austrian merchant ship off Cape Finisterre in September 1914). She was assigned to the East Indies and then to Egypt in 1914-15, serving at the Dardanelles (she sank the Turkish torpedo boat *Demirhissar* off Chios on 17 April 1915). She remained in Egyptian waters through 1916, helping to defend the Suez Canal against a Turkish attack. Once that threat had gone, she served in East African waters in 1916-18, and at the Cape in 1918. She was sold in 1920.

duction was centred in the Baltic. By the 1850s, however, the Ukraine, with its rich black soil, was growing three times as much as the Baltic. This grain was exported through the Bosporus, the Turkish straits between the Black Sea and the Mediterranean. Quite aside from the exports, the Russians had long sought control of the straits. However, by the latter part of the nineteenth century exports through the Bosporus were their chief source of foreign exchange. That certainly sharpened Russian determination to control the straits, inevitably at the expense of Turkey. The situation was further complicated by the Russians' position as the centre of Orthodox Christianity, hence as the protectors of many Christians living in Turkish territories in the Balkans on the edges of the Black Sea. The Russians viewed themselves as successors to the Byzantine Empire ('the third Rome'), hence chosen to reverse the Turks' victory over Byzantium (Constantinople) four centuries earlier. Byzantium had been a maritime empire controlling the eastern Mediterranean. Thus Russian interests made collision with the British inevitable, given British sensitivity to any challenge in the Mediterranean, on the other side of the Turkish straits.

In the 1890s speed became the great distinction between cruisers – ships which could operate with the fleet – and the mass of cruising ships which maintained good order at sea and in British possessions. Until about 1885, however, many cruisers (corvettes) were not very fast at all. The corvette HMS *Rapid* was originally classified as a sloop, then rerated as a corvette, illustrating the fluid state of warship designations in the 1880s. The formal distinction was that a cruiser was a Captain's command, a sloop a Commander's.
(Allan C Green via State Library of Victoria)

Probably because Russia was a key grain exporter, the Russians particularly well understood how dependent the British were on grain imports. It was the nineteenth-century equivalent of a key OPEC member contemplating the vulnerability of Western oil-consuming states to an interruption in the flow of oil. As early as 1863 (in the context of a crisis over Russian suppression of a revolt in Poland), the Russians saw commerce warfare as a natural part of any war against the British. That year Russian squadrons visited New York and San Francisco. Americans saw the visit as valuable support during the Civil War. However, the point of the visit was to show the British that Russian warships could leave the Baltic (to attack their commerce) without the British observing them at all (the British seem not to have gotten this point). Once outside Russian waters, moreover, the squadrons could raid British commerce despite any blockade the British imposed (Russian geography, then and later, made it relatively easy to block access to the open sea). During the 1877-78 crisis the Russians sought to evade British blockade altogether by assembling the Russian Volunteer Fleet of commerce-raiding merchant ships in foreign ports.

There was a counter-current to British fears of trade warfare: by the 1850s British governments increasingly interested in commerce were less and less anxious to seize private property on the high seas. That applied particularly to the greatest free-trade country of all, the United Kingdom. For example, during the Crimean War – which contemporaries called the Great Russian War – no blockade was imposed. (It might, however, be suggested that the main goods the Russians imported by sea were manufactured goods from England, and that the British government of the day was not anxious to damage its own economy.)

The great scourge of previous wars had been privateers, privately-owned ships carrying special authorizations (letters of marque). Any civilian ship could be used in this way, so the number of commerce raiders could be immense. Similarly, all existing ports could be used as privateer bases. In 1859 the Treaty of Paris, signed by all the major sea powers except the United States, outlawed privateers. The potential scale of the commerce-raiding problem was dramatically reduced; navies had to choose between devoting resources to battle fleets and devoting them to war against trade.

The Treaty of Paris might even be read as abandonment of blockade. The British surrendered their 'ancient right' to seize enemy cargo carried in neutral ships. It seemed that shipowners could protect themselves in wartime simply by fleeing to other flags (as many did in 1914). Many in the Royal Navy thought this abandonment of the ancient rights of the maritime power had rendered sea power almost pointless. The treaty also limited what goods could legitimately be interdicted, food being an important exception. As the nineteenth century wore on, few British naval officers continued to believe that a ruthless enemy would care about either new rule – for them, enemy attacks on commerce increasingly carried the threat of starvation. The First World War showed that they were entirely correct.

Liberals led by William Gladstone sometimes argued that there was no point in planning for trade protection because the threat had been so dramatically reduced. At the least that made Gladstone, no friend of the Royal Navy, inclined against a fleet designed for blockade operations. Gladstone's first administration spanned the period 1868-74, which was exactly when the presence role of cruisers was far more important than the trade protection role. Naval officers pointed to the depredations of raiders operated by the Confederates during the American Civil War to show that the threat to trade – to British food – was still very real. *Alabama* and other successful Confederate raiders showed just how effectively a steam-powered cruiser could attack merchant shipping, which in the 1860s was still overwhelmingly sail-powered.

Meanwhile the geography of British sea power changed. British naval dominance of Europe depended largely on the fact that the British Isles blocked the exits from the Channel and from the North Sea and, by extension, the Baltic. Fleets based in the British Isles could blockade enemy bases in all these places, as indeed they had during the Napoleonic Wars. Once Britain had Gibraltar, she gained control (at least in theory) of the outlet of the Mediterranean. Any potential enemy with bases *outside* the area blocked by the British Isles and Gibraltar presented a new and potentially devastating threat, particularly to British trade. At the least it was a much more expensive threat to counter. That was certainly the case with the United States, whose naval policy through most of the nineteenth century was to be prepared to counter Britain, her traditional enemy, with a combination of trade warfare and coast defence. The United States had to be taken seriously as a danger because of its potential threat to Canada, which it had exercised (albeit not successfully) in 1812. Once the United States reached the Pacific, the British also had to deal with threats associated with the US–British Columbia border there.

Russian expansion into East Asia similarly brought them outside European geography. During the Crimean War, the Royal Navy raided the sole Russian Pacific base, Petropavlovsk. It had only limited value, as it was not large and also as it was closed by ice for much of the year. In 1860, however, the Russians set up an ice-free Asian port, Vladivostok, which posed a year-round threat to British Pacific trade.

Once the Suez Canal opened in 1869, the route to India and points east through the Mediterranean became far more important. The opening of the Suez Canal unfortunately roughly coincided with Russian denunciation of the clauses of the Crimean War settlement barring them from recreating a Black Sea Fleet. The two guarantors had been the two wartime allies, Britain and France, and the Franco-Prussian War (1870-71) paralysed France. The British alone were unwilling to enforce what the Czar of the time considered a gross humiliation. Grain exports did not figure in the Czar's comments, and the Russians did not immediately build up the Black Sea Fleet. However, it must have been obvious that once they did they could exert considerably more pressure on the British in the Mediterranean.

The Suez Canal was a Franco-Egyptian venture, but once in office in 1874 Prime Minister Benjamin Disraeli saw it as a vital British interest; he bought a controlling share by buying up the Egyptian Government's holdings. Although nominally part of the Turkish (Ottoman) Empire, Egypt was effectively independent, its government constantly in need of money.

Not too long after Disraeli bought the Canal shares, the Russo-Turkish crisis of 1875-77 threatened to place a Russian satellite state (Bulgaria) on the Mediterranean, within range of the Canal.[1] In 1878, with Russian troops threatening Constantinople, a British battle squadron made the dangerous ascent of the Bosporus in a snowstorm. The Russians had no real Black Sea Fleet, but the British ironclads were placing themselves to shell the Russian troops if necessary (the threat forced a Russian withdrawal). This fleet was commanded by Admiral Sir Geoffrey Phipps Hornby, who had commanded the Flying Squadron, and who would be a key figure in the agitation leading to the Naval Defence Act of 1889.

Although the ascent of the Turkish straits was a great success, other aspects of the British response were not. In addition to the standing Mediterranean Fleet, the Admiralty decided to assemble a fleet to penetrate the Baltic. To so do without removing the Channel Fleet (i.e., without presenting the French with the opportunity to invade), it tried to mobilize reserve ships and form them into a Baltic fleet. Mobilization proved difficult and far too slow. Intelligence had been collected, but at the crucial moment it could not be found. It proved impossible to maintain contact with Russian cruisers, which would have preyed on British trade had war broken out.

Ultimately the need to secure the Canal helped draw the British into making Egypt a quasi-colony.[2] At this time British colonies (apart from India) were generally fairly distant from anyone else's, approachable only by sea. Egypt was a very different proposition. It was close to other European colonies in North Africa, and it could be approached through Africa. Britain and France almost went to war in 1898 because French troops probing north met British troops at Fashoda in southern Egypt, suggesting that some larger thrust was planned (war orders were drafted, and one consequence of the war scare was a supplemental naval program). In this sense Egypt was analogous to India; in both cases defence included the defence of land frontiers. In both cases the land frontiers were considerably less approachable than maps suggested to governments in London.

British seizure of Egypt without French involvement made it difficult for the British to resist attempts by other European powers to seize parts of Africa. This scramble for Africa provided colonies the Germans, previously without colonial possessions, hoped to use as bases for cruisers during the First World War. The British found themselves seizing the German colonies not because they had enormous inherent value, but to deny them as bases for use against vital British trade.

The Mediterranean became so vital that the Mediterranean Fleet became the most important British naval formation of the late nineteenth century. With French bases circling much of the Mediterranean, it faced unusual conditions which brought forth special tactical solutions, not least for cruisers. As CinC of the Mediterranean Fleet, Admiral Sir John Fisher conceived many of his key ideas, which led in turn to the revolutions he pushed through at the Admiralty at the close of the period covered by this book.

Through the mid-nineteenth century the Russians drove south into Central Asia towards India. It might not be possible to overthrow British power in India by sea; the country was just too large. However, the British thought that the Russians planned to turn both Persia (Iran) and Afghanistan into vassal states, and it was conceivable that Afghans pouring across the northern frontier of India might have begun its conquest. This land threat was the substance of the 'Great Game' celebrated by Kipling and others. The naval aspect was that the best way for the British to counter Russian moves in Central Asia was to apply naval pressure in the one place most vital to the Russians: the Baltic.

HMS *Egeria* was a *Fantome* class sloop, the size just below corvettes (which were later rated as cruisers). This class introduced the composite construction which DNC Sir Nathaniel Barnaby later applied to the *Satellite* class corvettes. Built at Pembroke, *Egeria* was launched on 1 November 1873. Designed displacement was 894 tons, but the ships displaced 949 as completed; the difference may have been due to miscalculation involving the new type of construction (dimensions: 160ft × 31¼ft × 12½ft). Armament comprised two 7in 90cwt and two 64pdr, all muzzle-loading rifles on slides (these were the largest British warships with an all-traversing armament). One 7in was between funnel and mainmast and one on the quarterdeck, both with ports so that they could fire on the broadside. The only major armament modification was to replace wooden with iron slides after the first commission (*Egeria* later had her armament reduced as a surveying ship). Ships like this needed sail power for endurance. As a sloop, *Egeria* was slower than Barnaby's corvettes: on trial she made 11.303kts on 1011 IHP. The class was rated at 1000nm at 10kts. Machinery comprised three cylindrical boilers and a two-cylinder compound engine (these were the first sloops with compound engines). Ballard described the class as easily handled under sail, free from yaw when running before a heavy sea, buoyant when lying-to, and stiff enough not to require any ballast. They did not hold a good lee, however. They were never faster than 11½kts even when scudding before a high wind. These sailing qualities mattered; like other Victorian sloops, they made their long passages under sail. Complement was 125. *Egeria* served initially on the China station (1874-81, receiving a relief crew in 1878). She grounded badly off Hainan in a fog in 1879, but was refloated successfully (she lost most of her false keel in the process). On her return she went into reserve for two years, and was then selected as a surveying ship, her 64pdrs and 7in guns replaced by four 20pdrs (to deal with pirates). She was ready in 1886, and she was not brought home until she had to be reboilered (in 1894). She was paid off at Esquimault in 1911.

The next Anglo-Russian crisis after 1878 (1885) was prompted not by a thrust towards the Turkish straits, but by a Russian probe into Afghanistan, which bordered India.³ Without a large standing army, the only response available to the British was naval. In 1878 a fleet was sent up the Bosporus while another was mobilized to enter the Baltic. In 1885 there was no Mediterranean response, but a Baltic squadron was again mobilized, this time commanded by Admiral Phipps Hornby. When the immediate threat dissipated, the squadron was retained for manoeuvres, which were intended to test new technology. By this time the Russians had invested heavily in torpedo craft, and some of the exercises tested the fleet's ability to seize and maintain a base in the Baltic in the face of torpedoes and mines. Lessons learned deeply affected cruiser development. The 1885 exercises were considered so valuable a test of tactics and technology that they were made a nearly annual event. As in 1877-78, mobilization was not entirely successful, although there were notable improvements. For example, this time the navy was able to shadow Russian ships, precluding a major Russian offensive against British trade.

The French gained an ability to operate outside blockadable waters as they seized colonies in East Africa (such as Madagascar) and in Asia (Vietnam). Among other things, in the 1860s both the Russians and the French built second-rate

HMS *Penguin* was an *Osprey* class composite screw sloop, Barnaby's follow-on to the *Egeria* class. She had another two 64pdr guns. The embrasures for stern fire ran about half way along her poop. They are barely visible in this photograph because the hull was painted black. These ships came out light, the surplus of 35 tons being used for more coal. In effect these ships were half-scale models of contemporary composite corvettes, with the same kind of profile and embrasures at bow and stern (for end-on fire) and with the corvettes' sharp end lines and full midsections. Like Barnaby's corvettes, they had knee bows. The sharp tapering to the ends was accompanied by sharp rise of floor. This combination made them handy (as intended) but did not confer the desired speed. The lines did, however, make them remarkably suitable for meeting weather from any direction. In the worst gale they would rise or scud equally well under steam or sail. They did, however, roll too quickly to be efficient gun platforms, which suggests that metacentric height was greater than expected due to too low a centre of gravity (underestimated weights). Initially the ships had a light poop and forecastle, both open at the break, the poop covering two cabins with a chaser between them, and the forecastle covering the heads and another chaser. After the first commission both were strengthened and fully enclosed and machine guns mounted on top. Machinery divided the hull in two lengthwise, a narrow communication passage running along the starboard side through the upper part of the boiler and engine rooms, with a watertight door at each end. This was the first class to have glass scuttles in place of the older square hanging ports or 'rat hole' plug scuttles. Like the larger cruisers, these ships started out with two heavy guns, in this case 7in 4½-tonners on slides, one between funnel and mainmast and the other on the quarterdeck, both intended to fire on the broadside. They had two 64pdrs on the broadside and two more under the forecastle and poop as chasers. This combination gave them a heavy broadside, but using it put so much weight on one side (the heavy guns would be traversed to bear) that the ship heeled. Of this class, *Wild Swan* and *Pelican* were rearmed with breech-loaders. They were given two 6in at quarterdeck broadside ports, four 5in at broadside ports, and two 5in chasers firing through embrasures at bow and stern. *Penguin* received a pair of 5in breech-loaders on her poop instead of the single 64pdr below it. *Osprey* and *Cormorant* were never rearmed, because new guns were not available until they were too old. Due to the unusual hull form, space for the horizontal engines could be found just half-way between bow and stern, so the engines were, unusually, forward of the mainmast rather than abaft as in other three-masted Royal Navy ships of this period. That made for an unusually long propeller shaft, a source of trouble, and the mainmast had to be stepped on the main deck instead of the keel. Like *Egeria*, *Penguin* was relatively slow (she was the slowest of the class, making 9.875kts with 666 IHP; her Devonport-built sister *Pelican* made 12.241kts on 1056 IHP). After her first commission her machinery was replaced by Devonport-built compound engines. Built under contract (by Robert Napier and Sons), *Penguin* was launched on 25 March 1876. Displacement was 1130 tons (170ft pp × 36ft × 15ft 9in). Complement was 150. *Penguin* went to the Pacific on completion in 1877, returning in 1881 to have her machinery replaced. Unlike her sister *Wild Swan*, which went into the yard at the same time, she was not rearmed at this time with breech-loaders due to a shortage of guns. She went into reserve, recommissioning in 1886 for the East Indies. On return in 1889, she was selected for conversion to a survey ship, all her guns except a pair of broadside 64pdrs being removed. Space left vacant by the 7in guns was used for deckhouses and her boat complement was increased. In this form she commissioned in January 1890, not being paid off until March 1907, in Sydney, where she was reduced to harbour depot ship – the last of her class to remain at sea. She was transferred to the new RAN.

HMS *Doterel* was the name ship of a class very similar to the *Penguin*s, distinguishable by their vertical stems. They displaced 1130 tons (170ft pp x 34ft x 15ft) and were armed with two 7in 90cwt guns plus four 64pdrs, all on pivoted slides, plus four machine guns. They had three cylindrical boilers feeding a horizontal compound engine: *Doterel* made 11kts on 900 IHP. Endurance under steam was 1480nm at 10kts. *Doterel* was launched at Chatham on 2 March 1880. She was lost on her maiden voyage, exploding and sinking off Sandy Point, Punta Arenas on 26 April 1881.

(Allan C Green, courtesy of State Library of Victoria)

armoured ships specifically to operate in Eastern waters, far from their concentrated fleets. Viable British presence in the Pacific required that cruisers be backed by armoured ships. This requirement created the first ships rated by the Royal Navy as armoured cruisers (though quite unrelated to the armoured cruisers of the late nineteenth and early twentieth centuries).

Given the emergence of foreign colonies as potential raider bases, British war planners of the late nineteenth century envisaged attacks on them. This was not the colonial warfare of the past, in which colonies were worth seizing for their rich resources; rather it was a coldly strategic counter to commerce raiding. Thus when the British contemplated war against France in 1898 their arrangements included convoys of troops (escorted by cruisers) to seize French naval bases abroad. This anti-raider mission is why, for example, the British were so anxious to seize Tsingtao in China and German East Africa in the opening phase of the First World War. Without bases, enemy raiders at sea would not last for very long, whether or not they were sucked into a focal area. The German squadron based at Tsingtao certainly caused considerable havoc when it was forced to sea, but it seems unlikely that it could have remained at sea for very long with limited resources – many of which the Admiralty indirectly controlled.

It was bad enough to face the French *or* the Russians, but beginning in the 1880s the two threats merged, particularly in the Mediterranean.[4]

In the 1850s and 1860s the British also faced the possibility of conflict with the United States due, among other reasons, to disagreements over the border with Canada. For example, in 1858 there was a considerable scare as the French seemed about to match or even to surpass British naval strength. First Naval Lord Admiral Sir Richard Dundas pointed to the possibility that the United States would feel encouraged to attack British possessions in North America in the event of a war with France.[5] Second Naval Lord Admiral Martin considered that the United States might fight if the Royal Navy imposed a blockade against France. At this time the French navy nearly equalled the Royal Navy in size, and France had more frigates (though fewer smaller cruisers). Thus it could be argued that France could blockade England (which was already importing much of her food) quite aside from the usual threat of a direct invasion by the large French army.

The US Navy had a long-standing war policy of raiding British commerce, as it had no hope of challenging the British fleet. In the past it had built unusually large fast frigates like USS *Constitution* in hopes of overwhelming British convoy escorts. In 1854 it announced plans for five new fast screw frigates and a screw corvette. The British were led to design their own fast screw frigates as answers to these ships; in the process they pushed wood hull construction as far as it could go. It turned out that the British frigates were much faster than their US counterparts, but also that their powerful engines overstrained their hulls. There was a real possibility of war against the United States several times during and immediately after the American Civil War, but it was always averted. The United States disappeared as a naval threat only when the large fleet built up to fight the Civil War was allowed to decline precipitously in the early 1870s.

Trade Protection
During the centuries leading up to the end of the Napoleonic Wars, the Royal Navy relied heavily on convoy to protect seaborne trade. Convoy Acts forced merchant ship owners to submit to Royal Navy orders and to join convoys with escorts. Many historians have observed that this apparently successful policy was discarded after 1815, and it is often suggested that the Royal Navy's failure to protect vital shipping from U-boats in 1914-17 could be traced to a lack of interest in trade protection and to the abandonment of a previously successful policy in favour of an emotionally satisfying offensive (rather than defensive) strategy. None of this seems to match reality. For the Royal Navy, perhaps the most interesting lesson of the American Civil War was the striking success of Confederate raiders. Blockade could not deal with them, because they were built and armed abroad (British connivance in Confederate raiding was a major source of post Civil War tension). The closest approach to blockade, which netted the very successful CSS *Alabama*, was to station the cruiser USS *Kearsage* off the port of Cherbourg, in the expectation that the Confederate ship would have to put into port for resupply. There was no hope whatever of patrolling the open Atlantic, and the Union Navy lacked resources for any kind of convoy strategy

It is difficult to trace the evolution of British thinking about trade protection, because responsible officers only rarely had to explain themselves to civilians, such as the First Lord of the Admiralty, who were not already familiar with their thinking. The considerable volume of the program to build small cruisers (frigate down to gun-vessel) during the 1840s and 1850s suggests an attempt to maintain the small-ship force which in the past had escorted convoys. In 1858 Surveyor Captain Walker commented that the size of the French steam frigate force, roughly equal to the British, suggested an intent to conduct trade warfare, and he decried the inability of the Royal Navy to concentrate its forces in the Channel due to the need to protect British trade as well as British possessions overseas.

In two cases British cruisers were built specifically to run down fast cruisers built by the United States explicitly to operate as raiders in wartime, in accordance with settled US naval policy. In 1854 the US Navy announced plans to build five large steam frigates and one large steam corvette, and the Royal Navy responded with large fast frigates of its own. It turned out that the US ships were not nearly as fast as had been expected. The British ships were not repeated because they were so expensive; commerce protection, certainly as then understood, demanded numbers. During the American Civil War, Confederate raiders like CSS *Alabama* devastated Union merchant shipping. The Union response was a series of what were expected to be very fast cruisers capable of running such raiders down. They were also potential commerce raiders, and again they demanded a British response. It came in the form of a program for six large fast steam frigates, only three of which were ultimately built (*Inconstant*, *Raleigh*, and *Shah*). Again they were too expensive to be constructed in any numbers.

It is not clear when British naval officers realized that the combination of an explosion in the sheer number of British merchant ships and the nature of steam power (in the 1870s and early 1880s cruisers could not match the endurance of merchant steamers) made the old convoy policy obsolete. Nor was the lesson of the Napoleonic Wars entirely clear. One witness before the Carnarvon Commission, an experienced and thoughtful shipowner, explained that a convoy attacked by overwhelming force would be annihilated – as had happened on several occasions. An effective convoy defence would have required that each convoy be escorted by a force capable of beating off the most powerful enemy ships. It may be that the ability simply to crush an enemy's ports seemed for a time a sufficient guarantee against large-scale commerce raiding.

The first internal document formally laying out the desired cruiser force seems to have been a statement prepared by First Naval Lord Admiral Milne in December 1874 for the First Lord, in connection with the First Lord's attempt to frame a rational naval program.[6] Milne's paper on unarmoured ships was written to help the First Lord frame estimates. It is impossible to say whether it reflected widely-accepted ideas, which were not expressed on paper because they were not worth writing down. Explaining the navy's thinking to a civilian First Lord was a different proposition.

Milne mentioned both the need to protect the trade on which the country relied, and also what might now be called presence missions, such as suppressing the slave trade and piracy. Milne distinguished between the main fleet, which for him included fast frigates and corvettes, for general war and also for commerce protection, and smaller unarmoured ships for foreign and home service, surveying, despatch duty, and coast guard service. He also produced a paper on trade protection, perhaps the earliest one formally to advocate what was later called a policy of patrolling focal areas. 'It is well known to foreign nations that our trade is our great point of weakness, and that it is open to the attack of the cruizers of any enemy.' Recent intelligence showed that the Russians had planned to attack the Australasian trade during the 1863 crisis.

Milne argued that any seaman trying to destroy British trade would know the main trade routes, and would seek targets in particular places where they were concentrated. He identified eighteen such places, Each of these eighteen stations should be occupied by two or three ships, making a total of forty to fifty cruisers. Adding reliefs 'and separate ships for obtaining information' gave the total of fifty to sixty cruisers he sought.[7] By cruisers Milne meant frigates and corvettes, which he thought would soon be rerated as cruisers of the first, second, and third classes. Only a few of them were really fast.

Milne proposed a fleet of 20 frigates, 25 to 30 first-class corvettes, and 30 second-class corvettes, aside from lesser craft (sloops and gunboats). He considered this a low estimate, and pointed out that a quarter would probably always be under repair or defective at any time. However, the figures seem to have been unaffordably high, so in a marginal note Milne called for a war establishment of 30 frigates and 25 corvettes, a total of 55 such ships. Actual numbers were falling rapidly. Of 26 frigates on the Navy List, 14 were fit only for harbour service, and of the remaining 12, 6 would have to be repaired or replaced within four years. Against a wartime requirement for 30 corvettes, 32 were on the list, but 11 had already been condemned. Of the remaining 21, 14 were in commission, and Milne expected three to be found unfit within three years. Another seven sloops had been commissioned as second-class corvettes, six of which had recently been repaired. No frigates were building, but three first-class and nine second-class corvettes were under construction, in addition to nine sloops and lesser vessels not considered in this book.

Milne pointed to the destruction of US commerce by Confederate raiders, most famously css *Alabama*, only about a decade before. He pointed to the failure of the US Navy to find sufficient ships to run down this Confederate raider. The British cruiser force was shrinking as the wooden ships of the 1850s and 1860s were being condemned much faster than they were replaced. Since 1 January 1868, 19 frigates had been stricken, and 3 built; 16 corvettes had been stricken, and 12 built; and 19 sloops had been stricken, and 12 built. As a minimum, Milne wanted an immediate program of six *Boadicea* class frigates to be laid down in 1875, another six following in 1876. The 1875 proposal was apparently vetoed by the Cabinet.

Focal area defence was part of a larger strategy. French bases abroad would be attacked so that they could not be used as bases for commerce raiders. The troopships used for such attacks would be convoyed, and some other unusually valuable ships might also be protected directly. The issue of convoy was whether such protection could be or would be extended to the mass of merchant shipping. The conclusion was clearly that such extension was impossible and unaffordable.

The enemy force which got to the focal areas had to be restricted; the British had to neutralize the French battleships. That was not too difficult in European waters, but it became far more difficult as the French gained colonies in Africa and in Asia. The British had to station their own armoured ships in the Far East specifically because a single French armoured ship could destroy the unarmoured cruisers which would execute the trade protection mission in wartime. Hence the British (and French) policy of building second-class armoured ships, many of them classed as armoured cruisers, for foreign service. The nature of these ships is obvious partly because their Ships' Covers are clearly marked 'second-class ironclad' rather than 'armoured cruiser'.

Milne also pointed to the varied peacetime (presence) roles of unarmoured British warships, such as presence missions for the Foreign Office and suppression of piracy and of the slave trade. He was embarrassed that he could not provide ships; there was no reserve apart from the Channel Squadron and the Detached Squadron.

It is not clear to what extent *Iris* and *Mercury* were intended to meet Milne's needs. Certainly he did not get the large cruiser program he wanted. The British cruiser program continued to consist mainly of relatively slow corvettes through the early 1880s.

In the aftermath of the 1878 crisis with Russia the Carnarvon Committee met to examine the ability of the Empire to maintain the food supply of the United Kingdom in the face of foreign attacks on British trade. It spent relatively little of its effort examining naval efforts to deal with enemy commerce raiders, concentrating instead on the defence of British colonies and coaling stations. Most of the world's steaming coal was in exactly these places. Without coal, an enemy raider would soon be rendered immobile.[8] The Carnarvon Committee did collect statements from some prominent shipowners attacking the earlier trade protection tactic of convoy, which had apparently already been abandoned.

In 1885 the Foreign Intelligence Committee (now in effect a naval staff) issued a comparison of trade protection by focal area patrol and convoy.[9] The unpleasant reality was that the Royal Navy had no cruisers capable of working with really fast merchant ships. Very few had the combination of speed and high-speed endurance needed to convoy even 10kt freighters, which were quite common by that time. Even sailing merchant ships would be difficult to convoy, because they might easily be becalmed. Their owners considered them so vulnerable that they would be laid up in wartime. The alternative of directly protecting the trade routes by flanking them with cruisers along their whole length had been already rejected as impossible. That left only the focal area concept Milne had laid out a decade earlier. The 1885 paper advocated employment of 83 cruisers and 75 merchant auxiliaries; it also offered a reduced version requiring 38 cruisers and 37 merchant auxiliaries. The main later development was to analyse trade routes to decide exactly what areas demanded cruisers. A formal Admiralty Memorandum on protection of British trade in wartime was drafted in November 1898 and printed in February 1900 so that it could be issued to merchant ships in an emergency. It restated the focal area policy: protecting squadrons would be stationed 'where the convergence of the important ordinary trade routes offers to the enemy great opportunities for making captures'. This pamphlet explicitly stated that convoys would not be formed except under special circumstances (i.e., of ships, such as troopships, whose loss could not be tolerated – but that was not said).

Milne's focal area strategy was not for public consumption: any offensive trade protection strategy implied that the British merchant fleet would face heavy losses early in a war. After a few months the enemy raiding force would have been destroyed, and losses would cease. That is what happened to the German cruiser force intended to destroy British commerce during the early months of the First World War. Things later went badly wrong because the anti-raider strategy, so little discussed pre-war, was ineffective against U-boats, which could not easily be hunted down. The economics driving the strategy – that there were too few ships for effective escort – explains the Admiralty's attempt to revive hunting in 1939, when it thought that the advent of Asdic had made the earlier strategy viable again. In each case the key failure was not to understand that a primary requirement, the ability of a cruiser or other ship on station to detect a raider at a distance and kill it, had been lost. The US Navy revived offensive anti-raider strategy when it sought to deal with Soviet nuclear submarines during the Cold War;

The *Doterel* class sloop *Espiegle* rearmed with ten 5in Mk III breech-loading guns in shields, four of them (in shields) on VC and six (on the broadside) on VB mountings. The *Mariner* class were similar but slightly larger, completed with breech-loading guns (eight 5in). They displaced 970 tons. Two ships of that class (*Mariner* and *Racer*) participated in the 1885 fleet exercise, proving that they were far too slow (rated at 11.5kts on 850 IHP) to work with a battle fleet. The *Mariner*s were laid down as gun-vessels, but reclassified as sloops on 26 November 1884, while under construction.

again, there was little prospect of building enough escorts of sufficient capability. Moreover, a convoy too lightly escorted became a tasty meal for a raider. That had become evident during the Napoleonic Wars, and the unpleasant experiences of such convoys were cited during the 1878 hearings of the Carnarvon Commission on colonial defence and on protecting British seaborne trade.

It did not help that the Royal Navy's rivals did not have to match its numbers. For example, the Royal Navy squadrons deployed in the Far East had to deal with a Russian threat to trade mounted from Vladivostok. A Russian raider might appear anywhere in the area, so any of the deployed squadrons there had, at least in theory, to be able to counter the most powerful of the potential raiders. British numbers were set by the number of places that had to be covered. It did not take large numbers of potential Russian (or, for that matter, French) raiders to force up the size of the ships the Royal Navy had to deploy in the Far East, hence the cost of the Royal Navy.

The number of vulnerable focal areas increased as the French and the Russians gained bases outside the area the Royal Navy could expect to dominate. Just before the turn of the century the French seem to have been particularly keenly aware that building limited numbers of armoured cruisers would place intolerable financial burdens on the Royal Navy. By that time a big armoured cruiser cost about as much as a battleship, so a Royal Navy forced to build a large number of such ships (to cover the focal areas) would be building, in effect, two battle fleets. It was time to find a new way to handle the problem. Admiral Sir John Fisher seems to have seen the way: use intelligence to find the enemy cruisers, and build overwhelmingly powerful large fast cruisers to run them down. That was a key rationale of the battlecruisers which Fisher hoped would replace armoured cruisers.

Conversely, it was argued that by stationing powerful cruisers at focal areas, the Royal Navy would be forcing enemies to limit their attacks on trade to their most powerful cruisers, and in that way much reducing the scale of the attack.[10]

When he became First Sea Lord, Admiral Fisher rethought trade protection.[11] He again rejected convoy, partly because an entire convoy could be lost if its escorts were overwhelmed. It would be impossible to keep formation of a convoy secret, and the mass of smoke it produced by day (and the lights it would have to show at night) would attract attack. Probably the worst problem was that there were just not enough cruisers to escort convoys and to do 'the far more effective work of hunting down the enemy's commerce destroyers'. It seemed that most of the large number of merchant ships, each proceeding unpredictably, would escape a small number of enemy raiders.

Recent analysis had shown that even famous raiders of the past, such as CSS *Alabama*, had not been very productive. A US analysis conducted after the Civil War showed that Confederate raiders had destroyed only about 5 per cent of the Union merchant fleet; another 32 per cent had been lost as shipowners fled to neutral flags. The latter loss proved permanent due to onerous post-war taxes rather than to anything the Confederates had accomplished directly. *Alabama* herself had accounted for about three ships each month of her raiding lifetime.

The Royal Navy was increasingly arguing that the main defence of trade was control of the sea, to be gained by seeking out and destroying the enemy's fleet. There had to be a fallback defence of trade to deal with enemy cruisers escaping from the British fleet, but it should be be minimized because the needs of the fleet came first.

For the moment, Fisher retained the focal area strategy. It was affordable, in terms of numbers of cruisers required and in terms of coal and wear and tear on the ships. It made concentration of force (when needed) practicable. Given a squadron operating in a focal area, the officer in command could readily react to information. Merchant ships under threat would know where to run. As pointed out above, Fisher soon became interested in an alternative to focal areas, using fast cruisers to run down raiders based on intelligence – a strategy which became possible with radio. This strategy in turn helped engender the battlecruiser, as a replacement for armoured cruisers.

Naval Presence
With its rise as the centre of world finance, the City of London became an important element of the British economy and hence a factor in policy-making. It did not speak with any single voice, but in effect it demanded that successive British Governments understand that they had a vital interest in keeping the peace abroad so that international trade, and British traders in particular, could flourish. That role was not too different from what is sometimes now called the vital peacetime mission of 'maintaining good order at sea'. In practice the Royal Navy had to maintain cruiser squadrons on foreign stations. Such squadrons were not necessarily a means of protecting trade. Rather, they were a way of maintaining what would now be called presence. For example, when the Peruvian ironclad *Huascar* mutinied and became piratical in 1877, she was hunted down and disarmed by the local British squadron headed by HMS *Shah* – which fired the first self-propelled torpedo to be used in action against the ironclad (it missed).

Shah was not defending British colonies, but rather the British-centred trading system which kept Britain alive. The City was in effect the centre of an informal empire defined by trade. Unlike the formal empire, it was not generally garrisoned by the small British professional army, and it did not figure in formal defence arrangements. In effect the City could and did apply pressure to maintain the naval presence which protected the British traders abroad and which reassured the governments of the informal empire when they favoured policies which helped international trade – which usually meant trade financed by the City. Whether Britain should have a formal empire at all was a matter of intense debate in mid-century, but the informal empire was not, and could not, be debated at all. It was the informal empire which demanded all those cruisers on foreign stations. The formal empire is largely gone, but not the City and therefore not the vital foreign trading interests. That should, but does not, suggest that the presence mission is still vital, quite unaffected by the demise of formal empire.

Ships intended primarily for the presence role did not necessarily have to be very fast, but they needed long endurance, heavy armament, and survivability. Nearly all the masted cruisers built for the Royal Navy before about 1880 shared these characteristics.

It was not obvious to all in British government that global naval presence was worth while. It was certainly expensive; battleships were often maintained in reserve at home, but cruisers on foreign stations had to be manned and maintained and refitted periodically. In times of crisis, the Admiralty also questioned the value of dispersed ships conducting presence operations. In 1858 the French navy approached the size of the Royal Navy, and in at least one category (frigates) they were superior. The naval members of the Board wanted the fleet concentrated in home waters to deter the French from any idea of invasion, some members suggesting in addition spoiling attacks on the French Channel ports (Cherbourg in particular was being fortified as a fleet base).

The Royal Navy was probably the largest single item in the British national budget of the time. William Gladstone, the Liberal prime minister during much of the late nineteenth century, was an ardent anti-imperialist hostile to naval spending. In 1861, well before he became Prime Minister for the first time, he argued since steam made it possible to reach out to the world rapidly and reliably, the bulk of the fleet could be maintained in home waters. Implicit in Gladstone's argument was that the ships (cruisers) on foreign stations were there to protect British colonies. Gladstone could accept a reduced fleet capable of responding to crises, but not naval presence. He would have dramatically reduced the peacetime British cruiser force, which provided presence. Once Gladstone was in office in 1868, he tested the idea. His First Lord, H C E Childers (who famously disregarded professional naval opinion) argued that money saved by eliminating most of the ships on station could be spent instead on more ironclads in home waters and in the Mediterranean. This idea corresponded to Gladstone's preference for home defence over Empire defence (he was a 'little Englander'). The idea was tested by sending a Flying Squadron commanded by Rear Admiral Geoffrey Phipps Hornby abroad in 1869. Among the drawbacks to the idea were the low speed of existing ships and their very limited coal endurance. Phipps Hornby later described the Flying Squadron as a valuable means of training officers and men (largely under sail) and of showing the flag (cruising under sail also minimized dependence on foreign coal). Despite its prestige, the squadron could not be in more than one place at a time: the United Kingdom still needed a large cruiser force continuously on station.

Presence, and the somewhat similar imperial police role, required large numbers of small ships, ranging downwards from cruisers capable of fleet operations to steam sloops, gun-vessels, and gunboats. About 1860, for example, large numbers of shallow-draught sloops and gunboats were required for China, even though China was not in any sense a British colony. These small units were never really expected to engage enemy cruisers, but they seemed absolutely essential; during the nineteenth century after 1815 they saw much more action than larger and more capable warships. They were caught up in the financial problems the Royal Navy faced by 1900, as the cost of adequate warships escalated while resources did not. Hence Admiral Fisher's famous call, upon becoming First Sea Lord in 1904, to scrap all the small ships abroad which could 'neither fight nor run away'.

In effect Fisher was saying that he could no longer include the cost of the Imperial maritime police force in the Royal Navy budget; in order to maintain a navy adequate for war, he could not continue to pay for assets really needed by the Foreign Office and the Colonial Office. He probably hoped that they would realize that they needed the small warships badly enough to be willing to pay for them, but that did not happen (on the other hand, surprisingly few of the sloops were scrapped). The problem has continued to haunt navies, when maritime solutions to national problems other than naval warfare pop up. If that seems abstract, think about strategic submarines. Both in Britain and in the United States, Polaris submarines and their successors did the national job formerly done mainly by land-based bombers. They did not contribute to conventional naval missions. However, in neither country did governments pay for the new strategic weapons out of the budgets formerly allocated to the land-based bombers. Instead, the submarines were paid for by cutting general-purpose naval forces.

The Shape of the Fleet and the Changing Role of the Cruiser
Nineteenth-century cruisers are often regarded as direct descendants of the frigates and sloops of the age of sail. That is not quite true. Sailing frigates and sloops were generally faster than the line-of-battle ships, to the point that they could escape from such ships. As long as steam engines were bulky and inefficient, steam-powered battleships were generally as fast as (if not faster than) most steam frigates and lesser craft. It took a large frigate (often filled with machinery) to outrun a steam-powered battleship when both ships were under steam. Frigates lost their place in fleet engagements, although they certainly retained their roles in trade defence and attack. Only in the mid-1870s did the combination of steel hulls and more efficient machinery restore the cruiser's speed advantage. It took about a decade more for the cruiser to regain a place in the battle fleet, partly because the nature of the fleet itself was changing.

Even the term cruiser (sometimes spelled cruizer) was not widely used as a ship type until the 1880s. Before that ships were classified as frigates, corvettes, sloops, gun-vessels, and gunboats, of which only the first three figure in this book. The categories were left over from the sailing ship era. In 1878 frigates and corvettes were first officially redesignated cruisers, but the earlier designations survived well into the 1880s in official documents. Sloops remained as a separate category, and so did the lesser cruising vessels.

The evolving roles of cruising ships were intertwined with radical changes in the character of the fleet and of naval warfare. There were three distinct naval roles. One was to protect trade, either directly (by convoy) or by denying an enemy the ability to deploy raiders (blockade and attack at source, i.e., raids on ports harbouring raiders), or by destroying the raiders individually at sea. A second was the destruction or neutralization of the enemy's main fleet. It made the first type of operation possible, by limiting the scale of threat that escorts or blockaders or harbour attackers had to face. A third was to capitalize on control of the sea (secured mainly by battlefleet action) to move troops to strategic places and thus to upset an enemy's position ashore. For example, the British fleet victory at Trafalgar (which effectively finished the French and Spanish battle fleets) secured free use of the sea, which the British used first for an unsuccessful descent on the Dutch North Sea coast and then to support Wellington's Peninsular campaign. Without Trafalgar, there could have been no Peninsular campaign. Trafalgar also made the blockade of various French ports effective. Despite Trafalgar, the Royal Navy had to keep hunting down French raiders until the end of the war.

Steam dramatically changed the situation. A steam warship was independent of the vagaries of the wind. It might no longer be necessary to operate ships in the dense line-ahead formations of the past. Until the 1880s or even later, steam plants were extremely inefficient. For example, it was common in the 1840s and 1850s to design steam warships with a coal endurance of about two weeks and a stores endurance of five months, the assumption being that the ship would spend most of her time cruising under sail. The protracted blockades of the age of sail were no longer practical.

Moreover, sailing ships had been governed by prevailing winds, so that in effect the winds created highways in the otherwise trackless sea. That is why we can read about a British fleet well out of sight of land waiting for the Spanish gold convoy to approach, or an attack on some other large convoy. Steamships could manoeuvre much more freely. In a world without radio, the best way to locate – to destroy – an enemy's warships was at or near their port. As in the sailing ship era, the alternatives were to enter the port (a cutting-out expedition) or to blockade it. The effect of the new steam and other (e.g., heavy gun) technology was to limit the number of ports which could support major warships, and thus to limit the number of ports which had to be dealt with. During the sailing ship era, blockade was far preferable to direct attack on a fleet in port because ships generally could not engage the fortifications protecting the port. Fortifications were, moreover, relatively inexpensive; the French fortified not only their fleet bases but also the ports which supported privateers preying on British trade.

The Crimean War changed this perception. French armoured floating batteries successfully engaged Russian forts (the British built similar batteries, but did not bring them into action during the war). Unarmoured British gunboats were also successful against forts. This lesson was repeated during the American Civil War. More powerful guns which appeared after 1865 presented the even more attractive possibility of destroying an enemy fleet by shelling it from just outside the protected port. It now became far more profitable to attack an enemy port than to blockade it. Both the Royal Navy and the French navy built 'coast defence' ships which might more properly be described as coast (or port) attackers.[12] The French wrote about their 'seagoing siege train'. To the extent that harbour attack became the favoured tactic in the Royal Navy and in its French counterpart, the fleet in the Channel was no longer the long-range seagoing entity of the past, with its scouts arrayed ahead of it. Because they had vital interests far from the British Isles, the British also needed seagoing armoured ships which would be deployed at long range. However, once they arrived at their destinations, they, quite as much as the shorter-range coastal ships, would be attacking an enemy fleet in port.

A fleet crashing into an enemy port to destroy everything inside had only a limited need for scouts. For example, the fleet

HMS *Dolphin*. *Dolphin* and her sister *Wanderer* were the first British sloops to be armed with breech-loading guns. Originally classified as gun-vessels, they were reclassified as sloops while under construction. These photographs were taken when the ship was completed, armed with two 6in and two 5in breech-loaders. The stern view shows closed ports (embrasures) on either side of the ship's stern, a feature of many British sail-and-steam warships of this period. Guns on slides could be moved between the embrasures and side ports. Embrasures made it possible to fire dead astern (there were similar ports forward) without fouling the trunk into which the ship's single propeller was hoisted when she was under sail. Sailing qualities were essential to ships which would spend much of their time under sail so as to conserve coal and thus to achieve the long endurance demanded of cruising warships. These ships displaced 925 tons (157ft pp × 32ft × 14ft). *Dolphin* had a 720 IHP compound engine and was rated at 11.3kts; endurance was 1700nm at 10kts. Both ships were built under contract by Raylton Dixon of Middlesbrough; *Dolphin* was launched on 9 December 1882. She became a sailing training ship in 1899, when the larger corvettes of the Training Squadron were discarded. In 1907 she was hulked as an accommodation ship for submarines; in 1912 she became a submarine depot ship.

which ascended the Turkish straits in 1878 included no cruisers (the sole cruiser in the area, HMS *Raleigh*, was among the ships which remained at Besika Bay).

This did not change the need to protect trade and interests abroad. Both the British and the French built second-class battleships (which in the Royal Navy were superseded for a time by armoured cruisers) for individual operations on distant stations. They had both a cruising role and a port defence role; they backed unarmoured cruisers.

The situation began to change as underwater weapons developed. The American Civil War showed that underwater attack, e.g. by mines, could damage or sink large ships in confined waters. It might be difficult or even impossible for the coast defence ships to approach an enemy port to destroy the fleet inside. With all its difficulties, a fleet operating well offshore might be the only viable means of wielding sea power. That in turn demanded creation of a steam equivalent to the earlier sailing battle fleet, capable of fighting in the open sea. The further from a port the fleet had to remain, the more it would need scouts – fleet cruisers.

A fleet forced (by the torpedo and mine threat) to stand well outside the port containing an enemy fleet badly needed scouts. The attacking fleet also wanted to be able to use torpedoes, and cruisers turned out to be better torpedo platforms than battleships: they enabled an admiral to wield his two disparate weapons, gun and torpedo, flexibly. Too, a British fleet waiting for an enemy fleet to come out might well find itself pursuing that fleet. In 1884 the *Mersey*s and their immediate successors were described as adjuncts to the ironclads capable both of scouting and of forcing a faster enemy fleet to action (the French in particular seemed to be building faster capital ships). That justified arming them with heavy guns. As the manoeuvre experience described below shows, the cruiser was soon seen primarily as a scout – and it was wanted in ever-increasing numbers.

The cruiser role changed again beginning in 1896, when DNC Sir William White sold the Admiralty Board the idea that new lightweight armour made it possible to produce a cruiser with battleship protection – in effect, the battlecruiser.

Fleet Operations: The 1884 Analysis
The rising role of cruisers within fleets is evident in an 1884 analysis of the fleet Britain would need in a war against France, at that time the most powerful potentially hostile sea power. It was conducted by Captain W H Hall, head of the Foreign Intelligence Committee.[13] Hall's work seems to have been an attempt to stave off increasingly loud voices arguing that the Royal Navy had fallen behind the French. Hall's analysis offers a contemporary professional picture of the sort of naval war the Royal Navy expected to fight.

There must still have been advocates of convoy operations: Hall took pains to reject both convoy and other proposed means of trade protection as impossibly expensive (and also as unacceptably defensive). A modern reader might be surprised by how little of the French navy was normally active. Most of it, like most of the British fleet, was in various levels of reserve, awaiting activation by called-up reservists (the idea of nucleus crews was far in the future). Thus the offensive concept was to deal with the active enemy fleet at sea while rushing blockading squadrons to seal the rest in before they could be activated to the point of steaming out. Since reservists came from the merchant fleet, and since the British had a far larger merchant fleet than the French, it was reasonable to imagine that the British could mobilize more quickly. For that matter, mobilization would be a war warning.

Hall advocated mounting an immediate offensive against French forces overseas and already active in the Mediterranean (which might otherwise attack British shipping) while blocking the main French ports (containing the bulk of the [unmobilized] French fleet), destroying French shipbuilding facilities, and also destroying overseas coaling stations and bases.

Aside from ships deployed on foreign stations, the active French fleet consisted of an Evolutionary Squadron based on Toulon and an Eastern Squadron based in the Levant, looking after French interests in Syria. The Evolutionary Squadron consisted of two first-class and four second-class armour-clads, one despatch vessel (to link it to the command ashore), a gun-vessel, and two torpedo boats (it seems unlikely that the latter could go very far to sea; they were presumably to ensure that the squadron could get to sea in the event a hostile fleet appeared). A fifth second-class armour-clad was in 1st Reserve at Toulon, hence could probably get to sea to join the squadron. To deal with this squadron Hall envisaged a British fleet consisting of two first-class and six second-class armour-clads plus two corvettes and six torpedo vessels. The corvettes were presumably the fleet's scouts, and the expectation probably was that the French would be caught in Toulon. The French Eastern Squadron consisted of a frigate and two corvettes, against which Hall envisaged a British squadron headed by a frigate and three corvettes (first-class rather than second).

Hall did not envisage sending fleets into French harbours. Each of his blockading fleets included both means of defence against the torpedo boats (torpedo vessels, which soon emerged as torpedo gunboats) and scouts (typically a frigate and two corvettes). Hall did not say so, but presumably the frigate would normally watch the port, the corvettes linking her to the armoured squadron further offshore. The exceptions were Cherbourg, for which Hall allocated one first-class and three second-class corvettes; Rochefort, for which he allocated two corvettes. At the time it appeared that the French were building much larger torpedo craft in the form of avisos, capable of operating well offshore on a sustained basis and thus denying all British ships, even corvettes, a clear view of the ships in a harbour or even of the harbour entrance.

Hall's strategy of trade protection required instant destruction of every French force abroad, because every such force could be used against British trade. Thus he listed each British foreign station with the ships normally present and the corresponding French foreign station. There were obvious imbalances, because the two countries valued their overseas possessions rather differently. For example, the British squadron on the Australia station consisted of a second-class ironclad, a corvette, two sloops, and three gunboats. Facing this force at New Caledonia, the French had a fast sloop, a gun-vessel, and two small gunboats, hardly a match. Hall thought a corvette, a sloop, and two gun-vessels would suffice to overwhelm the French. He clearly separated fleets into categories, seeking equality or superiority in each category. Thus he accepted that any ironclad could overwhelm every unarmoured ship, but he does not seem to have accepted that even several gunboats or gun-vessels would have no chance against a corvette or frigate, hence that the attacking British force did not have to include small unarmoured craft.

French foreign interests were clearly concentrated in China (their force included one second-class ironclad and three third-class, plus five corvettes) and in a second Pacific force based at Tahiti (one second-class ironclad, a corvette, and two sloops). At this time the British counted what would later be called armoured cruisers as second-class ironclads, so the apparent deficit in such ships was a deficit in cruisers.

Hall classified unarmoured ships as frigates (with a covered battery) of first or second class (speed at least 14½ or 10kts, respectively, and of at least 3000 and 2500 tons, respectively), as corvettes of first, second, and third classes (first: at least 3000 tons, speed not less than 14½kts; second, at least 1700 tons, speed not less than 12kts; and third class, at least 1400 tons, speed not less than 11kts), plus sloops, gun-vessels, and gunboats.

Hall's analysis showed the Royal Navy with a deficiency of 14 armour-clads (first and second class), 37 frigates and corvettes, 97 torpedo vessels, and also auxiliaries. The British had too many third-class armour-clads (10), coast defence armour-clads (5), small unarmoured ships (sloops and below: 37), and torpedo boats (20). The coast defence armour-clads could be employed in some of the operations envisaged, but not the old third-class armour-clads, whose belts could be penetrated by even moderate-calibre guns. They were in effect the left-overs of the building race with France twenty years earlier, and the deficit in more modern armour-clads could be blamed on the habit among successive governments to count the entire British armoured fleet as equivalent, hence to downplay obsolescence. The excessive number of small unarmoured ships could be traced to the need to maintain a maritime police force in a large maritime empire. Nine of them might replace second-class corvettes, albeit inefficiently.

The Royal Navy could not execute all of Hall's envisaged operations simultaneously, but it could begin by attacking all French ships in commission. The French ships active on foreign stations were clearly the most dangerous to British trade, as they could be sent on that mission 'by a flash of the telegraph'. With the exception of China, the British already had powerful enough forces on foreign stations to deal with the French; that was the case even in the Mediterranean. China was a worse proposition. Not only were the French more powerful, but some of their cruisers were faster than anything the British had. Thus the French had the options both of attacking Hong Kong and of attacking British commerce in the Far East. Hall's only solution was to commission six of the fastest British merchant steamers using crews taken from the collection of unarmoured ships already in the Far East. The merchant ships might not be as fast as the French cruisers on a short-time basis, but they would be able to sustain full speed for very much longer, and would not have to coal nearly as often. Once the French squadrons abroad had been dealt with, the remaining British forces would deal with French coaling stations and commercial ports, thus dramatically reducing further French ability to attack British trade.

The British armour-clads in home and Mediterranean waters could meanwhile attack the French ports. This was not blockade, but rather something more like the direct attack of the past. For example, Hall suggested that the five armour-clads in commission in the Channel and First Reserve Squadrons plus the coast defence armour-clad in commission at Portsmouth could form a squadron to attack Cherbourg, the strongest of the French Channel ports, by day, and then disperse to attack the rest simultaneously. After those attacks it would reform as an observation (not blockading, in Hall's words) force off Cherbourg, to prevent the ships there from coming out. If the initial bombardment sufficiently damaged the ships in Cherbourg, the squadron might proceed to attack Brest. Hall wrote that he deliberately avoided using the term blockade because he considered it impossible to establish a true blockade by any squadron which did not include torpedo vessels (i.e., torpedo gunboats).

The Mediterranean ships in commission would watch Toulon. Some of these ships might be sent to reinforce the China station. The Mediterranean would be reinforced by armour-clads in reserve at home and at Malta.

All of this suggests that at this time the French did not yet have sufficient ocean-going torpedo boats to prevent a force from bombarding a port from just outside, but that earlier ideas of actually entering the port in force to destroy the ships inside were no longer practicable.

In effect Hall showed that the existing British force could fight a naval war against France as long as it did not try to execute all necessary offensive operations simultaneously. There was one essential caveat. The necessary blockades could not be enforced so long as fleets had to stay well out to sea at night to avoid French torpedo boat attacks. Thus Hall's most important recommendation was the mass purchase of what he called torpedo vessels, anti-torpedo boat ships. He noted in passing that some of the French cruisers were considerably faster than their British counterparts, and the only solution he could offer in the near term was to take up and arm large liners. Hall also pointed out that his war plan required that several British squadrons keep the sea for a sustained period; to do that he advocated large fast auxiliaries carrying stores, ammunition, and, most important, coal. As there was no way of transferring coal in the open sea, Hall proposed doing so either in protected waters or in neutral ports (where the usual restrictions on what neutrals could supply in wartime would not apply).

Hall listed deficiencies in terms of his plan for simultaneous operations. They amounted to 5 first-class and 9 second-class armour-clads; 2 frigates; 8 first-class and 35 second-class corvettes; and lesser craft (these numbers did not take into account the replacement of some corvettes by sloops). Hall's program was not affordable, but it seems to have shaped what was done. For example, the need for nine second-class armour-clads may well have been met by the construction of the seven *Orlando* class belted cruisers plus *Imperieuse* and *Warspite*, which were seen as small battleships. The two frigates were, in effect, the big first-class cruisers *Blake* and *Blenheim*. Eight *Leander* and *Mersey* class cruisers, which Hall might have considered first-class corvettes, were already under construction. Within a few years the Royal Navy would have a substantial fleet of third-class cruisers which might fill Hall's requirement for second-class corvettes.[14] The deficit in ironclads was considerably reduced (but the cruiser situation complicated) as the French tried a new naval strategy (*jeune école*) based on a combination of base and harbour defence by torpedo boat and commerce warfare (*guerre de course*) abroad.

It was accepted that in wartime the Royal Navy would need far more cruisers than it could afford to build in peacetime. The solution often advanced was to take up merchant ships from trade and arm them. DNC Nathaniel Barnaby described what would be needed.[15] For a time the parsimonious Gladstone administration seems to have imagined that armed merchant ships were viable substitutes for all cruisers. The British first tested the armed merchant cruiser idea during the Anglo-Russian crisis in 1877-78, HMS *Hecla* being retained in effect as a test case. Several fast liners were chartered in 1885 during another war scare. The only one commissioned into the Royal Navy, *Oregon*, performed impressively. Within a year or so, possibly due to a change in administration, it seems to have been accepted that, although they would be useful in wartime, fast armed merchant ships were no substitutes for real cruisers.

Fleet Manoeuvres and Their Lessons

The first formal large-scale British naval manoeuvres (June–July 1885) provide an idea of contemporary tactics.[16] The fleet (the Particular Service Squadron) had been assembled for Baltic operations, and it was known that the Russians had large numbers of torpedo boats. The fleet was commanded by Admiral Sir Geoffrey Phipps Hornby, probably the most skilled living British operational commander. He had fourteen ironclads (the term battleship was not yet used). Six unarmoured ships were lookouts when the fleet cruised: *Conquest* (right ahead), *Mercury* (on starboard bow), *Leander* (on port bow), *Racer* (on starboard quarter), *Mariner* (on port quarter), and *Cormorant* (right astern). *Mercury* was the first of the new fast steel cruisers, and *Leander* was a larger and somewhat slower successor. *Conquest* was a considerably slower protected cruiser (corvette). *Mariner* and *Racer* were 970-ton sloops, and *Cormorant* was an 1130-ton sloop. The fleet was accompanied by the torpedo depot ship (converted merchantman) *Hecla* and eight torpedo boats. It was later joined by the torpedo ram *Polyphemus*. The 8kt average fleet speed while manoeuvring was too fast for the sloops *Mariner* and *Racer* to keep station.

Berehaven played the part of a Russian port the fleet might blockade. The fleet anchored outside, protected (it was hoped) by controlled mines it laid, by a boom, and by searchlights. The corvette *Conquest* was sent out with four torpedo boats to watch the port. The corvette squadron (*Conquest*, *Mercury*, *Racer*, *Mariner*) and four torpedo boats represented the inshore

HMS *Swallow* was a composite-built *Nymphe* class sloop. All later sloops had steel hulls. She was not too much smaller than ships classified as corvettes (cruisers) a few years earlier, displacing 1140 tons (195ft pp × 28ft × 12ft 6in), and she had about the same speed as *Calypso* class cruisers (13.5kts on 1570 IHP). She was armed with eight 5in guns and eight machine guns. *Swallow* was built by Sheerness, launched 27 October 1885. She was sold for scrap in 1904.

HMS *Mutine* was one of the last sloops built for the Royal Navy. She built under contract by Laird, launched on 1 March 1900. She was one of six *Condor* class, which were followed by six *Cadmus* class. These ships survived to fight during the First World War. Armament was six 4in QF: two on the forecastle, two in the waist, two on the poop. Twenty years before, her steaming performance would have matched that of a *Comus* class cruiser – 13.5kts (1400 IHP) – but by 1900 cruisers were making 20kts or more. Thus *Mutine* and her like were considered specialist maritime police ships. She was steel-hulled and entirely unprotected.

squadron of a blockading fleet. The ships in port were to sortie while torpedo boats (the other four first-class boats and four second-class from the ironclads) drove off the blockading squadron. The blockaders were to keep in touch with the escaping squadron long enough to be sure of their course. The three escaping ironclads were spotted by a torpedo boat. At daylight they had *Mercury* and *Mariner* on either side, out of gun range. A passage to Blacksod Bay proved that the torpedo boats working with the fleet could hardly be considered seagoing.

A temporary base would have been created so that an anchored fleet and its service vessels (including colliers and transports) could shelter from Russian torpedo attacks. The fleet tested a combination of booms and mines (both contact and controlled). Admiral Phipps Hornby wrote that 'a boom to [rams] is as a bit of pack-thread' – *Polyphemus* smashed the boom at Berehaven. It would take mines to deal with rams.

Existing torpedo boats (Nos *21* and *22*) were unable to attack *Mercury* when the latter was steaming in open water at 16kts. *Mercury* was deemed to have sunk one of the torpedo boats by the fire of her stern and machine guns.

In a second phase of the exercise, the fleet split into attacking and defending squadrons. The attackers had six ironclads plus the torpedo ram *Polyphemus*. Their six lookouts were the fast cruiser *Mercury*, the sloop *Racer*, the seagoing gunboat *Express*, the coastal gunboats (each with a heavy gun) *Medina* and *Snap*, and the tug *Seahorse*. One object was to see whether small handy ships like the gunboats and the tug could defend a fleet against night torpedo attack. The gunboats proved slow, particularly in a seaway (Admiral Phipps Hornby: 'during the forenoon we had striking evidence of what a clog on the speed of the squadron the heavy-gun gunboats become, invaluable as they are in narrow waters and for many purposes'). For the long passage the gunboats had to be towed by the armoured ships, badly reducing their speed. Finally the fleet included the torpedo depot ship *Hecla* with four first-class torpedo boats. The defenders (seven ironclads) had four lookouts: the fast converted liner *Oregon* (taken up from trade due to the war emergency), the corvette *Conquest*, and the sloops *Mariner* and *Cormorant*. It included two gunboats (*Medway* and *Pike*) and four first-class torpedo boats.

Other exercises had the attacking fleet running at night to elude surveillance by the fast armed merchant cruiser *Oregon*. Phipps Hornby noted: 'the only thought in everyone's mind was "Where is she?" If she caught sight of us our chance was gone, as we had nothing fast enough to prevent her from dogging our steps and acquainting her admiral what place we were steering for.' However, the exercise proved that no one

could prevent a squadron of ironclads from getting to sea in thick weather, even when nights were short. The enemy fleet's object was to get 30 to 35nm offshore before daylight, for which 8kts sufficed. The line of eight ironclads was only 8 cables long (one cable was a tenth of a nautical mile) and the width 2 cables, 'a small space to find in thick weather'. It was pointless to maintain a blockading squadron of ironclads at sea off a port, burning down their coal supply. They would be better off sheltering in a nearby port with bunkers full, waiting for a scout's report.

A few cruisers offshore were not enough. Ideally there should be a line of torpedo vessels (i.e., torpedo cruisers) between port and blockading fleet, at the least to warn the fleet that the enemy was sending torpedo boats against it. The line of patrols should be as far as possible from the fleet. Although sloops like *Mariner* and *Racer* were both handy and well-armed, they were not fast enough. *Mercury* was fast but too large and expensive to risk against a torpedo boat. She would have to move so far from the port mouth at night to avoid attack by a torpedo boat so as to make her a useless picket.

Phipps Hornby concluded that he wanted (i) fast vessels, (ii) seagoing torpedo boats in numbers, and (iii) the means to shelter the fast torpedo boats while coaling, so that they could accompany the fleet overseas. To some extent the first two requirements were combined in torpedo cruisers and also in faster cruisers.

Captain J A Fisher, the future First Sea Lord, accompanied the fleet as Captain of HMS *Excellent*, the gunnery school (and ordnance experimental establishment). He supplied both the detailed narrative in the official report and detailed conclusions. Ironclad squadrons (six ships) should be accompanied by at least four fast unarmoured ships (cruisers) with moderate heavy gun power but with numerous quick-firing guns (to deal with torpedo craft). They would serve both as lookouts and as supports for the torpedo boat destroyers (torpedo boats armed mainly with guns, the first time this term was used) working with the ironclads. 'It is obvious that they cannot perform these duties efficiently or avoid certain destruction by the modern fast ironclads unless their speed is also great and approximate to that of the first-class torpedo boats.'

Each ironclad squadron should also be accompanied by at least two seagoing torpedo boats plus a fast torpedo depot ship with commanding speed (such as the *Oregon*) carrying second-class torpedo boats, and also stores (mines and booms) to defend a temporary fleet anchorage. The torpedo boats should have an alternative gun armament to beat off torpedo boat attacks (Fisher used the phrase 'torpedo boat destroyer' for this role). Half the boats, equipped for defence, should be placed ahead of the squadron on going into action, the others (attackers) steaming astern of their ironclads, 'ready to act in the smoke and confusion when the opposing ironclads pass each other'.

Fisher foreshadowed much of the cruiser development which followed soon after. His fast cruisers were the *Medea*s and their successors. His seagoing torpedo boats were the torpedo cruisers and then the torpedo gunboats. Fisher specifically rejected building a special-purpose torpedo depot ship, but his idea for her was embodied in the depot ship/cruiser *Vulcan*.

There were no 1886 manoeuvres, but in 1887 they followed the Queen's Jubilee Review off Spithead.[17] The fleet was organized into three cruising squadrons (A, B, and C) and four coast defence flotillas. Squadron A was ten ironclads (including *Imperieuse*) and four cruisers (including *Curlew*); B was another ten ironclads and four cruisers, and C was six cruisers (including the slow *Calypso*). The coast defence units included both ironclads and first-class torpedo boats plus, in some cases, gunboats. The general idea was that British squadrons had lost touch with an enemy fleet which had put to sea to do maximum damage to English ports in the Channel and in the Thames and Medway while avoiding any engagement. The enemy was represented by the second divisions of A and B squadrons: five ironclads, *Archer* and *Curlew* (A) and five ironclads and the cruisers *Amphion* and *Mohawk*. The first division of A defended against the second division of A, the first division of B against the second division of B. C squadron was to try to pass through the North Channel without being discovered or, if so, attacked by the coast defence units. A second exercise had two cruisers entering the Irish Channel to attack commerce in the face of four British cruisers and the coast defence units. The defending element of B squadron spotted the attackers by their smoke and managed to use its cruisers to hold contact with them for 21 hours, so that it could bring the attackers to action. The A squadron defenders had no such luck (its enemy succeeded in attacking Falmouth, but failed to attack the Thames, where it would have been trapped). Torpedo boats proved effective in attacking the C cruisers during their first operation.[18]

The trade protection exercise must have been sobering. *Calypso* was soon captured by the faster cruiser *Rover*, but *Volage* was never captured (she narrowly avoided HMS *Inconstant*). She claimed 16 vessels off Liverpool, 5 off the entrance to the Clyde, and 36 in Kingstown harbour. Of the 57 in total, there were 14 steamers (but only 6 of any importance), 14 coasters, and 21 yachts. Most of the ships captured at Liverpool were lying off the bar waiting for the tide (capture required that the cruiser remain within a mile of the prize for half an hour, then stop for an hour, the latter representing the time to board a vessel, examine her papers, and put a prize crew aboard or sink the vessel). Umpires pointed out that *Volage* claimed 14 ships at the same time, which was unrealistic. Even simply sinking the ships would have taken longer. The umpires also doubted that *Volage* could have operated freely in the face of the coast defence flotillas envisaged in the other phases of the exercise. She had to get too close to them, and to fixed defences, to find her prey. Cruisers generally proved considerably slower than expected. Against trial (measured mile) speeds of 15.1kts and 16.2kts for *Volage* and *Inconstant*, actual speeds (when the ships were doing their best) were 12 and 11.8kts. However, *Rover* and *Calypso* attained 14¼kts and 13¼kts, respectively, which were much closer to trial speeds.

A, B, and C squadrons were attacked by torpedo boats. Anchored at Spithead, A squadron relied on nets, guns, and rifle fire, plus outlying small craft and torpedo boats. An attack by twenty-two torpedo boats led by the torpedo gunboat *Rattlesnake* failed. B and C were anchored at Portland, with a boom, wire hawsers, and mines laid across the mouth of the anchorage, plus fixed searchlight beams and small craft. Most of the torpedo boats managed to cut through the boom.

HMS *Avon* was a *Beacon* class composite gun-vessel, the category below a sloop. These ships and the larger *Plover*s were conceived as replacements for decayed Crimean War gunboats, particularly for action in China. About thirty of these earlier ships were sent to China to fight in the wars of the 1850s and 1860s. They proved useful, although the ten which attacked the Peiho forts were beaten off with the loss of three of their number. Because the Crimean War gunboats were built of unseasoned timber, they had to be discarded within about a decade. Thus by 1863 work on a replacement was urgent; the *Plover*s were the first new cruising vessels laid down after the mass cancellations of large screw frigates. The engines were still good, and they featured in the *Avon* class replacement ships (four ships did get new engines). The main lesson of the Chinese operations was that the 32pdr armament of the Crimean War gunboats was inadequate. On the one hand something heavier was needed to deal with forts; on the other something firing faster was needed to deal with armed junks and with pirates. Draught had to be limited, so Robinson and Reed selected twin rather than single screws. The *Plover*s were of conventional wooden type, but for the smaller follow-on *Avon*s Reed combined an iron frame with wooden planking – the first British composite hull. The hull was flat-bottomed and square-bilged for about three-quarters of her length; Admiral Ballard described her as almost on the lines of an elongated packing case. The result was a steady gun platform and a buoyant sea boat, and the flat bottom made it easier to deal with frequent grounding. On the other hand, the ships steered erratically in a following sea, and they could not avoid drifting sideways in a strong cross-wind. As the first ships below battleship size with iron frames, they were also the first such ships with watertight bulkheads. Planned armament was two 68pdr smooth-bore muzzle-loaders and two 20pdr breech-loaders at the ends, but ships had one 7in 6½-ton (between funnel and mainmast) and one 64pdr (between funnel and foremast: both muzzle-loading rifles) instead of the two 64pdrs (they retained the 20pdrs). The two different calibres of heavy guns were adopted because two 64pdrs would have been inadequate and

INTRODUCTION

However, they were considered put out of action either by the patrolling craft or by the guns of the outer line of ships. It seemed that the problems of torpedo defence raised by the 1885 manoeuvres had been solved.

The first conclusion was that a squadron needed more than two scouts, to search a wider area, to allow for breakdowns, and to allow for ships absent while coaling. Ships needed better-trained and more numerous signal staff, with more practice in distant signalling by day and night. Local defensive squadrons would greatly assist in the protection not only of British ports but also of trade, which would inevitably concentrate off the ports. Rapid coaling was essential, and the battleships of a squadron should all have the same speed. Above all, manoeuvres should be conducted on an annual basis.

The 1888 manoeuvres were staged while the Naval Defence Act of 1889 was being framed. They were far more sophisticated than those of 1887. At the sudden outbreak of war, two enemy squadrons (fleet B) in ports some distance apart were preparing for action.[19] The British (fleet A) established blockades of both bases, and the blockaded forces tried to emerge. Each fleet consisted of battleships, fast cruisers, and torpedo boats. The fleet A was numerically stronger than the enemy (B). A1 was based at Pembroke, A2 at Lamlash Bay; B1 was based at Berehaven and B2 at Lough Swilly. England and Scotland were friendly to A, Ireland to B. The object of the B fleet was (1) to attack commerce off the coast of Ireland, in the Irish and entrance to the Bristol Channels and in the English Channel, (2) to attack ports on the west and south coast of England, other than those counted as heavily fortified, and (3) to land troops on any unfortified position.

A1 consisted of seven ironclads and seven cruisers (including the torpedo cruiser *Rattlesnake*). A2 consisted of another five older ironclads, six cruisers (including the torpedo cruisers *Tartar* and *Mohawk* and the torpedo gunboat *Grasshopper*) and twelve first-class torpedo boats. In cruising order the A1 cruisers were dispersed ahead and astern of the two columns of ironclads. Those ahead were to stay 'within signal distance'; the two ships astern were to stay within two miles. A collier trailed the ironclads. When A1 and A2 steamed together, a column of six cruisers steamed alongside the main body, other cruisers being dispersed before and abaft the main body. Against A1, B1 had six ironclads (including the armoured cruiser *Warspite*) and five cruisers (including the torpedo cruiser *Cossack* and the gunboat *Sandfly*). B2 was four ironclads and five cruisers (including the torpedo gunboat *Spider*).

The blockading force off Berehaven consisted of an inner line of lookouts (six torpedo boats and a torpedo gunboat), an inner cruiser squadron, and an outer squadron of ironclads, plus one cruiser and one torpedo boat at each of two telegraphic centres, to which Admiralty intelligence would be sent.[20] If the enemy broke out without being followed, the two A fleet squadrons would rendezvous.

Once the enemy had broken out, in effect A adopted a focal area strategy. A division was assigned to watch Liverpool for two days, after which it would leave a force (two ironclads, a cruiser, and a torpedo boat) to guard that port, falling on Milford Haven in the face of a superior enemy force. The rest of this division was to guard the western part of the English Channel. Cruisers were detached to protect merchant shipping

two 6½-ton guns too heavy to carry; later the Admiralty planned to replace both with the new 7in 4½-ton (90cwt) gun, but that was done only for *Rocket*, *Lynx*, *Hornet*, *Flirt*, and *Rifleman*. *Avon*, *Elk*, and *Frolic* each had their 7in gun replaced by the lighter type. Although the ships were designed for river service, they first had to get to China (or other rivers: ships also served in West Africa and in South America) on their own bottoms, which meant sailing. These ships displaced 603 tons (they had been designed for 584); dimensions were 155ft × 25ft × 11ft. Eighteen were built under the 1867-68 program, and another four under the 1871-72 program. *Avon* was launched at Portsmouth on 2 October 1867, and discarded in 1890. She served in China, in West Africa, and in South America.

HMS *Ringdove* was a *Redbreast* class screw gunboat armed with six 4in guns. She displaced 805 tons (165ft pp × 31ft × 11ft) and could make 13kts (1200 IHP). She was launched on 30 April 1889, and was discarded in 1906 as part of Admiral Fisher's program of scrapping ships which could 'neither fight nor run away'.
(Allan C Green, courtesy of State Library of Victoria)

between the North Foreland and Land's End.

Objects were to determine (1) the most efficient distribution of a blockading squadron both day and night; (2) the best means of maintaining communication between scouts and the main body of a fleet; (3) the relative advantages and disadvantages of keeping the main body of a fleet off a blockaded port using an inshore squadron, or of keeping it at a nearby base, maintaining a cruiser and torpedo boat force off the blockaded port, 'with means of rapid communication with the Fleet' (radio did not yet exist); (4) the best means of keeping a blockading fleet supplied with coal; (5) the best means of using torpedo boats, both with and against a blockading fleet; (6) the best means of keeping track of hostile cruisers attempting to attack trade; (7) the best kind of identification signals for a fortified port and minefield; and (8) how to deal with the special dangers to which a blockading squadron would be exposed. These were not too different from the problems laid out in the 1885 manoeuvres.

A Squadron reported that the exercise rules much favoured the blockaded fleet: it was impossible 'to put a torpedo boat out of action except through the stupidity of the officer in charge of her ... and cruisers could with impunity brave the fire of the blockading force'. Fleet A considered its best blockade disposition to be with seagoing torpedo vessels innermost, then fast cruisers, and only then ironclads, the ironclads having cruisers on their flanks. The ships should be end-on to the shore, never exposing their broadsides, with their heads offshore if possible so that they could chase any emerging enemy force. This position would also make ramming much more difficult. To guard against ramming, ships should keep up full steam – which would run down their coal. Ships standing offshore should be able to protect themselves against torpedo attack using nets, but 'in the whole fleet there is not an efficient net defence that could, if down at sea, be raised quickly clear of gun fire; and very few nets that would be safe down, if steaming 4 or 5kts'.

Two torpedo boats and one catcher (torpedo gunboat) should be attached to each ironclad. The blockading fleet should have 50 per cent more ironclads than its enemy, and twice as many cruisers (and those of the highest possible speed). The inner blockade force should include a proportion of torpedo boats and catchers kept with the fleet to carry despatches, to scout, and for other purposes. Torpedo boats should work in pairs, if possible supported by catchers.

Given the fragility of torpedo boats, a refuge should be set up for them on the nearby coast. Torpedo catchers (torpedo gunboats) were far more serviceable than torpedo boats, and could work in much worse weather. They were not nearly as exhausting for crews. Commanding B Squadron, Admiral Tryon considered catchers 'of very great value. I have a very high opinion of them.'

Cruisers and certain ironclads should be assigned nightly to chase and run down any enemy ships that might escape, special care being taken to assign enough to make capture certain. The chasing ships should be accompanied by catchers, which could report back to the admiral commanding the blockading squadron.

Any enemy ship seen escaping should be followed by torpedo catchers (torpedo gunboats or torpedo cruisers), which would shine their searchlights on them while signalling the fleet, not giving up the chase until relieved by ships of the outer line. If enemy ships escaped in fog, a captive balloon would be a great help, determining which ships were still in harbour . It should be flown by a ship far enough offshore to be safe from enemy fire. In moderate weather, ships should be visible, particularly from aloft, three or four miles away.

A telegraph ship should be attached to the blockading squadron, and a cable laid from the home base to it.

It seemed most efficient to keep in touch with scouts via fast cruisers ('in which we are at present sadly deficient'). Unless there was a nearby anchorage, the ironclads had to be kept constantly under way. To keep them fuelled, the fleet should include 10kt colliers, which would coal ships at their temporary base. Ships should fuel at every opportunity. Seagoing torpedo vessels were vital to the blockading fleet, as they could prevent the enemy from launching harassing torpedo attacks designed to break up the blockade. The enemy would be forced to seek a general action, in which case the torpedo vessels would fall back on the main body of ironclads.

There was no real hope that the blockaders could rest in a nearby port while the enemy was watched by cruisers and torpedo vessels. Enemy ironclads could drive them off and then get away in fog.

The chief dangers facing a blockading fleet were (1) running out of coal, (2) torpedo attacks, and (3) surprise by a second fleet working with the blockaded fleet. Squadron A was weakened daily by ships detached to coal, sometimes in a bay 60 miles away. It had a cruiser at Lamlash waiting for telegrams, a torpedo boat away for repairs, and a ship watering torpedo boats in a sheltered area. This was quite aside from accidents. In good weather the blockading fleet could coal at sea, a ship taking on 20 to 30 tons an hour from a collier. Special fleet colliers might be built.

Ships were not fast enough, and the official fleet handbook (*Steamships of England*) overstated what they could do. The chief defects in the fleet were in boilers, generally due to using forced draught 'which in my [commander of A Squadron] opinion, is the ruin of them. Forced draught is not supposed to be used unless in emergency, but having the power, emergency is certain to arise some time or other. This, and a very inferior class of Stokers, as well as Engineer Officers being strange to machinery, which they have had to work at high speeds without much experience in many of the ships, were the causes of failure in boilers and engines.'

Of the cruisers, only *Mercury* maintained anything like her reputed speed. *Mersey* was reduced to 12kts after running 300nm at 17kts. *Thames* never attained more than 15kts, and stopped continually to deal with defects in steam pipes. *Arethusa* was good for 15kts. The *Archer* class torpedo cruisers were all reduced to 11 to 13kts. These ships were too heavily armed; the weights of their heavy guns fore and aft made them pitch excessively. In many cases (not just in cruisers) coal was very inferior and smoky. Tryon (B Squadron) commented that 'ships are now apt to be too complicated and unnecessarily so. Everything should be as simple as possible. There is often a want of good means of communicating with the engine-room ... Electrical fittings and arrangements have been largely used in substitution of mechanical fittings and appliances, and they failed far too often.' Tryon also complained that ships were too beamy, as a result of which they could steam well in a calm but not in even a moderate sea. He particularly cited the armoured cruiser *Warspite*, which he wrote had been criticized in comparison with foreign ships five years earlier.

In September 1888 the Admiralty appointed a special committee to draw lessons from the manoeuvres, presumably ultimately for Cabinet and parliamentary consumption.[21] The report was submitted on 21 November. The first key conclusion was that steam and torpedoes had made blockade so dangerous that a blockading fleet had to be in the proportion of 5 to 3 to the fleet being blockaded, to allow for casualties which the fleet in harbour would not be risking. An even larger margin would be needed if the area covered by the blockaders were extensive, since in that case the entire blockading fleet might not be concentrated in one place. If the blockading fleet could lie in a nearby port, the proportion might be reduced to 4 to 3. The proportion of cruisers should be at least 2 to 1 in favour of the blockaders, so that any enemy cruisers trying to break out could be run down without weakening the force off the port; at the least, there should be a cruiser to each battleship. Torpedo gunboats would be of 'incalculable value' to the blockading fleet, but first-class torpedo boats would be useful mainly to those being blockaded. They would be worthwhile if they could be carried on board a special ship (superior to *Hecla*; for some reason there was no mention of *Vulcan*, then being built). On occasion the second-class torpedo boats aboard battleships would be useful (but the committee much preferred the new picket boats, which could be armed with torpedoes, as they were better seaboats).

It seemed to the Committee that the A and B squadrons fairly represented the full British and French forces in home waters. These two squadrons together were the entire British naval force available for general purposes in wartime – to reinforce the Mediterranean and distant squadrons, to maintain superiority in the Channel, and to maintain a considerable light squadron off the Irish coast. The manoeuvres implied that the Channel Fleet had to be powerful enough to blockade the French Atlantic ports, leaving a sufficient reserve to hold the Channel and protect the coasts and commerce of the United Kingdom, with sufficient battleships and cruisers to reinforce squadrons abroad and to form detached squadrons.

As of July 1888, the British had in home waters (in commission or in reserve) 22 battleships and 23 cruisers and gunboats. In the Mediterranean were 8 ironclads (including the torpedo ram *Polyphemus*), 4 cruisers, 3 sloops, 4 gunboats, and a despatch vessel. Including ships in reserve but ready for commissioning in Toulon, the French Mediterranean fleet consisted of 15 ironclads, 2 armoured gunboats, 5 first- and second-class cruisers, 11 third-class cruisers and gunboats, 4 torpedo cruisers and avisos, and 7 seagoing torpedo boats.

Had war broken out, to give the Mediterranean Fleet equal forces, 9 ironclads and 13 cruisers would have had to go there, leaving 13 battleships (including 3 coast defence ships) and 10 cruisers in the Channel and reserve squadrons. They would be watching a French fleet in Cherbourg of 5 seagoing ironclads, 6 coast defence ironclads (including 2 gunboats), 6 cruisers, 8 avisos (including 4 torpedo avisos), and 4 seagoing torpedo boats. In addition, the French had ships at Brest (2 ironclads, 4 first- and second-class cruisers, 1 third-class cruiser), Lorient (7 cruisers, 6 of them third-class), and Rochefort (5 third-class cruisers and avisos).

The total British force was 'manifestly altogether inadequate' against France alone; 'and should the fleets of one other Power – say of that Great Power [Russia] whose Imperial interests may be said to clash most with those of the British Empire – have been joined to those of France against Great Britain at that time, the balance of maritime strength would have been most decidedly against her'. As an emergency measure, the old but still serviceable ironclads should be brought into condition to be activated in an emergency. The system, in force since 1870, of recommissioning ships abroad over and over again 'has, in great measure, brought about a dearth of reserves'.

None of the analysis took into account ships under construction, and the Committee thought the situation would be better in 1890-91; but no ironclads had been laid down since 1886 (i.e., since the Northbrook Program) and 'as there is nothing, in our opinion, to justify the belief that the days of ironclad battleships are over', further new construction was urgent. Since England could not control the question of peace and war, at any time a maritime power might challenge her; so 'we are decidedly of opinion that no time should be lost in placing the Navy of England beyond comparison with any two powers'.

'Putting Russia beside the question, there can be little doubt but that, were England involved in a war with France, and she were to resume her natural rights as a belligerent [i.e., rights of blockade and of seizing neutral ships with enemy cargoes on board], which appear to have been voluntarily laid aside by the Declaration of Paris, troubles with the United States would inevitably ensue, and her whole commercial position, and the immense carrying trade by which it is sustained, would be jeopardized at the outset were war to be forced upon her at a time when her Navy was weak.'

France had both military and naval power, but the British position depended entirely on naval supremacy, 'which has never seriously been challenged since the close of the last Great War [i.e., against Napoleon]. The defeat of her Navy means to her the loss of India and her Colonies and of her place among the nations.'

To the Committee, the arrangements made by A squadron to protect commerce, and those by B squadron to attack it, were much those that would be made in wartime by the admiral commanding the sole British Channel squadron and an enemy force. The B admiral at Berehaven judged that he was justified in breaking out both to attack trade and to attack major coastal cities, causing panic and inflicting great damage. He did so by attracting attention to his main body coming out of harbour while three of his cruisers escaped unobserved. He took a considerable risk, and almost lost two of his ironclads to torpedo attack, but the cruisers got out. B squadron cruisers also managed to break out of Lough Swilly unobserved; they also raided shipping and coastal towns. The British admiral blockading these fleets had decided that if as many as three ships broke out, he was unjustified in continuing the blockade and leaving the approaches to London, the heart of the Empire, uncovered. He also detached ships to cover Liverpool. That freed up the enemy forces, which merged and seized Liverpool. It seemed clear that the British fleet had not had enough cruisers to watch the enemy force, and thus to bring them to battle (as nearly happened off Liverpool, the British force having recently left). The British defending force had never had enough ships.

The blockaded force had an important advantage: continuous access to telegraph lines and thus to current intelligence, so long as it remained in port. Off Bantry the blockading admiral was 200 miles from the nearest telegraphic centre (and for purposes of the manoeuvres he was cut off from the natural source of intelligence, the Admiralty).

Overall, there could be no doubt that any maritime enemy 'would adopt every possible means of weakening her enemy; and we know of no means more efficacious for making an enemy feel the pinch of war than thus destroying his property, and touching his pocket'. The British admiral trying to protect British commerce was badly hampered by the lack of intelligence (under manoeuvre rules) and also by the absence, under his command, of coast defence ships which would otherwise have prevented single enemy cruisers from getting close to defended cities near which shipping would concentrate (i.e., he could not mount a focal area defence). The B fleet won. By definition, B had no floating commerce worth attacking, and the British could not spare any force to attack its capital and its coastal towns.

No cruisers could be spared to protect British commerce. Had Britain been fighting France, all such ships in commission would have been required by the Channel Fleet, watching the French naval ports, preventing their escape, and helping bring them to action if they broke out. Assuming that the enemy did not arm privateers, British commerce would have been relatively safe near British shores. It would be necessary to arrange convoys for the slower steamers (12kts or less); sailing ships would presumably be laid up. The Committee suggested further that groups of merchant steamers with strong bows, steaming together, might give a good account of themselves against unarmoured enemy cruisers, using their bows as a weapon. Without enough unarmoured cruisers to form detached squadrons off the entrances to St George's and the English Channels, and on the fishery grounds, merchant ships would have to be taken up from trade for that purpose.

The Royal Navy needed many more fast cruisers, in addition to the battleships the Committee obviously wanted. This mass of cruisers appeared in the Naval Defence Act of 1889, which might be seen as the outcome of the 1888 manoeuvres (and other efforts). A supplementary report examined the behaviour of various classes of ships; its remarks are given in the discussions of the *Leander*, *Mersey*, and *Archer* classes in later chapters.

The 1889 manoeuvres tested the extent to which a British fleet could mask an enemy fleet from strategic bases, its scouts keeping watch on the enemy's fleet in its own bases. This was very different from the close blockade envisaged earlier. It demanded much more numerous scouting forces plus ships linking the scouts to the main British fleet (there was no radio). In the first phase of the manoeuvres an enemy force trying to pass up the Channel was intercepted. In the second phase the enemy force evaded contact, passing around the north of Scotland into the North Sea, and bombarding East Coast towns before being defeated by a superior British fleet. [22]

The 1890 manoeuvres placed an enemy fleet on an important trade route.[23] The British fleet sought to engage it (the enemy fleet tried to avoid engagement). A secondary object was to find the best way to employ the considerable body of scouting cruisers on both sides. Each side could put cruisers to sea before the outbreak of war in order to watch the other fleet. At the outbreak of war the main British fleet was at Plymouth, a reserve British fleet was at Portland; it was allowed to move from one port to another as necessary. The enemy fleet was at Berehaven in Ireland (later it also used a base at Shannon). Upon declaration of war, the enemy fleet would enter the Channel from the West, the British fleet seeking to engage it. One artificial restriction was that cruisers, which in previous exercises had attacked trade directly, were limited to scouting and despatch (i.e., linking) services. The hostile fleet established a torpedo boat base (boats plus the cruiser [sloop] *Curlew*, other cruisers later joining) at Alderney in the Channel Islands to operate against any British fleet trying to use the Channel. The design of the exercise was somewhat complicated by the need not to interfere with actual shipping in the Channel.

The main British fleet was commanded by Vice Admiral Sir George Tryon, at that time the leading British tactician. He had nine battleships and thirteen cruisers and lesser craft, including the old unarmoured cruiser *Inconstant*, the armoured cruiser *Shannon*, and several torpedo gunboats. A second British fleet was created from the mobilized Reserve Squadron and based at Portland as a kind of coast defence force: six battleships and coast defence ships, the torpedo depot ship *Hecla*, and only three cruisers (the old cruiser *Active* and two torpedo gunboats). The Portland force also included twelve torpedo boats. The enemy had eight battleships, twelve cruisers, and twelve torpedo boats. The enemy fleet managed to get to sea unobserved. In the past, enemy fleets had generally been intercepted by British fleets lying off their bases, waiting for them to emerge. Once an enemy fleet lost itself in the trackless sea, the only hope of catching it was to guess its destination (or to gain intelligence of that destination). In 1798 Nelson found the French at Aboukir only by learning of their movements from ships in the Mediterranean, and it was crucial that they stayed at Aboukir long enough for him to get there. By 1890 the Admiralty was assembling operational intelligence, which could be distributed by telegraph to special signal stations around the British coast. Without radio, which did not yet exist, an admiral afloat had to rely on linking ships (or on ships steaming out from the coast) to provide him with that sort of information – i.e., on fast cruisers.

Tryon did have an important advantage. Like Milne, he knew that the only profitable place for an enemy to attack trade was in a focal area, so he concentrated his cruisers there. He also arranged to be in almost constant communication with the English coast, hence with the Admiralty intelligence centre. His first move was to send three powerful cruiser divisions to await the enemy fleet in the focal area. He soon sent a battle force out to back up the cruisers. Tryon's dispositions blocked a possible enemy run up the Channel. Tryon was thus the first to test the ability of modern materiel to combine an adequate defence of a vital spot of trade, to maintain regular and frequent communication with a base, and to keep the Channel clear of an enemy.

Tryon failed; he never brought the enemy fleet to battle. The two fleets were never closer than 300nm, and at the end of the manoeuvres they were 1700 nm apart. The umpires praised Tryon's use of his cruisers; the hostile fleet clearly did not consider cruiser scouting a primary object. The cruiser force Tryon wielded was not strong enough. An enemy who managed to get out of his port unobserved could still get away altogether. To the extent that there was a solution, it had to be more and faster cruisers, not least to link deployed scouts with the main body of a fleet.

The 1892 manoeuvres had a Red fleet in two separated divisions, trying to join up in the face of enemy (Blue) torpedo attacks – of the sort the French could and would mount from their side of the Channel against a British fleet whose bases were still dispersed (the Irish Channel played the part of the English Channel). The torpedo boats were backed by coast defence ships and cruisers. Opposite the Blue torpedo base was a Red base with torpedo boats, catchers (torpedo gunboats), and coast defence ships. This Red force tried to cover the juncture of the two Red divisions by attacking the Blue base and force.

Again, each fleet and each division included a large cruiser force. The Red first division consisted of eight battleships, two armoured cruisers, seven second-class cruisers, and two torpedo gunboats. Red's second division was seven more battleships, one armoured cruiser, six second-class cruisers, and two torpedo gunboats. The Red covering squadron consisted of four coast defence ships backed by a second-class cruiser, eight torpedo gunboats, and six torpedo boats. Blue had three coast defence ships, the three oldest armoured cruisers, six second-class cruisers, three torpedo gunboats, the depot ship *Hecla*, and twenty-one torpedo boats. Cruiser operations began even before hostilities, each side's cruisers watching the other's fleet in harbour. As long as the observers remained outside the three-mile limit, they could not be driven off before hostilities began. The umpires pointed out that not much could or would be seen, either, unless the observed party sent out ships to challenge the observers. Moreover, the observers always ran the risk that the observed party, having declared war, could jump them. It surprised the Blue commander that the Red Covering Force, which was not far from his own, made no pre-emptive attack using its own torpedo boats, but instead retired from the Irish Channel. Blue never engaged it at all; it might as well not have been present. The day of coast defence/coast attack ships was over: they could not live in the presence of torpedo boats.

Like the French fleet, Blue enjoyed a considerable superiority in torpedo boats. That had surprisingly little impact on Blue's behaviour, because the superiority counted for so little among Blue officers. The official report sympathized that there was no record of battle experience on which to base confidence or its lack, but he considered it important that Blue showed 'a tendency to consider the torpedo boat as something not to be included in the ordinary naval strength of a country ...' The Red divisional commanders certainly were impressed, the torpedo boat threat delaying their junction by about 43 hours (had it not been thought necessary to have a long period of daylight after the junction [to stave off a night torpedo attack], the delay would have been 37 hours). The delay could be attributed to caution considered necessary when entering waters in which hostile torpedo boats might be operating. Red was clearly impressed with the torpedo boat threat, which was probably exactly what the French hoped. The umpires thought this an important illustration of likely wartime behaviour.

Blue could have chosen either to concentrate its force (as it did) or to distribute its torpedo craft along the coast to harass Red. It concentrated and was destroyed. The exercise report suggested that the special characteristics of torpedo boats made dispersal the wiser course. It also seemed that Blue had been foolish to use its torpedo boats to search for the enemy; they should have been kept in hand for a surprise attack as the enemy approached. Torpedo boats were most successful, it seemed, when they were sent to attack an enemy whose location had already been found – most likely by a cruiser working with the torpedo boats. British and foreign exercises tabulated over five years showed that when the position of the objective was not known at all, the boats succeeded three times; when it was approximately known, six times; and when it was exactly known, sixteen times.

'The number of cruisers to be attached to a Fleet is fixed according to the service on which the Fleet is employed rather than the number of battleships which it contains.' A memo on cruiser organization (for the second division of the Red Fleet) distinguished lookout cruisers (which should be paired) from scouts. Scouts would form a Detached Squadron. There was no allowance for repeaters or links from scouts back to the main body: Scouts could never stray far from visual range.

In the 1894 manoeuvres, each fleet (Red and Blue) was split in half, each trying to unite its two squadrons before being destroyed in detail. Red had six and Blue had eighteen torpedo boats. Red had battleships in both its fleets, as well as strong cruiser forces. Each fleet was in three groups, with six ships each in the first two, and torpedo gunboats in the third. The first group consisted of three battleships and three fast cruisers (*Blenheim* was in the first group of the first Red fleet). Each of the second groups consisted of six cruisers. Note the disparity between cruiser and battleship numbers. One of the Blue fleets had seven battleships in its first group, with seven cruisers in the second; the other had only cruisers and torpedo gunboats. The four-fleet situation was something like that between Britain and France in the Mediterranean. In wartime the British would try to unite the Channel and Mediterranean Fleets, and the French their Brest and Toulon Fleets. The Brest fleet was weighted heavily towards cruisers, for raiding in the Atlantic, whereas a classic battle fleet (to contest control of the Mediterranean) was based at Toulon. As in 1892, much attention was paid to the effectiveness of torpedo boats. The commander of *TB 80* wrote that boats trailing a fleet in order to attack had been unable to regain position once lost due to the speed of the fleet. This may have been the first indication that high fleet speed in itself would be an important protection for a fleet passing through a narrow strait at night. It was again clear that torpedo boats had to work with cruisers which would find and report the enemy.

The 1896 manoeuvres again examined the problem of watching a hostile fleet in a nearby port. Red Fleet A watched Blue Fleet C, while Red Fleet B mobilized in another port. As in 1894, there was also a Fleet D, which would try to join Fleet C. This was not too different from the problem of the Mediterranean Fleet (A) watching the French Toulon Fleet (C) while the British Channel Fleet (B) tried to join it, and the Russian fleet (D), newly allied to the French, tried to even the odds. C's object was to destroy A before B could arrive or, failing that, to destroy B before the two Red fleets could join. The commander of A knew the strength of C, but not vice versa. His primary purpose was to defeat C by meeting it at sea. C did not know the strength of B, which was mobilizing, and D was also mobilizing, its strength unknown to A. Overall, A was superior to C and faster; C was superior to B; and B was faster than, and equal to, D. On meeting at sea, C would have to return to its port if it met A. Similarly, A could force D back into its port. However, C plus D were superior to A. If A met C after having defeated D, it would have to return to base. However, if it joined with B before meeting, C would have to withdraw. There would be no decisive result if B met D. 'Meeting' was taken to mean battleship squadrons within 3nm of each other for two hours.

All of this was very much a scouting problem, hence a cruiser problem. Thus Fleet A consisted of five battleships, seven second-class protected cruisers, four torpedo gunboats, and ten destroyers. Fleet B was four battleships (the cruisers *Blenheim*, *Hermione*, and *Charybdis* played battleships), two second-class cruisers, two third-class cruisers, four torpedo gunboats, and ten destroyers. Fleet C consisted of five battleships, two armoured cruisers, five second-class cruisers, and five torpedo gunboats. Fleet D comprised four slow battleships, three second-class cruisers, a third-class cruiser, and four torpedo gunboats. C was inferior to A 'so long as the Battle Squadron, which alone counts, is intact'. At the outset, cruisers and destroyers of Fleet A would be watching Fleet C in its base. An engagement between the cruiser *Thetis* and a torpedo gunboat leading a torpedo flotilla demonstrated once again that it was nearly impossible to execute a torpedo attack in daylight against a fast cruiser armed with quick-firing guns.

C joined D as soon as possible, A being unable to prevent that. Nor were A and B able to prevent the united enemy fleet from reaching the base it sought. The umpires added that 'with regard to the use made of cruisers and destroyers for obtaining and communicating information, nothing has reached [us] which enables us to give an opinion'. That was exactly the problem. The manoeuvres demonstrated a frightening failure of both scouting and communication.

The search problem evidently attracted considerable interest, because the instructions for the 1897 manoeuvres (held between roughly equal forces which had been mobilized for the Diamond Jubilee) include a discussion of the curve of search on the open sea for an enemy whose speed was known, and whose position at some particular time was known. In this case a fleet put to sea before the opening of hostilities, one cruiser being left behind to bring the news that war had begun. This cruiser was to meet the fleet at a set rendezvous. She was to be intercepted by two opposing cruisers intent on finding the enemy fleet, so that it in turn could be intercepted. Without wireless, the rub was that once they saw the enemy fleet those two cruisers had to turn back to report (the instructions for the exercise assume that the cruiser, once caught, would give up the rendezvous). The cruiser carrying the news would run at 12kts on an unknown track, the intercepting cruisers at 17kts. Hence the search curve. The test failed because the fleet commander chose to send a cruiser force back to escort the cruiser carrying the news of war. This was considered a hostile act before the outbreak of war.

The 1898 manoeuvres were intended to determine the best way of employing a large cruiser force with a fleet, with secondary objectives of helping indicate the relative advantages of speed and fighting strength, and also to obtain more information about the operations of destroyers and torpedo boats.[24] A convoy (C) of slow ships would be escorted by a fast cruiser from Halifax (in Canada) to Milford Haven. A fast hostile squadron (A) lying in Belfast would seek to intercept and capture the convoy. At some point a slower but superior British squadron (B) would be sent to protect C, meeting it at a prearranged rendezvous. The coast of Ireland was considered hostile (A) territory, containing A's torpedo boat bases. The English and Welsh coasts were B territory, including several destroyer bases. Obviously a great deal depended on intelligence available to A, and the manoeuvre instructions included special notes on the distribution of that intelligence, each fleet having its own Naval Centre with outlying despatch stations and signal stations. As yet there was no wireless, so once ships went to sea they could communicate with the land-based intelligence organization only via linking ships. Both fleets had numerous cruisers attached: Fleet A (Red) had three first-class cruisers and sixteen second- and third-class. Fleet B (Blue) had four first-class cruisers and sixteen second- and third-class. Fleet A also had torpedo boats led by torpedo gunboats; B had destroyers.

The result was another failed search exercise. It turned out that A was searching in the wrong place; the convoy was 63nm outside the area A planned to search, and at no time was any A cruiser closer than 120nm to the convoy. B met the convoy as planned, and brought it into port. Nothing was learned of the best way to employ a large cruiser force, but it seems clear that those planning the exercise hoped that by adding cruisers they could make A's search effective.

Further manoeuvres in 1901, in which two fleets fought for control of the Channel, showed that neither fleet had enough cruisers for the necessary scouting and look-out duties, particularly after a cruiser action notionally sank so many on each side.[25] 'This action points decisively to the great advantage either side would have obtained if supported by modern armoured cruisers.' Further, 'the fact of a heavy Cruiser action being fought on the first day of hostilities prevented, in a great

British shipbuilders, particularly Armstrong, constructed many of the world's cruisers between about 1880 and 1910. Armstrong built *Ching Yuen* for China. Completed on 23 July 1887, she was one of two sisters ordered for the Chinese Peiyang Fleet in October 1885. Like other Armstrong cruisers of the time, she was armed with unusually powerful guns, in this case three Krupp 8.2in (two forward, one aft), plus two 6in/36 Armstrong guns (in the waist), eight 6pdr QF, two 3pdr QF, six 1pdr QF, and four 14in torpedo tubes (two training tubes on the broadside and bow and stern tubes (the bow tube is barely visible above water). No other ships had the unusual combination of a twin mounting forward and a single mounting aft, although it featured in an abortive Armstrong design for cruisers for the Australian state of Victoria. Some of the 1pdrs are visible in the fighting tops fore and aft. She displaced only 2310 tons (250ft × 38ft × 15ft) and was designed to make 18kts under forced draught (5500 IHP). On trial she made 18.5kts on 6892 IHP. Under natural draught she made 15.26kts on 3733 IHP (she was designed to make 3300 IHP under natural draught). Here she flies an admiral's flag.

Initially Armstrong's great competitor was Thomson (Clydebank) of Glasgow. The company built the Spanish *Reina Regente*, seen here at the Columbian Naval Review (May 1893). Thomson became the John Brown shipyard, but the company's independent design capacity was abandoned. Thomson's last export success was the Japanese armoured cruiser *Chiyoda*, and the only other cruisers it built for export were the Confederate screw corvette *Canton* (which became the Spanish *Pampero*), the Chilean screw corvette *Abtao*, and the Spanish torpedo gunboat *Destructor*. The Armstrong (Elswick) design which lost out to Thomson was reportedly sold to the United States, to become the basis for the US cruisers *Baltimore* and *Philadelphia* (purchased through Humphreys, Tennant). Unfortunately, Armstrong records for the period before about 1910 have been lost, and it is impossible to say which foreign-built cruisers the company designed. For example, it is impossible to say whether ships built by the company's Italian subsidiary owed anything to the British home office. Later Armstrong records suggest that the company often acted as design agent for other yards. There was apparently a boom in British-built paddle warships through the early 1850s, after which most British warship exports were either ironclads or small gunboats. That would be consistent with the relative status of capital ships and steam frigates, the latter important mainly to attack or defend seaborne trade. Some British yards exported small numbers of cruisers after 1860; the list which follows is probably incomplete. R & H Green of Blackwall built the composite corvettes *O'Higgins* and *Chacabuco* (launched 1865-66) and *Magallanes* (1874) for Chile, and *Rainha de Portugal* and *Mindello* (1875) for Portugal. Thames Iron Works built the Spanish unprotected cruisers *Gravina* and *Velasco* (1881).
(Courtesy Ted Stone via NHHC)

measure, the necessary opportunities for practising one of the most important of a Cruiser's duties, i.e., scouting and getting touch of the enemy's Main Fleet.' The umpires much regretted that there had been no opportunity to test the value of a mass torpedo attack on a battle fleet, 'though often prevailing misty and foggy weather would seem to have been particularly favourable for such an attack, if either of the Fleets could have been quickly informed of the other's movements'.

Thus scouting was recognized as more and more important, and cruiser scouts would be opposed by the enemy's cruisers. They were unlikely to succeed unless they were backed by powerful armoured cruisers. Quite aside from any argument for trade protection against cruiser raiders, the 1901 manoeuvres showed that the main British fleet absolutely had to include a powerful fast armoured cruiser force of ships at least equal to any foreign counterparts.

Programs and Shipbuilders

Until 1889, the Royal Navy relied primarily on the Royal Dockyards for major warships such as cruisers: Chatham, Deptford, Devonport, Pembroke, Portsmouth, and Sheerness (Woolwich was closed as a dockyard, being confined to gun and boiler production, and in the 1880s Sheerness was closed altogether). The large commercial British shipbuilding industry, which often built warships for foreign governments, was considered a mobilization resource. For example, large numbers of gunboats were built under contract under emergency programs during the Crimean War. That mobilization bankrupted at least two builders, because it caused great wage and price inflation. Private builders were also brought in to introduce commercial technology not previously mastered by the Royal Dockyards, the most striking example being iron hull construction in the 1840s and 1850s. The effect of the 1889 Naval Defence Act was to stabilize warship construction programs and thus to attract private builders.

The British fiscal year began on 6 April. Through the 1860s the programs at the Royal Dockyards were generally described by a Program of Works (PW) dated by the fiscal year, e.g. PW 1860. PW 1860 was financed by the 1860-61 Estimates, which in this book is referred to as the 1860-61 program. Ships were typically ordered as early as possible in the fiscal year, although in some cases they were inserted later. In at least two important cases the planned programs were increased by Supplementals: 1884 (Northbrook Program) and 1898-99 (due to the Fashoda war scare). The 1885 crisis also brought forth a supplemental program, but it did not include new cruisers.

Changing Technology

During the period covered by this book ship design gradually changed from art towards science, one indication being the formation of the Institution of Naval Architects (later the Royal Institution) in 1860. The Royal Navy formed a series of professional schools for naval constructors, ultimately creating a course at Greenwich which educated not only important British constructors, but also many foreign ones. In 1883 it formed the Royal Corps of Naval Constructors, which was intended to design all British warships. All Directors of Naval Construction from 1923 on were products of the Greenwich course. Probably the most important development of this period was the work on resistance (to motion through the water) carried out by William Froude, who later ran the Royal Navy's experimental testing tank. Froude's work made it possible for the first time to predict (albeit not always precisely) how fast a ship of given dimensions, with a given hull form and with a given power plant, would be. The insights he gained made it possible to compare British ships with foreign ships which ran their trials under very different conditions conducive to much higher trial speeds. Without that insight, the Royal Navy would have found itself much more frequently pursuing higher speeds.

There were several waves of technology, beginning with steam power in its initial inefficient form (which greatly limited endurance under steam, and demanded that ships be powered by a combination of sail – for long endurance – and steam power). The next and roughly simultaneous waves were the telegraph and iron, rather than wood, hulls. The telegraph offered a new kind of naval strategy based on rapid reaction to events half a world away, and also (as indicated by the manoeuvre notes) to intelligence-based operations.

The next series of radical changes were the advent of efficient steam engines (compound engines), the appearance of breech-loading guns, the introduction of self-propelled torpedoes, and the advent of steel hulls, all about 1875-85. After that came a revolution in the rate at which guns could fire and shortly afterwards the appearance of lightweight (Harvey and Krupp) armour, in the 1890s. Although many of the cruisers in this book benefited from it, radio (introduced from about 1900 on) had little impact on their designs. The revolutionary impact of radio on the shape of the fleet, and on its tactics, came during the Fisher era, from 1904 on.

The most dramatic consequence of changing technology was that the effective life of a ship shrank, while the cost and complexity of individual ships increased. Although design and construction practices certainly evolved during the sailing ship era, they did so relatively slowly. HMS *Victory* could serve as Nelson's flagship at Trafalgar in 1805 although she had been launched in 1765. In 1900 it would have been inconceivable that a 40-year-old capital ship would have any first- or even third-line role; indeed, any 20-year-old capital ship was profoundly obsolete by that time.

These realities condemned the late nineteenth-century Royal Navy to a continuing financial crisis in which cruisers generally figured. Had technology not been changing, the size of the British cruiser force would have been the number bought each year multiplied by the lifetime of the ships. British naval administrators often grossly overestimated the important factor of lifetime, because they thought in terms of the durability of the ships, their hulls and their machinery. Unfortunately, in a time of rapid technological change the important issue was how quickly a ship became obsolete.

Guns
The Royal Navy designated its guns in three quite different ways: by nominal weight of projectile (e.g., 25pdr or 68pdr); by weight of gun (e.g., 95cwt, one cwt [abbreviation of hundredweight] being 112lbs, 20 of which made a standard [long] ton); or, as is now common, by calibre in inches. The latter seems to have become standard only after breech-loaders were re-introduced from 1881 on. One reason was that such guns could easily fire projectiles of different lengths, hence weights. In the 1830s, when the first ships in this book were begun, the usual designation was by nominal weight of projectile, based on round solid iron shot (guns did, however, differ in length). Projectile weight (hence gun calibre) was ultimately limited by what a gunner could lift. Much larger and more powerful guns were needed to penetrate armour, and they in turn required power loading or lifting. Guns were increasingly designated by their weight, so that in 1866 plans called for arming the new cruiser *Inconstant* with 12½-ton guns – at that time the heaviest in the Royal Navy.

The guns of the Napoleonic Wars, those mounted on board the earliest cruisers in this book, were smoth-bore muzzle-loaders, typically 18- , 24-, 32- and 42-pounders. Line-of-battle ships typically mounted 32pdrs on the gun deck and 18- or 24pdrs on the upper deck(s), plus short carronades (24- or 32-pdrs).[26] The first proposals for a uniform armament of 32pdrs (with shorter guns on the upper deck to save weight) came in the 1820s. The standard early nineteenth-century cast-iron 32pdr was 9ft 6in long and weighed 55cwt 2qr [quarters]. Beginning in 1830 many guns were bored out to 32pdr calibre (6.25in); some ships were rearmed. New types of 32pdr were being developed.[27]

Apart from carronades, these guns were all mounted on wheeled trucks, the entire truck recoiling with the gun. There were no fixed mountings. Ships' sides generally had gun ports cut into them, and guns were placed at the ports. Chasers (guns firing right ahead and astern, used when the ship was in chase or being chased) were placed at bow or stern ports, but were not fixed there. In some cases guns were wheeled from broadside positions to act as chasers. Chasers are sometimes described as pivot guns. That generally meant guns on slide mountings pivoted at one end, the gun recoiling along the slide. Typically the slide had rollers running along fixed deck racers. Most chasers of 64pdr size and below were on trucks which could be rolled to fire from ports in the bow or stern. This type of mounting made it simple to rearm ships; until ships had mountings built into them, armaments were hardly permanent. Needing less space to recoil, carronades were typically mounted on slides pivoted to the deck.

There was considerable interest in heavier solid-shot guns, but they required larger crews to manhandle them, and these extra men in turn crowded gun decks. The Royal Navy standardized on 32pdr solid-shot guns, with the sole exception of the 68pdr 95cwt (8in) gun introduced by Colonel Dundas, which was adopted in 1838. The 68pdr also became the Royal Navy's standard shell gun, firing a 51lb shell or a 56lb plugged solid shot. It was generally used as a chaser, but by the 1840s some ships mounted only 68pdrs on their gun decks.[28]

In the 1850s the argument about manpower was turned around. With men somewhat scarce, it was argued that ships should mount fewer heavier guns, all 68pdrs if possible. On this basis a large frigate (with a single gun deck) might be as powerful as a three-deck ship of the line armed entirely with 32pdrs and carronades.

Intense interest in large-calibre shell-firing guns dated back to proposals by French artillery officer Henri-Joseph Paixhans published in 1821-22.[29] Many agreed with him that shell guns

A 40pdr Armstrong breech-loader on a truck mounting on board the screw frigate HMS *Narcissus* (the standing officer obscures the breech). In battery the gun was lashed to the side of the ship, as shown, but the carriage could be wheeled to a bow or stern port. The 40pdr (4.75in) weighed 1 ton 15cwt (35cwt) and was 10ft 1in long (its bore was 22.39 calibres long); it fired a 40lb shell at 1160ft/sec. There was also a 20pdr breech-loader for sloops and for boats (3.75in calibre, muzzle velocity 1000ft/sec, bore 54in long, 15cwt; 13cwt for boats). The initial main deck battery of *Narcissus* was twenty-two 32pdr and eight 8in 65cwt shell guns. On her upper deck were one 68pdr 95cwt chaser on a pivoted slide plus two 8in shell guns and eighteen 32pdrs. All of these weapons were smooth-bores, but soon Armstrong breech-loaders like this one were available (the 40pdr was officially adopted in 1859). Apparently one 7in (110pdr) breech-loader replaced the chaser and eight 40pdrs replaced the other upper deck guns. Notes on the 1857 plan for the ship suggest that 110pdrs replaced the main deck 32pdrs (the numbers are not known and it is not certain the planned changes occurred). In November 1864 Controller Rear Admiral Robinson listed *Narcissus* among the first ships to be given the new 64pdr muzzle-loading rifled guns, 150 of which would soon be available. As refitted, the ship's main deck battery was fourteen 8in shell guns and the twelve 64pdrs. *Aurora* and *Liverpool* were first in priority for rearmament (12 guns each). Of the others, *Narcissus* was seventh. The remainder, in priority order (number of guns in parentheses), were: *Cadmus* (8), *Arethusa* (12), *Constance* (12), *Scout* (8), *Bristol* (12), *Octavia* (12), *Challenger* (8), *Jason* (8), *Satellite* (8), *Undaunted* (12), *Immortalite* (12), and *Topaze* (12), a total of 160. In 1865 a list of ships to have the new 6½-ton (7in) muzzle-loader included three screw frigates, each with four of them: *Mersey*, *Orlando*, and *Endymion*. Later the *Amazon* class screw sloops were added. On commissioning (20 December 1860) *Narcissus* joined the Cape of Good Hope station; in April 1865 she became flagship of the South East Coast of America (South America) station. Beginning in December 1870 she was flagship of the Detached (Flying) Squadron, described alternatively as a training squadron and as an attempt to replace the deployed units on different stations. She ended this service in May 1877. *Narcissus* was reduced to coast guard service at Greenock on 20 July 1877, paying off on 8 May 1878.

(National Maritime Museum A7807-019)

An Armstrong 7in 110pdr breech-loader on board HMS *Narcissus*. The gas seal consisted of the steel vent-piece (inserted from the top of the gun) screwed tight by the two handles (shell and charge were inserted through the opening between the handles). In action it was not always possible to be sure that the handles were tight enough, and vent-pieces sometimes flew out. The Armstrong breech-loaders, particularly the 110pdr, gained a bad reputation after Vice Admiral Kuper's squadron shelled Kagoshima on 14 August 1863: 21 Armstrong guns suffered 28 accidents while firing 365 rounds. The lead coating of their shells fouled the rifling, rendering them inaccurate. The 110pdr was officially withdrawn early in 1864, to be replaced by the lighter muzzle-loading 64pdr rifle, but some ships still had them as late as 1872 (by 1874 they were gone). In 1872 data for the 7in breech-loader were: weight 4 tons 2cwt (82cwt), overall length 10ft, projectile 90½lbs, muzzle velocity with maximum charge 1125ft/sec. Comparable data for the 7in muzzle-loader were: weight 130cwt, extreme length 11ft, bore 15.88 calibres, projectile weight 115lbs, muzzle velocity 1325 ft/sec. There were two different types of 64pdr, Mk I (71cwt) being a conversion of an existing 68pdr smooth-bore and Mk III (64 cwt) newly-built (Mk II was not used). Both versions were 6.3in calibre. Mk I was 10ft 2.72in long (bore was 16.42 calibres long) and had a muzzle velocity of 1260ft/sec with a full charge. Mk III was 9ft 10in long (bore was 15.47 calibres long) and had a muzzle velocity of 1390ft/sec with its heavier full charge (10 vs 8¼lbs). The true replacement for the 110pdr was the 7in rifled muzzle-loader (6½ tons or 130cwt; after 1872 there was also a 90cwt cruiser version). Guns like the 110pdr could not handle charges as great as those of contemporary muzzle-loaders because their breeches could not withstand as much pressure. Before about 1880 powder burned quickly, so a gun gained little or nothing from having a longer barrel (the longer the barrel, the more friction slowed the shell passing from it). The later slow-burning powders reversed the situation, since it took a long barrel to make full use of the available energy. According to the 1885 gunnery manual, the need for long barrels became clear in 1873-79. They could not be muzzle-loaders because long guns could not be run back far enough into a ship to be reloaded at the muzzle. That was quite apart from the lesson of the explosion of an accidentally double-loaded muzzle-loader on board HMS *Thunderer*.
(National Maritime Museum A7807-011)

could burn out or shatter wooden warships, which in the past had been able to absorb considerable damage from heavy solid shot (that is why so few large ships were sunk by gunfire during the age of sail). In 1839 the Admiralty decided to place shell guns on board thirty ships of the line and forty frigates. In addition to the 68pdr, the Royal Navy later adopted a 10in gun which fired only shells (84lb projectiles).[30] Armour was adopted largely to solve the shell problem, although in retrospect it is not clear how destructive shellfire really was.[31]

Quite aside from improved guns, the Royal Navy of the 1830s and 1840s benefited from systematic improvement in gunnery. The naval gunnery school HMS *Excellent* was established at Portsmouth in 1830; its improvements were evident during the Syrian crisis of 1840, which was also the first important operational use of British steam warships. In addition to training British gunners, *Excellent* was in effect the centre of British gunnery expertise (and also torpedo and mine expertise, until the foundation of HMS *Vernon*). Her CO was in many ways the Royal Navy's senior armament expert, and his opinions were sought when ships were designed. Future Admiral Sir John Fisher was CO of *Excellent* at a crucial time in the 1880s.

The other major new development was rifling, which considerably increased maximum accurate range. The Royal Navy adopted the Lancaster rifled cast-iron muzzle-loader in 1855. It imparted spin to its elongated shell using a twisted bore of elliptical cross-section. The Lancaster gun proved unreliable during the Crimean War. William Armstrong, later Lord Armstrong, was far more successful. In 1854 he proposed a built-up breech-loader to the Minister of War. It was tested in 1856, and adopted in 1859 on the 1858 recommendation of the Committee on Rifled Cannon. Types were 7in (110pdr), 40-, 20-, 12-, 9-, and 6pdrs. From 1861 on the 7in replaced the 68pdr as the standard navy chaser. The Armstrong guns can be recognized by the handle used to rotate the breech. There was no means of withdrawing the breech without removing it entirely from the gun, and the process of breech-loading and reloading was cumbersome. Unfortunately there was no way to be certain that the breech was fully closed, and there were serious accidents (Armstrong also produced rifled muzzle-loaders). In competition with Armstrong, Whitworth produced a muzzle-loader with a hexagonal cross-section. Armstrong's guns beat out Whitworth's in an 1863 trial, and in 1864 the British forces formally adopted rifled guns. Armstrong received the ordnance contract for both the Royal Navy and for the British army. However, a series of disasters showed that the adoption of breech-loading was premature. Armstrong was dismissed, but under the contract negotiated with him when he was hired, he retained the factory built for him. He turned to the export market, and began building cruisers as well as guns. Armstrong's cruisers figure prominently in this book.

Gun construction for both army and navy was then concentrated in the Royal Gun Factory at Woolwich Arsenal. Woolwich argued that only muzzle-loaders were safe. Its muzzle-loading rifles (MLR) were adopted about 1865. Other navies, such as the French, continued to use breech-loaders, and some Royal Navy officers wondered whether they had not taken the better decision. For example, Controller Rear Admiral Robinson visited the 1867 Paris world's fair, together with Reed and with the Admiralty's gunnery experts Admiral Cooper Key (DNO) and Captain Hood (Captain of HMS *Excellent*).[32] The naval exhibits provided by the Admiralty and by the French made it relatively easy to compare practices in the two navies. Robinson was clearly impressed with the French breech-loaders, which seemed (to him) to be well adapted to firing longer and therefore more accurate shells. Key took pains to claim that the British muzzle-loaders were superior, in part because they could be fired more rapidly. He pointed out that with their higher-powered powder, the British guns could be lighter than the French for the same penetrating power (which he measured by muzzle energy per inch of calibre).

As a means of quickly producing rifled guns, in the mid-1860s (i.e., as Armstrong was rejected) the Royal Navy adopted the Palliser system of inserting a steel inner tube into an existing cast-iron gun. The guns involved were the 32pdr 56 and 58cwt, the 8in 65cwt shell gun, and the 10in 95cwt shell gun. They survived into the 1870s. During that period they were extensively mounted on board cruisers and smaller ships. Prior to conversion they had flintlocks and muzzle notch fore sights, but upon conversion they were given friction tubes and drop fore sights, with rear sights modified for the new trajectories and greater ranges. Carriages were not changed. Note that the name Palliser was also associated with chilled iron armour-piercing shot, which the Royal Navy used into the 1890s.

Much more powerful (hence heavier) guns appeared as the Royal Navy adopted (and faced) ironclads. They could hardly be manhandled on wheeled trucks. Instead, they were mounted on slides, which could be moved about a ship's decks along racers, curved tracks let into the wooden deck. Some racers were laid in intersecting patterns, so that a gun could fire out of any of several ports cut in the ship's side. The gun recoiled along the slide, which was slightly inclined (so that the weight of the gun would return it to battery after it recoiled). When the Royal Navy reverted to breech-loaders, its first cruiser mountings were Vavasseurs (named after their inventor and manufacturer, Charles Vavasseur), which were, in effect, developed slides. Typically a Vavasseur was anchored at one end by a fixed pivot in the deck. The other end was wheeled, so the entire mounting could swing back and forth. The main part of the mounting was the steeply angled track up which the gun recoiled after it fired, gravity returning the gun to position. These were powerful guns, and they needed more than gravity to absorb the energy of firing. Vavasseur therefore provided a friction brake. Later centre-pivot and pedestal mountings were more compact.

As of 1875, British unarmoured ships mounted six types of gun.[33] The most powerful was the 9in 12½-ton MLR, essentially a capital ship weapon, which armed the armoured cruisers or second-class ironclads of the *Shannon* and *Nelson* classes. It fired a 250lb shell and was mounted on an iron slide. One step down were 7in 6½-ton and 4½-ton MLRs firing a 120lb shell, on a wooden or iron slide (these guns were often characterized as 110pdrs). The standard broadside gun was the 6.3in 64pdr 64cwt, firing a 64lb shell; there was also a 71cwt version. Two breech-loaders survived: the 4.75 in 35cwt firing a 40lb shell and the 3.75 in 15cwt firing a 20lb shell. Both were Armstrong types with screw breeches.

As of 1885, with rearmament with breech-loaders beginning, the heaviest MLR guns on board British cruisers were

10in of 18 tons (Mk I) or 20 tons (Mk II), 13 ft long (i.e., 15.6 calibre). They fired a 410lb projectile at 1370ft/sec. There were five Marks of 9in 12-ton MLR (initially described as 12½-ton), 12ft long (16 calibre). A typical 9in gun fired a 256lb projectile at 1440ft/sec. There were three Marks of 8in 9-ton gun, 11ft long (16.5 calibre), firing a 18lb projectile at 138 ft/sec (or a 181lb shell with a 17.7lb burster). There were three Marks of 7in 6½ tons, 11ft long (18.9 calibre), firing a 115lb projectile at 1525ft/sec. In 1885 these wrought iron guns were restricted to target practice. The newer 7in 90cwt gun (4.5 tons) was 10ft 11in long (18.7 calibre) and fired a 115lb projectile at 1361ft/sec or a 159lb shell (13.4lb burster) at 1161ft/sec. The smallest major guns then in use were 64pdrs. There were three Marks of 64pdr 64cwt guns (3.2 tons), about 10ft long (19.3 calibres); the latest Mk III fired a 6.22in projectile (65lbs) at 1200ft/sec. The 64pdr 71cwt gun (3.55 tons) fired a similar projectile at 1125ft/sec. There were also small-calibre 9pdrs and 7pdrs.

These guns were all short because they used high-explosive powder. Its energy was quickly exhausted, so making the barrel longer than necessary merely slowed the projectile by friction. The barrel lengths quoted are somewhat deceptive: they refer to the overall length of the gun, including considerable metal at the breech end to contain the explosion. Thus the 8in gun was 16.5 calibres long overall, but 14.8 long internally.

Given Woolwich's insistence that only its muzzle-loaders were safe, it was ironic that the Royal Navy abandoned muzzle-loading due to a major accident. The heavy muzzle-loaders of the 1870s demanded power-loading; typically a turret gun was depressed to line it up with a power rammer operating from below decks. HMS *Thunderer* was the first ship with such power-loading. On 2 January 1879 she accidentally double-loaded a gun (it was impossible to see whether a charge and projectile were in place). The gun could not possibly survive the resulting explosion. Neither could reliance on Woolwich and its muzzle-loaders. There was already considerable sentiment favouring a return to breech-loaders, and Woolwich itself was designing one. The return to breech-loaders was associated with the adoption of slower-burning powder. In 1878 Sir Andrew Noble began experimenting with the longer guns (which had to be breech-loaders) which could fully exploit slow-burning powder. Armstrong (Elswick) was already making such guns for export.

The Royal Navy found itself relying on commercial suppliers again. Both services joined in an Ordnance Committee formed in 1881 to determine which guns should be developed and which designs to adopt. Designs for 16.25in, 13.5in, 9.2in, and 8in guns were approved that year. The rearmament of the fleet began, but it was a lengthy process (according to the 1885 official gunnery handbook, it was expected to take fifteen years). Adoption of breech-loaders increased the rate of fire about five-fold in guns of the same weight. Because a breech-loader was heavier than a muzzle-loader (it needed much more material around its breech), the weight of fire for roughly comparable ships trebled. Rearmament of existing cruisers began in 1884. At this time the army continued to buy guns for the Royal Navy, a practice which ended in 1888.

As of 1885, the new cruiser guns were the 5in, for sloops, gun-vessels, and some corvettes; the 6in, for large cruisers (it was the largest gun in corvettes); and the 8in and 9.2in (for heavy cruisers). Internal lengths were about 25 calibres. For example, the 8in 11-ton gun was 18ft 6.5in long (outside dimension: 28 calibres). It fired a 210lb (rather than 180lb) projectile at 1953ft/sec. The most powerful of the new cruiser guns was the 24-ton 9.2in gun, 25ft 10in long (33.7 calibres externally, 31.5 calibres internally), firing a 389lb projectile at 2060ft/sec. As Robinson had pointed out in 1867, there was really no limit on the length of a breech-loader, since it did not have to be brought back inside the ship to be reloaded. The 31.5-calibre 9.2in gun replaced a 27-calibre gun, and later guns were 40 or even 50 calibres long.

Also in the 1880s, it became possible to combine projectile and powder in a single round, using a brass cartridge case. When the gun was fired, the case expanded to seal the chamber against gas leakage. When the cartridge case cooled, it contracted, and it could be extracted relatively easily. Since it no longer had to seal the chamber very completely, the breech mechanism could be simplified and could operate much more rapidly. Cartridge cases had first been used in breech-loading rifles. In 1881 the Admiralty sought tenders for a 6pdr gun firing 12 rounds per minute. It was classified as quick-firing (QF). Initially it seemed that QF guns and their smaller cousins, machine guns and multi-barrel guns, were vital mainly as a defence against torpedo boats. However, within a few years larger-calibre QF guns were being produced, a 4.7in type being tested at Portsmouth in 1887. Some cruisers had their 6in guns converted to QF operation as QFC guns. Ironically, it soon turned out that a 6in gun with a 'bare' cartridge (i.e., without metal) could be made to fire quickly enough, using an improved breech mechanism, that QF operation was no longer needed above 4in or 4.7in calibre.

A second important development was much-improved gun mountings, which made it possible to fire even heavy guns quite rapidly. In the 1880s or early 1890s it seemed that a fast cruiser armed with heavy QF guns might tear up the sides of a battleship whose 12in or heavier guns might fire only once in several minutes. Soon after 1900 the same gun could fire once or twice a minute, and the big cruiser was much less viable, at least in a fleet action.

Steam Power[34]

Cruisers demanded a combination of high power (for speed) and long endurance at lower speed. All but one of the ships in this book were powered by reciprocating (piston) engines, and most of these engines were coupled directly to paddle wheel or, in most cases, propeller. Until engines and boilers became efficient, long endurance meant endurance under sail. Propellers or paddles created undesirable drag, and early screw cruisers were designed to hoist (retract) their propellers when they were not needed, and often also to collapse their funnels to make it easier to handle sail. That limited them to a single screw, and it demanded that space be left above the propeller into which it could retract (this space made it difficult to mount stern chasers).

The idea of the screw propeller originated well before 1800, but it became practicable only in the late 1830s. In England Francis Petit Smith built a 6-ton demonstrator, which ran successful sea trials for the Admiralty in 1838. Before adopting screw propulsion, the Admiralty asked for trials of a ship of at least 200 tons; Smith had the *Archimedes* built. Successful trials included a race across the Channel against the fastest of the paddle mail steamers of the time. By the spring of 1840 the Board was clearly convinced that the future lay with the propeller, and by 1844 the Admiralty was ordering screw frigates, although it continued to buy paddle warships.

Combining screws with wooden hulls entailed problems. A wooden hull flexed in a seaway, but the propeller shaft and its bearings had to be kept rigid over a considerable length (the French solved the problem using universal joints, but the British did not). As the propeller turned, its blades bit into the stream of water coming off the hull, causing the hull to vibrate. That vibration could damage a wooden hull. Finally, a bluff stern, such as that in a line of battle ship, could block the run of water to the propeller and thus make it inefficient. Propellers turned at higher speeds than paddles, so the engines driving them had to run at faster rates, and vibration became a problem. Once protective decks were introduced, cylinders had to be kept short enough to fit under those decks (initially the requirement was that the machinery lie completely below the waterline, where it was relatively safe from gunfire). Pistons had to run faster, and that increased vibration. In some ships cylinders were set horizontally, their dimensions limited by the ship's beam.

Through the nineteenth century merchant ships, particularly the large Atlantic liners, led in engine and boiler development. The Admiralty naturally took a conservative point of view: it could not afford the consequences of large-scale failure. However, it did pioneer important improvements. In 1860 Engineer-in-Chief Thomas Lloyd told a Parliamentary Committee on marine engines that the Admiralty had led in the shift from flue to fire-tube boilers; the direct-acting instead of the beam engine; the screw propeller in place of paddles; and fast-running engines instead of slow-acting geared-up engines.[35]

The ships in this book burned coal. Each furnace was fed by hand, and a stoker could move only so much coal per hour. Boiler arrangements had to allow not only for stokers standing in front of them, but also for access to the mass of coal that each stoker used. Boiler spaces had to be massive, and high-powered ships needed large numbers of boilers. Coal was also an essential part of the protection of many British cruisers. Oil, whose advantages included ease of handling and a much higher energy content, was proposed as early as 1865, but was not adopted until after the turn of the twentieth century, mainly because coal was so much less expensive, and because large supplies of the best steaming coal were available in Wales.

As might be imagined, engines came in a bewildering variety of forms, which are not described in any detail in this book. Through the 1870s warship engines typically let into one or more cylinders (in parallel) and then condensed. Low-pressure steam did not have enough residual energy after the first expansion to be worth re-using. Some engines had double-acting cylinders, steam being let in alternately to one and then the other side of the single piston.

The associated boilers were, in effect, oversized teapots, vessels (often called boxes) filled with water and heated externally from below. Hot gas passed through flues below and around the mass of water and then up the funnel. Steam was drawn off at the top. These boilers could not withstand pressures much beyond 20lb/sq in (pounds per square inch, or psi); the boilers of the 1830s and 1840s operated at about 5psi. At such low pressures, engines operated by having their pistons driven by atmospheric pressure against a vacuum created when steam on the other side of a piston condensed. Boilers used sea water, which left a salt scale in them; it protected some iron parts (not

A 10in 18-ton muzzle-loading gun aboard HMS *Sultan*. This weapon armed the armoured cruisers *Shannon*, *Nelson* and *Northampton*. It was the heaviest muzzle-loader which did not require elaborate below-decks machinery for loading. The mounting is a pivoted slide, its rollers running along tracks (racers) laid in the deck. Slide carriages were common in the Royal Navy of the 1860s through the 1890s. Typically each gun port had a fighting bolt to which the front of the slide could be secured. In many cases guns could be rolled between sets of deck tracks (the installation in *Sultan* was clearly permanent, as it included a geared track) when the fighting bolt was disconnected. Often there was a permanent stowage bolt on the ship's centreline, around which a gun pivoted to be placed at different ports. Once at the port, the stowage bolt was disconnected and the slide connected instead to the fighting bolt at the port. Guns were connected to the fighting bolts by pairs of bars carried on the slide. The gun carriage ran along the slide on gunmetal rollers. External compressor plates helped slow the gun's recoil. The standard 64pdr 64cwt cruiser gun was mounted either on a truck or on a wooden (oak) slide, which moved on cross skids rather than on the metal rollers shown here. For the 18-ton gun, gearing elevated and traversed the gun, which recoiled along the slide. Ships later had more sophisticated Vavasseur pivot mountings in which gun and (shorter) slide were more integrated.

the steam spaces, which pitted due to oxygen liberated from the water surface as it boiled) but also reduced heat transfer from flues to the water inside.

It seems to have been understood by the mid-1850s that a boiler working at high enough pressure could leave considerable energy in the steam exhausted from a cylinder.[36] That turned out to be the key to greater efficiency. A double-expansion or compound engine exhausted the steam from its high-pressure cylinder into a low-pressure cylinder. The first practical double-expansion engine in the Royal Navy was installed in the steam frigate *Constance*, launched in 1862. She successfully raced her sister ships *Arethusa* and *Octavia* between Plymouth and Madeira in 1865. Compound engines first went to sea in the 1830s and were introduced in merchant ships in 1853. The French preceded the Royal Navy by ordering such an engine from its British inventors, Charles Randolph and John Elder, for the sloop *Actif* (which ran trials in 1862). *Constance* had an alternative type of compound engine, on 'Woolf's Principle'. The 1872 Committee on Designs strongly favoured compound engines for all future British warships.

Compounding became worthwhile for pressures above about 40psi. That in turn required stronger boilers and a more efficient way of turning heat into steam. By the 1850s a solution had been conceived in the form of a tubular or fire-tube boiler.[37] Hot gas passed through fire-tubes inside the mass of water, sucked up by a funnel or smokestack. The area of boiler water touched by hot gas was far greater than in a kettle boiler. Flat-sided box boilers could not take the higher pressure, so from the 1860s on boilers were being made oval or cylindrical. Oval boilers could handle pressures up to about 75psi; above that boilers had to be cylindrical. Designers resisted this change because the new cylindrical (Scotch) boilers wasted considerable space in a flat-sided stokehold.

By about 1890, most battleships and large cruisers typically had single-ended return-tube boilers with four furnaces each (some earlier cruisers had double-ended boilers). Second-class cruisers typically had three-furnace boilers, some with single and some with double ends. All had one combustion chamber per furnace. Single-ended boilers made it easier to subdivide power, but were heavier. Return-tubes meant that the nested fire-tubes passed back and forth through the water volume before exhausting. A typical fire-tube might be 2½ins in outside diameter, with a 7in water space down the middle of each nest of tubes. The grate area on which coal was burned was about 3 per cent of total heating area (i.e., the area of the fire-tubes), the latter typically amounting to 2.5 square feet per IHP at natural draught.

To generate more heat, hence more steam, boilers needed more air. Fans were used to build up air pressure and hence air volume in a closed stokehold. In mid-century advocates of such forced draught claimed that they could increase steam output by 30 or 40 per cent, even with low-quality coal. Greater temperatures in turn increased stress on the boiler itself. Typical British (and, presumably, foreign) naval practice limited machinery weight by using thinner boiler plating than in commercial practice. Boilers had to be rigid, to contain steam pressure, but they also had to expand at high temperatures (typically they were corrugated, to allow for expansion). This was not a good combination. To avoid bursting boilers, the Admiralty typically limited forced draught runs to a few hours, and it distinguished between a ship's performance using forced versus natural draught. During the 1880s and 1890s DNC Sir William White often claimed that foreign cruisers reached high speeds by using high rates of forcing which could never be repeated in service; the rated speeds of the cruisers he had designed for the Royal Navy were far more realistic because they reflected much more realistic conditions. In its 1892 report the Boiler Committee recommended that specified forced draught be limited to 25 per cent beyond specified natural draught power for standard navy boilers, and 45 per cent for torpedo gunboats (presumably meaning for locomotive boilers).

With high enough steam pressure, enough was left at the outlet of the second cylinder to make a third or even a fourth cylinder worth while: triple or quadruple expansion. Higher pressure and more cylinders meant greater efficiency and thus longer range. Each boost in steam pressure bought greater economy.[38] Because triple expansion increased the number of cylinders, it made crankshafts easier to balance and thus reduced vibration.

The most extreme fire-tube boilers were the locomotive boilers installed on board small fast ships from the 1870s on. In the Royal Navy, the first such boiler was on board the prototype torpedo boat *Lightning* (1879), and these boilers were later tried on board small cruisers. There was no pretension to efficiency; the object was to generate as much steam as possible in the smallest possible dimensions. Cylindrical boilers used relatively large-diameter fire-tubes, which could not easily be blocked by cinders from the coal fire. Locomotive boilers used the smallest possible tube diameters, for maximum heating area inside a cylinder filled with water. The tubes were straight, from firebox to smoke box (leading to funnel). Tubes could easily be blocked (and burst) by unwanted grease or cinders, but in the 1880s there seemed to be no other way to produce enough steam within small dimensions.

The alternative to fire-tube boilers was conceived (and used in a few cases) as early as the 1850s: the water-tube or tubulous boiler.[39] The relationship between water and hot gas was reversed. Feed water was led through tubes passing through the furnace. Much greater water surface could be exposed to heat. Limited diameter tubes could withstand greater pressure than a large cylindrical boiler. The outer skin of the furnace did not have to withstand steam pressure. Water-tube boilers could generate higher-pressure steam, which was exactly what high-powered warships needed. As early as 1873 some liners were operating at 100psi. Proponents argued further that because the mass of water in them was relatively small, it took less heat to start them: they could start much more quickly, and they could more quickly answer demands for more steam. They were also expected to be more durable, capable of longer runs at high power. The British found themselves unable to get enough power from the available heating space, using conventional boilers.[40] In 1892 the Boiler Committee recommended installing tubulous boilers in two ships for trials (Thornycroft on board the torpedo gunboat *Speedy*, Belleville on board the torpedo gunboat *Sharpshooter*), and that one at least of the new cruisers be so fitted if the trials proved successful. A third torpedo gunboat, *Spanker*, was fitted with French du Temple boilers. Bellevilles were chosen for the cruisers *Powerful* and

Terrible before the *Sharpshooter* trials were complete because they needed so much power. The only ones considered should have relatively large-diameter straight tubes which could easily be cleaned and examined. It happened that the French Belleville fitted this description.

When the Royal Navy adopted water-tube boilers, the great advantage cited was that it was no longer necessary to force boilers to reach and maintain high power (the Germans, however, wrote that water-tube boilers were more heavily forced than cylindrical ones). The 1902 report of the Boiler Committee explained that there was greater fire-grate area for the same floor space, hence less forcing to reach full power. There would be less damage if the boiler were struck by a projectile, since there would not be a large pressurized vessel to burst. A water-tube boiler could also carry a higher steam pressure, and it was lighter for the power it generated. However, it took relatively little scale or corrosion to ruin a water-tube boiler. The Royal Navy adopted fresh water as boiler feed and its ships had to carry stocks of reserve feed water for the first time.[41] With so little water in the boiler, there was no reserve to make up for slight irregularities in feed, so the rate of feeding had to be automatically controlled, and very quickly altered when more steam was demanded. Similarly, a water-tube boiler would react more sensitively to irregular stoking, and the type of fire used had to be changed. The boilers had to be fed more continuously, and with greater care than before. Water-tube boilers were not necessarily more efficient than their cylindrical predecessors – and cruisers needed efficiency as well as compact high power: the boilers worked best at a high fraction of their designed output. The solution to economical cruising was to have a large number of such boilers, only a few of which were lit off for cruising. Unfortunately, a ship in a combat zone would want most of her boilers lit all the time, so she would be quite uneconomical. Some British armoured cruisers designed about 1902 had a combination of cylindrical and water-tube boilers, the cylindrical boilers acting as, in effect, the ship's cruising power plant.[42] The agonizing period during which the Royal Navy decided both to adopt water-tube boilers and which boilers to adopt became the storied 'battle of the boilers'.[43]

The first practical water-tube boiler was the Belleville, invented in France in the 1850s and first adopted by the French Navy in the 1880s. Its water-tubes formed a series of flattened spirals built up of straight tubes with cast-iron junction boxes connecting them. They rose from a feed box in front of the boiler to a cylindrical steam drum at the top. Most ships had economizers, which preheated the feed water and controlled steam output when it had to be changed suddenly, for example to increase speed. Pressure inside the boiler was typically 350psi, reduced to 250 for the engine (the greater pressure inside the boiler was later considered a serious defect, though

A broadside 6in breech-loading gun on board HMS *Imperieuse*, on a Vavasseur pivot mounting with racers (tracks) laid in the deck. In contrast to earlier slide mountings, this one was a permanent installation not intended to be transferred from port to port. The Royal Navy adapted the Vavasseur for medium guns worked manually. Compared to the earlier types, it could be elevated and trained up to the moment of firing, and it required fewer men. Strain was also more evenly distributed than in earlier types of mounting. Vavassurs could be divided into broadside (as here) and central pivot mountings. The mounting consisted of a high slide with a considerable slope (7.5 deg for 6in, as here) carrying a top carriage, consisting of the cylinders of the hydraulic buffers to which the trunnions of the gun are pivoted. The carriage was a steel casting held together by transoms and a bottom plate. Elevating gear consisted of a hand wheel and shaft working in brackets on the slide, driving a worm wheel on the top carriage which in turn connected to the elevating pinion via friction plates. The friction plates isolated the gearing from any sudden blow, such as the muzzle striking the gun port on recoil. The elevating shaft did not move when the gun recoiled, hence the gun could be elevated while it was being fired. Training gear was arranged so that it could train the gun or run it in for housing behind the doors of a port. As in the past, the gun trained along a racer to which it could be clipped; the racer could hold the mounting when it fired. By the mid-1880s it seemed likely that (as happened) the simpler central pivot mountings would become standard. The Vavasseur mounting incorporated a hydraulic recoil buffer consisting of two cylinders connected by a pipe, each with a piston being attached to the slide of the gun. The trunnion boxes were part of the cylinders, so that the cylinders with their connections formed the gun-carriage, and recoiled with the gun. As the gun recoiled, liquid was forced through holes in the piston, the ports closing gradually as the gun recoiled. Compared to the big Armstrong breech-loader, the gun had a simpler breech using an interrupted screw, which requires only a fraction of a turn to open or close it.
(National Maritime Museum 59-209)

it came to be commonly accepted). Observation of Bellevilles on board the French mail steamer *Laos* prompted the Royal Navy to try it on board the torpedo gunboat *Sharpshooter* and then to adopt it for numerous large cruisers, such as the *Powerful* class. The Belleville used large water-tubes, and it was attractive because it appeared to be sturdy, and because it was already in successful service. It offered more fire grate area (for overall size) than any other boiler then known, and its small elements did not require a large opening in a ship's armour deck. The Admiralty did not appreciate that Bellevilles, introduced at the same time as much higher steam pressure (300psi or more instead of 160), were a considerable technological leap. There were serious breakdowns in service; HMS *Hermes* had to come home after only a year in commission. *Europa* showed extravagant fuel consumption on passage from Portsmouth to Sydney: of eighty-eight days she had to spend thirty coaling (partly due to leaky condensers and leaky steam joints). The big cruiser *Terrible* burned 200 tons a day on a 1902 voyage to China at an average of 11.8kts, but two years later she burned only half as much at an average of 12.6kts.

Early problems with the Bellevilles were critical because it was adopted so quickly for so many important ships. By 1900 there were calls for a Committee of Enquiry, one engineer calling the Belleville 'the worst boiler in existence'. In September 1900 the Admiralty formed a Boiler Committee under Admiral Sir Compton Domville.[44] All but one member (Chief Inspector of Machinery J A Smith) were associated with either the merchant fleet or with Lloyd's. The first interim report was issued in 1901 and the final one in 1904. In 1904 Domville was flying his flag in the Belleville-boilered battleship *Bulwark*; he considered her boilers entirely satisfactory. Many of the problems attributed to the Bellevilles turned out to be due to other changes, including machinery packed too tightly together because with higher pressure it could be made more compact.

The interim report recommended fitting both cylindrical and water-tube boilers and abandonment of the Belleville as it seemed to have no particular advantages over other types. The committee listed thirty-six other water-tube boilers, of which it favoured four, already being fitted on a large scale in foreign navies: the Babcock & Wilcox, the French Niclausse, the German Dürr, and the Yarrow large-tube boiler. Of these the first two had already been tested satisfactorily in the Royal Navy, and were being adopted on a limited basis – two sloops (*Espiegle* and *Odin*) and a second-class cruiser (*Challenger*) were receiving Babcocks, and one sloop (*Fantome*) and a first-class cruiser (*Devonshire*) were receiving Niclausse boilers. The Babcock & Wilcox was already being tested on board the torpedo gunboat *Sheldrake*, but the type now contemplated was different. At the committee's suggestion, the cruisers *Medea* and *Medusa* were reboilered with, respectively, Yarrow and Dürr boilers, as it was difficult to draw conclusions fully applicable to larger ships from torpedo gunboat trials. In addition, in 1897 and in 1899 the small cruisers *Barham* and *Bellona* were both reboilered with Thornycroft water-tube (small-tube) boilers (not as part of the Boiler Committee program). Similarly, in 1900 and in 1901 *Blanche* and *Blonde* were reboilered with Normand small-tube water-tube boilers.

For ships powered by piston steam engines output is expressed in *indicated horsepower* (IHP). IHP was measured using an indicator card which directly measured the work done by the engine. Although an engine produced a given IHP, by no means was all of that power transmitted to the shaft. The engine drove various auxiliaries and also had to overcome friction within it. Modern turbine engines are rated in shaft horsepower (SHP), which is the power actually available to drive the propeller. For ships described in this book it was typically 80 to 85 per cent of IHP. Yet another measure of power was *effective horsepower* (EHP), the power actually required to drive a ship at a given speed, which was estimated on the basis of model tests. The model basin also estimated the efficiency of a ship's propellers, to estimate the IHP required to achieve the EHP it calculated. The overall ratio between EHP and IHP was about 50 per cent, but errors in estimating efficiency helped make it difficult to predict exactly how fast a given ship would be, even in smooth water. *Blake* and *Blenheim* seem to have been particular cases of failed estimates.

Tonnage and Cost

Until the early 1870s, ships at the design stage were described more by their *burthen* tonnage rather than by their displacement, as has been standard ever since. Burthen tonnage – sometimes called builder's (old) measurement – was easy to calculate because it was based entirely on a ship's dimensions. It was given as (L-2/3B) x B x B/2 divided by 94; one indication that it was being used in design reports was that tonnage was given as tons plus some number divided by 94. This tonnage seems to have been used initially because designers could not precisely predict the displacement of ships, perhaps partly because weights (particularly those of machinery) were difficult to estimate (but by about 1860 displacements were generally calculated, and accounts of earlier steam warships often include their displacements as well as their burthen tonnage). Burthen seems to have been considered a good way to compare hull cost. It was probably not too bad as long as ships had similar hull forms. That fell apart for ships with unusually fine hulls, which might be long but not heavy, as in the comparison between *Volage*, *Raleigh*, and *Bacchante* in 1871. The following year burthen was abolished as the official measure of ship size (displacement replaced it). That estimates could still be quite faulty became obvious in the unfortunate *Orlando* class more than a decade later.

For much the same reason, until the mid-1870s design reports gave nominal horsepower (NHP) rather than the indicated horsepower (IHP) which determined a ship's performance. NHP was a measure of the size of the engine, not its output. It could be specified precisely, but actual engine performance seems to have been a very different matter, again until some time in the late 1860s or early 1870s. NHP was 7 x area of piston x equivalent piston speed divided by 33,000. Equivalent piston speed was based on the length of the stroke. NHP matched actual indicated horsepower for a steam pressure of 7psi and particular average piston speeds (piston speed clearly varied during a stroke). By 1866, British engineers were achieving about six times NHP in actual output (IHP).

The Admiralty in a Time of Radical Change

Alongside this series of dramatic changes in technology was an equally dramatic change in the way in which the Admiralty, which was ultimately responsible for the ships, operated. It took a much larger and more complex Admiralty to handle the new technology. The changing form of the Admiralty helps explain how decisions as to the shape of the fleet (including the size and nature of the cruiser force) and the shape of the ships themselves were reached at various times. There was no formal naval staff of the type created just before and during the First World War, hence no formal staff requirements for ships or weapons. This lack suggested to later writers that throughout the century ship development was determined primarily by the way in which technology evolved and thus by the views of technical experts such as DNCs. The reality was considerably more complex. There is certainly evidence of exactly the sort of strategic thinking later associated with naval staffs. It does not help historians that in a small Admiralty organization much of what happened was decided by face to face meetings which did not have to be written up.

The issue which most exercised naval officers was the balance between political control, exerted by the First Lord (who was responsible to the Cabinet) and professional naval thinking (represented by the Naval Lords, who were later called Sea Lords). A second issue, increasingly important as the pace of technological change accelerated, was the way in which the professional officers on the Board were connected to technological experts. The professionals on the Board set policy, but it had to be translated into ships.

The almost continuous wars ending in 1815 created an administration focussed on operations with a nearly independent Navy Board responsible for manning, supplies, and materiel. Once the war was over, operations receded. In 1832, at the outset of the steam revolution, the Navy board was abolished and the Admiralty was made responsible for both operations and resources. The new organization emphasized professional naval experience more than its predecessor. The new Board consisted of a First Lord superintending four Naval Lords (headed by a Senior Naval Lord, later First Sea Lord) and a Civil Lord (Fifth Lord), each of whom was responsible for a department through its separate chief. The First Lord was a political appointee responsible to Parliament (i.e., to the Cabinet). Although in practice he generally accepted the advice of the Naval Lords, the First Lord could issue commands without their advice or approval. Serving officers could sit in Parliament and experienced admirals were often chosen as First Lords.

The Senior Naval Lord (sometimes called First Sea Lord) was responsible for the distribution and composition of the fleet, for drawing up sailing orders, and for armament and complements of ships – as an advisor to the civilian First Lord. He performed much the same duties as his predecessor in the earlier all-operational Admiralty Board. However, he was also responsible for the Surveyor, who in turn was responsible for materiel, including ships.[45] The Surveyor was envisaged as an instrument of the Board, designing (or ordering the design of) ships when asked to do so; the Board even reserved for itself decisions on the dimensions of masts and yards. In later terms the Surveyor was more DNC than anything else. In the official list of Directors of Naval Construction, Surveyors precede the first formally appointed DNC (his office was not yet called that), Sir Edward C Reed. The Surveyor had senior shipwrights (of the Royal Dockyards) under him; he had to approve the designs they submitted.

The Board did not provide the general policy guidelines envisaged. From about 1837 on the Surveyor gained autonomy. The Board as a whole seems to have been too busy with routine matters to spend time on policy and ship design issues.[46] In 1837 a separate steam department, under a Comptroller of Steam Machinery, was set up to work alongside the Surveyor's department.[47]

The two major Surveyors involved in this book were Captain Sir William Symonds (appointed 1832, retired 1847) and Rear Admiral Sir Baldwin Walker. Symonds was interested in curing what he considered the inferiority of British designs manifested in the Napoleonic Wars, favouring a combination of great beam and extraordinary sharpness, which made for much larger ships than their predecessors.[48] He was not professionally trained, and he distrusted the new scientific naval architecture, preferring what he considered a more traditional or pragmatic approach. Symonds was unfortunate in holding office just as new technology, such as iron hulls and screw propellers, developed. From 1841 the Board of Admiralty lost confidence in him, subjecting his work to more and more scrutiny.

In contrast, Walker was a respected seaman who knew that he was no naval architect. He intended to supervise naval architects. He also had far more respect than Symonds had shown for technical expertise.[49] Walker became Surveyor in February 1848. That June he made Isaac Watts his Assistant Surveyor and, in effect, his chief warship designer. In many cases, however, the chief shipwright at a yard prepared the design for a ship built there, in contrast to later (and earlier) policy in which basic design was centralized. That policy seems not to have solidified until the 1870s, under Barnaby.

With the new role of superintending the materiel of the fleet, in the spring of 1848 Lord Auckland the First Lord approved the existing practice under which the Surveyor prepared an annual program of ship construction and repair, taking into account the state of the fleet and reserves of timber in the yards. Auckland wanted the Surveyor's projection to take account also of the number of ships currently at sea and of the numbers likely to be sent to sea during the year (Walker seems not to have gone that far). On this basis Walker was responsible for the program of steam battleship construction offered to the Board in response to French programs. Walker had been seconded to the Turkish navy in 1840 and was thus in an excellent (and appreciated) position to advise the Board when the crisis with Russia escalated in 1853, leading to the Crimean War (the Great Russian War). Walker also seems to have been co-author of plans for the Baltic amphibious assault, the threat of which may have been decisive in ending the war on Allied terms. In 1859-60 the Surveyor was finally formally authorized to submit monthly and annual programs to the Board, and he was also given the authority to issue direct orders to master shipwrights and engineers in the yards (Walker had actually issued such orders since the Crimean War, particularly when they were urgent).

In 1860 the Surveyor was formally redesignated Controller of the Navy.[50] Walker was transferred out his job in 1861 to the post of commander of the Cape Station. His successor Rear Admiral (later Vice Admiral) Spencer Robinson found that he could not control shipbuilding and repair costs, so he sought to expand his powers. Cost control became more urgent because, from 1858 on, the Royal Navy was engaged in a building race with France, initially in wooden steam warships and then in ironclads. Both were far more expensive than their sailing predecessors.[51] In the past, a much larger fraction of the budget had been operating costs (including repairs to existing ships), and the size and shape of the fleet had not been urgent issues. Now they were. Robinson found himself trading off the cost of repairing existing wooden ships against that of new construction. Because the building program was now so large a fraction of the overall naval budget, changes (up or down) in the budget were often concentrated on new construction.

Robinson revived an earlier idea, that the Controller should sit on the Board. That did not happen at once, but he was regularly invited to Board meetings, as he was in effect the Board's expert on the new technology (particularly on guns and armour). He found himself disagreeing with his Senior Naval Lord, Admiral Sir Frederick Grey (in office 1861-66), who seems to have considered Robinson far too outspoken, and barred him from Board meetings. Even so, Robinson had a considerable impact on the Board in the form of comments on circulated papers. Moreover, Robinson made a very favourable impression on Civil Lord Hugh C E Childers (in office 1864-65), who shared his views on the need to centralize the Controller's authority to enforce financial discipline.

As Controller, Robinson made his chief shipwright his deputy for ship design and construction. This deputy was initially designated Chief Constructor, and then Director of Naval Construction (DNC). The connection to Controller shows in the later formal title of Assistant Controller and Director of Naval Construction. DNC was formally the professional advisor to the Board on warship design. In a period of rapid technological change, DNC's position had to include considerable advice to the Board as to what sorts of ships were needed, because no one on the Board had anything like the technical knowledge to translate policy into ships (though several senior naval officers tried, as will be seen). Watts retired in 1863, and Robinson chose 33-year-old Edward C Reed, who had gained prominence by publishing several ship designs in an engineering journal he edited. That Reed was a professional engineer (naval architect) rather than a product of the dockyard system (like the earlier chief shipwright, Isaac Watts) was held against him (and, presumably, against Robinson, too).

Alongside DNC was the Director of Naval Ordnance (DNO).[52] Under the 1832 reorganization, Second Naval Lord was responsible both for personnel and for artillery, including the work of the gunnery establishment HMS *Excellent*. The guns themselves were provided by the army.

The post of Engineer-in-Chief (EinC), responsible for ships' machinery, lapsed some time before 1870.

In December 1868 William Ewart Gladstone became Prime Minister. He was determined to cut naval spending by 10 per cent, partly by curtailing the building program. Having become First Lord, Childers pushed through the reform Robinson had advocated: Robinson became Second Naval Lord. The naval part of the Board was reduced to First Naval Lord, Second Naval Lord (Controller), and Junior Naval Lord, the latter only a Captain (previously a Rear Admiral). The Parliamentary Secretary (who became, in effect, a Board member) was responsible for finance. The Civil Lord became his assistant. Childers represented Gladstone, and neither man seems to have taken professional naval advice very seriously. In effect Childers simply dictated his reorganization (and other plans) to the Board, which met only rarely when he was First Lord. To contemporaries, the professional views of the navy, normally reflected by the Naval Lords, were being swept aside. Gladstone and his creature Childers were the enemies of British sea power. It happened that Gladstone's long-term adversary Benjamin Disraeli was not much more anxious to raise the naval budget.

Childers enthusiastically supported Captain Cowper Coles, who proposed a new kind of ironclad (built as HMS *Captain*) in the face of Reed's disapproval. The fight wore down Reed, who resigned in July 1870. He became both a commercial warship designer and, eventually, a Member of Parliament. His bitterness probably explains his public criticism of the designs produced by both Barnaby and Barnaby's successor Sir William H White. As for Coles, Reed was vindicated when HMS *Captain*, Coles's ship, capsized on 7 September 1870 (with Coles aboard). The key issue had been the ship's stability under sail. Childers blamed Robinson and Reed, but a full parliamentary inquiry into British warship design (which survives as a useful account of designs, including that of the new large cruisers) vindicated both.[53] The report was not published until 1872, and Reed's post as Chief Constructor was left empty. By that time Robinson had left, his position impossible given Childers' attacks. Childers left at about the same time, exhausted. The extent of Robinson's downfall is evident in his replacement by a Captain (Robert Hall), who remained as Controller until his post was removed from the Board the following year (May 1872).

A Select Committee of the House of Lords reviewed Admiralty procedures. Childers' successor George Goschen (appointed in March 1871) could not simply undo Childers' reorganization, because that would have been an admission that Gladstone himself had failed. Robinson was seen by many naval officers as an interloper on the Board. His position became the obvious victim; Goschen split off the Controller from the Second Naval Lord position and dropped it from the Board. That increased senior naval representation on the Board; Goschen also created the position of Naval Secretary. It was probably far more important that he stipulated regular Board meetings and also very frequent informal meetings including the Controller (to exchange views but not to take formal decisions). He recognized that he was no Childers.

Goschen appointed a new Chief Constructor: Reed's brother-in-law Nathaniel Barnaby, who had been running the department in Reed's absence. Barnaby was initially styled Chief Naval Architect, and some of Reed's powers were given to two other officers: a new Surveyor of Dockyards and a revived Engineer-in-Chief. For a time the three formed a Council of Construction, with Barnaby as chairman, but in 1875 Barnaby was appointed Director of Naval Construction (DNC). The other two offices remained, Engineer-in-Chief advising DNC and working with him.

Goschen's First Naval Lord was Sir Alexander Milne, who had already served as Senior Naval Lord in 1866-68.[54] He survived the change of administration in 1874. The new First Lord G Ward Hunt asked Milne and other senior officers for advice as to the proper size and shape of the fleet. Neither Childers

Until well into the 1880s, any Royal Navy ship intended to cruise for long periods had to rely on sail much of the time. This was not simply a question of steaming endurance. A ship on a foreign station for months at a time would use up her coal no matter how efficient her engines. Until there were plentiful coal supplies throughout the world, the ship would be unable to remain at sea under steam. Much the same consideration affected the shift from coal to oil fuel (it explains why the First World War *Hawkins* class cruisers, conceived for distant service against raiders, were designed with both coal- and oil-burning boilers, well after the Royal Navy shifted to all-oil-burning in cruisers designed to work with the main fleet. The cruiser was very different from a steamer making a point-to-point voyage of limited duration. The need for excellent sailing qualities much affected all design decisions, such as the restriction to single screws and usually to two-bladed screws (so that they could be raised). This photograph of the corvette (cruiser) HMS *Calypso* was taken by Cdr Robinson (HMS *Active*) when the Training Squadron was 'chasing' down the Trade Winds between the Canary Islands and Barbados. The squadron consisted of HMS *Active, Volage, Calypso*, and *Ruby. Calypso* was unique in the squadron for having a disconnecting propeller (which revolved when the ship exceeded 4kts); the others all had lifting screws. (National Maritime Museum, photograph courtesy of Mrs Craig-Waller, whose husband was a midshipman in *Calypso* from December 1889 to June 1891).
(National Maritime Museum L5403)

nor Goschen seems to have done so; the senior officers wrote as though this was an entirely new issue. Like Gladstone, Disraeli was interested in economy, so his First Lord asked what sort of fleet Britain needed in a time of profound and protracted peace. His naval officers rather more realistically estimated what sort of fleet the country would need in war, which they assumed meant war against France. That made sense: soon after 1874 it became clear that the world was becoming considerably more dangerous. The surprise, if indeed there was one, was that the immediate threat was Russian.

The change to a more modern Admiralty, with a war planning staff, began with the embarrassments of the Anglo-Russian crisis of 1877-78: mobilization problems and the absence of a vital intelligence report on Russian Baltic defences, prepared shortly before the war, which could not be found. A Mobilization Committee and a Foreign Intelligence Committee (FIC) were formed after the crisis ended.[55] The crisis made evident the global threat the Russians posed both to British trade and to isolated British colonies. Former First Naval Lord Admiral Milne was appointed to head a Colonial Defence Committee (CDC), which in turn led to the formation of the investigative Carnarvon Committee. In its wake the CDC was revived; among its successors was the Committee on Imperial Defence formed in 1902.

Key, who had commanded the 1878 Baltic fleet, became First Naval Lord on 15 September 1879, serving until 1 July 1885. The experience of botched mobilization (i.e., poor staff work) and poor intelligence support undoubtedly led him to turn the FIC into the Naval Intelligence Division and to entrust it with staff as well as pure intelligence duties. The need for intelligence was further emphasized when the Royal Navy found itself bombarding Alexandria in 1882 without sufficient information on the defences of the port.

The Controller once again sat on the Board (as Third Naval Lord) from 1882 on, perhaps also as a result of the lessons of the 1877-78 crisis. This was the final major change to the Board during the period covered by this book.

The most important thing did not change at all. The First Lord accepted the advice of the Naval Lords, but he was responsible to the Cabinet, which could and did veto proposed programs (such as an 1875 proposal for six fast cruisers). By the early 1880s some key British naval officers were convinced that no Government, either Liberal (Gladstone) or Conservative, was likely to solve the navy's problems of gross obsolescence (too few new ships to embody enough new technology) and limited numbers (in an era of growing foreign fleets). The public, or at least that portion of the public to which the politicians listened, had to be engaged, not least because the cost of naval growth would be considerable. In May 1881, for example, Captain J C E Colomb RN, who became famous as a strategist, complained to the Royal United Services Institution that few in the United Kingdom understood that their lives depended on seaborne trade; if it was interrupted, they were only a few months from starvation and penury. Most Britons imagined that sea dominance had been settled at Trafalgar (or even by the victory over the Armada), and that the defence of the British Isles themselves against invasion was all that mattered.[56]

Admiral Phipps Hornby, the hero of the straits ascent (and the commander at Portsmouth), orchestrated a campaign to reach public opinion over the head of the hostile Gladstone government. In September 1884 the journalist W T Stead, who was sympathetic to the navy, began publishing a series of articles called 'The Truth About the Navy' in the influential *Pall Mall Gazette*. Phipps Hornby's covert conduit to the press was Captain John Fisher, the future First Sea Lord.[57] Initially First Lord Northbrook was unrattled, saying that he had no idea what he would do with any large supplemental budget. Naturally First Naval Lord Admiral Cooper Key felt that he could not say that his resources were inadequate. As the campaign gained momentum, Gladstone's government felt compelled to give way. On 10 November Northbrook admitted in a speech at the Guildhall that more armoured ships and cruisers were needed, and that it was particularly important that the smaller ships be faster. On 2 December the government announced an additional £5.5 million for imperial defence (£3.1 million for the navy, £2.4 million for the army, naval ordnance and base fortifications) over the next five years, beginning with the 1885-86 program (reduced from the Admiralty estimate that £11 million was needed). Public opinion was so aroused that this rather large program was widely considered inadequate, Cooper Key becoming extremely unpopular within the navy for supporting the earlier government position.

The Northbrook Program amounted to 1 ironclad, 2 torpedo rams, 5 armoured cruisers, 10 torpedo cruisers, and 30 torpedo boats, beyond the normal annual programs. The money was later redistributed to buy 2 battleships (*Victoria* and *Sans Pareil*), 5 armoured cruisers (*Orlando* class), 6 torpedo cruisers (*Archer* class), and 14 torpedo boats (presumably including 4 torpedo gunboats). Among the first indications that the Northbrook Program would be carried out was the announcement of requests for tenders for six of the ten projected torpedo cruisers. Any backsliding on Gladstone's part was prevented by the 1885 war scare, which reinforced Stead's point that the navy was not powerful enough. From the navy's point of view the greatest success was that Stead made the strength of the Royal Navy a permanent and prominent public concern.

The British situation was exacerbated by a gun crisis: given the recent shift from Woolwich muzzle-loaders to Armstrong breech-loaders, there was a strong perception in 1884 that guns, particularly heavy ones, were not being produced nearly rapidly enough. The French seemed far ahead, and that sense contributed to the feeling of impending naval crisis.

After the Gladstone administration fell in 1885, new First Lord Hamilton determined on a large sustained program to ensure British naval superiority over both France and Russia (which were increasingly seen, realistically, as a combined threat).

Hamilton fired DNC Barnaby, who had been associated with the penny-pinching of the past. For example, Barnaby seems to have been fascinated with the idea of pushing down the size (hence the cost) of protected cruising ships. He also became associated with the idea of arming large fast merchant ships, which in Gladstone's terms might well be seen as a way of avoiding building expensive fast cruisers. Gladstone's aversion to spending probably explains why, in 1885, Captain Fisher pressed for a fast torpedo depot ship, but only as a conversion of a merchant ship – because building a special warship for that purpose would cut construction of more vital ships. Under the new regime, fast merchant ships were still worth arming in wartime – but only as supplements to the core of specially-built warships.

Hamilton was looking forward to a more expansive future. He needed a visionary DNC who could and would design the large modern warships he expected to finance. He appointed William H White, who had been Barnaby's assistant before being hired by Armstrong to design spectacular export cruisers.[58] White designed so many of the ships in this book that its subtitle might almost have been 'The White Era'. Having made a name at Armstrong (Elswick), White returned to the Admiralty as DNC, accepting a considerably reduced salary. In compensation the Admiralty shipped Barnaby's deputy Philip Watts to Armstrong as chief naval architect. Watts in turn replaced White in 1902.

Although Gladstone returned briefly to office in 1886, Hamilton was soon back, remaining in office between 9 August 1886 and 25 August 1892. He reached his goal with the 1889 Naval Defence Act. White worked with Hamilton to develop a rolling program which would maintain a modern Royal Navy. To that end White assigned ships effective lifetimes, which were formally proposed in 1891: 22 years for armoured, protected, and partially protected ships (including nearly all cruisers), i.e., depreciation of 4 per cent per year; and 15 years (6 per cent) for corvettes, sloops, torpedo cruisers, gun-vessels, gunboats, troopships, etc.[59] Lifetimes implied a regular replacement program.

White also prepared a report showing that 72 ships should be discarded between 1888 and 1891. That transformed Hamilton's major new construction program into a far more acceptable 70-ship replacement program. On the eve of the 1888 manoeuvres, the Naval Lords were asked for a confidential report showing what the navy would need in the event of a war with France. It was to include the requirements of a war against France and Russia, should it be necessary (as in 1885) to defend Constantinople. This was Hall's war, with Russia added. On this basis the Naval Lords asked for 65 ships – 8 first-class and 2 second-class battleships, 8 large cruisers, 25 second-class cruisers, 4 third-class cruisers, and 18 torpedo gunboats. The Naval Lords also wanted the building program reviewed no later than 1892-93, to prevent any break in construction. A program was submitted to the Cabinet about October 1888. It was soon buttressed by the post-manoeuvre report described above, which (with parts of the manoeuvre report itself) was released to Parliament in February 1889

On 7 March 1889 Lord George Hamilton introduced the Naval Defence Act: 21.5 million for 70 ships, including 8 first-class and 2 second-class battleships, 9 large *Edgar* class cruisers, 29 second-class cruisers (21 *Apollo* and 8 *Astraea* class), 4 third-class cruisers (*Pallas* class), and 18 torpedo gunboats. This multi-year program became possible when the British national debt was refinanced on favourable terms (the 32 ships to be built by contract were paid for out of the Consolidated Fund, to be spread over the seven years ending 31 March 1896, but the 38 ships to be built in Royal Dockyards were paid for out of annual votes).

By this time both the Russians and the French had bases outside Western Europe from which they could raid British territory in the Pacific. Australia was clearly increasingly at risk if war broke out. The key issue, revived again and again, was how to distribute the burden. The first Colonial (defence) Conference, meeting in 1887, proposed a deal in which the Australians would subsidize a British squadron. On this basis ships, including *Pearl* class cruisers, were ordered in 1888. The same conference released portions of the report of the earlier Carnarvon Committee (on colonial defence) which cast doubt on the Royal Navy's ability to protect the Empire.

The 1889 Act (and to a much lesser extent the 1884 Northbrook Program) was treated at the time as the dawn of a new Royal Navy, rejecting the sluggish and retrograde thinking of the past. That was natural. Until 1884 the Admiralty failed again and again to get across to its political masters what was needed to maintain British naval supremacy. In 1956 Dr Oscar Parkes labelled the pre-Act period 'the Dark Ages of the Admiralty' in his history of British battleships. In fact there was considerable continuity, particularly in strategic thinking. There was less continuity in technology, but that was simply because the technology kept changing at breakneck speed. The main darkness of the dark ages was political: the Admiralty's failure to gain political traction, hence the money it needed.

The 1889 Act included provision for a review of the building program not later than 1892-93, engendering the Naval Defence Act (Spencer Program) of 1893. Gladstone was back in office by this time, but he was unable to resist. Early in 1893 it seemed that no battleships at all would be included in the 1893-94 program. The public opinion which had swept in the 1889 Act was still potent. Spencer felt compelled to prove that his fleet was sufficiently more powerful than the French. The French announced a large program, including four new battleships ordered in January 1893. Spencer asked DNC White to prepare a statement listing new ships which might be laid down over the next five years to match the French. White considered six new battleships the absolute minimum to avoid critical weakness in 1896-97. When Spencer defended the existing fleet as adequate, the naval members of the Board threatened to resign as a body. Spencer found himself proposing a large program for 1893-98 (8 December 1893): 7 battleships, 2 large cruisers (*Powerful*s), 6 first-class cruisers (*Diadem* class), 12 second-class cruisers (*Talbot*s), 4 third-class cruisers (*Pelorus* class), 6 ram cruisers (*Arrogant*s), 7 torpedo gunboats, 2 sloops, 82 destroyers, 30 torpedo boats, and one torpedo depot ship. The cruisers were reduced, the *Diadem*s being deferred and only nine *Talbot*s being built. The program for ram cruisers seems to have been dropped, the *Arrogant*s having been bought before the Spencer Program began. The torpedo depot ship was also dropped. This program was financed at least partly by fiscal reform, the death duties being readjusted.

The multi-year approach did not quite capture the effect of headlong changes in technology. For example, in 1891 the Royal Navy had not one effective cruiser completed before 1878-79, and at least fifteen of the twenty built between 1879 and 1884 would be obsolete in 1894. Ships became obsolete long before they wore out. To make matters worse, the unit size, hence the unit cost, of ships continued to rise; what had paid for an adequate first-class cruiser in 1890 could hardly pay for a second-class cruiser in, say, 1898. Ships' machinery was a particular problem. Guns could be replaced by better ones, but it was entirely impractical to re-engine (and re-boiler) a ship in order to maintain her speed relative to more modern ships. The speed issue particularly affected cruisers.

Battleships did not grow very much over the decade following the Naval Defence Act, but cruisers did. Once battleships also began to grow the Royal Navy felt increasing financial pressure. Until 1909 there was, moreover, no corresponding change in British finances to relax that pressure. Admiral Sir John ('Jacky') Fisher was appointed First Sea Lord in 1904 specifically to solve the problem. In the Mediterranean he had shown that he could prevail over the French and the Russians with limited forces, relying on fast striking forces directed by intelligence rather than on the blocking concepts of the past. In the Admiralty Fisher sought to cut costs by ending the focal area cruiser strategy, substituting a limited number of large fast cruisers working with smaller ones. Fisher also sought deep cuts in the smaller deployed ships which were used mainly to police the Empire and to deal with peacetime threats to shipping, such as pirates. He was certainly aware that these roles mattered, but he also probably felt that they should have been paid for out of the Foreign Office budget.

Fisher's savings on cruisers made capital ships the single largest item in the British naval budget. They followed the same trajectory as the cruisers. Successive classes grew larger and much more expensive, so that by 1913 the Royal Navy again faced crisis, despite changes in its financing. The attempts to resolve this problem are beyond the scope of this book.

1 STEAM, SAIL, AND WOODEN HULLS

Ship Classification

During the age of sail the Royal Navy used two parallel forms of description. One was physical, based on the number of covered gun decks, meaning that a row of guns could be mounted on the deck above. The largest line-of-battle ships (liners) were three-deckers; frigates were single-deckers (although by the early nineteenth century the forecastle and quarterdecks of most large ships had been joined to form a complete flush deck above, capable of carrying an additional tier of guns). Sloops came in two forms: one with a single uncovered gun deck; and another with a light quarterdeck and forecastle above it. In both cases sloops were characterized by having a CO of Commander rank, as distinct from the Captain in charge of all larger ships.

Below them were gunbrigs and gunboats, usually commanded by Lieutenants. The frigate was the largest type of cruising warship, broadly corresponding to the later first-class cruiser.

However, formally the fleet was classified by Rates, from First to Sixth, with lesser vessels described as 'unrated', the divisions fixed by the number of guns carried. The first three rates were ships of the line, and below them were three rates of frigates, the smallest ships commanded by Captains. In 1817 the larger sloops were reclassified as Sixth Rate frigates (supposedly in order to give the experience of command to young Captains); mounting only 24 to 36 guns, they were disparagingly called 'donkey frigates'. They later came to be described by the borrowed term 'corvette', which the French had applied to warships of the size of the smallest Sixth Rates since the eighteenth century, though increasingly it applied to vessels with a single open gun battery. The corvette category was formally

Topaze was one of five 51-gun *Liffey* class frigates. In 1868 she was armed with five 7in breech-loading rifles on her upper deck (one revolving, four side) and with twelve 64pdr rifles and fourteen 8in smooth-bores (firing shells) on her main deck. At this time only she, *Mersey* (with 12), *Arethusa* (1), *Constance* (1), *Octavia* (1), *Doris* (4 on the upper deck and 4 on the main deck), *Endymion* (3 revolving guns), *Narcissus* (1), and *Aurora* (1) still had 7in rifled breech-loaders. She still had the same battery in 1872. By 1874 *Topaze* had been rearmed with the new standard frigate battery: four 64pdr on her upper deck (4 chase, 2 side) plus four 7in 6½-ton guns and eighteen 64pdr on her main deck. Upon commissioning in June 1859 she served in the Channel squadron, but was sent to the Pacific in October, serving there until September 1869. She was part of the Detached (Flying) Squadron between June 1871 and May 1877, then was coast guard at Kingstown until decommissioning in June 1878. She was sold for breaking up in February 1884.
(National Maritime Museum D2178)

established in the Royal Navy only in 1854, *Highflyer* and *Esk* being classified as corvettes, and other frigates later being placed in this category. However, the term 'corvette-built', meaning having a single open gun deck, was already well established by that time. Below corvettes in the steam era came sloops, still commanded by Commanders, and below them gun-vessels and gunboats. Gun-vessels carried their principal armament on one deck amidships on revolving slides; gunboats were low-powered gun-vessels intended only for coastal operations.[1]

This system broke down with the advent of armoured ships and individually powerful guns. The first armoured ships built for the Royal Navy, beginning with *Warrior* in 1861, were rated as frigates because they had a single covered gun deck. For cruisers the break came with the big *Inconstant* of 1866. She mounted most of her guns on an open gun deck, the idea being to limit splinter damage if they were hit. On this basis she was a corvette; because *Inconstant* was as large as many ironclads, the corvette classification must have seemed ludicrous, and she was redesignated a frigate. She and her near-sisters were very expensive, so an attempt was made to design a less expensive alternative, the *Boadicea* class, still with a heavy battery on an open gun deck, and still with the high speed of the *Inconstant*s. To show that these ships were not equivalent to *Inconstant*, they were rated as corvettes. This is much the same as the modern practice of calling ships frigates rather than destroyers, or destroyers rather than cruisers. To make matters more confusing, the corvette rating was also applied to much smaller ships.[2]

Into the 1860s annual programs of construction at the Royal Dockyards (but *not* contract construction) were defined by Programs of Works (PW), which are described in what follows. As with later programs, the fiscal year began at the end of March.

Warship design was somewhat decentralized: some designs were by the Surveyor of the Navy, but many were by Master Shipwrights at the Royal Dockyards. Those most important to steam cruiser design between 1830 and 1860 were:

Richard Abethell: at Portsmouth from July 1852
John Edye: at Pembroke from September 1837 and then at
    Plymouth and Devonport (single appointment,
    December 1843)
John Fincham: at Sheerness from February 1835, at
    Chatham from April 1839, at Portsmouth from October
    1844, then at Deptford from May 1860
Oliver Lang: at Sheerness from January 1823, then at
    Woolwich from July 1826
Oliver W Lang: at Pembroke from April 1853, and at
    Chatham from October 1858
Thomas Roberts: at Plymouth 1813-15 and 1830-37
    (he designed *Rhadamanthus*)
Joseph Seaton: at Sheerness from July 1826

In 1841 the Admiralty Board convened a committee of the Master Shipwrights to critique designs by Symonds (Surveyor) and Edye. Its criticisms were taken seriously enough that a new Committee of Reference was set up in 1846 to review Symonds' designs. Its chairman, Captain Lord John Hay, was supported by two Master Shipwrights (i.e., naval architects), Fincham and Abethell. It altered almost all of the ships not already well advanced, and it developed some of its own: the paddle frigate *Leopard*, the paddle sloop *Barracouta*, and the screw sloop *Brisk*.

When Symonds resigned in June 1847, Edye became acting Surveyor until the appointment of the new Surveyor, Captain Sir Baldwin Wake Walker, on 5 February 1848. During this time the Committee of Reference took responsibility for construction policy; it actively advocated steam power. Once Walker took office Edye and Isaac Watts acted as his constructors.

A few ships were designed by naval officers: *Sidon* by Captain Sir Charles Napier and *Janus* by Lord Dundonald (Admiral Thomas Cochrane).

Hulls

Although Britain had the world's first major iron industry, and although the first iron barge was demonstrated in 1787, the ships described in this chapter had wooden hulls. Iron plate was clearly stronger and lighter than wood, and once problems with magnetic compasses were solved, it became the predominant merchant shipbuilding material. The Royal Navy expected to follow suit, and ordered five iron frigates (four screw ships and one paddler).

While the iron frigates were being built, sceptics expressed doubts that iron hulls could withstand gunfire. Secret trials began in August 1845 with a 32pdr. A high-velocity shot would make a clean (pluggable) hole in an iron ship. However, a spent shot would create a hole with ragged edges, difficult to plug. These results could be used either to support or to condemn the new building material. Symonds was apparently quite hostile.[3] To clarify matters, the small worn-out iron tender *Ruby* was fired upon at HMS *Excellent*, the gunnery school. As before, the holes made by the shot were clean, but shot striking her ribs tore up the iron plating; the side opposite the entry of shot was badly damaged, and very dangerous splinters were created. The Board became nervous, and asked Symonds what it would cost to cancel the four steam frigates. In March the British Consul in New York was asked for details of US trials against iron plates at Sandy Hook, but that month it was decided simply to use the four frigates (*Greenock*, *Birkenhead*, *Megaera*, and *Simoom*) as transports.

Beginnings: Paddle Warships

The first British steam warships were paddlers. The British built the first seagoing steam warship in the world: the 907-ton (displacement) HMS *Dee*, launched 5 May 1832 and completed that year. She was eventually rated a second-class sloop, and falls outside the subject of this book.

Paddle frigates, intially classified as steam vessels first class, were reclassified as steam frigates first or second class on 31 May 1844, the exception being HMS *Gorgon*, which became a first-class sloop. The difference between first- and second-class frigates was complement, 200 or 175, respectively. Without the new heavy guns they would have been virtually useless, since the paddle wheel boxes covered a significant part of their sides. Once classifications had been set, armament was (in theory) standardized:[4]

First-class frigate: two 8in 112cwt, four 8in 65cwt, four
    32pdr 25cwt (crew 200)
Second-class frigate: two 8in 112cwt, four 8in 65cwt, two
    24pdr (crew 175)

First-class sloop: two 42pdr 84cwt, two 68pdr 64cwt, two 42pdr 22cwt (crew 145)

Second-class sloop: two 10in 84cwt, two 32pdr 25cwt (crew 100)

Third-class sloop: one 68pdr 65cwt, four 32pdr 17cwt (crew 100)

The sheer size of the program shows how strongly the Admiralty supported the new kind of propulsion. However, it was not the first to buy steam frigates: Egypt bought the world's first, *Nile*, which was built in London.[5] Five of the six large steam warships in the world in 1840 had been built in England, four of them for the Royal Navy. France had only laid down her first steam warship, *Infernal*. Hiccups in the British program, particularly the enlargement of so many ships to make up for unexpectedly large and heavy engines, show how experimental steam still was.

The British steam warship program began in earnest with the launch of the *Gorgon* and *Cyclops* in 1837-38 (1100 tons burthen, 320 NHP). Ordered on 25 June 1836, *Cyclops* was originally rated a steam vessel first class, and then a frigate. She was ordered with *Gorgon*, but in July 1838 was lengthened by 12¼ft.[6] Three slightly improved versions (*Vulture*, *Firebrand*, and *Gladiator*) were ordered on 18 March 1841.[7] HMS *Sampson* (Woolwich) was a lengthened version (by 13½ft) with a modified hull form, ordered the same day. Also on the same day two more ships, *Centaur* and *Dragon*, were ordered to a *Firebrand* design lengthened by 10ft.[8]

Dragon was renamed *Janus* in July 1843. She was built (PW 1843) to an experimental double-ended design produced by Admiral Cochrane, Lord Dundonald.[9] The *Cyclops* design became the basis of the next paddle frigate, work on which was authorized in March 1842: a large steam frigate of not less than 500 NHP armed with the new 8in (112cwt) gun. Maudsley (the machinery builders) offered 800 NHP using a double-cylinder engine as in HMS *Devastation* (which they said would fit the same space planned for 500 NHP), and 600 tons of coal. Drawings were submitted on 28 May 1842. This ship was ordered 26 March 1842 as *Dragon*, and then renamed *Watt* and finally *Retribution*.[10] The engineers had been over-optimistic. The ship was launched on 2 July 1844, and it became clear that her machinery was 131 tons overweight (displacement was not reported; she was 1641 tons burthen). Worse, proposed modifications to the engine would make it heavier, and the proposed installation of a lighter tubular boiler would take too long. The existing boilers were too large to allow for coal stowage in the bottom of the ship. The enormous paddle wheels were inefficient because they were too deeply immersed. The proposed solution was to install instead the 560 NHP engines bought for HMS *Leopard*, which could be done in about two months. *Leopard* herself was delayed pending availability of a new set of engines (she was not ordered until 26 March 1846, well after *Retribution* had been completed, and in January 1847 construction was suspended pending the *Odin* trials).

HMS *Dauntless* was ordered on 19 February 1844 as a repeat *Sampson*, but on 13 August the Surveyor was asked to prepare alternative paddle and screw versions, the screw version being chosen on 15 November. Before that could happen, designer John Fincham had to prove that the ship was large enough for her function.[11] In the process, her building yard was switched from Portsmouth to Deptford. Because she had not been designed from the outset for screw propulsion, her stern was too bluff, and she had to be lengthened 10ft in 1850 (her performance did not improve).

Meanwhile a design was prepared to convert 46-gun *Hebe* class sailing frigates to paddle frigates as a way of quickly enlarging the British steam fleet. Only *Penelope* (launched 1829) was modified in this way (conversion was ordered on 26 March 1842, the design being approved in May). Further conversions were dropped because policy shifted to converting frigates to screw propulsion.[12]

PW 1843 included one wooden and one iron paddle steamer. The wooden one was HMS *Terrible* (originally *Simoom*), built at Woolwich. *Terrible* was an unusually large frigate, exceptionally strongly built, with four double-ended tubular boilers, each with six furnaces and its own funnel (she was the first four-funnelled ship in the Royal Navy).[13] The iron one was *Birkenhead* (ex-*Vulcan*), the first of the five projected iron frigates (the others were screw ships). She was built privately, because the Royal Dockyards did not have iron shipbuilding capability. Ordered in April 1843, she was reordered as a troopship. She became famous for the exemplary conduct of her crew and her troops when she grounded and sank in 1852.

PW 1844 included six paddle frigates: *Avenger* and five frigates similar to *Sampson* (above): *Niger* and *Odin* to be built at Woolwich, *Conflict* and *Desperate* at Pembroke, and *Dauntless* at Portsmouth. In August 1844 the Admiralty ordered the Surveyor to prepare alternative plans for these five, as paddle or screw ships. In April 1845, *Dauntless* and *Conflict* were both ordered built as first-class steam sloops.[14] *Odin* was later transferred to Deptford and reordered to a new design. Two later ships, *Sidon* and *Leopard*, were to have been sisters. *Niger* ended up as a screw sloop, conceived specifically for comparison with the paddle sloop *Basilisk*.[15]

The 1845-46 program seems to have been devoted largely to screw ships, amounting to a kind of false dawn, as Surveyor Symonds clearly felt screws were a risky proposition (see below). *Sidon* (ordered April 1845) was an improved *Odin* with greater depth of hold and capacity for 400 more tons of coal. *Leopard* (ordered March 1846) was originally to have been a second *Odin*, but in 1848 she was lengthened by 10ft.

PW 1847 included the last British paddle frigates, the five modified *Sphinx* class, of which *Resolute* was cancelled in 1850.[16] Originally rated as first-class sloops (and planned as repeat *Driver*s), they were rerated as second-class frigates between 1847 and 1852, being completed in 1852-53. They fell into groups with different designs: *Magicienne* and *Valorous*, both at Pembroke; *Tiger* at Chatham; and *Furious* and *Resolute* at Portsmouth. Compared to *Sphinx*, they were enlarged (presumably to handle the increased weight of their engines): they were expected (as of June 1847) to displace 240 tons more than *Sphinx* and 139 more than *Bulldog*, making them 1200-tonners, which made them frigates rather than sloops (the sloops displaced 1055 and 1124 tons). Depth of hold would be a foot greater.[17] No further paddle frigates were built.

Alongside these paddle frigates were paddle sloops, originally steam vessels second and third class. The first of them, ordered in 1831, predated the paddle frigates. On 10 January

1831, less than two months after taking office, the new First Lord Sir James Graham ordered four built to competitive designs, one (*Phoenix*) by the Surveyor (Robert Seppings) and the other three by the Master Shipwrights of the Royal Dockyards. All were to have 220 NHP engines, at the time considered quite powerful, and all were to be schooner-rigged. Each would carry a 10in 80cwt gun. They were *Salamander* (Joseph Seaton, Sheerness [Seaton was Master Shipwright at Portsmouth, where she was originally to have been built]), *Phoenix* (Seppings, built at Chatham), *Rhadamanthus* (Thomas Roberts, built at Plymouth), and *Medea* (Oliver Lang, Woolwich). These ships were rerated as second-class sloops under the Admiralty Order of 31 May 1844, except that *Rhadamanthus* and *Medea* were classed as transports until 1846.[18] *Phoenix* was unique in later being converted into a screw sloop (at Deptford). She was reinforced for ice operation in 1854-55 specifically to attack Russian targets in the White Sea.

PW 1834 included three more paddle sloops: *Hermes* (Portsmouth, ordered January 1834), *Volcano* (Portsmouth: November 1834), and *Megaera* (Sheerness: November 1834; she was wrecked in 1843, freeing her name for the iron frigate mentioned above). A fourth, *Acheron*, was ordered in September 1837 from Sheerness.[19] *Hermes* was originally described as a (mail) packet. The Royal Navy took over post office mail service in 1836/7; it was soon returned to civilian hands. However, by 1840 there was interest in arming fast mail steamers in wartime. PW 1834 also appears to have included an abortive plan to build a steam vessel at Plymouth, using the teak frames originally produced at Bombay, and assembled at Plymouth for a planned 46-gun *Andromeda* class sailing frigate, laid down in 1822 and cancelled in August 1832. Construction was ordered in April 1834, and in July she was assigned two 110 NHP engines. This seems to have been the origin of HMS *Gorgon*, which was not, however, built at Plymouth.

PW 1834 included the much larger *Gorgon* (ordered from Pembroke in July 1834).

PW 1837 included *Hydra* (Chatham), and PW 1838 included two sisters: *Hecla* (Chatham) and *Hecate* (Chatham).[20]

Two PW 1838 ships planned as repeat *Medea*s were redesigned based on *Gorgon*: *Stromboli* (Portsmouth) and *Vesuvius* (Sheerness).[21] They were conceived specifically to carry 10in 84cwt guns fore and aft. Somewhat later they were assigned two 140 NHP engines each.

The PW 1839 paddle sloops were the *Alecto* class: *Alecto* (Chatham), *Prometheus* (Sheerness), *Polyphemus* (Chatham), and *Ardent* (Chatham). *Rattler* of this class was ordered under PW 1841 and then reordered as a screw sloop in February 1842, to become the first true warship propelled by screw. She and *Alecto* conducted a famous tug-of-war on 3 April 1845, in theory to show that screws were superior to paddles – but by that time the Admiralty was already ordering screw ships. A sixth ship, *Argus*, was ordered from Portsmouth under PW 1847, but then redesigned (lengthened by 6ft, with 11in more depth, adding 183 tons to displacement). *Ardent* was similarly modified.[22] *Polyphemus* was employed as a packet, armed with only one 32pdr 56cwt gun.

The PW 1840 class was six *Driver*s: *Driver* (Portsmouth), *Styx* (Sheerness), *Vixen* (Pembroke), *Devastation* (Woolwich), *Geyser* (Pembroke), and *Growler* (Chatham).[23] The repeat PW 1841 class comprised *Thunderbolt* (Portsmouth), *Cormorant* (Sheerness), *Spiteful* (Pembroke), *Eclair* (Woolwich), *Virago* (Chatham), and *Sphinx* (Woolwich). Plans for PW 1841 called for ten *Driver*s, but *Rattler* was built to the *Alecto* class, becoming a screw sloop. *Bulldog* (Chatham), *Inflexible* (Pembroke), and *Scourge* (Portsmouth) were lengthened at the bow (to add machinery space) to become the *Bulldog* class. A fourth ship of that class (*Fury*, Sheerness) was added under PW 1844. Another five *Driver*s were included in PW 1847: *Furious*, *Magicienne*, *Resolute*, *Tiger*, and *Valorous*) but *Resolute* was cancelled and the others reordered as paddle frigates.

PW 1846 included the paddle sloop *Basilisk* (Woolwich), intended specifically for comparison with her screw-powered half-sister *Niger*, with which she competed in, among other things, a tug-of-war like that between *Alecto* and *Rattler*.[24] Comparative trials were held between May and August 1849 – by which time the Royal Navy had already decided to adopt screws. The last Royal Navy paddle sloop was *Barracouta* (PW 1847, Pembroke), designed by the Committee of Reference.[25]

In parallel with the iron frigates, the Royal Navy ordered the iron paddle sloop *Trident* (initially as a steam yacht, then rerated as steam vessel third class, and then as a steam sloop in 1844). Three iron paddlers ordered as mail packets for the Ionian Islands, Malta, and Greece were briefly sloops third class.

The paddle warships particularly distinguished themselves during the first post-Napoleonic crisis between Britain and France, in the Mediterranean in 1839-40. It began when Mehmet Ali, pasha of quasi-independent Egypt (nominally part of the Ottoman Empire), decided to declare Egypt and his own dependency Syria (seized from Turkey in 1832) independent in name as well as in fact.[26] The British feared that the Ottoman Empire would break up, the Turkish part becoming a Russian satellite, bringing the Russians to the Mediterranean, with large forces in Asia Minor placed to march east to India. The Turks decided to crush Ali's rebellion by retaking Syria, but their June 1839 attack failed. In July their fleet defected to Egypt. On paper Ali now had the strongest fleet in the Mediterranean. His French backers envisaged a combined French-Egyptian fleet as a counter to British sea power. British Foreign Secretary Lord Palmerston declared the survival of the Ottoman Empire a vital British interest, to preserve the balance of power and the peace of Europe. French control of Egypt, the land link on the route to India, loomed. Increased Russian and French power would upset the balance of power in Europe, which guaranteed British security. Egypt already nominally controlled the North African and Arabian parts of the Ottoman (Muslim) Empire, and hence could also be seen as a threat to India (via the Gulf). Palmerston warned the Egyptans that they would be ejected from any naval base they created in the Gulf.

Palmerston sought unified European action backing Turkey, which he hoped would detach the Turks from an earlier treaty with the Russians. He backed his diplomacy by moving the Mediterranean Fleet near the Straits in 1839. The Russians, the Austrians, and the Prussians were willing to back Palmerston, but not surprisingly the French preferred to take their chances with the Egyptians. Palmerston used his European backing to manoeuvre his Cabinet into support.[27] In July 1840 he ordered the British fleet to prepare for action in Syria. British intelligence assured Palmerston that the French would not fight to support Mehmet Ali; their Mediterranean trade was already disappearing for fear that if war came it would all be seized by the Royal Navy.[28]

The new British steamers – HMS *Gorgon*, *Stromboli*, and *Vesuvius* – fought for the first time, as part of the mainly sailing Mediterranean Fleet. The most important action was an attack on the Syrian fortress of St Jean d'Acre. New gunnery training proved its value as even the smaller British ships managed to disperse Egyptian troops. HMS *Gorgon* fired the decisive shot that blew up the magazine at Acre and ended the battle. In this pre-telegraph campaign, steam was invaluable because it allowed Palmerston in London to keep in close touch with the local commander, Admiral Stopford of the Mediterranean Fleet. Palmerston considered Stopford too cautious. He later wrote that the attack on Acre would not have been mounted had he not been able to prod the Admiral on a timely basis, via HMS *Vesuvius*. It was essential to attack at once, because the French were playing for time, hoping to force a more favourable settlement as their own mobilization was completed and as the four-power agreement collapsed. Overall, steamers proved themselves by their sturdiness and manoeuvrability, even in rough seas. They landed troops (both British Marines and Turks). Paddle tugs towed sailing line of battle ships into the best positions for attack.

British naval steamers were also important in the Chinese campaigns of this time, but the Syrian campaign had the greatest impact. The French suddenly realized that the new technology offered a great opportunity: the British enjoyed a far greater lead in the existing technology of sail than in the new one. The blockades that had frustrated the French during the Napoleonic Wars were no longer practical, because it was no longer true that the wind which could blow a French fleet out of harbour could also propel the British fleet watching it. Because they could steam against the wind, the new ships could easily cross the Channel.

The Prince de Joinville, the French king's admiral son, suggested a steam-powered descent on the British south coast in an 1844 article, *Note sur l'etat des forces navales de la France*. De Joinville also argued that French paddle warships could effectively attack British trade, to an extent impossible in previous wars. He was mainly interested in encouraging the French

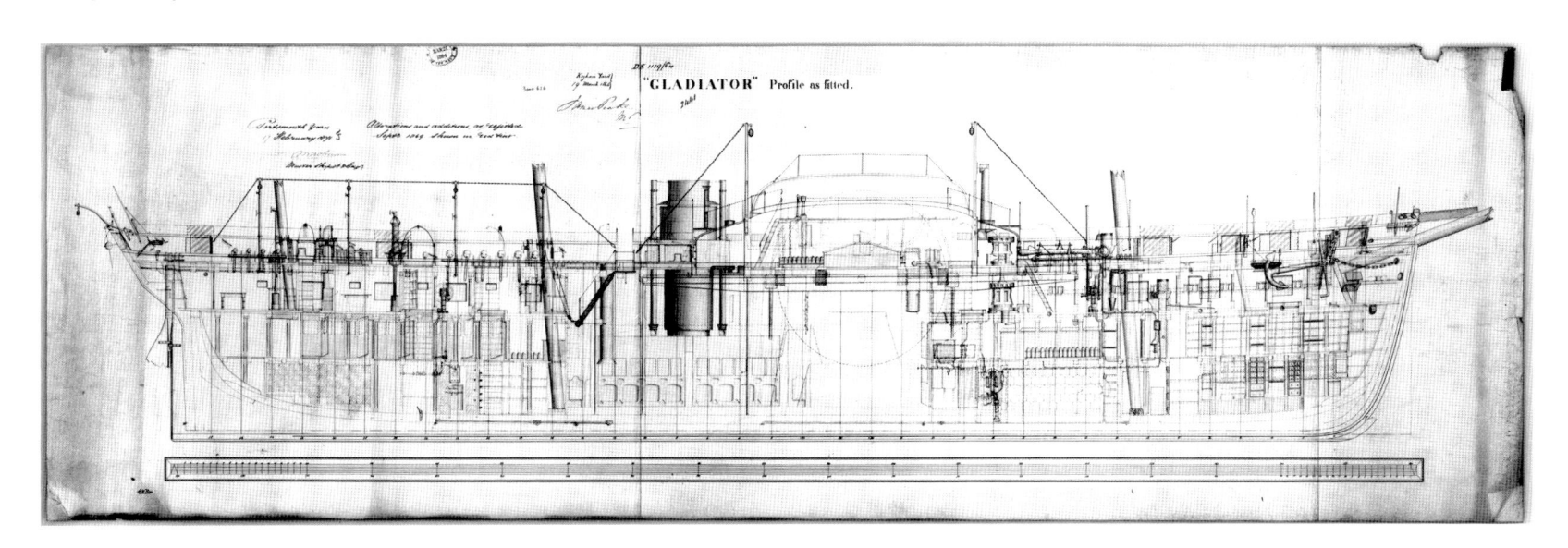

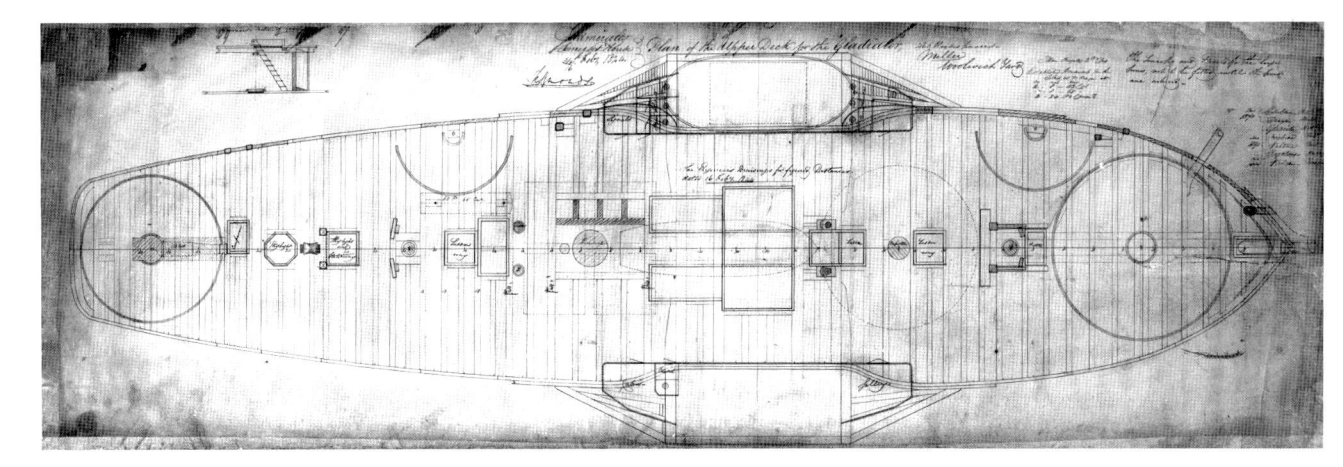

HMS *Gladiator* was a later *Cyclops* class paddle frigate, typical of a large group of ships. The deck view clearly shows how much of her length – which in early steam warships typically determined how many guns could be carried – was taken up by her paddle boxes. The circles and partial circles in the deck plan (dated 6 February 1844) were racers along which a slide pivoted at one end could traverse. The after racer shows one such slide, extending forward of its pivot. Presumably two of the starboard side pivots and racers have been omitted from the drawing. *Gladiator* was armed mainly with heavy-calibre shell-firing guns: two 8in (112cwt) and four 8in (65cwt), plus two 24pdr carronades. She had nothing but an upper-deck battery. Paddlers like this one were expected to use their power to manoeuvre and to maintain long range, since they could not stand up to the heavy broadsides of sailing warships (or of the later screw warships). *Gladiator* was completed on 25 April 1846 (launched 15 October 1844), and survived until 1879. Upon completion she was assigned to the Channel squadron and then to the Mediterranean. In 1855 she went to the Black Sea to fight in the Russian (Crimean) War. In 1859 she was commissioned for the North America and West Indies station, and upon her return she was commissioned for particular service (March 1864), including trials for the Floating Obstruction Committee (1865). Between August 1869 and February 1872 she served on the South East Coast of America station, paying off on 20 February 1872.
(National Maritime Museum DR3000626 and DR7580)

Aurora was one of five *Imperieuse* class 51-gun screw frigates. Her single funnel is down. Even with their funnels retracted, steam frigates could be distinguished from their sailing relatives by the greater separation between their fore- and mainmasts, the heavy steam machinery being placed as close as possible to the ship's centre of buoyancy, the cylinders clearing the base of the mainmast. These ships had two-cylinder single expansion engines; *Aurora* was rated at 400 NHP but on trial produced 1576 IHP for 10.21kts. In 1868 *Aurora* was armed with one 7in and eight 40pdrs on her upper deck (all rifled guns) and with twelve 64pdr rifles and fourteen 8in smooth-bores on her main deck. The 40pdrs and 20pdrs were Armstrong breech-loaders. Only she, *Arethusa*, *Constance*, *Octavia*, and *Narcissus* had the 40pdrs. In 1872 *Aurora* had the new standard frigate battery: six 64pdr on her upper deck (4 chase, 2 broadside) plus four 7in 6½-ton and eighteen 64pdr on her main deck. Ordered on 4 April 1851, she was laid down on 5 September 1854, but not launched until 22 June 1861. Her career illustrates rapid changes in British naval policy due to the perceived French build-up of the 1850s and early 1860s. After the demobilization following the Crimean War, the sole remaining large British naval formation was the Mediterranean Fleet, which in 1856 comprised six steam battleships ('liners') and eight cruisers (presumably frigates). This fleet was well situated to swing between the Channel and the eastern Mediterranean, but it could not deal with any rapid mobilization of French naval forces in the Channel (in 1856 the main French fleet was based at Toulon, in the Mediterranean). The cry in the late 1850s was therefore for a permanent Channel squadron or fleet. It was formed late in 1858, initially with five steam battleships and three cruisers. After war broke out between France and Austria (over parts of what would now be called Italy) in April 1859, four reserve battleships were commissioned to replace ships sent from the Channel squadron to reinforce the Mediterranean. Because the Royal Navy had demobilized so completely after the Crimean War, and because it had to rely on volunteers, the recommissioned ships were considered ineffective, as their

to embrace the new technology, but many in Britain saw the article as a warning. British budget cuts had considerably reduced the active fleet. A French naval attack on Tangiers (August 1844) commanded by de Joinville seemed to show increasing French aggressiveness. British Prime Minister Robert Peel had to contemplate mobilization. Among the measures considered was arming the growing British steam merchant fleet.

The perceived French threat (and British inadequacy) became a major political issue between the Tories and the Liberals.[29] In July 1845, in opposition, Lord Palmerston told the House of Commons that a 'steam bridge' had turned the Channel into a viable invasion route. The British had more steamers than the French, but they were deployed globally.[30] The French could concentrate their smaller fleet to attain local superiority in the Channel. The British relied on their greater mass of merchant seamen to mobilize their large reserve fleet. The French had an organized naval reserve, which could be deployed more quickly.

British responses to the threat included the creation of defended harbours at Dover, Harwich, and Portland as centres of naval concentration in the event of war.[31] In August 1845 the Admiralty ordered the first conversions of old ships of the line and frigates into self-propelled 'blockships' (mobile floating batteries).[32]

In January 1847 the public outcry reached its peak when, without permission, *The Times* published a letter from the Duke of Wellington, by far the most authoritative British military man, to Sir John Burgoyne.[33] Steam ships could quickly place a large body of men on the south coast. They could capture a harbour, land their cavalry and artillery, and march on London. Against a 40,000-man French army, the British could probably concentrate only 5000 men. This kind of invasion threat was raised frequently through the nineteenth and early twentieth centuries

crews were inexperienced. By 1863, when *Aurora* was completed, new ships were often going to the Channel rather than the Mediterranean. Thus HMS *Aurora* served initially in the Channel squadron (November 1863 to September 1865), including a voyage in which she took the Prince and Princess of Wales to Copenhagen and the Baltic. In January 1865 she was sent to the North America and West Indies squadron. In August 1866 she was one of three screw frigates in the West Indies (the others were *Doris* and *Constance*). She visited Quebec that year. She paid off in December 1867, and was a sea-going training ship for boys in 1872. She was briefly in the detached squadron in 1873, and then temporary flagship at Queenstown, before being reduced to coast guard duty at Greenock in May 1874. She was finally paid off on 19 June 1877, and discarded in 1881.

(Allan C Green, courtesy of State Library of Victoria)

HMS *Salamander* was the first substantial Royal Navy steam warship, ordered on 12 January 1831 and completed on 12 February 1833. She was rated as a second-class steam sloop, armed with two pivoted 10in 84cwt shell guns and two (later four) 32pdr 25cwt guns. In this she was part of a trend towards relatively small ships armed with unusually powerful weapons, which might counter the massed fire of more conventional warships. She displaced 1018 tons and could make 7kts under steam. *Salamander* was designed by Joseph Seaton, who was Master Shipwright at Sheerness (where she was built) in 1826-30. Through August 1841 she was assigned to particular service. In June 1842 she was commissioned for the South America station, then between July 18509 and August 1854 she was on the East Indies station. She was assigned to the Mediterranean between August and November 1854, then to the West Coast of Africa (November 1855 – February 1857). She was then on the Australia station, beginning no later than 1860 and serving there at least through 1865.

(National Maritime Museum A0501)

as an argument for army as opposed to navy expenditure.

The panic evaporated when Chancellor of the Exchequer Lord John Russell proposed more than doubling income tax to pay for increased defence. The downfall that year of French King Louis Philippe (and consequently of his son) contributed to the sense of relief, and a committee of the House of Commons was appointed to recommend reductions in military and naval expenditure.

Screw Steamers
The screw sloop *Rattler* ran her first trials in 1843. The next year bids were invited for four iron screw frigates and it was decided to order HMS *Dauntless* as a screw frigate rather than as a paddler (she and screw frigate HMS *Termagant* were ordered in 1845, together with the iron screw frigates).[34] Sceptics led by Surveyor Symonds considered the new screw warships risky experiments. In October 1846 Symonds wrote that *Termagant* and *Dauntless* were unusually long narrow ships designed specially to carry a heavy main deck armament. Neither had sufficient displacement to allow for enough stores, provisions, etc for the complements required to work their heavy armament. If the openings in their decks were sufficiently enlarged to properly ventilate their engine rooms and stokeholds, there would not be sufficient space on deck to operate their guns. Symonds wanted the experimental ships completed and tested before any further screw ships were built or converted. On this basis, the planned sister ships of the two prototype frigates, respectively HMS *Euphrates* and HMS *Vigilant*, ordered in January 1846, were suspended a few months later. Both were cancelled on 22 May 1849. The frigate *Fervent*, conceived as a screw equivalent to the large paddle frigate *Terrible*, ordered a month after *Termagant* and *Dauntless*, was suspended six weeks later (7 April 1845) and cancelled with the others in 1849.

Galatea was one of two 26-gun *Ariadne* class corvettes, which were rerated frigates (two more were cancelled). They and the *Orlando*s were known as 'Walker's big frigates', designed specifically for speed through a combination of high power and great length. Rated at 800 NHP, *Galatea* made 3061 IHP (11.796kts). Her sister *Ariadne* made 13.087kts on 3350 IHP. The reduced number of guns was balanced by much greater individual power: she had twenty-four 10in shell guns on her broadside and two 68pdr chasers (soon replaced by slide-mounted Armstrong 110pdr breech-loaders). The ship in the background is the *Pearl* class corvette HMS *Challenger*, soon to become famous as a scientific survey ship. They were photographed together in Sydney in 1867. She had been repaired the previous year. In 1868 *Galatea* and *Ariadne* were both armed with four 64pdr muzzle-loading rifles on her upper deck and with four 7in muzzle-loading rifles and eighteen 10in muzzle-loading smooth-bores on her main deck. They retained this battery to the end of their careers. She was commissioned in May 1862 for the Channel squadron, then going to the North America and West Indies station. Beginning in January 1867 she undertook an extensive world tour commanded by Captain the Duke of Edinburgh. Decommissioned in June 1871, she was broken up in 1883.
(Allan C Green via State Library of Victoria)

The 1845 program included four iron screw warships, bids for which were requested in 1844 (received November 1844). In February 1845 contracts were let to private builders already experienced in building iron merchant ships: *Pegasus* (completed as the commercial *Greenock*), *Vulcan*, *Megaera*, and *Simoom*. *Megaera* and *Pegasus* were ordered as first-class screw sloops rather than frigates but later rerated.[35] In later terms, all were sailing ships with auxiliary steam power. After the unfavourable firing tests at Portsmouth, the program collapsed. An early sign was the November 1846 decision to rename *Pegasus* as *Greenock* (where she was built). On 1 December the Admiralty asked for cancellation costs. In April 1847 it decided to complete all four as troopships with reduced power.

Parallel experiments with screw propulsion were the conversion of the frigate *Amphion* and the screw line of battle ship *Blenheim*. HMS *Amphion* was ordered as the sailing Fifth Rate *Ambuscade* in 1828 (renamed in 1831), but was not laid down until 1840. She was initially rated steam vessel first class, then rerated as a steam frigate on 9 May 1845. At this point steam machinery was so massive that it limited space for provisions and ammunition. *Amphion* was very much a sailing ship with an auxiliary steam engine; she made only 6.75kts under steam.[36]

A second frigate conversion soon followed: HMS *Arrogant* (1872 tons, 360 NHP). Ordered as a sailing frigate, she was reordered as a steam frigate in February 1845.[37] Like *Amphion*, she was very much a sailing warship with auxiliary steam power; she developed 774 IHP, for 8.6kts under steam. Her important innovation was direct rather than geared drive connecting engine and screw. Its success led to adoption in the next conversion design, *Imperieuse*, and in later screw frigates. Armament amounted to 28 main deck guns (twelve 8in 65cwt and sixteen 32pdr 56cwt) plus 18 upper deck guns (two 68pdr 95cwt and sixteen 32pdr 32cwt), a total of 46.

HMS *Encounter* (reclassified as a corvette) was the first steam sloop built from the outset with a propeller.[38] She was ordered in March 1845 (PW 1845, Pembroke) and lengthened aft while under construction. In accordance with the Surveyor's view that only single prototypes should be built, her sister ship *Harrier* (ordered March 1846 under PW 1846, also from Pembroke) was suspended in September 1846; she was cancelled in April 1851, presumably because by then she was obsolete.

Roughly parallel to these frigate conversions was the conversion of the paddle sloop *Phoenix*, ordered in March 1843 and begun in April 1844.[39] PW 1845 also included two *Conflict* class sloops (never reclassified as corvettes), both built at Pembroke: *Conflict* and *Desperate*.[40] Two sisters ordered from Pembroke under PW 1846 were cancelled: *Enchantress* and *Falcon*.

PW 1846 included another single corvette, *Niger* (Woolwich), a screw equivalent of the paddle *Basilisk*, intended specifically for comparative trials. Again, in accord with Surveyor's dictum, her sister ship *Florentia* (ordered at the same time from Woolwich) was suspended in October 1846 and then cancelled in May 1849.

PW 1847 included five screw sloops (ordered 17 February 1847) to the *Rattler* design: *Brisk* and *Highflyer* from Woolwich, *Archer* and *Parthian* (renamed *Wasp*) from Deptford, and *Grinder* (renamed *Miranda*) from Sheerness.[41] Compared to *Rattler*, these ships were intended to be 3ft 6in longer and 12in beamier, adding 198 tons to their displacement. *Highflyer* was later built to a larger design, rated as a corvette (see below). Two others were built to different improved *Rattler* designs: *Miranda* by Lord John Hay, *Brisk* by the Committee of Reference. *Archer* and *Wasp* were built to a separate John Edye design. They had been ordered as gun-vessels (*Rifleman* class) in 1846 and reordered as screw sloops on 25 April 1847. As an indication of how fluid the situation was, in March 1849 the Admiralty ordered the 250 NHP engine of *Wasp* replaced by a 60 NHP engine; she ended up with a 100 NHP engine (which produced 280 IHP, for 8.2kts). Her sister *Archer* had a 202 NHP horizontal geared engine, which produced 347 IHP, for 7.8kts. *Archer* was reclassed as a corvette in 1862, but her sister *Wasp* remained a sloop.

One more screw sloop, *Malacca*, was ordered built under contract in Moulmein, Burma, where there were abundant sup-

Orlando was one of two *Mersey* class frigates, the longest wooden ships ever built for the Royal Navy. With the *Ariadne*s, the *Orlando*s comprised 'Walker's big frigates', the difference being that they were rated as frigates from the outset, which meant they had covered gun decks. Gun deck armament was twenty-eight 10in shell guns; their upper decks had twelve slide-mounted 95cwt 68pdrs. On trial, *Orlando* made 13kts on 3617 IHP (she was rated at 1000 NHP). As one of the most powerful British cruisers of her time, upon commissioning (December 1861) *Orlando* went to the North America and West Indies station as part of a build-up of British naval forces occasioned by the Union seizure of two Confederate envoys on board the British mail steamer *Trent* (8 November 1861). The CinC on the station was Rear Admiral Sir Alexander Milne. His plan, had war broken out, was to break the Union blockade of the Confederacy, hopefully destroying the main Union fleet in the process, then enforce his own blockade of the North. Early in December orders went to the Cape, Brazils, and Pacific stations to be ready to attack US commerce. At the outbreak of the American Civil War in July 1861, Milne had two capital ships and seven cruisers. In October three capital ships and two cruisers were added, but they were earmarked for allied representation in Mexico. By 6 December three capital ships, a frigate, and a corvette had been transferred from the Channel and the Mediterranean to the North America and West Indies station, and a frigate from the reserve had been ordered to Bermuda. Three more Mediterranean frigates were placed on standby status at Gibraltar. Two of them escorted troop ships (11,000 men) to Canada, and a sloop was taken from reserve. Milne then had eight capital ships and thirteen cruisers (frigates and corvettes), the latter including all four of Walker's big fast frigates (*Mersey*s and *Ariadne*s) plus *Diadem*, his earlier large frigate (her sister *Doris* did not join the station). The big cruisers were intended specifically to deal with the sort of commerce raiding which had marked US strategy during the War of 1812. Tensions eased in 1862, and although the increased military strength in Canada was maintained, the North America and West Indies station was drawn down. *Orlando* went to the Mediterranean in 1863, remaining there until she returned to be paid off at Plymouth on 3 January 1866; she was sold for breaking up in 1871. Great length was a problem. In January 1862 Milne wrote to Senior Naval Lord Admiral Grey that he had had 'very bad accounts of the state of the *Orlando* ... I feel assured that these long ships will prove unsatisfactory to the service as sea boats, and will work themselves to pieces, nor can the rudder exert power over them, the leverage is too great and they fall off into the trough of the sea.' The dockyard at Bermuda required six months to make good the ship's defects. She had just broken the knees bracing the sternpost, and iron ones had to be fitted. Caulking placed in the hull in Halifax had all been driven out, presumably by the flexing of the hull, and the holds were 'in a beastly state'. The next year Milne wrote that the after sternpost had separated about ten or twelve feet above water; he suspected that the whole after body of the ship was weak 'and it will not do to keep the ship out here'. He worried that once the ship was drydocked the damage would become invisible, as once on the blocks the stern piece would be forced up into position. *Orlando* had to be sent home so that her sternpost could be repaired again (Milne correspondence courtesy of Professor John Beeler). *Orlando* was sufficiently valued to be first in line for new ordnance. She and *Mersey* were each given four of the new 7in muzzle-loaders under the 1865 rearmament program, although they were not on the list for first installation of the new 64pdr muzzle-loading rifles (in August 1866 both ships were on the refit list). In January 1868 *Orlando* was armed with twelve 64pdr muzzle-loading rifles on her upper deck and with four 7in and thirty 64pdr MLRs on her main deck. Her sister *Mersey* had an earlier battery: twelve 7in breech-loading rifles on her upper deck plus four 7in muzzle-loading rifles and twenty 10in smooth-bore shell guns on her main deck.

(National Maritime Museum 9077)

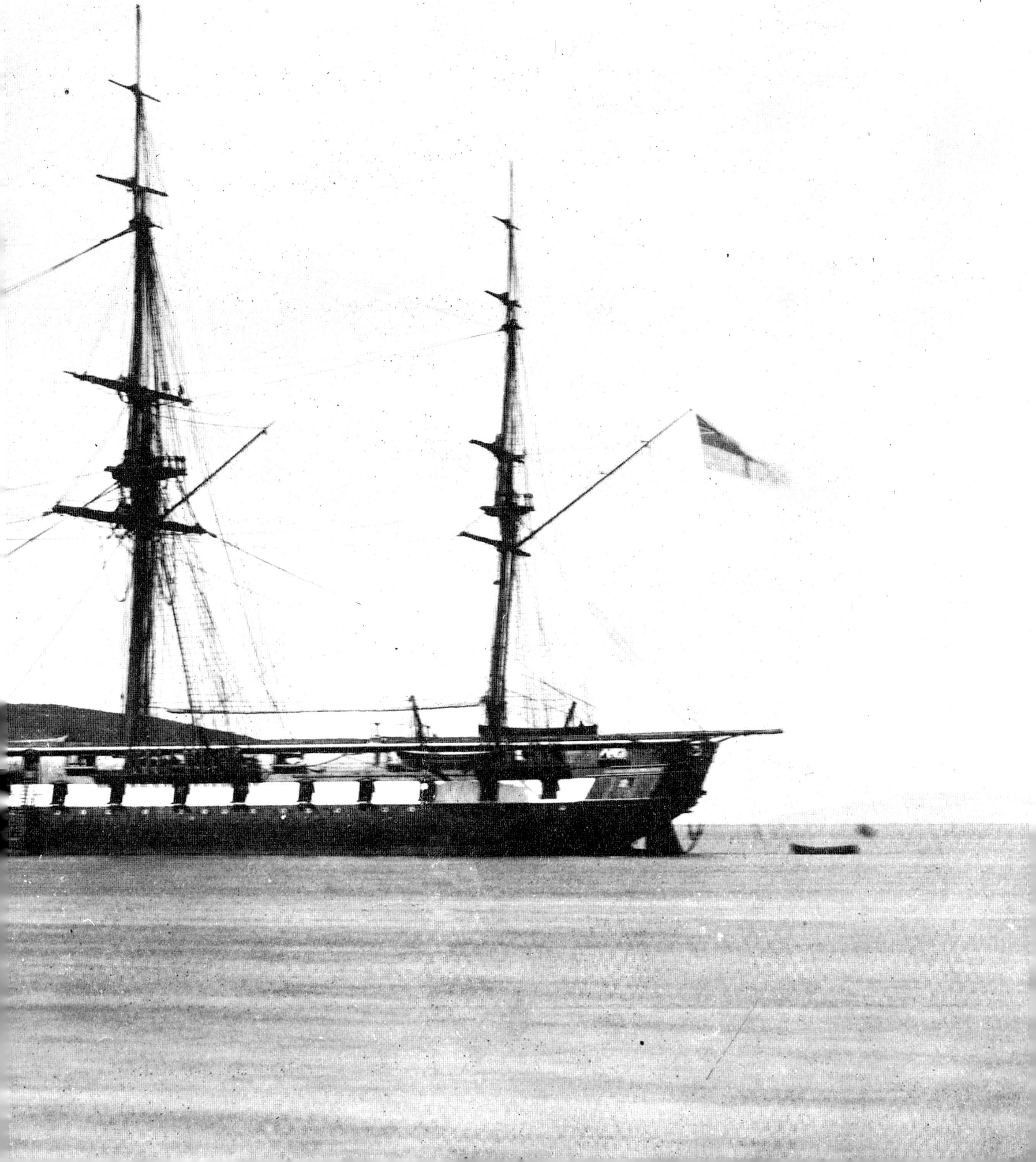

Walker's big fast frigates were inspired by a US program of six large steam warships authorized on 6 April 1854: five steam frigates and the steam corvette *Niagara*. Armament was unusually powerful (one 10in, twenty-six 9in, and fourteen 8in muzzle-loaders) and the ships were large for their time (*Minnesota* displaced 4833 tons, compared to 5385 tons for *Orlando*). Although the US ships were intended as fast sailers, they were slow under steam (about 9kts). There was also a French threat, which has usually been ignored. In September 1852 the French announced a project for a first-class steam frigate to make the highest possible speed, with enough coal to steam for 10 to 12 days. The designers at Brest chose fine hull forms like those then being adopted for big transatlantic liners, so on a displacement of 4000 tons they were 80m (about 291ft) long. Toulon offered a more conservative hull form. The French chose five Brest-type frigates (the *Imperatrice Eugenie* class, 3800 metric tons, 56 guns) and one Toulon-type frigate (*Souvereine*). On trials these ships exceeded 12kts, but according to a French account their sailing qualities left something to be desired, and they suffered from the speed with which they were built. Even so, the six big French frigates must have been even more daunting than the six slower US ships. In October 1858 the Minister of Marine asked his constructors at Brest and Toulon for designs for a 'cruising frigate' (*frégate de croisière*) intended specifically to operate against trade from foreign stations. He received nine proposals, the ships ranging from 4000 to 5200 tons; this large size was due to the requirement that the ships be able to cruise for as much as six months at a time. All proposals were rejected as too expensive, but by this time the French, as much as the British, were probably finding it impossible to afford a cruiser program alongside a substantial ironclad program.

plies of superior teak wood. She was conceived as a duplicate *Tiger*, i.e., a second-class paddle frigate, but was completed as a screw sloop. The incomplete (unpowered) ship sailed for Britain in May 1853. That November she was assigned the 200 NHP engine of *Active*.[42]

PW 1847 also included four 'steam gun schooners': the *Cracker* class (*Cracker* and *Hornet* at, respectively, Deptford and Woolwich), *Plumper* (Portsmouth), and *Reynard* (Deptford). *Reynard* and *Plumper* were alternative 8-gun sloop designs by, respectively, Fincham and Edye.[43] Both *Cracker* and *Hornet* were cancelled and reordered, *Cracker* to the larger *Cruizer* design. Another four steam gun schooners were in the projected PW 1848, two each being ordered from Deptford and Chatham, but they were not built in that form.

The Admiralty saw steam as a useful supplement to sail. For example, in 1847 the commander of HMS *Rattler* reported her underpowered, faster under steam plus sail than under steam. The Board replied that there was no point in increasing the ship's steam power. She should sail from point to point, adding her steam power for battle, much as later ships with combined powerplants lit off their boost plants only for combat. The Admiralty Board was still interested in pure sailing warships: in mid-1848 there was protracted discussion of the design of a new class of large sailing frigates (50 to 60 guns). However, in July 1848 the Board instructed the Surveyor to design the ships so that they could be converted to steam if so desired. Any decision would await more evidence as to the capability of steam screw warships.

At just this point the blockship *Blenheim* and the screw frigate *Amphion* demonstrated excellent seagoing capabilities. Squadron operations off Lisbon made it obvious that screw ships were much superior to paddlers.[44] On 5 January 1848 three existing ships of the line were ordered fitted with engines originally ordered for the abortive iron screw frigates, but the conversions were soon cancelled. However, beginning in 1849 both the British and the French began to build screw capital ships.

The French 'steam bridge' threat had apparently evaporated with the 1848 revolution deposing Louis Philippe (and therefore the Prince de Joinville), but in April 1849 British fears were renewed when the French managed to deploy a substantial army to Italy from Toulon within ten days.

Impérieuse, ordered as a 60-gun sailing frigate in March 1848, was reordered as a screw frigate on 14 June 1850. She became the first of a class of five (*Impérieuse*, *Euryalus*, *Aurora*, *Forte*, and *Chesapeake*). This seems to have been the result of a June 1850 submission by the Surveyor.[45] Like *Arrogant*, these were conceived as low-powered frigates with auxiliary steam engines, in this case of 360 or 400 NHP. Although conceived as 50-gun frigates, these ships ended up as 51-gunners, with a 68pdr (95cwt) chaser on the upper deck.[46]

Tribune, an 'auxiliary power screw frigate', was the second conversion ordered at this time. Ordered as a 28-gun sailing frigate in 1846, in 1850 she was reordered as a smaller screw frigate, to be built at Sheerness under PW 1850. A design submitted on 31 October 1850 showed 30 guns plus a chaser forward.[47] Her 300 NHP engine was hardly powerful for the time (1068 IHP for 10.4kts). Later a second ship, *Curacoa*, was built to the same design with a somewhat more powerful engine (350 NHP); see below.

On 30 November 1849 a new considerably enlarged design

for the sloop *Highflyer* was approved. She had originally been ordered from Woolwich, then shifted to Chatham in March 1849, and then to a contract with C J Mare & Co of Blackwall – a very unusual procedure at the time.[48] In March 1852 she was rerated as a Fifth Rate frigate (i.e., a corvette under a later rating system). A second ship, *Esk*, was ordered from Deptford on 23 March 1850 (i.e., under PW 1850), but the order was shifted in August 1852 to J Scott Russell of Millwall in exchange for the iron frigate *Greenock* (ex-*Pegasus*), which Russell sold to the Australian Royal Mail Co. Deptford built the sloop *Fawn* instead. *Pylades* (below) was originally to have been a sister ship, but was given 2ft more beam. This was the first class of steam corvettes in the Royal Navy.

In May 1850 the Surveyor, Captain Walker, listed the steam strength of the Royal Navy: 3 liners, 4 liner blockships, 4 frigate blockships, 22 steam frigates (paddle and screw), 64 steam sloops, and 26 steam gun-vessels. There were also 91 sail liners, 82 Fourth and Fifth Rate sailing frigates, 31 Sixth Rates (sailing corvettes), 58 sailing ship-rigged sloops, and 27 sailing brig-rigged sloops. Most of these ships were out of commission in reserve.

PW 1850 included five large new screw cruisers, but no money was initially appropriated for them, so in March 1851 Walker ordered that they not be included in the Navy List until they were named and ordered built. Four of them were 1500-ton (burthen) frigates. They remained in the 1851-52 list, and then became 1161-ton (burthen) corvettes in the 1853 list. They were built as the 50-gun frigate *Aurora* (see above) and the corvettes *Pylades*, *Pearl*, and *Cadmus*.[49] The fifth ship was the sloop *Fawn*, built at Deptford as a unit of the *Cruizer* class (see below): names and yards were chosen before designs were fixed. Only in December 1852 was the order given for *Pylades* (Sheerness) to be a *Highflyer* class corvette, but with 2ft more beam.

PW 1850 included the first of the *Cruizer* class of large sloops (later corvettes): *Cruizer* (Deptford) and *Hornet* (Deptford), the first two in effect replacing the two steam schooners cancelled in 1847, and *Fawn* (built later at Deptford).[50] The others in the class were ordered under PW 1851 (*Harrier*, Pembroke) and PW 1853 (*Falcon* and *Alert*, both at Pembroke). *Mutine* (PW 1852, below) was to have been of this class, but was built instead to an enlarged design adapted to 200 NHP rather than 150 NHP engines. The first of this new type was *Greyhound* (PW 1854, Pembroke); *Mutine* was changed to the new design in 1856. The *Cameleon* class (see below) was a lengthened *Cruizer* with the 200 NHP engine, intended for higher speed. In October 1850 the Surveyor proposed a smaller screw

Melpomene was one of three *Emerald* class frigates converted on the stocks from sailing frigates. All were ordered as 60-gun sailing frigates in 1848 and laid down in 1849, but reordered as screw frigates in 1854-6. They were lengthened by 52ft to accommodate their 600 NHP machinery, the fore and after parts being launched separately (the after part was launched on 9 August 1856, the entire ship being launched on 8 August 1857). On trial, *Melpomene* made 12.4kts on 2323 IHP. In January 1868 *Melpomene* was armed with six 64pdr muzzle-loading rifles on her upper deck plus four 7in muzzle-loader (6½-ton guns) and another eighteen 64pdrs on her main deck. Her sisters *Emerald* and *Immortalite* were similarly armed. By July 1859 she was part of the Channel Fleet. By April 1862 she was on the North America and West Indies station.
(National Maritime Museum N05334)

sloop intermediate between *Reynard* and *Plumper* of the 1847 program. It became the *Swallow* class ordered under PW 1852.[51]

Parallel to this new construction was a continuing conversion program; in March 1851 Chatham was ordered to convert the 2356-ton frigate *Euryalus* along the same lines as *Impericuse*, with a 400 NHP engine. She had been ordered in 1848 as a 50-gun sailing frigate of the *Narcissus* class, and was reordered before being launched.

PW 1851, submitted on 26 March 1851, included the new steam frigate *Curacoa* (Pembroke, 1560 tons) on the lines of the 30-gun frigate *Tribune*, then building at Sheerness. She used frames originally ordered for 36-gun sailing frigates. She was to have been one of the 1500-tonners of PW 1850.

The steam sloop *Harrier* was ordered built at Pembroke on the lines of the cruiser building at Deptford (i.e., *Cruiser* class), using portions of the frames built for three earlier ships cancelled as part of PW 1851 (*Enchantress*, *Falcon*, and *Harrier*).

Five more frigates were converted on the slip: *Shannon* (Portsmouth, 2356 tons), *Bacchante* (Portsmouth, 2356 tons), *Liffey* (Devonport, 2356 tons), and *Aurora* (Pembroke, 2356 tons, 400 NHP). Of the five, *Liffey* was to have been one of the 50-gun *Constance* class, the largest British sailing frigates ever built. She was laid down but never completed, and was reordered as a steam frigate. *Shannon* was laid down to a slightly smaller 50-gun frigate design, but reordered as a steam frigate. Both ships were ordered in 1844, to designs dated 1843. *Aurora* and *Bacchante* were ordered as 50-gun sailing frigates in 1848. As converted on the slip (having hardly been begun) these ships fell into two classes of steam frigate: the 51-gun *Impericuse* class (design approved 14 June 1850: *Impericuse*, *Euryalus*, *Aurora*,

Undaunted was one of a planned fourteen *Bristol* class frigates whose design was approved on 12 August 1858. They were intended to help redress the frigate balance against the French; fourteen were ordered, but ten were cancelled, and *Undaunted* was placed in reserve when completed in 1861. On trial she made 11.8kts on 2261 IHP, which barely placed her in the modern category a few years later. As completed, ships had one pivoted (slide) 68pdr and twenty 32pdr on the upper deck and thirty 8in shell guns on the main deck, all smooth-bores. In January 1868 *Undaunted* was armed with six 64pdr rifles on her upper deck and with four 7in and eighteen 64pdr on her main deck, at that time the standard new frigate battery. Her sisters *Glasgow* and *Newcastle* had the same battery. *Bristol* had four 64pdrs on her upper deck and twelve on her main deck, plus ten 8in smooth-bore shell guns on her main deck. In 1873 DNC was asked to assess planned rearmament of *Newcastle* and *Undaunted*: adding one 6½-ton (7in) revolving gun and two additional 64pdr on the quarter deck. The revolving 7in gun replaced two 64pdr bow chasers, these guns being moved into side positions. The resulting upper deck battery was one 7in and eight 64pdr (6 side, 2 chase); the main deck battery was unchanged (four 7in and fourteen 64pdr). *Undaunted* was one of eight wooden frigates still on the Royal Navy list in January 1878, serving as flagship in the East Indies. The other seven were in various categories of reserve: *Doris*, *Topaze*, *Immortalite*, *Newcastle*, *Glasgow*, *Narcissus*, and *Endymion*. These ships, the big iron frigates, and the *Bacchante*s were all classified at that time as first-class frigates. The three big iron corvettes constituted the second class. The third class were corvettes: the new *Comus* class, the *Opal*s, the *Amethyst*s, the *Druid*s, the *Blanche* class, the *Eclipse* class. *Undaunted* apparently spent most of her life in reserve. She was commissioned on 2 March 1875 as flagship East Indies station, remaining in that role until October 1878 (she was paid off on 21 December).

(Allan C Green via State Library of Victoria)

Endymion was the only one of five *Ister* class 36-gun screw frigates completed. Hers was the last class to be designed before the mass cancellations. In August 1866 she was under repair. Designed armament (which must have been set in 1863-64) was eight 64pdr muzzle-loading rifles and twenty-two 32pdr. In January 1868 she was armed with three 7in (110pdr) breech-loading rifles on her upper deck and with four 7in muzzle-loading rifles (6½-ton guns) and fourteen 8in smooth-bores on her main deck. In 1874 she had the standard frigate armament: four 64pdr on the upper deck (2 side, 2 chase) plus four main-deck 7in and fourteen main-deck 64pdrs. *Endymion* was one of the eight wooden frigates still on the Royal Navy list in January 1878. By that time the main-deck 7in guns had been removed. She was commissioned in September 1866 for the Mediterranean, remaining there until May 1869, when she was assigned to the Detached (Flying) Squadron, in which she remained until November 1870. She was a training ship for cadets from April 1872, then in 1873 assigned again to the Detached Squadron, which she left in July 1874. She was then coast guard in the Humber until 31 July 1879, being sold as a hulk in 1885.

(Allan C Green via State Library of Victoria)

Forte, and *Chesapeake*) and the 51-gun *Liffey* class (*Liffey*, *Shannon*, *Topaze*, *Bacchante*, and *Liverpool*). The *Imperieuse* class had 400 NHP engines (*Imperieuse* had 360 NHP); the *Liffey* class had 600 NHP engines. Typical actual output in the *Imperieuse* class was 1159 IHP (*Chesapeake*) for 9.7kts; in the *Liffey* class it was 2490 IHP for 12.1kts (*Bacchante*).[52] Thus the *Liffey*s were the first British frigates designed to exceed 11kts, and presumably the first conceived as steam warships rather than as sailing warships with auxiliary steam engines.

The British became nervous when Louis Napoleon gained power after a 2 December 1851 coup. The British press and then the public decided that his predecessor Louis Philippe had been a quietist, but that Louis Napoleon was an aggressive threat (due both to his rhetoric and to a name which the British still found fearsome). In opposition, Lord Derby argued the need for increased military power to preclude invasion. Once in office (presumably helped by the panic), he introduced a Militia Bill. Palmerston again spoke of the 'steam bridge' and the possibility that 50,000 or 60,000 men might land from Cherbourg in one night. Parliament then dissolved. Before it could meet again Louis Napoleon had made himself Emperor (crowned in December 1852), with all the echoes that carried of the last major war. As in 1848, the panic collapsed when it was translated in budgetary – tax – terms, the Derby government being ejected from office.

PW 1852 (orders dated 27 March 1852) included three more big steam frigates converted on the slip to the new designs: *Chesapeake* (Chatham, 2356 tons, 400 NHP), *Forte* (Deptford, 2356 tons), and *Topaze* (Devonport, 2356 tons), plus two *Cruiser* class steam sloops: *Fawn* (Deptford) and *Mutine* (Deptford).

Forte and *Chesapeake* were to the existing *Imperieuse* design; *Topaze* was a *Liffey*. In October, the existing frigate *San Fiorenzo* was ordered adapted for steam power at Woolwich (2066 tons). Work was suspended in December 1851 and cancelled in April 1856.[53] The frigate *Narcissus* was converted instead under the PW 1856 program.

A need was felt for smaller sloops: *Swallow* (Pembroke) and *Curlew* (Deptford) were ordered as gun-vessels (later sloops). They were built using the remains of the frames of even smaller ships now cancelled. At 485 tons burthen (625 tons displacement) they were at the low end of the sloop scale.[54] PW 1853 included two more ships, *Ariel* (Pembroke) and *Icarus* (Deptford). Later ships were built to a lengthened *Racer* class design (861 tons displacement) and were designated from the outset as third-class sloops rather than gun-vessels: PW 1853 included *Lyra* (Deptford), *Cordelia* (Pembroke), *Gannet* (Pembroke), and *Racer* (Deptford). Construction resumed in PW 1857 with *Pantaloon* (Devonport), *Rosario* (Deptford), and *Peterel* (Devonport). *Rosario* was to have duplicated *Icarus*, but under the PW 1858 program she was a repeat *Racer*.[55] Later the three PW 1857 ships were considered a separate *Rosario* class, in effect further enlarged *Racer*s (913 tons displacement) Two more were built under PW 1858: *Shearwater* (Pembroke) and *Royalist* (Devonport), followed by *Columbine* (Deptford, PW 1859), and four PW 1860 ships: *Africa* (Devonport), *Enterprise* (renamed *Circassian*: Deptford), *Bittern* (Devonport), and *Acheron* (Deptford). Of the 1860 ships, only *Africa* was completed, the others falling to the wave of cancellations in 1863. Similarly, none of the PW 1861 ships (*Fame*, *Cynthia*, and *Sabrina*) was completed.

In October through December 1852 a large program of new construction (or the adaptation of considerably modified existing hulls) and relatively inexpensive conversions of existing ships was ordered specifically to overmatch the French: twelve steam capital ships, but only one frigate (*San Fiorenzo*) – which was never, in the event, converted (she was replaced by *Narcissus*). PW 1853 was more balanced between capital ships (two) and cruisers (presumably many capital ship slips were occupied by the previous program). It included three corvettes (*Pearl*, Woolwich, 1390 tons; *Satellite*, Devonport, 1300 tons; and *Cadmus*, Chatham, 1300 tons, ex-*Coquette*, two of them left over from PW 1850), and the *Cruiser* class (748-ton) sloops

Severn was one of the sailing frigates converted into steam frigates under a program announced in 1859 by First Lord Pakington. Initially he wanted to convert (presumably including cutting down) twelve or fourteen 80-gun sailing ships, which were too lightly armed to remain effective as battleships. This plan was abandoned in favour of converting twelve or thirteen relatively new sailing frigates. In mid-1859 Pakington hoped to have five new frigates afloat by the end of the year, and to re-launch another four converted ships. Only eight ships were converted, and the demands of the capital ship program crowded out the frigates. Conversion was ordered on 4 March 1859 and begun the next day. *Severn* went into reserve as soon as she was completed (by installing her 500 NHP machinery). Her only active service was with the East Indies division (as senior officer's ship) between 19 July 1862 and 12 June 1866. On trial she made 11.696kts on 2092 IHP, which made her obsolescent by 1865. In August 1866 she was on the ineffective list, but in January 1868 she was credited with the new standard frigate armament of six 64pdrs on the upper deck and four 7in muzzle-loading rifles and eighteen 64pdrs on the main deck. Planned armament had been one 68pdr (pivoted slide) and twenty 32pdrs on the upper deck plus thirty 8in smooth-bore shell guns on the main deck.
(National Maritime Museum N05333)

Falcon and *Alert*, both at Pembroke.[56]

By mid-1853 British attention was shifting from France to Russia, as it seemed the Russians were making a new attempt to destroy Turkey and gain direct access to the Mediterranean. France and Britain became allies. By this time the French were more wholeheartedly adopting steam power. Alongside the French in the Black Sea, the British saw the superiority of their ships.[57] The successful invasion of the Crimea demonstrated the reality of the 'steam bridge' which had so exercised British and French imagination. The British found that they were able to maintain a large steam fleet in the Baltic, far from bases. Fears that it would be difficult to supply sufficient coal proved entirely unfounded.

The British continued to build large steam warships during the Crimean War, although considerable effort went into shallow-draught gunboats intended to attack Kronstadt and St Peterburg in the Baltic. Thus PW 1854 included three steam frigates (*Ariadne*, Deptford, 2479 tons; *Diadem*, Pembroke, 2479 tons; and *Doris*, Pembroke, 2479 tons). *Diadem* and *Doris* were ordered as 'special type (frigate-) corvettes' of 30 guns.[58] The number of guns was down, compared to other large steam

Racoon was one of ten *Pearl* class corvettes, the first Royal Navy steam corvettes to have been built in any numbers. Designed armament was one bow 68pdr on a pivoted slide plus twenty 8in smooth-bore shell guns on broadside trucks, an early application of the idea that a few shell guns might be as effective as a larger number of guns firing solid shot. In January 1868 she had two 64pdr on her spar deck and eight on her main deck, plus eight 8in shell guns. *Challenger* had the same armament. Others in the class varied. *Charybdis*, *Pearl*, *Pelorus*, *Satellite*, and *Scout* all had a single 7in breech-loader. In *Charybdis*, *Pearl*, and *Satellite* and it was backed by eight 64pdr and eight 8in shell guns. *Pelorus* and *Scout* had four 40pdr breech-loaders and sixteen 8in shell guns. *Scylla* and *Cadmus* had a single-calibre battery of sixteen 64pdr, presumably the planned ultimate battery for the class. *Clio* had a spar deck above her main deck carrying two revolving 64pdrs (plus sixteen on the full deck below). In 1870 *Challenger* had two 7in breech-loaders on revolving mountings on her spar deck plus eight 64pdr and eight 8in shell guns on her upper deck. In 1874 the planned battery for ships on re-commissioning was one revolving 64pdr and sixteen on the broadside. Except that they had two revolving 64pdrs, this was the armament planned for big iron corvettes such as *Volage*. *Racoon* and *Challenger* were unusual in having two revolving 64pdrs. By this time the only active units of the class were *Charybdis* and *Clio*. *Racoon* was commissioned 22 November 1867 into the Channel squadron, then served in the Mediterranean (1 May 1860 – 21 January 1862), then on the North America and West Indies station (beginning 29 January 1863), then (April 1864 – March 1866) in the Mediterranean, then at Queenstown in March 1866. On 3 November 1866 she was commissioned for the Cape of Good Hope station, but then went to the North America and West Indies station some time before May 1870, remaining there until she was decommissioned on 2 July 1873.
(National Maritime Museum N05245)

frigates, because the individual guns were more powerful. Plans were submitted in January 1855. Because these large ships were armed with so few guns, initially they were classified as corvettes; they were reclassified as frigates only in 1856. Their 800 NHP engines were a step up from the 600 NHP of the *Liffey* class. *Diadem* produced 2979 IHP for 12kts, and *Doris* produced 3087 IHP for 12.865kts. These two ships are sometimes counted as the first of Walker's 'big frigates' intended to counter big US frigates.

Ariadne was redesigned as part of Walker's fast frigate program described below. There were also three *Pearl* class corvettes (*Scylla*, Sheerness; *Scout*, Woolwich; and *Charybdis*, Chatham). The Treasury seized two corvettes under construction for Russia, which the Royal Navy named *Cossack* and *Tartar*, in April 1854.[59]

Three second-class PW 1854 sloops (*Pelican*, Pembroke; *Cameleon*, Deptford; and *Greyhound*, Pembroke) were later grouped with *Mutine* and with later second-class sloops as a single class. They had been rated third class, under a system based on NHP rather than hull size. Four more PW 1854 sloops (*Lyra*, Deptford; *Cordelia*, Pembroke; *Gannet*, Pembroke; and *Racer*, Deptford) had been rated as gun-vessels first class, and were rerated third-class sloops beginning with *Cruizer*. In February 1855 the Surveyor wrote that the smaller steam vessels should have higher power (using higher pressure, so dimensions would not change) to give them the desired 11kts speed despite their shorter length. Ships would be lengthened. The three *Cruizer* class would be given 200 NHP engines and the three *Swallow* class 150 NHP. In 1856 *Icarus*, *Racer*, *Cordelia*, and *Gannet* and later third-class sloops formed a single class. In 1858 *Pelican*, *Zebra*, *Rinaldo*, and the PW 58 ships were made a single class (950 tons burthen), joined in 1860 by *Perseus* and *Cameleon*.

In addition, on 23 February 1855 (towards the end of the 1854-55 fiscal year), *Bacchante* and *Topaze* were ordered from Portsmouth and Devonport, respectively, to duplicate *Shannon* and *Liffey*.

In May 1854 the Board approved the Surveyor's suggestion that the frigate *Emerald* be lengthened (by 52ft) and converted into a *Liffey* class steam frigate with a 600 NHP engine. Like the earlier ships, she was still on the slip. She became name ship of a class of 51-gun 2852-ton frigates (the others were *Melpomene* and *Immortalite*, both at Pembroke).[60] All had been ordered in 1848 as 60-gun frigates. A fourth sister ship, *Imperieuse*, had already been converted to a different design. Given advances in steam machinery, 600 NHP bought much more in these ships: in *Emerald* actual power was 2323 IHP, for 12kts.

PW 1855 included another six steam frigates: the 2651-ton (600 NHP) *Liverpool* (Devonport: *Liffey* class), *Glasgow* (Portsmouth), and *Newcastle* (Deptford); the 2355-ton (400 NHP) *Mersey* and *Tweed*, and the 2479-ton *Orlando* (to be a repeat *Doris*). *Glasgow* and *Newcastle* and the later *Bristol* and *Undaunted* formed the *Bristol* class, along with many ships later cancelled. They were the now somewhat old-fashioned slow frigates.[61] *Tweed* was later ordered to duplicate *Aurora*, and still later she was ordered to be armoured (and then cancelled). *Orlando* and *Mersey* were built to a different design (see below).

PW 1855 also included four 1462-ton corvettes: *Pelorus* (Devonport), *Racoon* (Chatham), *Challenger* (Woolwich), and *Clio* (Sheerness), of which *Challenger* later became famous as a scientific survey ship. In May 1856 the Surveyor wrote that some of the large screw corvettes on order should have a light deck covering their gun deck carrying a pivot gun fore and aft. He submitted a design of such a deck on board HMS *Pearl*; the idea applied specifically to *Challenger* and to *Racoon*. *Clio* was later added. These ships are generally counted with the *Pearl* class.

PW 1856, submitted at the end of the Crimean War (ships were ordered on 9 April 1856), included three frigates and three corvettes. The frigates were the 2852-ton 600 NHP *Melpomene* (Pembroke) and *Immortalite* (Pembroke), and *Bristol* (Woolwich), all of existing classes. *Melpomene* was to be modified with an additional three gun ports amidships. The corvettes were the 1462-ton *Jason* (Devonport), *Galatea* (Woolwich), and *Barrosa* (Woolwich). *Barrosa* (and later *Jason* and *Galatea*) and the corvettes ordered under PW 1857-59 were reclassified in 1859 into a new class of 21-gun corvettes with open batteries, the design of which was approved on 10 February 1858.[62]

With the end of the Crimean War in March 1856, British relations with France cooled, and the threat of the 'steam bridge' revived. PW 1857, the first post-Crimea program, included only one frigate (*Ister*, at Devonport) and two *Jason* class corvettes (*Orpheus*, at Chatham, and *Orestes*, at Sheerness), together with capital ships and smaller craft. New drawings for *Ister* were approved on 23 February 1860.[63] She was cancelled in December 1864, and her engine installed in the corvette *Thalia*. The other ships were *Endymion*, *Blonde*, *Astraea*, and *Dartmouth*, of which only *Endymion* (Deptford) was completed, having been suspended in 1862-63.

The end of the Crimean War made it possible to focus on other threats. In 1854 the US Navy announced that it planned to build five large fast steam frigates (*Merrimack* class) and one large fast steam corvette (*Niagara*), all of which were clearly intended to raid British commerce. In June 1856 Surveyor Baldwin Walker wrote that he considered it essential to have a certain number of 'steam vessels of great speed carrying the heaviest armament'. He submitted designs for a 36-gun screw frigate and a 26-gun covered-deck corvette, both powered by a 1000 NHP engine and armed with the heaviest guns. He recommended building two of each type. Four ships already authorized were built: the frigates *Mersey* and *Orlando* and the corvettes (soon rerated frigates) *Ariadne* and *Galatea* (originally to have been a *Jason* class corvette).[64]

'Walker's big frigates' were much more successful – much faster – than their American counterparts. Walker got his desired speed (13kts) by stretching wooden hulls as far as post-Napoleonic innovations, such as diagonal framing, would take him (*Mersey* made 13.75kts on trial). The long hulls of the 'big frigates' were not rigid enough to support long propeller shafts, and the ships had considerable problems in service. This experience helps explain the adoption of iron for the next fast British cruisers, *Inconstant* and her successors (see the next chapter). In hull form *Mersey* was in effect a wooden prototype for the first British ironclad, HMS *Warrior*.

The new frigates were as large and expensive as a capital ship. In some ways their long-range heavy armament (comparable to that of the new American ships) was superior to that on board conventional line of battle ships. It would take an entirely new kind of heavy capital ship to deal with the new gen-

Wolverine was one of seven *Jason* class corvettes, one of which was cancelled. As a 21-gun ship, she was typical of steam corvettes of her time. By the time the ships were being built, the Royal Navy had adopted the Armstrong 7in breech-loader. Thus the initial armament was one such gun plus the twenty 8in shell guns of the previous class. In 1868 *Wolverine* and her sister *Barrosa* each had seventeen 64pdrs. Her sister HMS *Rattlesnake* had nine 64pdr plus eight 8in shell guns. *Jason* had the 7in Armstrong plus eight 64pdr and eight shell guns. Sister ship *Orpheus* had been wrecked on a bar in New Zealand in 1863, and *Orestes* had been broken up (in 1866) after only five years' service. By 1872 the planned battery for the class was one rotating and sixteen broadside 64pdrs (*Jason* still had her 7in Armstrong). Surviving ships (*Jason* was no longer considered suitable for sea service) all had the planned battery by 1875. With this battery *Wolverine* was given to the New South Wales colonial government in 1882. She is shown in Australian waters. On commissioning (7 May 1864) *Wolverine* was assigned to the North America and West Indies station, paying off on 27 February 1868. On 25 October 1870 she was commissioned for the East Indies station, after which she was made commodore's flagship on the Australia station (commissioned for this purpose in August 1876). She was paid off in Australia on 16 February 1882, having been given to the New South Wales Naval Brigade the previous 16 January. She was hulked in February 1893, but was not sold until 1923. (Allan C Green via State Library of Victoria)

eration of big heavily-armed frigates: late in 1858 the Board considered plans for a 100-gun screw liner (line of battle ship), over half of whose armament would be 10in guns and 68pdrs. The project was aborted by the advent of the French ironclad *Gloire* and by trials at Portsmouth which demonstrated the value of armour.

PW 1857 included two second-class sloops: *Perseus* (Pembroke) and *Rinaldo* (Portsmouth) and four third-class: *Zebra* (Deptford), *Pantaloon* (Devonport), *Rosario* (Deptford), and *Peterel* (Devonport). In 1858 *Rosario*, *Peterel*, and third-class sloops of the PW 1859-61 programs were made a new class.[65]

By this time the Royal Navy had accumulated considerable experience with fast steam warships. On 18 December 1857 Walker wrote that both theory and experience showed that high speed required great length and fine lines. Walker argued, moreover, that increasing length was the only path to ensuring that ships would achieve speeds proportionate to their power, either steam or sail. Great length and fine lines could not be combined in heavily armed warships, within the limits of length previously accepted. New designs should be considerably longer, and existing ships lengthened. Longer, finer ships could gain the appropriate firepower only by mounting smaller numbers of the new powerful guns. In February 1858 plans were submitted to lengthen the frigate *Immortalite* and the corvettes *Jason*, *Barrosa*, *Orestes*, and *Orpheus*.[66] At about the same time these ships were rerated with 20 rather than 22 guns (*Charybdis* was rerated with 20 rather than 21 guns). In August 1858 plans were submitted to lengthen two classes of 50-gun frigate.

Sketch Estimates for 1858-59 (i.e., including PW 1858) were introduced into the House on 18 May 1857. They were higher than ever before in peacetime. The First Lord justified them on the ground that the French were nearly matching British strength in ships of the line (40 to 42, omitting the British blockships) and in frigates (37 to 42, again omitting blockships). No crash program was approved.

Cruiser construction continued in PW 1858: two *Bristol* class frigates (*Undaunted*, Chatham; and *Dryad*, Portsmouth) and three corvettes, all repeats of previous ships: *Rattlesnake* (repeat *Orpheus* at Chatham), *Wolverine* (repeat *Barrosa* at Woolwich), and *North Star* (repeat *Orestes* at Sheerness). Few of these ships were completed, owing to the mass cancellations from 1862 on. In May 1865 the Surveyor ordered *North Star* broken up on the slip and her material used to build a corvette of *Challenger* class. *Harlequin* and *Dryad* were broken up at Portsmouth to build HMS *Danae* of the new *Amazon* class.

PW 1858 included three second-class sloops: *Chanticleer* (Portsmouth: repeat *Rinaldo*), *Reindeer* (Chatham), and *Rattler* (Deptford: repeat *Cameleon*). The three third-class sloops were: *Rapid* (Deptford: repeat *Racer*), *Shearwater* (Pembroke: repeat *Gannet*), and *Royalist* (Devonport: repeat *Pantaloon*)

The opposition Tories rejected the increased expenditure proposed in 1857. The situation exploded when they entered office in February 1858.[67] New Prime Minister the Earl of Derby was determined to cut defence spending, and the new Foreign Secretary Lord Malmesbury hoped to reduce tensions with France.[68] They were forced to confront the fact that the French were exploiting the chance steam had given them.[69] Malmesbury's calculation of relative British and French naval strength showed that the situation was critical. He sponsored intensified intelligence-gathering, particularly at the French port of Cherbourg, from which any attack against England would be mounted. Before any new course of action could be chosen, the new Ministry (a minority government) submitted its reduced Estimates, which passed the House of Commons in April, in time for the 1858-59 fiscal year. The new government had to accept that it would not have the naval edge to back diplomacy in Europe. As a stop-gap, new capital ship construction was suspended in PW 1858 to provide men and money for quick conversions of existing capital ships (three-deckers cut down to two-deckers). PW 1860 was the attempt to redress the naval balance.

HMS *Dido* was one of seven *Blanche* class corvettes, scaled-up versions of the *Amazon*s. The two 7in guns were placed on slides nearly amidships, supplemented by four 64pdrs on trucks – two at ports at the forward end of the waist, and two at ports on the quarterdeck. Guns on trucks could be run forward or aft to fire through two bow ports and three stern ports (one on the centreline). Soon end-on fire was of much greater concern. After their first commission, ships were given two truck-mounted 64pdrs as chase guns, using the same ports as before, but permanently sited near them. Later still the 7in guns were replaced by 64pdrs in accord with a policy of arming cruisers entirely with lighter faster-firing guns. That added three 64pdr on each side, for a total of twelve including the chasers (*Dido* is shown with this armament, evident in her six broadside ports plus additional ports visible forward and aft). All the 64pdrs were of the wrought-iron Mk III type on trucks. *Dido* was originally ship-rigged, but she was later reduced, as shown here, to barque rig (*Eclipse*, *Danae*, and *Sirius* were all completed with barque rigs). *Dido* began her career in Australian waters (1871-75), spent 1876-79 in reserve went to the Cape station (1879-86) and then to the North America and West Indies station. She was converted into a mining stores hulk upon returning home.
(National Maritime Museum A3666)

Sea power was measured largely in ships of the line, but they were increasingly expensive, particularly in terms of manpower – which the British lacked. The war in China had absorbed too many British naval seamen, and there was no organized naval reserve (as the French had). The Royal Navy was too widely dispersed, largely for presence missions, to concentrate enough power in the Channel against the French. The capital ships needed large crews mainly to service their numerous guns. First Naval Lord Admiral Dundas (appointed November 1857, relieved March 1858, but returned to office June 1859) pointed out that large frigates like Walker's could deal with such capital ships by mounting smaller numbers of more powerful guns. In June 1858 the Admiralty decided to arm the large frigate HMS *Diadem* entirely with 68pdrs.

The strategic situation worsened as the French completed the fortified port at Cherbourg, facing the British south coast. Their invitation to Queen Victoria to visit was seen as attempted intimidation. The Queen, Prince Albert, Foreign Secretary Malmesbury, and First Lord Pakington visited in August, accompanied by Admiralty technical experts including chief constructor Isaac Watts, the Queen being convinced that the British had to do much more to maintain their maritime position. By late August 1858 the Cabinet was willing to boost the naval program, although Chancellor Disraeli, who had led the Tory fight against the Liberals' naval estimates the previous year, was opposed. Rear Admiral Milne proposed using the fleet of gunboats built during the recent war (to attack Kronstadt) to deal with the French port. This seems to have been the first formal proposal to substitute port attack for blockade.

The 1860-61 program presented to the Cabinet in November 1858 showed a budget-breaking increase of £700,000. To cover his flank against opposition by Chancellor of the Exchequer Disraeli, Prime Minister Lord Derby ordered a formal report of the causes for the great increase since the 1852-53 budget. This December 1858 report completely discounted the accumulated capital of sailing battleships: 'as sailing ships could not be opposed to steam-ships with any chance of success, the latter must now be considered as the only ships really effective for purposes of war'.[70] The French had decided to convert all sailing ships fit for the purpose to steam.

In 1850 the British had had 86 ships of the line against 45 French; in 1858 the British had 50 steam line of battle ships built and building to 40 French; the gap was closing (in completed ships it was 29 each). Another 6 British liners were proposed for steam conversion (the Surveyor thought they could be ready in 1861). Nothing more could be added through 1863. The 5 French liners under construction were further along than the 10 British (progress was measured in eighths, and the French program was 31/8 complete vs 27/8 for the British). Against that, 3 of the 10 British ships were of the most powerful, three-decker, type. Two remaining French sailing liners were suitable for conversion, but it was not clear whether they would be converted to steam or cut down and armoured.[71] The British had 34 steam frigates (17 screw and 9 paddle completed) to 46 French (15 screw and 19 paddle completed). Of the British ships, 28 had been completed; of the French, 37. The situation had been far better in 1852, when the British had 176 steam warships compared to 122 French, including 17 ships of the line vs 6 French, 29 frigates to 21 French, 59 corvettes and sloops to 31 French, and 67 smaller warships to 64 French.[72]

Much worse, four of the eight French frigates under construction (compared to six British) were iron-sided (no one yet used the term ironclad). To the British agent in France, they could be substituted for line of battle ships; 'so convinced do naval men seem to be in this country [France] of the irresistable qualities of these ships, that they do not mean to lay down another ship of the line, as they say that in ten years they will have become quite obsolete.' Two more iron-sided ships were planned. Adding the six ironclads to the French line-of-battle ships would make a total French force of 46; if the remaining two ships were converted, to 48, compared to a British maximum of 56. On 22 June 1858 Surveyor Captain Walker advised the Admiralty to begin building ironclads.

The disparity in steam frigates was seen as a particular threat to British commerce. It was not clear to what extent the gross British superiority in the next lower category, corvettes and sloops, made up for the disparity in frigates, since seven of the British corvettes had previously been rated as frigates. The French had declined in this category (from 31 to 22), while the British had grown from 59 to 82.

The only quick way to produce more steam frigates, to match the French, was to convert already completed sailing frigates.[73] In 1857 plans called for converting two during 1860 (i.e., PW 1859) and two in PW 1860. This program was accelerated: towards the end of the 1858-59 fiscal year orders were given for four frigate conversions: *Sutlej* (Portsmouth), *Phaeton* (Sheerness), *Severn* (Chatham), and *Phoebe* (Devonport). Four more were ordered in January 1860: *Octavia* (Portsmouth), *Leander* (Sheerness), *Arethusa* (Chatham), and *Constance* (Devonport). They were later treated as a single group, although they were not sister ships. All received 400 or 500 NHP engines, and thus may be grouped with the earlier slow frigates intended as sailing ships with auxiliary steam power. The fastest was *Phoebe* (1780 IHP, 11.9kts). Displacements were up to 3800 tons. All were armed with thirty 8in 65cwt guns on the main deck and twenty 32pdr 56cwt plus one 68pdr 95cwt chaser on the upper deck. Ships were about 180ft long on the gun deck, and conversion involved cutting them in two amidships and lengthening them by 60 to 70ft to accommodate boilers, engine, and bunkers.

Three conversions, *Arethusa*, *Constance*, and *Octavia*, were intended specifically to test the relative merits of plans proposed for superheated steam by three firms: Maudsley, Penn, and Randolph & Elder of Glasgow. *Constance* had the first Royal Navy compound engines, with six cylinders in triplets, each comprising one high-pressure cylinder between two low-pressure ones. It was rated at 500 NHP (2301 IHP, 10.8kts).

PW 1859 included only a single frigate (the *Bristol* class *Belvidera* at Chatham, which was never completed) and a single corvette (*Favourite* at Deptford) in addition to three sailing line of battle ships and smaller craft. In February 1863 *Belvidera* was ordered armoured, but instead she was cancelled on 16 December 1864. HMS *Warrior* was ordered this year from Thames Iron Works.

PW 1860 was the attempt to redress the balance. It included the last class of unarmoured line of battle ships the Royal Navy ordered, plus an extraordinary eight steam frigates: the repeat *Belvidera*s *Raleigh* (Pembroke), *Barham* (Portsmouth), *Briton* (Portsmouth), and *Pomone* (Chatham); and the repeat *Ister*s *Dartmouth* (Woolwich), *Endymion* (Deptford), *Blonde* (Woolwich), and *Astraea* (Devonport). There were also six corvettes: *Dido* (Deptford), *Alligator* (Woolwich), *Menai* (Chatham), *Ontario* (Woolwich), *Weymouth* (Sheerness), and *Falmouth* (Chatham). Of these, *Weymouth* and *Falmouth* were repeat *North Star*s. This program was slowed by the lack of well-seasoned timber in the dockyards.[74]

The program included four second-class sloops: *Harlequin* (Portsmouth), *Sappho* (Deptford), *Trent* (Pembroke), and *Tees* (Chatham); and four third-class sloops: *Africa* (Devonport), *Enterprise* (Deptford), *Bittern* (Devonport), and *Acheron* (Deptford). In addition, in February 1860 the Surveyor proposed converting two 36-gun frigates then in the program, as they were to be partly built in 1861 plus the frames of two more, which were then in the 1860-61 program.[75] The design was quickly approved.

Although he had designed a wooden ironclad the previous year, based on the big frigate *Ariadne*, by mid-1858 Walker considered an iron hull essential. His iron ships had to be contracted out to private yards with experience building iron merchant ships; the Royal Dockyards as yet had no iron shipbuilding experience.[76] The ironclads were hugely expensive, and the size of the French program ensured that many would be ordered in rapid succession. Upgrading the Royal Dockyards to build iron ships ate further into the budget available for cruisers.

An *Amazon* class corvette. This class was built specifically to counter raiders comparable to the Confederate *Alabama* – which was an enlarged version of a Royal Navy gun-vessel. The ram bow gained buoyancy forward. This picture was taken in Australian waters. The ship is unidentified; it is any of the class except the name ship. As designed, the ships had two 64pdr and two 7in 6½-ton guns on each side, the latter on traversing slides. They were paired, the starboard pair forward of the port pair, and the port 64pdr further aft of the port 7in guns than the starboard 64pdr was forward of the starboard 7in. Only *Dryad*, *Nymphe*, and *Vestal* were rearmed in the 1870s. They received a uniform battery of 64pdrs: a chaser in the bow and four on either broadside, symmetrically, with the after gun well abaft the other three on each side. Unusually, the bow gun could fire from any of three bow ports: one on the centreline and one on each side (it could be trundled to any of the three). Ports in the poop allowed for stern fire by any of the after 64pdrs. *Daphne* was considered too old for full rearmament, but on returning home she was given a bow 64pdr. *Amazon* and *Niobe* were both lost before any armament conversion was done, one by collision and the other by running onto rocks. All had single-expansion engines with steam (at 30 to 33psi) from rectangular boilers. They were the largest wooden sloops, and the first large sloops with barque rather than ship rig. *Amazon*, *Niobe*, and *Vestal* were completed with pole topmasts (devoid of sail), but *Vestal* and later ships had fidded topmasts.
(Allan C Green via State Library of Victoria)

This took time to sink in; PW 1861 included a cruiser program. Of its five frigates – *Boadicea* (Chatham), *Bucephalus* (Portsmouth), *Dextrous* (Pembroke), *Acasta* (Deptford), and *Hyperion* (Woolwich) – the last two were of the *Ariadne* class (described as a new type intermediate between *Galatea* and *Ister*). There were two corvettes: *Nereide* (Woolwich) and *Ganymede* (Chatham); four second-class sloops: *Diligence* (Portsmouth), *Circassian* (Deptford), *Imogene* (Portsmouth), and *Success* (Pembroke); and three third-class sloops: *Fame* (Deptford), *Cynthia* (Devonport), and *Sabrina* (Pembroke). *Circassian* had the unusual fate of being armoured (she was the smallest British ironclad of her time) as HMS *Enterprise*.

In 1862 the large sloops *Archer*, *Brisk*, *Encounter*, *Malacca*, *Miranda*, and *Niger* were rerated as corvettes. Rerating made it possible to fill out the needs for corvettes despite cancellations. First-class sloops *not* rerated were *Conflict*, *Desperate*, *Phoenix*, and *Wasp*.

No frigates or corvettes or sloops were included in PW 1862. By the time that program was being framed, the ironclad program was crowding out all other construction, and numerous cruisers were being cancelled. Work did not even begin on many ships, which were simply dropped from the Navy List. The only frigate suspended but later completed was *Endymion*, the only corvette suspended and later completed was *Wolverine* (with engines originally intended for *Adventure*), and the only sloop suspended and later completed was *Reindeer*.

Cancellations were also partly due to the Board's decision that wooden corvettes armed with 8in 65cwt guns, and with speeds of no more than 11kts, 'necessarily deficient in the strength required of a screw-ship to resist the wear and tear of powerful engines', were obsolete for war, as were even slower first- and second-class sloops, as well as the paddle frigates and sloops.[77] To Robinson, that meant discarding large numbers of exactly the types in which the Royal Navy was most deficient.

Cancellations of steam screw frigates in 1863-64 (many in December 1863) amounted to ten *Belvidera* class (**Tweed*, **Dryad*, **Belvidera*, **Pomone*, *Raleigh*, *Briton*, *Barham*, *Boadicea*, *Bucephalus*, and *Dextrous*, of which only the starred ships were laid down); four of the five *Ister* (*Endymion*) class (*Ister*, *Blonde*, *Astraea*, and *Dartmouth*, all laid down); and two of four *Ariadne* class (*Acasta* and *Hyperion*; only *Acasta* was laid down). All ten *North Star* class corvettes were cancelled (*North Star*, *Favourite* [reordered as an ironclad, and completed as such], *Ontario*, *Weymouth*, *Alligator*, *Menai*, *Dido*, *Falmouth*, *Nereide*, and *Ganymede*). Six of thirteen *Rosario* class sloops were cancelled (*Circassian*, *Acheron*, *Bittern*, *Fame*, *Cynthia*, and *Sabrina*).

Continued armament development affected the big frigates. In September 1864 it was proposed to arm the as-built steam frigates with sixteen (later changed to fourteen) 8in and twelve 64pdrs on the main deck, and five 110pdrs on slides on the upper deck. Converted ships would have the same main deck battery, but three 110pdrs on the upper deck. The Surveyor found that of the conversions, all but *Phaeton* were better able to take five 110pdrs than the *Aurora*s and the *Chesapeake*s. These ships were given three 110pdrs. The only problem in installing these weapons was to find sufficient clearance for the 11ft 6in slides, which had to clear hatchways. The super-corvettes *Mersey* and *Orlando* would easily take four 6¼- ton guns on the main deck and twelve 110pdrs on the upper deck on slides. *Doris* could have four 110pdrs on slides on her upper deck (she had two such there on her last commission).[78]

By 1866 the fleet preferred heavy armour-piercing guns, even in unarmoured ships. By that time the standard cruiser armour-piercing gun was the 7in 6½-ton type. Later in the 1860s opinion reversed, ships being fitted instead with 64pdrs of a new wrought-iron 64cwt type, weighing less than half as much as the 7in gun. Some ships could carry many more guns. This was the difference between HMS *Inconstant*, designed with heavy guns, and her near-sisters *Raleigh* and *Shah*, with lighter ones.

Two cruisers based on Royal Navy designs were built for the Confederacy during the Civil War. The first Confederate cruiser, CSS *Florida*, was built by William C Miller & Sons, which had just completed HMS *Steady* of the *Philomel* (*Ranger*) class.[79] The larger and more famous CSS *Alabama* was a slightly enlarged *Roebuck* with more powerful engines.[80] The Confederates bought HMS *Victor*, a sister of HMS *Roebuck*, in November 1863, but she was interned by the French government (February 1864) before she could become operational. The British attributed Confederate success to the lack of fast enough US warships. Could the same thing happen to the British? They knew that *Alabama* was based on the *Roebuck* design, somewhat enlarged. Her more powerful engines were intended to drive her at 12kts (it was not certain that she ever reached that speed at load draught, however).

Confederate operations inspired the Royal Navy to return to building cruisers, beginning with a new class of small sloop intended specifically to deal with commerce raiders like the famous CSS *Alabama*: *Amazon* and *Osprey* at Pembroke and *Niobe* at Deptford. PW 1865 included another three: *Nymphe* at Pembroke and *Dryad* and *Daphne* at Devonport.[81] The principal requirement was speed under steam, 13kts being the goal (to overtake 12-knotters like *Alabama*). *Amazon* was conceived as a light sloop commanded by a Commander, with a complement of 100, armed with four guns (two 7in MLR and two 40pdr Armstrong). Arrangements were similar to those of *Alabama*, and the rig was much like that of *Roebuck*. *Amazon* made only 12.3kts, though her sister *Vestal* slightly exceeded 13kts on trial.[82] *Daphne* and *Dryad* were built of teak.

These ships had an unusual ram bow, which give them additional buoyancy forward.[83] The ram bow was not a weapon, but rather a means of lightening the submerged part of the bow by reversing the slope of the bow above it. These ships also copied the new battleship ('cruiser') stern. The *Amazon*s were the first major British warships to break from the long tradition of the knee (clipper) bow, which had been adopted to support the bowsprit. The first to do so was the French naval architect Dupuy de Lôme, in his ironclad *Gloire* in the 1850s (his next step was to add a ram).

Under PW 1865 Chatham was allocated a new *Amazon* class sloop (*Blanche*). Another (*Danae*) was later allocated to Portsmouth.[84] They became the first of a new class. Five of the six sloops in PW 1866 were built to the *Blanche* design: *Eclipse* (ex-*Sappho*, at Sheerness), *Sirius* (Portsmouth), *Spartan* (Deptford), *Dido* (Portsmouth), and *Tenedos* (Devonport).[85] Two more were planned in December 1866 (presumably under PW 1867) but never ordered: *Proserpine* and *Diomede*. In the usual way that designs expand, later ships intended as repeat *Amazon*s were larger, heavier, and slower. Because the speed of the *Amazon* was considered unsatisfactory, the ships were lengthened, the armament changed (64pdrs replaced the 40pdrs), the complement increased, the rig was altered, and stores and boats added. The result had the nominal tonnage intended, but was in effect of the old and rather different type. The class became a Captain's command (a corvette, although they were originally rated sloops). For Robinson, 'all trace of the original idea has disappeared' except the ram bow. This class introduced iron cross-beams, though the ships retained wooden frames. Robinson later described them as the type needed for foreign service in the colonies, in China, and 'to clear the seas of privateers or pirates'. They would displace about 1250 tons, mount 4 heavy guns, and be capable of 13kts (like

HMS *Thetis* was one of three *Druid* class corvettes based on the earlier *Blanche* class. Apart from the large *Active* and *Volage* and the paddle corvettes, they were the first British corvettes to have a permanent stern chase gun, on a non-shifting pivoted slide. Many ships had such guns in their bows, but the *Druid*s were unusual for their size to have a similar gun aft. They were also the first medium-size wooden corvettes with poops. This combination presented a problem. A hoisting screw was normally protected by bulkheading. That had to extend up through the poop – exactly where a stern gun would be mounted. Placing the stern gun atop the poop, as in *Active* and *Volage*, would have entailed too much topweight. The later solution was to provide a pair of embrasured ports with intersecting curved tracks on deck sufficient for a gun to move between them and also to fire from side ports. The gun was always forward of the propeller well. The *Druid*s had a single port right aft with ports on either side facing towards the broadside, tracks on deck making it possible to move the gun between the three ports. To solve the problem, the screw was made non-hoisting. Initially a special device was provided to remove blades in situ (it proved impractical). *Briton* and *Druid* both had 7in 6½-ton bow and stern chasers (the 4½-ton version had not yet been made) plus eight 64pdrs on the broadside. After their first commissions both ships were rearmed with all-64pdr armaments, the chasers being replaced by new 64pdr Mk III weighing about half as much as the 7in guns. The weight saved went into two more 64pdr (all Mk III) on each side, for a total of fourteen. *Thetis* was completed with this armament. In contrast to the later *Amethyst*s, the *Druid*s floated at their designed waterlines (the later ships floated nearly a foot deep). They rolled more uneasily than their successors, suggesting insufficient metacentric height or restoring arm, and they yawed more easily in a following sea. However, according to Admiral Ballard, like all corvettes of their time, they rode beautifully when lying-to in a gale. They were fast and handy under steam, but slow (and sluggish in steering) under sail. Poor sailing performance was attributed to the non-hoisting screw. They also had a light draught in comparison to their sail area, giving them a poor grip when sailing close-hauled. *Thetis* went to China on completion in 1873 and was transferred to the East Indies station in 1874. She returned to pay off and refit in 1877, and in 1879 went to the Pacific. She returned home and decommissioned in 1887, and was immediately sold for breaking up.
(National Maritime Museum N05352)

Amazon, as conceived).[86] This design figured in the program Robinson proposed in August 1866 to new First Lord Sir John Pakington.[87] He wanted six more ships under PW 1867-69, and ultimately a total of twenty.

Robinson disliked the *Blanche* as neither a true sloop nor a fast corvette. He submitted a new design in December 1867. It would be a Captain's command (i.e., a corvette) from the outset, with ten guns, a complement of 175, ship rigged, and all the boats, spars, sails, stores etc of the *Blanche* class. Armament would be two 7in on revolving slides and carriages plus eight 64pdrs, one of which could fire right ahead and one right astern. Ships would be built at Deptford and Sheerness during the coming year (i.e., under PW 1868).[88] Three were built: *Druid* (Deptford) and *Briton* (Sheerness) under PW 1868 and *Thetis* (Devonport) under PW 1870. Like the *Blanche*s, they had wooden frames with iron reinforcing cross-beams, and ram bows.[89] They were the first small British corvettes (other than paddlers) with permanently-placed stern guns. Earlier ships with much lighter guns ran them from broadside to a stern port. This operation was the subject of a standard drill. The 64pdr 71cwt was much too heavy, and even heavier guns were coming; and steam ships could change bearing rapidly, so stern fire mattered more than in the past. Guns were therefore mounted on permanently centred revolving slides, provided with three or four ports through which they could fire. The poop was a complication. The pocket into which the ship's propeller was raised (when she was under sail) extended well up through the poop, blocking any potential fire from any gun not atop the poop. In later ships the solution was to embrasure the stern ports – to provide a position alongside the bulkheading for the propeller. In the wooden ram-bow corvettes the solution was not to hoist the screw at all, leaving space over the counter for the stern chaser (with a port right aft and one on either side, the slide moving back and around on racers – on tracks laid on the deck).

Five of the ten ram-bowed corvettes (*Blanche* and *Briton* classes) had the old type of single-expansion engine; five had compound engines. The latter required nearly twice the boiler pressure achieved in the earlier type of box boiler, hence led to the design of the cylindrical boilers standard in later classes (steam pressure increased from 20–30psi to 60psi). *Briton* and *Thetis* had six cylindrical boilers each, and achieved 13¼kts and 13½kts, respectively, on trials. However, different compound engines in two smaller ram-bowed corvettes were not successful, so *Druid* had single-expansion machinery with four rectangular boilers. She could steam only about two-thirds as far as her sisters, even though she carried 30 tons more coal.

In an August 1866 memorandum for First Lord Pakington summarizing the needs of the Royal Navy, Robinson pressed for three different classes of cruiser to defend British trade. The greatest threat was posed by the new American cruisers (*Wampanoag* class, which Robinson called the *Pampanoosuc* class), against which the *Inconstant* (see the next chapter) had been designed. Robinson wanted six such ships within the next three years (proposed 1866-67 through 1868-69 programs), and a total of twelve. Next came the *Blanche*s. Below them came a third (*Plover*) class of gunboats (second-class sloops) for river service (twin screws for shallow draught, 670 tons burthen, with one large and two small guns).[90] One had already been ordered, and Robinson wanted eleven more, a total of twelve in three years. Ultimately there should be twenty.[91] Rated as gun-vessels and not sloops, these were the first small British warships to be built after 1863.

No substantial unarmoured ships were included in the 1868-69 and 1869-70 programs. On leaving office in 1871, Robinson proposed building another three *Blanche*s (presumably meaning *Briton*s). They materialized as the first three of the *Amethyst* class, described in the next chapter.

Some time before leaving office in July 1866, the Admiralty Board asked Robinson for two cruiser designs: the big *Inconstant* (see the next chapter) and also a screw ship armed like the old paddle frigates and capable of all of their services (*Juno*). The latter apparently referred to the ability to transport troops, which was important for colonial and China service. Ordered under PW 1866, *Juno* (Deptford) was not included in Robinson's trade protection fleet. Her sister *Thalia* (Woolwich) was ordered later (some time after September 1866), also within PW 1866.[92] This class was not in the mainstream of British masted cruiser development.

In August and September 1866 Robinson reminded the new Board that many wooden ships had, or soon would have, worn out.[93] Of thirteen frigates in commission (15 considered effective), one was on the Home Station (*Liverpool*), one in the Mediterranean (*Arethusa*), three in the West Indies (*Aurora*, *Constance*, and *Doris*), one on the South East Coast of America (*Narcissus*), one in the East Indies (*Octavia*), one on the Coast of Africa (*Bristol*), one on Coast Guard service (*Dauntless*), and one in Australia (*Curacoa*). Six more were refitting (*Liffey*, *Mersey*, *Orlando*, *Galatea*, *Ariadne*, and *Endymion*). *Undaunted* had been completed but she went directly to reserve; *Newcastle* and *Glasgow* had been laid up incomplete (they were completed in, respectively, 1874 and 1871). The two remaining blockships *Hastings* and *Pembroke* were assigned, respectively, as hospital ship at Queenstown and to the Coast Guard; neither would last much longer. Another fifteen frigates were considered ineffective, meaning that repairs would be too expensive to be worthwhile.

Of five paddle frigates still on the list, one (*Terrible*) had recently been thoroughly repaired. It was unlikely that two others (*Leopard* and *Valorous*) would be repaired on returning from foreign service. *Magicienne* was in dock being repaired, and *Gladiator* would probably continue through 1870 with moderate repairs (she was ordered broken up in 1877). That four (of five) paddle frigates were in commission suggests that these elderly ships were easily maintained and considered valuable – hence the need for *Juno* and *Thalia*.

Eighteen of the twenty-three corvettes were in commission: one on the Home Station (*Racoon*), one in the Mediterranean (*Cossack*), five on the West Indies Station, with one ordered home (*Pylades*, *Cadmus*, *Wolverine*, *Niger*, and *Jason*), three in the Pacific (*Clio*, *Malacca*, and *Scout*), one on the East Indies Station (*Highflyer*), four in China, with one ordered home (*Barrosa*, *Pelorus*, *Scylla*, and *Pearl*), and three in Australia (*Esk*, *Brisk*, and *Challenger*). Two (*Barrosa* and *Wolverine*) had never been repaired. Three were currently refitting (*Satellite*, *Rattlesnake*, and *Charybdis*), and two (*Miranda* and *Orestes*) were worn out. Eight recently repaired would probably last until 1870 (*Cadmus*, *Scout*, *Scylla*, *Highflyer*, and *Malacca* in

1865, and *Challenger, Pearl,* and *Jason* in 1866). *Clio* had been repaired in 1864 and would be repaired again in PW 1866; she might last until 1870. Five (*Racoon, Cossack, Esk, Pylades,* and *Pelorus*) had been repaired and were unlikely to last beyond 1868. Two (*Brisk* and *Niger*) were obsolete and had been repaired more than once; they would not be serviceable after 1868.

Of a total of eighteen first-class sloops, nine were in commission: one in the West Indies (*Fawn*), two in the Pacific (*Alert* and *Mutine*), one in the East Indies (*Wasp*), one on the West Coast of Africa (*Greyhound*), two in China (*Rattler* and *Perseus*), one in Australia (*Falcon*), and one on the Home Station (*Cruizer,* now renamed *Cruiser*). Three were modern screw ships (*Reindeer, Vestal,* and *Niobe*), and three had never been repaired (*Pelican, Perseus,* and *Rattler*). Four more were refitting (*Cameleon, Chanticleer, Lyra,* and *Rinaldo*), and three more had recently been repaired (*Greyhound, Mutine,* and *Cruiser,* all in 1865). The remaining four (*Wasp, Alert, Falcon,* and *Fawn*) were not worth repairing.

Special provision had to be made for the considerable force of second- and third-class sloops and gunboats to be maintained in China. All eleven second-class (and all four third-class sloops) were in commission. Two were on their way home. All would probably remain serviceable through 1870. Five second-class sloops (*Cordelia* in 1864, *Gannet, Icarus, Peterel,* and *Racer* in 1865) had recently been repaired. The other six (*Pantaloon, Rapid, Rosario, Royalist, Columbine,* and *Shearwater*) had never been repaired.

Of ten paddle sloops, eight were in commission. Four, repaired in 1862-63 (*Argus* in 1862, *Buzzard, Hydra,* and *Salamander* in 1863) were unlikely to last past 1868. Four more repaired in 1865-66 (*Basilisk, Spiteful,* and *Sphinx* in 1865, *Barracouta* in 1866) were likely to last through 1870. *Virago* was currenly refitting, and *Devastation* was already worn out.

Apart from new construction, then, by 1870, 14 corvettes, 13 first-class sloops, 11 second-class sloops, one paddle frigate, and 5 paddle sloops would remain, plus smaller craft. Thirty-three ships would be discarded. In August 1866 Robinson proposed a three-year program comprising 6 *Inconstant*s, 12 first-class sloops (*Blanche* class), 12 second-class sloops or gunboats (*Plover* class), 3 *Juno* class (which were distinguished from sloops), and 2 paddle despatch vessels, a total of 35 ships. Moreover, the ships to be added would be far superior to those being discarded. On this basis, after 1870 no ship of earlier type and low speed should be repaired.

Robinson also pointed out that much of the expense of maintaining the large British steam fleet went into small slow ships which could not fight a war against a maritime power – an early version of Admiral Fisher's complaint about ships which could 'neither run nor fight.' The replacements should be able to meet the smaller ships of France, America, or Russia (in that order, as written) on equal terms.

HMS *Thalia* was designed to combine corvette and troopship duties, replacing earlier paddle frigates in the latter role. Armament was two 7in 6½-ton and four 64pdr (2 chaser, 2 side). As of January 1874 *Juno* (but not *Thalia*) was to be rearmed when recommissioned with one 7in and another two broadside 64pdr. As of June 1876 *Juno* had the new armament, but *Thalia* still had her 7in guns. The following January *Thalia* was being rearmed like *Juno*. Both ships were included in the list of 'Ships for Special Service' in the 1 January 1878 official list. At that time *Thalia* was in reserve at Devonport, and *Juno* was in China. Despite the 'special service' classification (which they shared with *Iris* and *Mercury* and with the torpedo boat *Lightning*) they were 'considered as Fighting Ships'. *Thalia* was repaired in 1879-80. In 1882 she was listed on 'Particular Service,' which suggests trooping duty. *Thalia* was given two more 64pdrs in exchange for her 7in guns, and *Juno* had four more 64pdrs when her 7in guns were landed. Completed in 1870, *Thalia* was reclassified as a troopship in October 1886; she became a powder hulk in 1891 and a depot ship in February 1915. *Juno* was sold in 1887.
(Allan C Green via State Library of Victoria)

2 IRON HULLS

In mid-1863 the US Navy announced in its *Annual Report* that it would build a series of fast cruisers (with a sustained speed of 15kts, an unprecedented speed at the time) to 'sweep the seas' of enemy ships. That could be read as a counter to Confederate raiders, but it could also be read as a potential threat to British seaborne trade.[1] The classic US approach to war against Britain was a combination of commerce raiding and coast defence. Britain and the United States had nearly come to blows over issues as disparate as the Oregon border (1846) and private American attempts to attack Canada (which continued after the American Civil War). It did not help that the Confederate raiders had been built in the United Kingdom. Of the US ships only USS *Wampanoag* was really successful. She ran trials in February 1868.

The Admiralty was aware of the planned performance of the US ships by 1865, and by April 1866 a British counterpart, which became HMS *Inconstant*, had been designed.[2] The designed speed (15kts) and probably the battery were intended to match those of the US ship, which also mounted ten main-battery guns on her gun deck. The great design problem was the

Inconstant is shown about 1890. Her size and her great complement made her as expensive to maintain as a capital ship, and she was difficult to combine with other ships because she sailed and steamed so much faster; she was outrun under sail only by the wooden screw frigate *Immortalite* (*Emerald* class, but lengthened by 14ft while building). After service with the Channel Fleet, in 1871 she was made part of the 'Flying' Squadron, returning home to pay off in 1872. She was recommissioned in 1880 to carry relief crews to the Mediterranean, then made flagship of a new Flying Squadron (the rest of which were corvettes). The squadron was diverted to the Cape of Good Hope for possible emergency service during the 1881 Boer War, and then to Alexandria when trouble broke out in Egypt in 1882. Although too late for the bombardment, she arrived in time for her crew to land in the city and help control it. She paid off on returning home, having been in full commission for only slightly over five years, the shortest for any Victorian ship not lost while in service. She was temporarily commissioned for several fleet manoeuvres, and later was overflow ship at Plymouth. She was removed from the effective list in 1904 and then converted into a gunnery hulk for the boys' training ship *Impregnable*, then transferred in 1920 to serve as accommodation hulk for the Plymouth Torpedo School.

(National Maritime Museum L5407)

Inconstant, probably as built (she shows no new shielded guns). She had unusually fine lines at her ends with considerable rise of floor, her stem receding slightly as it rose and her stern, as shown here, round and sloping outwards, with false ports and no quarter galleries. Internally she resembled contemporary iron battleships, with three decks and watertight compartments (but she lacked their double bottom). She was described as a good sea boat and a steady gun platform, easily handled despite her great length, though sluggish when tacking or wearing in light winds (perhaps due to her unusual balanced rudder).

USS *Wampanoag* created the scare to which the big British iron frigates responded. Renamed *Florida*, she is shown laid up at the New York Navy Yard in 1874, her four funnels suggesting how much of her hull was filled with machinery. She was ordered in July 1863 as a 'screw sloop of great speed'. Of three groups of steam sloops ordered that year, *Wampanoag* and others of her group were described as sacrificing some armament for great speed. They were designed to make 16kts and 'to sweep the ocean and chase and hunt down the vessels of an enemy' – which could apply to British commerce as well as to Confederate-type raiders. Underwater her hull was a lengthened (by 35ft, without increasing beam) version of that of the more conventional steam sloop *Guerriere*. She was lengthened another 10ft in September 1863 to accommodate her engines and boilers, which took up 166ft of her length. Claimed trial performance (February 1868) was an average of 16.6kts for 38 hours, which made her the fastest ship in the world (the British considered the speed an over-estimate, as the trial was not run on a measured mile). Her sister *Madawaska* had an identical hull but Ericsson (as in the monitor *Dictator*) rather than Isherwood machinery; she sustained only 12.73kts for 41 hours, but made 15.25kts for five hours. Two more cruisers, *Ammonoosuc* and *Neshaminy*, had the same machinery as *Wampanoag* but slightly fuller lines and somewhat lighter construction. *Ammonoosuc* averaged 17.11kts on her June 1868 trials for nearly three hours. Construction of her sister was abandoned because her hull was badly twisted by the time machinery was installed. Two *Pomponoosuc*s were similar but four feet beamier, but they were never launched (only engines were ever ordered for the second ship, *Bon Homme Richard*). Two smaller ships were not successful steamers: *Idaho* and *Chattanooga*, of which *Idaho* was ordered before *Wampanoag* (May 1863). *Idaho* made only 8.27kts under steam (May 1866), but her fine lines made her a very fast sailer once the engines were removed (she logged over 18.5kts). *Chattanooga* reportedly had engines identical to those of the Russian armoured cruiser or second-class ironclad *General Admiral*, and averaged 13.2kts for 24 hours. By 1874, when this photograph was taken, she had been sunk by floating ice while in reserve at League Island (Philadelphia), and *Madawaska* (renamed *Tennessee* in 1869) had had half her boilers and their two funnels removed, a complete spar (upper) deck added, and a ship rig fitted. The US Navy's Board on Steam Machinery Afloat recommended this refit for the whole class. The remaining boiler power was insufficient to turn over the ship's engines. The ship was again refitted in 1871-75 with new cylindrical boilers and new four-cylinder 3200 IHP engines (her original engines produced 2143 IHP; *Wampanoag*'s produced 4049).

need to combine heavy machinery with a long narrow lightweight hull. The US Navy opted for the usual wooden hull, which required it to accept unusually light construction. Ultimately it was clear that the choice had been disastrous, but that was hardly evident in 1865-66. Through 1870 the potential threat of American commerce raiders seems to have dominated British thinking about large commerce-protecting cruisers.

Reed solved the hull weight problem by adopting iron, a much lighter material. Robinson (possibly not Reed) was well aware of the experiments which had convinced the Admiralty not to use iron in fighting ships except when it was well protected by armour.[3] He was particularly impressed by the dangers of end-on fire, because at the time it seemed that ships would fight mainly end-on due to their ability to manoeuvre. Shot running the length of the ship would be slowed well enough to be particularly devastating. Hollow and solid shot fired with weak charges at 400yds were even more destructive, creating clouds of splinters, which produced large irregular holes that would be difficult or impossible to patch in action. Oak filling between the ribs did not solve the problem.

It would be impossible to adapt an unarmoured iron ship for close action by using watertight bulkheads or other devices. At close quarters an iron ship would be sunk more quickly than a wooden one, which could better be patched in action. Robinson's solution was to avoid close action. His ship would be armed with long-range guns, the 9in 12½-ton type then then planned for battleships. Given her unusually high speed, she could choose her range. When she was completed, HMS *Inconstant* was the third most powerfully armed ship in the Royal Navy, but she had many fewer guns than contemporary wooden steam frigates. The rub was only solid shot could reach long range; the lighter shells exploded at relatively short ranges, because their fuzes, ignited as they were fired, burned out in a short time. Yet it seemed that solid shot could not quickly destroy a wooden warship (though heavy shellfire could). *Wampanoag* would probably be different. Her machinery, well above water, represented a large area vulnerable to solid shot. Her lightly-built hull would also be vulnerable, whereas most wooden warships had heavily-built hulls which were difficult to destroy. It seems unlikely in retrospect that Robinson's long-range battery made much sense, given the state of naval gunnery. In evidence given before the 1871 Committee on Designs, Captain Charles Waddilove of HMS *Inconstant* thought that he would engage an enemy at short range, i.e., in traditional fashion.

As completed, *Inconstant* mounted both the planned ten 9in guns and four 7in (6½-ton). The additional guns, mounted on the upper deck, were first planned for her successor HMS *Blonde* (later renamed *Shah*). In 1866 the US ship was (incorrectly) credited with sixteen 9in shell guns (smooth-bore) and two 100pdr rifled guns on the main deck, and one 60pdr rifled pivot gun and two 30pdr rifled guns on the upper deck. Her near-sisters were to carry 17 rather than 21 guns. *Inconstant* would have been outgunned, with ten 12-ton (9in) MLR on the main deck, two pivot 6½-ton (7in) MLR on the upper deck, and two broadside 6½-ton MLR on the upper deck (all upper deck guns could bear on either broadside). The British ship would have nine guns on her broadside compared to nine, ten, or eleven on the American ships, The key question was whether US smoth-bores were as effective as the British muzzle-loading rifles – which should be far superior at longer range. In fact the US ship carried fewer guns.

Because the ship's ends were so fine, the entire main-deck battery was concentrated amidships. Because she could not be beamy, there was not much space behind each gun, although space to either side was ample. In 1871 the ship's captain agreed that such an undivided battery could be put completely out of action by a single 9in shell. Transverse partitions could not be placed between the guns because they would have been forced towards the ends of the ship, which were too narrow for them or their weight. Above this deck there was a chaser on the forecastle, which fired a little ahead and 4 degrees across the ship; one of the bow port guns (6½-ton) could be moved to the forecastle. The very narrow forecastle made it impossible to work two guns side by side.

Unless she could destroy an opponent at long range, *Inconstant* could be in trouble. The 1871 Committee on Designs asked her captain how he would fare against the wooden US steam frigate *Franklin* credited with 36 guns. He thought that whichever ship managed to get in a waterline broadside first would probably sink the other. With equal gunnery, the ship with more guns would have a far better chance. However, *Inconstant* had much more powerful guns, firing shells with a bursting charge of 18½lbs compared to 3½lbs for the US ship. The ship's captain agreed that the difference greatly favoured his ship. He also admitted that the difference in construction would count. The US shells would penetrate the wood and thin iron on his ship's side and burst inside, 'and that would rather be in our favour'. The British shell would burst as it passed through the wooden hull of the US ship 'and make an enormous hole.' The main protection against waterline hits was his ship's ten watertight bulkheads, continuous from the orlop deck (slightly below the waterline) up to the main deck. The two end bulkheads were completely watertight, the others being pierced by watertight doors. The ship's captain was not sure whether the bulkheads offered sufficient security if the ship took one or two waterline hits.

Reed incorporated sheathing below the waterline, the hull being coppered like a wooden ship, so that she could keep the sea without fouling, to operate for a protracted period in tropical waters without docking. At Robinson's insistence, the double layer of 9in oak sheathing was extended above the waterline as partial protection against the shattering effect of shellfire, deadening the effect of blows (Reed did not mention the possibility in his design report). The wood would also support the skin against the effect of shot passing through the ship to hit the other side. However, clearly Robinson did not think it would make the ship viable in a short-range action.

Robinson refused to guarantee 15-knot speed for fear that weights had been underestimated and the 'extreme difficulty' sometimes encountered in attempts to reach six times the NHP of the best recent engines 'and the very different manner in which such a result has been finally obtained'. No armed seagoing ship in the world had yet attained 15kts (*Wampanoag* had not yet been completed). He was willing to guarantee 14kts, expecting it to be exceeded. Robinson's faith was justified. On trials *Inconstant* averaged 16.512kts on full power on the measured mile and 13.701kts at half power at a displacement of 5328 tons. Unlike *Wampanoag*, she had a hoisting screw (and retractable funnels) and a full rig for cruising. She was an unusually fast sailer: she once made 13½kts, and her captain thought she was good for 14½. At her most economical speed, 6.4kts, she could steam 3020nm, about the breadth of the Atlantic. At higher speeds endurance fell considerably: 1170nm at her full speed of 16.2kts, 2700nm at 10kts.[4] *Inconstant* proved what she could do when she carried back the sad news of the loss of HMS *Captain* from Cape Finisterre in November 1870. She averaged 15kts throughout, albeit not in really rough weather.

Technically *Inconstant* was a corvette, because her main battery was carried on an uncovered gun deck (she carried a few more guns on forecastle and poop above it). However, she was much larger and more powerful than wooden steam corvettes; she was soon designated a frigate. She and her two immediate successors, *Shah* and *Raleigh*, were the last frigates in the Royal Navy until the category was revived in 1943 for ASW ships.

Robinson wanted at least six *Inconstant*s in the 1866-67

HMS *Shah* was to have been named *Blonde*, but was named instead to honour Shah Nasr-ed-din of Persia, who was being courted by the British government (and feted in London) at the time. Like the other two iron frigates, she was an excellent sea boat, very steady in all weather and under all wind directions. She steamed easily (and dryly) into a head sea, and was considered handy for her length (in a 1936 article Admiral Ballard credited this to her conventional rather than balanced rudder). Like *Raleigh*, she had deep bow and stern embrasures for 9in chasers (one gun, two ports, at each end; the gun could be moved to fire out of either port). Her 6½-ton 7in guns gave her somewhat better armour-piercing firepower than *Raleigh*. She was among the first British cruisers armed with torpedoes, ejected from carriages firing through ports forward of her 7in guns (she had twelve 14in torpedoes). *Shah* was commissioned in 1876 (as shown here) as flagship of Rear Admiral De Horsey in the Pacific. For the previous decade the British Pacific flagship had been an ironclad, to face the ironclads of South American navies, but in 1876 the Royal Navy was concentrating its ironclads in European waters to meet the ongoing Turkish crisis (which nearly led to war with Russia in 1878). In May 1877 a Peruvian revolutionary seized the ironclad *Huascar*. British ships dominated the carrying trade along the Pacific coast of South America; the rebels interfered with it as they pressured the Peruvian authorities. They were attacking what would now be called 'good order at sea'. The Royal Navy was its main guarantor — 'good order at sea' was key to British prosperity. No other navy could operate on a global scale. On 29 May 1877 *Huascar* rejected a demand to surrender. *Shah* repeatedly hit *Huascar*, wrecking her upper works, but she was unable to penetrate her belt or her turrets. *Huascar*'s shots all went high. *Shah*'s only ironclad-killing weapon was her torpedo: she was the first warship to fire a self-propelled torpedo in anger, during this engagement (it missed because it was so slow). At nightfall *Shah* bottled up *Huascar*. De Horsey planned to send in a boat to torpedo her (at anchor she would have been an excellent target), but as it approached he learned that *Huascar* had surrendered to the Peruvian authorities. The Admiralty concluded that the flagship on any station facing ironclads should be an ironclad; HMS *Triumph* replaced *Shah* after two years rather than the usual four of this commission. En route home, *Shah* called at St Helena, to discover (by mail steamer; there was no telegraph connection) that the Zulu War had broken out; the governor of St Helena promptly loaded all his troops on board and despatched *Shah* to the Cape of Good Hope. They were joined by 400 officers and seamen from *Shah*, who spent five months in the field helping fight the Zulus. On returning home in October 1879, a year after starting from Valparaiso, *Shah* went into reserve, emerging only in 1892 for harbour service in Bermuda.

Shah 1876

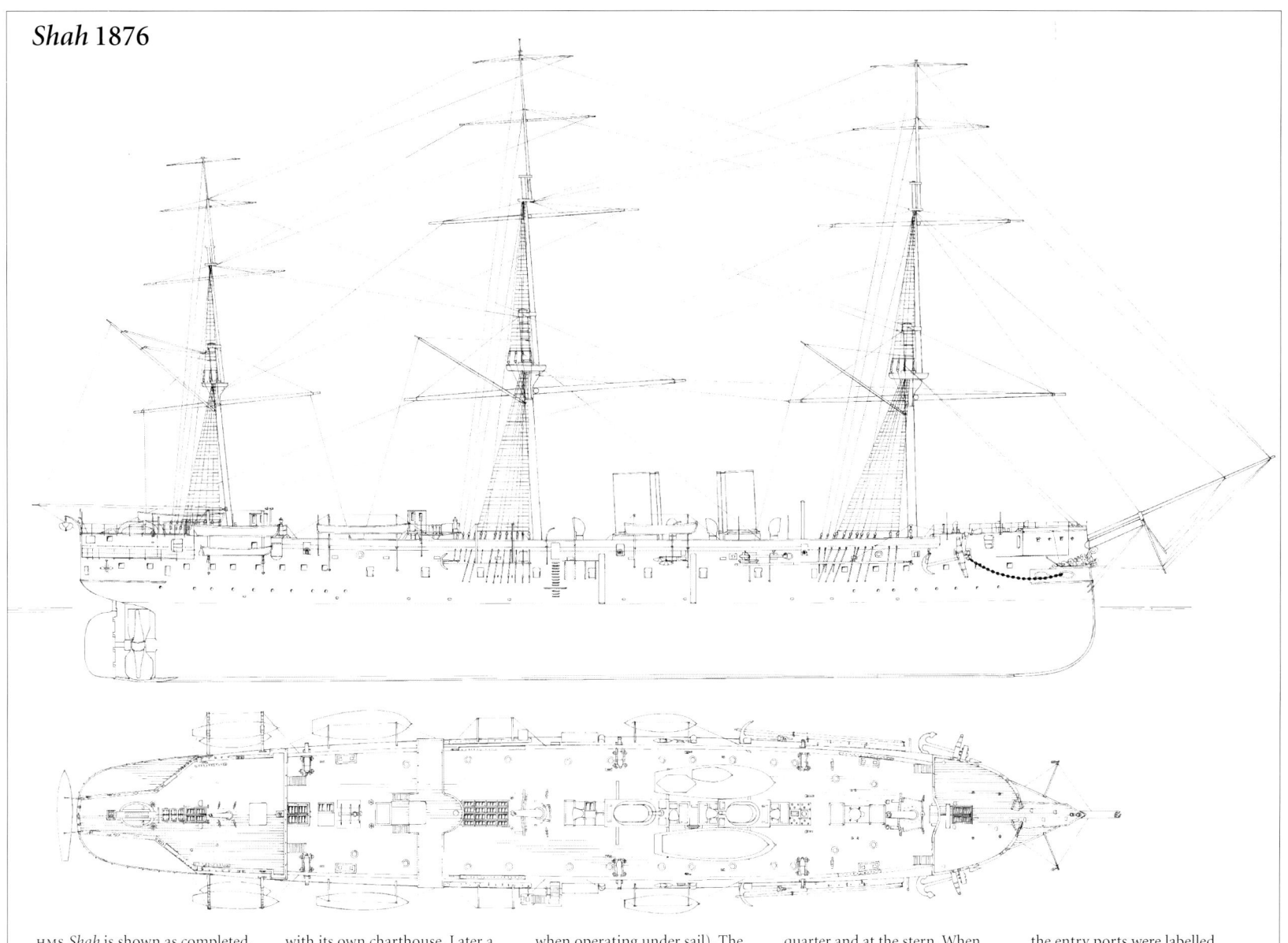

HMS *Shah* is shown as completed, December 1876. Her hull was copper-sheathed (over wood) up to the line shown on the drawing. Prior to completion she was altered in several ways. Her poop was extended forward 7ft, and 4ft diameter 'conning towers' were added on either side at its fore end. The original charthouse on the poop was retained, but an entire new flying bridge, supported only by pillars, was added 45ft forward of the poop, with its own charthouse. Later a fore and aft catwalk was added to connect the two conning positions, and a second small deckhouse was added on the flying bridge. The rigging plan is based on a drawing prepared prior to completion. In service *Shah* carried only three yards on each mast, and each of the three masts was moved about 7ft forward of the originally planned position. The funnels were fixed (*Inconstant* could retract hers when operating under sail). The 9in guns were mounted on slides, and could traverse to fire through forward- or aft-facing ports on either side. The forwardmost and aftmost of the six upper deck 64pdrs could be moved to fire forward or aft on the opposite side of the ship from the traversed 9in guns. The other two 64pdrs were normally mounted abaft the line of 7in guns on the lower deck, but could be moved to fire through ports on the quarter and at the stern. When firing on the broadside, the lines of fire of the two 9in guns converged only 150yds away, which may indicate expected battle range. *Shah* had no fixed torpedo tubes, relying instead on torpedo carriages, similar in concept to gun carriages. She also had two spindle shaped 'buoys' for Harvey torpedoes slung on her sides amidships. The platforms jutting from the ship's sides abaft the after funnel and the entry ports were labelled 'sentry platforms' on the plans. They were probably dismounted when the ship was underway. The 36ft gig boats slung from davits across the stern were stowed on raised skids atop the poop when the ship was at sea. Note that the davits are of the quadrantial type and that the after sets were used to stow two boats each. Unlike her near-sisters *Inconstant* and *Raleigh*, *Shah* was never rearmed.
(A D Baker III)

through 1869-70 programs, presumably including the first ship (1865-66 program).[5] Three were proposed in December 1866 for the 1867-68 program, but in February 1867 it was decided that only one would be built. The new First Lord (H T Lowry Corry took office on 8 March 1867) decided to build one smaller corvette (*Volage*), to free up money. A second ship, *Active*, was later added. Robinson thought that the 1867-68 iron cruiser would be less expensive to build under contract, and both the *Volage*s were contracted out to Thames Iron Works. Like *Inconstant*, these were iron ships sheathed in wood. The design requirements seem to have been that they should be half the size (hence cost) of *Inconstant* with the same 15-knot speed (*Inconstant* had not yet been completed).[6] Reed pointed out that the two corvettes would cost more than a single *Inconstant* both initially and in running cost. He was not at all sure that they were a great bargain. A sketch design was submitted on 9 April 1867, but further detailed designs were prepared at least through May 1867. By 1871 the *Volage*s were rated at 15¼kts, but *Inconstant* was rated at 16½. *Volage* made 15.128kts on trial.

An initial sketch design in the Ships' Cover (28 March 1867,

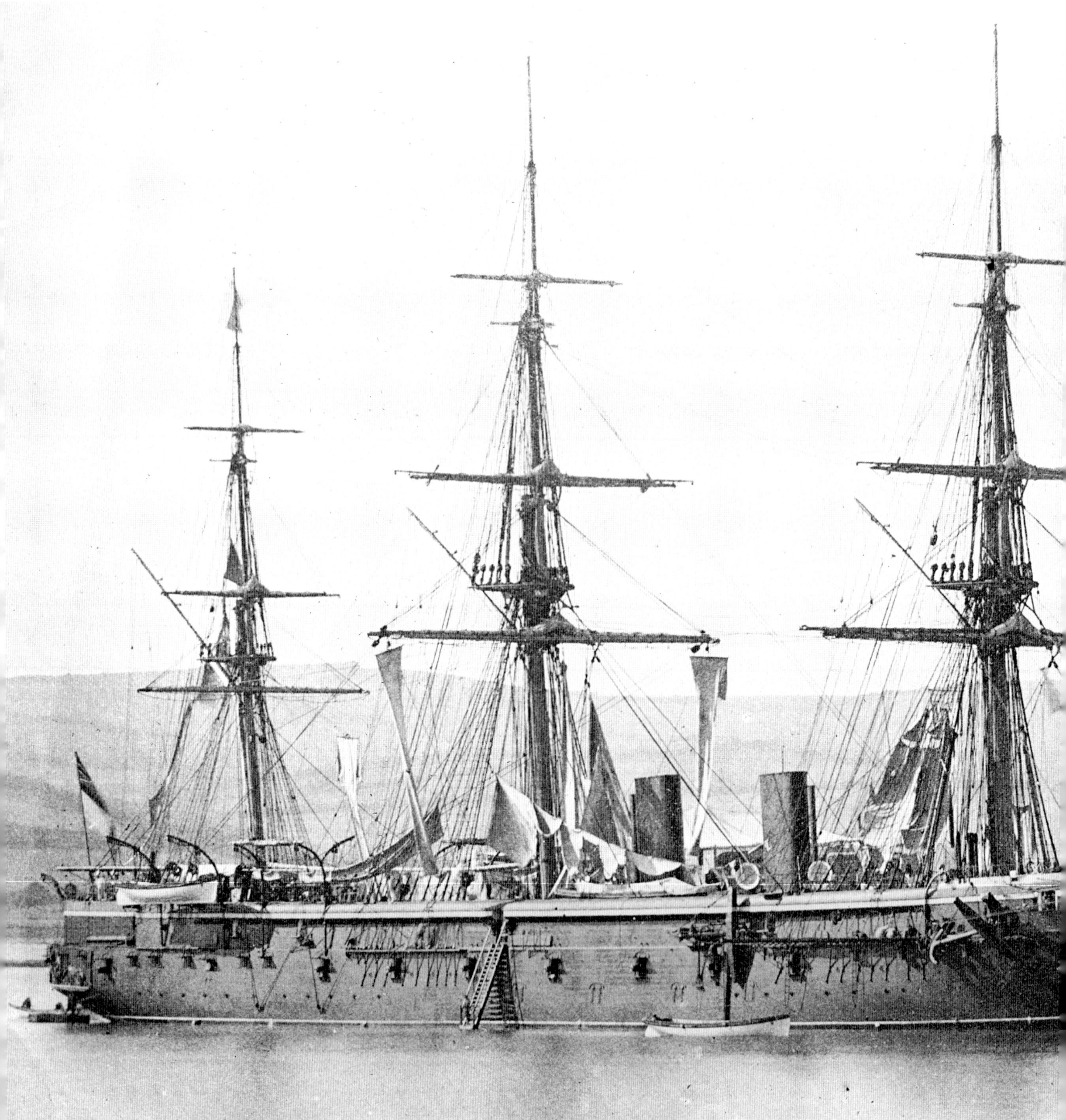

headed 'Small ship in lieu of one of the size of *Inconstant*', shows an armament of two 12½-ton guns, two 6½-ton, and two 64pdrs, but as submitted the design showed six 6½-ton guns and the two 64pdrs. The only difference in the completed ship was another two 64pdrs. The 6½-ton guns were all on the broadside, in slides, with one 64pdr on each broadside and one each as bow and stern chasers. These guns armed HMS *Shah*.[7]

Corry apparently decided to cease building ships after the 1867-68 program, presumably in order to cut budget costs. In 1869 the new First Lord (Childers) decided to resume construction.[8] The proposed 1870-71 program consisted of the second *Inconstant*, a repeat *Volage*, and a small corvette (*Druid* type). Childers ordered the design of a smaller new frigate called the *Raleigh* class. The ship would be a knot slower, armed with twenty-four 64pdrs and one 12½-ton gun. Initially he substituted two such ships for the *Volage* and the small corvette.

As required, Robinson reduced the size and speed of the new frigate. He was unhappy to do so; he thought Childers and his First Naval Lord Dacres were making the same penny-pinching mistake an earlier Board had made with ironclads.[9] Having built the superior *Warrior* and *Defence*, they demanded smaller, hence less capable, ships. Size was vital, and the French seemed to be the only ones who understood.

Reed submitted his first design for an improved *Inconstant* in November 1866.[10] The main new feature was watertight coal bunkers forming a protective layer outboard of the engine and boiler rooms, separated from them by longitudinal bulkheads. The bunkers added coal capacity (for a total of 750 tons, 180 more than her rated capacity), and they were a pointer to later forms of protection based on coal. Wing bulkheads separated the coal from the machinery. Reed rejected a proposed double bottom due to its weight and the consequent loss of speed. He considered the wood sheathing and a wooden keel sufficient protection against grounding. The ship added six 6½-ton guns on her upper deck, a feature adopted for *Inconstant* while under construction.

Dacres agreed that an *Inconstant* would be best to fight the new American cruisers, but she was more expensive than a *Raleigh* to build and operate, and only a knot faster. Dacres thought he could have four *Raleigh*s for the price of three *Inconstant*s. He rejected Controller's claim that a *Raleigh* would be so inferior in fighting power. Compared to *Inconstant*, she would have a larger number of guns firing much faster. The total weight of burster delivered to the target would make all the difference against an unarmoured ship. Numbers mattered for commerce protection. Childers agreed. On 11 February he ordered that one of the two frigates be a repeat *Inconstant*, the other a *Raleigh*. The repeat *Inconstant* was ordered as HMS *Blonde* and later renamed *Shah*. The smaller frigate was HMS *Raleigh*. Dacres' argument shows in the lighter-gun armament chosen for the new frigate: sixteen 6½-ton guns (7in, 112pdr) and two 64pdrs (64cwt, 6.3in) on the main deck, plus two 9in 12½-ton chasers and six more 64pdrs on her upper deck. The new frigates would be rigged more heavily (in proportion) than *Inconstant* or the *Volage* class. *Raleigh* was considerably smaller than *Inconstant*.[11]

Compared to *Inconstant*, *Shah* incorporated several of the improvements Reed proposed. She was not laid down until 1870, presumably so that her detailed design could reflect lessons

Raleigh is shown as built. She had much the same lines as *Inconstant*, but added a poop and deeply embrasured stern (to accommodate stern chasers). Like *Inconstant*, she was an excellent sea boat and a steady gun platform. Externally she was more decorated, with one of the last portrait-type naval figureheads. Not only was she armed mainly with lighter guns than *Inconstant*, but her 7in guns were of the light (4½-ton) rather than the heavy (6½-ton) type, the former being considered battleship armour-piercing weapons and the latter suited more to lower-velocity explosive shells (both guns fired shells of the same weight). Thus the lighter gun differed from contemporary muzzle-loaders in having a heavier shell in proportion to its overall weight: one and a quarter pounds per cwt of gun compared to the usual one pound per cwt. *Raleigh* was partly converted to breech-loaders after a decade of service. Her original battery was two 9in chasers (one each forward and aft) and four 64pdr (6.3in) on broadside trucks on the upper deck, plus fourteen 7in and two 64pdr on trucks on the main deck. On rearming, she retained only eight 7in on her main deck. To them were added eight 6in breech-loaders (half on the upper and half on the main deck) and eight 5in (all on the upper deck), the upper deck 6in guns being chasers. Two of the main deck ports were used for torpedo carriages. *Raleigh* replaced *Inconstant* in the Flying (Detached) Squadron, which began a two-year cruise after she joined. After returning home she sailed for Australia with relief crews; she was the last British frigate to round Cape Horn under sail. On returning home she paid off for the refit during which her armament was changed. In 1884 she became flagship on the Cape of Good Hope and West Africa stations, staying for three full commissions (i.e., for three changes of crew). On that service in 1895 she became the last British full-rigged warship to carry an Admiral's flag. On returning home she led the Training Squadron, the last square-rigged organization in the Royal Navy. *Raleigh* was put into reserve when the Training Squadron was abolished in 1899, having had nineteen years of seagoing commission – nearly the longest commissioned sea service of any Victorian warship. She was sold for breaking up in 1905 during the general clear-out of obsolete tonnage under Admiral Fisher.

(National Maritime Museum N05360)

Volage as built, with her funnel down. According to Admiral Ballard, she and *Active* were unsteady gun platforms. When driven into a head sea they tended to pitch deeply due to their fine entry and limited flare. In a beam or following sea they rolled badly. Ballard attributes the rolling to a poorly located centre of gravity and to the absence of a false keel (which would have raised the centre of gravity, and which was an Edward Reed innovation). *Volage* needed 75 tons of pig iron ballast (*Active* had 50 tons). Ballast was added after inclining experiments, and increased draught by 8in and 6in, respectively. Eventually the ships were fitted with wide bilge keels. They were wetter than the average British warships of their size. *Volage* was rearmed twice, *Active* once. Both ships began with six 7in 6½-ton guns on slides on their broadsides plus two 64pdr

Active in 1895 when she was flagship of the Training Squadron. She was placed in reserve upon being completed, being commissioned as flagship of the Cape of Good Hope and Africa station in 1873. Operations there included the Ashanti War of 1874, including a boat attack on Gemina. She returned to pay off (and be rearmed) in 1879, after which she went into reserve until 1885. She was then selected as flagship of the new Training Squadron, remaining in that service until 1898. She was sold in 1906. Admiral Ballard remembered her as the last British warship to leave Portsmouth harbour under sail.
(National Maritime Museum N01228)

learned from the trials of HMS *Inconstant*. *Inconstant* needed 180 tons of solid ballast. *Shah* was given slightly greater beam to provide enough stability that she needed no ballast at all.[12] HMS *Shah* famously fought the mutinous Peruvian ironclad *Huascar* in 1877, firing a torpedo at sea (albeit unsuccessfully) for the first time in history.

Perhaps not surprisingly, the next step was an attempt to design a reduced *Raleigh*, much as *Volage* had been a reduced *Inconstant*. Reed was gone, Nathaniel Barnaby already acting in his place. In August 1871 one of the naval draughtsmen was asked to sketch a new ship with displacement (hence cost) intermediate between *Volage* and *Raleigh*, with the speed of *Volage* and the same draught aft. The ship could have increased beam and horsepower, and unlike *Volage* she was to have a continuous upper deck (which in theory made her a frigate). The main deck guns were to be 90cwt rather than 8-ton, and the arrangements of bow and stern guns would match those of *Raleigh*. An internal design report, dated 16 September, describes the new ship as *Volage* with a complete deck over her guns, and topsides like *Raleigh*'s above that. Armament would consist of eight of the new 90cwt guns, four on each side, one of them on a revolving mount at bow or stern as a chaser, as in *Raleigh*. Complement would be about 350, and speed 15kts. The ship would be given as much sail as stability would allow. The form at bow and stern (entrance and run) would match that of *Volage*, but the ship would be enlarged to 280ft x 48ft x 20ft (18ft 6in forward, 21ft 6in aft). The projected powerplant was compound engines producing 5250 IHP.

A preliminary Legend, later cancelled, was dated 16 September 1871. It compared the projected ship with both *Volage* and *Raleigh*. She was about the size of the initial *Volage*

broadside guns on trucks and two 64pdrs on traversing mountings (slides) as chasers, the latter on forecastle and poop. Before her second commission *Volage* was rearmed with fourteen 64pdrs on trucks, the 7in being landed. That reflected the shift away from armour-piercing guns for cruisers, which was also reflected in the armament of HMS *Raleigh* compared to HMS *Inconstant*. In 1880 she was rearmed again with breech-loaders: her main deck battery was replaced by ten 6in, but she retained the 64pdrs on poop and forecastle. According to Ballard, these latter guns were retained because they were lighter than the new 6in; presumably the ships could not take additional topweight. Two 14in torpedo tubes were fitted on the fore part of the main deck. *Active* was never rearmed with the all-64pdr battery, but she was rearmed with breech-loaders. Both ships had low-pressure rectangular boilers and single-expansion engines; trial speed was about 15kts. The best recorded speed under sail was 13kts (*Volage*; *Active* made 12½kts). As completed *Volage* joined the Channel Fleet in 1870, and was then transferred to the Flying Squadron, returning to England in 1872 for her first rearmament. Ready for sea eighteen months later, she was chosen to carry astronomers to the Kerguelen Islands to observe the transit of Venus across the sun. She then became senior ship in South American (Atlantic) waters, returning home for her second rearmament in 1879. The refit included new boilers. She then served in the Training Squadron, remaining until that organization was disbanded in 1899.

(National Maritime Museum N05845)

Volage after her final rearmament, possibly at Portsmouth.

design, but displaced nearly as much as *Raleigh* in burthen terms (3169 64/94 tons compared to 3210 46/94; *Volage* was 2321 59/94). Nominal horsepower was given as 700, compared to 800 for *Raleigh* and 600 for *Volage*. That was expected to translate into 5250 IHP (6000 for *Raleigh*) and a speed of 15kts (15 to 15½ for *Raleigh*). Armament would have been eight 90cwt broadside guns and two 64pdr chasers (bow and stern) on the main deck plus two 12½-ton guns in revolving mountings, two 64pdrs in broadside mountings, and two 64pdr chasers on the upper deck. That was 16 guns compared to 22 for *Raleigh*, which had fourteen 64pdr broadside guns on her main deck but otherwise matched the new ship. Both ships completely outclassed *Volage*. Complement was given as 450, compared to 500 for *Raleigh*.

A preliminary design was submitted to the Board on 13 October 1871. The ship was expected to make 15kts, to carry a full rig, and to have a covered battery of the new 90cwt guns. She was described as the smallest ship which could meet the conditions laid down, but she was nearly as large as HMS *Raleigh*. She displaced 650 tons less and needed less power (by 750 IHP), and she needed 100 fewer men. She was expected to have the same steaming range with much less coal consumed, probably mainly because she would use a compound engine. While the ship was being designed, the Board was considering doing away with burthen (builder's measurement) tonnage. The ship's designer pointed out that under the old calculation the new ship was larger than HMS *Raleigh*, although she displaced more than 10 per cent less. Since the old measurement no longer counted, the designer had been able to adopt a better form for speed, both under steam and under sail, in which the ship was fuller at the waterline amidships than was usual.

There were attempts to shrink the ship to cut her cost. Thus a memo dated 18 October showed 270ft × 46ft, with the note that a Minute of 26 October called for further reduction to 240ft. The 18 October memo gave a battery of ten 90cwt guns on the main deck and two in revolving mountings on the upper deck, i.e., two more 90cwt. A few days later four 64pdrs were to replace four of the main deck 90cwt guns, arranged as chasers (bow and stern); later still two of the 90cwt were added back in, for a total of eight. The four 64pdrs would be placed forward and aft on truck carriages with ports cut so that they could be moved to fire fore and aft, to fire along the centreline as chasers. The two 90cwt guns on revolving mountings were still to be fitted on the upper deck. This armament was retained.

Weight would be saved by making the upper deck very light in the wake of masts and guns. Speed was still given as 15kts. A few days later the designers complained that the shorter hull had so little space that they were compelled to carry coal on the lower deck, thereby losing stability. Lengthening the ship back up to 280ft (with a 45ft beam) would not increase burthen tonnage very much (2671 rather than 2561 burthen tons), but it would allow all coal to be stowed deep enough to solve the stability problem.

A Legend dated 17 February 1872 describing this fast unarmoured cruising ship was prepared for the Board. Two of these iron corvettes sheathed in wood were built at Portsmouth under the 1872-73 program: HMS *Boadicea* and *Bacchante*. They were somewhat oddly (presumably for political reasons) described as modified *Volage*s, the main changes listed being 90cwt guns,

Bacchante in 1880. Note the deep embrasure forward for a bow chaser. As corvettes, these ships carried nearly their whole armament on the main deck (fourteen 7in), with chasers on forecastle and poop. All guns were on iron slides, and the chasers could be moved to fire from either port or starboard ports. *Boadicea* and *Euryalus* also had two 64pdr on trucks, which could quickly be shifted to fire from any port with side bolts sufficient to take their breeching and tackles. There were six suitable main-deck ports other than those for the 7in guns. Later all three ships received two or four 6in breech-loaders to replace an equal number of 7in. Two wheeled 14in Whitehead torpedo carriages occupied main deck ports forward of the guns. *Bacchante* alone received torpedo net defence after her first commission. In 1886 *Boadicea* and *Euryalus* each had four 5in on the upper deck and twelve 6in on the lower deck. *Bacchante* alone retained muzzle-loaders: two 7in 90cwt on her upper deck and eight on her main deck, plus four 6in on her main deck, the remnant of the earlier rearmament. Each ship had six 14in Whitehead torpedoes aboard. Unlike the three iron frigates, these ships had cylindrical 'Scotch' boilers operating at higher pressure (70psi) to feed compound engines: a high-pressure cylinder between their two low-pressure ones. These more efficient engines could drive them about twice as far (per ton of coal) as the earlier single-expansion iron frigates. With the exception of HMS *Rover*, they were the first British cruisers of more than 2000 tons to have cylindrical boilers and compound engines. The ships were considered fast under steam but slow under sail. Thus they made about 15kts on steam trials, but the best hour's run under sail was 11½kts for *Bacchante* (9½kts for *Euryalus*). *Bacchante* began her career with a year of independent service, followed by two years in the Flying Squadron formed in 1880 (with *Inconstant* as flagship). On returning home she was refitted and partially rearmed, then sent out in 1885 (relieving *Bacchante*) as flagship of the East Indies station. She was paid off in 1888 and sold for scrap in 1897.
(National Maritime Museum N05359)

IRON HULLS

Boadicea as refitted and partly rearmed in 1888. Like her predecessors, she was steered and handled from aft; there was no bridge amidships as in more modern ships. Note the closed embrasure for a bow chaser, visible almost directly under the funnel.
(National Maritime Museum G10329)

IRON HULLS 93

Boadicea in the white tropical livery in which she spent most of her career. She began her career in the fleet assembled for the Baltic in 1878, but then became flagship of the Cape of Good Hope and West Africa station. Relieved (by *Raleigh*) in 1885, she was refitted and partially rearmed at Portsmouth. She was recommissioned in 1888 as flagship in the East Indies (relieving *Bacchante*), returning home in 1894 to be decommissioned. *Boadicea* and *Euryalus* spent their entire careers as flagships on foreign stations, and *Bacchante* about half her service that way.
(National Maritime Museum N01232)

Euryalus in 1882. Upon completion in 1878 she became flagship of the East Indies Squadron, serving until 1885. Although refitted and partly rearmed at that time, she was laid up. Admiral Ballard recalls her as the first ship in the Royal Navy to wear white tropical livery; both her sisters began life in the usual dark livery, and were not painted white until middle age.
(National Maritime Museum N05358)

Rover was slightly slower in smooth water than *Active* and *Volage*, but faster in rough. Most importantly, she was the first large British warship with higher-pressure boilers and compound engines, which gave her 60 per cent greater endurance (*Constance* and the armoured *Pallas* had been experiments with no real follow-up). According to Admiral Ballard, navies resisted the shift to compound engines for fear of the consequences of battle damage to higher-pressure boilers. The winning argument was that higher-pressure cylindrical boilers had lower crowns, hence would lie entirely beneath the waterline, where they were safe. In contrast to commercial practice (vertical cylinders), *Rover* and other warships had their cylinders horizontal, where they were also safe below the waterline. Her single high-pressure cylinder lay between two low-pressure ones. She had two funnels to serve her ten cylindrical boilers; the earlier corvettes *Active* and *Volage* had one funnel serving five low-pressure rectangular boilers. According to Admiral Ballard, she was an indifferent performer under sail, noticeably slower than *Volage*; she never logged more than 11kts under sail. Ballard attributes this to the drag due to her uneven trim; she sailed better after being rearmed, which corrected her trim.

Compared to the earlier ships, she had a square bow profile rather than a knee, and narrower convergence fore and aft above the waterline, both to save weight at the ends. The cross-section was modified to change the metacentric height, and she had a false keel, both to reduce rolling. She did trim excessively by the stern, which affected both her sailing qualities and her steering. As built she had two 7in guns on slides as chasers, firing through bow and stern embrasured ports, and sixteen 64pdrs on trucks on her broadside. As rearmed after her first commission she had fourteen 6in breech-loaders, all on slides. Twelve were on her broadside. One each fired through bow and stern embrasures. These Elswick-built 80pdrs (6in Mk I) were the first modern breech-loaders supplied to the Royal Navy (Woolwich produced the Mk II gun). At the same time two 14in torpedo tubes were mounted on the main deck. *Rover* spent her first commission (1875-79) on the North American station, returning to be rearmed and refitted. She then joined the new Training Squadron (1880), serving until 1889. Ballard attributes her relatively short service to her unhandiness under sail. She was sold in 1893.

(Allan C Green, courtesy of State Library of Victoria)

a covered gun deck, and compound engines – which made the ships grow from 3080 to 3912 tons, still well below the 4762 tons of HMS *Raleigh* or the 5782 tons of HMS *Inconstant*. As an indication of firepower, the new ship had a 796lb broadside, compared to 537lbs for *Volage*, but far below the 1676lbs of *Shah* or the 1710lbs of *Inconstant*. Total bursting change per broadside was 88lbs, compared to 46lbs for *Volage*, but 130lbs for *Shah* and 123lbs for *Inconstant*. Neither of these figures took into account the greater rate of fire of lighter guns. The new ship was more impressive in weight of ahead fire: 218lbs, compared to 64 for *Volage*, 314 for *Shah*, and 115lbs for *Inconstant*. Normal coal capacity was 400 (recently raised from 350) tons, equivalent to 3½ days at full power. That compared to 2½ days for *Volage* (with the same 400 tons), to 2¾ for *Shah* (700 tons), and 2½ days for *Inconstant* (670 tons).

The 1872-73 program included the corvette *Rover*, which was really an improved *Volage*. Like *Volage*, she was built by Thames Iron Works. She was armed with two 7in 112pdr 4½-ton (90cwt) chasers on bow and stern slides plus sixteen 64pdr 63cwt on broadside trucks. After her first commission, she was rearmed in 1879-80 with a uniform armament of fourteen 6in 80pdr 81cwt breech-loaders – two chasers and twelve on the broadside.

Euryalus, was ordered from Chatham the following year (1873-74 program) as a 'new *Bacchante*'. Admiral Milne had recently become First Naval Lord, and he considered cruisers – the large fast ships then coming into service – a priority for trade protection, the *Bacchante*s being the standard cruisers of the near future. In 1873, presumably looking ahead to the 1874-75 program, he tried but failed to convince First Lord Goschen to order another three *Bacchante*s. In 1875 he tried again, this time proposing six to be ordered that year and six the next; he had no luck. A fourth *Bacchante* was ordered from Portsmouth on 26 August 1878 (1878-79 program), presumably as part of the reaction to the Russian commerce-raiding threat of the 1877-78 crisis. She was cancelled in favour of the two smaller cruisers *Canada* and *Cordelia* described in a later chapter.

The two *Bacchantes* each had eight 7in (90cwt) guns and six 64pdr on the main deck, plus two 90cwt guns (bow chasers) on the upper deck in revolving mountings. For *Euryalus*, in May 1873 DNO proposed a main deck armament of twelve 7in guns and two 64pdrs, for which gun ports had to be rearranged. The remaining 64pdrs would retain their quarter (aft) ports as before, so that they could be used as stern chasers. That would increase the weight of broadside by 102lbs (from 882 to 984lbs) at a total cost in weight of 26 tons. DNO wanted the same change made to the two earlier ships. *Boadicea* was a particular problem, because she had no surplus of weight to work against. The other two were lighter because they had only one thickness of wood sheathing. All three were changed during construction.

The *Bacchantes* ended the era of iron cruisers in the Royal Navy. All of these ships can be traced back to HMS *Inconstant*. The best guide to forward thinking is probably the proceedings of the 1871 Admiralty Committee on Designs, convened in the aftermath of the embarassing loss of HMS *Captain*. As might be imagined, *Inconstant* was the starting point, too expensive to be built in sufficient numbers. Her CO Captain Waddilove preferred the smaller *Volage*, which cost only half as much. The Committee pointed out that abandoning covered gun decks would make for smaller ships less liable to demoralizing (and devastating) splinter damage from shells bursting in the gun decks. The smaller the unarmoured ship, the smaller the target she represented. Future cruisers should be split into two types, one with much the sail power (for endurance) of the *Inconstant*, the other with still higher speed under steam (perhaps 18kts on trial) with less canvas and more coal. The first would be best for distant seas, the second nearer home. *Iris* and *Mercury*, conceived only three years later, fit the second requirement. A dissenting opinion appended to the report recommended, among other things, a 3in underwater armour deck to protect magazines and boilers, protecting ships

HMS *Encounter*, 1879. She was unique in having a vertical stem and in being barque- rather than ship-rigged. Soon after first commissioning (21 August 1873), she recommissioned with a new captain on 1 September, assigned to the West Coast of Africa station and then (January 1878) to the North America and West Indies station. She was paid off on 14 December 1877, but recommissioned on 8 January 1879 for the China station, on which she remained until 15 June 1883 (this was the date of paying off, not the date she left the station). She was sold in October 1888.
(National Maritime Museum N07783)

at long ranges (it was assumed they would avoid fighting at close quarters). The dissenters envisaged wartime commerce protection and peacetime trooping roles.[13]

The much smaller (and slower) cruising ships, from smaller screw corvettes down, were were built of wood because there was no vital need to limit hull weight or to maintain strength in unusually long hulls built for high speed.

Smaller Cruisers

The 1871-72 program included the first three *Amethyst* class corvettes (*Encounter* from Sheerness, *Ameythyst* from Devonport, and *Modeste* from Devonport), the other two (*Diamond* from Sheerness and *Sapphire* from Devonport) being included in the 1872-73 program. They were the last all-wood corvettes. Unlike the *Amazon*s and their successors, they had knee (clipper) bows. *Amethyst* was ship-rigged, the others (and the successor *Opal* class) being barque-rigged. The last pair had frigate sterns.[14]

The captain of HMS *Encounter* wrote about her behaviour at sea in a 24 July 1874 letter sent from off the Cape of Good Hope.[15] She had, he thought, undergone a fair trial, considering that she had already made two passages to the Cape, once partly under steam and the other wholly under sail (because her screw had been disabled when the banjo frame supporting it carried away). She was 'the easiest and driest ship I have ever been in, very stiff under canvas and sails well on a wind which is her best point; with the wind on the quarter she is sluggish unless with a strong breeze after her – owing to the small amount of canvas she spreads for her tonnage. We sadly feel the want of stouter topmasts and top gallant masts, but with

The *Amethyst* class corvette HMS *Sapphire* with her funnel most of the way down. She and *Diamond* differed from the others in having frigate sterns. Designed armament was fourteen 64pdrs (probably Mk III), of which two were on rotating slides as bow and stern chasers. *Sapphire*, *Modeste*, and *Diamond* all had their two of their twelve broadside 64pdrs removed by about 1882, for their second commissions (the change was inked into the May 1881 armament list). *Modeste* seems to have been unique in that, at least as of 1882, her broadside guns were all converted 68pdrs (71cwt) rather than Mk IIIs. *Sapphire* was completed in August 1875. As commissioned, she was assigned to the Australia station (through 7 July 1879). She was commissioned for the China station on 18 January 1883, remaining until 25 September 1889, when she was the last wooden ship in full commission in the Royal Navy. In 1890 she was in reserve at Sheerness until discarded in 1892.

our present lower masts that is impossible ... The up and down stern and the Barque rig are admirable. The eye soon gets accoustomed to the look and they are certainly more serviceable, the former has no extra weight, which makes her easy in pitching; while the latter as she always carries good weather helm makes her very handy in working ... Coming in here the other day with the wind off the Dockyards, light and baffling, we worked up in seven tacks leeward of the Roman rocks, picking up moorings without anchoring. I merely write this to shew what a handy ship she is.'

The *Amethyst*s were followed by six *Emerald* (or *Opal*) class.[16] Unusually, the first ship, *Opal* (1873-74 program) was built under contract (by Doxford). So were three of the four of the 1874-75 program: *Turquoise* and *Ruby* by Earle's, and *Tourmaline* by Raylton Dixon. *Emerald* was built by Pembroke, and *Garnet* (1875-76 program) by Chatham. The decision to build by contract apparently predated the design. The *Emerald*s began as composite-hulled (wood on iron frames) *Amethyst*s. In his July 1873 design report, Barnaby explained that he had to switch to composite construction (first tested in the *Fantome* class sloops designed in 1871-72 and built under the 1872-73 program) because it was impossible to get a suitable wood frame from a contractor. Only the Royal Dockyards could bear the cost of storing and seasoning wood, but without that wooden hulls rapidly decayed.[17] Compared to the previous all-wood construction, composite construction offered the resistance to sagging and distortion of an all-iron hull, and it was better able to resist perforation from grounding or collision. However, wood-skinned hulls were more comfortable than iron.

Tank tests, including comparisons with the French corvette *Infernet*, convinced Barnaby to retain the length of the earlier ship but to increase beam by 3ft and draught by 6in in order to give better lines for speed. Displacement was a little less, but Barnaby expected cost to be about the same. Barnaby chose the fullest possible midships section and very fine entry and run.[18] To carry a sufficient load, a short hull had to have an unusually long parallel body amidships: the extremities were short and most of the hull was bulky. The resulting ship was slow but handy; an officer remarked of this class that she looked like a pregnant thoroughbred mare. The ships apparently had unusually good seagoing performance, among a generation of warships considered excellent seaboats.[19] The hull form would

HMS *Emerald* in 1877-78. She and her sisters had an unusually long knee bow, an outward-sloping stern, and a very full midships section. That imposed strains on the hull, as they had considerable weight but little buoyancy at the ends. Even the iron-framed *Garnet* hogged when rearmed with four rather than two chasers. Plans called for an armament of fourteen 64pdr, but the first ship, *Opal*, was overweight, and the others all had only twelve guns. All were on iron slides previously used for heavier-calibre guns. There were two chasers, each provided with embrasured ports on both sides of poop and forecastle, the rest being on the broadside. The ships of this class all had six 60psi cylindrical boilers driving two-cylinder horizontal compound engines. *Emerald* was unique in having return connecting-rod drive instead of direct drive The unusual lines gave poor speed under steam. Ships of this class were originally ship-rigged, but that was unsatisfactory (they had a tendency to carry excessive weather helm). They were therefore rerigged as barques. They also proved insufficiently stable. That was reflected in steadiness (a slow roll) and what Admiral Ballard called indifferent stability against wind pressure aloft. Forty tons of ballast had to be added. Under sail they were slower than all but a few British wooden corvettes, but sailing trials to windward showed that they could point higher when close-hauled, holding a better lee than other ships.
(National Maritime Museum N05364)

have been impossible without composite construction: the fine entry and run provided insufficient buoyancy to support the weights of bow and stern, and that would have ruined a wooden ship with insufficient longitudinal strength. Composite construction also made it possible to provide iron watertight bulkheads rising the whole height of the hull.

As in all wooden corvettes built after 1865, these ships had two complete decks, with poop and topgallant forecastle rising above them. The crew lived on the main deck, the upper deck being used for the armament. Ammunition was stowed below the main deck, evenly divided before and abaft the engines.

Like the *Amethyst*s, these ships were designed for fourteen 64pdrs, but only *Opal* was so armed. Two of her guns were landed following her first commission. The other five had twelve guns (all 64pdr 64cwt, two chasers, ten on the broadside, all in slides), but *Tourmaline* had her sides cut with twelve ports (as in *Opal*).[20] The others all had only ten ports. In the early 1880s *Emerald* and *Tourmaline* were modernized with four 6in (100pdr 81cwt) and eight 5in (50pdr 38cwt) breech-loaders.

Emerald as rearmed. She, *Tourmaline*, and *Garnet* were all rearmed with breech-loaders. *Emerald* and *Tourmaline* received four 6in 100pdrs on broadside sponsons allowing end-on fire plus eight 5in in the waist between the sponsons, all on Vavasseur mountings. That eliminated the weight of chasers. *Garnet* was rearmed with fourteen 5in, of which two were mounted at each end as chasers, the others occupying the original broadside ports. That entailed less work, and the new battery was lighter, but it gave her more weight at the ends, causing her to pitch more deeply in a head or a following sea. None of the ships ever carried torpedoes. *Emerald* began her service on the Australian station in 1878. On her return to England in 1882 she became the first of three ships of the class to be rearmed and rerigged. She went into reserve upon completion of the refit, but in 1886 went to the North America and West Indies station, where she remained until 1892. In 1896 she was cut down to serve as a powder hulk at Portsmouth.
(National Maritime Museum N05365)

3 THE FIRST ARMOURED CRUISERS

HMS *Shannon* was the first British armoured cruiser, as distinguished from second-class ironclads which might be assigned to foreign duties. When she was being built in 1875, the official British list did not distinguish between different kinds of ironclads, except by type (e.g., broadside vs turret). In 1875 *Nelson* was credited with two 10in (18-ton) guns in a central battery and with seven 9in (12-ton) guns: one revolving gun and six side (broadside) guns. By 1877 *Shannon* was also credited with six broadside 20pdr breech-loaders 'for saluting etc', a type not even in the 1875 armament list. Later lists did not include the note about saluting. By 1880 *Shannon* also had twelve 16in Whitehead torpedoes aboard, a standard load-out for British ironclads of the time (but most carried 14in torpedoes). In 1880 she also had two 0.45in Gatling guns and six 1in Nordenfelts, mainly to deal with attacking torpedo boats. In 1882 *Shannon* had eight Nordenfelts, and her torpedoes were the standard 14in calibre. Gatlings had been superseded by Gardner machine guns. As a coast guard ship upon returning home after her first commission, *Shannon* lacked the new QF guns other ships received to deal with the torpedo threat. *Shannon* joined the Channel Fleet in March 1878 and then went to China, but was sent home in July 1878 for further changes. She was recommissioned in December 1878 and spent some time in the Mediterranean before going to the Pacific in July 1879. She returned to Devonport in July 1881 and went into reserve for a long refit, after which she became tender to HMS *Warrior* at Portsmouth, then becoming a coast guard ship at Greenock and then Bantry Bay. Her only later sea service was as part of the Particular Service Squadron formed in June 1885 for possible Baltic operations under Admiral Phipps Hornby. It was disbanded in July 1885.
(National Maritime Museum 58-3450)

Shannon with funnel down.
(National Maritime Museum C5840)

By 1865 the French were building *cuirassés croisières*, cruising armoured ships (second-class ironclads) specifically for service on foreign stations. They were not cruising commerce destroyers, but rather a means of destroying British ships and naval bases abroad as a prerequisite for successful raiding – just as ironclads in European waters would have attacked fleets in or near their ports. Asked the following year by First Lord Pakington to list classes in which the Royal Navy was deficient, Controller Robinson focussed on, among others, this second-class category. He had Reed prepare a design within a 3000-ton limit, referring to burthen tons, not displacement (which was considerably greater). Reed offered ten guns (eight 9-ton and two 6½-ton) with 6in armour and a speed of 12kts. The ship would have carried an unusually large spread of sail and 330 tons of coal, with a complement of 400. Mean draught would have been 22ft. The large spread of sail was required by the Board specifically because the ship was intended to serve on a distant station, where coal might be difficult to obtain.[1]

Reed took special pains to reject ideas, then current outside the Admiralty, of fast (15kt or 16kt) ironclads: 'it must now be clear to everyone, I imagine, that it is impossible to combine a very high speed – by which I mean a speed of 14kts or more – with heavy armour and armament on small dimensions, whether a ship be on the broadside or the turret principle ...' If foreign powers stationed small ironclads on foreign stations, the Royal Navy had to produce its own. They could not combine the fast cruiser (*Inconstant*) and small ironclad roles. A foreign station needed both types. In the 1870s the British built both second-class ironclads later classed as armoured cruisers and fast unarmoured cruisers, in similar numbers.

According to Robinson, neither he nor Reed was happy with the 6in armour or the limited armament. The first French second-class ironclads (*Alma* class) had only 5.9in armour, but in 1866 they reportedly ordered ships of the same type with 7.6in armour. By 1873 it was known that the French ships all had 6in belts with lighter armour (4¾-4in) over their guns. They had six 7.6in (9½-ton) guns, which the British considered inferior to their 12½-ton gun, let alone the new 18-ton gun. Their speed was 12kts.

Moderately increasing displacement (to 3774 burthen tons) in Reed's 1866 design made it possible to carry 8in armour and 12½-ton guns. The ship incorporated Reed's great innovation, a central battery with embrasures at the ends so that guns could be fired end-on. They had ten 12½-ton guns, the same number as in *Inconstant*, of which four were on the upper deck and six on the main deck, the latter including two broadside guns. Reed stayed inside the draught limit set by the Board partly by adopting twin screws. Given the need for high performance under sail, they should have been retractable, but that proved impossible. Unfortunately, when the ships were designed no one knew how much drag the propellers would create when the ship ran entirely under sail.

There were also four upper deck 64pdr (6in) chasers, two forward and two aft, perhaps added as a result of visits to the 1867 Paris World's Fair, which had both British and French naval exhibits. Robinson, Reed, Admiral Cooper Key (DNO), and Captain Hood of HMS *Excellent* (the gunnery school and experimental establishment) all attended and reported. In criticizing the French barbettes, Key admitted that guns in embrasures would be ineffective against an enemy who got close enough. He proposed adding bow and stern chasers.

The Board very reluctantly approved the project; Robinson and Reed most disliked the limited draught and the combination of large sail power and twin screws. Four *Invincible* class (or *Audacious* class) second-class 6000-ton ironclads were built under the 1867-68 program. Although always classed as full ironclads or battleships, in fact they were the first of a series of British armoured ships intended specifically for overseas service, and in that sense the progenitors of the first generation of ships the British later classified as armoured cruisers.

When Robinson and Reed were finally compelled to give up any attempt to make twin screws lift, they managed to convince the Board to retreat on the draught limit so as to make a single lifting screw practicable. Two ships thus modified were built under the 1868-69 program as HMS *Swiftsure* and *Triumph*.

By 1873 new First Lord Goschen considered all of these ships too expensive to waste on distant stations: India, Australia, China, and the Pacific. He wanted 'a certain number of ironclads of the second rank, which may be good cruizers under sail, draw less water than our large ironclads, yet be defended by thicker armour at the waterline and armoured with heavier guns than the second class ships [*Audacious* Class] of an earlier period'. Goschen also wanted very thick athwartships bulkheads, presumably on the theory that a ship operating by herself would often be end-on to her enemy, chasing or being chased. Therefore they should have the most powerful possible bow fire (i.e., 18-ton guns). The ships should be inexpensive enough to be built in numbers in a shorter time than the bigger ironclads.

On 11 March 1873 DNC Nathanial Barnaby formally asked his assistant to design an ironclad to cost half as much as *Superb*, with the same coal endurance as the second-class ironclad *Swiftsure*, 'in accordance with arrangements with the First Lord, the Controller, and myself this day'.[2] To further complicate the problem, in 1873 the ship needed thicker armour than *Swiftsure*. To get all of this, Barnaby gave up protection for the ship's broadside guns and also belt armour near the bow.

He must have been working on this project for some time, since that day he was able to send his assistant a sketch with dimensions of 260ft × 54ft × 21ft mean (20ft 6in fwd, 21ft 6in aft) and details of gun arrangement and armour protection. Reed's central battery was gone. Like *Audacious*, the ship had eight 12½-ton guns, the end pairs in armoured boxes near bow and stern, their bulkheads protecting the ship from raking fire from either end. These guns had ports both broadside and end-on; as in the earlier central battery ships, the guns would move to fire through either port. The other two guns were in the open on the broadside, their only protection the 9in athwartship bulkhead protecting the forecastle guns and the 8in athwartship protection abaft the poop guns. The ship had a narrow belt, her sides bare above that, except for the three-sided armour boxes fore and aft. The four broadside guns were entirely unprotected. Enough weight was saved to thicken the belt to 9in (rather than 8in) at the waterline. Barnaby also saved weight by ending his belt 60ft short of the bow, using a 3in armour deck (as mentioned by the Committee on Designs) 5ft under water to protect the bow. The bow would be as sharply curved as possible to limit the volume (hence weight) of water which could flood into her fore end. A 1in deck covered the belt amidships, protecting machinery and boilers from plunging shots.

Barnaby hoped to achieve the same coal endurance as *Swiftsure* by using more economical compound engines. The ship would have a single lifting screw and full sail power, with a speed of 13kts on the measured mile.

Barnaby forwarded a sketch to Controller (Captain Hood) on 24 March. By this time he had replaced the two bow 12½-ton guns with the new 18-ton (10in) type, leaving six 12½-ton guns, two of them in the after protected battery. Gatling guns were placed at intervening ports on the broadside.

Based on the cost estimate for *Superb* (£421,000) Barnaby expected hull, armour, and engines to total £214,400, just over half. *Swiftsure* had sufficient coal for 2.7 days at full speed, but with her more efficient compound engine (with about half the fuel consumption) the new ship should have enough for 3 days – or for 19 days at 5kts (2280nm).[3] Since she would operate in the tropics, the ship would be fully sheathed (with wood) and coppered. The amidships hull armour of the new ship would be impenetrable by *Swiftsure*, but she would penetrate the hull armour of the earlier ship out to about 4000yds. For ahead fire the new ship would have a pair of 18-ton guns protected by 9in armour, compared to two 12½-ton guns in *Swiftsure* behind 5in armour.

Compared to the French, the new ship had thicker armour, she was much better armed, and she was a knot faster. Barnaby wrote that she would even match the French *Flandre* class first-class broadside ironclads (the most numerous French class), which were armed with 24cm (9.4in) guns. The French ship could not penetrate the armour of the new British ship, but the British ship could penetrate the thickest French armour out to about 4000yds, i.e., at any reasonable battle range. Similarly, all of the guns of the new British ship could penetrate the 4¾in armour over the French ship's guns out to nearly 3000yds – again, at any likely battle range.

Captain Hood liked the design overall, agreeing that on the limited dimensions it would have been impossible to protect the guns as well as the vitals. He was unimpressed by the 1in deck over the belt, and thought too much weight had gone into protecting the stern battery, and also to protecting the ship from being raked from astern – which was most unlikely unless the ship lost power and steering. It would be better to give

The French *Alma* helped inspire the British belted cruisers. She was the first of seven armoured corvettes (the first such ship was the different *Belliqueuse*). The advent of these ships convinced the Admiralty Board to make armoured ships for distant waters its first priority in framing the 1867-68 program. The result was the two *Audacious* class second-class ironclads. HMS *Shannon* was conceived as a less expensive equivalent. *Alma* displaced about 3600 tons and was armed with six 7.6in and smaller guns. Armour was a 6in wrought iron belt. She steamed at about 11kts. *Alma* was laid down at Lorient on 1 October 1865 and was completed in 1869.

up the after armoured box altogether. Similarly, Hood saw little value in stern chasers. There should be only one of them, arranged so that it could fire both right aft and on either side, as in *Shah* and *Raleigh*. The broadside battery was increased to six guns. Eliminating the after armoured bulkhead would save about 100 tons, which could go into the additional gun (33 tons), another half an inch of deck armour (60 tons), and 8in rather than 6in side armour over the 18-ton guns forward (about 9 tons).

Shannon was built under the 1873-74 program and was completed on 19 July 1877.[4] She was described alternatively as an ironclad corvette and as a second-class ironclad. She seems to have suffered from engine trouble. After entering Plymouth Sound in July 1876, she immediately went into dockyard hands, emerging only in September 1877, and then spending another eight months in the dockyard for engine repairs. It is unlikely that she was ever completely reliable after that. She went out to the Pacific as flagship, her intended role, but she did not last long; she was relegated to coast guard duty in 1883 after a refit.

After two years in command (28 July 1879), Captain Grant wrote that he was 'much impressed when in company with other Ironclads at [the] great advantage *Shannon* presented, as all her guns could be fought with ease and precision when the weather precluded the main deck batteries being used with any sensible effect. [She] can take her place in line of battle, and hold her own always ready to advance as [a] skirmisher of the most formidable description, being able to play 10in guns right ahead sheltered by 9in armour, by which means she might possibly bring a fleet at bay, which otherwise might elude a combat.' The value of the upper deck heavy battery deserved better recognition. Earlier Grant had written, 'I consider I am justified in believing there is no ship at present, with a combination of so many good qualities.' She answered her helm instantly, was buoyant, and made good weather. As for the open battery on the upper deck, a shell bursting in it would dissipate most of its energy in the air. Grant saw the armoured box

Nelson bow and stern. In 1875 these ships were credited with four 10in guns in a central battery plus eight 9in guns in broadside mountings. The 1877 list added eight (later changed to six) 20pdr breech-loaders 'for saluting etc'. Each ship was also credited with two Gatling guns. By 1880 they also had six Nordenfelts and twelve 14in torpedoes. By 1882 there were eight Nordenfelts, and the Gatlings had been replaced by Gardner machine guns. In 1883 there were ten Nordenfelts and three Gardners – the torpedo threat was growing. On the Australia station in 1887, *Nelson* had six 6pdr QF guns to back up her machine guns; she now had six Nordenfelts (one four- and one two-barrel 1in plus four- and five-barrel 0.45in), plus two five-barrel Gardners. *Nelson* was commissioned in July 1881 as flagship on the Australia station, serving there until January 1889. She underwent a three-year refit at Chatham, emerging to become guard ship at Portsmouth in October 1891. She was transferred to the Fleet Reserve in November 1894. Her only further active service was trooping runs to Malta. She was reduced to Dockyard Reserve in April 1901, and was hulked to become training ship for stokers.

forward as a refuge for the crew either when the ship was running to ram, or when her battery was set for remote ('director') fire, the guns being set off electrically.[5] Admiral Hood was unimpressed: Captain Grant 'ignores how entirely unprotected the crews of the guns would be from the fire of machine guns and riflemen in action, a most important point when within 1000yds of an enemy's ship'. Barnaby retorted that the captain's views accorded with current French, German, and Italian practice. 'They will not sacrifice the power of using their armament for the purpose of securing their men against the effects of rifle and Gatling fire.'

Two more ships, *Nelson* and *Northampton*, were ordered under the 1874-75 program. In effect they were *Shannon*s with a very different kind of battery.[6] Instead of continuing to the stern, the belt was limited to the length of the battery, with a 3in underwater deck aft similar to that forward. The deck over the belt was thickened to 2in. Now much more of the side of the ship could be riddled, and flooding fore and aft would be much more dangerous. To deal with this threat, the ship's side near the waterline was filled with cofferdams, iron boxes themselves filled with material it was hoped would swell up when wet to block the flow of water. Such cellular cofferdams were an important feature of cruiser design in the 1880s and 1890s.

The after armoured box eliminated in *Shannon* was restored (presumably using weight freed by eliminating the after part of the belt), so the ship had the athwartship armoured bulkheads Barnaby had originally planned. Moreover, the armoured boxes fore and aft were complete rather than three-sided, as in the forward box on *Shannon*. An armour screen divided the battery in two. The armament was considerably heavier than in *Shannon*: two 18-ton guns at each end in the armoured boxes, and four (rather than six) 12½-ton guns on the broadside. The forward 18-ton guns could fire right ahead as well as on the broadside, but the after guns were on slides, and could only fire at an angle to the centreline. Compared to *Shannon*, the new ships had a complete upper deck (which had been advocated when the *Shannon* design was reviewed). Given this considerably increased weight, the ship had to be lengthened to 280ft and given greater beam (60ft). Displacement increased by 40 per cent, which can hardly have kept cost down. The ships had twin screws instead of a single hoisting screw. That change greatly improved protection to steering gear. Because she had a hoisting screw, *Shannon* had her steering gear well above water, though behind belt armour. The two *Nelson*s had theirs underwater, below a 3in deck. Presumably moving the steering gear underwater justified limiting the length of the belt armour. Rated speed increased to 14kts. Coal capacity, hence range, was considerably increased, to 1150 tons (normal capacity was 540 tons). Rated endurance was 3500nm at 12½kts, or 5000nm at 10½kts. The two ships had different engines.

In 1879 DNO commented that *Shannon* was less likely to be disabled by shellfire than *Nelson* thanks to her open battery; he had seen a shell burst at the foot of the mizzen mast of a corvette, doing nothing more than confusing a man hit by a splinter. A shell exploding in the enclosed gun deck of a frigate (like *Nelson*) would kill and wound many of the crew, because it would create a shower of splinters. It was true that the open

Nelson after her 1889-91 refit. Note the muzzle of the 10in rifle in the casemate. As refitted she retained her main battery but received additional anti-torpedo weapons. She received four 4.7in QF to supplement six 6pdr and fourteen 3pdr QF guns (her sister had only eight 3pdrs). Her machine gun battery was cut to two two-barrel and two five-barrel Nordenfelts and to one (later six) Gardners. The refit included replacing her rig with a single military mast and adding torpedo nets.

Nelson with HMS *Raven*
(Allan C Green via State Library of Victoria)

THE FIRST ARMOURED CRUISERS

Imperieuse being docked in 1886 for rerigging after unsuccessful sailing trials. She was commissioned in July–August 1887 for the Jubilee Review, then went into reserve until she was sent to China as flagship (March 1889–94). She was then refitted at Portsmouth. She went to the Pacific as flagship (March 1896 to August 1899), going into reserve after a refit. She was commissioned for the 1904 manoeuvres, but in February 1905 became depot for destroyers at Portsmouth as *Sapphire II*.

Imperieuse as completed in 1886, with brig rig. She was armed with four 9.2in guns (22-ton Mk V rather than 24-ton Mk III), with six 6in (89cwt Mk III), and with four 6pdr QF, plus the usual machine guns: ten 1in Nordenfelts (six four-barrel and four two-barrel), two 0.45in Nordenfelts (five-barrel), and two 0.45in Gardner (five-barrel), and she had eighteen 14in Whitehead torpedoes on board. By 1890 she also had four 3pdr QF guns, and her machine gun battery had been increased to four four-barrel and six five-barrel Nordenfelts, all of 1in calibre; the 0.45s were gone. By 1892 she and her sister both had another four 6in guns (three Mk IV, one Mk VI), all breech-loaders like the original six, having been refitted in the Far East. They also had eight Hotchkiss 6pdr QF guns and nine (*Warspite* ten) 3pdr Hotchkiss QF – anti-torpedo guns. By 1900 all ten 6in guns had been converted to QF (as QFC guns). By that time they had four Mk VA trainable torpedo launchers and two fixed tubes on the broadside.

Imperieuse 1896

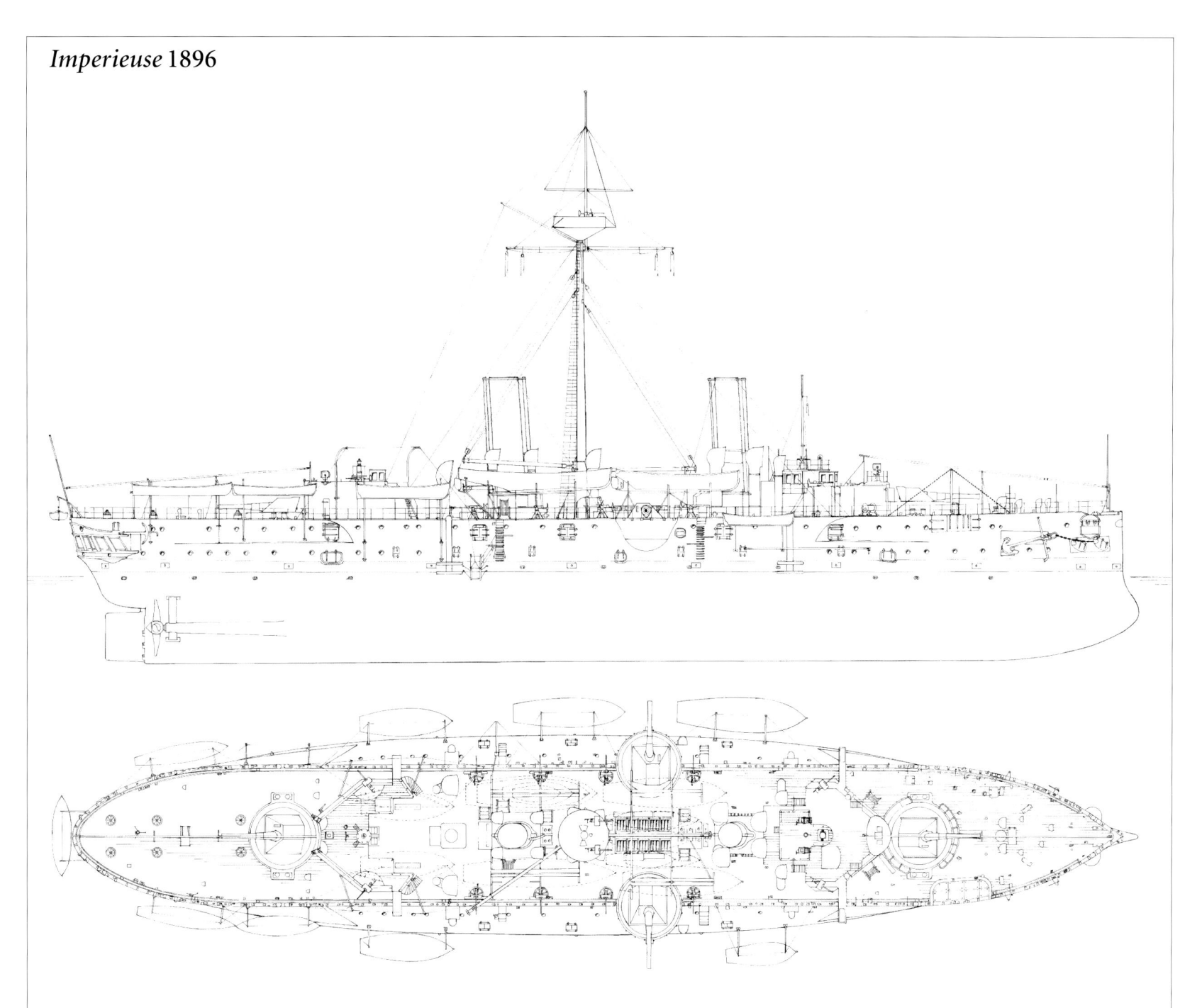

The armoured cruiser HMS *Imperieuse* is shown in March 1896, nearly a decade after completion. Each 9.2in gun had 50 ready-use projectiles stowed around the inner wall of the upper barbette. The ship was completed with a brig rig but during an 1886-88 refit bowsprit and masts were removed and a new mainmast (with fighting top) replaced her original boat derrick kingpost. The single mast was supported by six splayed auxiliary legs because it was not possible to fit adequate staying. These legs are not visible in the drawing due to depiction of the fighting top in the plan view and the clutter of boats and ship's fittings in the elevation. The otherwise highly detailed surviving as-fitted drawing (as modified in 1896) shows no bilge keels fitted to the hull. During the 1886 refit, all six torpedo tubes had to be raised two feet due to the ship's excessive draught. The two amidships tubes were fixed, firing at a 45-degree angle off the bow. The four tubes forward and aft could pivot through an 80-degree arc. The upper edge of the 10in belt created the knuckle or crease seen in the elevation. About 1887 *Imperieuse* was fitted with torpedo defence boom gear; it was removed during her 1895-96 refit. The mounting positions for the booms are the small rectangles just above the waterline in the elevation view. Also during the 1895-96 refit the original 6in BLR were replaced by 6in QF (presumably the guns were simply converted). They remained on their pivoting carriages with limited (120-degree) firing arcs. An armoured torpedo fire control 'tower' atop the after superstructure was replaced with a 24in searchlight, but the two small armoured torpedo fire control blisters on the hull sides just forward of the two midships 9.2in barbettes were retained. The former provision for two 9pdr artillery pieces on carriages (one at the extreme stern and one to port of the after funnel) seems to have been deleted. The 1896 as-fitted drawing shows locations for eight 6pdr QF, although standard references credit the ship with only four (the official January 1900 armament summary shows eight such guns, four on frame and four on recoil mountings, for *Imperieuse*, but none for *Warspite*). Other modifications included replacement of ship's boats by smaller versions of the same types, and removal of the 37ft steam pinnace and its davits to starboard of the after funnel. Her sister ship *Warspite* was completed with only the single mast and had elaborate scrollwork at the bow. On both ships, the quarter lights were only decorative. Both ships used combined ash elevator/cowl ventilation trunks, six of which were fitted. The forward pair, abreast the charthouse, were canted inboard to allow the midships 9.2in guns to fire dead ahead. An unusual feature of the boat arrangement was that the two 30ft cutters were slung beneath outboard davits when the ships were at sea, and had to be transferred by the davits to a second outboard set for harbour use. That was necessary due to the extreme tumblehome and also to the fact that neither of the two boat derricks could reach these boats.

(A D Baker III)

Imperieuse in tropical livery, a photo collected by ONI.
(NHHC Farenholt Collection)

Imperieuse with experimental torpedo nets. Note the bow boom, which was not used in later operational installations.

THE FIRST ARMOURED CRUISERS 111

Imperieuse in March 1886 after being rerigged with a single mast carrying a military top. These photos emphasize her tumblehome amidships.

gun deck would be exposed to small arms fire (and machine gun fire), 'but a ship must be very close before her topmen can fire down on the guns' crews on the engaged side'. The Americans nearly gave up building frigates after shell guns were introduced, preferring corvettes (i.e., ships with open gun decks). *Shannon* would have been nearly perfect had her after battery been protected. First Naval Lord Cooper Key disagreed; men in a covered battery would be far steadier, 'their attention not being diverted by the work on deck or aloft or by objects around them'. He did not consider it enough of an advantage that *Shannon* carried her guns very high.

Comments in the *Shannon* Cover do *not* touch on the switch from directly protecting most of a ship's waterline to protecting only the vitals amidships, which might be considered the most significant difference between the *Shannon* and *Nelson* designs.

No new second-class ironclads were included in the programs for 1875-76 through 1880-81. Action on the 1880-81 program was deferred so that improvements in guns, engines, etc could be incorporated. The Royal Navy was abandoning muzzle-loaders in favour of breech-loaders, with somewhat unpredictable consequences. Nor was it clear how large torpedo ships such as the torpedo ram *Polyphemus* would fit into a battle fleet.

For years the French had been mounting their breech-loaders in open-topped barbettes; perhaps it was time for the British to follow suit. The British first encountered the idea at the 1867 Paris World's Fair.[7] A model of the new battleship *Marengo* showed four 14-ton guns in upper deck barbettes, plus another four on the main deck (as built the ship had more powerful guns in the barbettes and less powerful ones on the main deck). DNO Cooper Key argued that the upper-deck barbette guns did not really provide end-on fire because they were inside the line of the hammocks (i.e., well inside the outer edge of the

Warspite in Victorian livery, with torpedo net booms installed. She was Pacific flagship (February 1890 – June 1893 and March 1899 – July 1902). She was commissioned for the 1888 manoeuvres but afterwards went into reserve before going to the Pacific.

upper deck). The upper deck had to be cleared completely when they were manned. The guns' great height was a disadvantage, as they could not be much depressed when firing nearly end-on, hence would be almost useless against an enemy at close quarters ahead or astern. They were only a 'formidable addition to the broadside armament', as their height made them usable in all weather, but they were limited. By 1880 it was clear that by adopting barbettes the French were managing to mount small numbers of unusually heavy guns, the weight of the usual gun protection going into the guns themselves.

Also attracting attention was the Italian *Italia* class, which achieved unusually high speed by eliminating side armour altogether, retaining only a cruiser-style protective deck. The latest British battleship, the turret ship *Ajax*, mounted four 38-ton guns in two turrets. She had far less freeboard than the French ships, and was not nearly as fast as the Italians (which had much more powerful guns). The closest British ship to the French type was HMS *Temeraire*, which had some of her guns on disappearing mounts in barbettes. In August Barnaby proposed building a revised *Temeraire*. It became the prototype British barbette ship HMS *Collingwood*.

Whatever was designed to match the Italians would have to be something new and unusual, with a speed of 17 or 18kts – extraordinary figures at the time. Barnaby thought that anything so sophisticated would have to be built under contract rather than in a Royal Dockyard. This project foundered.

A new belted cruiser was also wanted. Barnaby compared new French cruisers, proposed modifications to *Shannon* and *Nelson*, and New *Temeraire*. He recommended two 6000-ton ships of a modified copper-sheathed *Shannon* type: 14kts, with eleven 8in breech-loaders, with a 10in waterline belt over its machinery (as in the *Nelson*s) and with 9in over its guns. This was one gun fewer than in a *Nelson*, with a homogenous battery (presumably including a single stern chaser, as in *Shannon*, but with a four-gun battery on each side, as in *Nelson*). At a 24 November 1880 meeting Barnaby was told that the ship should be a knot faster. He would have to lengthen the ship 30ft, to 300ft, so to stay within 6000 tons, he would have to reduce vertical protection over the guns and vitals by 22½ per cent and reduce the underwater deck so that it would resist nothing more than 7in shot. To keep the same thicknesses, he would need another thousand tons (7000 tons).

There was very little prospect of repeating *Shannon* on a somewhat larger scale. DNO wanted barbettes like those of the two latest French overseas ironclads, laid down in December 1878 and February 1879, *Vauban* and *Dugesclin*, but somewhat heavier. They were armed with four 9.4in guns in barbettes, two side by side forward of the funnels, and two on the centreline abaft the funnels. Belt armour was 10in thick, which may be why New *Shannon* (*Imperieuse*) used that thickness. Rated speed was 14kts.

Members of the Board liked the French barbette arrangement in which fewer guns were mounted, but their training gear and slides were protected by armour. Barnaby disliked barbettes; he thought armour arrangement would be worse, for the same weight, than in *Shannon*. He offered three alternatives, all with about the same total of armament and its protection. Version I had barbettes for nine guns, three covered against rifle fire; II had cross bulkheads at each end of the upper deck, with six of the ten guns carried covered; III had eleven guns, two in barbettes and three covered.

Barnaby contrasted these large expensive ships with the fast (16kt) *Leander* he had recently designed (see next chapter). A 7000-ton ship with armament arrangement II and with full protection would cost £400,000. *Leander* was expected to cost £150,000. She was much smaller, carrying a total of 330 tons of armament and protection, compared to 1850 tons in the 7000-tonner. It must have seemed clear that scaling up a *Leander* might be a worthwhile alternative to modifying the existing type of belted cruiser.

By late November there was a requirement that the new cruiser make 16kts. Barnaby's chief assistant William H White (later DNC) offered two alternatives. One was a *Shannon* capable of 16kts. White had to go to 7000 tons. On that he could have a 10in waterline belt. He needed slightly more power than the alternative enlarged *Leander*, 7200 to 8000 IHP, compared to 7000 to 7500. The other possibility was a 6000-ton version of the new fast (16kt) cruiser *Leander* with a thicker protective deck. To stay within 6000 tons, White had to abandon belt armour in favour of a thick protective deck over the machinery, 2in on the flat, 2½in and 3½in on the inclined part. The two foremost guns were covered with armour. In another alternative the weight of armour over the guns was used instead to extend the protective deck all the way fore and aft. Both of these alternatives corresponded more or less to the modified *Leander*. All of these ships would have been 300ft between perpendiculars, a step up from the *Nelson*s. Projected armament was eleven 8in (11½-ton breech-loading) guns, six 20pdr anti-torpedo and saluting guns, four 1.5in Nordenfelts, and two Gatlings.

The Board liked the 7000-ton belted cruiser, whose guns were protected by 9in armour. Its armour arrangement was more like that of the *Nelson*s than that of the *Shannon*, the belt extending only over the machinery. One question was whether (and with what thickness) the belt might be extended fore and aft in place of the underwater decks there.

At a December 1880 Board meeting DNC thought he received full support for a mixed arrangement of barbettes and a conventional battery. The design was accepted on the understanding that dimensions (300ft × 61ft × 24¼ft), displacement (7200 tons), and cost (£400,000 for hull and engines) might have to be modified as the design was worked out. However, the situation suddenly changed, so that a 14 December 1880 Legend showed a radically different armament ordered by the Board: four heavy guns in barbettes (18 tons, 9.2in calibre).[8] These new guns were considered more powerful than the 38-ton 12.5in MLR which armed recent British turreted battleships. They were arranged as in contemporary French battleships, one forward and one aft on the centreline, and one on each side. The double bottom was extended up the side through the length of the machinery; Barnaby later wrote that provision of this double bottom made it possible to put the barbettes as far out to the sides as they were, so that they provided end fire without unduly encroaching on the deck. There was also a lower-calibre broadside battery (six 6in), one on each side forward of the midships barbette and two abaft it.[9]

Now the mountings had to be designed. The British had no details of the French mountings, and they were only beginning to arm their ships with breech-loaders. They knew that the charges for the guns came up a central tube, and presumed that the guns were run out for loading. Remarkably, the solution was simply to ask the French naval attaché in London for details of the French mountings. The French provided drawings of the mountings in the *Bayard* class then being completed, and these drawings formed the basis for those in the two new British armoured cruisers. Detail design was assigned to Armstrong.

Armour thickness matched that of earlier belted cruisers, but the armour was the new steel-faced type equivalent to the thickest iron hull armour (12in) on the turret ironclads *Thunderer* and *Devastation*.[10] Unlike the earlier belted cruisers, in this design all the fighting elements of the ship – machinery, armament, and personnel – were protected by the heaviest armour. Protection to steering gear was better than in battleships.

Like the earlier belted cruisers, these ships were intended to carry sail for auxiliary propulsion. However, by this time engines were far more efficient, and coal was far easier to come by in distant waters. To achieve maximum range, each of the two shafts was driven by two sets of engines, one of which could be unclutched at cruising speed. The after (working) set would be supplied with 90psi steam from conventional salt-water boilers. The foremost (auxiliary) engine would be powered by a compact locomotive type boiler operating at 120psi fed by fresh water evaporated by the heat of the other set of boilers from salt water. With 900 tons of coal, the ship was expected to steam for 4½ days at 16kts (1720nm) and for 18 days at 10kts (4320nm).

Tank tests showed that it would take 8800 IHP to drive the 300ft ship at 16kts, but that a 315ft ship (7400 rather than 7000 tons) would make that speed with 8000 IHP. However, at speeds below 13kts she would burn more coal, because the frictional resistance of the hull would count more than wave-making. Money could be spent either on a longer hull or on more powerful machinery. Since endurance mattered enormously, Barnaby opted for the shorter hull. Controller argued that the longer ship would keep her speed in a seaway, and that she would be less crowded. Barnaby's deputy White argued that extra length was useful mainly to limit required power in smooth water at maximum speed. There would be no real advantage in a seaway: this was not like choosing between a 300ft and a 400ft ship. Given the fineness of the ends, very little stowage space would be gained. The longer ship would be noticeably less handy, and her finer hull fore and aft would make her pitch worse, particularly since the weights of the barbettes were near her ends. At about 16kts the curves of engine power vs speed were nearly parallel, the longer ship beginning its steep increase (in power required for a given speed) about a half knot further up than the shorter. 'In other words if on the measured mile greater engine power is developed than is contracted for, the consequent gain in speed will be about equal in both ships.' Controller agreed for the moment, but in the end the ships were 315ft long.

Barnaby submitted the design for approval on 8 March 1881. Controller described it as 'a partly protected cruiser whose speed and protection makes her superior to any Unarmoured Cruiser, her protection, armament, and speed make her a match or superior to what at present constitutes the 2nd Class Battle Ship of other powers'. By this time Portsmouth was arranging to begin work on the first ship, so approval was urgent. The design was formally approved by First Lord Northbrook on 19 March.

Two ships were included in the 1881-82 program: *Impérieuse* (Portsmouth) and *Warspite* (Chatham).

By this time, as a Member of Parliament, Reed had made himself his brother-in-law's most aggressive critic. The Cover includes his offer of a new design (for submission to First Lord Northbook, in effect the navy's representative in Parliament) offering the same armament and protection but a much larger coal supply – 1200 tons at normal draught with a capacity for 1800, compared to the 400 and 900 tons of the new cruiser design. He thoughtfully added that the ship was poorly protected, her belt covering only 40 per cent of her length (he offered 60 per cent). With the longer belt it was no longer necessary to provide cofferdams at the ends. He claimed that he could offer higher speed with the same power (16½kts rather than the guaranteed 15½kts), and that the Admiralty design showed excessive freeboard. To get all of this, Reed wanted a much longer ship: 380ft x 50ft x 24ft rather than 315ft x 61ft x 24ft 11in. He also claimed that his ship would be less expensive to build 'for reasons which will be obvious'.

Reed's comments carried weight both because he had preceded Barnaby as DNC and because in 1880 he was a professional naval architect designing warships for foreign navies. Barnaby was compelled to produce a formal comparison with Reed's proposals. Reed's sketchy details (such as the position and character of deck protection) had to be filled in. Controller was particularly interested in Reed's claim that his ship, but not Barnaby's, could carry 1200 tons of coal. Barnaby replied that there would be no problem, apart from limiting accommodations; the bunkers might permanently be built for 1200 tons at the cost of half a knot.

Barnaby remarked sarcastically that this was the same Reed, advocating a ship as long as HMS *Warrior*, who had recently criticized the same ship as far too long to be manoeuvrable (with a length chosen only to extend her coal endurance), and who was pushing hard for short manoeuvrable ships suited to ramming. He had attacked HMS *Inflexible* (length 4⅓ times the beam) as too narrow, but now a cruiser 5⅓ as long as her beam was too beamy. Reed had even advocated round armoured ships, the Russian *Popoffka*s. Barnaby pointed out that width was a considerable virtue in a ship which might be torpedoed or rammed. Not only did it provide protection in the form of the extended double bottoms, but it reduced the heeling effect of underwater damage. Reed had deliberately missed the point of the 400-ton normal coal load: it was what the ship would carry on the measured mile for trials, not what she would carry in service. Barnaby doubted that Reed could carry the weights required within the same displacement as the Admiralty design. There was no question but that a ship of the dimensions proposed by Reed, displacing 7330 tons, could make 16.5kts on 8000 IHP – but Reed's ship would actually have to displace 8780 tons. It was Barnaby's great misfortune that none of this could be made public.

The next armoured cruisers, the *Orlando*s, seem to have been seen as a compromise tilted further towards cruiser duties. They failed. The next time the Royal Navy built armoured ships specifically for foreign stations, they were scaled-down battleships of the *Barfleur* class. These were clearly seen as follow-ons to the *Imperieuse* class, their Legends comparing them to that earlier design.

Barfleur was a second-class battleship built under the Naval Defence Act of 1889. Although she was a scaled-down battleship, in effect she was the direct successor to cruisers like *Imperieuse*, to the extent that in her Cover her details were compared with those of *Imperieuse*.

4 FAST STEEL CRUISERS

Iris and Mercury

A key conclusion of the 1871 Committee on Designs was that the sort of speed achieved at very great cost in ships like HMS *Inconstant* would soon be available from much smaller ships with better hull forms and more compact engines. Barnaby undoubtedly contributed to it. Once Gladstone was out of office in March 1874, it became possible to imagine a larger building program that might include such ships, although First Naval Lord Admiral Milne still seems to have assumed that it would take something massive like a *Bacchante* to achieve high speed.

Barnaby seems to have conceived the really fast cruiser while working on an enlarged version of the *Fantome* class sloop, having been asked merely to lengthen them to berth more men.[1] In April 1874 he wrote to Controller Captain Hood that the new sloops were too slow and carried too few guns 'to be satisfactory for the protection of our commerce

Mercury at the 1887 Jubilee Review.
(Symonds via NHHC)

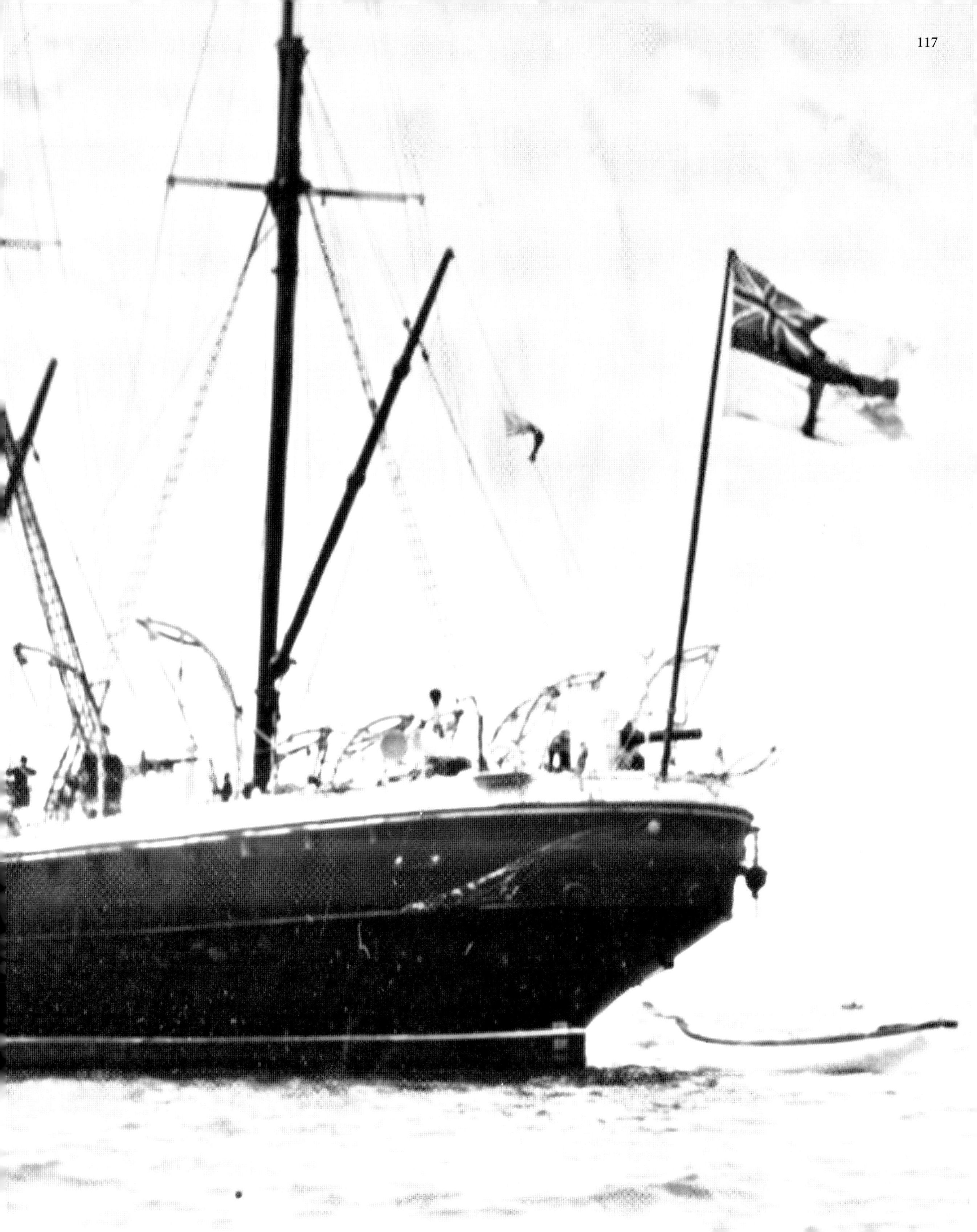

on Foreign Stations, with no intermediate class between them and the *Magicienne* [*Opal*]'. Their 11kts on trials (10kts at sea) was 'decidedly insufficient in cruisers for the protection our trade in time of war from privateers'. New ships should have a speed of 12 or 12½kts under steam, having good sail power, and a lifting screw, with an armament of 64pdrs, two of which should be mounted as revolving chasers, the rest on the broadside. Such a ship could be built on about 1500 tons, slightly smaller than the existing *Nymphe* (*Amazon* class). Such ships would be ideal for commerce protection, the *Magicienne* class being too large to be built in numbers.

In a more formal submission to Controller, Barnaby argued that speed was 'of the utmost importance' in an unarmoured steam fighting ship. 'In the days of sailing ships, skillful seamanship and good gunnery made up for the difference in speed; but the use of steam greatly reduces the values of these qualities, and speed and coal endurance take the first place ... A difference of two knots in speed between two unarmoured vessels sighting each other in daylight must almost ensure the successful attack of the faster, if she is properly and proportionately armed. This consideration, standing alone, is almost paralyzing, and would prevent the formation of any satisfactory *un*armoured Navy. We must therefore consider practically what speeds we should have to contend with in our adversaries and what speeds are most suitable for the general work of the Navy, including the training of men, and diplomatic and police services in time of peace.'

Most British unarmoured ships were very slow. Of 93 in service the previous February (84 on foreign stations, which shows how important such ships were), half had trial speeds of less than 10kts, which meant working speeds of less than 9kts. Only 13 recently-built ships had trial speeds of 13kts or more; the fastest steam frigates, corvettes, and sloops existing six years ago (1868) hardly reached 13kts. The Royal Navy had built or was building 24 unarmoured corvettes and sloops with speeds of 13kts and above, which exceeded the equivalent number of all other navies together, and more were planned for 1874-75 (presumably the *Emerald* class). The fastest of such ships were rated at 15kts, which was just enough to catch existing merchant ships and to evade 14kt ironclads.

No one else was complaining that British unarmoured ships were too slow. Barnaby inferred that officers considered their ships fast enough, compared with merchant ships and the foreign cruisers they met. That tallied with known details of foreign cruisers. This happy situation was about to change. In 1874 he wrote that in a future war many of the big fast passenger ships would be converted into unarmoured cruisers with trial speeds of 13 to 14½kts; higher speeds would be 'quite exceptional'. This would be the most suitable speed for future unarmoured fighting ships. Not all ships could be this fast, so the unarmoured fleet had to be split between fast ships intended mainly for war and slow ones, liable to be swept away in war, but vital for general peacetime work. In order to limit the cost of the peacetime ships, their speed should be fixed at 9½ to 10½kts. In effect Barnaby was marking the formal split between the sloops, which were primarily peacetime ships, and the cruisers intended for commerce protection in war, with speeds of at least 13kts.

By the fall of 1874 Barnaby was interested in higher speed, because European powers were already building 15-knot cruisers of their own, which were far smaller and less expensive than the British 15-knot cruisers. He probably had in mind the French *Infernet* and *Sané* classes, completed between 1871 and 1876, the German *Ariadne* and *Leipzig* classes, and the Italian *Cristoforo Colombo*. By the autumn of 1874 he was sketching a 17-knot cruiser. Barnaby concluded that he could get what he wanted on about 280ft x 40ft x 17ft (fwd)/23ft (aft) and 2500 tons – about the size of a *Volage* class corvette, but displacing much less, with twin screws for 6000 to 7000 IHP. In so narrow a hull, the engines driving one shaft would have to be abaft those driving the other. The ship would have a very light fore and aft rig. High-powered machinery would be heavy, so the

Iris as completed, in a photograph taken before 1883, with minimal bridge structure. When the cruiser category was established in 1878, she and *Mercury* were counted as Special Service ships rather than as cruisers. About 1890 they were finally included in the unprotected cruiser category. Given their limited endurance, neither ship was ever assigned to an overseas fleet or station. As built, both ships were armed with ten 64pdrs: two on upper-deck pivots as chasers fore and aft, and eight on the main deck. About 1880 Iris had her main-deck guns replaced by breech-loaders: four 6in and four 5in. In 1886-87 both were rearmed with thirteen 5in (40cwt) Mk III breech-loaders, four 3pdr QF, seven machine guns (two two-barrel and two four-barrel 1in Nordenfelts, two five-barrel and one two-barrel 0.45in Gardner), and four torpedo carriages (two Mk IV and two Mk VII) with ten 14in torpedoes. This was their final armament.
(National Maritime Museum C5849)

Iris 1888

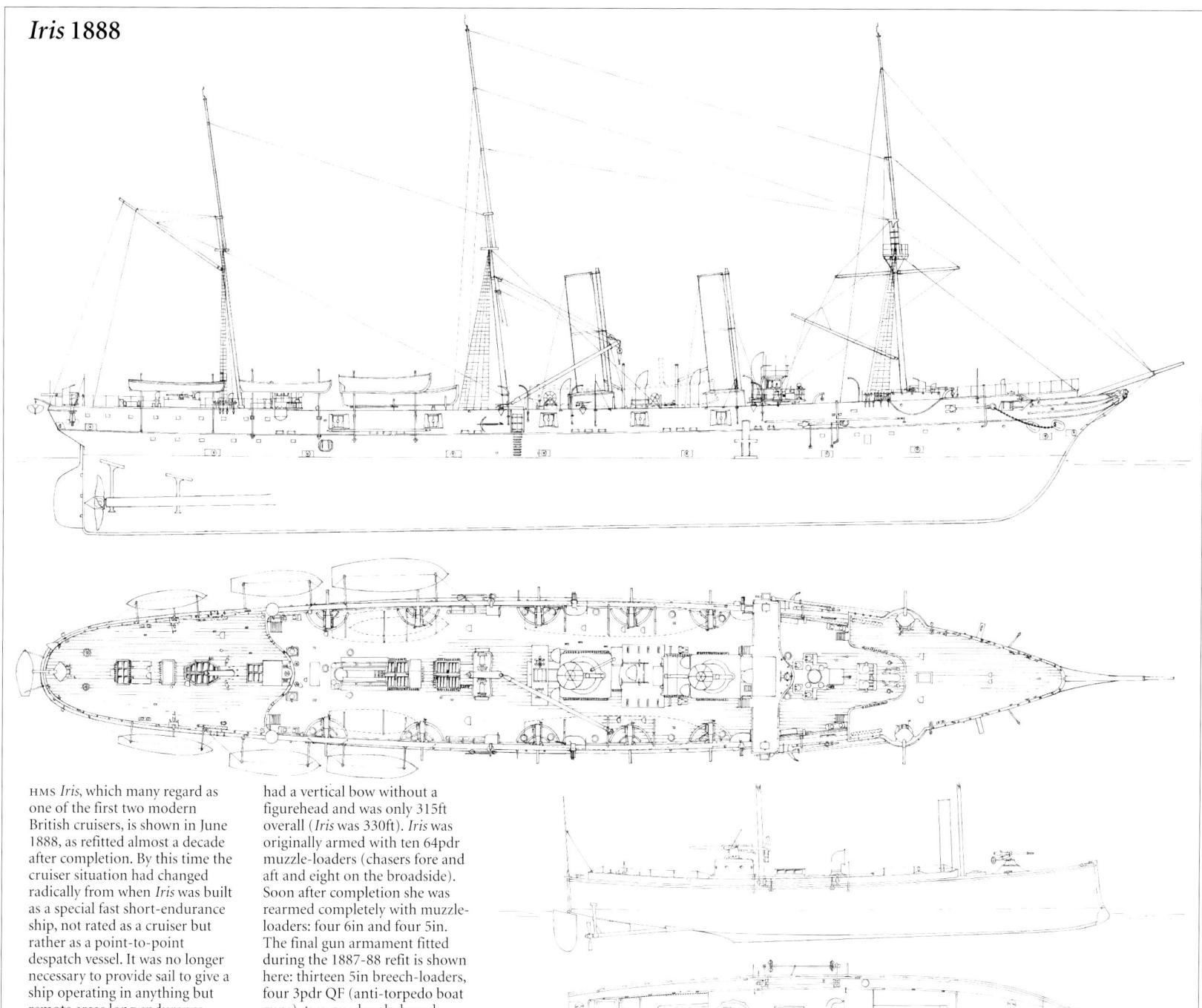

HMS *Iris*, which many regard as one of the first two modern British cruisers, is shown in June 1888, as refitted almost a decade after completion. By this time the cruiser situation had changed radically from when *Iris* was built as a special fast short-endurance ship, not rated as a cruiser but rather as a point-to-point despatch vessel. It was no longer necessary to provide sail to give a ship operating in anything but remote areas long endurance, because the rise of steam merchant ships had made steaming coal plentiful abroad. That nearly all the suppliers were British offered the possibility that in a crisis the Royal Navy could retain its mobility, whereas foreign navies would be badly hampered. *Iris* was reclassified as a second-class cruiser after her 1888 refit. Originally she was barque-rigged with yards on her fore- and mainmasts. The mainmast yards were deleted prior to completion, and after 1888 she carried only one yard on the foremast, for signal flags. Her bowsprit was reduced to a stub, and her upper topmasts on fore- and mainmasts were replaced by single masts. Her sister *Mercury* had a vertical bow without a figurehead and was only 315ft overall (*Iris* was 330ft). *Iris* was originally armed with ten 64pdr muzzle-loaders (chasers fore and aft and eight on the broadside). Soon after completion she was rearmed completely with muzzle-loaders: four 6in and four 5in. The final gun armament fitted during the 1887-88 refit is shown here: thirteen 5in breech-loaders, four 3pdr QF (anti-torpedo boat guns), two quadruple-barrel Nordenfelts, and two five-barrel Gardner machine guns. She was also fitted with four torpedo launchers (two Mk IV on carriages forward, two trainable Mk VII aft, total of 14 torpedoes). The Mk IVs fired through small ports forward. Tubes could be mounted on the second-class torpedo boats she carried. An 1888 photo shows one of the boats equipped with a single tube aft, and they could also carry two 14in torpedoes in drop gear. The two small circular conning towers protruding from the hull sides at the fore end of the poop were added in 1888; they flanked the main steering wheel.
(A D Baker III)

TB 12, a 56ft wooden second-class torpedo boat, is of the type carried on board *Iris* and many other British cruisers. This particular boat was completed by J Samuel White in May 1888. She displaced 14 tons (56ft overall × 9ft 3in × 4ft 9in) and was powered by a 200 IHP triple-expansion engine (15.5kts). Armament was one 3pdr QF, one twin 1pdr Nordenfelt, and two 14in torpedoes in drop gear. She had a crew of nine. Three boats of this type were built (*TB 10-12*). This design evolved into the much more versatile 56ft steam picket boat. Some comparable boats, including a Thornycroft-built boat carried by *Iris*, had a single trainable 14in torpedo tube aft. The torpedo drop gear on *TB 12* is shown mounted to starboard in the elevation view and to port in the plan view. The spindle-shaped torpedoes were held within two sets of padded tongs, which were opened by a lever to launch the torpedo (which was started by lanyard). The torpedoes were not gyro-stabilized, range during the 1880s being less than 900yds, and hitting probability low. The funnel folded aft, and the masts were dismountable. They could be fitted with a light sailing rig in an emergency. There were no sleeping or cooking arrangements. Two rudders were fitted, one on the transom and one forward of the propeller. This was White's 'turnabout' design for increased handiness. The craft could be steered from the wheel in the cockpit aft or by a smaller wheel inside the lightly armoured conning tower, which doubled as support for the 3pdr.
(A D Baker III)

Iris in December 1890, as rearmed with shielded breech-loaders on her upper deck.

FAST STEEL CRUISERS 121

Iris in July 1895.

Iris in July 1895.

Mercury about 1887-89. Note the shielded breech-loader visible forward of her foremast. (Symonds via NHHC)

ship's hull had to be as light as possible. Barnaby chose steel and minimum scantlings. For strength, he would have a long forecastle and poop. The ship would have one 4½-ton gun on a turntable at each end, firing through any of several ports cut in the side, with additional guns on turntables on the main deck amidships. The ship would normally carry 400 tons of coal (800 tons capacity). A crude sketch showed two funnels.

Barnaby sent his sketch and estimates to his assistant on 26 November. He got back a design for a 300ft x 43ft x 17ft/22ft 6ft ship to displace 3420 tons, with 7000 IHP engines. She might make as much as 18kts if her hull form was as good as that of *Inconstant*, or 17.28kts if she matched *Volage*. Since twin screws were likely to be more efficient than single, she would probably do somewhat better. Weight would be saved by minimizing the rig. The ship would cost about as much as *Boadicea* – i.e., as the ships Admiral Milne was then trying to convince his First Lord to buy.

Barnaby submitted the design to Controller on 6 January 1875. He proposed an armament of ten accurate long-range guns: eight broadside 64pdrs in addition to the bow and stern chasers originally envisaged (the Board later decided to change the chasers to 64pdrs). The Board also added provision for torpedoes (initially four Harvey). Eventually the ships were armed with four torpedo launchers for Whiteheads. The only protection would be coal bunkers completely surrounding engines and boilers.

Barnaby argued that the Royal Navy should have a few really fast cruisers of the proposed type. The fast European cruisers and their faster successors could evade the British 13- to 15-knot cruisers, and they could capture mail steamers and the despatch vessels which linked a fleet at sea with the Admiralty. In addition to her cruiser function, the proposed fast ship would be ideal for despatch duty, since she could outrun any pursuer. She was not a cruiser as generally understood, because her range was limited: she could not sail very fast with her unretractable twin screws and limited rig. Barnaby envisaged operating her from a naval station or attaching her to a fleet. He called his ship an armed despatch vessel of high speed, but she was something quite different: a fast limited endurance combatant. Over the next few years the meaning of 'cruiser' changed in such a way that Barnaby's fast ship was definitely a cruiser. Moreover, it evolved directly into the steel cruisers of the later Victorian period.

Controller (Rear Admiral W Houston Stewart) submitted Barnaby's proposal to the Board on 18 January 1875. Milne liked it but wanted something smaller and less expensive. Despite unhappiness with the absence of sails, the Board approved the project, and Controller decided to order two of them from Pembroke under the 1875-76 program (First Lord Ward Hunt approved on 25 January 1875).

Estimates of coal endurance were not reassuring. At full power (17-18kts) the ship would burn all 400 tons of coal in one day and 18 hours; at half power (14kts) that would extend to 3 days and 21 hours. With a full load of 700 tons, the ship could steam for 3 days 3 hours at full power and 6 days 19 hours at half power. Capacity was increased to 500 tons (maximum 750) and more efficient compound engines adopted. To provide enough stability for the increased load, the poop and forecastle were closed in.

Machinery filled the mid-part of the ship. A sketch showed four large hatches, one each for the boiler rooms and one each for the two engines in tandem on the centreline. Barnaby planned to use rectangular rather than cylindrical boilers so as to save space, presumably accepting that they could not stand as much pressure (he planned to operate them at 40psi). The boilers would be given thick tops to protect them against shellfire. That changed to 8 oval and 4 cylindrical boilers (65psi) with the adoption of compound engines. There was some difficulty over complement, which did not seem to provide enough stokers until it was realized that the ship would never carry a full spread of sail. DNC limited complement to 250 to limit the size of the ship.

A full Legend prepared for the Board (25 May 1875) was labelled Armed Despatch Vessel to distinguish it from the usual fast but unarmed ships of that type. Nearly a third of the displacement of 3615 tons (3693 tons as indicated by the ship's lines) would be devoted to machinery (1100 tons plus 20 tons of engineers' stores and 450 tons of coal). Armament weighed only 120 tons. Despite considerable efforts to save weight, the hull was expected to consume nearly half the ship's weight, 1595 tons. The Legend compared the new ship to HMS *Volage*, which was shorter and narrower (270ft x 42ft vs 300ft x 46ft) and displaced less (3080 rather than 3650 tons), Even so, her iron hull weighed nearly as much as the steel hull of the new ship (1485 vs 1580 tons), and she did not carry much more armament (135 vs 120 tons). The weight of rigging was dramatically reduced (116 vs 74 tons). The real difference was machinery weight: 610 tons for *Volage*, 1120 for the new ship.

The ship was expected to burn 10 tons of coal per hour at maximum speed: endurance would be only 787.5nm at maximum speed, or 1312.5nm with bunkers full. At a cruising speed of 8kts she would burn only 1.2 tons per hour, giving her an endurance of 3000nm. Barnaby admitted that endurance would be very limited: 'high speed in a vessel of moderate dimensions would be impossible if it were attempted to give the same number of days' supply to the powerful engines required as to the engines which are sufficient for [the usual] low speed ... every thing has been cut down to the lowest limit in order to provide engine power and fuel'. In 1880 Captain Seymour of HMS *Iris* reported that he had learned to limit fuel expenditure by cruising on one screw and trailing or locking the other, accepting the yaw that produced. The following year he reported that he had managed a rate equivalent to 3120nm at 15kts under excellent conditions, a lot better than Barnaby had imagined.

The sketch design showed a double bottom under the whole of the boiler and engine rooms, and a double side (forming coal bunkers) around them. That had not been possible in any previous unarmoured ship. Steel was cheaper, ton for ton, than iron, and because it was stronger the hull was thinner and lighter. During detail design, it proved possible to reduce machinery weight from 1100 to 1064 tons, and later to 1025 tons. As a result, it was possible to increase normal coal capacity to 500 tons and to extend the double bottom to the ends of the ship. An additional survivability feature, apparently unusual for the time, was to place boilers in two separate boiler rooms and engines in two separate engine rooms. Given separate steam pipes for each boiler room, one could still operate if the other flooded.

The design was formally approved on 10 June 1875. The ships were HMS *Iris* and *Mercury*. By September, when Barnaby decided that their funnels should not be retractable, they were designated 'swift corvettes', which might translate as fast cruisers. By February 1876 complement had grown to 300, and the broadside armament was six 6½-ton guns. By way of comparison, in the 1 July 1876 armament list *Active* had two more 64pdrs, and *Volage* had a uniform battery of eighteen 64pdrs.

Protected Corvettes

After producing *Iris* and *Mercury*, Barnaby designed the *Comus* class steel corvettes, the conventional cruisers of their day. They were given the 12½-knot speed Barnaby considered the minimum for an acceptable cruiser. Barnaby added a new feature, a protective deck. There is every evidence in the Cover that the deck was Barnaby's idea, at least as it applied to cruisers, and not a requirement imposed by Controller or by anyone else on the Board. In this sense the *Comus* class, more than *Iris* and *Mercury*, were progenitors of the mass of Victorian steel cruisers.

Comus, *Champion*, *Cleopatra*, *Carysfort*, and *Conquest* were built under the 1876-77 program (all under contract by John Elder), *Constance* (Chatham) under the 1878-79 program, and *Canada* and *Cordelia* (both by Portsmouth) under the 1879-

HMS *Cleopatra* at Sydney 1881. She had the original battery of two 7in 90cwt and twelve 64pdr Mk III, all muzzle-loaders.
(Allan C Green, courtesy of State Library of Victoria)

HMS *Conquest* as built, with broadside guns only. She was armed with two 7in 90cwt and twelve 64pdr Mk III, all muzzle-loaders, plus four 1in Nordenfelts, two 0.45in Gardner machine guns, and she was assigned six 14in torpedoes (not yet supplied as of 1884).
(Allan C Green, courtesy of State Library of Victoria)

80 program. The two 1879-80 ships replaced a larger cruiser ordered under the 1878-79 program. Two modified *Calypso*s were built under the 1881-82 program: *Calypso* at Chatham and *Calliope* at Portsmouth. These were the last fully rigged British cruisers, and also the last slow ones (rated speed was 13.75kts). The decision not to build repeat *Calypso*s marked the beginning of the late Victorian force of fast cruisers. HMS *Calliope* was famous for having ridden out the Apia (Samoa) hurricane of 1889, US and German warships in the harbour sinking.

The design began as a modified version of the *Opal* class corvette (*Champion*) described in a previous chapter. In January 1876 Barnaby expected only to change framing and to add 100 tons more fuel, but then he decided to add protection, mainly in the form of an iron protective deck (1½in thick, 2½ to 3½ft under water) to cover the boilers, engine, and magazines. Coal atop the deck would add more protection. The lower deck would be kept at its earlier height. Between it and the iron deck (i.e., upper deck) fore and aft, deep beams would form supports for both decks. The chamber thus formed could be filled with fuel and with stores. The outside of the chamber would be kept empty or filled with water-excluding material. This was somewhat similar to a 'raft body protection' proposed for large armoured ships in mid-January by Admirals Elliot and Ryder. Barnaby pointed out that all vital parts, including steering, would be protected, even though some large heavily armoured ships had no better protection to crew or openings to machinery and magazines, nor was their steering gear protected (his was

HMS *Comus* as rearmed. In 1884 she was receiving four 6in 81cwt (Mk II) breech-loaders plus eight 64pdr Mk III in place of her original battery of two 7in and twelve 64pdr Mk III. In 1886 she was the only ship of the class to have been rearmed.
(Allan C Green, courtesy of State Library of Victoria)

under water, covered by a deck).

The result would be somewhat larger than *Opal* (5ft longer and 4½ft broader, 2383 rather than 2144 tons), and she would need more power (2300 rather than 2100 IHP) to maintain the 13kts of the earlier ship. Endurance would be comparable; at 10kts, with bunkers full, both the new ship and *Opal* would steam 2440nm. The new ship had greater reserve bunker space (100 tons), so with that fuel she would steam 3340 rather than 2800nm. Armament would be heavier. Both ships had the same twelve 64pdrs on the broadside, but the new ship would have two 90cwt revolving guns rather than the two 64pdrs of *Opal*. Armament would also be heavier because all the guns would be on slides. Eliminating the lifting screw made it possible for a gun to fire right aft. The ships would be designed so that they could act as rams, having heavy stems like those of the ironclad rams. Estimated cost of hull and machinery rose from £91,462 to £100,000.

The design was submitted to Controller on 6 June 1876.[2] Some of Barnaby's innovations went too far. A cruiser would spend much of her time under sail, and to reduce drag she should be able to retract her propeller (the alternative, feathering, had not yet been tested). That in turn would require a trunk up which the propeller could retract, so it would be impossible to have Barnaby's stern port. Instead, the ship should have two embrasures aft, guns being placed alongside the trunk. The non-retracting propeller was associated with Barnaby's underwater steering gear, which was also untested. The protective deck was attractive; could it be extended to the ends? The coal belt was also untested. If a shell exploded in it, would it pulverize the coal, creating an explosive mass?

Extending the protective deck all the way fore and aft would cost 70 tons (later recalculated as 84 tons), about half the weight of the armament. Surely subdivision of the ends would do. Controller liked the fuller deck, but was not willing to cut armament to buy it, particularly in view of the increasing power of the 90cwt (7in) heavy cruiser gun then in sight. One ship would have a feathering screw, the others having the usual lifting screws (and embrasured ports). The structure would be strengthened as much as possible.

Barnaby pointed out that the existence of the protective deck

HMS *Cordelia*. On the China station in 1888, she was armed with ten 6in Mk II instead of the original breech-loaders.
(Allan C Green, courtesy of State Library of Victoria)

HMS *Curacoa* with shielded 6in guns. In 1888 she was armed with four 6in Mk IV (5-ton) and with eight 5in 40cwt Mk III breech-loaders. She had two Mk VII discharges (torpedo launchers) for 14in Whitehead torpedoes, of which she carried the standard class allowance of six. Minor armament comprised three four-barrel and two two-barrel 1in Nordenfelts, two five-barrel 0.45in Nordenfelts, and two five-barrel 0.45in Gardner machine guns. Most ships of the class had four four-barrel 1in Nordenfelts and two Gardners, but the other weapons were being installed.

made it desirable to build the ship of iron or steel plates covered with two thicknesses of wood and sheathed with copper, like HMS *Boadicea*. That would be much stronger than the composite construction of the *Opal* class and even more durable, but also more expensive and heavier. The combination of protective deck and stronger hull explained the jump in size from the 1864 tons of *Opal* to 2377 tons. Barnaby later calculated that the weight of the 1½in deck was equivalent to that of a 6½in belt (6ft wide) with wood backing (without any covering deck, of course). If the belt were covered by a ¾in deck, it would have to be reduced to 3¼in. Reducing all the guns to 64pdrs would free up enough weight to make the platform decks fore and aft of steel and watertight (otherwise only the bulkheads could be made watertight). That was not done; the ships kept their two 90cwt guns.

By the time *Canada* and *Cordelia* were being built, the Royal Navy was abandoning muzzle-loaders in favour of a new generation of breech-loaders.[3] *Comus* was completed with the original battery, but by 1887 she had been armed with four 6in in sponsons instead of her chasers, but she retained eight 64pdr Mk III MLR (by 1895 she had ten 6in). Others were being rearmed: *Cleopatra*, *Champion*, and *Carysfort* were all scheduled to have their original batteries replaced by four 6in and eight 5in on the broadside. *Curacoa* already had the new battery. *Carysfort* and *Conquest* were never rearmed.[4] From the outset, *Canada* and *Cordelia* had ten 6in, four of them in sponsons (as indicated in a Legend dated January 1881). At least *Comus* and the last pair also had two torpedo carriages (not tubes).

The six Elder-built ships had ship rigs and three-cylinder engines (one high-pressure, two low-pressure). Royal Dockyard

FAST STEEL CRUISERS

The *Satellite* class sloop (later classed as a corvette) *Heroine*, probably in the Hamoaze, Devonport. On the China station in 1888, she was armed with eight 6in Mk II, as were *Satellite*, *Hyacinth*, *Royalist*, and *Rapid*. In 1884 she had the same armament. However, *Royalist* and *Rapid* had two 6in Mk II and ten 5in Mk I. *Satellite*, *Heroine* and *Hyacinth* all had eight 6in Mk II. Only *Caroline* and *Pylades* had the later fourteen 5in gun armament. In 1895 *Heroine* and *Hyacinth* still had eight 6in, and *Caroline* and *Pylades* both had fourteen 5in Mk II, but other ships of the class had reduced armaments. *Rapid* had two 6in Mk IV plus ten 5in (five Mk V, four Mk III, one Mk II). *Royalist* had a similar battery (two 6in, ten 5in) of different Marks of guns (one 6in Mk VI, one Mk IV; four 5in Mk V, 6 Mk IV). *Satellite* (Pacific station) had two 6in and only six 5in.

HMS *Pylades* in Hobsons Bay, 1895. In 1881 she was armed with fourteen 5in Mk II. She had no torpedo tubes; *Caroline* was the same. In March 1891 she was assigned to the North America and West Indies station.
(Allan C Green, courtesy of State Library of Victoria)

HMS *Rapid* (*Satellite* class).
(Allan C Green, courtesy of State Library of Victoria)

ships had barque rigs and four-cylinder engines (two high- and two low-pressure).

First Naval Lord Admiral Sir Cooper Key required the two 1881-82 ships (initially called New *Cordelia*) to be faster, with greater accommodation. DNC proposed to lengthen the ship 10ft and to use larger boilers (power increased to 3000 IHP) to increase speed from three-quarters to one knot, so that they would achieve about 14kts on trial (the Legend figure was 13¾kts). Complement would increase from the previous 264 to 280, including 36 Marines. The new ships were given a different battery: four 6in on Vavasseur central pivot mountings in sponsons plus twelve 5in on Vavasseur B (battery) mountings turning on racers in the deck, on the broadside. In addition they had four four-barrel Nordenfelts, two two-barrel Nordenfelts, two five-barrel Gardner machine guns, two two-barrel Gardners, and six 14in Whitehead torpedoes. Legend displacement was 2835 tons.

The seven *Satellite* class sloops (rerated as corvettes in 1884) were in effect smaller wood composite equivalents to the *Comus* class: three built under the 1880-81 program (*Satellite* from Sheerness, *Heroine* from Devonport, and *Hyacinth* from Devonport), three under the 1881-82 program (*Royalist* and *Rapid* from Devonport and *Caroline* from Sheerness), and the final ship apparently under the 1882-83 program (*Pylades* from Sheerness). They were the only British wooden warships with steel protective decks.

These ships began early in 1880 as follow-ons to the *Cormorant* class sloops. Initially Barnaby was asked just to add more coal. He protested that every ton of coal added had to be paid for. The British currently carried as much coal as the

HMS *Calliope* was famous for riding out the disastrous Apia (Samoa) hurricane of 1889. Her survival, while US and German warships in that harbour foundered, was a tribute both to seamanship and to the quality of her hull and her machinery. She managed to steam very slowly out of the harbour into the safety of deeper water, sometimes making no more than half a knot over the ground. In the process she managed to thread the narrow passage through the reef. In 1888, on the Australia station, she had four 6in Mk IV and twelve 5in 38cwt Mk II.
(Allan C Green, courtesy State Library of Victoria)

French, but they had the greatest command of coaling facilities. They should sacrifice the least for their coal. Barnaby had to step down: normal fuel capacity was increased from 125 to 150 tons. As in the *Cormorant*s, the engines were horizontal compound expansion. Initially maximum capacity was 300 tons, but during design that was increased to 400. On that basis endurance was over 3000nm at full speed and about 8000nm at 8kts. Sail power would be increased to provide the same sort of performance under sail as in *Cormorant*. All of this would raise the cost per ship from £49,700 to about £61,000.

Barnaby wrote that any change increasing first cost should provide greater firepower 'so as to increase the usefulness of these vessels when employed with heavier ships, and that in the same view there should be some protection for the machinery and magazines against the explosion of shell'. He proposed the 1½in protective deck of the *Comus* class, but complained to his assistant (Mr Morgan) that the deck added 30 per cent to the ships' cost.[5] Engines and boilers were well protected by their placement and by the coal bunkers on the sides of the ship even without any deck. Empty space above the boilers could be filled with additional coal, which would act as protection. Barnaby could accept the additional cost if deck thickness were halved (to ¾in). The weight saved went into more powerful armament. There was just enough weight to substitute six 6in breech-loaders for both the 90cwt muzzle-loaders and two 64pdr on each side. It cost 6 more tons to provide eight 6in (two revolving, six broadside). As built the ships were armed with two 6in and eight 5in. To accommodate the stern chaser, the ship had a non-hoisting (feathering) screw. Controller (William Houston Stewart) considered the protection offered by the steel deck well worth the additional cost of the ships, and First Naval Lord Admiral Cooper Key agreed.

HMS *Calliope* in 1900-01, in Victorian livery. At that time she was armed with four 6in Mk IV and with twelve 5in Mk II, plus four four-barrel 1in Nordenfelts, two two-barrel 1in Nordenfelts, two five-barrel 0.45in Gardners, and one two-barrel 0.45in Gardner machine guns, plus two Mk VIA torpedo discharges (14in) with six torpedoes. Torpedoes and discharges were landed while she served as tender to HMS *Northampton*.
(National Maritime Museum N07792 and N01250)

Barnaby submitted his sketch design in February 1880. The July 1880 Legend reflected an important difference between a corvette like *Comus* and a sloop: speed. The new design was credited with a speed of 11kts rather than 13kts.[6] When the second series (*Caroline* etc) were ordered, the *Comus* class (*Calliope*) was being redesigned with 6in guns in sponsons, adding to their bow and stern fire. In September 1881 Barnaby proposed redesigning the new sloops to match, giving them two bow and stern guns instead of one, with the other four guns on the broadside. The three ships already being built could also be modified. In fact the 1881-82 ships (*Caroline*, *Royalist*, and *Rapid*) were given two 6in and ten 5in breech-loaders. The earlier trio had eight 6in.[7] None of these ships had sponsons like those of the *Comus* class.

The 1882-83 program included 'New *Caroline*', which became HMS *Pylades*. Barnaby proposed that she have the same dimensions as the earlier ones, but with 1600 IHP for 13kts (i.e., cruiser speed). In fact if machinery were rated at 1500 IHP (12¾kts) under forced draught it could fit within the existing space and nearly within the existing weight (200 rather than 194 tons), and it would probably actually produce the desired 1600 IHP. Requiring the higher rating would entail larger machinery and considerable redesign. According to the official *Steamships of England* (1892 edition) the 950 IHP rating was at natural draught. All ships (including *Pylades*) were rated at 1400 IHP rating (12.6kts) under forced draught. *Pylades* had a uniform battery of fourteen 5in guns.

These were the last slow British cruisers; all later sloops were an entirely separate category not intended to work with a fleet. Sir William White's first sloops (*Nymphe* class) were faster (14.5kts in some), but by that time cruiser speed was closer to 20kts.

New *Iris* and *Leander*

Iris and *Mercury* were completed in 1877-78, just as the Russians demonstrated the need for fast cruisers to protect British trade. Fast Russian cruisers converted from liners carried a large coal supply. A British cruiser trying to run them down might lose too much time coaling. Controller wrote in 1880 that the Royal Navy badly needed ships which could steam at high speed for long distances without needing frequent coaling. Work on a new cruiser seems to have begun well before February 1879. There were apparently two alternatives. One was to reduce power (cutting speed to 16kts) to provide space for a lot more coal. In February 1879 Barnaby decided that the 16-knot ship should be armed with ten 6in breech-loaders, those on the poop and forecastle on turntables and those on the broadside on pivoted carriages, to give them large arcs of fire. Any increased armament weight would be deducted from the normal coal supply.

The alternative (New *Iris*) was to lengthen the ship (to make

LEFT HMS *Leander* as completed, probably at the 1887 Jubilee Review. This photo is labelled *Amphion*, but a card in the Brass Foundry indicates that she is actually *Leander*. Although contemporary drawings showed cross-yards and sails on the main and mizzen masts, surviving photographs show square sails only on the foremast. She was part of the Particular Service Squadron mobilized as a potential Baltic Fleet in 1885, and then served in China (1886-95), followed by a Chatham refit (1896-97). Then she went to the Pacific (1897-1901). She was converted into a destroyer depot ship in 1902-4, serving in the Mediterranean (1904-5), the Atlantic (1905), the Nore (1906), Devonport (1907-14), and the Grand Fleet (1914-19).

RIGHT *Leander* drying her sails, 1885.
(National Maritime Museum N01263)

Leander as modernized, about 1902 (the date is based on the grey livery).

space), to 360ft (rather than 300ft). She would make the same 18kts as *Iris*, in this case on 6400 IHP (the longer hull was easier to drive).[8] That would have cut machinery weight from the 1032 tons (*Iris* as built) to 930 tons. The larger hull could accommodate more coal: 800 tons (1200 tons maximum) – normal capacity of would have exceeded the maximum capacity of *Iris*. More economical machinery would have burned 7 rather than 10 tons per hour at full speed. Complement would have been 250 compared to the 257 of *Iris*, and armament would have matched that of *Iris*. By this time *Iris* had been completed and her actual, as opposed to estimated, displacement, was known: 3727 tons, rather more than had been expected. New *Iris* was expected to displace 4015 tons. In each case standard procedure was to compare the total of weights in the ship (as

Arethusa as completed. On completion she went into reserve at Chatham (1886-93) and then served with the Mediterranean Fleet (1893-97). After a further period in reserve at Chatham (1897-99), she served in the Pacific (1899-1903; she was temporarily assigned to the China Fleet during the 1900 Boxer Rebellion). She went into reserve at Chatham on returning in 1903, and was sold in 1905.

noted) with the displacement indicated by the hull form, which was 3735 tons for *Iris* (i.e., she drew more water than expected) and 4060 tons for New *Iris*. A specification for New *Iris* was approved on 10 March 1880.

While New *Iris* was being sketched, the Royal Navy was building the fast torpedo ram *Polyphemus*, which became (in effect) a test-bed for new lightweight machinery. In January 1880 Barnaby's assistant William H White asked the Chief Draughtsman to prepare drawings of New *Iris* using the new lightweight machinery (perhaps 700 tons or less for 6500 IHP). The weight saved could go into a protective steel deck (say 1½in, 150 tons) over the engines and boilers, as in the corvette *Comus* (see above), and into more coal (80 tons). This was a considerable step towards a fast survivable cruiser.

Some time in the spring of 1880 New *Iris* was dropped in favour of the 16-knot design with a normal load of 1000 tons of coal. Early in February Barnaby offered Controller Rear Admiral Houston Stewart a design with the desired speed and coal, with protected boilers, engines, and magazines, within the *Iris* hull lines. Controller approved. By April Barnaby hoped that reducing speed to 16kts would cut required power to 4500 IHP, freeing 270 tons for ammunition and the protective deck (and saving about £24,000 on engines).[9] A 15 April 1880 Legend showed the ten 6in BLR and the 1½in deck Barnaby had introduced in the *Comus* class. Ships' boats were expected to include two second-class torpedo boats (one had been added to *Iris* and *Mercury* after completion). At maximum speed with normal coal load the ship could steam 3200nm, and at 14kts

Amphion 1900

HMS *Amphion* is shown in September 1900. The 6in guns were normally withdrawn behind the doors on the hull sides (note that the forward set was larger). The forward pair of broadside guns had a 108-degree arc of fire, the midships guns 102 degrees, and the after pair 112 degrees. The four shielded upper deck 6in on pivot mountings were normally covered by folding metal panels on the sides. The original light armament included eight quadruple-barrel Nordenfelt guns (replaced by 3pdrs about 1897-1900) in the eight semi-circular small embrasures. The guns were not centred in the projections, so that they did not protrude when the covers were closed, but that somewhat limited arcs of fire. Originally four more quadruple-barrel Nordenfelts and two five-barrel Gardner 0.45in machine guns were located on the upper deck. In the drawing the twin 1in Nordenfelt is shown mounted to port amidships. The ship originally carried two second-class torpedo boats, each with dropping gear for two 14in torpedoes. About 1897-1900 the second boat was replaced by a 48ft steam pinnace, which also had dropping gear. *Amphion* and her sisters were completed with a barque rig, but that was reduced to schooner rig during the early 1890s (the jibboom was deleted) and the bowsprit was completely eliminated about 1897-1900, while the foremast lost its upper topmast and retained only two yards from which signal flags could be flown. Funnels were raised on completion. By 1900 the ornamental scrollwork at bow and stern had been removed. No rigging plan for this period has survived, so the masting and rigging shown were taken from contemporary photographs and from an analysis of deck fittings; it is probably incomplete. Note that a modern stockless anchor had replaced the original starboard anchor, while a stocked anchor was originally stowed amidships, partially protruding through the bulwark.
(A D Baker III)

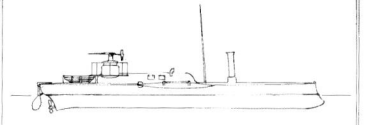

(two-thirds power) she could steam 4000nm. Controller much liked the design, which he immediately submitted to the Board.

This was an unusually fast handy ship, so early in 1881 someone suggested replacing the existing battery with a single massive 80-ton gun. It might add about 100 tons, immersing the ship about 5 inches. Barnaby thought the ship would have to be a bit beamier to add stiffness. If masts and many other weights could be dispensed with, the gun might be accommodated without any additional immersion.

By the time the design was submitted the 1880-81 program already included three cruisers, for which the names *Leander*, *Phaeton*, and *Arethusa* had been chosen. One more ship, *Amphion*, was included in the 1881-82 program.

Like earlier sailing warships, the *Leander*s had a single magazine, powder from which was brought to the gun deck and then passed forward or aft. In this case the magazine was aft. Similarly, the single shell room was forward. That made less sense for a ship using heavy ammunition, so in March 1882 Barnaby's assistant William H White suggested modifying the ship to place a magazine and shell room at each end. Given their limited volume, the magazines could be kept under the length of a protective deck restricted by the available weight. As the design was developed, the gun arrangement was changed to place one 6in on each side at each end, with a clear forward (or after) arc instead of one gun on the centreline, where its fire might be blocked (for example by the bowsprit). That left six guns on the broadside. *Leander* and *Amphion* both had closed stokeholds for forced draught.

The ships came out heavy, drawing 10in more than designed, even though the normal coal supply was reduced to 550 tons as compensation for overweights. From a later perspective, the worst flaw was that the steering gear was wholly unprotected because the deck covered only machinery and magazines.

According to the supplementary report of the 1888 Manoeuvres, the CO of *Arethusa* considered his ship a good seaboat, steaming well against a moderate head sea and a strong wind, but rolling heavily with the sea abeam or abaft. She was therefore an unsteady gun platform under these conditions (and machine gun fire from her tops would be useless). The square rig on the foremast and the fighting tops should be eliminated to reduce topweight. The rudder should be enlarged, the upper bridge extended to the sides to obtain a view right aft, and a searchlight fitted on the poop, to catch a torpedo boat coming up from astern. The committee reviewing the manoeuvre reports concurred with Admiral Baird (who commanded A Squadron) that these ships (and the *Mersey*s, below) were overarmed.

The *Mersey* Class
By 1882 the Board was interested in another kind of cruiser, a protected seagoing torpedo ship. It was already clear that torpedoes had to be integrated into the fleet. To be used during a fleet engagement, they should be protected, which meant placed under water. An attempt to add underwater tubes to existing battleships had been abandoned in the late 1870s as far too expensive. The alternative was to place the torpedoes on board smaller fast ships working with the battleships. The first attempt, the torpedo ram *Polyphemus*, was ordered under the 1878-79 program. First Naval Lord Cooper Key, who took office in September 1879, considered the idea sound but wanted more conventional ships. They could both deliver torpedo attacks and beat off enemy torpedo boats. He asked for 'a cheap *Polyphemus*' armed, like her namesake, with 40 torpedoes and four underwater tubes.

The constructors began working on this problem some time in 1880 (their sketch design apparently has not survived). On 31 December 1880 DNC wrote that the ship could not be built for much less than £100,000. Because she could not be protected against light quick-firing guns intended to defend against torpedo boats, she would find it difficult to get close enought to torpedo a battleship. However, something larger, the size of a cruiser, could keep going even after being riddled in this fashion. Barnaby much preferred the fast *Polyphemus*, whose minimum size and immersion offered a small target. A simplified slower (16kt) *Polyphemus* would cost no more than an unprotected torpedo ship – but she would lack the 6in guns First Naval Lord later wanted.

In 1882 Barnaby pointed to a recent design competition for a fast (16kt) despatch vessel as an indication of what high speed required. The ship was simpler than the desired warship, because its machinery, boilers, and steering gear required no protection, and no space had to be found below decks for torpedo tubes. All the main British shipbuilders were invited to bid.[10] They offered small fast merchant ships, typically 275ft long, typically displacing about 2100 tons, with 3500 IHP engines, stowing 750 tons of coal (400 to 500 tons normal supply). To Barnaby, the typical cost of £80,000 confirmed his £100,000 cost estimate of a 16-knot torpedo ship, either a simplified slow *Polyphemus* or a scaled-down *Leander*.

Barnaby argued that Cooper Key would do better to adopt a big fast merchant ship, 400ft to 500ft long, carrying four first-class torpedo boats. She would have the coal endurance and seakeeping for long transits, and when she arrived the boats would attack the enemy battleships. In peacetime she would be a normal merchant ship, and in wartime she would be leased. The White Star Line was proposing to build exactly such a ship, an 18-knot liner with unusually great beam and with twin

HMS *Forth*, in nearly her original configuration, with small charthouse. Note the bridge wing semaphore. She spent her entire career as a cruiser in Devonport Reserve, emerging in 1903 to be converted into a submarine depot ship.

HMS *Severn* in Far East livery. She served in the China Fleet (1889-95), then went into reserve at Chatham on her return (1895-98). She later served as coast guard at Harwich (1898-1904) before going into reserve at Chatham and being sold.
(NHHC collection)

HMS *Severn*, 1897, with enlarged pilothouse and semaphores on both bridge wings.
(National Maritime Museum N01271)

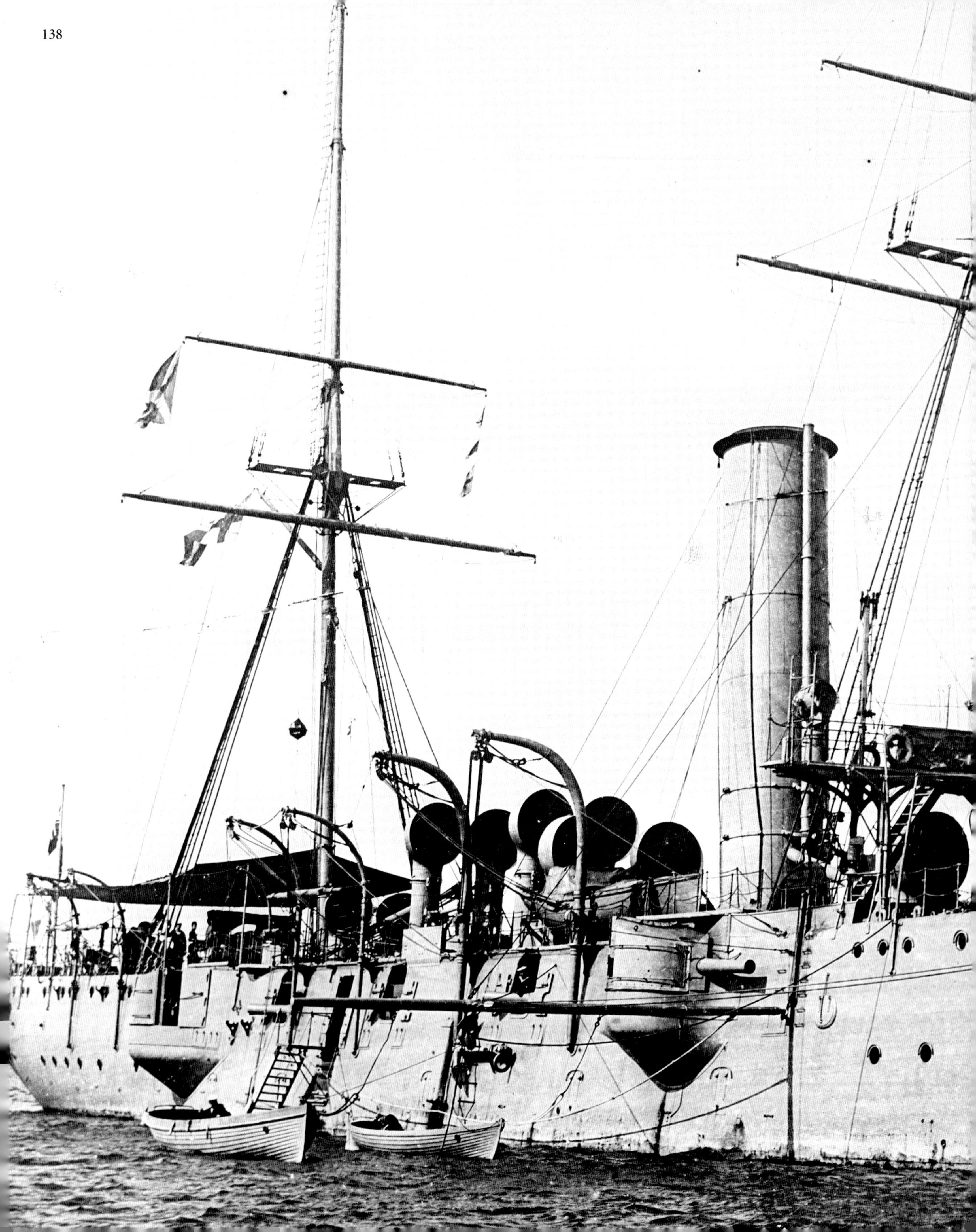

HMS *Mersey* in 1904, shortly before her demise as a fighting ship. She went from completion into reserve at Chatham, emerging in 1893 to become coast guard at Harwich (1893-98) and then going back into reserve at Chatham, emerging only to be sold in 1905. As this photograph shows, reserve did not mean being laid up; ships were periodically put into service, for example for fleet exercises. This photograph was taken just before Admiral Fisher changed the basis of the reserve from ships waiting for whatever reservists might be available to ships with dedicated nucleus crews and assigned reservists.
(National Maritime Museum N01269)

screws. She would cost the Royal Navy very little in peacetime. The first priorities should be to build some large torpedo boats suitable for hoisting in and out of a large ship, and devising the necessary cranes, suitable for mounting on the deck of a merchant ship. Once that had been done, and as soon as *Polyphemus* had proved herself, either a smaller cheaper version could be built in quantity, or – a much less attractive alternative – *Leander* could be modified with underwater torpedo tubes.

Cooper Key was less than enthusiastic about Barnaby's carrier, because he saw problems in hoisting large torpedo craft in and out. The second-class torpedo boats, specially designed to be carried on board cruisers and battleships, had not yet been fully tested, and Barnaby's big boats would present further problems. The idea was revived after the 1885 manoeuvres, resulting in the design and construction of HMS *Vulcan* described in the next chapter. For the present, Cooper Key wanted a cruiser. Not only was it expensive to integrate torpedo tubes with battleships, it was also unwise. Cooper Key later wrote that it would be a mistake to think underwater weapons (ram and torpedo) as important as the gun; instead the commander of a squadron should be able to manoeuvre the two weapons independently, on board two separate kinds of ship.

On 2 January 1882 Cooper Key formally asked Controller for a seagoing 16-knot torpedo ship to 'do the torpedo work for [the ironclads], and thus avoid the risks incidental to this warfare in the more costly ships:' the modified *Leander*. The speed was chosen so that the unarmoured ships could bring a faster enemy fleet to battle, or to prevent their escape. The light ships would also carry the fleet's searchlights, so that enemy torpedo craft attacking at night might be illuminated without the lights giving away the positions of the battleships. On 12 January Cooper Key recommended that both of Barnaby's options, the cut-rate *Polyphemus* and the torpedo *Leander*, be pursued, and one of each included in the 1883-84 program.

Barnaby offered one more, much cheaper, option: converting one of Armstrong's big-gun China gunboats, which were a great sensation at the time. She could be armed with one 6in gun forward and broadside torpedo tubes, with a crew of only

80. The gunboats were far smaller than a *Leander*, 220ft long. With stoke holds closed for forced draught, the craft might well sustain 16kts for up to 3 hours. The maximum sustained speed was 13kts, for which they had 5 days of coal on board (10 days at 10kts, 2400nm). These ships had ½in protective decks. The gunboat would be handier than a *Leander*, but the better-protected cruiser would have a better chance of closing with a 14- or 15-knot ironclad under that ship's fire. She would also be a much better seaboat. Barnaby pointed out that the gunboat would be far more versatile than a modified *Polyphemus*, which could perform no peacetime service other than training. The Board was uninterested. The modified *Leander* went ahead.

At the beginning of January, Barnaby asked his deputy William H White to sketch a 16-knot ship carrying four 6in guns on revolving mounts and 500 tons of coal. Hull and engines should cost £100,000. He chose the same length as *Iris* (300ft) but a much narrower beam (36ft) and a mean draught of 18ft. These dimensions were scaled down from those of the 360ft New *Iris*, which was apparently considered a particularly good hull form, giving a displacement of 2500 tons. The ship would have a 1in protective deck. Barnaby thought he could save a great deal of power, so he suggested 2000 IHP (natural draught). White also tried a thicker deck (2 to 2½in). In mid-January 1882 he reported that a 2800-ton ship with 4000 IHP machinery would be perfectly feasible. His sketch showed a full upper deck (forecastle and poop joined) and one funnel (two 30ft boiler rooms forward of two engine rooms). One of two 20ft torpedo rooms would be forward of the coal, itself forward of the boiler rooms (the magazine was forward of this room), the other abaft the machinery. Each torpedo room contained two tubes, one pointing to each side, staggered. Above each were two 6in guns on revolving mounts between the main and upper decks. Between them were between-decks mountings for 1in quick-firing Nordenfeldts, the standard anti-torpedo boat guns. Three were mounted on each side in the waist, plus one on each side at each end of the ship. An armoured pilothouse was set just abaft the forward pair of 6in guns.

Torpedo range was very short: the ship would take considerable fire as she ran in to attack. She therefore had a much thicker deck than *Leander*'s: 2in on the flat, 3in on the slope, with 9in screen bulkheads at the fore end and a 10in conning tower. Barnaby offered to design a larger ship with any desired thickness of deck, but argued that the proposed deck was already enough.

By May 1882 a detailed Legend for a 3150-ton version of White's design was ready.[11] It incorporated a comparison with *Giovanni Bausan*, a torpedo ram Armstrong was then building for Italy. The Armstrong ship was somewhat shorter than the British ships, but faster, with more powerful engines. She was also much more heavily armed, with a 10in gun at each end, six 6in on the broadside, and torpedoes. All of that weighed a lot: estimated armament weight was 233 tons, more than twice that of the Royal Navy design. Some of the weight came out of protection: 146 rather than 415 tons of deck armour. Armstrong's ship was expected to displace 3107 tons.[12] *Bausan* seems to have so impressed the British that on 29 June Barnaby produced a Legend of a Protected Seagoing Vessel, essentially his torpedo ship rearmed with two 10in guns and four 6in (85 rounds per gun for both calibres), with much the same dimensions. The new armament weighed 235 tons.

One major gap remained. In 1882 the Royal Navy still had no workable underwater torpedo tube. If none materialized very soon, the ship would have to be modified as a gun cruiser. In June White pointed out that the gun version would be nearly identical to the torpedo ship up to the level of the protective deck. He proposed suppressing the poop and forecastle, building up the central part of the ship (for a length of about 140ft) and covering it with a spar deck. This ship would mount the same four 6in guns as the torpedo ship, but more importantly she could match the *Bausan*. Heavier armament would add about 120 tons (5in or 6in greater draught). It might be desirable to add 6in to the depth of the hull below the protective deck. Load displacement would then be about 3350 tons (originally the estimate was 3300). The heavy-gun version was now pursued in parallel to the torpedo version.

The Board met early in July to consider the cruiser program. Probably its most important decision was to abandon plans to build a follow-on to the slow *Calliope*. From now on the Royal Navy would build only fast cruisers. Both the torpedo ship and a gun cruiser (with armament arranged as in *Bausan*) would be pursued. The latter would replace the follow-on *Calliope* in the program.[13]

The British considered development of a viable broadside submerged torpedo tube stalled (other navies used bow tubes), so the cheap *Polyphemus* was no longer a near-term proposition and was dropped altogether. That left the modified *Leander*. The Board decided that the ships should be convertible, their primary armament either torpedoes (if the underwater tubes were successful) or guns. As work progressed without any dramatic success in underwater tube development, space reserved for torpedo rooms was released. Cooper Key considered the gun version admirable, though somewhat large and costly. Without a protected torpedo battery she could not normally risk a close encounter with an ironclad, but 'might on occasion inflict considerable damage on an ironclad and would be useful as a frigate attached to a squadron for chasing and bringing on an action – or picking up disabled ships – and this in addition to her value as a cruizer'.

The gun ship equivalent to *Bausan* had 6in guns at the ends plus six 6in in a battery amidships under a spar deck. An alternative version sacrificed two 6in to upgrade the end guns to 18-ton 9.2in. To Cooper Key the 9.2s were wanted mainly to fight ironclads. The ship was more likely to be chased by an ironclad rather than to chase her. To save herself, she should retain the 9.2in gun aft, but replace the forward gun with a pair of 6in in sponsons on a raised forecastle, plus two more 6in in the midships battery.

George W Rendel joined the Board in 1882 as Civil Lord, probably specifically to provide the Royal Navy with the experience he had gathered during a long career with Armstrong. Probably *Bausan* figured so prominently in discussions because she was Rendel's last design. Rendel preferred to retain the forward 9.2in gun. The new cruiser was conceived, perhaps for the first time, as part of a composite fleet 'which, it has been agreed, value for value, will have more fighting efficiency than a fleet of ironclads alone'. Unless the cruisers could attack ironclads they would be valuable only as scouts. Bringing a fleeing enemy fleet to action required chasing enemy ironclads.

FAST STEEL CRUISERS 141

HMS *Australia* at the 1893 Columbian Review in New York. She had probably just completed her period of service in the Mediterranean Fleet (1889-93), her only substantial sea service. Upon returning home she became coast guard at Southampton Water (1893-1903) before going into reserve at Chatham. In this photograph the ship still has the short funnels with which she was completed. The two tall poles on the bridge wings are semaphores used to communicate with other ships in company.
(Ted Stone via NHHC)

HMS *Orlando*. Note her two bridge semaphores, the arms of the starboard one at right angles, and the 3pdr QF gun in the embrasure at her bow. The latter was a feature of many Victorian Royal Navy cruisers. It was placed right forward on the theory that torpedo boats would usually attack from ahead. Other guns were behind the closed ports in the waist. The military tops visible here were occupied by machine guns, which were valued as anti-personnel weapons. *Orlando* was flagship of the Australia station 1888-98, returned to Portsmouth for a refit in 1898-99, and then was assigned to the China Fleet in 1899-1902. She returned to enter Portsmouth Reserve (1903-5).

Rendel thought that two such ships working together could successfully engage an ironclad if their armament was protected from machine gun fire. Presumably this was much the argument which had convinced the Royal Italian Navy to buy Rendel's *Bausan*. Rendel particularly discounted the value of the 6in gun against armour.[14] In another context Barnaby had drawn the Board's attention to the heavy stern chasers of French ironclads the cruisers might have to chase: 'it would be of special value to have a powerful bow fire in some swift vessels of the English fleet in order to bring an action.'

Rendel's views must have carried considerable weight. Not only had he designed recent successful export cruisers, but his firm was one of the greatest producers of guns in the world. Early in November Cooper Key opted for two parallel designs. One was the ship already being designed, with two 9.2in and six 6in. The other had an all-6in battery, with two 6in sponsons on poop and forecastle and ten more in an enclosed midships structure. White suspected that the additional weight

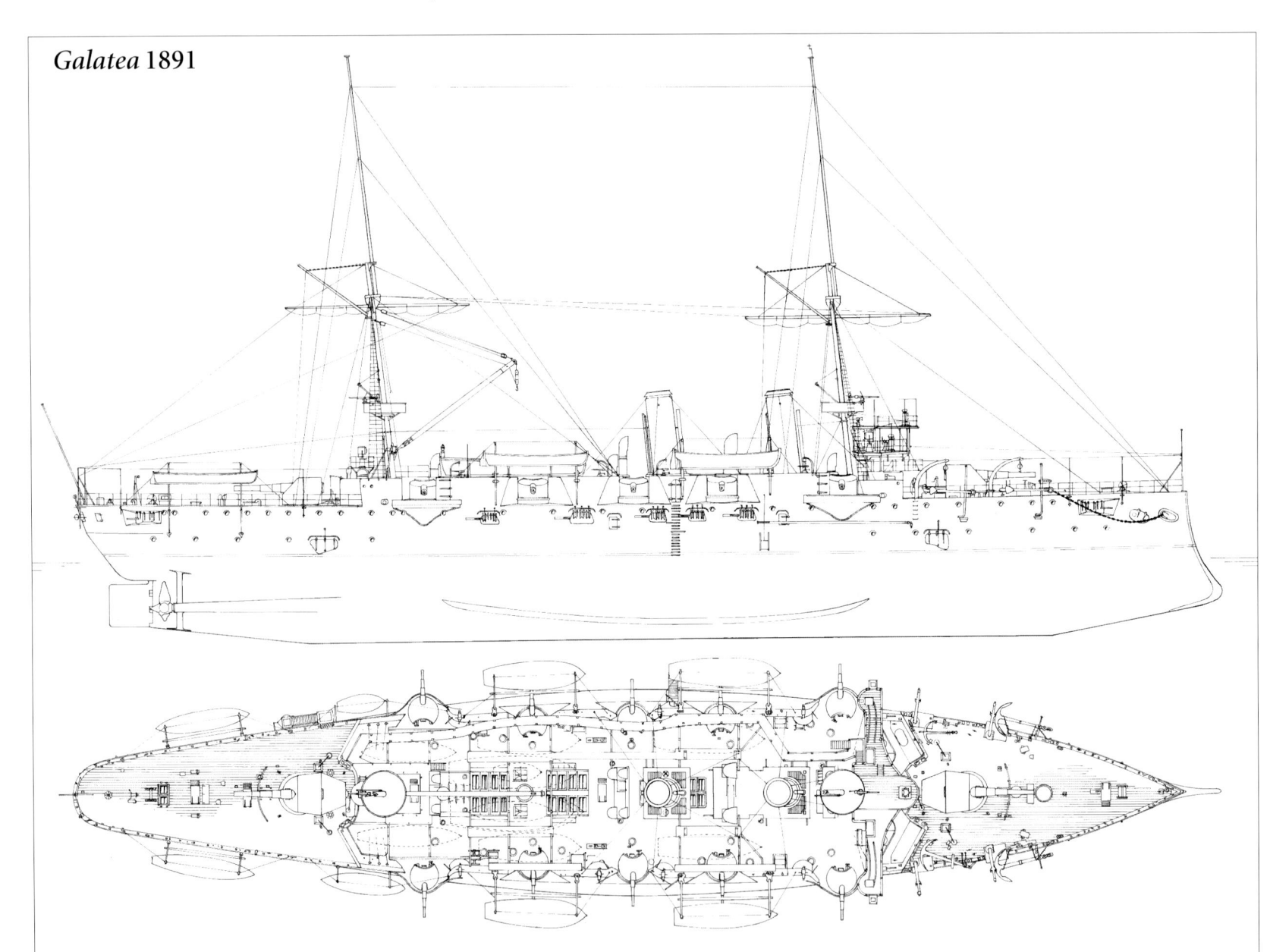

Galatea 1891

HMS *Galatea*, an *Orlando* class belted cruiser, based on an as-fitted plan dated 27 January 1891; the ship was completed in August 1889, so this drawing shows minor post-completion alterations, including installation of a catwalk between the forward superstructure and the rudimentary after superstructure. Note that there was no after bridge, just a raised searchlight platform aft. At this time, too, the hawse pipe fittings were enlarged. During an 1895 refit, the ship's funnels were raised and the 6in BLR guns converted to quick-firing (as QFC). One of the two 9.2in Mk Vs was replaced by a Mk VI gun (*Narcissus* had two of the latter). Doors in the bulwarks forward and abaft the sponsoned 6in guns could be opened to increase their firing arcs. The three rectangular structures on deck at the breech ends of the 9.2in guns were elevators for projectiles and powder. Each was served by a davit, and the open platforms could accommodate half a dozen ready-service projectiles each. Note that there were four Nordenfelt machine guns to starboard, but only three to port. Two of them could be mounted on the two single-axle carriages for shore use. The two 9pdr shore artillery pieces were stowed on the upper deck atop their four-axle carriages. Of the six 6pdr QF, four were on the main deck at bow and stern and two were abaft the second funnel (behind the doors seen low on the hull). They were barely above the waterline, a situation aggravated by the ship's gross overweight. They pivoted at their muzzle ends over about a 60-degree arc. At least eight reload torpedoes could be carried in the single magazine forward, beneath the torpedo tube compartment. The funnels had no covers. Instead, internal rotating flues were rigged near their tops, controlled by cables from the base of the funnels. A rigging plan prepared in 1896 showed two additional yards on the masts, but none show in any photo of ships of the class. The gaff on the foremast was seldom fitted. 'Sentry platforms' could be rigged at the upper deck level on either side just abaft the enlisted men's gangway (the portside location is shown). Some boats seen in the plan view have been omitted from the profile for clarity.

(A D Baker III)

of the all-6in battery would have to be paid for out of the protective deck.

The 1883-84 program included two cruisers, by this time called first class, one at Chatham (*Mersey*), one under contract. As described for Parliament in February 1883 the 'protected torpedo ship' to be built at Chatham was, like *Polyphemus*, designed to work with a fleet. It implied that for the first time the new cruiser would combine the ram (clearly popular in Parliament) with the new and rapidly-developing torpedo,

HMS *Aurora* as completed, without a shield to her 9.2in gun. Note that the gun was shielded rather than enclosed in a gunhouse, as in many later cruisers. *Aurora* went from completion into reserve at Devonport, then joined the Channel Squadron (1890-92). She then returned to Devonport (1892-93) and was made coast guard at Bantry Bay (1893-95). She went back into Devonport reserve (1895-99), emerging to join the China Fleet (1899-1902). She was refitted on Clydebank in 1902-3 and then went to Devonport in 1904 before being laid up in the Holy Loch in 1905.

HMS *Aurora* as fully fitted out.

HMS *Narcissus* in the Far East after her funnels were raised. At this time tall funnels were a way of increasing draught to boilers, hence increasing power by pulling air through them. Only later, when ships were given spotting tops, was smoke interference with tops an important issue. *Narcissus* went into Chatham reserve on completion (1889-92), then joined the Channel Squadron (1892-94), and after an 1894 Portsmouth refit (probably when her funnels were raised) went to the China Fleet (1895-99). On her return she became tender to HMS *Excellent* (the gunnery school) as Gunnery Training Ship at Portsmouth (1901-5).

overcoming the defects of limited habitability and endurance of the *Polyphemus*. The new ship would not be as manoeuvrable nor as fast, but she would be much less expensive and a much better seakeeper.

The Chatham ship would have Cooper Key's 6in battery. The contract ship would mount the heavy-gun battery, which Barnaby called the Elswick (i.e., Armstrong) battery. In fact both ships were built at Chatham, the second (*Severn*) being laid down in January 1884, very late in the 1883-84 fiscal year. The Elswick battery was abandoned for the time being; both were to have the same all-6in battery. However, in December 1883 it was suggested that the four end 6in guns be replaced by new 7in guns (which would have added about 60 tons in all). Another possibility was to have one 7in at each end working with two 6in chasers, the amidships battery being six 6in. Subject to approval by First Lord, on 5 December the Board decided that both of the 1883-84 ships should be armed with 7in sponson guns. The planned 7in gun never materialized, because in March 1884 DNO reported that it was needed only for the two *Mersey*s.

The 1884-85 program included two more, *Thames* and *Forth*. Their armament had not yet been settled as late as January 1884. About August 1884 Cooper Key wrote that unless 7in guns were required for *Thames*, she should mount either 8in guns fore and aft or pairs of 6in in sponsons. He rejected the 9.2in gun because the ship would require a special lightweight type (18 tons rather than 22 or 24). This gun would be too long for any ship to mount on the broadside, and if only a few ships mounted it, spares would have to be retained on several distant stations. Moreover, it seemed to him that it did not offer enough advantage over the existing 12-ton 8in gun or even over two 6in (4½ tons each). All-6in, characterized as a return to the original battery, was specified for HMS *Thames*.

However, by late July 1884 plans called for 8in guns in the two *Mersey*s: two 8in at the ends and ten 6in in the broadside battery. Instead of the forty torpedoes envisaged in the original torpedo cruiser project, they would have ten. Ultimately the same battery was chosen for *Thames* and *Forth*, but it is not clear exactly when the decision was taken to make all four ships identical sisters.

According to the supplementary report on the 1888 manoeuvres, the *Mersey*s proved themselves good seaboats and handy, steady gun platforms, and able to fight their guns 'longer [i.e., in increasingly bad weather] than most ships.' The CO of *Severn* wanted the 8in guns on forecastle and poop removed and replaced by lighter guns. Admiral Baird, who commanded the A squadron (representing a British fleet), considered cruisers in general too heavily armed.

First Lord Northbrook seems to have considered these and proposed larger cruisers an impediment to his first priority of building ironclads. In mid-1883 he listed as his second priority (after building new ironclads), the conversion of the big

*Warrior*s and the 400ft ironclads to cruisers. No more large cruisers should be built until that was done (it never happened). That may explain why the *Orlando* class belted cruisers (in effect small ironclads) were acceptable.[15]

New *Mersey* and the *Orlando* Class

As of June 1884 the proposed 1885-86 program included a follow-on New *Mersey*. Rendel wanted a total of four ships (with two in 1885-86), but in the wake of the 'truth about the navy' scare that fall the Gladstone Administration was compelled to accept the large supplemental Northbrook Program. The shape of the program was probably influenced by Captain Hall's 1884 report on British naval weaknesses, in which second-class armourclads were a particular problem.[16] Although the new ships were really cruisers with some thick waterline armour, they qualified as ironclads. The first five were ordered under the supplementary Northbrook Program of the 1884-85 fiscal year (actually in 1885), the last two being the 1885-86 ships. They formed the *Orlando* class.

The Elswick armament was not dead. Rendel revived his argument for heavy guns. This ship would have 9.2in guns at the ends (and twelve 6in on her broadside) and much thicker deck armour (2in flat as before, but 6in slopes). She had to be larger, 350ft rather than 300ft long, displacing 4150 tons.[17] By August 1884 New *Mersey* had been superseded by what became the *Orlando* class, a growth version with the same armament (but using a standard 9.2in gun) and a 10in belt as in the *Imperieuse* class armoured cruisers instead of the thick sloping armour of New *Mersey*.[18] The modified ship now had the waterline protection of a second-class ironclad, but many of the attributes (such as speed) of a cruiser. There could no longer be any question but that she ought to be armed with the most powerful possible armour-piercing guns, at the time still the 9.2in which had been considered for the *Mersey*s. Barnaby designed the modified *Polyphemus* Cooper Key had requested as an alternative to the *Mersey*s, but it went nowhere.

All of the guns were unprotected, except against machine-gun fire. Existing armour-piercing guns fired slowly. Those loading them were vulnerable mainly to machine-gun fire, given the very short ranges then envisaged, so thin shields pro-

HMS *Medusa*, William White's attempt to give the Royal Navy an equivalent of the fast new export cruisers Armstrong was building. Built at Chatham, she was somewhat less sophisticated than her contract-built sisters, with horizontal rather than vertical engines. She was also built relatively slowly, so that she was obsolescent when completed. Upon completion she became RNR drill ship at North Shields (1895-1901). After refitting at Jarrow in 1901-2 she joined the Cruiser Training Squadron (1902-3), and then became seagoing tender to the training ship *Impregnable* at Devonport in 1904 before being laid up in 1905-8. Although placed on the sale list, she was refitted at Pembroke in 1909 and then towed to Bantry Bay as a calibrating ship for fire control systems in 1910. She was assigned to Queenstown for harbour service in 1917-18; the timing suggests a connection with convoy operations.

tected crews at the 9.2s at the ends and the four 6in at the ends of the battery. Like the *Mersey*s, the ship was described as both a ram and a torpedo vessel. By this time the underwater tubes in *Polyphemus* were finally successful, and Barnaby expected the new ship to be similarly armed. Control of both underwater weapons would be exercised from a heavily armoured conning tower.

This ship was shorter (she reverted to *Mersey* or *Leander* class length) but beamier (53ft and then 55ft), displacing 4650 tons – more than 1000 more than *Mersey*. A sketch and Legend were ready for the Board late in October 1884. A striking improvement over previous ships was mounting the end 6in guns of the midships battery in sponsons, giving them end fire. There was some question as to the value of the belt as opposed to the protective deck. The only substantial change ordered by the Board was elimination of two of the twelve 6in.

The initial Legend showed slightly more power (6700 rather than 6000 IHP) for the same speed as the *Mersey*s.[19] Tank tests suggested that a 321ft x 55ft 6in x 20ft 6in hull of 5000 tons would be best for propulsion, but the shorter hull was chosen. It would be handier, and it offered a greater proportion of armoured to unarmoured side and greater buoyancy under the heavy guns at the ends of the superstructure. The magazines under the guns would be further from the ship's sides because her lines would not be so fine. The shorter ship would also have a somewhat smaller chance of being hit by a few projectiles or a torpedo. About 100 tons would be saved on the hull, and it might be about 6in deeper amidships, with somewhat more space for engines and boilers. Compared to the longer ship, the shorter one would pay a speed penalty of about half a knot over a wide speed range, and it would find it more difficult to maintain speed in a seaway.

The design proved over-optimistic. Alternations made in 1886-87, reported in February 1887, included an increase of complement from 350 to 421. A bridge and charthouse were added forward and a torpedo director tower aft. Plans were made to fit electric lighting internally and electric searchlights externally. Installation of net defence (against torpedoes) was being considered.

Virtually all the British warships of this era suffered from overweight due to poor estimates of weights, but usually that made no great difference except for some loss of speed. The *Orlando*s were not so fortunate, because they had relatively narrow (5½ft) waterline belts. The design called for the top of the belt to be 3½ft above water with 950 tons of coal on board. A May 1887 weight statement showed *Orlando* 800 tons overweight on a 5000-ton designed displacement, putting the top of her belt 2ft underwater (with 750 tons of coal on board) – where it was altogether useless. Since the belt was not covered by an armour deck, the ship was to all intents a totally unarmoured cruiser with an unusually powerful armament. Contributing to the overweight was heavier than expected armour (950 tons).

The fiasco made the Board of Admiralty particularly sensitive to overweight. It was attributed mainly to the practice of accepting additions during construction. Until this time the Legends – the design descriptions – of British warships showed two displacement figures. One was the total of calculated weights. A second was the 'displacement on lines', meaning the displacement implied by the underwater volume of the hull. The two generally did not match. When the displacement by lines was considerably greater, the difference seems to have been considered a safety margin. Now it was clear that such practices had to be abandoned – calculations had to be a lot better, and weight had to be controlled.

Changes during construction were inevitable. To accommodate and, more importantly, to control them, ships were assigned a Board Margin, a percentage of the calculated displacement. Ships would be designed on the basis that they might grow by up to the Board Margin during construction, so, for example, armour belts were designed on the basis of the draught at the total allowable displacement. Ships' Covers were required to show every change as a deduction from the Board Margin. Explicit Board approval had to be sought for anything more. The first major cruisers affected were the big *Blake* and *Blenheim*, described in a later chapter.

White and the Armstrong Cruisers
Armstrong hired Barnaby's chief assistant William H White in 1883, just before work began on the *Orlando* class. He had been Barnaby's presumptive heir. Now he became chief naval architect of the leading cruiser building company in the world, and also superintendant of their Elswick yard.

Barnaby faced increasing criticism. His Admiralty designs did not seem to offer anything like what Armstrong was showing it could deliver. The theme of superior private designs compared with hidebound Admiralty practice lasted through the twentieth century. Reed's sniping cannot have helped. The Admiralty case was that private builders could achieve better results – on paper, but often not in reality. Their ships ran trials at unrealistic displacements at rates of forcing which could not have been maintained for long, relying on specially chosen stokers using hand-picked coal. They might mount more or heavier guns, but they sacrificed ammunition capacity. Unfortunately for Barnaby, appearances particularly affected politicians, and he made little effort to defend his ships. On 1 July 1885 a change of Government brought a new First Lord, Lord George Hamilton. He fired Barnaby and appointed the man who was building the hottest cruisers: White. The same change of Government removed George Rendel, who might have defended Barnaby, from the Board. Ironically, once in office White found himself explaining both to the outer world and to the Royal Navy exactly the facts of life which Barnaby should have used to defend himself.

When the Admiralty hired White back as DNC, as compensation Armstrong was allowed (perhaps encourged) to hire Philip Watts, who might otherwise have succeeded Barnaby in White's absence. Watts became DNC upon White's retirement in 1902.

Armstrong's products were impressive.[20] The firm began not as shipbuilders, but as gun-makers. They used a barge to test their largest guns offshore, and their engineer George Rendel realized that a self-propelled version could be built as an inexpensive coast defence craft. It became the basis for a series of 'flat-iron gunboats' in both British and foreign (particularly Chinese) service. They were promoted on almost the same basis as the much later missile boats. They could strike heavily, but they offered small targets, and several could (at least in theory) work together. The next step was to make the gun platform much more mobile, mounting unusually heavy guns on board small fast seagoing ships. Like the *Mersey*s, these were not cruisers in the accepted sense; they were something new. They were protected by a thin underwater deck and by water-excluding material at the waterline. The first such ship, *Arturo Prat*, was laid down for Chile in 1879 and then bought by Japan as *Tsukushi*. China, which had previously bought Armstrong gunboats, bought two more. The Chilean *Esmeralda* and Italian *Bausan* were much-expanded versions.

White's Fast Cruisers: The *Medea* Class

White understood that he had been hired to produce spectacular cruisers. During his brief tenure at Armstrong he had been responsible for several small fast cruisers, beginning with the Italian *Dogali*. Just as his predecessor Barnaby had developed a series of ships based on the *Iris* and *Mercury*, White produced a series based on his new fast cruisers *Medea* and *Medusa*.

Some time in the autumn of 1885 the new DNC White met the Board in the Controller's room, offering a very fast cruiser on roughly the displacement of the existing *Comus* class. Referring to that class, he called the new design the 'modern corvette'.[21] Much attention had been lavished on large cruisers, but little had been done to modernize corvettes: the only small fast cruisers were torpedo cruisers. The proposed ship would have three times the power of a *Comus* (for a trial speed of 19kts rather than 15kts), and much more efficient triple-expansion engines fed by boilers which could use forced draught. The partial deck (1½in) of the earlier ship would be replaced by a full deck (1in flat, 2in slopes). With slightly more bunker capacity (200 tons normal, 500 maximum), she would have three times the range at the same speed. To get all of this White lengthened the ship by 35ft, eliminated sheathing over his steel hull, eliminated the heavy rig (which made sense given the great steaming range of the new ship), adopted twin screws, and reduced armament weight.[22] She still had an impressive six 6in, plus no fewer than six above-water torpedo tubes in four torpedo rooms, all protected by the ship's upper deck.

The new cruiser would be the first of a standard type suited both to trade protection and to fleet work as a super torpedo cruiser (the Board was unhappy with the torpedo cruisers described in the next chapter). Finally the Royal Navy would have a cruiser which could outrun big liners: White claimed that only four ships in the entire British merchant fleet were as fast, and they were nearly twice as long and five times the displacement. No other merchant fleet in the world had more than two or three ships approaching the speed of the new cruiser. The cruiser would cost no more than half as much as the liner (but that also meant that she was about two and a half times as expensive per ton. In wartime an enemy might seize the fastest British liners and turn them into commerce raiders, but White's new cruiser was a good antidote. The liners were faster in bad weather, but they were entirely unprotected. White's ship had a high forecastle to enable her to drive into a sea at high speed, plus a high poop. The combination of high speed and extreme steaming range suited the new ship to trade protection.

At this time 19kts or 20kts was considered an extraordinary cruiser speed, just as 15kts had been twenty years earlier. A first sketch design showed a length of 250ft and a displacement of 2070 tons (weight added up to 2018). Output would be 7500 IHP at forced draught or 5000 IHP at natural draught; speed was given as 18kts or 19kts. Under natural draught, which could be sustained, this ship would be as fast as *Mersey* or even *Iris* when the latter was under short-duration forced draught. Under forced draught the new cruiser would be faster than any warship yet tested – except for those White had designed and built at Elswick for the Austrian and Japanese navies.[23] White wanted to guarantee 19kts, so he told his assistant to lengthen the ship by 10ft (from 250ft to 260ft between perpendiculars) and to increase displacement to 2200 tons.[24] The ship had two boiler rooms (one funnel each) forward of an engine room divided by one transverse bulkhead. Magazines were at either end of the machinery spaces (duplicate magazines fore and aft were apparently still somewhat novel). A double bottom extended between the fore and aft magazines, under boilers and engines. It continued up around the machinery in the form of vertical bulkheads enclosing coal bunkers. The ship had a belt of coal extending up to the protective deck plus another such belt between the protective deck and the upper deck. The bunkers were all subdivided, and they were supplemented by cofferdams.

Two 6in guns were mounted side by side on forecastle and poop, with two more on the broadside. Oddly, the conning tower was placed between and just abaft the two forward guns, presumably to place it as far forward as possible and to keep the weights of the guns as far aft as possible. Nine 6pdr anti-torpedo (boat) guns were in ports under poop (two on the sides, one firing right aft) and forecastle, plus three on each side under the hammock berthing on the broadside. The ship also had two Gatlings in the tops, and six torpedo tubes.[25] While the design was being prepared, DNO suggested moving two of the chasers fore and aft to the broadside. White argued against sacrificing ahead fire. The added broadside guns would be much closer to the water, hence less useful in a seaway. Moving the bow chaser to the centreline would also block the conning tower. DNO argued that if the two forward waist guns were on sponsons, ahead fire would be strengthened. First Naval Lord Admiral Hood decided to keep White's gun arrangement first because he considered two guns high above water much better than one high and two low guns for chasing; because a single centreline gun would interfere with vision from the conning tower, wherever it was; and because a second broadside gun would interfere with the 6pdrs there. Hood also rejected the argument by Junior Naval Lord Captain William Codrington that the conning tower was so far forward (40ft from the stem) that steering from it would be difficult.

The hiccup was sufficient space for the crew: the designer balanced weights but not volumes. The smaller the ship – and this was an unusually small ship – the worse the space problem, partly because so much of the ship had to be filled with machinery. The greater the complement, the worse the problem. When White's assistant completed a sketch design in December 1885, it seemed that the ship would need a complement of 160 to 170, but there was space for only 140 men in hammocks, even when the torpedo rooms and the protective deck above the engines were included. Even then it might be necessary to remove the inner ends of the torpedo tubes

Armstrong Cruisers

The Chilean *Blanco Encalada* typified the Armstrong cruisers, with a pair of heavy guns at the ends and a protective deck (which is shaded here). This sketch shows her as built; it is taken from a paper by Philip Watts, Elswick's chief naval constructor, on the Elswick cruisers, published by the *Transactions of the Institution of Naval Architects* in 1899.

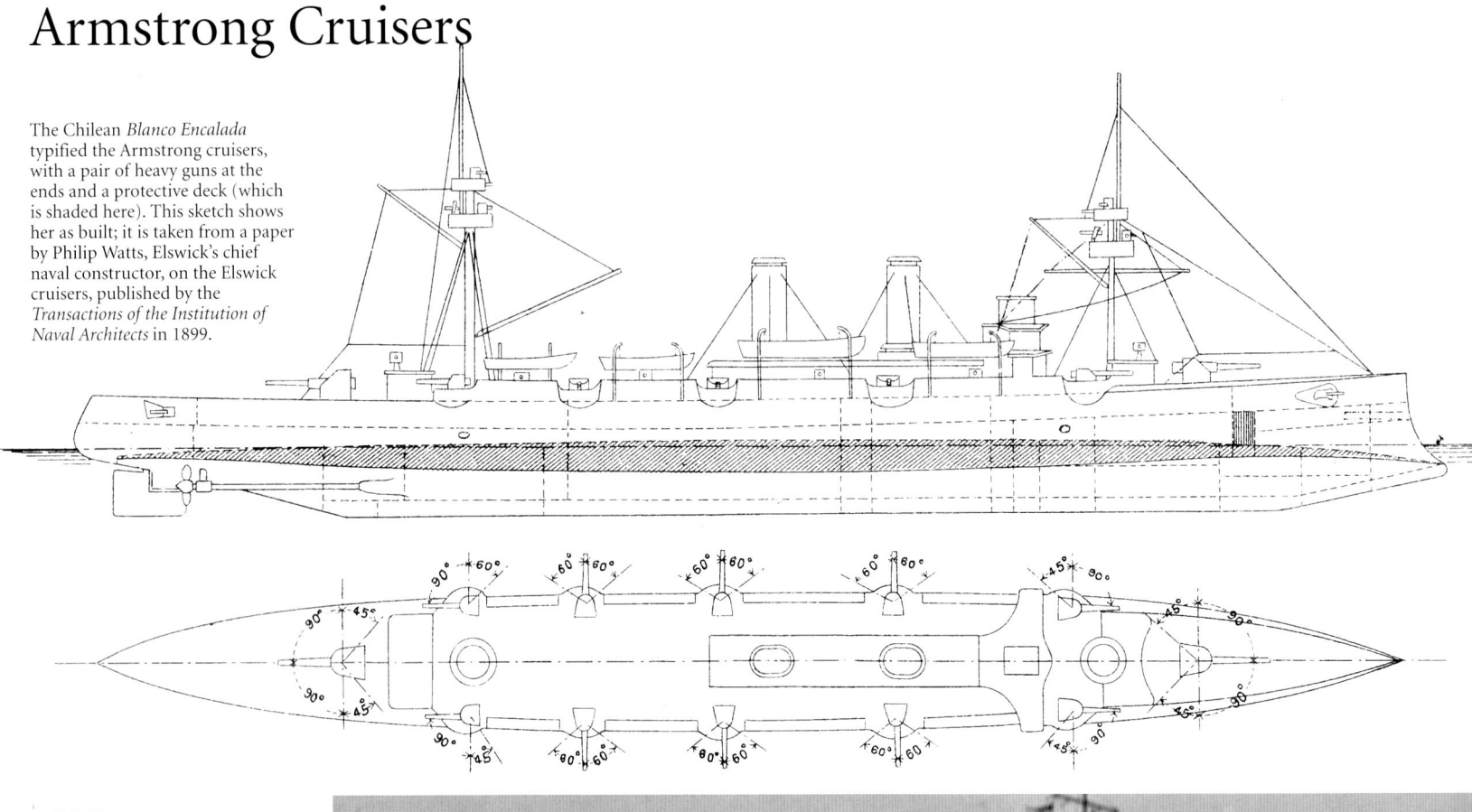

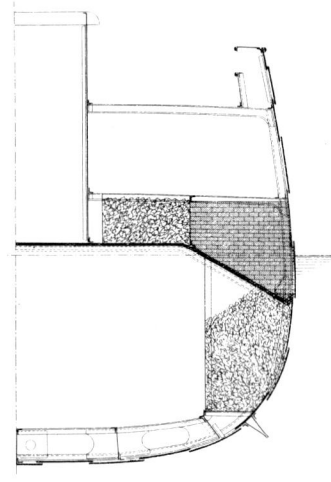

Blanco Encalada is shown in the 1930s (this photograph was submitted by the US Naval Attaché in Santiago on 6 November 1942). In effect she was a modernized equivalent to the heavy-gun Elswick cruisers of the 1880s: she had two 8in/40s at her ends plus ten 6in QF, twelve 3pdr QF, and ten 1pdr (in, among other places, her military tops) plus five 18in torpedo tubes. She displaced 4403 tons (but 4568 on trials: 380ft × 45ft 9in × 18ft 5in). On trial she made 22.78kts under forced draught (14,500 IHP). She was launched on 9 September 1893 and ran final trials on 29 May 1894. The Argentine *Buenos Aires* was similar, laid down as a stock ship in February 1893.

A cross-section shows the protective system adopted by Armstrong and, incidentally, by William White for Royal Navy cruisers. The fuzzier shading indicates coal to be used immediately, both above and below the protective deck. The brick-like shading outside an internal longitudinal bulkhead is either tightly packed coal (in White's Royal Navy cruisers) or water-excluding material, often called a raft body (in Elswick cruisers). In either case, it was not armour, which was limited to the deck below. This cross-section probably represented that of the Japanese fast cruiser *Yoshino*. It is taken from the 1899 paper on Elswick cruisers published in the *Transactions of the Institution of Naval Architects*.

FAST STEEL CRUISERS

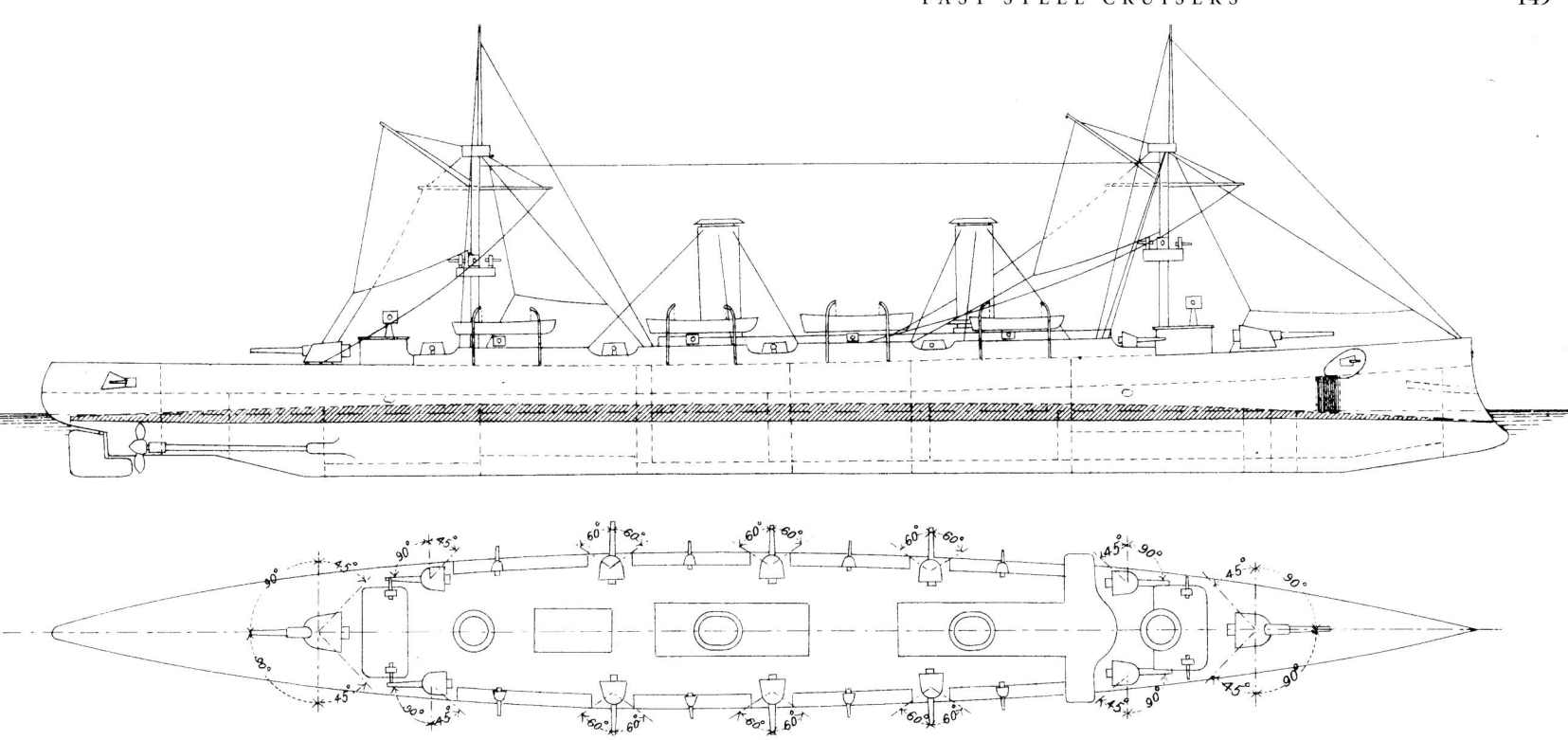

The Argentine *Buenos Aires* was broadly similar to the Chilean *Blanco Encalada*, with a similar battery headed by two 8in/45 with four 6in/45 and six 4.7in/45, all QF. She displaced 4620 tons (4788 tons on trial: 396ft pp × 46ft 6in × 17ft 4in). Estimated maximum power (forced draught) was 17,000 IHP, and natural draught power was 12,500 IHP. On trial she was not forced, making 14,000 IHP under natural draught for a speed of 23.2kts on a 12-hour run – the opposite of the typical totally unrealistic trial performance. The 8in/45 guns were semi-automatic (i.e., the force of recoil opened the breech), credited with a rate of fire of one round every 15 seconds, compared to one every 20 seconds for *Blanco Encalada*. *Buenos Aires* was laid down as a stock ship. This drawing is from the 1899 paper on Elswick cruisers by Philip Watts.

The Japanese cruiser *Yoshino* was a more lightly armed ship of unusually high speed. She was designed to meet an 1891 invitation to tender for a 4200-ton cruiser; the Japanese accepted Armstrong's proposal (modified in some ways) that November. She was longer than her predecessors, and introduced a full double bottom into Elswick cruisers. *Yoshino* had a 3ft deep raft body between her lower and protective decks. Design displacement was 4158 tons (4180 on trial: 360ft pp × 46ft 6in × 17ft). Armament was four 6in/40, eight 4.7in/40, twenty-two 3pdr, and five 18in torpedo tubes. She was designed to make 22.5kts on 15,750 IHP (forced draught). On trial she actually reached 23.031kts on 15,818 IHP. Natural draught output was 10,000 IHP for 20kts (on trial, 10,320 IHP for 21.614kts). For a time *Yoshino* was the world's fastest cruiser. During the Sino-Japanese War she was flagship of the 'flying squadron' that turned the flank of the Chinese line at the Yalu. She made a considerable impression with her all-QF armament, and it probably helped considerably that she was the only warship present with smokeless powder. The Japanese *Takasago* and the Chilean *Chacabuco*, both laid down as stock cruisers, were near sisters.

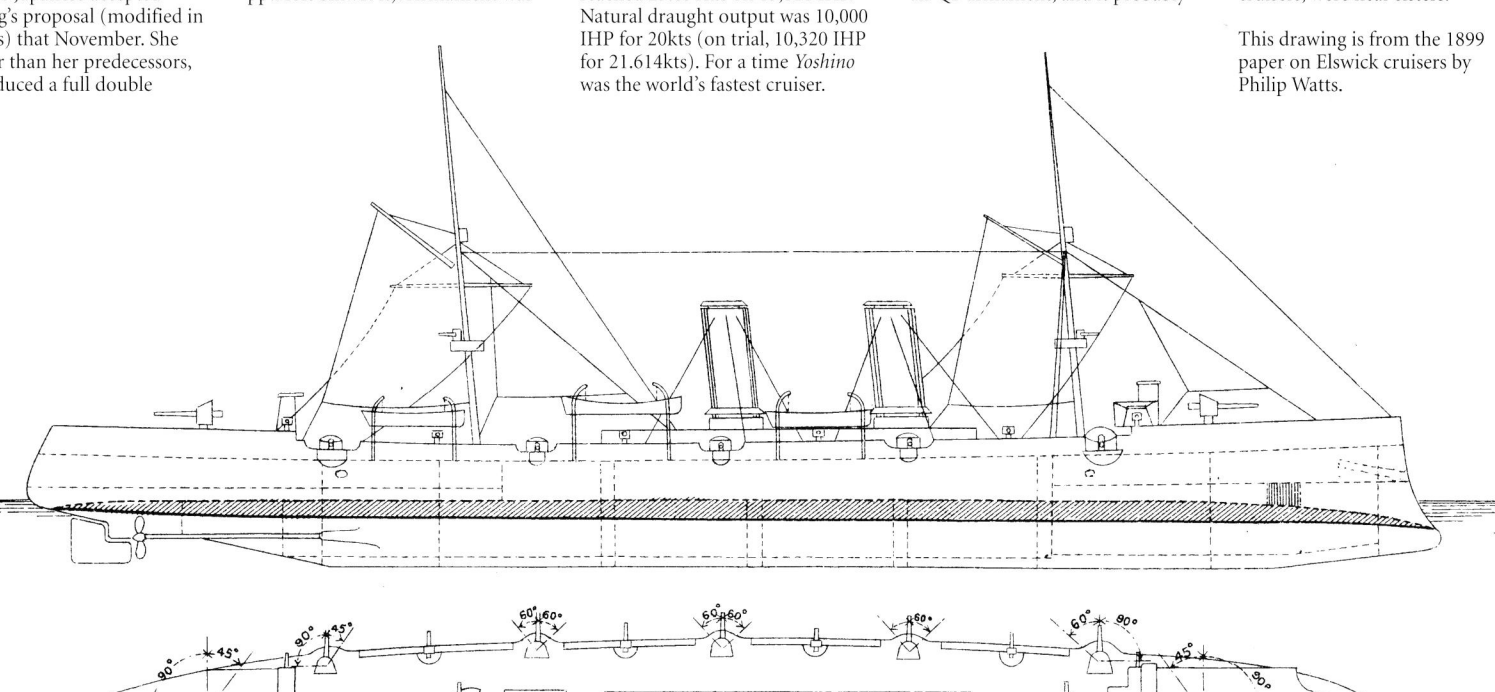

This drawing is from the 1899 paper on Elswick cruisers by Philip Watts.

RIGHT The Chinese cruiser *Yang Wei* in the Tyne before delivery. In effect she was the progenitor of Elswick cruisers. Armstrong began as a gun-maker, not a shipbuilder, and chief engineer George Rendel was initially interested in building the smallest platform which could support the most powerful gun – in much the way more modern designers have sought to place the most powerful anti-ship missiles on the smallest, cheapest platforms. The first step was a series of powerful coastal gunboats, some of which were built for China. The next step was an ocean-going gun platform. Although generally described as a cruiser, it was not intended for the usual cruiser duty of long-endurance oceanic patrol. *Yang Wei* was armed with two 10in and four 4.7in breech-loaders; she was credited with a speed of 16.5kts under forced draught. She was launched on 29 January 1881 and completed on 14 July of that year. The two Chinese ships (the other was *Cha'o Yung*) were preceded by the Chilean *Arturo Prat*. The latter was not delivered, either because the Chileans no longer needed her (after their success in the War of the Pacific against Peru) or because they ceased payment. She was sold to Japan and renamed *Tsukushi*. These ships displaced 1350 tons (210ft x 32ft x 15ft).
(National Maritime Museum PM2931-02)

LEFT The Romanian cruiser *Elisabeta* is shown at the opening of the Kiel Canal in 1895. She was at the low end of Elswick cruiser size, 1325 tons (222ft x 33½ft x 12ft). Her armament comprised four Krupp 5.9in guns backed by four 6pdrs and four 14in torpedo tubes. All of the guns were on the broadside (their shields are visible here). On trial she made 18.3kts under forced draught. *Elisabeta* was launched on 29 December 1887 and ran her final trials on 19 September 1888. The only smaller cruisers built by Elswick were the Spanish *Isla de Cuba* and *Isla de Luzon* (1038 tons, 185ft x 30ft x 11½ft) and the Brazilian *Republica* (1314 tons, 210ft x 35ft x 12¾ft).

RIGHT The Italian *Giovanni Bausan* was in effect a higher-performance *Yang Wei*, making 17.4kts under forced draught. Like the Chinese ship, she had two unusually powerful guns (10in/30), in this case backed by six 6in/26 and four 6pdr QF. There were also three 14in torpedo tubes (one submerged at the bow, two above water on the broadside). She displaced 3082 tons (280ft x 42ft x 18½ft). The Italians liked her enough to order four sisters built in Italy as *Etna*, *Vesuvio*, *Stromboli*, and *Ettore Fieramosca*. She was launched on 15 November 1883 and completed on 9 May 1885. She was slightly larger than, but overall similar to, the Chilean *Esmeralda* (completed 15 July 1884), which was sold in 1894 to become the Japanese *Izumi*.
(National Maritime Museum N05756)

FAST STEEL CRUISERS

ABOVE The Argentine *Nueve de Julio* began as a stock ship intended specifically to maintain the steady pace of work at Elswick. She was conceived as a repeat *25 de Mayo* (Elswick Yard No 541) rather than a repeat of the lower-performance HMS *Pandora* the yard had just built. She was laid down in February 1891 and offered to Argentina (which had bought the earlier stock ship which became *25 de Mayo*) in May 1892; she was launched on 26 July 1892. Unlike the earlier ship, she was armed entirely with QF guns: two 6in at each end and four 4.7in on each broadside, plus twelve 3pdr anti-torpedo guns and twelve 1pdrs, plus five torpedo tubes (bow and four broadside). She displaced 3557 tons (354ft × 44ft × 16½ft) and made 22.74kts under forced draught on trial (14,185 IHP). *Neuve de Julio* is shown at the Columbian Naval Review of 1893.

ABOVE In addition to *Dogali*, DNC William H White used the Austro-Hungarian *Panther* shown here as a demonstration of the kind of performance he could produce. *Panther* was launched on 13 June 1885 and ran final trials on 16 December. She was designed to make 18kts under forced draught (6500 IHP). White hoped for 19kts under forced draught, but neither *Panther* nor her sister *Leopard* attained it, the best result being 18.94kts on 6520 IHP (*Panther*). As a torpedo cruiser, she could be compared to Barnaby's *Archer*s. She was armed with two 4.7in (Krupp) and with ten 47mm Hotchkiss revolver cannon, plus four above-water torpedo tubes (bow and stern plus training tubes amidships). She displaced 1352 tons (224ft × 34ft × 14ft).

ABOVE USS *New Orleans* after her rearmament with 5in guns in 1907-8. She was typical of the small fast cruisers Armstrong built in the 1890s. She was laid down as *Amazonas*, the third of a batch of three cruisers for Brazil. Having left the Tyne for Gravesend on 3 March 1898, she was sold to the US Navy on 16 March; the United States was then in the midst of the diplomatic crisis which would soon lead to war with Spain. She was a sister to the Brazilian *Barroso*. A third ship, which never received a Brazilian name, was acquired by the US Navy as *Albany*. These ships displaced 3438 tons (330ft × 43ft × 16ft 10in); trial speed was 20.5kts on 7520 IHP (forced draught). Original armament was six 6in/50 (ends plus four sponsons), four 4.7in/50, and ten 6pdr QF plus three 18in torpedo tubes (one bow, two broadside).

ABOVE USS *Charleston* was built to Elswick plans as modified by Union Iron Works. Her two Elswick-built half-sisters were the Japanese *Naniwa* and *Takachiho*. All shared the basic Elswick formula of two heavy guns at the ends with lighter ones in the superstructure between them. *Charleston* herself was not particularly successful, her engines not performing very spectacularly. Her heavy guns were 8in/35s; the Japanese had 10.2in Krupps. Commissioned on 26 December 1889, *Charleston* was wrecked on Camiguin Island in the Philippines, 2 November 1899.

RIGHT The Italian *Dogali* (Armstrong Design 16) exemplified the new emphasis on small fast cruisers adopted by William H White as chief at Elswick. Unlike her predecessors, she had no very heavy guns, but only six 6in plus nine 6pdr and four 14in torpedo tubes. She displaced only 2050 tons (250ft × 37ft × 14½ft). On trials she made 19.66kts under forced draught. White laid down *Dogali* as a stock ship, i.e., without any order. He may well have seen her as a way of demonstrating what Elswick could do, hence of attracting widespread business. She was launched with the Greek name *Salaminia* because in December 1885 (she was launched 28 January 1886) the Greeks had an option on her. The Turks later also had an option, but she was completed in May 1886 without any owner. The Italians made the offer which secured her in January 1887. As DNC, White used *Dogali* to show that he could build a very fast cruiser for the Royal Navy; the result was the *Medea* class.

when the ship was not cleared for action. White seems to have hoped that the high forecastle and poop would provide sufficient accommodation, with natural light and ventilation. The irreducible part of the complement was an engine room complement of 71.[26]

First Naval Lord was pleased with the result, and recommended that two ships be built under contract under the 1886-87 program. The two ships would be contract-built, but there was no money that year, so the ships were shifted a year to 1887-88. Now the design could be developed further, before there was any need to produce detailed plans for bidders. By this time the ship was growing, and adding power to make up for greater displacement. A Legend dated 19 January 1886 showed another 5ft of length and a displacement of 2340 tons; the same power would drive the ship at the same speed, 19kts.

Deferment to the 1887-88 program suspended design work. In September 1886 White offered a somewhat larger hull carrying a 9000 IHP powerplant sufficient for 20kts with full (400 rather than 500 tons) rather than normal (200 tons) bunker load.[27] Extra power required longer piston strokes. Past engines had horizontal cylinders, which could fit below the protective deck. That limited piston stroke. High power demanded unacceptably high piston speeds within limited stroke length. White's solution was longer strokes: the cylinder heads would come above the protective deck. Vertical engines were described as more efficient and economical for continuous steaming.

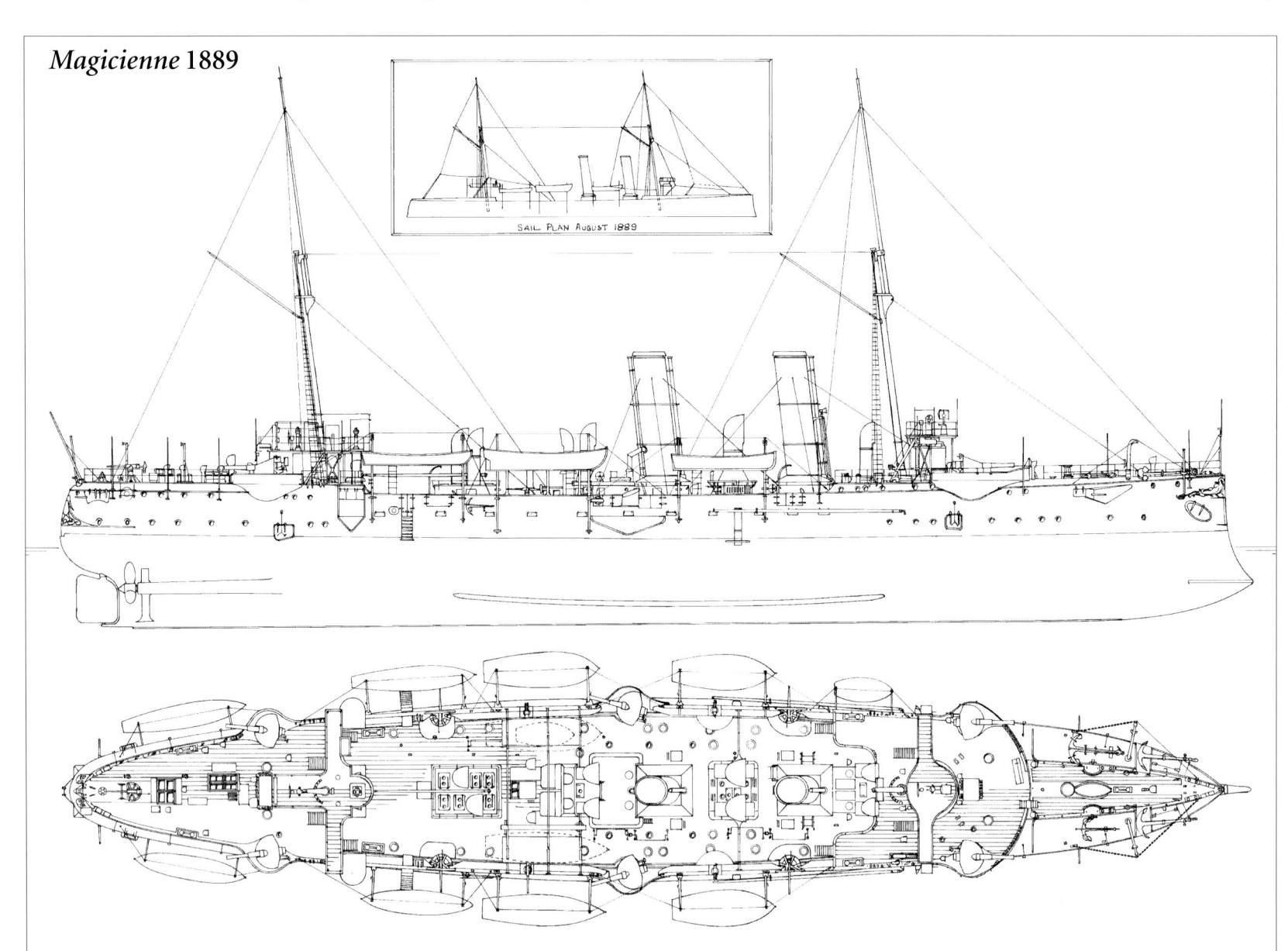

Magicienne 1889

SAIL PLAN AUGUST 1889

HMS *Magicienne* is shown as completed, August 1889. Unlike the first two ships of the class (*Medea* and *Medusa*) she had horizontal (vice vertical) compound engines. She and others of her class were normally conned from the after bridge. This class had the original 6in guns replaced by QF guns during refits in the 1890s, at which time the aftermost deckhouse in the waist was replaced by a low engine room skylight, and the 30ft steam cutter replaced by a 32ft steam cutter. The protective deck was 1ft above the mean waterline at its flat crown, the outer edge of the slope being 5ft below at the side. The 9pdr field gun was stowed on the forecastle deck to starboard of the foremast, and could alternatively be mounted on one of the pintles on either side of the foredeck. The 3pdr QF could be mounted on a steam launch or on a carriage (four light gun mountings could carry either a 3pdr or a machine gun). Two searchlights were mounted on short athwartships rails within the semi-circular embrasures at the fore end of the poop, a third being mounted on the forward bridge. Fixed torpedo tubes were mounted at bow and stern, with two swivelling mountings on each broadside. The light boat boom aft was usually dismounted and stowed on the starboard boat platform.
(A D Baker III)

Magicienne was contract-built and embodied all of William White's approaches to fast cruiser design. Upon completion in 1889 she went to the Cape station (1890-91) and then the North America and West Indies station (1891-6). After a short period at Devonport (1896-7) she returned to the Cape (1897-1901), returning to Devonport and to reserve (1901-4).

Making the cylinders vertical freed space below the protective deck for auxiliary machinery (such as generators), some of which had previously been unprotected. White later claimed that making the engines vertical also made for roomy stokeholds and a better arrangement to supply coal to them. White protected the protruding cylinder heads by wrapping 100 tons of vertical armour around them, to back up the protective coal.

The ship had to be made beamier to offset the topweight of the taller engines and their protection (initially 39ft). That in turn would cost a fraction of a knot (estimated speed with full bunkers was 19.6 rather than 20kts). The 39ft beam ship would displace 2720 tons, compared to the 2420 tons of the earlier version. Other improvements made by this time were provision of four rather than two trainable torpedo tubes on the broadside, electric lighting, and extended cofferdam protection.

The crucial issue was volume – space had to be found for everyone in the crew. White considered his ship a reasonable compromise. Any great increase in complement beyond 150 or 160 would demand a much larger ship. The powerplant would have to grow, and a point of balance would not be reached until the ship became much larger and more expensive. DNO challenged White's logic by demanding 188 men to serve the ship's weapons, more than in the entire complement White envisaged. White thought DNO based his figure on experience of large ships with ample space. With much the same battery, and with more torpedo tubes, HMS *Archer* made do with 140 men. The new ships should need even fewer, because they had better arrangements for passing ammunition. White's way out was to use some of the engine room complement to handle ammunition. In action about thirty engine room men would be used for other purposes, such as damage control and moving ammunition. On this basis, out of his complement of 160, White offered 81 men to man the guns, without counting 6 idlers. DNO still wanted another 107. Third Naval Lord (Controller) Admiral William Graham suggested 170 as a viable minimum complement.

Worse was coming. To serve the hungrier boilers of the new more powerful plant (9000 IHP), Engineer-in-Chief wanted 20 more men: complement rose to 190. The ship was so cramped that messing and sleeping space was found by sleeping some of the crew in the passage between the officers' cabins on the lower deck, and by messing as many as possible in the after torpedo room (which had been reserved for the ERAs). This arrangement was considered acceptable only because it was nearly impossible that the entire crew would have to find hammock space at the same time.

By late 1886, many new foreign cruisers could make 18kts or more, and the French were reportedly building fast second-class (2600-ton) cruisers. White could point directly to Armstrong cruisers (which he had designed) for China, Japan, and Austria, not to mention the new Armstrong stock cruiser (soon bought by the Italians as *Dogali*). He now considered 20kts imperative, so he offered 1½kts more with the previous full load of 400 tons of coal (carrying that much would have cost half a knot in the previous design). The ship could probably sustain full forced draught – full speed – for about 8 hours (there was enough coal for 48). The ship would sustain 17 to 17½kts indefinitely under natural draught: 400 tons

Medea in 1904 at the end of her career. Like *Medusa*, on completion she became RNR drill ship (in her case at Southampton), and she joined the Cruiser Training Squadron (1902-3) and then became seagoing tender to *Impregnable*.
(National Maritime Museum N01301)

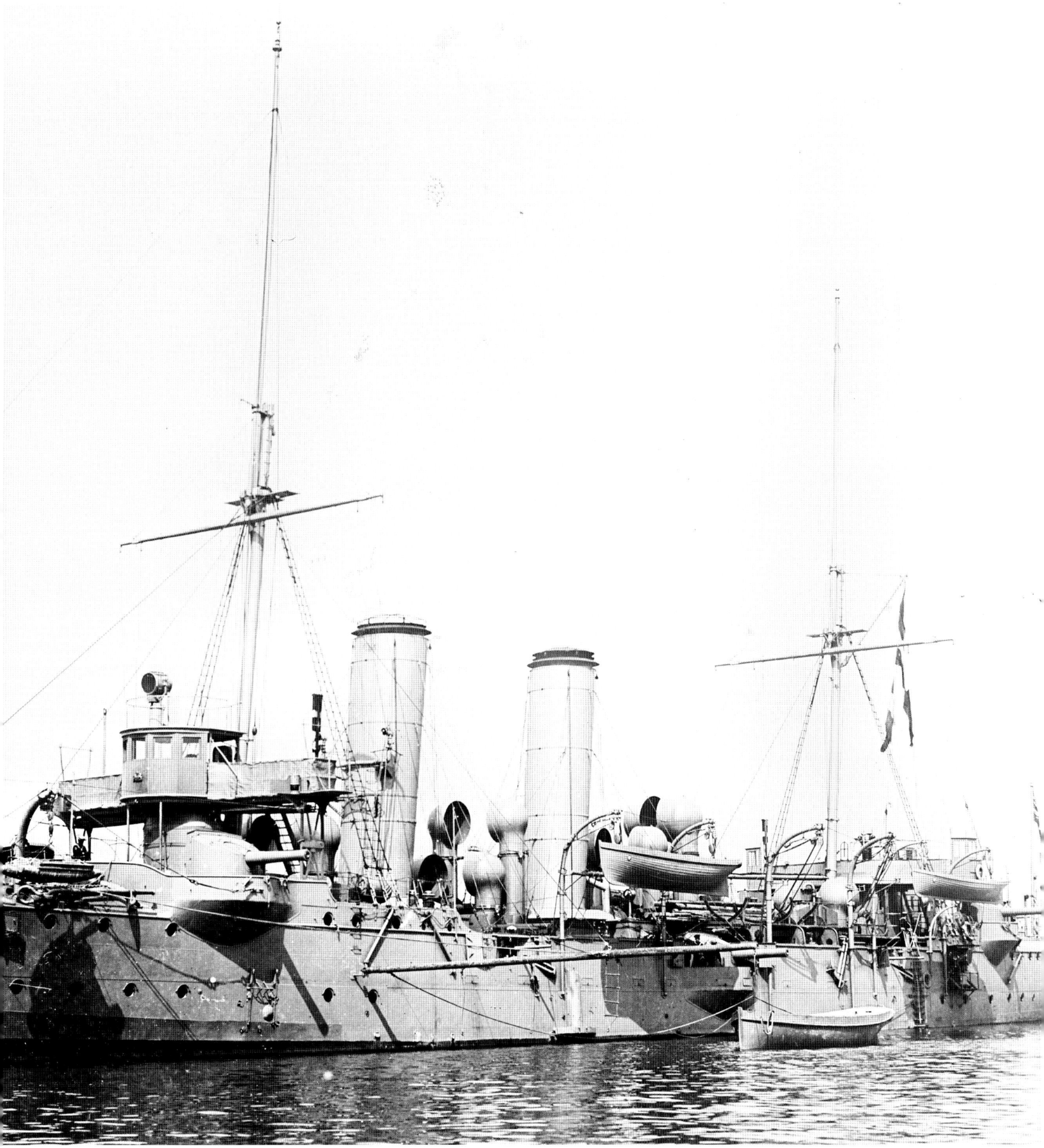

of coal would last 4 days, perhaps 1680nm.

Submitting a new (even if only a revised) design reopened the questions previously considered. New DNO Captain John Fisher (the future First Sea Lord) preferred six 4in guns to the two waist 6in, and 3pdr rather than 6pdr QF guns. Third Lord Graham preferred White's six 6in. First Sea Lord Hood approved the design, which he thought would be invaluable to protect trade against fast enemy cruisers. He was somewhat nervous about the new engine arrangement: if three ships were to be built, two should have horizontal engines (and anti-fouling sheathing) and one should have vertical engines and an unsheathed bottom. Lord Charles Beresford, by this time Junior Naval Lord, agreed: vertical engines were unproven, and it would be best to build different ships with both types of engine. Only the first two ships, built at Chatham, had vertical engines: *Medea* and *Medusa*.

The 1887-88 Estimates provided enough money to build, not three, but five ships, the first two at Chatham. Three ships built under contract were Admiral Hood's alternative: horizontal engines and sheathing (which added a foot to their beam and cost a quarter-knot). The horizontal engines weighed 20 tons more and the ships had considerably heavier hulls (totals of hull and protection were 1490 rather than 1360 tons), so displacement of the three contract cruisers was 2950 rather than 2800 tons. HMS *Medusa* (vertical engines) maintained 18kts with natural draught, with all 400 tons of coal on board.

Because the ships carried most of their guns on forecastle and poop, in theory they were sloops (Commanders' commands), but that was unrealistic. First Sea Lord Hood understood as much, classifying them in the Fourth Rate (corvettes), as Captains' commands. This discussion may have helped motivate the classification of such ships simply as cruisers. Initially the ships were grouped with the *Mersey*s and *Leander* as second-class cruisers, but they were so much smaller that on 23 May 1890 First Lord Hamilton decided that they should be grouped with the small cruisers of the next chapter in the third class. However, the *Medea* design led directly to the designs of a series of increasingly powerful second-class cruisers, with which they are properly grouped.

Apollo Class
No further small cruisers were included in the 1888-89 program, but by late 1888 the 1889 Naval Defence Act had been proposed to the Cabinet. That October it included 9 first-class cruisers (described in a later chapter), 29 second-class cruisers, and 4 third-class cruisers (*Pallas* class, described in the next chapter), plus torpedo gunboats.

Work on a follow-on to the *Medea* class began in the summer of 1888, looking forward to the 1889-90 program. By this time the Royal Navy had quick-firing 6in and 4.7in guns. The Board wanted DNO's single 6in guns at the ends (QF rather than the slow-firing BL of the past), but with three 4.7in QF on the broadside instead of two 6in. The QF guns had considerably more ammunition.[28] White later said that armament weight increased about 30 per cent. More guns required more men, and QFs needed their ammunition passed much more quickly. Estimated complement grew to 210.

All of this meant a ship somewhat longer and larger than *Medea*, but with the same speed and coal endurance. Displacement increased further because for the first time a Board Margin was demanded. The new hull could either be scaled up from the new Australian third-class cruiser (see the next chapter) or modified from *Medea*. White thought she would be longer, perhaps 285ft rather than the 265ft of *Medea* (or the 215ft of the Australian ship), which would make up for the additional displacement; in August he wrote that the 9000 IHP of the *Medea* would surely suffice.

This modified *Medea* (3200 tons, 290ft long) was presented to the Board on 27 September 1888.[29] Greater length would make it easier to maintain speed in a seaway. It was now possible to insert an athwartships coal bunker between the two midships stokeholds, making it easier to keep steaming for an extended period. Bunker capacity was equal to the Board Margin. If White could keep the margin from being expended, the ship would have enough coal to steam more than 10,000nm at 10kts, an extraordinary figure.

Junior Naval Lord (Admiral Charles F Hotham) considered the ship too short; he wanted 315ft (and 2ft less beam), so that she could steam against a head sea and maintain her speed. The bow was too low: he wanted more sheer for driving into a head sea. Speed had to be more than what was achieved on trials in smooth water. White countered that lengthening the ship without increasing beam would make her too weak. Anything beyond 300ft (which he accepted) would be too expensive. The ship's 90ft forecastle (with 5ft sheer) should be enough for seakeeping. The extra 10ft added 5ft to the engine room and another 5ft to the store rooms.

Hotham also wanted an auxiliary boiler to drive the ship's generators, pump up her torpedoes, wash decks, water ship, work fire mains, and condensing. 'Otherwise one of the main boilers will always be at work causing a larger consumption of coal and much more heat than necessary from the quantity of hot water in the ship, a very important matter in the Tropics.' White considered it impossible to provide an auxiliary boiler in so small a ship. Hotham also considered the ship undermanned: no provision was made for men out of action due to sickness. On most stations the percentage of sick was 8 to 10. That would add another 20 to a complement already well beyond that which had squeezed the *Medea*s so badly. First Naval Lord Admiral Hood wanted four 6pdr QF substituted for the 3pdrs under the forecastle and poop. That was no problem.

By this time the Naval Defence Act was well in train. The cruiser now being designed would be built in considerable numbers – 25 were planned. When he reviewed the Board's comments, White could point to a need to limit unit cost.

The sketch design received the Board Stamp on 24 October 1888, details being left to further discussion with DNC. The Board approved the sheer draught and midship section on 18 December.[30] Including wood and copper sheathing (and Board Margin) the ship would displace 3600 tons, far from the 2200 with which the *Medea* design began. Due to delays in completing the 6in QF gun, the first fifteen ships would have the earlier slow-firing BL gun, which weighed 20 tons less. Moreover, the designers had not taken the details of the QF gun sufficiently into account.[31] There was abortive interest in substituting two 4.7in QF for each 6in gun. Due to delays, only two ships of the new class, *Aeolus* and *Brilliant*, received the 6in QF gun.

Twenty-one of these *Apollo* class cruisers were built under the 1889 Act. They were considered successful. They could steam continuously at over 16.5kts. Additions after design were held to about 80 tons, including heavier boilers and increased complement. As a result, ships could carry 550 tons of coal at the intended draught.

On an experimental trip to Malta in May 1891, *Latona* rolled only 6 or 7 degrees, albeit in a way (attributed to vibration at high speed) that made some veteran officers and men unexpectedly seasick. After rounding Cape St Vincent she encountered a short head sea, which she rode comfortably without racing her engines or taking anything more than spray forward; she had to reduce speed by only a knot. On passage home through the Bay of Biscay, she was very steady; Controller (who was embarked) thought most ships would have rolled more with so heavy a swell on her beam and quarter. He thought her roomy, well ventilated, and comfortable, with plenty of room for her crew. On a later run in Brazilian waters HMS *Sirius* was overrun by a sea on her quarter, shipping much water over her bulwarks. With all doors shut and with no men on the upper deck she would have been perfectly comfortable, but as it happened one man was swimming on the quarter deck, and many others were up to their middles on the other side, hanging on to what they could clutch. 'But she is a beautiful ship, her motion so easy – so steady compared with what the *Cleopatra* would have been. Her motion is quick, but very easy – she rolled 30 degrees to one side and 24 degrees to the other but so easy were her rolls that you could scarcely credit she was rolling so much. She steered beautifully and every place below was tight and dry.' She was so free of vibration that her captain could write easily while she ran at 19.4kts, his table being near the 6pdr gun port aft, immediately over the screws.

White was particularly proud that the ship lost so little stability if she retained her waterline coal – her protective belt – while burning the coal lower in the ship.

Astraea Class
The other eight Naval Defence Act second-class cruisers were built to an improved *Apollo* design, forming the *Astraea* class. White was already aware that the waist of the ship might be wet, so in November 1889, before any *Apollo*s had been completed, he suggested joining poop and forecastle with what he called a spar deck.[32] The 4.7in guns in the waist would go up to that deck, and screens fitted to protect guns, ventilators, and boats from the blast of the 6in guns when they fired at extreme angles. Raising so much weight (130 tons) from main to spar deck (i.e., upper deck) demanded 3ft more beam for stability. To preserve a hull form adapted to high speed the ship had to be lengthened by 20ft. These changes would cost 400 tons, but the extra length would very nearly balance off the greater displacement: the engines used in HMS *Apollo* would still drive the ship at nearly 20kts. White considered it unreasonable to protect a 4000-ton ship no better than a 2900-ton *Medea*, so he proposed thickening the deck over boilers and engines to 1½in on the flat and 3in on the slope. That would cost 100 tons. EinC wanted heavier boilers (50 tons).[33] Lengthening the ship by 10 or 15ft and increasing her beam to 46ft (to gain sufficient stability) would provide the necessary weight. White submitted his plan for an Improved (flush-decked) *Apollo* in January 1890. The change would cost £25,000.

DNO (Fisher, who would become Controller in February 1892) fastened on the wetness DNC mentioned. He would have preferred to keep the waist guns below any flush upper deck, because there they were protected from splinters generated when shells hit the boats and other gear above, but the guns were not on sponsons (which were considered impractical), and they needed large ports. The ships would be a lot larger than the *Apollo*s, so Fisher asked whether they could carry a more powerful torpedo armament, as in the *Medea*s. These ships had the new 18in torpedoes, ordered about August 1889.

As of early 1890 plans called for twelve ships, of which three were to be laid down at Royal Dockyards under the 1891-92 program. A sketch design was quickly submitted, followed by a sheer draught and midships section for Board Stamp (April 1890). By that time model tests had shown that the beam amidships should be increased (by 2ft 10in) to secure a fine entrance, adding about 100 tons. White increased scantlings, since the longer hull would be more highly stressed. He expected 18¼kts using natural draught (7000 IHP) and 19½kts using forced draught with moderate air pressure (9000 IHP). In smooth water continuous speed should be 15½kts (3750 IHP). Compared to a sheathed *Apollo* the new cruiser would lose only about a quarter-knot. There was much more space than in an *Apollo*, so although normal coal capacity (the amount carried on trial) was the same 400 tons, full capacity was 800 (later that was increased to 1000 tons). Roominess made it possible to accommodate more men. Complement was set at 265, but there was space for 20 per cent more as supernumeraries. The design received the Board Stamp on 2 May 1890.[34] By this time the 6in QF was available. Ships carried 250 rounds per 6in and 300 per 4.7in gun. There were eight 6pdr QF guns. The torpedo battery was two fixed tubes (one in the bow) and two trainable tubes, with 12 torpedoes.[35]

White was right: the ships were no slower than the *Apollo*s. On forced draught trials, HMS *Cambrian* made 20.44kts on 9259 IHP. With natural draught (7164 IHP), she made 19.4kts. The first captains were enthusiastic. For example, Rear Admiral Kennedy flew his flag in HMS *Bonaventure* on the India station. He described her (October 1894) as 'a perfect fighting machine', her only defects being poor accommodation for officers and poor ventilation in the engine room ('not fit to live in ... the efficiency of the ship is imperilled because the stokers cannot stand the terrible heat and succumb and are invalided wholesale') and in some officers' cabins aft ('really uninhabitable in this climate ... not one can sleep below – they sleep on deck which is pleasant enough whilst the weather is fine but would be impossible in the wet season'). The faults 'in this beautiful ship' were minor: 'she is fully able to wipe out the whole of the French squadron in these seas, either collectively or individually ... it is a grand thing to be able to steam from one end of the station to another at good speed regardless of weather etc.'

Talbot Class
The *Astraea* seemed like such a good design that it was further developed into a New *Astraea* (*Talbot* class). Looking toward the 1893-94 program in August 1892, White told his assistants to sketch a 5000- to 5500-ton improved *Astraea* with a heavier armament, including, if possible, submerged broadside torpedo tubes. The main limit was that total outlay, including

armament (not ammunition), should not exceed about £250,000 – something over twice the price of a *Medea* less than a decade earlier (the cost of an *Apollo* was given as £185,000, and that of a sheathed *Astraea* as £210,000 to £213,000). Initially it was intended that the new cruiser should be as fast as the *Astraea*s and *Apollo*s. The machinery would be similar to that in the earlier classes, which was considered unusually successful in giving long endurance at high speed. Greater dimensions should give the new cruisers a greater bunker capacity than the *Astraea*s, about 1100 tons – as in 7700-ton *Edgar* class first-class cruisers.

The *Apollo*s were just coming into service, so White was still looking back at the seakeeping problems of the *Medea*s. He wanted a long high forecastle plus a flush deck (over the waist, extending into the poop) as was being provided in the larger cruisers *Royal Arthur* and *Crescent*. That would give about 4ft more freeboard forward, for all the chase guns.

White went out of his way to reject the side armour the French were beginning to place on their large cruisers (beginning with their *Dupuy de Lôme*). He emphatically preferred his combination of coal, decks, and water-excluding material.

The question was how to allocate the working margin of cost compared to an *Astraea*, £35,000 to £40,000. White thought the best way would be to increase armament and to thicken the protective deck over boilers and engines by about 50 per cent. He proposed to add three more 6in guns, for a total of five, retaining the six 4.7in QF of the earlier ship. She would keep the single bow chaser (but on the high forecastle), backed by two sided upper deck 6in guns, with cut-outs allowing them to fire right ahead. The much lower poop would carry a pair of 6in guns, on the sides, as stern chasers. White also hoped to get two submerged torpedo tubes forward.

To get all of this White would lengthen the ship again, to 350ft, and accept the draught of an *Orlando*. The much larger ship could accommodate more powerful machinery; White hoped for (and Engineer-in-Chief said he could get) 9600 IHP at forced draught and 8000 IHP at natural draught.[36] White hoped for 19kts using natural draught, as in the *Astraea*. The sketch design was submitted to the Board for approval on 25 May 1893. By this time the Royal Navy was experimenting with water-tube boilers; the new cruisers might use them in place of the usual cylindrical fire-tube type. White compared the new

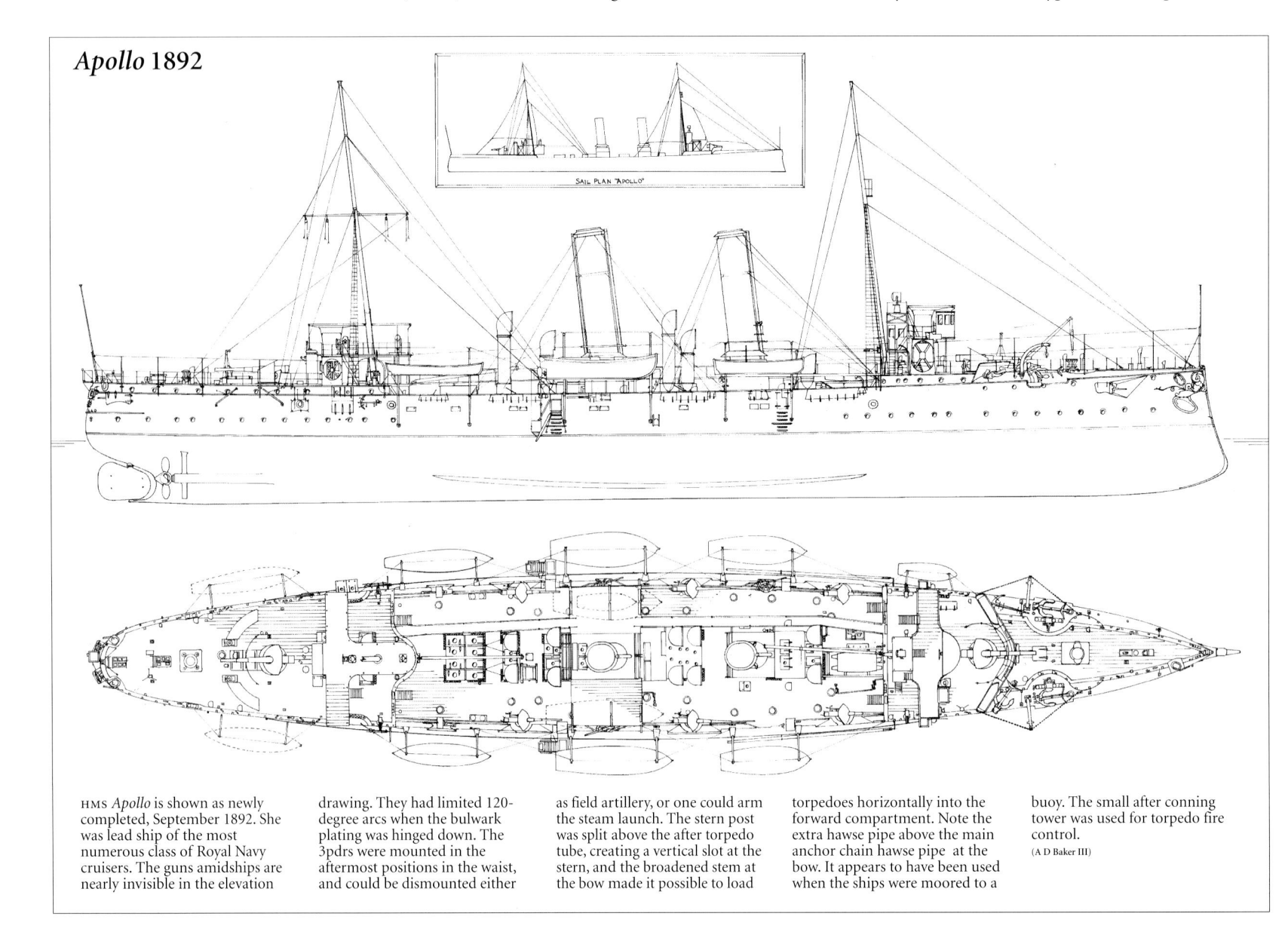

Apollo 1892

HMS *Apollo* is shown as newly completed, September 1892. She was lead ship of the most numerous class of Royal Navy cruisers. The guns amidships are nearly invisible in the elevation drawing. They had limited 120-degree arcs when the bulwark plating was hinged down. The 3pdrs were mounted in the aftermost positions in the waist, and could be dismounted either as field artillery, or one could arm the steam launch. The stern post was split above the after torpedo tube, creating a vertical slot at the stern, and the broadened stem at the bow made it possible to load torpedoes horizontally into the forward compartment. Note the extra hawse pipe above the main anchor chain hawse pipe at the bow. It appears to have been used when the ships were moored to a buoy. The small after conning tower was used for torpedo fire control. (A D Baker III)

ship with French and US second-class cruisers, particularly USS *Olympia*, Dewey's flagship a few years later at Manila Bay.[37] Four *Talbot*s were built under the 1893-94 program.

By this time private builders were producing faster cruisers. White felt compelled to explain that Royal Navy requirements limited maximum speed. Private firms accepted risks on trial which the Royal Navy would not and could not. Royal Navy trial speeds might appear moderate, but they were far more meaningful: British ships could sustain their speed. Export and other foreign cruisers used fast-running lightly-built short-stroke engines, typically placed completely under the protective deck, where they were not accessible. British engines ran more slowly (hence tended not to fall apart), and they were far more accessible, as their bigger cylinders rose out of the protective deck. Because export builders provided a smaller reserve of boiler power, their boilers were more highly forced on trial, which much reduced their lifetime. In some foreign ships (including those for export), the boilers nearly filled the ship, much of their outside surfae being only a few inches from the outer skin. That precluded the cellular double bottom which had saved British ships from serious damage when they grounded, as HMS *Apollo* recently had. Overall, foreign ships were more lightly built, hence much less durable. White's own examination of recent French cruisers showed him that 'French designers have gone much further than we should be prepared to follow in the reduction of scantlings; and it is a matter of common knowledge that troubles have arisen in many ships'. Similarly, equipment and armament weight had been cut:

The *Apollo* class cruiser *Latona* as completed. Like the *Medea*s, she initially had no charthouse. Ships of this class seem to have had charthouses by 1897-98. Upon completion *Latona* was placed in reserve at Portsmouth (1892-1902), though she made a special voyage to Bermuda in 1900. She was made a submarine depot ship in 1902-3, then used for particular service in 1904 and for the Newfoundland Fishery Squadron in 1905-6. She was converted into a minelayer at Portsmouth in 1906-8, then laid up with a nucleus crew until 1912. She joined the minelaying squadron of the Second Fleet in 1912-14. She was based at Dover in 1914-15, and then in the Mediterranean in 1915-18. There she laid the mines which damaged the German battlecruiser *Goeben* and sank the cruiser *Breslau* on their 1918 sortie. She was sold at Malta in 1920.
(ONI Farenholt collection from NHHC)

Brilliant is shown in 1904 with a new wireless gaff and a bridge semaphore (a 1902 photo, in which she is in Victorian rather than grey livery, shows the gaff but not the bridge semaphore; she does have a searchlight atop her charthouse). Other photographs of ships of this class suggest that gaffs were generally fitted by about 1905-6 (*Melampus* showed it with funnel bands in a photograph dated, possibly in error, 1904; she had no bridge semaphore). Upon completion *Brilliant* was held in reserve at Chatham in 1893-1901. She was then assigned to the Cruiser Squadron (1901-3) and to the South Atlantic (1903-4). On her return she became RNR drill ship at Southampton (1904-5). She was assigned to 4th Cruiser Squadron on the North America and West Indies station (1906-11) and then to the new Third (Reserve) Fleet 1911-14. After war broke out, she was assigned to North Sea patrols. She became a depot ship on the Tyne in 1914-15 and at Lerwick in 1915-18, and was then expended at Zeebrugge as a blockship.

(National Maritime Museum N01321)

Sappho shows tall masts for wireless (no gaff) in 1912 (they were already present in 1908). Note the canvas windscreen to the compass platform atop her charthouse. On completion she was held in reserve at Chatham (1892-1901), during which time she carried troops in 1895-96. She was then assigned to the Cape station in 1901-2, returning to Chatham in 1902-3 and becoming the RNR drill ship in the Firth of Forth in 1903-5. She was then assigned to the Newfoundland Fisheries in 1906. She returned to reserve with a nucleus crew at Chatham in 1906-7, and was mobilized for the North America and West Indies station in 1907-10. She returned home to the 4th Division (reserve) at Portsmouth (1911). After that she was tender to the flagship of the First Battle Squadron of the Home/Grand Fleet (1912-15), being laid up for subsidiary duties with the Grand Fleet in 1915-18. She was converted into a blockship, but broke down en route to Ostend in May 1918.
(National Maritime Museum N01350)

Iphigenia with a charthouse, probably about 1897-98. Her trials photograph (1896) shows the charthouse. An 1899 photograph of HMS *Pique* seems to show the semaphore on top of the charthouse in 1899. After completion she remained in reserve at Portsmouth 1892-97 until assigned to the China Fleet (1897-1900). She then returned to Portsmouth (1900-1903, with special service in 1901-2) before returning to China (1903-6) followed by special service. She was converted into a minelayer at Chatham in 1906-7, then laid up with a nucleus crew at Portsmouth (1907-8) and the Nore (1909-12). She was then assigned to the minelaying squadron of the new Second Fleet (1912-14). She was based at Dover in 1914-15, then in North Russia in 1915-16 and in the White Sea in 1917. In 1918 she was stripped as a blockship for the 23 April 1918 Zeebrugge Raid, being expended with her sisters *Brilliant*, *Intrepid*, and *Sirius*. The Admiralty selected a total of five *Apollo* class cruisers as potential blockships, three for Zeebrugge (*Intrepid*, *Iphegenia*, and *Thetis*) and two for Ostend (*Brilliant* and *Sirius*). As modified for Zeebrugge the blockships were armed with their three foremost guns (one 6in, two 4.7in). This represented rearmament in the case of minelayers. Additional conning and steering positions were fitted. Masts were cut down, and smoke generators installed. Scuttling charges were emplaced in the double bottom. The ships were given additional protection in the form of concrete at the bows (with more concrete aft to balance it) and around the machinery and the steering lines. Bags of dry cement were placed so that they would become sodden as the ships sank, hampering salvage. Open spaces amidships were filled with rubble. They were stripped of auxiliary machinery and also of metals which the Germans needed, such as copper and brass. Weight had to be controlled, because for Zeebrugge maximum draught was 18ft 6in; for Ostend it was 22ft.

Hermione 1896

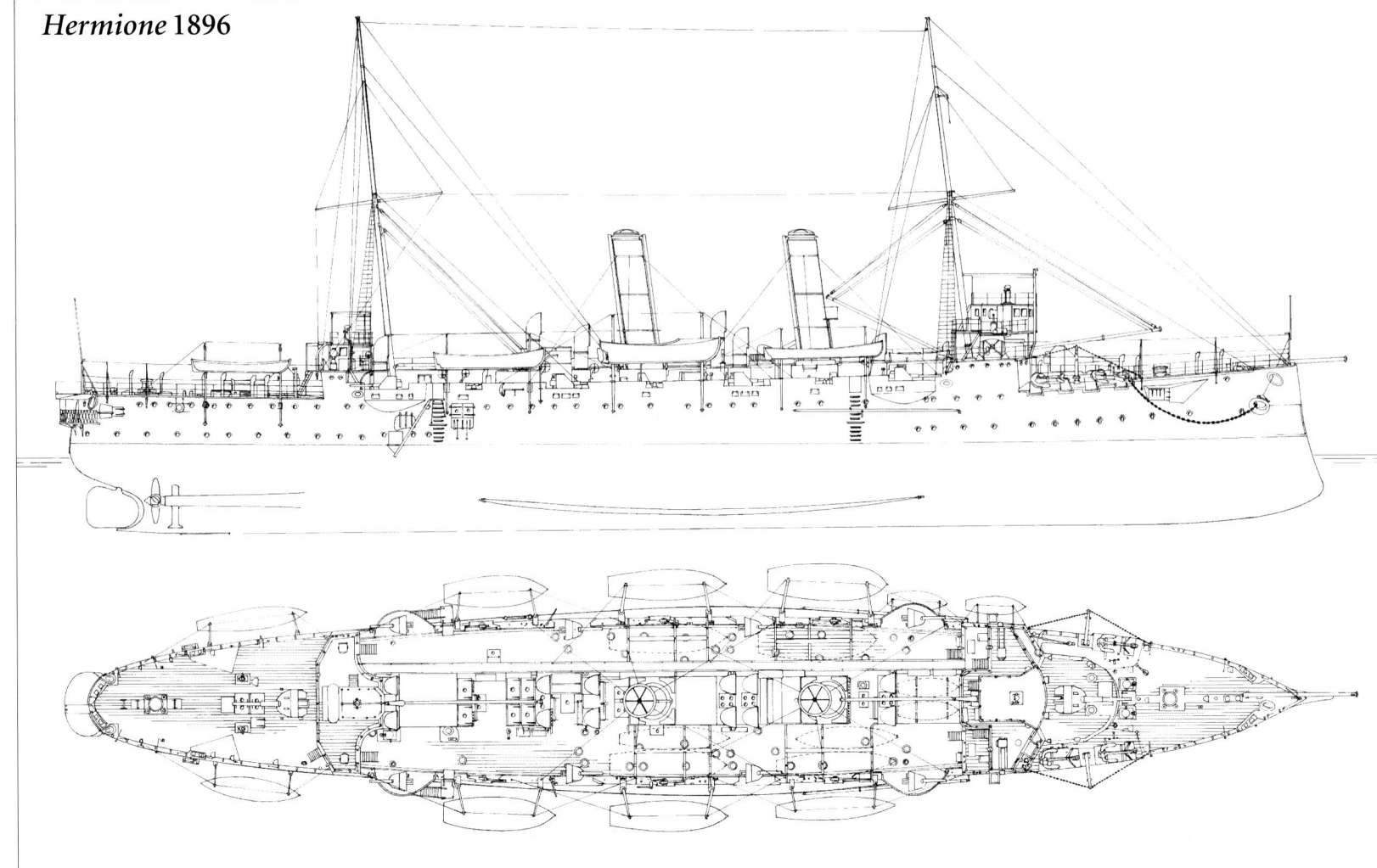

HMS *Hermione* is shown in January 1896, as completed. Bow torpedo tubes were removed soon after completion. Few changes were made while on active service, other than adding radio aerials and equipment. At times small upper yards were fitted to both masts. By 1907 a crow's-nest or rudimentary fire control platform was fitted to the foremast. Two searchlights were mounted behind the doors shown on the ship's sides. Those on the after superstructure were fixed, but those on the bridge forward could be moved outboard on rails for use. There was a small torpedo fire control tower atop the after superstructure. In the plan view, boats are shown in solid lines as swung out for harbour use and in dotted lines in their stowed positions. One of the two 16ft dinghies could alternatively be slung from portable davits on the starboard side of the hull abreast the bridge.
(A D Baker III)

foreign cruisers often carried many fewer rounds than did the British.

Having been in the business of producing flashy export cruisers, White spoke with real authority. Foreign navies which bought or built lightweight speed machines were well aware of their limitations, and they were never worked hard after running trials. In some cases (not specified) ships never developed even half the nominal power achieved on trial.

Later ships, beginning with HMS *Juno*, formed a sub-group (initially called New *Talbot* class). The chief potential improvements were water-tube boilers and fighting tops. With water-tube boilers the centre of gravity of the machinery was about 1¼ft higher, so the ship had to be made a foot beamier, 55ft (the stability of the *Talbot*s was considered 'none too good'). In January 1894 it was decided that, although the first ships would have conventional boilers, all of the New *Talbot*s would have the increased beam. Displacement would be about 5750 tons. It was estimated that on the same machinery weight (900 tons) water-tube boilers would generate 10,000 IHP.

Five New *Talbot*s were built under the 1894-95 program:

Forte is shown in 1909 with an extemporized spotting top forward, and a canvas-covered foretop. *Hermione* had no top, but had an aft-facing range drum on her foretop (to give ranges to the upper deck battery). On completion she went to the Mediterranean (1895-98, detached to the Cape 1897), after which she refitted at Chatham (1898-99) and then returned to the Cape (1899-1907). She was reduced to reserve with a nucleus crew at Portsmouth (1907-9) before returning to the Cape station (1909-13). She was laid up in the Medway (Kethole Reach) in 1913 and sold the following year.
(National Maritime Museum N01387)

The *Astraea* class cruiser *Hermione*, prior to 1904 when she was painted grey. Upon completion she joined the 'Flying Squadron' (1896), after which she served with the Channel fleet (1896-98) and then the China Fleet (1898-1901). She was refitted at Malta in 1901-2, then assigned to the Mediterranean Fleet 1902-4. She was reduced to reserve with a nucleus crew at Portsmouth (1904-7), but then sent out to the Cape station (1907-9). She returned home to the new Third (reserve) Fleet (10th Cruiser Squadron, 1909-13), service including airship trials at Barrow in 1910-12. She was on the North America and West Indies station in 1913-14 (4th Cruiser Squadron). Beginning in 1914 she was depot ship for patrol vessels at Southampton; she was burnt out in 1916, but remained in service.

Cambrian in Australian waters. She went to the Mediterranean upon completion (1894-97) and was refitted at Devonport upon her return. She was then assigned to the Cruiser Training Squadron (1899-1900) and was flagship of the South East Coast of America squadron (1901-3), after which she was assigned to the South Atlantic station (1903-4). After a Haulbowline refit (1905) she went to the Australia station (1906-13; she was flagship in 1913). She was paid off in 1914 to become stokers' training ship at Devonport (renamed *Harlech* in 1915).
(Allan C Green, courtesy of State Library of Victoria)

Bonaventure in tropical livery. Upon completion she became flagship of the East Indies station (1894-97). She returned home for a refit (1897-98), then went to the China Fleet (1898-1901), during which she grounded on the east coast of Korea on 5 July 1899 (she was repaired at Hong Kong). After a Devonport refit (1901-3) she went to the Pacific (1903-4) and then to the China Fleet (1904-6). She was converted to a submarine depot ship at Haulbowline in 1906-7.

Talbot is shown rearmed with an all-6in battery, with both her previous fighting tops removed. In 1909 *Talbot* showed only the fore spotting top, and no fighting top aft. *Dido*, *Minerva*, and *Talbot* had large spotting tops on their foremasts. Some ships (*Diana*, *Dido*, *Doris*, *Isis*, *Juno*, *Minerva*, and *Venus*) had small canvas tops protecting somewhat enlarged foretops (but no permanent vertical-sided structure). The after fighting top (emptied by 1905) may have been used as an after spotting top. In 1911-12 *Dido* had curtains atop her forward fighting top.
(National Maritime Museum N29433)

Venus, *Diana*, *Juno*, *Dido*, and *Isis*. Plans to equip them with water-tube boilers were dropped partly to allow construction on time. They did have fighting tops carrying 3pdr QF guns.

Hermes Class

The next stage was an Improved *Talbot* (*Highflyer*) built under the 1896-97 program (the gap after the *Talbot*s was due to construction of the four *Arrogant*s described in the next chapter). In effect the 1896-97 ships were the last three *Talbot*s. By 1896 considerable experience had been gained with water-tube boilers, particularly the French Bellevilles in the torpedo gunboat *Sharpshooter* (the big cruisers *Powerful* and *Terrible*, the first large British warships so equipped, had not yet been completed). The three ships, which formed the *Highflyer* class, had the new type of boiler. Individual Belleville boilers were more compact than the cylindrical type, so the modified design had three stokeholds and three rather than the previous two funnels. As previously estimated, water-tube boilers offered 10,000 rather than 8,000 IHP with natural draught, and full power for 8 hours instead of 9600 IHP with moderate forced draught for four hours. That might increase speed to nearly 20½kts, about ¾kt faster than what the *Talbot*s could achieve under forced draught. The ships could probably steam continuously at 7500 IHP, giving 18½kts in smooth water with a clean bottom, about half a knot faster than a *Talbot*.

Similarly, experience with four-cylinder engines showed that they were a desirable substitute for the three-cylinder type of earlier ships. They ran at higher speed, hence with a shorter stroke, and therefore could be placed entirely under the protective deck, saving weight and money. Given the more compact

Juno 1897

HMS *Juno* is shown soon after completion, September 1897. This class was unusual among British pre-1900 cruisers in having most of the conning tower forward of the bridge structure to give the occupants a much less encumbered view. A small lightly protected torpedo fire control tower was located at the after end of the after superstructure. The 6in mounts on the stern could be trained 30 degrees (19 degrees after the 1904 rearmament) across the centreline, so that at least three 6in could be trained on nearly all bearings. The broadside 4.7in guns were limited to 120-degree arcs. The six 12pdrs in the waist and the 3pdrs in the fighting tops were apparently normally fitted with shields. All ships of this *Eclipse* (or *Talbot*) class except HMS *Eclipse* were rearmed with eleven 6in guns in place of the original mixed battery. Rearmament required adding small sponsons to the waist positions to provide clearance for the larger gunshields. The after four sets of boat davits had to be moved slightly aft from the positions shown in the drawing. A rangefinder was added atop the charthouse. *Juno* was reboilered (with B&W water-tube boilers) when she was refitted (completed 1904). The anchor-handling boom stepped to the fore edge of the conning tower is omitted in the plan view.

(A D Baker III)

Eclipse, the name ship of her class. On completion she became flagship of the East Indies station (1897-1900). She returned home for a Chatham refit (1900-1901), and then went to the China Fleet (1901-4). She returned to the Devonport reserve (1904-5). After that she was the cadet training ship (based at Bermuda) attached to the North America and West Indies station (in the 4th Cruiser Squadron, 1905-6). She returned to the Portsmouth reserve (1906-7). She was then attached to the Royal Naval College at Osborne (1907-12). She then joined the new Third (reserve) Fleet at Portsmouth in 1912-13. Assigned to Devonport in 1913-14, she escorted the new Australian submarines *AE 1* and *AE 2* to Singapore in 1914. On the outbreak of war she joined the 12th Cruiser Squadron in the Western Channel, capturing two German merchant ships (on 10 August and 10 September 1914). She was accommodation ship for submarine flotillas in 1915-18.

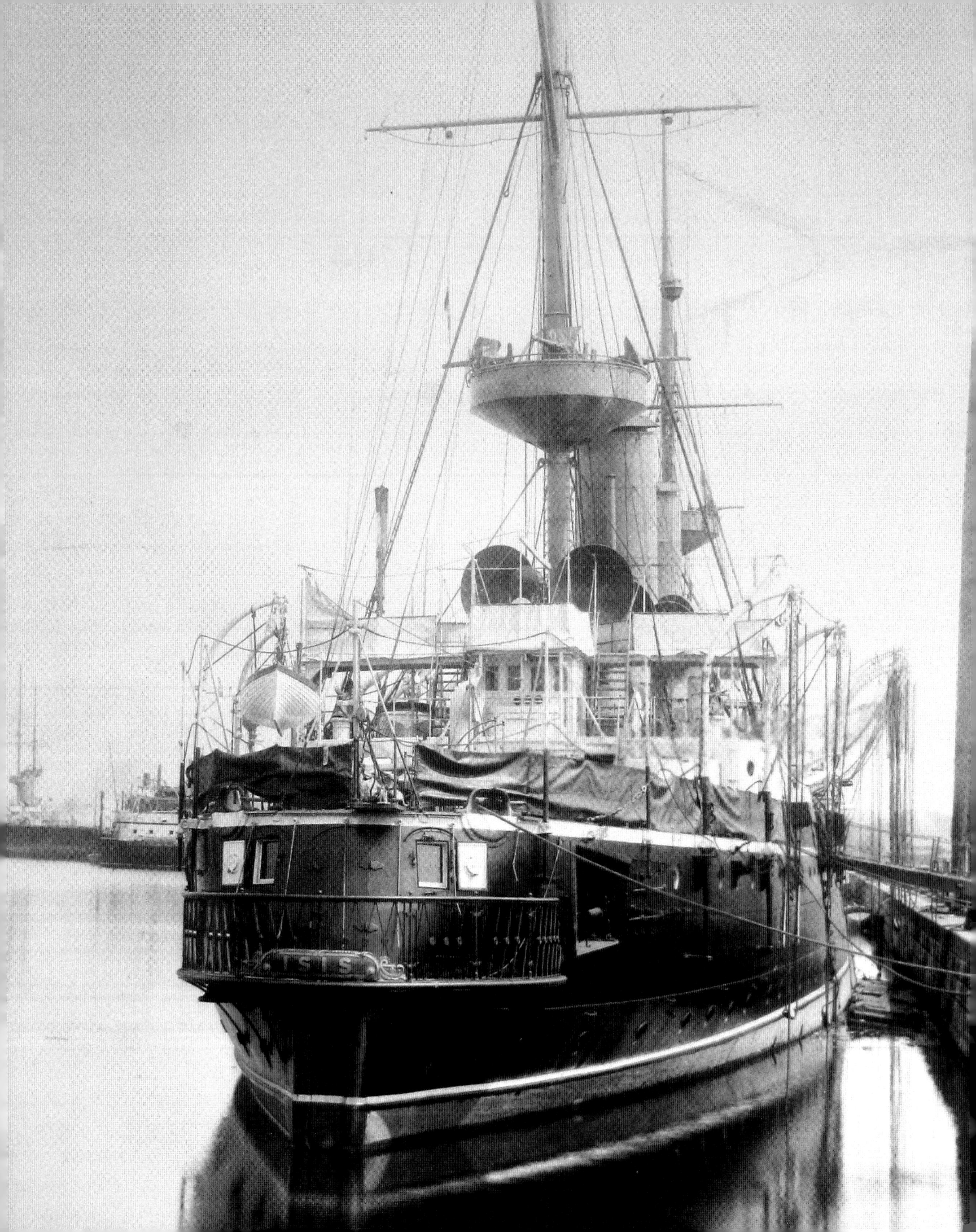
ISIS

Isis, showing bow and stern details. On completion *Isis* was assigned to the Mediterranean (1898-1901); she was detached to China in 1900 to help put down the Boxer Rebellion. She returned to Chatham (1901-2), and became tender to HMS *Britannia* as cadet training ship in 1902-5. She was then assigned to the North America and West Indies station (4th Cruiser Squadron: 1905-7) and to the Home Fleet Battle Squadrons in 1909-10. She was then assigned to the new Third (reserve) Fleet in 1911–14 at Devonport (attached to the 7th Battle Squadron in 1912). On the outbreak of war she joined the 11th Cruiser Squadron (West Coast of Ireland patrol), capturing a German merchant ship on 10 August 1914. She was assigned to the North America and West Indies station in 1915-18, and in 1919 was at Invergordon.

Highflyer as built in Victorian livery. On completion she joined the Cruiser Training Squadron (1899-1900). She then became flagship of the East Indies station (1900-1904) and later cadet training ship for the North America and West Indies station (1904-6). After a brief period of reserve with a nucleus crew at Devonport (1906), she went to the East Indies station (1906-8). She was then reduced to reserve with a nucleus crew at Devonport (1908-10) and became part of the new Third (reserve) Fleet (1910-11). She was flagship of the East Indies squadron (1911-13) before returning to the Third Fleet (this time at Chatham) in 1913. She was training ship for Special Entry cadets in 1913-14. On the outbreak of war she joined the 9th Cruiser Squadron in the mid-Atlantic, disabling the German armed merchant cruiser *Kaiser Wilhelm der Grosse* on 27 August 1914. In 1914-16 she was part of the 5th Cruiser Squadron (based in the Cape Verde Islands) operating in mid-Atlantic. She served in West African waters in 1916-17, and was flagship of the North America and West Indies squadron in 1917, and then on the East Indies station in 1918-21 (flagship in 1919-21). She was sold at Bombay in 1921.

powerplant, bunker capacity might be increased to 1200 tons.

There was clearly no space for more guns on the upper deck, and it was 'most undesirable' to carry them on the main deck. However, 100 tons could be used to substitute 6in for 4.7in QF guns in the broadside positions, giving a total of eleven such guns and far more firepower. That also greatly simplified ammunition stowage. DNO needed 20 more men, so estimated complement rose from 450 to 470. In so large a hull, that was no problem. The normal coal supply in a *Talbot* was 550 tons, but if the Board wanted to carry 50 per cent of the total on trials, then it could easily be increased to 600 tons.

White and his colleague Engineer-in-Chief Durston submitted the project to the Board in an October 1896 memo. The net increase of 30 tons was drawn from the unallocated Board Margin. The ships were counted as repeat (but modified) *Talbot*s, the design receiving the Board Stamp on 12 November 1896.[38]

In 1898 DNC proposed rearming the *Talbot*s and the *Arrogant*s, which were about the same size. DNO proposed rearming the *Talbot*s with new Vickers 6in guns. Both proposals were dropped as too expensive (for all the *Talbot*s, about as much as buying a new cruiser) and because it seemed undesirable to put ships out of action for long enough. First Naval Lord Admiral Sir Frederick William Richards suggested that money be provided in the 1899-1900 Estimates to rearm two ships of each class (it is not clear what the final battery was to have been). Controller was less enthusiastic. The plan died because there was no urgent need, and no money.

Challenger Class

Work on a further second-class cruiser, to be built under the 1899-1900 program, began in mid-1899, with estimates for a modified *Hermes* (*Highflyer*) with more powerful machinery (12,500 IHP, 1020 tons). Remarkably, this ship replaced a project for a small fleet scout cruiser, as explained in the next chapter. Several modified hull forms were considered, the hope being that the ship would make 21kts on her higher power while also recovering sufficient stability, given the high centre of gravity of the water-tube machinery. By February 1900 a 355ft hull had been sketched, and expected power was 13,000 IHP.[39] Bellevilles had not yet realized their promise, and the US-developed Babcock & Wilcox (B&W) was an attractive alternative. Although it required more space, Engineer-in-Chief was impressed by its success on board the torpedo gunboat *Sheldrake*. That justified installation in the sloop *Espiegle*. The new second-class cruiser seemed to be the appropriate trials ship. Compared to Bellevilles, B&Ws required about 10ft more length and 200 tons displacement, costing ⅓kt in speed.

A single design was prepared, suited to either B&W or Belleville boilers. It was 5ft longer than *Hermes*, and 2ft beamier (to preserve stability), and it would displace about 250 tons more. They were expected to cost no more than £300,000 – £50,000 more than the outer limit set for *Talbot*, the basis of the design. The output of 12,500 IHP would be barely enough for 21kts, so the designers gave full speed as 20¾ to 21kts. Anything more would have required another full boiler room.

Hermes 1903

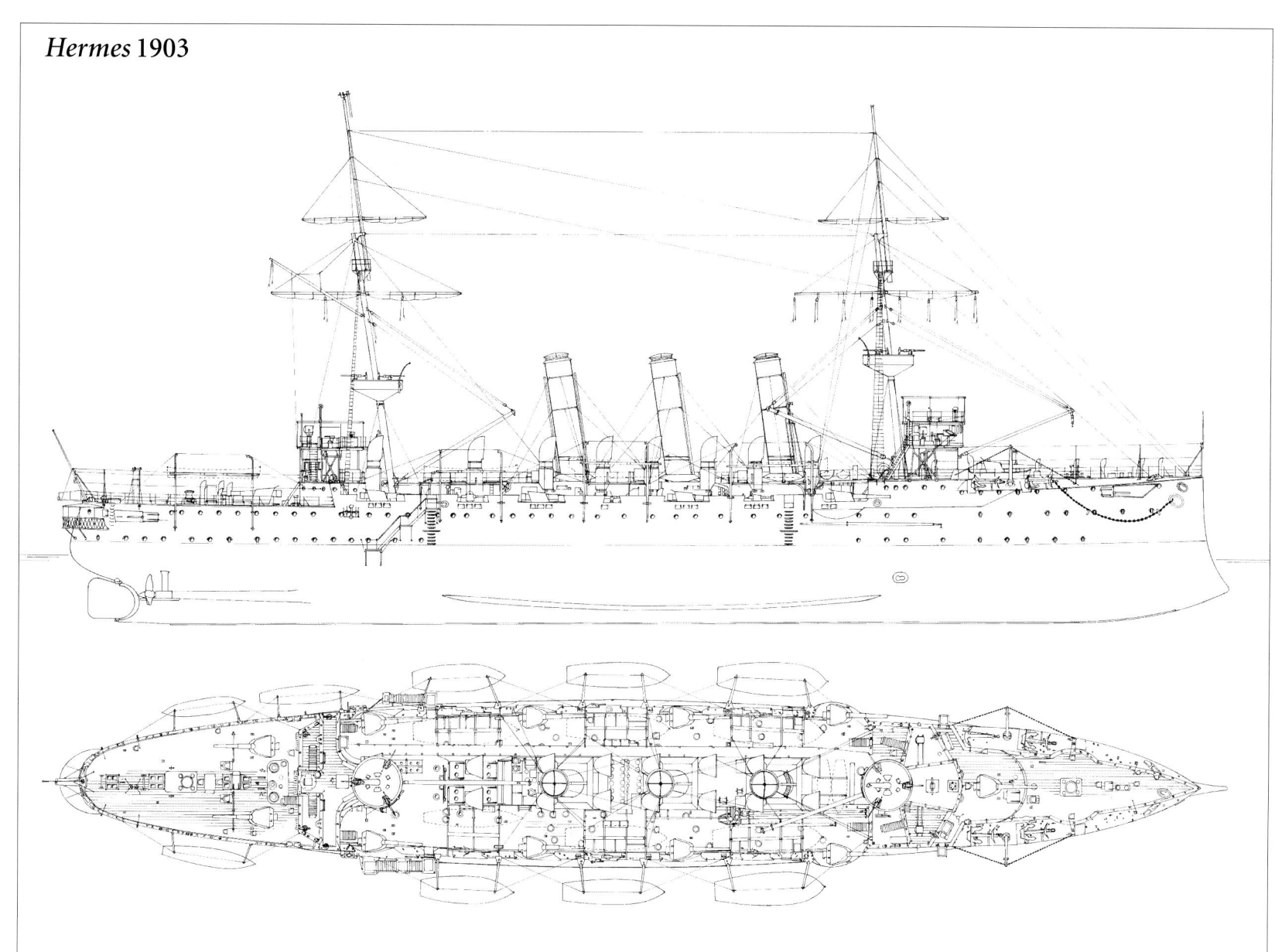

HMS *Hermes* is shown as fitted, April 1903; she had been completed in October 1899. She was in effect an *Eclipse* using water-tube boilers (hence her three funnels), with the engines of the *Arrogant* class, and with 6in more beam. She had two fighting tops and she lacked the fixed stern torpedo tube of the earlier ships. Photographs show that the hull was copper-sheathed to the trim line of the elevation drawing. The four 12pdrs in the waist had topless shields, but not the dismountable 12pdr 8cwt gun, which could be mounted to port or, as shown here, to starboard. Although the ship was given two Maxim machine guns, as-fitted plans show six mounting positions. Note the sixteen identical-height cowl ventilators to the engine and boiler rooms. In the plan view, the circular shapes abaft the second and third funnels are stowage for the smaller cowl ventilators used when the ship went to action stations. Also visible on the plan view are one boat mounting for the 12pdr 8cwt gun and four for 3pdr or Maxim guns. At sea the 27ft whaler was stowed with the 13.5ft balsa raft atop the 36ft pinnace to port of the fore funnel. The two 30ft cutters were carried slung outboard and could not be stowed on the boat skids. No rigging plan for this class has survived, and the plan views did not show the fittings for standing rigging for the mainmast. These were therefore estimated based on the rig of the *Eclipse* class and photography. By 1904 or shortly thereafter, radio antennas had been fitted, with the attendant gaff topmast to the mainmast. It was needed to provide clearance for the rotating semaphore at the masthead.
(A D Baker III)

Model tests showed that the hull form was slightly more efficient than that of *Hermes* above 16kts, and slightly less efficient (i.e., needing more power) below. Continuous sea speed was given as only half a knot greater than that of *Hermes*, because the B&W plant was expected to produce only 70 per cent of maximum power on a sustained basis, compared to 75 per cent in *Hermes*. Longer machinery spaces in much the same hull length left no great margin for magazines and holds. Armament matched that of *Talbot* and *Hermes*, except that the new ship would have a more recent type of 6in gun, and 7 rather than 10 torpedoes.[40]

The design received the Board Stamp on 8 June 1900, two *Challenger* class cruisers being built under the 1900-1901 program. *Challenger* had the planned B&W boilers, but some time after mid-1900 it was decided that *Encounter* should receive Dürr boilers instead.[41]

The *Challengers* marked the end of the series of medium fast cruisers begun with the *Medea*s about fifteen years earlier. In the process their size and cost roughly doubled, under what seems to be an iron law of warship development.

Challenger in Milford Sound, New Zealand, some time before 1919 (and probably before 1914). Note the forward-facing range drum on her foretop. She has her full armament of eleven 6in guns, though not all of the waist guns are easily distinguished.
(Allan C Green, courtesy State Library of Victoria)

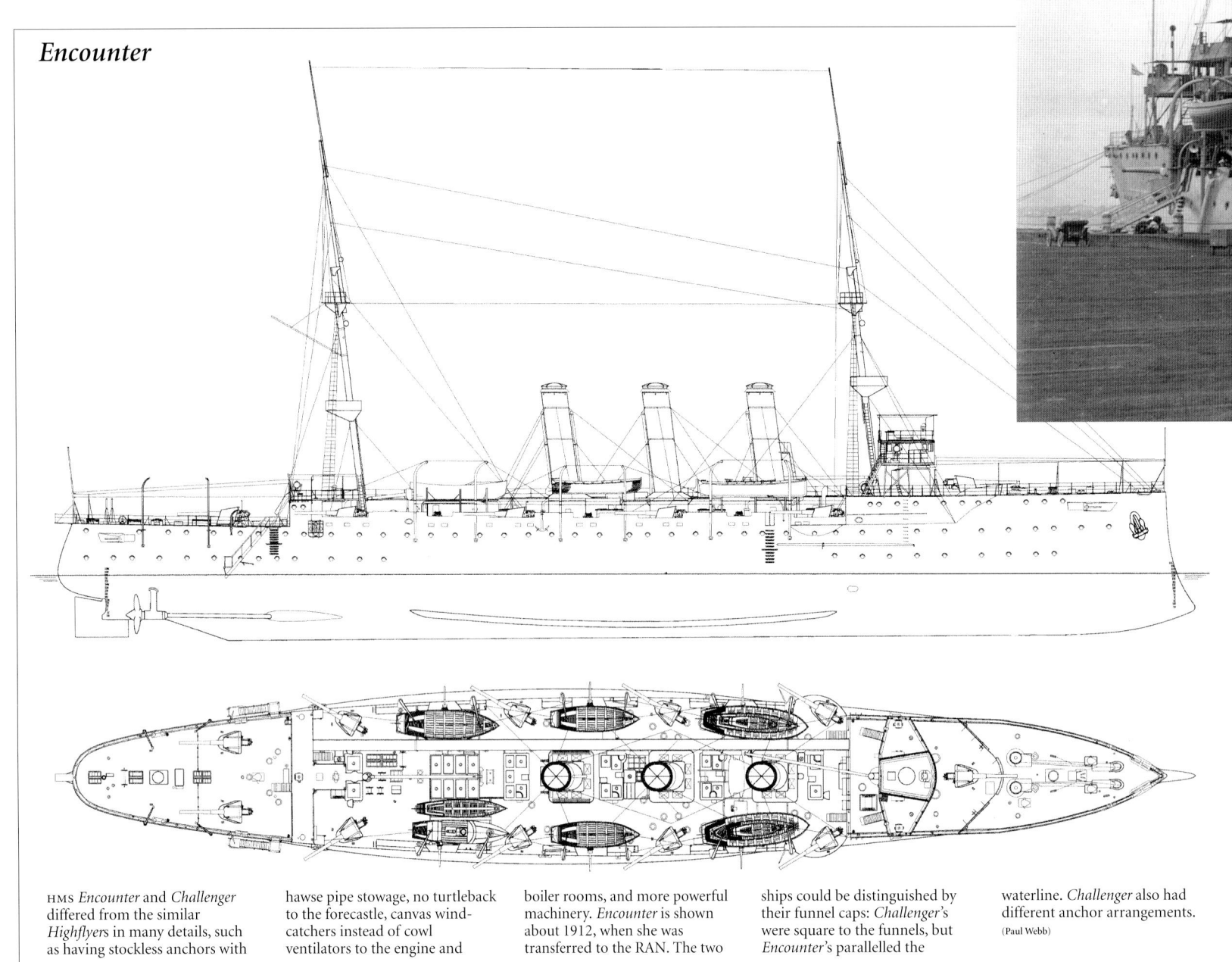

Encounter

HMS *Encounter* and *Challenger* differed from the similar *Highflyer*s in many details, such as having stockless anchors with hawse pipe stowage, no turtleback to the forecastle, canvas wind-catchers instead of cowl ventilators to the engine and boiler rooms, and more powerful machinery. *Encounter* is shown about 1912, when she was transferred to the RAN. The two ships could be distinguished by their funnel caps: *Challenger*'s were square to the funnels, but *Encounter*'s parallelled the waterline. *Challenger* also had different anchor arrangements.
(Paul Webb)

Challenger. On completion she went to the Australia station, where she remained until 1912. She then became part of the new Third (reserve) Fleet at Devonport. On the outbreak of war she joined 9th Cruiser Squadron, based at Portland and operating in mid-Atlantic, capturing a German steamer in the Bristol Channel in September 1914. She was detached to West Africa for the Cameroons campaign of 1914-15, and operated in East African waters in 1915-19. Operations included helping run down the German cruiser *Königsberg* and (with *Pioneer*) bombarding Dar-es-Salaam on 13 June 1915.
(Allan C Green, courtesy State Library of Victoria)

LEFT *Encounter*. Note the range drum facing aft, so that it could be read from the upper deck battery. On completion she went to the Australia station, being transferred to the RAN in 1912. During the First World War she served on the Pacific (1914-15, 1916-18) and China (1915-16) stations, and was permanently transferred to Australia in 1919.
(Allan C Green, courtesy State Library of Victoria)

Encounter with reduced armament as a training ship. The forward waist 6in gun positions have been plated in and the after 6in guns removed; only three guns are left, including two in the waist just abaft the third funnel. The compass platform carried what seems to be an empty support for a rangefinder. This photograph was probably taken at Sydney about 1920 (the ship was disarmed in 1923).
(Allan C Green, courtesy State Library of Victoria)

5 THE TORPEDO AND SMALL CRUISERS

Torpedo Cruisers

The failure of the *Mersey* project did not change Cooper Key's vision of smaller fleet cruisers armed with torpedoes working with the battleships. In battle they would lie in the lee of the line of ironclads, dashing out to attack. They could also beat off enemy torpedo boat attacks, and at night they would help protect a fleet anchored off an enemy port. They are best seen as direct predecessors of the fleet destroyers of the twentieth century. Work on such craft began before the *Mersey* design (whose Cover makes no reference to the smaller ship). DNC seems to have sketched a small torpedo ship, armed with submerged tubes (like *Polyphemus*), in November 1880 (details have not survived). In 1881 a paper describing a fleet torpedo ship was circulated among the Board. It may have helped lead to the *Mersey* design. Naval members of the Board considered the torpedo ship so important that they convinced First Lord Northbrook to insert it into the program as a high priority. Northbrook became so impressed with torpedo craft that in 1884 he gave a speech suggesting that the day of the ironclad might be over. Presumably he was promoting Prime Minister Gladstone's hope of cutting the navy budget, which at the time meant cutting battleship construction.

By 1883 Cooper Key still wanted small fleet torpedo vessels with submerged torpedo tubes; Barnaby reminded him of the November 1880 project. In mid-March 1883 Barnaby wrote to Cooper Key and the Controller that the French had just contracted with a British firm for a set of 3200 IHP engines for one of four fast 1365-ton ships, to be 224ft long, with an estimated maximum speed of 17kts and enough fuel for 3000nm at 10kts, and with a light fore and aft rig. They were armed with machine guns and with above-water torpedo tubes. They were exactly what Cooper Key had in mind, 'designed to accompany a fleet, but to operate against the torpedo flotilla of the enemy'. The French ships were the *Condor* class, armed with five 100mm (3.9in) guns. Laid down in 1882-83, they were completed in 1886-89.

Cooper Key proposed a British equivalent, which became the torpedo cruiser – and the progenitor of a series of third-class cruisers.[1] He seems to have envisaged a small ship with one large gun in her bow, plus submerged torpedo tubes, displacing no more than 1200 tons. In April 1883 Barnaby offered a sketch design with 5in guns fore and aft plus ten machine guns, at the time the only weapons suitable to deal with a fast torpedo boat. Tubes were all above water. Like Barnaby's larger cruisers, she had a protective deck (only ⅜in thick) over her boilers and machinery, plus the usual coal protection. A sketch showed twin-screw 2800 IHP engines, two funnels (the ships ended up with one), and two masts with full sail.[2] Barnaby sketched a parallel fast despatch vessel.[3] It too could be armed with guns and torpedoes. Both of Barnaby's designs were probably related to his 1882 design for a 15-knot despatch vessel.

Detailed design of the new torpedo vessel was well underway by 1 June 1883. Third Naval Lord (Controller) liked Barnaby's scaled-down cruiser, which could also function as a gun-vessel and as a despatch vessel. She could maintain her speed better in rough weather, and could remain at sea for much longer. Rendel, who had actually designed scaled-down cruisers (like his famous Chinese gun boats), liked them, and Civil Lord Thomas Brassey considered them more important than the large cruisers and slow gunboats the Royal Navy already had. He hoped that they could replace the despatch vessel and schooner already in the 1883-84 program. First Lord approved the program on 13 July 1883. The 1883-84 program was modified and HMS *Scout* and *Fearless* ordered.[4] The French had chosen the alternative of a scaled-up torpedo boat; such ships were offered by both British specialist builders of fast small ships, Thornycroft and Yarrow. The two fast despatch vessels, *Surprise* and *Alacrity*, were designed virtually without armament, but they were completed armed virtually as torpedo cruisers, with the same four 5in guns and with four 6pdr QF rather than eight 3pdr QF of the torpedo cruisers.[5] The Cover gives no indication as to when or why the ships were armed, but it seems likely to have been a consequence of the 1885 Russian war scare and the threat of Russian commerce raiding. Despite their armament, the ships were never reclassified as cruisers.

In October 1884 First Naval Lord Admiral Cooper Key proposed that the 1885-86 program include construction (by contract) of twenty small 16-knot unarmoured cruisers of about 1000 to 1200 tons. They would be valuable auxiliaries to the fleet and also valuable for trade protection. They would replace existing gun-vessels and sloops in peacetime. Unlike torpedo boats, they would always be in commission, hence would always be ready when needed.[6] Cooper Key's plans coincided with the big 1884-85 supplemental Northbrook Program. It included six follow-on torpedo cruisers, with a further two in the 1885-86 program.

Work began early in 1884. In February the new *Archer*s were described as *Scout*s with 6in instead of 5in guns, and with two additional guns on the broadside. The bow tube

The despatch ship (actually small cruiser) *Alacrity*.

Fearless as built. Note the closed torpedo tube whose mouth is visible in the hull forward, below the conning tower, and the muzzle of the bow tube half way down the bow. The embrasure of another broadside tube is visible aft, abaft the sponson for the after gun. Soon after completion she was assigned to the Mediterranean (1888-1900). After a refit at Sheerness (1901) she went to China (1901-4) and was discarded on her return.

Scout as completed with fore-and-aft rig and, presumably, her original armament of four 5in breech-loaders. She and her sister also had eight 3pdr QF guns and two machine guns, plus two torpedo carriages and one bow torpedo tube. Like guns on trucks, which could fire from multiple ports, the torpedo carriages could turn to fire out of embrasures on both sides of the ship. Thus the ships showed four such embrasures, but had only two carriages. In 1896 the 5in guns were ordered replaced by 4.7in QF once guns were available. By January 1898 *Fearless* had the new guns, but *Scout* did not have hers. She finally had the new guns in the January 1900 armament summary.

was eliminated, and the four torpedo carriages replaced by two submerged broadside tubes. The ram was strengthened, probably by running the steel protective deck all the way to the bow, to be more effective against unarmoured ships. The complement was increased from 120 to 140, and even that was acceptable only because First Sea Lord (Cooper Key) was willing to allow manning only half the guns (one broadside) at a time. Profile and specifications were ready in December 1884. The ship grew slightly during design, so that by August 1885 six above-water tubes had been added (with a total of 12 torpedoes).[7]

Six *Archer*s participated in the 1888 Manoeuvres. Their COs considered them good seaboats, but incapable of maintaining speed in a head sea. Due to the great weight (of armament) in their bows, they pitched heavily. They were quick rollers and unsteady gun platforms, but were considered handy. All the

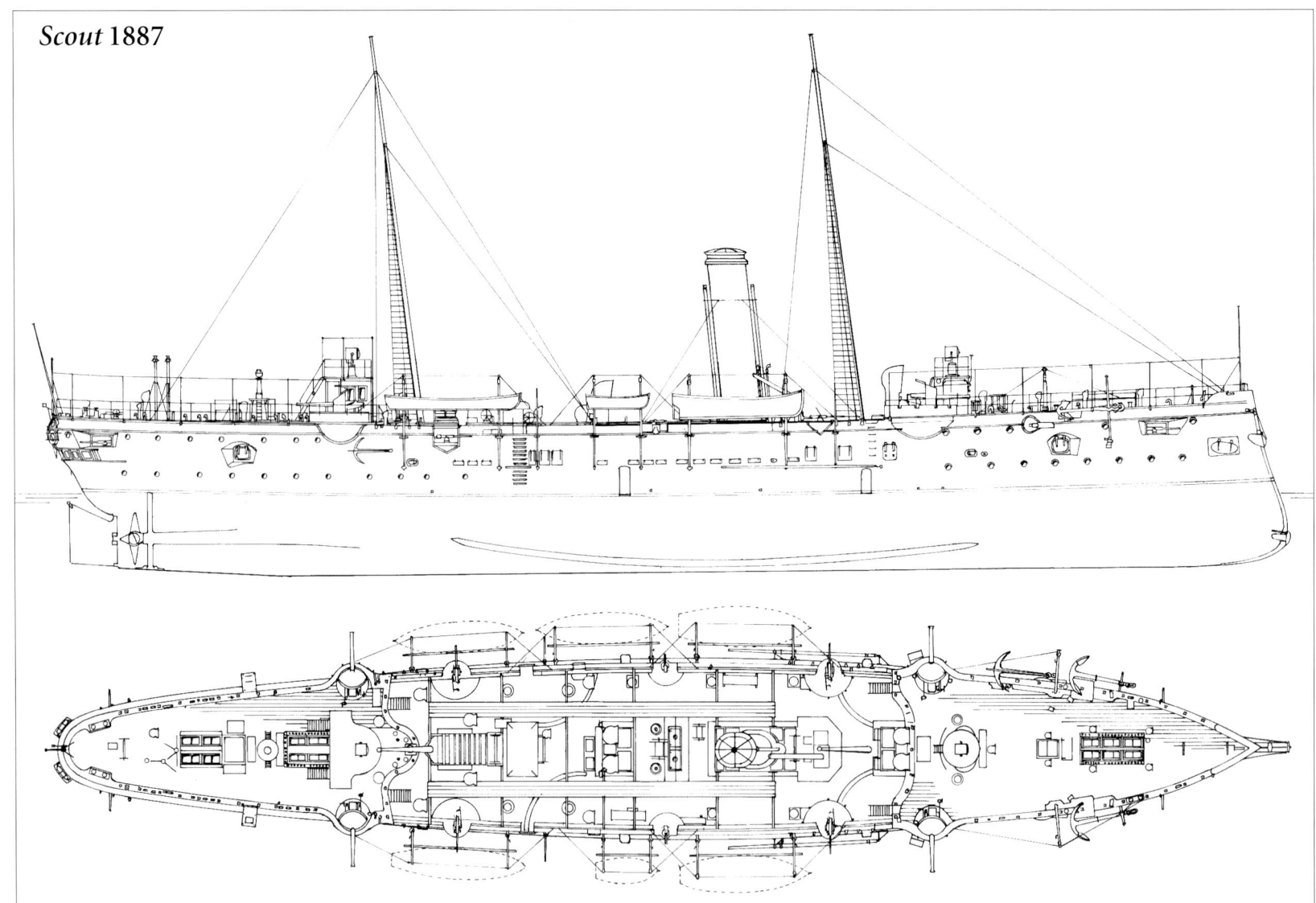

Scout 1887

HMS *Scout* is shown as completed in 1887. The above-water bow and stern tubes had been deleted by January 1900. The stern centreline tube was on the main deck in what was later the Commanding Officer's quarters. The sailing-ship type stern gallery was a dummy, and there was scrollwork at the bow. Armament was originally four 5in 40cwt Mk III, eight 3pdr QF, two five-barrel 0.45-calibre Nordenfelts, and 20 torpedoes (four Mk VD discharges firing through ports and three tubes: one bow, one stern, and one submerged bow tube). During 1899 the 5in guns were replaced by four 4.7in QF. The original sail plan was only three triangular sails, including the single jib, but a photo taken in the late 1880s shows two gaffs added. When the sailing capacity was deleted, a single yard was fitted to each mast to support signal halliards. A single semaphore was fitted on the after bridge, and the small searchlight platform forward was later fitted with short wings. No breakwater was originally fitted, but one is shown on the January 1900 revisions to the plans. *Fearless* carried her two 3pdr guns abaft the forecastle break at the main-deck level, firing through ports. (A D Baker III)

COs considered the armament too heavy, making the ships 'crank' [lacking stability]. The forecastle was not strong enough for the weight on it, which included two 6in guns (a little more than 25½ tons). *Racoon*, the only one which had experienced a heavy sea, in a moderate swell at 10 or 11kts once took on board a sea which carried away everything moveable on the forecastle, broke in the battened-down fore-hatch, tore away the iron stanchions supporting the forecastle, and bent the beams down 3 inches. The committee proposed replacing the two 6in forward by 5in (saving over 15 tons) and stowing the anchors further aft. In fact 5in guns might usefully be substituted for all the 6in on board. The rearmament was never carried out.

Making the Cruiser Smaller: *Curlew* and *Landrail*
Could an even smaller torpedo ship be designed? On 10 May 1884 Barnaby wrote that 'in view of the success which has attended the application of protective decks and forced draught to vessels even as small as *Heroine*, *Scout*, and *Swallow* we have been led to wonder whether the same features might not be applied to still smaller vessels such as those of the Gun Vessel Type'. *Heroine* was a *Satellite* class composite screw sloop (reclassified as a corvette – i.e., a cruiser – in 1884). *Swallow* was a somewhat smaller *Nymphe* class composite screw sloop. Barnaby sketched the result, intended to obtain maximum offensive and defensive power in a ship no larger than existing gun vessels (the class below sloops). He offered a 775-ton twin-screw ship capable of 14kts with forced draught (corvette speed) with 10,000nm range at moderate speed.[8] She had one 6in on the forecastle with clear arcs nearly all around, and pairs of single 4in in sponsons forward and aft. Barnaby argued that with a speed of 14kts she would have many chances of delivering torpedoes during a fleet

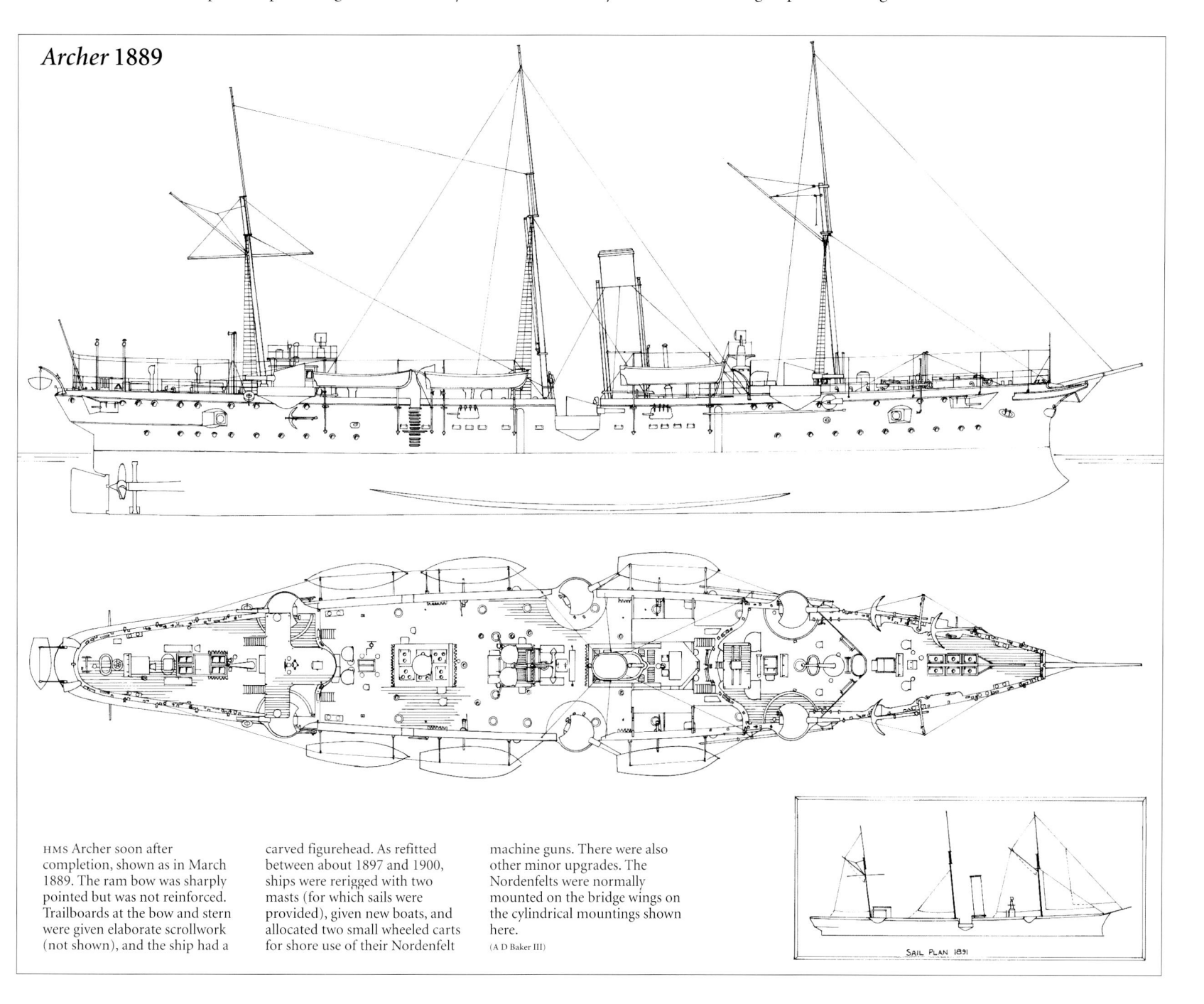

Archer 1889

HMS *Archer* soon after completion, shown as in March 1889. The ram bow was sharply pointed but was not reinforced. Trailboards at the bow and stern were given elaborate scrollwork (not shown), and the ship had a carved figurehead. As refitted between about 1897 and 1900, ships were rerigged with two masts (for which sails were provided), given new boats, and allocated two small wheeled carts for shore use of their Nordenfelt machine guns. There were also other minor upgrades. The Nordenfelts were normally mounted on the bridge wings on the cylindrical mountings shown here.
(A D Baker III)

SAIL PLAN 1891

178

Fearless at the end of her career in 1904 in the new grey livery. The embrasures of her 3pdr QF guns are visible right aft and in the waist (the other photographs show the embrasure right forward).
(National Maritime Museum N01277)

Fearless in Mediterranean livery in 1900. Her only bridge was aft, in the position from which sailing ships were conned; note the semaphore atop it. Note the addition of yardarms and a masthead semaphore on her mainmast.
(National Maritime Museum N01275)

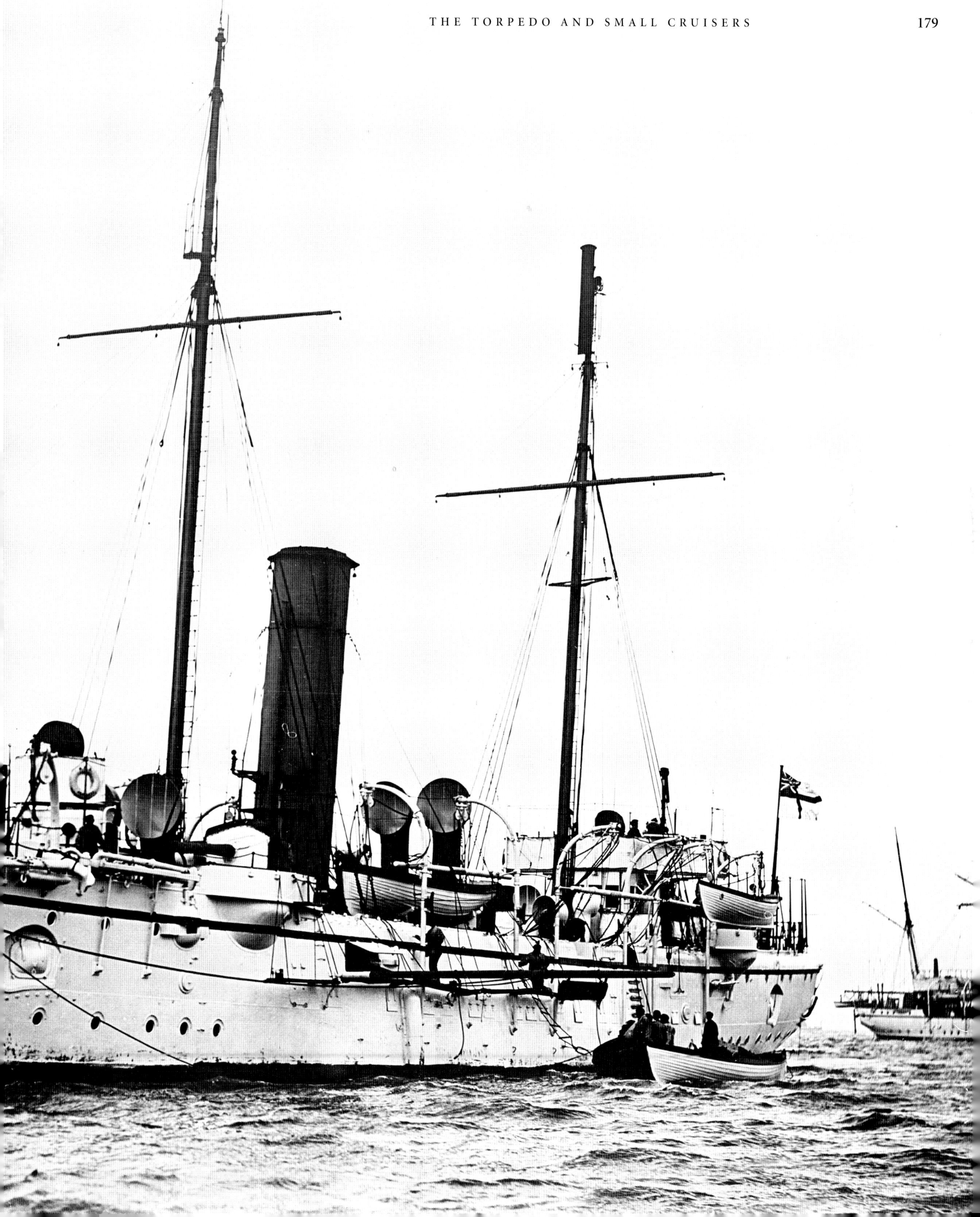

Landrail (with her sister *Curlew*) was an attempt to produce the smallest fleet torpedo ship, in effect a forerunner of the torpedo gunboats, which in turn were ancestors to the later fleet destroyers. Both were rated as sloops, but their connection with the larger torpedo cruisers merits inclusion here. The sheer size of the 6in gun forward suggests just how small she was for her armament. Note that she had a conning tower forward, but that her only bridge was well aft. The view from aft shows that the ship retained a fore-and-aft sail on her mainmast, if not her foremast. Armament was one 6in and three 5in (two amidships, one aft) plus seven machine guns (one is visible amidships), the bow torpedo tube, and four torpedo carriages firing on the broadside through ports (unlike the larger torpedo cruisers, these had no embrasures).

action; in effect she was a less expensive torpedo cruiser. To do that she had one above-water tube right forward, one on each bow, and one on each quarter. As in Barnaby's other protected cruiser designs, she also had coal protection. The entire crew was accommodated under a long forecastle, and all officers under the poop. To get all of this Barnaby proposed using an unsheathed steel hull and to give up sail altogether (to work sails, the ship would need more men than she could accommodate). Like the torpedo cruisers, the ship was described both as a replacement for gun vessels in peacetime and as a powerful element of a wartime fleet.

This was very much Barnaby's own idea, which he considered so attractive that it should be inserted into the program if at all possible. DNO (Captain J O Hopkins) considered the ship 'a step quite in the right direction' because he wanted to modernize the British small-ship fleet to deal with foreign navies which were building small fast steamers. Rendel thought the small ship an unusually good combination of fighting power, speed, survivability, and habitability. Like Hopkins, he felt that the navy's smaller ships had to be replaced with something modern. He suggested a different battery oriented more to the broadside. Controller (Admiral Brandreath) went further. He thought Barnaby's proposed ship a better approach to Cooper Key's ideal than the larger torpedo cruiser. Not surprisingly, Cooper Key was enthusiastic: 'a small number of such vessels on each station would be valuable during peace and invaluable during war.' Civil Lord Thomas Brassey, an enthusiast for unarmoured ships, wrote that 'it has been my earnest wish to see the principles represented in this design introduced in our unarmoured construction'. The main change in the design was Rendel's: the 4in guns in sponsons were replaced by three 5in guns, one on the centreline aft and two in sponsons

Like *Fearless* and *Scout*, *Archer* had two torpedo tube embrasures on each side and a bow tube. She had two Mk VD2 torpedo carriages, each of which could fire from either beam, and a total of twelve 14in torpedoes. Both classes of torpedo cruiser were considered too heavily armed, with too much weight near their ends. *Archer* was assigned to the Cape on completion (1888–91) and then to China (1891–99). After a Chatham refit (1900) she went to Australia (1901-4). She is shown in Australian waters.
(Allan C Green, courtesy of State Library of Victoria)

in the waist, plus the usual anti-torpedo guns.

Barnaby's design received the Board Stamp on 10 July 1884, and two 'gun and torpedo vessels' were ordered laid down at Devonport (under the 1884-85 program) instead of the planned ships of the *Mersey* class.[9] They were HMS *Curlew* and *Landrail*. They are often considered the direct ancestors of the even smaller torpedo gunboats.

Barnaby was clearly fascinated by the idea of pushing down the minimum size of a ship with a protective deck and forced-draught power. The Cover includes an undated cross-section for a Protected Gun Boat with dimensions of 155ft × 26ft × 10ft (500 tons) showing an arched protective deck and a double bottom extending all the way up to the waterline. This ship would develop 800 IHP under forced draught.[10] Another (presumably later) sheet gave a speed of 12½kts and a displacement of 515 tons. Barnaby thought the ship would need special lightweight (torpedo boat) engines. A Legend dated 3 June 1884 compared this composite gunboat with *Curlew*, the gunboat having interchangeable gun and gun-torpedo armaments (the latter with the same 5 tubes as in *Curlew*), in each case with one 5in gun on the centreline forward.

HMS *Porpoise* in tropical livery. Note that, like the earlier *Scouts*, her only bridge was well aft. On completion she went to the China station (1888-97); she is probably shown en route to China, with an old *Bacchante* class corvette in the left background. After China she went to Australia (1897-1901), was refitted at Sheerness (1902-3), and then went to the East Indies (1903-4). She was sold at Bombay.

Barracouta and *Barham* Classes

The next year, before either ship had been completed, a new DNC much more concerned with high speed entered office: William H White. He scaled *Curlew* up (to the *Barracouta* class cruiser) and down (to torpedo gunboats), both of which were considerably faster. Like Barnaby, White was interested in an alternative to the latest sloop (he called her *Buzzard*, but she was a sister of *Swallow*, to which *Curlew* had been compared). In October 1886 he proposed a ship armed like *Buzzard* (eight 5in) but carrying torpedoes like *Curlew*, and provided with a protective deck, 1in on the flat and 2in on the slopes amidships (¾in fore and aft). Like *Scout* and *Curlew*, the ship would have light masts and rig. White wanted a forecastle and poop, as in the gunboat, and he estimated that she would displace 1200 tons.[11] On that displacement he thought he could get 250 tons of machinery, with double-ended boilers (or at least boilers larger than those of the gunboat) for 3000 IHP – which ought to give 17kts. Early in 1887 White asked what 4000 IHP machinery would weigh, and how much weight he could save on the 3000 IHP plant by using lighter-weight locomotive boilers (65 tons on a total then given as 260). He also asked

Barracouta 1891

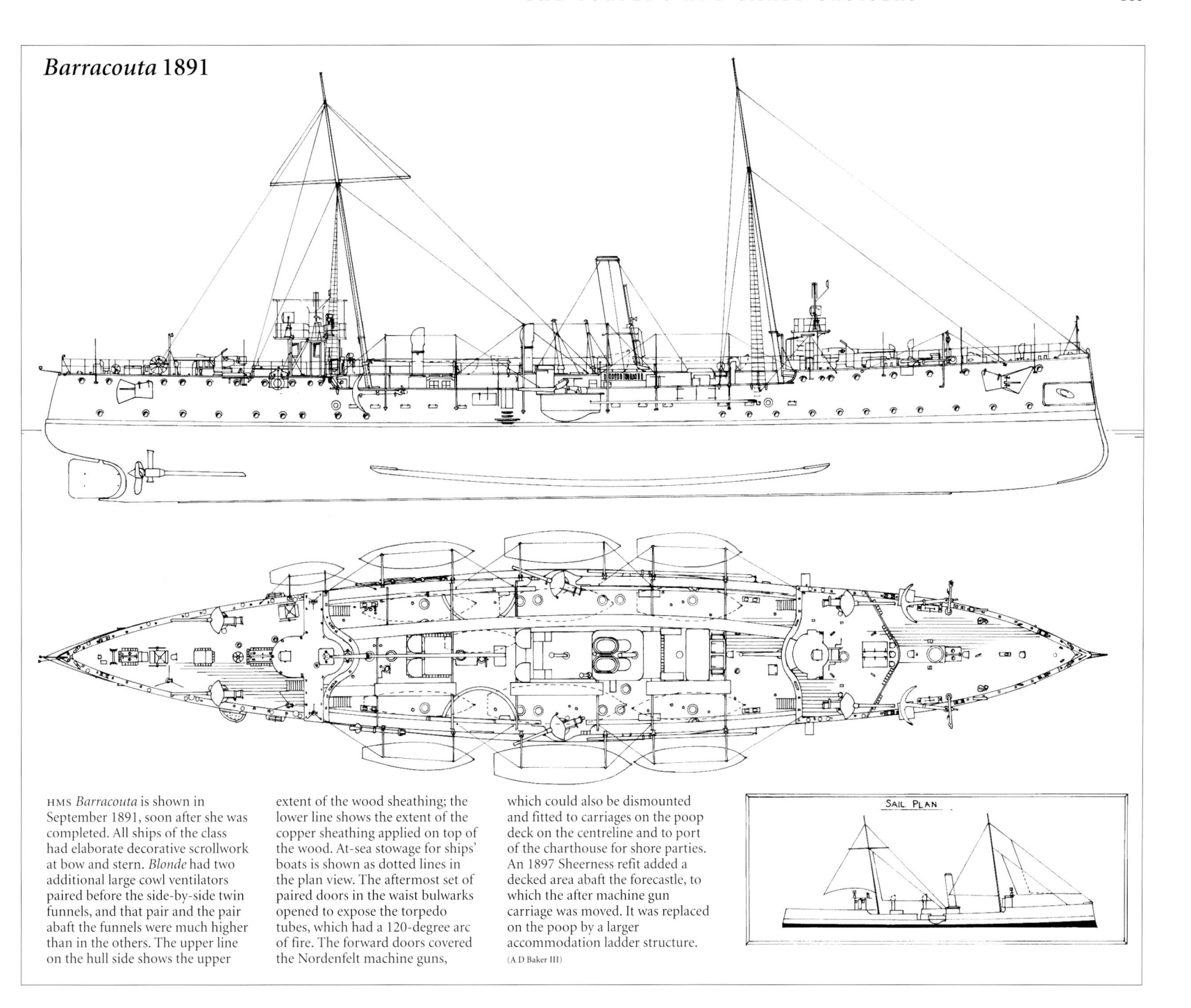

HMS *Barracouta* is shown in September 1891, soon after she was completed. All ships of the class had elaborate decorative scrollwork at bow and stern. *Blonde* had two additional large cowl ventilators paired before the side-by-side twin funnels, and that pair and the pair abaft the funnels were much higher than in the others. The upper line on the hull side shows the upper extent of the wood sheathing; the lower line shows the extent of the copper sheathing applied on top of the wood. At-sea stowage for ships' boats is shown as dotted lines in the plan view. The aftermost set of paired doors in the waist bulwarks opened to expose the torpedo tubes, which had a 120-degree arc of fire. The forward doors covered the Nordenfelt machine guns, which could also be dismounted and fitted to carriages on the poop deck on the centreline and to port of the charthouse for shore parties. An 1897 Sheerness refit added a decked area abaft the forecastle, to which the after machine gun carriage was moved. It was replaced on the poop by a larger accommodation ladder structure.
(A D Baker III)

what would be required, with such boilers, for 4000 IHP – that turned out to be 225 tons, less than the original machinery estimate, provided that the boilers were forced more. Although early papers called the ship New *Buzzard*, she could more reasonably be called a cruiser with about half the displacement of the *Medea* he was then designing. At this time *Buzzard* was credited with 15kts on 2000 IHP, rather more than the *Swallow* with which *Curlew* had been compared.

In effect this was White's equivalent to Barnaby's *Scout*, using technology, particularly engines, three years newer. For example, adopting triple-expansion engines made it possible to thicken the protective deck and extend it to the ends of the ship. The hull form was essentially the same, which made it relatively easy to estimate the ship's speed for various machinery. On this basis estimated speed was 17kts on 3000 IHP and 17½kts on 3700. A more conservative estimate, based on increased tonnage (1500 tons) was 16½kts on 3000 IHP.

By the fall of 1887 the armament of the 'new twin-screw sheathed ship' was that of *Buzzard* (eight 5in and smaller guns) plus four torpedo tubes. Soon it was changed to six 36pdr QF (4.7in), four Hotchkiss 4pdrs, two 0.45in Nordenfelts, and four 14in torpedo tubes with 10 torpedoes. Numbers were cut drastically compared to those in *Buzzard* because QF guns needed so many more rounds per gun: 300 rather than 85 or 105 (the 3pdrs had 500 rounds per gun).[12] The single bow and stern chasers were paired side by side, the other two guns being in waist sponsons. The 4pdr anti-torpedo (boat) guns were in bow and stern embrasures. As in many other ships, it was assumed that torpedo craft would attack from ahead or astern because they were unlikely to have enough speed in hand to attack from the side.

The Board approved White's project for a new fast sheathed steel sloop by Minute dated 16 August 1887. In those terms it was a spectacular advance on previous practice. Terms were malleable; the ship was more than half the size of White's *Medea*, and it was about as fast as most existing cruisers. All other sloops were of composite construction; White argued in his October 1887 Board submission that the speed and engine power he was using precluded that. Perhaps the greatest departure from sloop practice (except for *Curlew*) was the protective deck over the machinery and the boilers. In that sense this was a midget protected cruiser. Moreover, because the new ship had little or no rig, she lacked the endurance of sloops, which had considerable sail power to supplement their engines. White's ship might more properly be classed as a torpedo cruiser.

On 7 November 1887 the Board approved inclusion of four of White's Improved *Buzzard*s in the 1888-89 program plus two further improved versions.[13] The only changes were to lengthen the ship ten feet and to increase coal capacity from 140 to 160 tons. The proposal to include a submerged bow torpedo tube was finally killed, provision to be made for 'possibly' four above-water tubes. Without any tubes, the ship as modified was expected to displace 1580 tons and to make 16½kts under forced draught.[14] In January 1888 the Board reviewed torpedo batteries, and decided that the 'sheathed *Buzzard*s' and a follow-on class of 'steel *Buzzard*s' would have two tubes each.[15]

The four 'sheathed *Buzzard*s' were now the *Barracouta* class. As completed, they were classed as third-class cruisers rather than sloops. They were the first British cruisers with large-calibre QF guns and with triple-expansion engines. In effect they were White's approach to the torpedo cruiser, though not described as such, and no faster than a *Scout* or *Archer*.

Two improved *Barracouta*s were included in the 1888-89 program: *Barham* and *Bellona*.[16] They were initially described as 'steel *Buzzard*s' to distinguish them from the 'sheathed *Buzzard*s' of the *Barracouta* class. The important change was far more powerful (5000 IHP) machinery, for much greater speed (19.5kts). As the calculations early in the *Barracouta* design showed, on the same weight White could get twice the power achieved a few years ago by using locomotive rather than conventional cylindrical boilers (torpedo gunboats were being

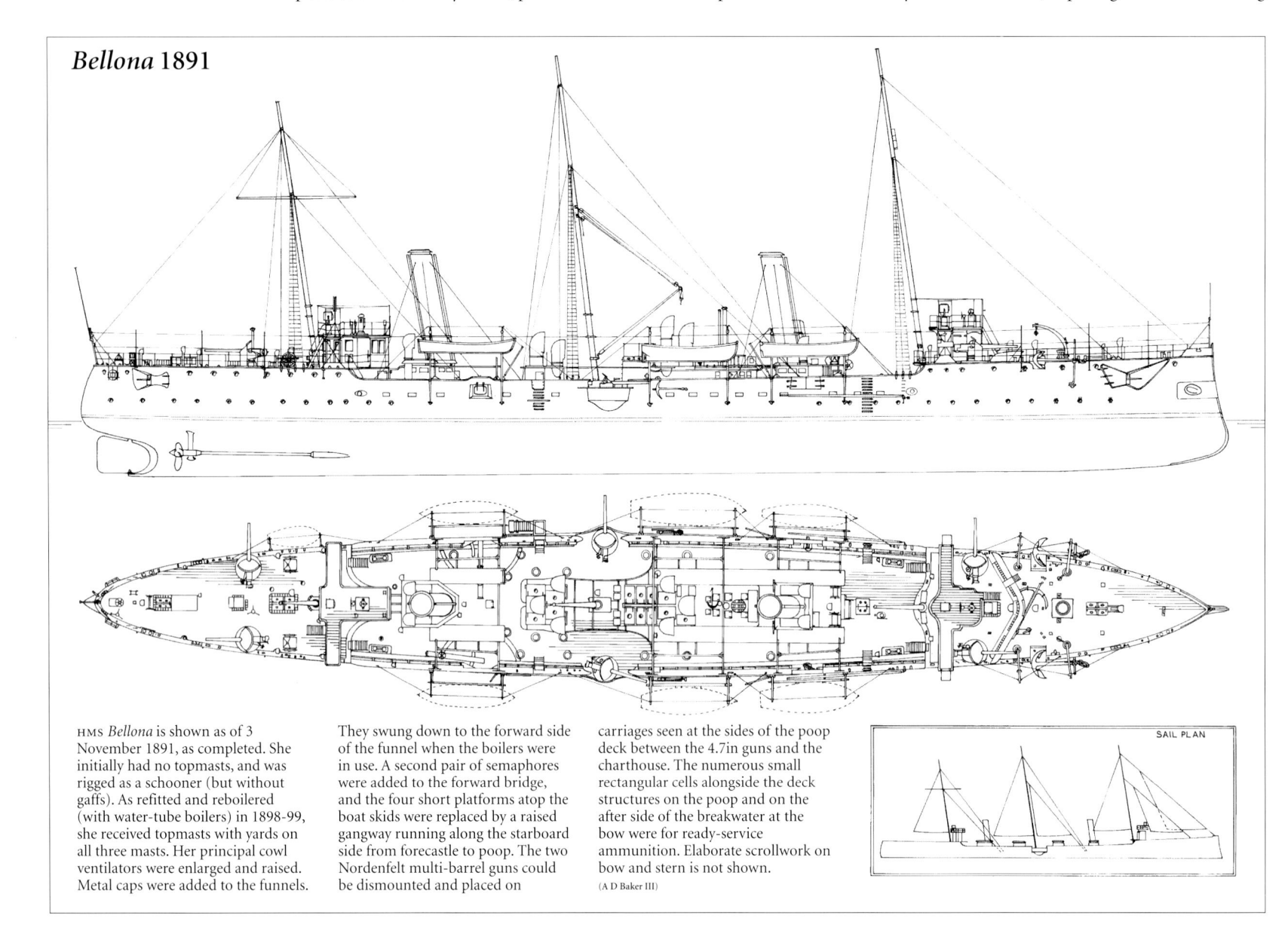

Bellona 1891

HMS *Bellona* is shown as of 3 November 1891, as completed. She initially had no topmasts, and was rigged as a schooner (but without gaffs). As refitted and reboilered (with water-tube boilers) in 1898-99, she received topmasts with yards on all three masts. Her principal cowl ventilators were enlarged and raised. Metal caps were added to the funnels. They swung down to the forward side of the funnel when the boilers were in use. A second pair of semaphores were added to the forward bridge, and the four short platforms atop the boat skids were replaced by a raised gangway running along the starboard side from forecastle to poop. The two Nordenfelt multi-barrel guns could be dismounted and placed on carriages seen at the sides of the poop deck between the 4.7in guns and the charthouse. The numerous small rectangular cells alongside the deck structures on the poop and on the after side of the breakwater at the bow were for ready-service ammunition. Elaborate scrollwork on bow and stern is not shown.
(A D Baker III)

SAIL PLAN

similarly powered). In November 1887 the Board approved his proposal to gain speed by adopting locomotive boilers, the goal being 18kts. A memo dated 10 January 1888 indicated that 5000 IHP could be attained on 235 tons.

White submitted his design, which he called a third-class cruiser or steel sloop, on 18 January 1888. White had lengthened the hull 20ft at a slight cost in displacement (20 tons), doubling the power. He had surrendered 20 tons of coal at normal draught. Locomotive boilers produced so much more steam that it had not been necessary to add machinery weight. Greater power required more men in the machinery spaces, so complement increased by 10.

More could be done. White offered a 19½kt alternative intended to match the new French cruiser *Forbin*, although he considered her over-rated, making her speed only in smooth water using highly-forced engines. The British ship carried much more numerous guns. He had to add another 20ft and increase power to 6000 IHP. Though superior to the French, this ship would cost a lot less: £96,000 instead of the reported £120,000 of the French ship.[17] The Board liked the design: the ships became the *Bellona* class.

During the detail design process, White asked how much power would be needed for 20kts, the speed he was then promising for second-class cruisers. At the end of May 1888 he submitted a new sheer draught and Legend, offering 20kts if power was increased to 6000 IHP (which did not require heavier machinery); at the same time coal stowage was increased to 200 tons. This increased stowage was actually necessary to provide the desired coal protection alongside the machinery (the Board had considered 140 tons sufficient for the Mediterranean). Full capacity, including coal protection, was 240 tons. Endurance would exceed 4000nm at 10kts, about 50 per cent better than what the Board had envisaged. The *Bellona*s were long and light but high-powered, so White designed them to trim about 3ft by the stern (to immerse their propellers) with their normal 140 tons of coal on board in the most convenient position to be shovelled into the boilers. However, the larger load changed the ships' trim (it did not help that reserve feed water was carried well forward). It turned out that the set by the stern would be reduced as coal and feed water were consumed. The successor (*Pallas*) class had a trim tank at the bow, which would give the captain greater control over trim in the light condition.

The new design needed more coal protection because locomotive boilers required longer boiler rooms. In the *Barracouta*s the four double-ended cylindrical boilers were paired side by side, each pair feeding a funnel: the two raked funnels were side by side. Locomotive boilers were fed from one end, gas emerging into a funnel at the other. In the new design, the engines were placed between the boiler rooms, the boilers exhausting into funnels at the opposite ends. That spread the two funnels far apart. A single officer in the engine room could supervise both sets of stokers. This arrangement offered the incidental advantage of minimizing vibration when engine revolutions coincided roughly with the natural period of vibration of the ship's structure. To get the required additional power, the ships had unusually fast-running engines; White later characterized their powerplants as scaled-up versions of those in torpedo gunboats.

In service the boilers proved troublesome, and the ships did not reach their designed power. During manoeuvres they maintained 19 to 19½kts for 2 or 3 hours. A few years later water-tube boilers had been proven in the torpedo gunboat *Speedy* and in new destroyers. White thought that within about the same weight ships with the new more reliable boilers could realize the intended 6000 IHP and therefore the designed speed of the *Bellona*s. This perception was the basis of the follow-on *Pallas* design of 1894-95 described below. By 1899 the *Barham*s had been refitted successfully with water-tube boilers which did produce the maximum power originally planned.

White also claimed that commanding officers found the ships' sea-keeping qualities and accommodation excellent, the only suggestion for improvement being to lift the waist guns about 2½ to 3ft, placing them on platforms or high pedestals so that they could be fought in rougher weather. He later characterized the *Barham*s as swift protected despatch vessels for the Channel and Mediterranean Fleets, intended specifically to match the French *Forbin* class, six of which were being built. The French later added three improved *Forbin*s with more powerful armament. Early in 1894 the Improved *Barham* (*Pelorus* class, described below) was conceived as an answer. The ships were not always assigned as envisaged: of six in commission in 1899, two were with the Channel Squadron and the others on foreign stations.

Colonial Cruisers: *Pearl* Class
In effect the *Bellona* design became the basis for a new kind of cruiser about half the size (hence cost) of emerging second-class cruisers based on HMS *Medea*. A Colonial Conference called in 1887, partly to settle defences in the event of another Russian crisis, reached an agreement in which the Australian colonies would subsidize British warships to protect them. That included a new class of small cruisers ordered in 1888. The ships would revert to the Royal Navy after ten years. The conference sought some existing cruiser which might be of the right size and cost, and seized on the *Archer*s. As the design developed, the stipulation that the new ship be a modified *Archer* somewhat complicated matters, as any basic change had to be referred back to the Australian authorities – which meant, at the time, several distinct colonial governments.

White sketched a cruiser specifically for the Colonial defence meeting at the Admiralty on 29 April 1887. A Legend compared *Archer* to a follow-on New *Archer* and to the 20-knot cruiser (*Medea*). New *Archer* was a 5000 IHP ship displacing slightly more than *Archer* (1650 rather than 1630 tons); it was roughly what White was about to offer the Admiralty as the 18-knot 'steel sloop'. Speed increased from the 17kts of *Archer* to 18kts.[18] White used weight savings in engines to provide the same sort of thick protective deck he was using in the broadly comparable *Bellona* class (*Archer* had only a ⅜in deck). To compensate for somewhat heavier engines, the coal supply was reduced from 185 to 150 tons, so endurance at 10kts would have been reduced from 3300 to 2800nm. Armament was the same: six 6in, eight 3pdr, and 12 torpedoes (6 tubes). As in the *Bellona* class, by November 1887 the armament was revised, in this case eight 4.7in QF guns replacing the six 6in slow-firing ones. It was soon clear that the new ship needed greater endurance, so coal capacity was increased to 250 tons (for a radius of 5000nm).

Mohawk in the new grey livery in 1904. Upon completion she went to the Cape (1890-92) and then to the North America and West Indies station (1892-97). After refitting at Chatham (1897) she went to Australia (1897-1901). After another Chatham refit (1902) she went to the Mediterranean (1903-4), and was then sold in 1905.
(National Maritime Museum N01281)

Blonde as completed, in tropical livery. Note the closely paired side-by-side funnels (for side-by-side locomotive boilers) and the absence of a forward bridge, as in the torpedo cruisers. These were the first British cruisers with QF guns and triple expansion engines. *Blonde* went into reserve at Devonport upon completion in 1890, and then went to the Cape (1892-99, including the M'wele operations in 1895-96, and Sierra Leone operations in 1898-99). She was at Devonport in 1899-1905, including reboilering in 1901-2.

THE TORPEDO AND SMALL CRUISERS   187

Barrosa as completed. She went into reserve at Portsmouth (1890-94) and then was temporarily assigned to the Channel Fleet in 1894. She was then assigned to the Cape station (1894-1901, including the Brass River operation in 1895 and the M'wele operations in 1895-96). She was refitted at Haulbowline in 1902-3 and then returned to the Cape in 1903-5.

Pearl 1892

HMS *Pearl* is shown as completed, October 1892. The structure on the poop deck surrounded by an oval rack for ready-use projectiles is labelled a 'director tower' on the as-fitted plans. It may have been a torpedo director, but in 1892 the Royal Navy still had gun directors which could fire a whole broadside electrically (this device was very important in the design of the earliest belted cruisers). Ready-service rounds for the forward pair of 4.7in guns were arranged around the conning tower, and additional rounds for the midships quartet of such guns were placed beneath overhanging structures, hence are not visible in the drawing. In the plan view, the location of some navigational and engineering control equipment on the two open bridges is not shown, due to the unavailability of plans showing these fittings. The two amidships searchlights were run out on rails on hinged platforms which folded down when in use, as shown on the drawing (the *Apollo*s were similarly fitted). The 28ft sailing cutter and 14ft dinghy were replaced about 1901 by a 30ft sailing cutter and a 16ft dinghy. Otherwise few changes were made during the ships' careers except for the addition of semaphores at the ends of the fore and aft bridge wings. The five ships built for Australian service had topmasts and slightly less powerful engines.

(A D Baker III)

Blanche is shown in 1899, reboilered with Laird boilers, hence with a single fatter funnel. On completion she went to the East Indies (1890-91) and then to the Cape station (1891-94, including the Witu operation in 1893 and Juba River in 1894). She returned for a refit and reserve at Devonport (1894-96) and was then assigned to the Mediterranean in 1896-7. She returned to Devonport for a refit (including reboilering) in 1898-1900, after which she went back to the Cape (1900-1903) and then to the South Atlantic (1903-4). She returned to be laid up at Devonport (1904-5).
(National Maritime Museum N01292)

As in *Bellona*, adopting QF guns added considerable ammunition weight (300 rounds per gun). Not surprisingly, the ship became heavier (2100 tons) and beamier (40ft), but estimated speed was still 18kts, on the same horsepower.[19] Bow submerged tubes having been abandoned, the ship was credited with four torpedo tubes (as completed, *Archer* had three) but the same 12 torpedoes. The new colonial cruiser was not far from White's 2800-ton 265ft *Medea*.

White formally submitted the new design, described as an Improved *Archer*, in January 1888. As in the case of the 'steel sloop', he argued that, although he had agreed to provide an 18-knot ship, the possibility of increased speed should not be dismissed, considering what was being done 'in France and elsewhere'. He admitted that the French were unlikely to send their few very fast ships to Australian waters, but 'these vessels, though primarily designed for service in Australian waters may hereafter be employed elsewhere'. He therefore offered both a 19-knot alternative (265ft rather than 240ft, 2500 rather than 2100 tons, endurance at 10kts of 6000 rather than 5000nm) and the *Medea* class (at that time 285ft, 2800 tons, 20kts, endurance 8000nm). The estimated cost of the 18-knot cruiser was £91,500, compared to £110,000 for the 19-knot cruiser and £125,000 or more for *Medea*. Both 18- and 19-knot alternatives were larger than *Bellona* because they offered much greater coal endurance. White wrote that the result 'will very closely resemble the improved *Buzzard*s (or third-class cruisers) but they have the advantages of a much larger radius of action, a somewhat heavier armament, and a higher speed (18kts against 16½kts)'. Compared to a *Barracouta*, the new design had an additional stokehold (hence two funnels in line ahead) and more men to provide the boilers with more coal. Projected complement was 185, compared to 150 for an *Archer*.[20]

Barham shows her characteristic widely separated funnels (with engines between her boiler rooms) and charthouses fore and aft, in contrast to the *Barracouta*s. A masthead semaphore is visible at the head of her mainmast. Both ships were rebuilt in 1898, Thornycroft water-tube boilers replacing the previous locomotive boilers. Both ships were employed as despatch vessels in the Channel and Mediterranean Fleets. *Barham* was employed for trials at Portsmouth upon completion (1890-93) and then went to the Mediterranean (1893-96). She returned to enter the Portsmouth Reserve (1896-98) and was then reboilered for further service (1898-99). She went to the Mediterranean (1899-1902), returning to the Portsmouth Reserve (1902-4) and then joining the Fishery Protection Squadron (1905-6). She was later attached to the Mediterranean Battle Squadron in 1907-12, fighting in Somaliland in 1908-10. She was sold in 1914.

In view of the intended employment and large coal endurance, White proposed two double-ended return-tube boilers of conventional type and a small auxiliary boiler (rather than, as he did *not* say, the more delicate locomotive boilers of the *Bellona*s). The auxiliary boiler would run electric generators and provide harbour service, and its steam could be fed into the main engines to add power in battle. White's design showed forecastle and poop; each carried two guns abreast. As with the *Medea*, there was sentiment in favour of putting only one gun at each end, on the theory that the forward or after guns in the waist could be sponsoned out to provide a measure of bow and stern fire. Two *Archer* class ships plunged heavily during the 1887 manoeuvres, and did not rise as they might to the sea, apparently because they had so much weight (two 6in guns side by side) on the forecastle given their fine form forward. White argued that the new 4.7in QF gun was much lighter (10 vs 25½ tons) and it was much further aft (65 rather than 41ft from the forward perpendicular). As in the *Medea*

Bellona in 1904 in grey livery, but otherwise little changed from her original appearance. On completion in 1891 she remained at Portsmouth for trials (1891-92), and was then assigned to the Channel Fleet (1892-97). She was reboilered at Portsmouth in 1898-99, and was then assigned to the Fishery Protection Squadron (1899-1905), with a temporary assignment to the Mediterranean in 1900. She was sold in 1906.
(National Maritime Museum N07804)

design, the arrangement with two guns side by side won out, since the waist guns could not really fire too close to the centreline, and also since they were considerably wetter than the forecastle and poop guns.

First Naval Lord Admiral Hood much preferred the 19-knot ship, if money were available. The Admiralty would have to pay anything over what the Australian colonies were willing to pay. The ships would be used to protect trade against fast enemy cruisers, so the faster the better, within limits. Hood understood that they would never be used 'in the ordinary Pacific Islands cruizing duties, for which they are in my opinion eminently unsuited'. DNO (Captain Fisher) argued that the ten-year contract required the Admiralty to look far ahead. It would be better to jump to the *Medea* class, 'as the ship most likely to maintain for the longest period a supremacy over all comers, and to be a modern ship at the end of ten years'. The 19-knot design was approved, and the ship was designated the Colonial Cruiser. A Legend for the 265ft 19-knot design was issued in March 1888.[21]

Amethyst 1905

The 'Gem' class cruiser *Amethyst* is shown as fitted in March 1905, newly delivered. She was the first Royal Navy cruiser to have turbine propulsion; her three near-sisters had reciprocating engines. She had Normand-Laird boilers. The drawing shows the original two-wire wireless array, and she had a large rotating semaphore atop her mainmast. By 1909 she and her near-sisters had more elaborate cage arrays strung between their masts, the mainmast semaphore was gone, and semaphores had been fitted to the bridge wings. They were not given anti-aircraft weapons during the First World War. In the plan view, note that the port cut-out permitting the after pair of 4in guns to fire astern was about 7ft longer than that to starboard. A mine magazine was fitted below the waterline beneath the bridge.
(A D Baker III)

Diamond as built. On completion she was assigned to 4th Cruiser Squadron on the North America and West Indies station (1905-7), followed by attachment to the Atlantic Fleet Battle Squadron, and later to the Channel Fleet Battle Squadron, 1907-9. She was Senior Officer's ship 3rd Destroyer Flotilla (Nore) 1909-12 and then 5th Destroyer Flotilla (Nore) 1912-13. In 1913-15 she was attached to the Battle Squadron of the Channel (2nd) Fleet. She was attached to the 5th Battle Squadron of the Grand Fleet in 1915-18. In 1918 she went to the Mediterranean as a CMB (coastal motor boat, i.e., motor torpedo boat) carrier with six 40ft boats in davits.

Sapphire in 1909 with spotting top and compass platform shielded. On completion she became flagship of Rear Admiral (D, i.e., destroyers) at Portland (1905-7), and then of Capt (D) of the Channel Fleet in 1907-9 and then Senior Officer's ship of the 5th Destroyer Flotilla (Devonport) in 1909-12, and of 7th Destroyer Flotilla (Patrol Flotilla) in 1912. She was attached to the Battle Squadron of the Channel Fleet in 1912-13 and to 4th Battle Squadron Grand Fleet in 1914-15. She went to the Mediterranean in 1915-16 and to the East Indies in 1916-19.
(National Maritime Museum N01484)

Diamond in 1913 with prominent spotting top forward and covered compass platform.
(National Maritime Museum N01482)

THE TORPEDO AND SMALL CRUISERS

Topaze. On completion she was attached to the Atlantic Fleet Battle Squadron (1905-7), then to the Home Fleet (with a full rather than nucleus crew) in 1907-9. She was Senior Officer's ship of 4th Destroyer Flotilla (Portsmouth) in 1909-12, and was attached to 6th Battle Squadron (2nd Fleet) in 1913, then to 5th Battle Squadron (Channel Fleet) in 1914-15 and assigned to the Mediterranean in 1915-17 and to the Red Sea in 1917-18.

Five ships were ordered for Australian waters: *Pandora*, *Pelorus*, *Persian*, *Phoenix*, and *Psyche*. In 1890 they received Australian names instead: *Katoomba*, *Mildura*, *Wallaroo*, *Tauranga*, and *Ringarooma*. In the fall of 1888, the projected Naval Defence Act program included four more ships specifically for the Royal Navy: *Pallas*, *Pearl*, *Phoebe*, and *Philomel*. The Colonial Cruiser design was chosen over an enlarged versions of *Bellona* (20kts) described in a Legend dated that September.[22]

Pelorus Class

The Spencer Program (1893) included four more third-class cruisers envisaged as follow-on *Barham*s (*Bellona*s), not follow-on Colonial Cruisers. White's assistant Henry Deadman was in charge of the design; in January 1894 he proposed a flush-deck alternative. Armament would consist entirely of 4in (25pdr) QF guns, total weight being the same as in *Barham*. In May DNC decided to pursue two alternatives. One was a 300ft (rather than 280ft) *Barham* with greater freeboard amidships (7ft 6in instead of 5ft). The other was Deadman's 300ft flush-deck ship. Both versions had water-tube boilers and an armament of eight 4in QF instead of six 4.7in, representing an increase of about 14 per cent in armament weight.[23] Draught aft was not to exceed that of *Barham* (14ft 9in). An undated Legend offered both 280ft and 300ft versions.[24]

White submitted a sketch of this modified *Bellona* in June 1894 (for the 1895-96 program). The major issues were the new armament, the question of retaining deck torpedo tubes, the choice between the 280 and 300ft designs (he preferred the latter, which gave higher speed and greater endurance at minimal additional cost), and the flush deck (which would make the ship larger and more expensive). The flush-decker offered greater accommodation, but would be 'much more visible, and therefore less adapted for the special purpose in view'. A new ship with the long forecastle of the *Bellona* would have no difficulty driving through seas at a considerable speed. In January 1895 Junior Naval Lord Admiral Gerard H Noel wrote that 'vessels of this description are very much needed as look outs with a fleet, specially in the Medterranean, for which their dimensions are particularly suitable, and where it will not perhaps be necessary to overload them with coal'. Only the *Bellona*s were currently available for this role. The *Apollo*s could also be used, but because of their size they were valued more for independent operations.

Water-tube boilers having been proven, they were adopted for the new class, combined with the quick-running engines of the *Bellona* class. The ships were expected to make 20kts on trials and to maintain 18½kts during 8-hour trials. Like the *Bellona*s, the new ones had a normal coal capacity of 250 tons. However, by increasing freeboard about 2ft 9in it was possible to allow for a total bunker capacity of 550 tons, sufficient for twice the endurance of the *Bellona*s: 6000nm at 10kts. Comparable French ships were understood to stow 200 to 250 tons (never more than 300), giving the new British design a considerable advantage in running them down. Even with the 550 tons on board, freeboard would be greater than in the

Phoebe as completed. She went to the Cape station (1892-99, including the 1894 Benin River operation, the M'wele operation in 1895-96, and the Benin operation in 1897), returning for a Devonport refit and reserve (1899-1901), and then went to Australia (1901-5), being paid off in 1905 and sold the following year.

Pioneer 1900

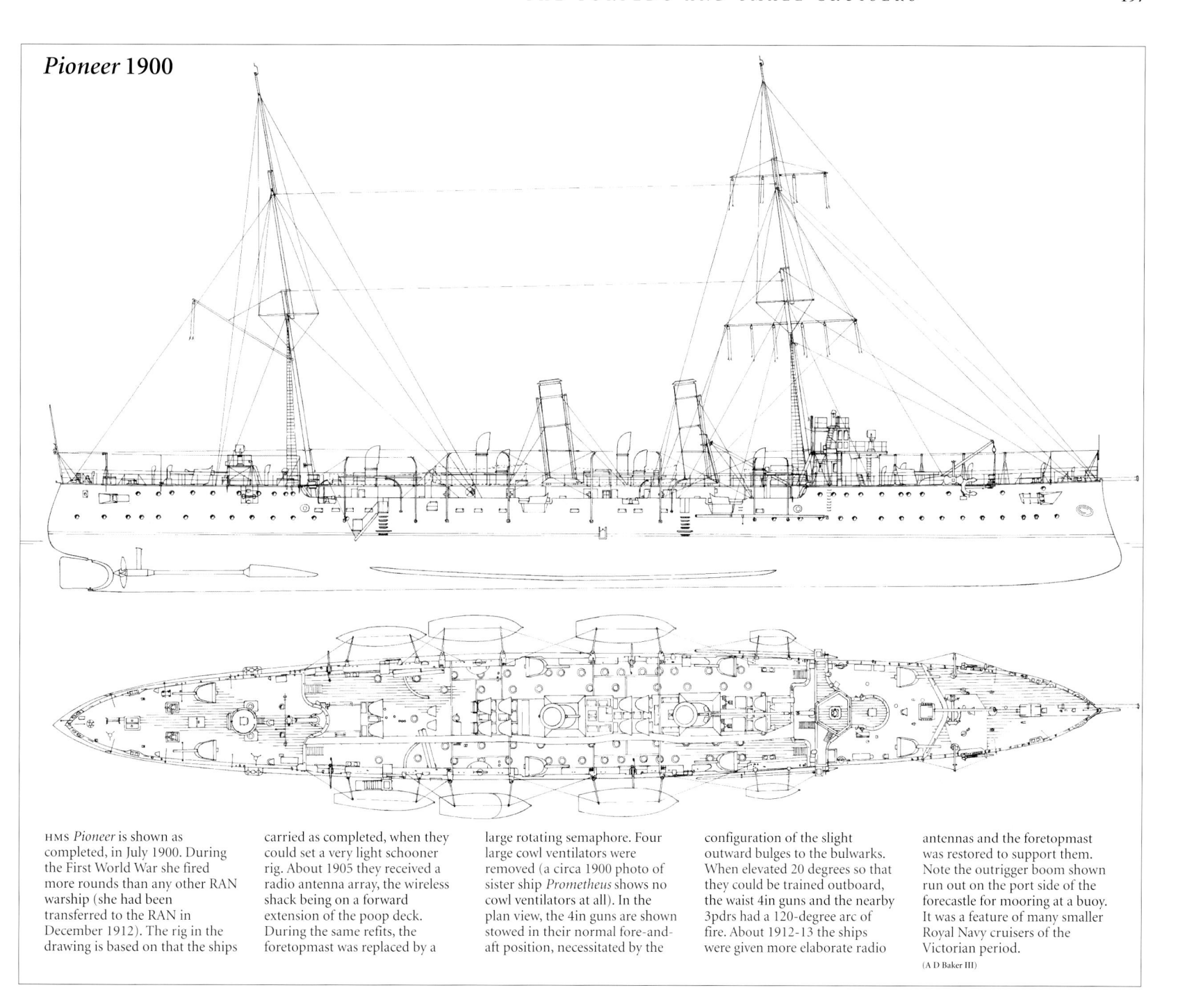

HMS *Pioneer* is shown as completed, in July 1900. During the First World War she fired more rounds than any other RAN warship (she had been transferred to the RAN in December 1912). The rig in the drawing is based on that the ships carried as completed, when they could set a very light schooner rig. About 1905 they received a radio antenna array, the wireless shack being on a forward extension of the poop deck. During the same refits, the foretopmast was replaced by a large rotating semaphore. Four large cowl ventilators were removed (a circa 1900 photo of sister ship *Prometheus* shows no cowl ventilators at all). In the plan view, the 4in guns are shown stowed in their normal fore-and-aft position, necessitated by the configuration of the slight outward bulges to the bulwarks. When elevated 20 degrees so that they could be trained outboard, the waist 4in guns and the nearby 3pdrs had a 120-degree arc of fire. About 1912-13 the ships were given more elaborate radio antennas and the foretopmast was restored to support them. Note the outrigger boom shown run out on the port side of the forecastle for mooring at a buoy. It was a feature of many smaller Royal Navy cruisers of the Victorian period.

(A D Baker III)

*Bellona*s. As in White's other protected cruisers, the bunkers above the protective deck formed a belt of coal subdivided by longitudinal bulkheads and cofferdams. The coal inside the longitudinal bulkhead could be worked without disturbing the outer layer, which provided the protection. Captains were encouraged to leave the upper outer layer of coal for last as they burned their fuel, and the ship had enough stability even if all but the upper outer layer was used up.

The Legend went to the Board in January 1895.[25] Work on the design was pushed because Sheerness, which was to build the first ship (*Pelorus*), needed the work. Soon a second ship was assigned to Sheerness (*Proserpine*). Three more 1895-96 ships were privately built: *Pegasus*, *Perseus*, and *Pactolus*. Six more were built under the next two programs: four in Royal Dockyards (*Pioneer* at Chatham, *Psyche* at Devonport, *Pandora* at Portsmouth, *Pomone* at Sheerness) and two privately (*Prometheus* and *Pyramus*). Of these, *Pandora* and *Pioneer* were built under the 1897-98 program.

Experience with *Pelorus* showed that the cylinder heads should be further below the armour deck; that required shorter-stroke (quicker-acting) engines. Engineer-in-Chief Durston considered the existing low-pressure cylinders large, so in May 1897 he suggested replacing each with two smaller cylinders. A four-cylinder engine would also be better balanced. Machinery would be slightly lighter (370 rather than 381 tons), which helped balance an unexpected 34-ton increase in equipment. Engine rooms had to be slightly longer. DNC offered modifications for the ships to be built at Portsmouth (*Pandora*) and Chatham (*Pioneer*). Any change to the ships being built under contract would have been much more expensive. The two ships had to be 5ft longer (305ft).²⁶ Later in 1897 the same modification was extended to the Chatham ship (*Pioneer*). The modified design was called New *Pelorus*.

Pelorus had Normand boilers. *Prosperpine*, *Perseus*, *Pioneer*, *Psyche*, *Pandora*, and *Prometheus* had British Thornycroft boilers (which the Royal Navy eventually adopted as standard). *Pegasus* and *Pyramus* had Reed boilers. *Pactolus* and *Pomone* had Blechynden boilers, which were so unsuccessful that the ships were removed from the effective list after a few years.

In 1901 the captain of the recently-completed HMS *Perseus* reported that his ship behaved well, but was poorly ventilated, employing an elaborate system of ventilators with electrically-driven fans. They could be used only when steam was up, but in the hot climate in which the ship was operating fires were kept out as much as possible, not only to economize on coal, but also to keep the ship as cool as possible. Even when it was used the system could adequately ventilate only one or two compartments at a time; if air was diffused through the ship, the compartment furthest from the fans naturally got little benefit. He wanted old-fashioned windsails instead, which he considered the most satisfactory way of getting fresh air below decks. He found it almost impossible to lead a windsail down to the lower deck compartments, except by taking them down ladderways, which was quite unsatisfactory. He asked permission to cut holes in the decks (with coamings to prevent water from getting down the same way). When moving head to wind, 'the difference made by these shoots is enormous, and helps greatly to cool and clean the atmospheres of cabins, mess decks, and store-rooms. At present desperate people rig out choots on their own account – often of cardboard or old charts, and equally unsightly things – anything to catch a breath of air, and those monstrosities grown to such proportions that one has to forbid them unless they are made of uniform pattern ...'

Amethyst Class ('Gems')

Three more third-class cruisers were included in the 1899-1900 program, to be built by Royal Dockyards at Portsmouth, Chatham, and Devonport. To frame characteristics, White

Tauranga in grey livery showing semaphores on her bridges fore and aft. She served in Australia between 1891 and 1905, and was sold for breaking up in 1906.
(Allan C Green, courtesy of State Library of Victoria)

THE TORPEDO AND SMALL CRUISERS

looked at the two comparable types the French were building. One was a 2400-ton 'station cruiser' (i.e., for foreign service – such as commerce raiding) armed with two 5.5in and four 3.9in guns, with an estimated speed of 20¼kts. They had about twice the coal capacity of their predecessors (480 rather than 200 to 225 tons).

The other new French type was a projected pair of 23-knot 4000-ton *Croiseurs Estafette* ('Despatch Cruisers') armed with six 3.9in guns and twelve 3pdrs (much the armament of the British *Pelorus*) with great bunker capacity (600/800 tons) for long range. According to the published French program, each ship would cost £316,000.[27] The ship's water-tube boilers would produce 15,000 IHP. Claimed endurance would be 8000nm at 10kts, and 1300 at maximum speed (which was only theoretical, since her boilers could develop maximum power for only 4 hours at a time). On the basis of British experience, White expected the French ships to have a continuous sea speed of 20kts and to be able to steam 7000nm at 10kts. The new ships seemed comparable in speed and endurance to the new *Montcalm* class armoured cruisers. White concluded that they were probably intended to work with the *Montcalm*s in a scouting group. In his view they sacrificed armament and protection for speed and endurance. They were inevitably long and therefore unmanoeuvrable. They could also attack British trade from French bases.

If all the small fast French cruisers were attached to their home fleets, the French would have 11 such ships against the 13 of the Royal Navy.

The Royal Navy also had to take the Russians into account. The radical Russian scout cruiser *Novik* (3000 tons and about 25kts) was under construction in Germany (Schichau, otherwise usually a torpedo-boat builder). A second somewhat slower ship was on order in Copenhagen, and the Russians had approached British firms for similar ships. *Novik* was unusually long, 350ft x 40ft x 16ft (about 3100 tons), with a protective deck like that of *Pelorus*, and much the same armament as *Barham* (six 4.7in QF, six 3pdr). Her boilers would be similar to the British Thornycroft water-tube type, and her quick-running

Pearl in 1896. Note the absence of a charthouse (the exposed chart table is visible on the bridge wing). On completion in 1892 she went into Devonport Reserve (to 1897), and then to the North America and West Indies station (1897-1901) and to the Cape station (1901-4), after which she was laid up and sold in 1906.
(National Maritime Museum N01308)

Phoebe in grey livery in Australian waters, 1901-5.
(Allan C Green, courtesy of State Library of Victoria)

engines would drive triple screws. Reported power was 17,000 to 20,000 IHP. Her 350 tons of coal would give her an endurance of 5000nm at 10kts. The design could work only by using ultra-lightweight type destroyer boilers, and the maximum speed could be attained for only 2 or 3 hours. No one else had crammed so much machinery into a relatively small ship; White expected her to be expensive to operate and to maintain. In White's view, *Novik* showed that the Russians were more interested in high sustained sea-speed than in anything else. The boilers could certainly develop 9000 to 10,000 IHP continuously, for a continuous sea speed of 21 to 21½kts. White expected *Novik* to be attached to the Russian Pacific squadron specifically to maintain communication between its two bases, Vladivostok and Port Arthur, or to swiftly cover the distance between Japanese and Russian bases (e.g., to transmit a warning that the Japanese were emerging – this was the pre-radio era).

What should the Royal Navy do? White could produce a British equivalent of the *Croiseur Estafette* to work with the 21-knot *Cressy* class armoured cruiser. She would cost about twice as much as a *Pelorus*, but would have no greater fighting value (in terms of protection and armament). She would be about 80ft longer than a *Pelorus*, and 2½ to 3kts faster. A ship matching the current *Drake* in sea speed (21kts) and endurance (2500nm at 21kts) would probably displace about 5500 tons. White could hardly justify that kind of expense, nor could he justify a British equivalent to *Novik*. He thought his *Monmouth* class armoured cruisers were a superior alternative to the *Croiseur Estafette*, combining speed and endurance with much superior armament and protection – at about twice the cost, say £625,000. If side armour were omitted, a modified *Hermes* could achieve the 21-knot sea speed and the endurance at a cost of less than £400,000. The Russians were currently building exactly this type in the United States and Germany, and White considered them a far better bargain than the French ship.

Controller (Rear Admiral A K Wilson) did not share White's view. Of course the Board wanted neither the *Croiseur Estafette* nor *Novik* nor the 5500-tonner. It did want something to work with the new *Drakes* as look-outs, linking them back to the main fleet they served, as well as with signal stations or with other cruisers. To do that they had to be as fast as possible, not in smooth but in rough water, within reasonable dimensions and cost. The Board wanted something affordable in quantity: a ship with *Pelorus* armament and protection, and with the highest possible fair-weather speed, with at least the same coal endurance at the same speeds as *Pelorus*. Durability and sea speed were more important than short-term high speed. Boilers might be Bellevilles or the newer small-tube type. Given a sketch design, the Board could decide whether the increased speed was worthwhile. If the answer was yes, given the greater size of the new scout, the question was whether the ship should be more heavily armed, probably with two 6in QF at the ends.

White's assistant William Whiting had already sketched a flush-decked ship whose hull weight would be based on those of torpedo gunboats, *Bellona*, and *Pelorus*. He wanted something much faster than the earlier ships, so he asked for power estimates for a 360ft to 380ft ship making up to 25kts. The ship would be deeper and narrower than *Pelorus* (as far as stability would allow). A triple-screw 4000-ton ship could make 23kts on about 14,000 horsepower. Another calculation showed that a 3000-tonner (380ft x 39ft x 14½ft) could make 25kts on 17,400 IHP using fast-running machinery. Yet another set envisaged a 3250-tonner (375ft x 42ft x 14ft).

Both Belleville large-tube and Normand small-tube boilers (both French) were considered.[28] The ship might have twin or triple screws. White hoped to limit the overall cost of the new ship to between £200,000 and £225,000, of which £90,000 might be available for machinery. Maximum power (4-hour

Philomel is shown newly refitted (at Haulbowline) in 1908 with charthouse and fore spotting top with range drum visible to those on the upper deck. The next year the top was enlarged and given a roof. She was probably the only one in the class with the spotting top. By 1909 (as recounted in that year's notes by DNO to his successor), 56 older cruisers had been fitted with a rudimentary fire control system consisting of a single control position forward with voice-pipe communication to a Barr & Stroud rangefinder. Range and deflection drums were placed aloft to provide range data to the upper deck. Guns were arranged in groups for salvo firing, a gong being fitted at each gun. Ships involved were 2 *Crescent* class, 2 *Challenger* class, 8 *Talbot*, 8 *Astraea*, 4 *Amethyst*, 1 *Barham*, *Vulcan*, 7 *Sappho* class, 6 *Edgar* class, 3 *Hermes* class, 3 *Arrogant* class, 9 *Pioneer* class, 1 *Philomel* class, and 1 *Medea* class. In later ships range drums were a means of passing ranges from ship to ship for concentration firing: they pointed outward instead of inward.

trial, *not* on the measured mile) would be 10,500 IHP, and coal endurance at 10kts and 17kts should match that of *Pelorus*. White estimated that the ship would be about 375ft long (14ft mean draught), displacing about 3300 tons. On the 4-hour trial the ship would make about 21½kts. White chose twin screws because triple screws would make for excessively long machinery spaces, and they in turn would interfere with stowage in the after part of the ship. The protective deck would have to be raised somewhat, and there would be no space for a double bottom, even though every British 3000-ton cruiser had one. Bunker capacity would have to be 600 to 620 tons for Belleville boilers or 700 to 720 tons for small-tube boilers, 300 or 350 tons being carried at normal draught. Although they would consume more coal, small-tube boilers would be 75 tons lighter. Bellevilles would offer more power in continuous steaming (7000 vs 5250 HP). Continuous speed would then be 18½ to 19kts for Bellevilles and 17 or 17½kts for small-tube boilers. *Pelorus*, which had small-tube boilers, had run to Madeira developing 60 per cent of her maximum power; small-tube boilers of new design achieving that sort of performance would drive the ship at 18¼kts. A trickier question was whether the engines should be optimized for the steam available on 4-hour or on 8-hour trial (natural draught for a Belleville, moderate forcing for a small-tube boiler).

White thought that adding two 6in guns would require a ship about 15ft longer and £8000 to £10,000 more expensive. She would need somewhat heavier scantlings, and she would be somewhat slower. Overall, White was less than enthusiastic.

Controller rejected the slighty improved *Hermes*. Only about half as many ships could be bought, and they would represent too large a fraction of the overall fighting force to be used to carry messages. They could not deal with enemy armoured cruisers, but they were too expensive to be used as auxiliaries. On the other hand only they could meet the four new Russian 6000-ton (23kt) cruisers on equal terms. If the only issue was war with Russia, it would be worthwhile to build the improved *Hermes*. However, the French were building a large armoured cruiser force. The preferred policy was to keep building British armoured cruisers (to deal with the French) while also building the 3300-tonner. The result, with the desired pair of 6in guns, would be nearly the size of *Apollo*, but two knots faster. Wilson accepted Engineer-in-Chief's preference for the Belleville boiler, and decided that 8-hour power at natural draught should be the rated power of the ship. Turbines could be left to next year's program. Wilson rejected DNC's argument that construction should be deferred.

However, at an 11 June 1899 meeting, the Naval Lords decided *not* to recommend the 3300-tonner, but to have DNC prepare a sketch design of his modified *Hermes*, to cost from £280,000 to £300,000. She would be a knot faster than *Hermes* on the 8-hour trial, and would make 21kts on the measured mile. This decision led to the construction of HMS *Challenger* and HMS *Encounter*, described in the previous chapter. That ended the fast cruiser project within the 1899-1900 program.

The fast small cruiser issue was revived the following year. White thought they were overrated: the fast armoured cruisers (which could maintain high speed under worse conditions) would run them down. Once the big French armoured cruiser program had been completed and the ships distributed between Toulon, Rochefort, Lorient, Brest, and Cherbourg, it would be impossible to assign second- and third-class cruisers for duty on the enemy coast.

Director of Naval Intelligence Captain Custance saw things differently. In November 1900 he reported on foreign development of unarmoured cruisers specifically to support destroyer attacks. The Royal Navy was interested in this mission, which was emerging in the Mediterranean Fleet. For Custance the problem in the North Sea, in which he was increasingly concerned, was that the small fast foreign cruisers could evade slower British cruisers and attack the mass of British shipping. Confined waters favoured destroyer attacks. Their threat would push back the British armoured cruisers, which might otherwise block fast enemy cruisers.

The issue was how to block the enemy's torpedo craft, because those craft made his small cruisers viable in the face of British armoured cruisers. The initial solution had been the destroyer, which was intended to loiter outside enemy bases. When the torpedo craft emerged, British destroyers would run them down. The new small fast cruisers might brush those destroyers aside. Custance argued that the British needed their own fast cruisers to counter the enemy's – to keep their destroyers alive. This was not the destroyer support ship the Mediterranean Fleet wanted, because it did not have to run with the destroyers: it only had to be fast enough to handle the new enemy cruisers (the Mediterranean Fleet wanted destroyer leaders, running with the destroyers, which materialized as the 'Scouts').[29]

Custance argued that any cruiser intended to support destroyers in a war against France had to be at least as fast as the

Perseus, probably in 1896. She spent her entire active life (1901-13) on the East Indies station.
(Allan C Green, courtesy of State Library of Victoria)

BRITISH CRUISERS OF THE VICTORIAN ERA

THE TORPEDO AND SMALL CRUISERS   205

French 21-knot armoured cruisers which might pursue her and had to overmatch French third-class cruisers. That entailed a speed of 21.5kts. Against new German cruisers 21.5 to 22kts would suffice. In theory the new Russian cruisers also should be matched, but a 25kt cruiser was unaffordable.

By concentrating on narrow seas, Custance solved a major design problem: his cruiser did not need the sort of endurance which made White's design so difficult. Probably the greatest distance from a base at which the cruisers would have to support destroyers would be 500 miles, about half the distance between Malta and Gibraltar. First Naval Lord Admiral Walter Kerr supported Custance. The new cruiser was included in the 1901-2 program.

In mid-January 1901 Wilson laid out specifics: two 6in guns

FAR LEFT AND ABOVE *Psyche* early in her career. Note the masthead semaphore atop her mainmast. Two other semaphores are visible on her bridge. The single line barely visible between her topmasts may have been an early wireless antenna, with leads down to transmitter and receiver offices. On completion *Psyche* went to the North America and West Indies station (1900-1902), and then went to the Australia station (1903-13) after refitting at Hawthorn Leslie. She was in the New Zealand Division in 1913-15, then to the China station in 1915, and then lent to the RAN, becoming training ship for seamen and stokers in Sydney in 1915-20.

Prometheus. Note the high mainmast yardarm for her wireless antenna, and the light-coloured funnel identification stripes. The object visible atop the canvas protecting her compass platform (atop her charthouse) is the cover of a chart table. Note the covered-in bow mounting for an anti-torpedo gun. She does not show the usual searchlight atop her conning tower, forward of her charthouse. This photograph was probably taken about 1908-10. On completion she went to the Channel Fleet (1901-4), then to the Australia station (1904-12). She was detached temporarily to the China station in 1912.
(Allan C Green, courtesy of State Library of Victoria)

and six 4in guns (200 rounds per gun) plus smaller guns and torpedoes as in *Pelorus*.[30] Protection would be similar to that of *Pelorus*, but there would be no need for her armour around the torpedo tubes. Speed should match that of the new German *Nymphe* class cruisers. *Niobe*, the last ship of the class, made 21.6kts on 8631 IHP on trials.[31] White decided to aim at a 'safe' 21kts as a minimum, hence try for 21½kts 'which is what *Niobe* is said to have maintained for 6 hours on a forced draught trial.' Coal capacity of the German cruiser was 500 tons (but her 'legend' capacity was not known), so White decided to aim for 600 tons at least, and see what normal capacity he could provide on about 3000 tons displacement.

By this time it was obvious that turbines might be replacing conventional reciprocating powerplants. White was to consider using them in one of the ships.[32] The others would have machinery and boilers similar in type to those of the *Pelorus* class.

White decided to start with a length of 350 to 360ft and a displacement of 3000 tons. He thought he might dispense with the poop of the *Pelorus* class, in which case he wanted to know whether he could still have enough accommodation, and good enough seagoing qualities. Model data showed that a 360ft x 42ft x 16ft hull (3000 tons) could be driven at 21½kts on about 9000 IHP, based partly on what had been achieved by HMS *Barham*. That was somewhat awkward. Boilers (of fixed output) were arranged in blocks of fixed size, set by the size of a ship. The desired output would have entailed adding more than half a block of boilers to the *Pelorus* plant.

A first sketch design was ready at the end of January 1901. There was still some question as to machinery weight (the initial estimate seemed to be somewhat high). Boilers would be arranged in two rooms, as in *Pelorus*, but slightly larger (42ft x 28ft rather than 40ft x 24ft), and the engine room would be somewhat longer (45ft compared to 38ft for the three-cylinder engine in *Pelorus* and 40½ft for the four-cylinder engine in *Pioneer*). To provide enough coal (600 tons), an 8ft block had to be provided across the fore end of the machinery spaces. Careful internal design made it possible to fit in the magazines and store rooms within a length of 325ft (25ft longer than *Pelorus*), well below what had been expected. Volume was so tight that the ship had to have a poop as well as a forecastle. What speed the ship would attain on 9000 IHP depended on her propulsive coefficient, which in turn depended on factors such as the way in which propellers and hull interacted. Given a typical cruiser figure (46 per cent) the ship would make 21¼kts; given a large-ship figure (49 per cent), that would rise to 21½kts.

In effect the 325-footer was the smallest which could meet Controller's requirements. Whiting then tried a slightly narrower 340ft x 39ft x 14½ft hull (2745 tons), which needed less power (8400 rather than 9000 HP) to attain 21kts. It traded off lighter machinery against a slightly heavier hull. Since machinery cost a lot more per ton than hull steel, that cut the cost of the ship while adding space. Both hulls needed about the same power to make 17kts. Power ratings for continuous sea speed and cruising were taken as fixed percentages of maximum power, so the larger ship would have a somewhat lower continuous sea speed. She would need a smaller complement (because of her reduced power). White chose the shorter ship, because it was also important to limit freeboard (i.e., target

New Orleans 1898

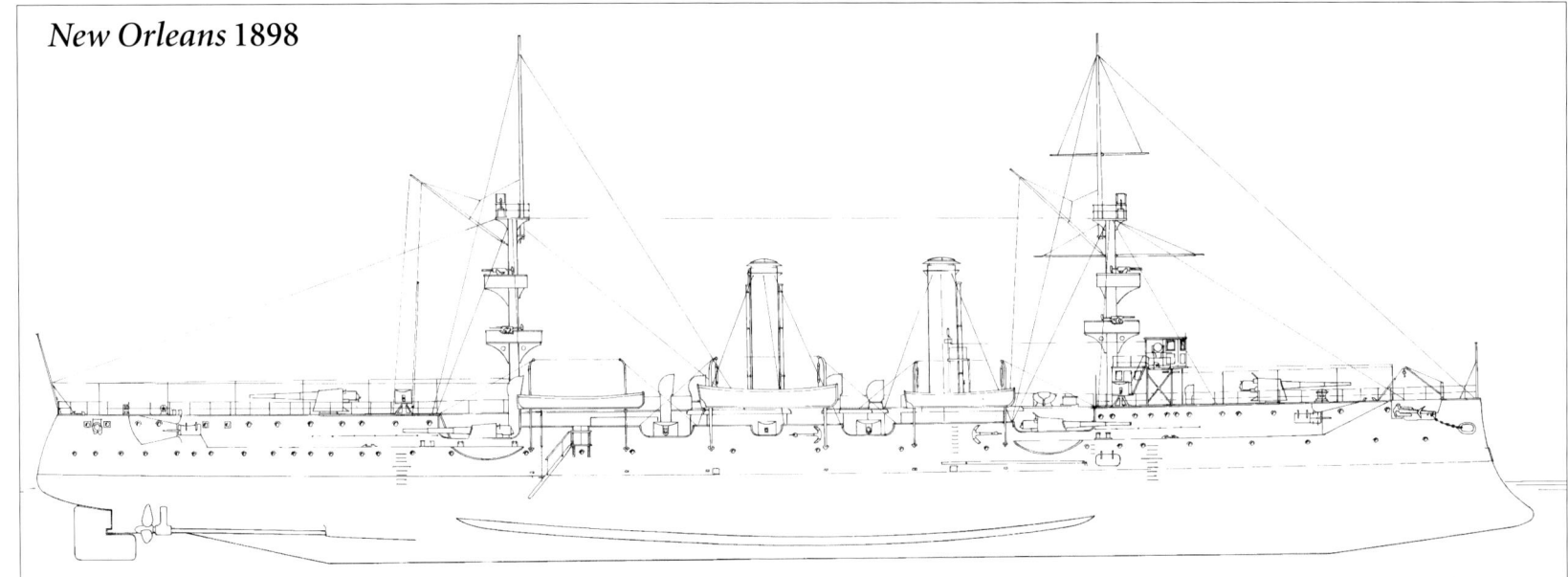

The Armstrong-built USS *New Orleans* is shown as commissioned into the US Navy, 18 March 1898. She and her sister were bought on an emergency basis due to the crisis which was building into the war against Spain. As such, *New Orleans* was typical of small fast Armstrong export cruisers of her time. Both ships had sheathed and coppered hulls, which treatment added 9 inches to their beam. Near-sister *Albany* had shorter, larger-diameter funnels. Both completed refits in 1907 in which they were rearmed with ten 5in/50 in place of the previous mixed battery of six 6in and four 4.7in guns. The three above-water 18in tubes were removed. In 1918 the foremost 5in mounts in the waist were removed, so the final armament was eight 5in, one 3in AA gun, two 3pdr QF, and a portable mine rail which could be emplaced running diagonally the full length of the poop, starboard to port. As of 1922, the complement was 12 officers, 20 chief petty officers, 265 enlisted personnel, and 15 Marines. That compared to 22 officers, 201 enlisted, and 42 Marines as initially in US service. The ship had a normal displacement of 3430 tons, compared to 3438 as designed. Coal capacity had been reduced from 808 to 693 tons in the 1907 refit. Note that these ships had much smaller diameter portholes than contemporary Royal Navy cruisers. The US Navy reclassified *New Orleans* as a gunboat in July 1920, but then as a light cruiser in 1922, when she was decommissioned.
(A D Baker III)

Pegasus Note the range drum at the foretop, facing aft. Note also the rangefinder and chart table on the compass platform. *Pelorus* had a similar fitting. On completion *Pegasus* went to the South East Coast of America station (1899-1900), then to the Mediterranean (1901-4), and then to the Australia station (1905-12). She was temporarily detached to the China station in 1912. She then went to the Cape station in 1913-14. She was sunk by the German cruiser *Königsberg* in East African waters on 20 September 1914.
(Abrahams of Devonport via RNHB).

area), and the shorter ship could make do with less.

White submitted a sketch design early in April 1901.[33] To achieve 1¼kts more than *Pelorus*, to have a heavier armament, and to have about 20 per cent more coal, the new ship was 30ft longer and had a 9000 rather than 7000 IHP powerplant. She had quick-running engines (which were considerably less durable) and small-tube boilers (as in *Pelorus*). Displacement including 300 tons of coal and a 50-ton margin was 2750 tons, about 25 per cent more than that of *Pelorus*. Estimated cost would rise from the £135,000 of *Pelorus* to £150,000 to £190,000, but the *Pelorus* class had been ordered when prices were relatively low. Compared to the German cruisers, this one was about as long, but slightly broader, and it would draw less water; the broader beam had been chosen for better stability. White expected his new cruiser to match the Germans in speed at a given horsepower. The new British cruisers had a greater maximum coal bunker capacity.[34]

Palmer and Armstrong were invited to offer alternative proposals including designs with Parsons turbines. Parsons offered an arrangement similar to that it proposed for destroyers.[35]

This was not the end of the story. In April 1901 DNC was asked for an entirely new design for a 21½–22-knot cruiser armed with ten 4in guns (of the new pattern) and eight 3pdr anti-torpedo guns. The speed was chosen specifically to surpass the German *Nymphe* class. Controller Rear Admiral May later explained that 6in guns had been dropped from the design because they were considered more powerful than needed, and because it was considered important to increase the number of guns (hence the chance of hitting a fast, agile target). A uniform main battery made for better ammunition supply. Furthermore, it was considered desirable to have more guns

Pyramus in 1914. Note the shields for the waist guns, which are present (but less visible) in the photograph of *Prometheus*. Note too the extemporized fore spotting top. On completion *Pyramus* went to the Mediterranean (1900-1904); on her return she went into reserve at Chatham with a nucleus crew (1904-6). She then went to the Australia station (1906-13), and to the New Zealand Division in 1914. She served in the Persian Gulf and the East Indies in 1915, and was then depot ship at Mudros in the Mediterranean in 1915-18.
(Allan C Green, courtesy of State Library of Victoria)

Almirante Grau 1907

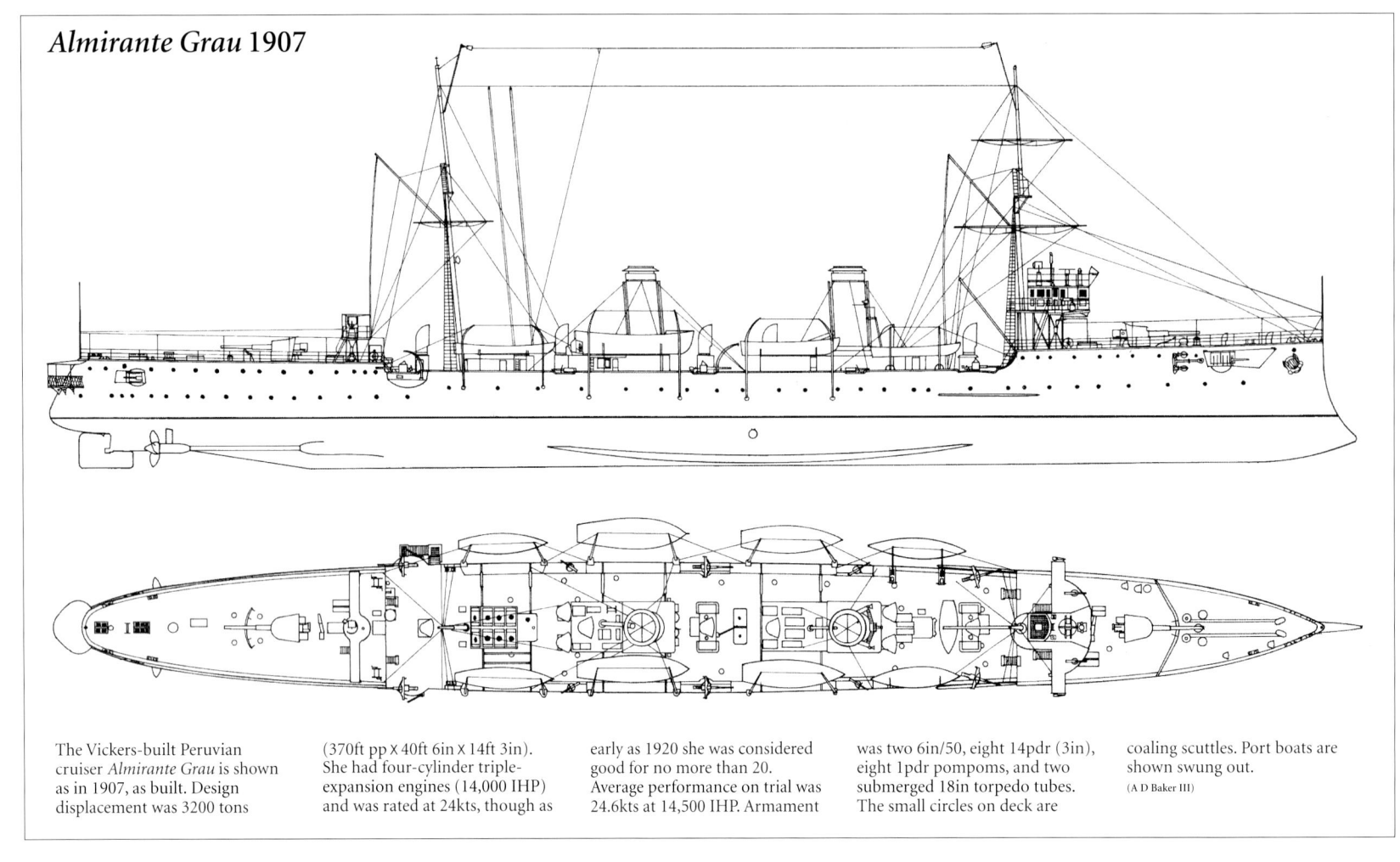

The Vickers-built Peruvian cruiser *Almirante Grau* is shown as in 1907, as built. Design displacement was 3200 tons (370ft pp × 40ft 6in × 14ft 3in). She had four-cylinder triple-expansion engines (14,000 IHP) and was rated at 24kts, though as early as 1920 she was considered good for no more than 20. Average performance on trial was 24.6kts at 14,500 IHP. Armament was two 6in/50, eight 14pdr (3in), eight 1pdr pompoms, and two submerged 18in torpedo tubes. The small circles on deck are coaling scuttles. Port boats are shown swung out. (A D Baker III)

Almirante Grau 1944

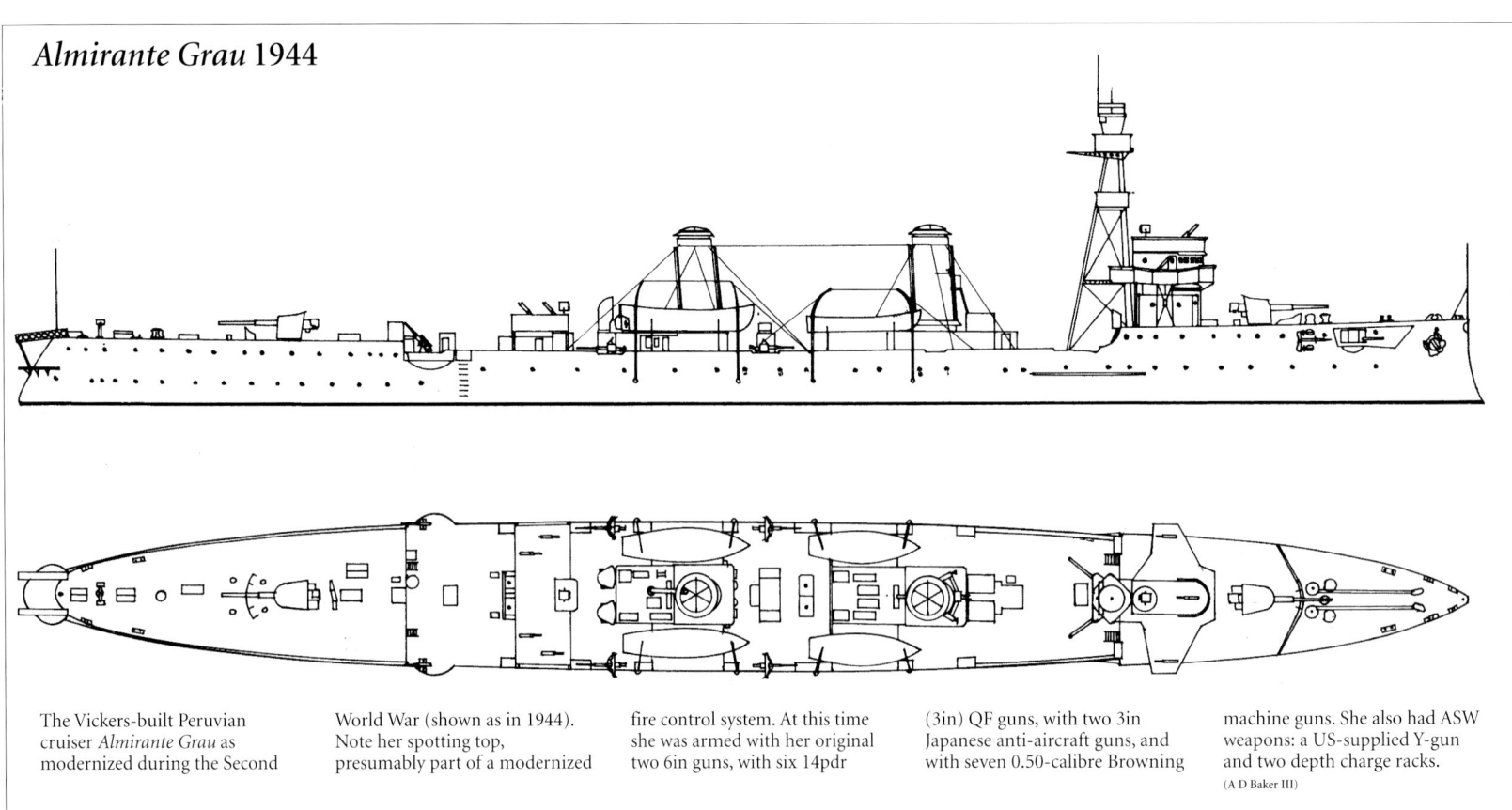

The Vickers-built Peruvian cruiser *Almirante Grau* as modernized during the Second World War (shown as in 1944). Note her spotting top, presumably part of a modernized fire control system. At this time she was armed with her original two 6in guns, with six 14pdr (3in) QF guns, with two 3in Japanese anti-aircraft guns, and with seven 0.50-calibre Browning machine guns. She also had ASW weapons: a US-supplied Y-gun and two depth charge racks. (A D Baker III)

than the *Nymphe* class.

The new armament required more length, and DNC realized that needed more power. In May he asked for the extra weight and space involved in adding 1200 IHP to the existing ship. Late in May the naval members of the Board met and again boosted requirements. Now they wanted twelve 4in (but of the existing pattern, because it appeared that the new type would not be ready in time), one each on the centreline on poop and forecastle, plus the 3pdrs and two 14in torpedo tubes, the type carried on board third-class cruisers. The twelve 4in were two more than the German *Nymphe* carried, but the British projectile was lighter than that of the German gun (which was a 4.1in).[36]

Boilers should be of the new small-tube type, for a speed of 21¾kts (with the word 'safe' in parentheses in DNC's notes, meaning that his calculated speed had to be higher).[37] Protection should match that of *Pelorus*, with a normal coal supply of 300 tons. Maximum coal stowage should provide an endurance of 5000nm at 10kts (Engineer-in-Chief estimated that 780 tons would be needed).

The day after the Board meeting (28 May) White estimated that to give the increased speed and to carry the heavier armament, the new cruiser would have to be about 30ft longer, and would have to displace at least 3000 tons, with 10,000 to 10,500 HP. White later explained that he had chosen the great length both to accommodate the machinery and to obtain a hull form adapted to the desired high speed. Freeboard was held down to limit hull weight and also to gain stability. A high forecastle would assure good seagoing qualities. Inevitably the ship would not be as handy as shorter cruisers, and White did not want to cut away the deadwood aft to make the ship more manoeuvrable (he considered a normal balanced rudder best). Structural design benefited from years of experience with the lightly-built *Barham*s. These ships used destroyer-type high tensile steel, which had already been used in some first-class cruisers. The longer ship should be about a third of a knot faster than the 330-footer. White aimed at 22kts in order to be sure of the required 21¾.[38] Controller approved and ordered that work begin. By August 1901 a Legend had been prepared, comparing the new ship with HMS *Pelorus*.[39]

In September, First Naval Lord Admiral Walter Kerr approved the design. Controller considered that the ship compared favourably with the German *Nymphe*, although the Russian *Novik* and *Boyarin* were faster, if not as well armed. The design received the Board Stamp on 18 November 1901. The most important post-approval change was a shift from 14in to 18in torpedoes, four (rather than the earlier five) being carried.

By late November 1901, the 1901-2 program included two third-class cruisers. Ultimately four ships were built as the 'Gem' class: *Amethyst*, *Diamond*, *Sapphire*, and *Topaze*. *Amethyst* was the turbine trials ship, the first ship larger than a destroyer so powered. *Sapphire* reached 22.4kts on slightly over 10,000 IHP. *Amethyst* made 23.6kts on trial and was rated at 23.4kts (12,000 SHP). Her power output on trial is not certain, because at the time it was difficult to measure turbine output.

Further third-class cruisers were planned for the 1902-3 program; in April 1902 White began preparing a modified design.[40] Estimates were prepared in July 1902 for an *Amethyst* deepened 18 inches (increasing displacement to 3080 tons, beam from 40 to 41ft, and draught from 14½ft to 15¼ft). By November the earlier program had encroached on the 1902-3 program, so the design for a new third-class cruiser had slipped to 1903-4. The main new requirements were a speed of 22kts and 400-ton coal capacity at normal displacement. The new ship would be flush-decked. Whiting suggested a much larger ship: 420ft x 42ft x 16ft. On 2 December 1902 the Naval Lords formally decided that they wanted an entirely new design. It should have high freeboard and 'thoroughly good seagoing qualifications, especially for steaming at high speeds at sea', and it should combine the 22-knot trial speed with an endurance of 2900nm at 18kts (but it should also be stated how far the ship would go at economical speed). Armament was again revised, this time to ten 4in guns (of the new higher-powered 50-calibre type, not the type in the 'Gems') and two 18in torpedo tubes. At the end of January 1903 Whiting decided to try a more conventional (poop and forecastle) hull the same length as a 'Gem', but beamier if necessary (360ft x 42 or 43ft x 15ft), with three boiler rooms. That was apparently too small, but a slightly later calculation sheet described a ship 20ft longer 380ft x 43ft x 14½ft /18ft, 3500 tons, making 22½kts on 12,000 HP).[41] Protection would match that of a 'Gem'. A Legend comparing the new cruiser with *Topaze* (reciprocating-engine 'Gem' class) was dated 28 February 1903.[42] It was marked 'this design need not be proceeded with for the present. It will be taken up again probably as soon as the general work of the office permits.'

The ship was formally dropped from the program in mid-June 1903. That was the end of the line of third-class cruisers White began with the *Bellona*s and *Barracouta*s.

Vulcan

Two other cruiser designs figure in the story of British cruisers intended for underwater warfare. The first is the cruiser-torpedo depot ship *Vulcan*, which in effect realized Captain Fisher's 1885 idea, derived from the manoeuvres, that the fleet could and should have a very fast cruiser, which might also act as a torpedo boat carrier. Instead of Fisher's converted merchant ship, she was designed from the outset as a cruiser. Probably the merchant ship conversion idea died with the Northbrook administration; Lord Hamilton's much more expansive Admiralty wanted a ship designed and built for the purpose.

The design was begun in 1887. The fleet already had a slow torpedo depot ship, the ex-merchant ship HMS *Hecla*, which was taken over on the stocks in 1878 during the Russian war scare that year. Initially the new ship was referred to as New *Hecla*. It is not clear when discussion began, but when he submitted the sketch design DNC William H White mentioned providing estimates for hull and machinery in June (a total of about £255,000) not including the hydraulic machinery associated with the torpedo depot role. The Board formally set requirements in mid-August 1887, deciding to build the ship at Portsmouth under the 1888-89 program, the last before the Naval Defence Act.

White described her as a fast but lightly armed protected cruiser with special equipment to lift and service torpedo craft, and also to carry the fleet's mining and torpedo stores.[43] A fleet operating near an enemy base, waiting for the enemy to come

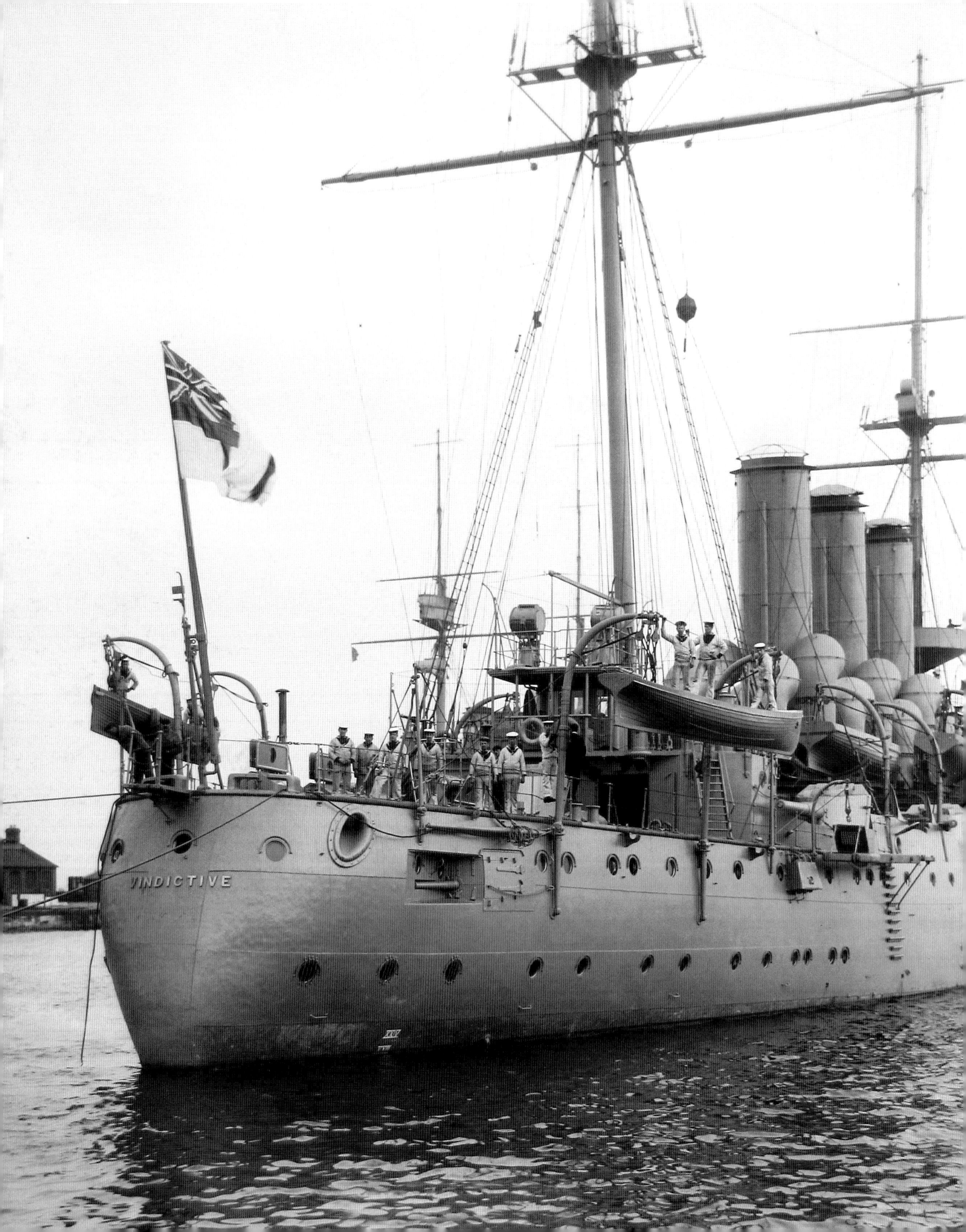
VINDICTIVE

out, would spend considerable time at anchor, using controlled mines to create a moveable defence. It might also want to raid the enemy base using its own portable torpedo craft, the second-class boats carried on board many battleships and cruisers. The special cruiser carried more of them, but more importantly it could keep these fragile craft in working order, and it could maintain their torpedoes.[44] This was an entirely new kind of ship, but White recalled that he had designed a somewhat similar ship while at Armstrong, incorporating that company's new hydraulic lifting equipment.

White offered two armaments, one with 6in guns and one with the new 4.7in QF guns. He preferred the latter, assuming that the War Office (which still supplied Royal Navy guns) approved the long-standing request for them. To White the armament offered both great offensive power and 'perfect defence' against torpedo attack.

One key to the design was the recent decision, in the *Medea* class, to adopt vertical engines, which could be placed abreast, saving length. They were separated by a longitudinal bulkhead, as in large armoured ships. In addition to the four main boilers, an auxiliary boiler powered cranes and the mass of other hydraulic machinery.

White justified the high (expensive) speed of the ship on the ground that, were she any slower, she could have been run down by the numerous foreign protected cruisers capable of 19 to 20kts in smooth water for limited periods. The new ship would also be more than a match for any fast converted liner. She could cruise for 6000nm at 14kts, a speed 'not likely to be maintained by the fastest squadron of armoured ships that could be brought together'.

The Board approved the design on 7 November 1887, with an armament of eight 4.7in (36pdr) QF. The ship would not have a proposed underwater bow torpedo tube. White submitted the finished sheer draught and midships section on 4 February 1888. By this time the Board had decided that the ship would have two submerged broadside tubes plus above-water bow and stern tubes. That eliminated a proposed pair of trainable above-water tubes.

The ship was built as HMS *Vulcan*. She was, in effect, the victim of rapidly-changing technology. Within a few years the idea of anchoring a fleet for a protracted period of observation was less and less attractive, as potential enemies had too many seagoing torpedo boats. Conversely, the small torpedo boats a cruiser could carry seemed less and less formidable. No further torpedo boat carriers were built, but the *Vulcan* design lived on as the basis for a series of first-class cruisers. When money became available (on a Supplemental basis) in 1898, there was considerable interest in building a repeat *Vulcan*. It took substantial effort by Controller Rear Admiral A K Wilson to stop it.

The *Arrogant* Class Fleet Rams

The other special underwater-attack cruiser was the *Arrogant* class 'fleet ram', generally classified as a second-class cruiser, but unrelated to contemporary ships of that type, such as the *Talbots*. She seems to have been the brainchild of First Naval Lord Sir Frederick William Richards, who took that position in November 1893 after having served as Second Naval Lord in the previous administration (in office 25 August 1892). He remained in office until August 1899.

Richards and other ram enthusiasts wanted a pure ram, her freeboard reduced as far as possible to make her less vulnerable (and to reduce the size of the target she presented), her upperworks eliminated so that they could not easily be waterlogged, and the remaining structure well armoured. They wanted to repeat HMS *Polyphemus*, which looked like a pure ram – but they did not realize that she had been turned into a torpedo ship by Barnaby, because he considered ramming a rather limited tactic. White took much the same point of view, trying to design a useful cruiser while following orders to produce a ram. He considered it was most undesirable to produce a pure ram. No repeat *Polyphemus* had ever been built, and the closest foreign equivalent, the USS *Katahdin*, had clearly been designed only for harbour defence. It seems clear that many senior officers agreed with White. Thus DNO Captain Compton Domville wrote that 'if it is necessary to have a special vessel for this purpose, the proposals made by the DNC seem the most useful way of carrying it into effect.'

In the early 1890s ramming made some sense. Advocates of ramming pointed out that only underwater damage (by ram or torpedo) could quickly sink a ship. Effective torpedo range was only about 800yds, and effective gun range was probably understood as 1500 to 2000yds. Heavy guns fired slowly, in some cases one round every four or five minutes. It was by no means clear that lighter quick-firing guns could so shred a ship's structure as to stop her. A fast cruiser might close with a target at an effective speed as high as 10kts, a nautical mile

Vindictive (*Arrogant* class) in grey livery, with a wireless gaff, but otherwise little altered since completion. She appears to have had a foremast range drum as of 1913, and may have been unique within her class in this regard. She was the only one of three surviving ships of this class to serve as a cruiser in 1914. Upon completion she went to the Mediterranean (1900-1904), then was rearmed at Chatham on her return. She remained in reserve at Chatham, eventually as part of the new Third (reserve) Fleet, until 1912. That year she became seagoing tender to HMS *Vernon*, the torpedo school and experimental establishment. On the outbreak of war she joined the 9th Cruiser Squadron on mid-Atlantic patrol, capturing two German merchant ships (7 August and 8 September 1914). She was assigned to the South East Coast of America station in 1915-16 and to the White Sea in 1916-17. In 1918 she was fitted out as an assault ship for the Zeebrugge Raid; she was expended a few weeks later at Ostend, 10 May 1918.

HMS *Vulcan*, the torpedo boat carrier, as designed. (NMM)

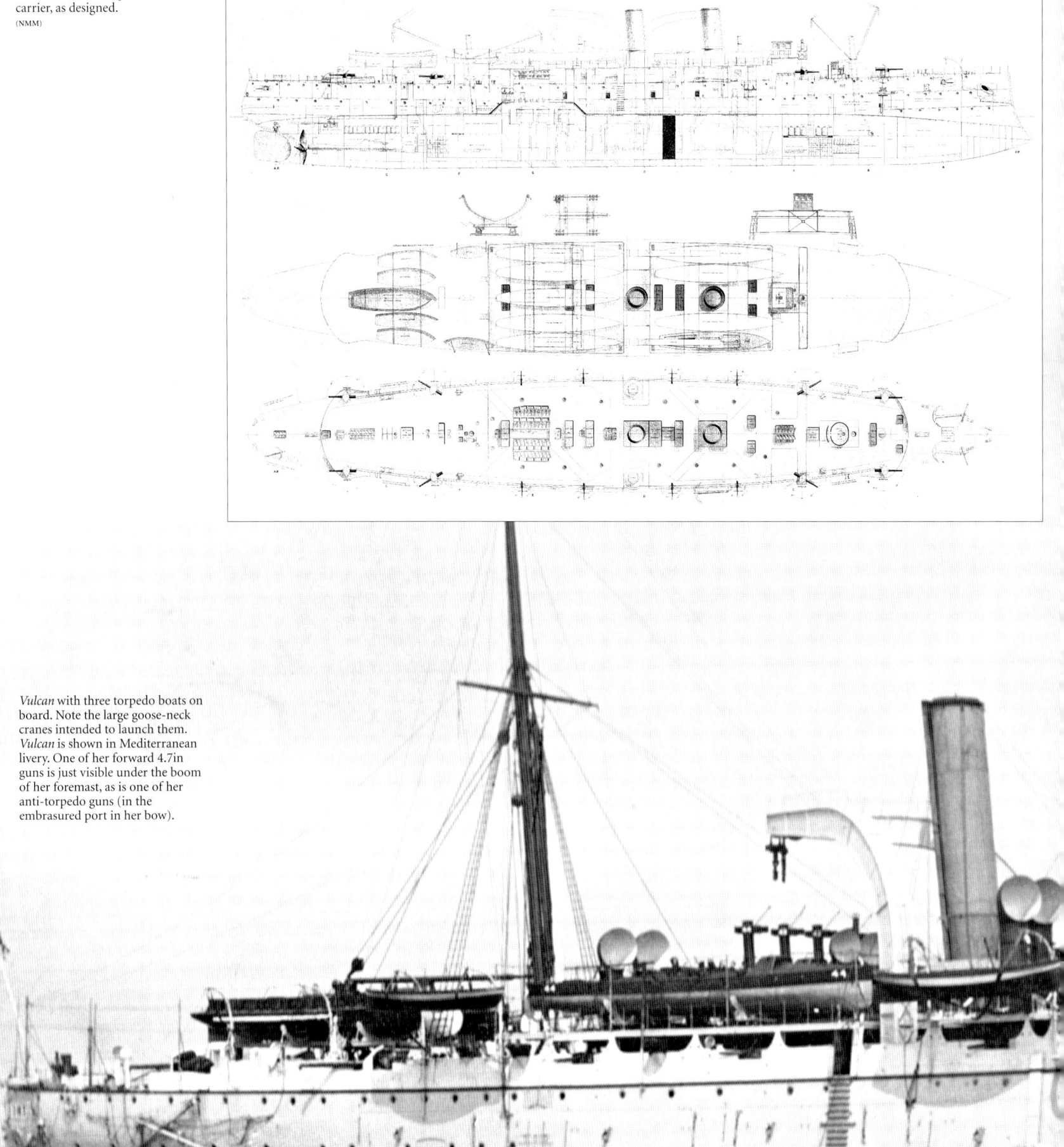

Vulcan with three torpedo boats on board. Note the large goose-neck cranes intended to launch them. *Vulcan* is shown in Mediterranean livery. One of her forward 4.7in guns is just visible under the boom of her foremast, as is one of her anti-torpedo guns (in the embrasured port in her bow).

THE TORPEDO AND SMALL CRUISERS

every six minutes. She might well escape damage from an enemy's heavy guns, each firing only about twice during her approach. The *Arrogant* class 'fleet rams' were soon described as 'fleet cruisers', as though no other cruisers had been conceived specifically for fleet work (although at the time that they were being compared to other cruisers which often worked with the fleet).

Design work began soon after Richards took office as First Naval Lord. White wrote the Controller that on several occasions he had discussed with First Lord (presumably meaning First Naval Lord) the construction of rams to accompany the fleet in European waters. The demands of the 1894-95 program precluded new cruiser construction. However, ram cruisers might be included in the next (1895-96) program.

Controller (Rear Admiral John Fisher, later First Sea Lord) laid out preliminary requirements in mid-November 1893. No happier than anyone else with a pure ram, Fisher added that this ship would be an efficient cruiser as well as a valuable auxiliary in a fleet. *Polyphemus* had died because, however valuable she might be in a fleet action, she was useless for anything else. To keep up with the new *Royal Sovereign* class battleships, the ship had to be large enough to accommodate sufficient coal for sustained fleet cruising, and she needed considerable freeboard. She also needed a strong protective deck and a reinforced bow. Her bow would be lightly armoured back 60 to 80ft, so that the ship could not be stopped by being riddled by QF fire. She would have to deal with foreign second-class

TB 39-48

A Yarrow second-class torpedo boat (*TB 39-48* class) as delivered in 1889. HMS *Vulcan* was intended to carry six boats of this type. The boat displaced 16.5 tons (60ft overall x 9ft 3in x 18in) and was armed with two 14in torpedoes in lever-operated dropping gear, with provision for one 3pdr QF or one machine gun aft. She was powered by a 240 IHP engine (16.5kts) with a locomotive boiler. There was no accommodation, but the low forward and after compartments had two wooden benches each. The steering wheel was in the pilothouse, the rudder being controlled by metal tubes and chains running down the sides of the upper deck. The forward life rails were fixed, the after ones being portable chains. The craft is drawn fully equipped for local service. The sidelights and navigation light supported by the funnel were portable, and the funnel and 16ft mast hinged down when the boat was stowed aboard ship. The similar *TB 49-50* had one 14in torpedo tube and a 200 IHP engine. These were the last second-class torpedo boats built for the Royal Navy. (A D Baker III)

cruisers, so it might make sense to arm her about as heavily as HMS *Apollo*. Fisher proposed one QF gun on the forecastle and one aft on the centreline, both with good shields, plus six 4.7in on the broadside, the two at each end of the battery able to fire dead ahead and astern. In addition there would be ten 3pdr (anti-torpedo guns) in tops and in selected deck positions. Torpedo armament might be dispensed with, on the theory that above-water tubes in a ship designed for close action might well be disabled before the ship came within range (and underwater tubes would be difficult to accommodate on limited dimensions). White characterized the ship as a ram cruiser with reduced gun armament (and without torpedoes) 'while the features necessary for successful ramming have been developed to an exceptional extent. While primarily designed for service with a fleet, they would be capable on occasion of separate service, and this adaptability for enlarge employment would not fail to add to their value.'[45]

Early in December Richards emphasized that the ship herself would be the projectile, albeit (bowing to White) with a suitable cruiser armament. The ram should be protected against lateral wrenching when the target was rammed, and there should be a special collision bulkhead to protect the ship. To maintain control during the approach, she should have a roomy well-armoured conning tower. Since the ship would have to come within torpedo range to attack, a small torpedo armament would be desirable, though that might not be feasible.

Obviously manoeuvrability would be crucial. White proposed to cut up the deadwood at both ends and to use the 'turn-about' rudders (bow as well as stern rudders) that the shipbuilding firm of J S White (no relation) was then using to give small torpedo craft great manoeuvrability (the torpedo gunboat *Jason* particularly demonstrated what could be done).

DNO Domville suggested eliminating the forecastle gun to clear the view from the conning tower as those inside aimed at the ship's target. Both 6in guns should be in casemates with arcs allowing them to fire right ahead. White interpreted this as adding a third 6in to the two 6in of an *Apollo* class cruiser, adding the third gun as a stern chaser. Unfortunately the guns and their protected casemates and their ammunition would add about 110 tons, about 45 per cent of the armament weight of an *Apollo*. White disliked the restricted arcs of the two forward guns, arguing that as the ram cruiser manoeuvred violently (to keep pointed at her target) the guns should be able to manoeuvre to stay on target.

White formally ordered preparation of a sketch design on 11 December 1893, about six weeks after Richards took office. Work was delayed; he may have been stalling in hopes the ram project would die. White was giving basic instructions as late as the end of April 1894. The ship would be about the size of the old *Orlando* (about 6000 tons), but with extremely hollow lines at the waterline for speed. The bow would be cut up (as in *Orlando*) but 'swelled out' in the wake of the ram, as in battleships, to give lateral strength.

The outline design was submitted on 8 June 1894, with the ships described not as rams but as fleet cruisers.[46] The Legend compared the new ship to *Orlando* and *Talbot*. The ship would cost about 10 per cent more than *Talbot* (about £275,000), which was acceptable. White claimed that she would be as capable as a *Talbot* in performing second-class cruiser duties,

and that her armament would compare favourably with that of many existing second-class cruisers – though armament had been sacrificed for protection and strengthening (for ramming).

The ship was 20ft longer than *Orlando* and 30ft shorter than the fast *Talbot*. White had tried to limit length to make the ship as manoeuvrable as possible, but he was unable to go below 320ft because he had to provide space for a submerged torpedo room (two tubes) as well as the usual machinery, boilers, magazines, steering gear, and so on. He hoped that his special rudder arrangements would make the ship at least as handy as a 300-footer, and (due to the bow rudder) handier when going astern. When the ships ran trials, it turned out that tactical diameter was 380 *feet*, compared to 650 yards for *Astraea* (of the same length) and 556yds for *Orlando* (which was 20ft shorter). This handiness was combined with steadiness on course.

Armour (3in reduced to 2in underwater) covered nearly the whole of the bow, narrowing as it ran aft. That 160 tons was both a defence against enemy gunfire as the cruiser ran towards her target, and as reinforcement for the ram; White claimed this was the strongest ram bow yet built. Abaft the ram was a pair of collision bulkheads running up to the upper deck, unpierced by doors or holes to a height of 15ft above water. The space forward of the collision bulkhead would be subdivided, and the two bulkheads were separated by a frame space, cork-filled cofferdams filling the space between them. Conning tower armour was 9in thick, compared to 6in in *Talbot* and 3in in *Astraea*.

White suggested using Belleville water-tube boilers, which promised the power he needed for high speed: 10,000 HP on trial with natural draught. They could not be 'forced' like the usual cylindrical type, but they would probably provide 80 per cent power on a sustained basis, giving 18½ to 19kts (at least equal to *Talbot*). The same weight of boilers and water in conventional (cylindrical) boilers would probably give no more than 6000 HP, for a smooth-water sustained speed of 17kts. It was also much easier rapidly to change the output of a water-tube boiler, which would be very important for a cruiser working with a fleet – especially for one which might suddenly have to accelerate in order to use her ram. Coal endurance must have been a particular problem. A battleship had 2000 tons of coal on board. The cruiser would need about half as much to match her endurance at cruising speed. Coal capacity was 1200 tons (7200nm at 10kts).

The Bellevilles turned out to burn coal much less efficiently than had been imagined. White argued that too much energy was going to auxiliaries. On their 30-hour trial at 12½kts they burned about 66 tons each day, which translated (for 1250 tons) to 19 days, nearly 5700nm. At 17.8kts they burned about 172 tons per day (3000nm). They hardly matched the battleships.

White chose to improve his usual coal protection. In addition to the usual transverse partitions, he planned to install longitudinal ones, dividing the bunkers above the protective deck on each side into two sections. In each, the coal in the inner layer could be worked down to the protective deck without disturbing the outer layer of coal. As in White's other designs, all of the coal below the protective deck could be burned without serious loss of stability.

Controller Rear Admiral Fisher proposed that the design be

Furious

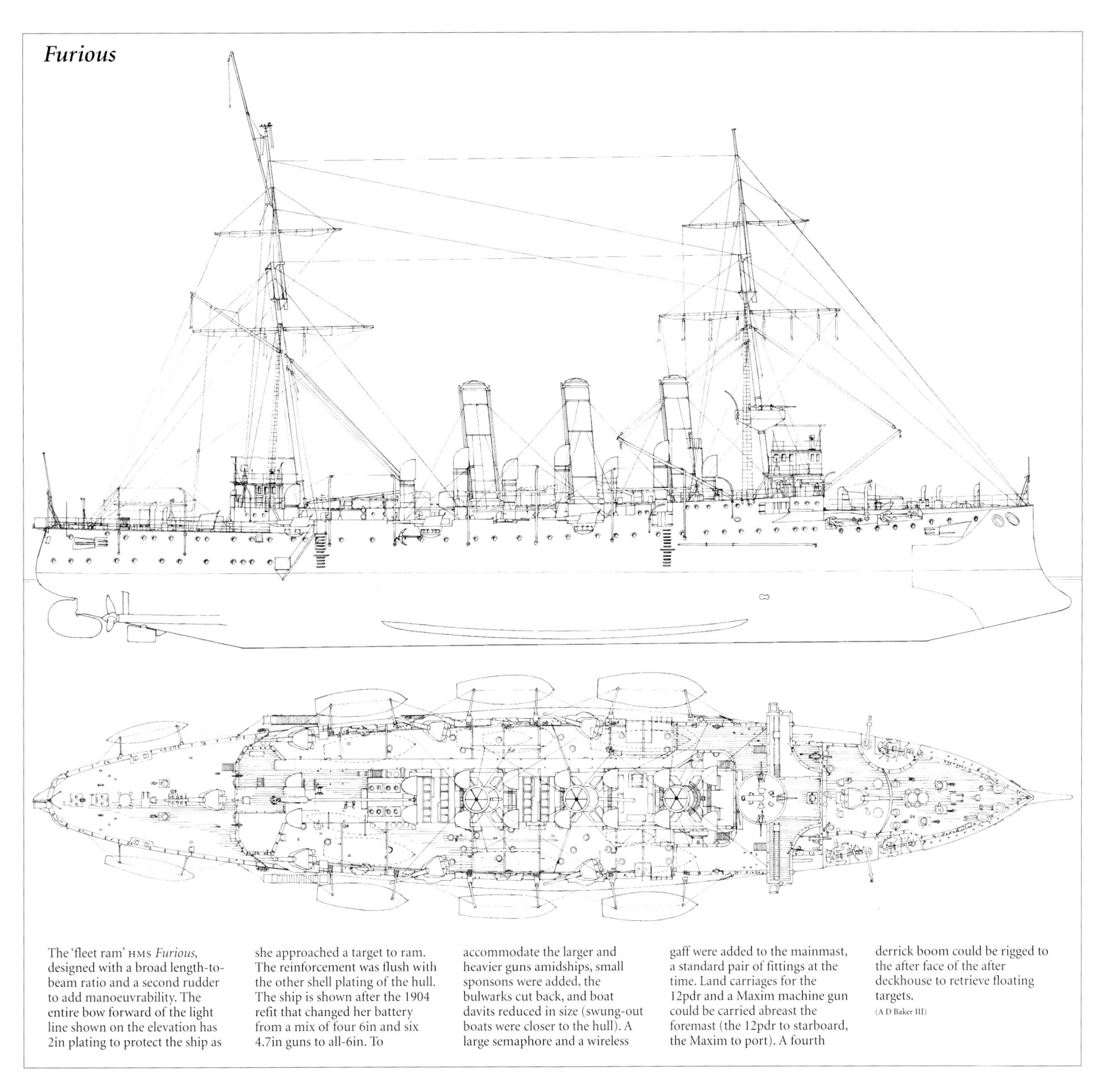

The 'fleet ram' HMS *Furious*, designed with a broad length-to-beam ratio and a second rudder to add manoeuvrability. The entire bow forward of the light line shown on the elevation has 2in plating to protect the ship as she approached a target to ram. The reinforcement was flush with the other shell plating of the hull. The ship is shown after the 1904 refit that changed her battery from a mix of four 6in and six 4.7in guns to all-6in. To accommodate the larger and heavier guns amidships, small sponsons were added, the bulwarks cut back, and boat davits reduced in size (swung-out boats were closer to the hull). A large semaphore and a wireless gaff were added to the mainmast, a standard pair of fittings at the time. Land carriages for the 12pdr and a Maxim machine gun could be carried abreast the foremast (the 12pdr to starboard, the Maxim to port). A fourth derrick boom could be rigged to the after face of the after deckhouse to retrieve floating targets. (A D Baker III)

approved. As a last step before ordering ships, on 19 October the Naval Lords, DNO, and DNC met to consider the ship's armament. They decided to add a gun forward on the centreline, for a total of four 6in. Compared to a *Talbot*, the ships had one 6in on the quarterdeck instead of two. They were supplemented by six 4.7in QF in the waist, by eight 12pdr, six 3pdr, and two submerged 18in torpedo tubes. All of this added about 100 tons. White later pointed out that, in a *Highflyer*, adding 100 tons would buy six 6in instead of the 4.7in in the waist. The same argument applied to an *Arrogant*.

Four of these *Arrogant* class second-class cruisers were included in the 1895-96 Estimates, rather than the six originally planned. One of them, HMS *Vindictive*, became famous for her attacks on Ostend and Zeebrugge in 1918. It seems likely that she was selected for the raids because of her bow protection.

6 BIG CRUISERS TO PROTECT COMMERCE

Blake and Blenheim

Having designed a small fast cruiser, in June 1887 White offered the Board a very large fast one with extraordinary range – the largest and (at 22kts) fastest in the world. It was so much larger than the others that a separate category – the first-class cruiser – had to be created for it, the others naturally becoming second- and then third-class.[1] White cited the threat, which had certainly been appreciated in 1885, of fast long-range liners (much larger than the new cruiser) converted into commerce raiders. A British cruiser capable of catching such a ship might have to drop out periodically to coal, letting the longer-legged raider get away. A forced-draught 22kts would buy the much more important ability to maintain 20kts, and thus to deal with foreign cruisers even when the latter resorted to forced draught to get away. 'Anything less [than 22kts] could scarcely be accepted under existing conditions in a vessel intended to be the most powerful of her class afloat.' As with the decision to build *Vulcan* as a cruiser rather than as a converted merchant ship, it seems likely that White, and probably First Lord Hamilton, saw White's super cruisers *Blake* and *Blenheim* as built-for-the-purpose (hence far more satisfactory) equivalents of liners converted into cruisers, capable of running down and killing foreign fast converted liners.

White began with a sketch of a ship with two 9.2in guns (later one) at each end, side by side, and five medium guns in the waist, plus four small QF guns above them behind a bulwark, and QF guns (to beat off torpedo boats) at bow and stern. The ship would have two boiler rooms, hence two funnels, with three double-ended cylindrical boilers side by side in each. Internal arrangement was simplified by having only one set of magazines, forward of the boilers. White envisaged a 375ft 7000- to 8000-ton ship developing 18,000 IHP for 22kts, at the time a remarkable speed.[2] He wrote that the maximum speed exceeded by 2kts 'what has been obtained or contemplated hitherto in any seagoing warship when *fully laden*. The *maximum ocean speed* required for the cruiser to be averaged in fair weather, as long as her coal could last, is 2kts greater than the *forced draught speed* which any cruiser built or building could maintain for *6 hours* with her full coal supply on board.'

Blenheim in Victorian livery as completed. Like many other Victorian cruisers, she went into reserve upon completion, remaining at Chatham in 1891-94. She was in the Channel Fleet in 1894-98, then in reserve 1898-1901, and in the China Fleet 1901-4. On her return she was converted into a destroyer depot ship (1905-6), serving in the Home (1906-13) and Mediterranean (1913-20) Fleets, and then as depot ship for reserve minesweepers at Harwich and later Sheerness (1921-5).
(National Maritime Museum N00997)

Instead of the belt in HMS *Orlando*, the ships would have White's preferred combination of protective decks (3in on the flat, 6in on the slope amidships, 2 to 2½in fore and aft). Except for size and speed, this was the upgraded *Mersey* dropped in favour of the belted *Orlando* – on a much larger scale, to achieve much higher speed, and greater range. This was among the first designs under the new weight rules, with an assigned Board Margin (4 per cent). White increased designed power from 18,000 to 20,000 IHP specifically to insure that the ship would make her speed at a displacement including the margin, 9000 tons.

The Board approved the project on 16 August 1887, probably the same day the *Vulcan* design was ordered. White submitted the design on 11 January 1888. One was to be laid down at Chatham during the 1888-89 financial year. Model tests convinced White that the ship would make her speed. He had doubled the power to gain the 3kts from 19 to 22. Great length made it easier to drive a very large ship. Thus White wrote that although a third heavier than the torpedo depot ship, the new cruiser would need only about 1500 HP more to attain 20kts; and although more than twice the displacement of the cruiser *Medea*, the new ship would require only 10 per cent more power to achieve 21kts.

The great length was chosen to balance the needs of propulsion (greater length cut resistance) and protection (which added weight by the length of the ship). White claimed that it was about the same 'as the heavier class in our Navy, and the latest large cruisers of the French Navy', but in 1887 no other British or French warship approached it. White admitted that the new ships would not be as manoeuvrable as armoured ships 325ft long (British battleships). He could make up some of the difference by cutting away deadwood, using a large balanced

Blenheim at the end of her cruiser career in 1904, in the new grey livery, looking somewhat beaten-up. Note the semaphore at the head of her mainmast (the thicker part of the mast at its head).
(National Maritime Museum N000998)

rudder, and providing a more powerful steering engine, but handiness was not so important in a fast ship intended for solitary operations protecting trade.

To produce all that power, White planned to put two vertical triple expansion engines in tandem on each shaft, in two engine rooms, arranged so that one or both of the after set could be disconnected to save power (up to 15 or 16kts). The hull was so deep that the cylinders would not protrude above the protective deck. The cylindrical boilers would work at high pressure, 150psi. As in other protected cruiser designs, this one had coal stowed between the skin and the boiler and engine rooms, providing additional protection. To produce the vast power required, White planned to use four separate stokeholds, each with its own cross-bunker. He appreciated that it would be difficult to load so much coal on board, and he provided special coaling ports. White wrote that protection over the vitals would equal the large Italian ships then building, which probably meant the two *Italia*s (just completed).

The January 1888 design showed heavy (70pdr) QF guns, but by this time their trials were disappointing, to the point where White later argued against considering them for his cruiser-depot ship *Vulcan*. The 70pdr would have been intermediate between the 5in gun of smaller ships and the 6in of cruisers and battleship secondary batteries, and it was no longer clear that it was worthwhile. By this time White thought it better to adopt either the existing slow-firing 6in or the 36pdr (4.7in) QF. Armstrong, which was developing the 70pdr, had decided to drop it in favour of a 6in QF (100pdr).

Blenheim 1894

HMS *Blenheim* is shown as newly completed, May 1894. The reference as-fitted drawing, dated 26 August 1893, shows fold-down bulwarks abreast the six upper-deck 6in guns, but they were omitted by the time the ships were completed. Note that the casemates had flat armour panels rather than the curved panels used on board later ships. The two 9pdr field artillery pieces were stowed on the upper deck amidships on their carriage wagons and with their two ammunition wagons. Two of the eight Nordenfelt machine guns could be fitted to two other wagons stowed on the upper deck abreast the mainmast. The crown of the protective deck was 18in above the waterline (at the centreline), and the lower edges of the slopes were 6ft 6in below the waterline at the sides. *Blenheim* and her sister *Blake* were the first Royal Navy ships to have torpedo net defences that included booms supporting nets rigged across bow and stern. Instead of platforms along the sides to carry the rolled-up nets when not in use (as in later ships), these ships stowed their nets on the slatted platform shown to starboard of the larger boats amidships. They were handled by the main boat booms. The ships had a very large water ballast tank just abaft their pronounced ram bows. In the plan view, the boats shown slung outboard for harbour service are also shown inboard in their seagoing positions. The original rigging plan for *Blenheim* shows that a single large jib could be carried by the foremast. All four 24in searchlights were mounted on the main deck behind the rectangular doors shown in the elevation. They were slid out on rails when in use, giving them 180-degree coverage. What appears to be a fifth searchlight is labelled on the as-fitted plan as a signal lamp. It could be mounted on either wing of the after bridge. It was normally stowed just to port of the centreline. By 1895 both ships had been given topmasts. Both ships had very elaborate bow scrollwork that unfortunately could not be reproduced in the drawing.
(A D Baker III)

When the design was before the Board, White compared it with known fast foreign cruisers under construction: the French *Tage*, *Dupuy de Lôme* and *Cecille*; the Russian *Admiral Kornilov*; and the German *Irene*. None was anything like as large (the French ships, the largest, displaced, respectively, 6930, 6200, and 5670 tons. The fastest of them, the French *Dupuy de Lôme*, was credited with no more than 20kts. None had a gun anything like as powerful as the new ship's 9.2in.

The Board found the design remarkable, the only change being a decision not to introduce a new calibre (70pdr) and to fall back on the combination of 36pdrs and 6in slow-firers, possibly in combination. Initially it was decided not to tender for the second ship (to be built under contract) until the armament had been decided. On this basis the design received the Board Stamp on 31 January 1888. By April, the armament had been chosen: two 9.2in, ten 100pdr (6in) QF on the main deck, eighteen 3pdr (upper and main decks), and four 14in torpedo tubes (two above and two below water).

The speedsters did not quite match White's hopes: *Blenheim* made 21.8kts under forced draught. They were, however, good for high sustained speeds. On trial *Blenheim* made 20.4kts on 14,924 IHP.

The lesson was probably that really high speed was an elusive and very expensive goal. *Blake* and *Blenheim* were not repeated in the large program enacted in 1889. That program included a ship tentatively called Improved *Mersey*, which merely meant a powerful protected cruiser. White based it on the next largest cruiser hull he had developed, *Vulcan*. The choice may have been forced on him by the sheer number of designs that had to be produced in a short time under the impetus of the Act.

Edgar Class
Meeting with the Board on board the Admiralty yacht *Enchantress* on 17 August 1888, DNC White proposed combining the armament of the *Blake* and the hull, protection, machinery, and coal supply of his next-largest cruiser design, *Vulcan*. To the extent possible, armament would match that of *Blake*: two 9.2in at the ends, ten 6in (but with six on the upper deck and four on the main deck), and 3pdrs interspersed with the 6in on both decks. It might be necessary to reduce the number of 3pdrs. Complement would be based on that of *Blake*, but with the engine room complement of *Vulcan*. Given experience with *Vulcan*, White estimated that the ship would cost (exclusive of armament) £250,000. This figure was about that suggested for an 'Improved 19½-knot *Mersey*' contained in a July 1888 confidential printed memo sketching the new naval program.

Things were not quite that simple. The *Vulcan* hull had to be enlarged somewhat, to 7000 tons and 360ft x 60ft rather than 350ft x 58ft and 6600 tons. A Legend was produced in October 1888.[3] The only armament sacrificed was six 3pdrs (later 6pdrs were substituted, to deal with increasingly large torpedo boats).[4] The protective deck was that of the *Vulcan*: 5in rather than 6in slopes amidships, but with 6in vertical armour around the cylinder heads, which in this case did protrude from the armoured deck. The flat of the deck was 2½in thick. The conning tower was 12in thick, as in *Blake*. Casemate protection (desired by the Board) was added to the main deck 6in guns (at a cost of 100 tons). To simplify coal supply at high speed, and to make it unnecessary to take coal from bunkers above the protective deck while in action, another cross-bunker was added, compared to *Vulcan*. This was not a bad bargain.

The Board asked for thicker shields for the 9.2in guns and greater coal capacity (for wartime: 1000 tons). There was also some interest in making the casemates thicker, and in providing protected ready-use magazines (which had been approved for *Blake* and *Blenheim*). That might have added another 160 to 180 tons. To preclude changes, Financial Secretary (Arthur Forwood) suggested that, rather than expend the 4 per cent margin, the ship should be enlarged – which no one was willing to do. The design received the Board Stamp on 6 November 1888. It later proved possible to thicken the deck over the magazines (2½in flat, 4in slope instead of 2 to 2½in) and at the bow (2in horizontal instead of 1 to 1½in) at a cost of less than 100 tons.[5]

The ships were protected by a protective deck and a belt of coal extending below the waterline, in subdivided bunkers. White's critics argued that against the relatively new threat of high-explosive shells the ship needed thin side armour. They cited recent trials against the old ironclad *Resistance*. White argued that the coal would stifle explosions above it. It also kept water out of the ship, whatever damage was done to the ship's thin side. Even if the side was shattered, the amount of water she would take on would be limited because the coal would fill nearly all of the space available (White estimated that only about 40 or 50 tons could enter the ship that way). It had always been assumed that in action the outer skin would be freely perforated or severely damaged, so any leak-stoppers in contact with the skin (e.g., cofferdams or other packing) would simply be shattered or blown away. He therefore put his cofferdams behind the longitudinal bulkhead dividing the outer bunkers from the inner ones.

White also thought that the *Resistance* experiments had not settled the issue. Moreover, within two years there would be further advances both in explosives and in HE shells. A 3in belt over 1in skin plating, to cover the boilers and machinery (a length of about 130ft) of the new first-class cruiser would cost 280 tons, nearly the whole Board Margin. He therefore proposed a fallback, a way of building the ships without giving up the possibility of adding side armour later on. Both the new cruisers and *Blake* and *Blenheim* would be built with doubled plating over the area a belt might cover. If side armour were wanted, the thicker side could support it. If not, he was adding only 45 tons to the new cruisers and about 55 to *Blake* and *Blenheim*. These figures were well within the Board Margins.

White did his best to make side armour a painful prospect. It should not merely cover a strip amidships, but should extend to the bow (if not to the stern). This was not just protection to the vitals, but to the buoyancy and trim of the ship. That meant real weight: 650 tons in the new ships, 700 for the *Blake*s. Unless the Board Margin, so recently introduced, was discarded, such figures were impossible. Moreover, it was impossible to thin the slopes of the thick part of the deck, because they really did protect the ship's vitals, and the thin belt would not. The *Blake*s had already grown by 300 tons. In May 1889 the Board approved the thin additional plating but not the proposed belts.

By January 1889 the effect of various changes approved by the

Gibraltar in February 1894. Note the booms of the torpedo net defence, and the after bridge. Until the advent of the steel hulls, British cruisers were generally conned from aft. Many classes retained after bridges, often with charthouses, well after the now-standard forward bridges were introduced. Upon completion in 1894, *Gibraltar* was assigned to the Particular Service squadron in 1894-95 and then to the 'Flying Squadron' in 1896. She was assigned to the Mediterranean in 1896-99. After refit and reserve at Portsmouth in 1899-1901 she became flagship of the Cape station (1901-4). She then went to the North America and West Indies station (1904-6) before going into the Devonport reserve (1906-13). During that time she carried troops to Australia in 1908 and escorted the new destroyers *Parramatta* and *Yarra* there in 1910-11. In 1914 she was assigned to the anti-submarine school at Portland. She then joined the Northern Patrol enforcing the blockade of Germany (10th Cruiser Squadron), and was disarmed early in 1915. She was depot ship for the Northern Patrol in the Shetlands in 1915-18, and then destroyer depot ship and anti-submarine school ship at Portland in 1919-22.

Gibraltar about 1912, showing her foretop and the range drum abaft it, its read-out visible from her upper deck. By 1907 *Endymion* had a similar top, and *Grafton* had a large square top with flat sides. At the time of her collision with ss *Olympic*, *Hawke* had a large round top. It was in place by 1907. She and other cruisers were given high topmasts to increase radio range. These masts replaced the earlier wireless gaff on the mainmast. The 'flat top' antenna itself was strung between the masts. It is barely visible in the form of leads and insulators strung from the upper yardarm of the foremast. Note too the canvas protecting the compass platform atop the charthouse, from which the ship was increasingly conned. A pelorus and a chart table are visible emerging from the canvas.

Board plus detailed design brought displacement to 7350 tons.

Boiler power was insufficient. The key requirement was a sustained sea speed of 18kts, the power available being defined as two-thirds of full natural draught power (which says a great deal about what contemporary boilers could do). Since 18kts required 8000 HP, the ship needed 12,000 HP at full natural draught. In June Engineer-in-Chief Durston pointed out that four boilers of the projected size would not suffice. To accommodate the six needed, the ship would have to be enlarged. However, the ship could achieve 10,000 HP if four larger boilers were substituted. White offered to make the necessary space by cutting back the coal bunker bulkheads and accepting a slight loss of stability. The engines would not be able to use all the steam the boilers would produce under forced draught. To exploit that, the engines would have to be enlarged, and the ship might make as much as 21kts on trial. If the engines were *not* enlarged, 'we shall be practically giving to Foreign ships an advantage in speed under critical conditions which may be of serious importance'. The real question was not whether British cruisers had adequate boiler power, but whether the existing Admiralty policy favouring large numbers of cruisers of moderate size and cost would continue. White seems to have been responding to criticism that British cruisers were substantially slower than fast liners which might be converted into raiders in wartime. Such ships, far larger than the cruisers, devoted so much of their capacity to engines and boilers that even the best of them would be ineffective warships. The Board took up the issue on 1 July 1889. All new first-class cruisers (and the *Apollo*s) were to be given increased boiler power.

These ships became the *Edgar* class, nine of which were built

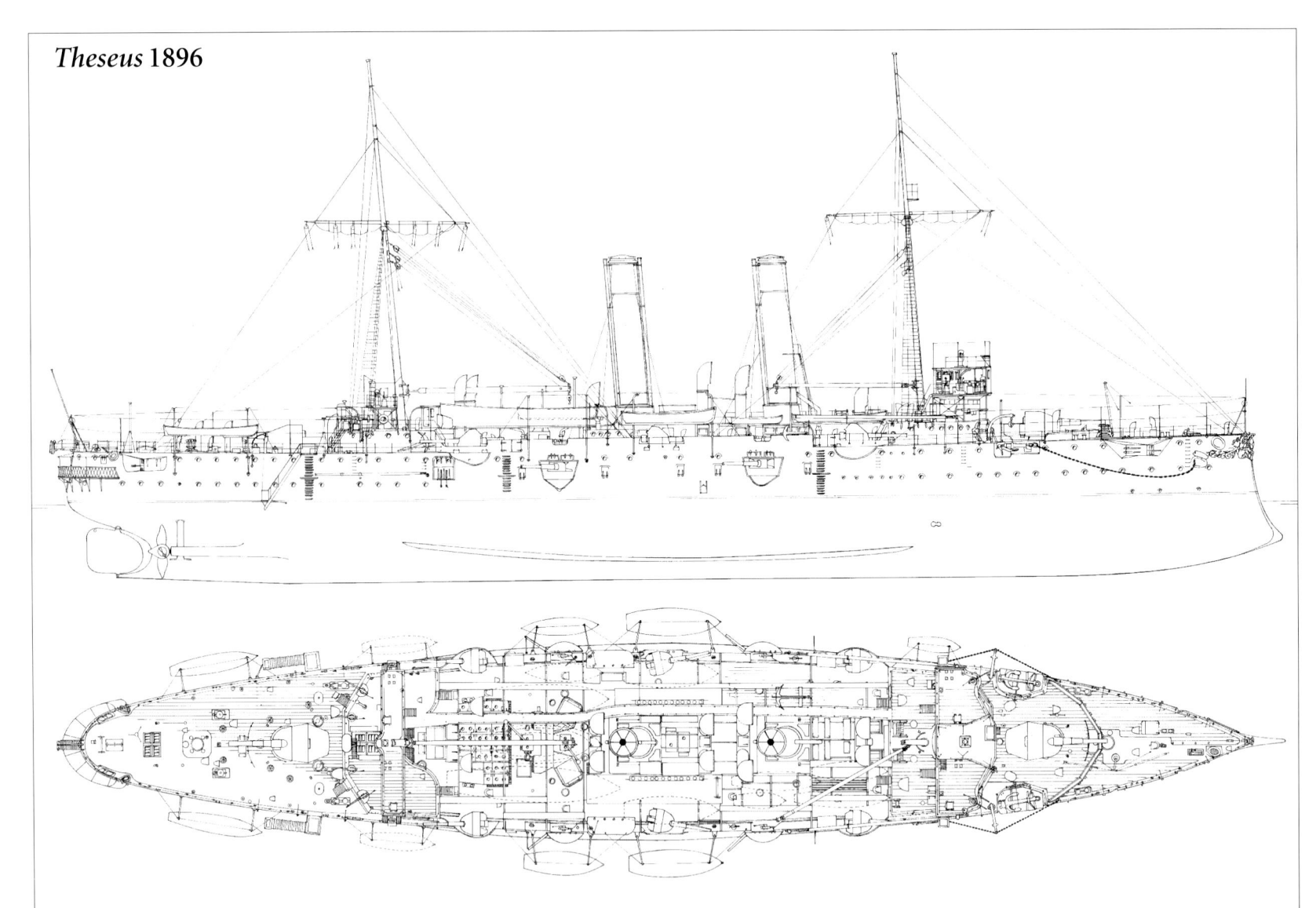

Theseus 1896

HMS *Theseus* is shown as completed, February 1896. By 1912, two 12pdr QF had been mounted on the forward corners of the after deckhouse, while the positions for the Maxim machine guns were relocated to platforms atop the latrine deckhouse amidships (with two alternate mounting positions). The rows of small circles abreast the second funnel in the plan view are stowage positions for small cowl ventilators used when the ship was cleared for action. What appears to be a second, narrower catwalk between the main superstructure blocks to port of the larger one was actually a stowage platform for collision mats. While most British conning towers were oval in plan form and had a domed top, in this class it was circular and had a flat top. A smaller conning tower was installed at the aft end of the after superstructure. Post-completion they were given four semaphores on the bridge wings. Later a large semaphore was added atop the mainmast. By 1912 it had been removed and a topmast added for radio antenna arrays. The searchlights are shown stowed to port and in their operating positions to starboard: there were no rails on which to move them. For clarity, some of the numerous ship's boats were omitted in the profile view, and some of boats are shown in both their stowed and harbour locations (the 16ft skiff could be carried either to port or to starboard of the forward bridge).

Crescent 1904

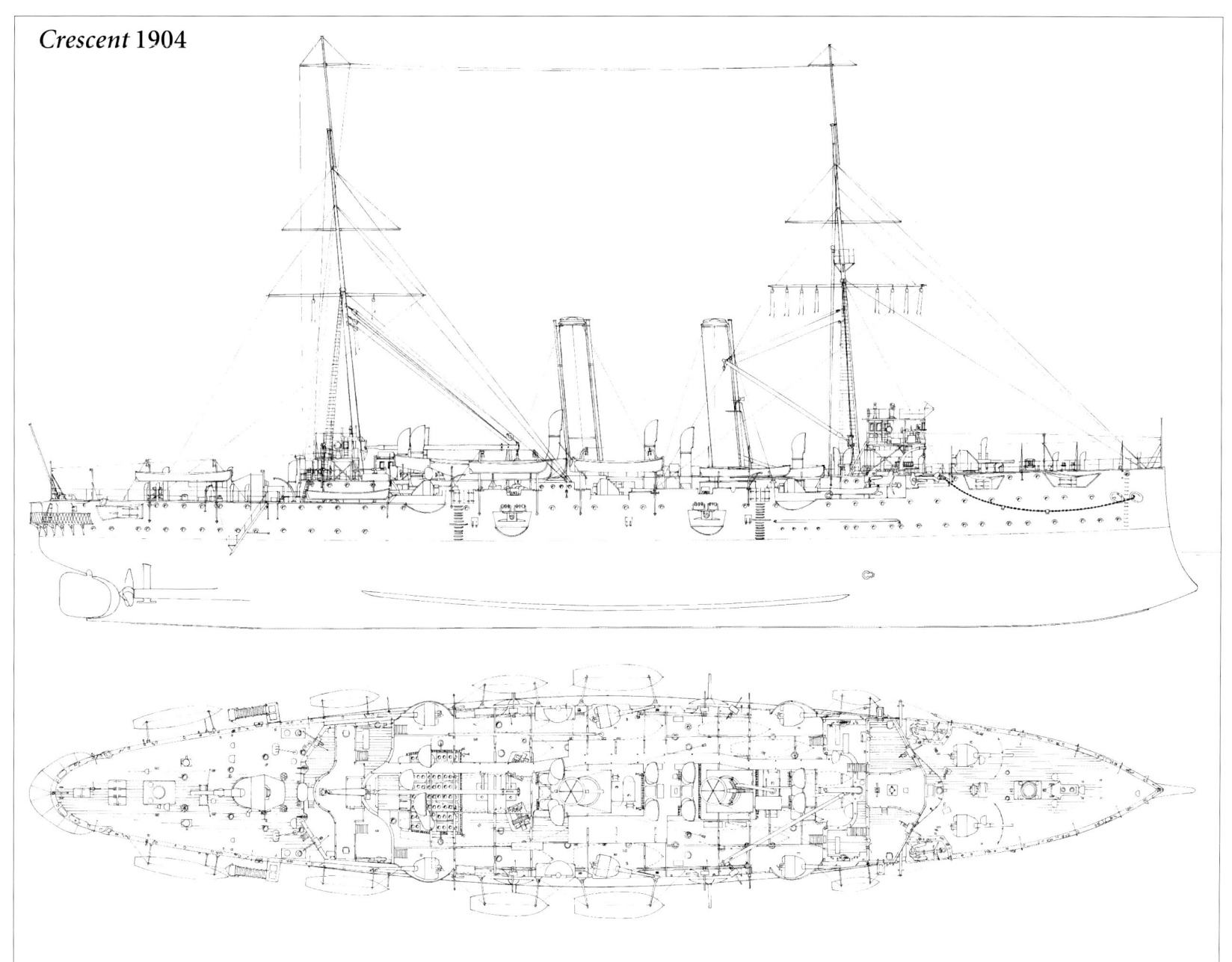

HMS *Crescent* is shown in February 1904, about a decade after completion. Changes made during the 1903-4 refit included removal of two 18in torpedo tubes in single mounts (formerly on the main deck abreast the torpedo fire control tower), removal of two 24in searchlights on the main deck (which had deployed through doors in the side of the hull), and addition of topmasts to support a radio antenna. The new radio room was fitted on the main deck to port, just forward of the 9.2in gun. Also removed was the torpedo net boom outfit, including the shelf along the side of the ship which she had carried since completion. The original elaborate bow scrollwork was also deleted. According to the 27 February 1904 as-fitted plan, the 25ft cutter shown in the drawing slung from davits to starboard was removed, but it continued to appear in later photos. Note the extensive clutter of ventilators and other gear that had to be taken down before the main battery guns could be trained. The heavy anchor davits could not be folded down and stowed on deck as in earlier British cruisers. In addition to the change in battery and the higher forecastle, she and her sister *Royal Arthur* differed from the *Edgar*s in having three- instead of four-bladed propellers, and in carrying a second-class torpedo boat rather than a 56ft steam launch (which had portable drop gear). In addition to the main conning tower beneath the bridge structure, these ships had a small armoured torpedo control tower at the after edge of the after superstructure. The two *Crescents* and the *Edgar* class cruisers *Gibraltar* and *St George* were intended for deployment abroad, hence had their underwater hulls sheathed in wood and coppered. (A D Baker III)

under the Naval Defence Act.

In the spring of 1890 Controller proposed a further change: a high forecastle about 100ft long, increasing freeboard forward from 20 to 27ft. It was requested primarily to provide additional internal space for flagships. The way in which the space was provided made it easier to drive the ships against a head sea. To compensate for the added weight (and also for the added moment of guns higher in the ship), the forward 9.2in gun was replaced by two 6in, leaving the 9.2in gun aft. The Board approved the change on 1 April 1890. White seems to have seen it as a vote favouring lighter cruiser guns (which seems not to have been the case). Later he rationalized it: the ship would probably find herself chasing unarmoured ships, in which case 6in bow chasers would suffice, whereas the 9.2in gun aft would still be available to defend the ship should something heavier chase her. He may also have had in mind Rear Admiral Hotham's earlier remark that a 9.2in gun was too heavy for a fast cruiser. White also later wrote that the changes had been discussed earlier, but had not been incorporated for the rather odd reason that it had been decided to follow the *Blake*s in armament and in general features such as freeboard and external appearance. Two ships, *Centaur* (later renamed *Royal Arthur*) and *Crescent*, were at a very early stage and hence could easily be modified.

Powerful and *Terrible*

Meanwhile the Russians were building large fast armoured cruisers, which the Royal Navy considered direct threats to British trade. The new *Rurik* (launched in November 1892) in particular seemed to offer sensational performance.[6] She was

Endymion. In the absence of fighting tops, machine guns were mounted on the bridge wings, as here. Note the absence of bridge semaphores, which are evident in the 1894 photographs of *Gibraltar*. On completion in 1894, she was assigned to the Channel Fleet (1894-95) and then to the Particular Service Squadron (1896-97). She was held in reserve at Chatham in 1897-99, and then assigned to the China Fleet in 1899-1902. After a refit at Harland & Wolff (1902-3) she was assigned to the Channel Fleet in 1904. She then became tender to HMS *Wildfire* as gunnery training ship at Sheerness in 1905-12, and was assigned to the Third (reserve) Fleet at Portsmouth in 1912-13. In 1913-14 she was flagship of the training squadron at Queenstown. In 1914 she was assigned to the Northern Patrol (10th Cruiser Squadron). Late in 1914 she was withdrawn to be rebuilt as a bombardment ship for the Dardanelles, where she served in 1915-16. She remained in the Mediterranean thereafter, and was in the Aegean in 1918.

credited with the same 18-knot sea speed as the *Edgar*s, but with a much greater coal capacity (1900 tons nominal, 2150 tons full capacity), and a heavy armament (four 8in, sixteen 6in, six 4.7in, all unprotected). The coal capacity, far greater than that of earlier Russian belted cruisers, was the problem. The Russians were building two more ships, and there were reports of a large program.[7] Aside from her value against the new Russian cruisers, his proposed British cruiser could run down any French liner converted into a cruiser, as well as all the steamers the Russians had collected (or could collect) in their Volunteer Fleet for wartime raiding.[8]

White thought the Russians had deliberately *understated* sea speed. On the basis of current British practice, the ships should have enough machinery weight to realize 19,000 to 20,000 IHP at natural draught (12,000 on a continuous basis), corresponding to a sea speed of 19kts. For the stated 18kts, 10,000 should have been enough. That would represent too great a margin between continuous and maximum power 'and the fact that it has been taken points to the desire of the Russian authorities to under-state the sea speed of the *Rurik*, and to give her an actual speed exceeding the published estimates'.

White was not sure that the Russian ships could steam quite as far as advertised. Kronstadt to Vladivostok was 16,000nm via the Cape and 12,740nm via the Canal. The Royal Navy had gained extensive experience of sustained steaming at the typical cruising speed of 10kts. White thought the Russians based their claims on the performance of merchant ships running at full power, in which case they would burn 1.5 to 1.7lbs of coal per IHP per hour. A cruising warship was less efficient, a typical British figure being nearly 3lbs per IHP per hour. On this basis White estimated that *Rurik* would cover about 8500nm on her 2000 tons of coal, rather more than half the distance

BIG CRUISERS TO PROTECT COMMERCE

Royal Arthur shows her raised forecastle, with two 6in instead of a single 9.2in gun. Upon completion she became flagship of the Pacific station (1893-96). After refitting at Portsmouth (1896-97) she joined the Particular Service Squadron in 1897, then became flagship of the Australia station (1897-1904). Upon returning home in 1904 she refitted and became flagship of the 4th Cruiser Squadron on the North America and West Indies station (1905-6). She then returned to reserve at Portsmouth; her duties included trooping in 1908. She was in the training squadron at Queenstown in 1913-14, and then in the Northern Patrol (10th Cruiser Squadron). In 1915 she was guardship at Scapa Flow, after which she was a submarine depot ship.

from her base to Vladivostok via the Cape. Even then she had an enormous coal endurance for a cruiser; *Blake* could steam only 7300nm at 10kts, and *Edgar* about 5300.

On 3 February 1893 White was ordered to design a new super-cruiser for the 1893-94 program specifically to be individually superior to the Russian ships.[9] It was left to a later meeting to decide just how superior she should be in speed, coal supply, armament, and protection. White understood that his ship had to be at least one knot faster on a continuous basis. At the least she should have a sea speed of 20kts, the figure in the sketch design he submitted. In that case the ship would make 22kts on natural draught trials (i.e., as much as had been hoped for from *Blake* under forced draught), and 23kts in smooth water with moderate forcing.[10]

As with the *Blake*s, despite gross British superiority in coaling stations, a British cruiser chasing one of the Russians might not be able to afford a day-long stopover to coal. Compared to the Russians, a huge fast British cruiser would need more power for 10kts, so she would burn more coal. The ratio of consumption might be 8 to 7 – so she would need about 2300 tons (in round figures, 2500) for the same endurance. With 3000 tons a cruiser could keep the sea for 46 days, enjoying a 30 per cent advantage over *Rurik*. White suggested a normal load (Legend or trial displacement) of 1500 tons, with capacity for 3000. Reducing coal capacity would make a smaller, less expensive, ship. The higher-powered British engines (for higher maximum speed) would be less efficient at lower speed: the British cruiser would always need more coal than the Russian for a given speed.

White offered a battery of twenty 6in QF, one at each end, plus ten 4in (25pdr) QF, ten 3pdr QF, and four submerged torpedo tubes. He explained the single bow and stern chasers on the ground that their positions, while the most commanding, were also the most exposed. A British ship armed with QF guns would pour out far more fire than *Rurik* (with her slow-firing unprotected guns), and also would enjoy greatly superior arrangements for handling ammunition. To accommodate all those guns on the broadside, White introduced two-storey casemates at the ends of the battery. The ten re-

Royal Arthur in later life, about 1904.
(Allan C Green, courtesy of State Library of Victoria)

maining 6in guns were in double-deck casemates (25pdr above, 6in below on the main deck) between the two two-storey 6in ones on each side. Adopting a single main calibre would much simplify ammunition supply. In offensive power his cruiser would compare favourably with 'many so-called battleships when the character of the armament and its protection are taken into account'. White understood that this was satisfactory to the Board.

White defended his preferred type of protection against both the thick narrow waterline belt of the Russian ships and the thin plating the French were then spreading over much of the sides of their new armoured cruisers, beginning with the *Dupuy de Lôme*. For him the key was protecting the vitals of the ship, which were underwater. That required a strong protective deck. A narrow waterline belt cost weight that could and should go into the deck. Because she had a belt, *Rurik*'s deck was half as thick as that White planned for the new ship, and only a quarter as strong. Coal and other material could protect against the effects of riddling the unprotected side of the ship. In the *Arrogant* class White had introduced a sophisticated form of coal protection in which a longitudinal bulkhead in the bunkers divided an outer protective layer from an inner layer from which coal could be taken without loss of protection. He claimed that experiments, presumably most prominently those against HMS *Resistance*, showed that coal stowed in bulk was 'one of the best possible "shell stiflers"' and that it would keep water out and so help maintain buoyancy and stability. White entirely rejected the idea that the belt offered serious protection to buoyancy and trim.

Advocates of thin armour generally claimed that it made sure that high-explosive shells burst on the side of a ship instead of inside. White pointed out that delayed-action fuzes could burst a shell inside a ship. Even if the shell did not make it inside, solid armour-piercing shot, even from 12pdr and 25pdr QF guns, could penetrate to do enormous damage. White cited the *Resistance* trials, which had inspired individual protection to guns in the form of casemates, introduced in the *Powerful*s. The *Resistance* experiments also showed that a high-explosive hit on thin side plating tended to do only local damage when the plating was well-supported by girders or frames.

Some read the experience of the Battle of the Yalu (1894) as proof of the value of light belt armour. White disagreed. The Chinese lost both a belted and a protected-deck cruiser, but the losses proved little: that the ships had been much neglected and their watertight subdivision was probably non-existent. The Japanese lost none of their protected cruisers. Perhaps most important of all, the two Chinese battleships had large unarmoured ends and underwater protected decks. They were

HMS *Terrible* as refitted with double casemates amidships. She participated in the 1897 manoeuvres before her completion. Upon completion she was assigned to special service in 1898-99, and then to the China Fleet (1899 - 1902); like her sister she was detached to the Cape (1899-1900) for the Boer War. Her battle honours included both the Boer War and the Boxer Rebellion. She was refitted (with the new casemates) on Clydebank in 1902-4, and then placed in commission in reserve at Portsmouth in 1905. She escorted HMS *Renown* for the cruise to India by the Prince and Princess of Wales in 1905-6 and then carried troops to China in 1906. She was then reduced to reserve with a nucleus crew at Portsmouth in 1907-12, moving to the Pembroke Reserve in 1913-14. She was disarmed, but was used for trooping to the Dardanelles in 1915-16. She then became an accommodation ship at Portsmouth as part of the *Fisgard* establishment (1916-31).

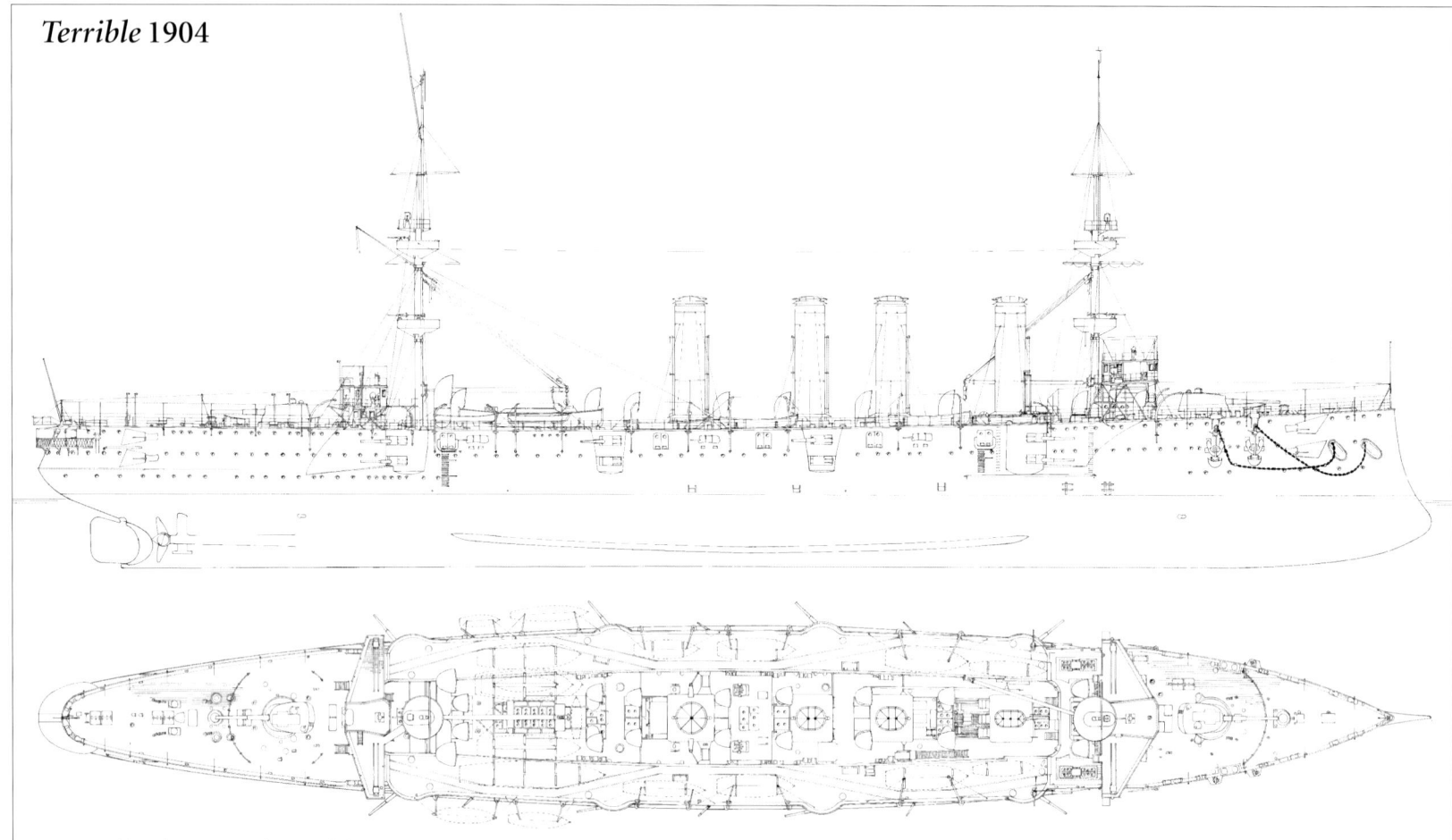

Terrible 1904

HMS *Terrible* is shown in March 1904 after her 1902-4 refit, during which she was given two-storey casemates between her end two-storey ones, although the lower 6in guns were not fitted (they were mounted in her sister *Powerful*). Four additional 3pdr positions in the two upper fighting tops were not occupied. To fit in the four upper casemates amidships, several 12pdr positions and coaling ports and the officers' heads had to be relocated. Coaling ports were required in the sides because most coal scuttles on the upper deck were beneath the overhanging boat deck. Given the ship's anti-raider mission of sustained pursuit with the most limited stops to coal, special attention was paid to measures allowing faster coaling, such as the side scuttles. During the Boer War, the ship carried ten Maxim machine guns in place of 3pdrs on the boat deck. The parallel diagonal lines on the boat deck in the plan view denote the brass strips which held down coir matting to improve footing on the bare-steel deck. As in the *Drake* class, the anchor-handling capstan was on the upper deck rather than on the weather deck. The armoured tower atop the after control superstructure was the torpedo control tower for torpedo tubes mounted forward and aft below the waterline. The torpedo magazines were loaded via hatches on the weather deck abaft the forward 9.2in turret and just abaft the after superstructure.

(A D Baker III)

riddled badly, but mainly well above the waterline; they survived. Advocates of QF guns and thin armour had predicted that both would quickly be sunk.

White considered a range of sizes between 450ft (12,500 tons) and 500ft (14,000 tons). This was a battleship-sized cruiser, which would probably cost almost as much as a battleship. The smaller ship was cramped, so he preferred the 500-footer, unless limits on docking facilities precluded that.[11] She would be easier to drive, particularly at high speed, and she would maintain her speed better in a seaway – important if she were running down one of the Russians. The extra 50ft would add comparatively little cost – perhaps £20,000 to £25,000 – because there was no side armour. A 500ft cruiser could already be drydocked at Portsmouth, Birkenhead, and Belfast, and one of the new Portsmouth docks could be completed with the desired length. A dock at Chatham would have to be lengthened. No existing dock at Devonport was long enough, but that yard was about to be modernized. Docks being built at Southampton and Glasgow (to take transatlantic liners) would take the new ship. Abroad there were large enough docks at Malta (if slightly altered), at Halifax, at Hong Kong (if slightly altered), at Sydney, and at Melbourne. The dock at Auckland could be adapted. White expected the standard for warship speed to rise. Ships would grow longer, and 500ft would no longer seem remarkable. Docks throughout the Empire would have to be enlarged, whether or not the 500ft cruiser was built. Docking facilities would surely keep improving in order to handle the large new liners.

The Russian cruisers, denied any British commercial docks in wartime, would not find anything like the same facilities. Large docks existed at Sevastopol and at Vladivostok, and the French had one at Saigon, but none of the European powers had any others. The United States, which would be neutral in a war between the United Kingdom and Russia, had one or two suitable docks.

High power demanded the most efficient type of boiler. This was the first design for which White recommended the new (for the Royal Navy) water-tube type. He soon extended the recommendation to the wide range of smaller cruisers described in previous chapters. White's design combined water-tube and cylindrical boilers (the latter possibly for cruising), but some time before construction the cylindrical boilers were eliminated, the ships emerging with 48 Bellevilles. They proved

HMS *Powerful* as completed, with double-storey casemates only at the ends of her 6in battery. Note the double military tops for anti-torpedo (boat) guns. By this time her funnels had been lengthened. *Powerful* and *Terrible* could easily be distinguished from other four-funnelled British cruisers of their era by the unequal spacing of the funnels, the middle two being noticeably closer together. The ships' boiler rooms were of unequal length, the forward room having been intended for cylindrical boilers. During the Boer War *Powerful* and *Terrible* landed the naval brigades which supported the relief of Ladysmith. Capt Percy Scott of HMS *Powerful*, the famous gunnery expert, further distinguished himself by landing heavy naval guns and providing them with extemporized carriages. Their great range was widely publicized, and the fact that similar guns on ships could not reach nearly so far inspired Arthur H Pollen to develop the first analogue computer fire control system. *Powerful* spent her first two years in trials and alterations (including raised funnels), and was then assigned to the China Fleet in 1898-1902. She was detached to the Cape in 1899-1901. On returning she was refitted in 1902-3 (when additional casemates were fitted) and then placed in the Portsmouth reserve in 1903-5. She became flagship of the Australia station in 1905-11. On her return she was assigned to the Third (reserve) Fleet in home waters (7th Cruiser Squadron: 1912). She was placed on the subsidiary list as a training hulk at Devonport in 1913 and renamed *Impregnable* in 1919.
(Allan C Green, courtesy of State Library of Australia)

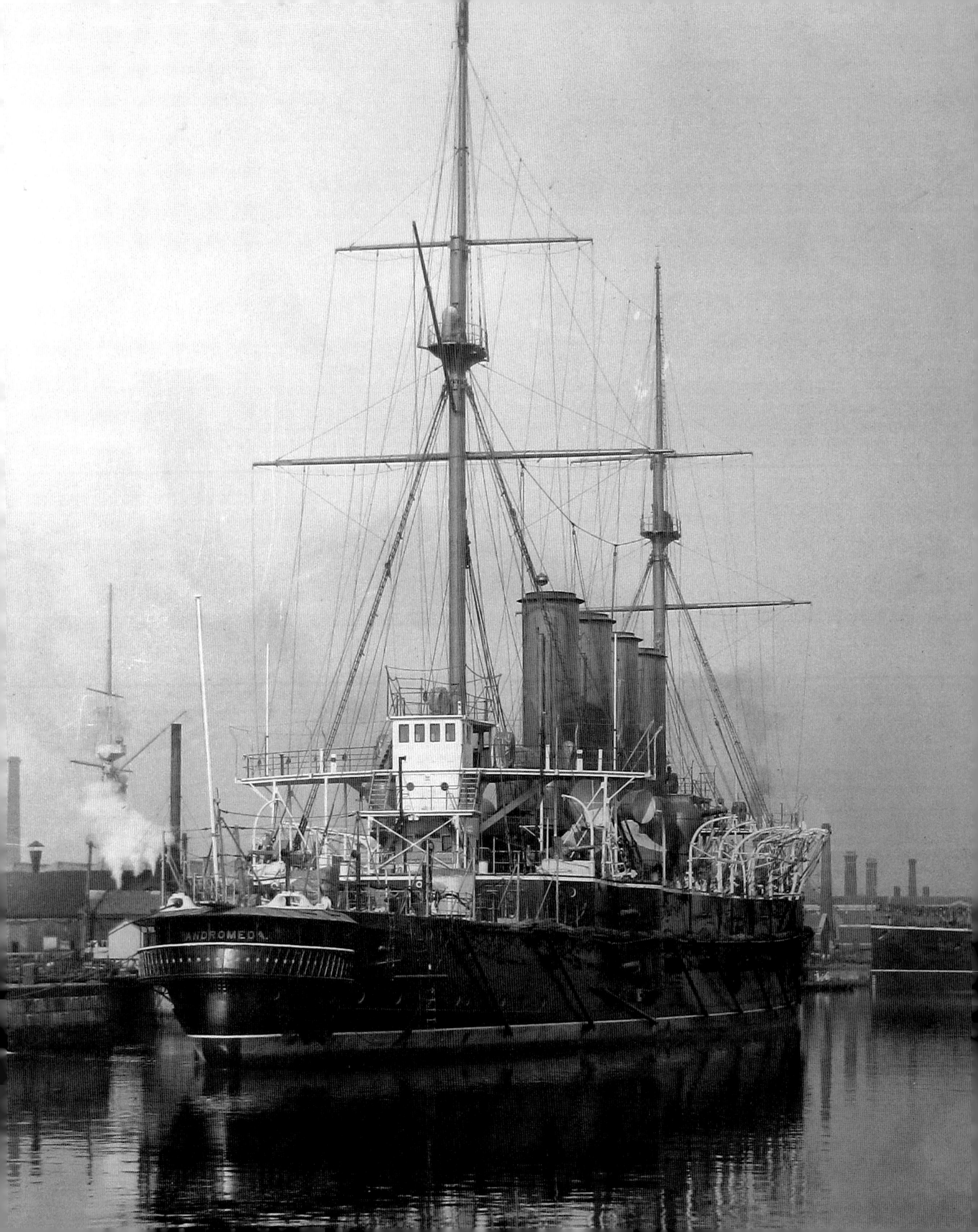
ANDROMEDA

LEFT AND FAR RIGHT *Andromeda* in July 1899. The view from aft shows her large after bridge with its charthouse. On completion she was assigned to the Mediterranean (1899-1902), then refitted (1903-4) before going to the China Fleet (1904-6). Then she was reduced to reserve at Chatham, going to Devonport with a nucleus crew (1907-11). She was then assigned (1912) to the new Third (reserve) Fleet 9th Cruiser Squadron. She was a Boys' Training Ship at Devonport 1913-29, renamed *Impregnable II* in 1919. She became part of the torpedo school in 1931 as HMS *Defiance*, surviving until 1956.

Andromeda as refitted, March 1904. Note the wireless gaff high on her mainmast.

The after bridge of HMS *Andromeda*.

unexpectedly inefficient both in these and in other ships. For example, the ships were rated at 8200nm at 14kts on 3000 tons of coal, but it took 2200 tons to take them 4400nm at 12½ to 14kts in relatively calm weather.

The Board approved White's 500ft ship on 24 February, after considering 450 and 470ft ships. It found little difference between 450 and 500ft as far as docking facilities were concerned. The critical issue was not length but rather the width of entrance (the ships would be quite wide because of their 6in casemates) and depth of water over the sill. The Board dropped a proposal to increase cruising speed to 21kts, as that would have required 25 per cent more boilers and machinery (the ship was on the steep part of the power vs speed curve), another 50ft of length, and probably 15,700 tons. White defended the size of his ship by comparing her to a new 600ft Cunard liner with a sea speed of 21½ to 22kts, which carried no armament, and probably needed 7000 tons of coal for an Atlantic passage at that speed. His displacement and length nearly matched those of the White Star liners *Teutonic* and *Majestic*, which crossed the Atlantic at an average of 20½kts. Estimated cost was about £800,000.

Controller (Rear Admiral Fisher) and DNO (Captain Compton Domville) rejected the all-6in battery; they wanted much more powerful bow and stern chasers. White thought that the *Crescent* episode showed that the Board considered a 6in gun powerful enough, but DNO explained what had really happened. DNO emphasized the greater smashing power of the heavier shell, and its much greater explosive content.

Controller (Rear Admiral Fisher) considered DNC's ship a particularly bad bargain compared with the new American armoured cruisers *Brooklyn* and *New York*, with their twin 8in turrets and 8in wing guns (twins in *Brooklyn*) firing right ahead. Like *Rurik*, these ships also had waterline belts. Fisher also listed for comparison the US protected cruisers *Olympia* and *Minneapolis* and the French *Dupuy de Lôme*. All had guns heavier than 6in, but they were considerably smaller than DNC's ship. *Brooklyn* was a particular sore point. She could fire six of her eight 8in guns ahead, and she had twelve 5in in casemates. DNO agreed. DNC particularly dismissed *Brooklyn*, on paper

Spartiate as completed in March 1903, with wireless gaff and torpedo defence net booms. Construction must have been much delayed, as she had been launched in October 1898. On completion she went into reserve at Portsmouth (1903-4), then at Chatham (1905), and then at Portsmouth with a nucleus crew (1906-9). The latter period included trooping in 1907. She was in the 4th Division at Portsmouth in 1909-11, and then was part of the 7th Cruiser Squadron of the new Third (reserve) Fleet in 1912-13. Beginning in 1913 she was a stokers' training ship (renamed *Fisgard* in 1915).

the most formidable of the lot. Her list of guns might look formidable, but she suffered from poor ammunition supply. DNO responded that ammunition supply might be poor, but it would be quite enough to decide an action. How could the Royal Navy build cruisers 6000 tons larger, supposedly superior to any other cruiser in the world, yet inferior to the American armoured cruiser, at least in armament?[12]

Controller and DNO both accepted that the alternative to the all-6in ship was one with heavy guns (either paired 8in or single 9.2in) at the ends, plus a reduced number of 6in, the double 6in casemates fore and aft being retained. Armstrong was installing an 8in/40 in cruisers for foreign navies, and Fisher wanted it for the new cruiser. It seemed an excellent compromise between weight of shell and rate of fire, offering nearly the same muzzle energy (a measure of armour penetration) as the existing service 9.2in gun. DNO preferred two 8in to one 9.2in at each end because he thought an 8in shell (about 200lbs instead of 380) could be lifted by hand, hence the gun could fire more rapidly. Too, the 8in gun was the largest whose breech could be completely hand-operated 'without recourse to extra leverage for starting the breech screw'. Because it needed this extra power, the 9.2in breech operated much more slowly. The longer-range 9.2in or 8in gun would cripple an enemy at distance, making it possible for the cruiser to close in and use her 6in QF guns.

The Board chose 9.2in guns at the ends at an 8 June 1893 meeting; 8in guns did not add enough, and no modern gun of that calibre had yet been approved for Royal Navy service. The heavy guns would have 6in protection and steam power for turning their turret shields.[13] That added weight. This version therefore had only twelve 6in guns (two on each side between the double casemates), plus sixteen 12pdr (8 upper deck, 8 main deck), twelve 3pdr, and smaller guns. There would be four submerged torpedo tubes in two rooms. By this time the 12pdr had, in effect, replaced the 6pdr as the standard anti-torpedo (boat) gun.

A sheer drawing and midships section received the Board Stamp on 12 October 1893.[14] Two super-cruisers, HMS *Powerful* and *Terrible*, were built to this design under the 1893-94 Estimates.

Soon after the ships had been completed, the question arose of whether the two waist casemates on each side (between the double casemates) could be replaced by double casemates. Nothing was done at the time, because the ships would not become available for major changes for some time.[15] The Board raised the idea again in May 1900.

Weight was no great problem, as the ships had enormous freeboard and thus could accept a few more inches of draught. Volume below the armoured deck, which would be needed to increase ammunition supply, was a different matter. Volume also governed personnel; extra 6in guns needed crews. Controller Rear Admiral Wilson argued that in practice rate of fire would be governed by the ammunition supply, and that could not change by much. First Naval Lord Admiral Walter Kerr agreed; the complement was already enormous, and there was no room for more ammunition. First Lord George Goschen had to agree, but reluctantly, as he had heard from so many quarters that 'it is a pity not to have more guns in so large a ship'.

Goschen's point kept the idea alive, Controller (still Wilson) raising it again in May 1901. The four additional guns were added in 1902-4.

Diadem Class

By the time the *Powerful*s were being designed, the Spencer Program (1894-95 through 1898-99 Estimates) was being drafted. It included six first-class cruisers intermediate in size between the *Powerful* and *Blake*, to cost £500,000 each; they were referred to as New *Blake*s and in effect they were follow-ons to the *Edgar*s. It was probably clear from the outset that the new ship would have to be somewhat longer and heavier than *Blake*.[16]

It was understood that First Naval Lord Admiral Sir Frederick W Richards (the same man who had inspired the *Arrogant*s) wanted armament arranged like that of the *Royal Arthur*, with its high forecastle carrying a pair of 6in guns. Not only could the ship go head to sea and still fight the two 6in bow chasers, but it later became clear that her captain preferred those guns to the 9.2in aft. Armament should be protected against small QF guns, meaning casemates for all 6in guns (except the shielded pair on the forecastle) and a shallow barbette and closed shield (as in *Powerful*) for the 9.2in gun aft. That meant the new double-storey casemates. As in the *Powerful*s, the anti-torpedo battery would probably be 12pdrs rather than 6pdrs. Another feature was to be two ammunition passages under the protective deck, as in *Powerful* (but not the *Blake*s). Ships without such passages had to have their ammunition transported to their side guns above the protective deck, although their passages might still be behind the upper coal bunkers. In armament the ships would be *Powerful*s with the forward 9.2in gun replaced by 6in guns.

Work began in November 1893. Like White's other cruisers of this time, the ships would have water-tube boilers, offering offer higher speed. A series of design alternatives began with a modified *Blake* with Belleville boilers, adding such improvements as casemates. It led to a considerably longer ship.[17] Engineer-in-Chief wanted a single set of four-cylinder engines on each of the two shafts. Coal supply was set at 1250/2000 tons.[18] A Legend was produced in April 1894.[19] The sketch design was discussed by the Naval Lords on 15 June 1894, the ships to be built under the 1895-96 Estimates. In July the Board approved proceeding with drawings of three ships.

The initial design showed two shielded 6in on the forecastle (White feared that they would be unusable if the nearby main deck casemate guns fired), one 6in in a casemate on either side nearby and below on the main deck, and two two-storey casemates on each side further aft, plus the single 9.2in guns. That gave four 6in firing ahead and four 6in plus one 9.2in firing dead astern. DNO (now Captain Kane) wanted more powerful ahead fire, reviving the 8in gun idea (for bow and stern chasers). About October 1894 five armament alternatives were considered. DNO's 8in ships were alternatives A and B. As weight compensation for the two 8in guns in A, upper deck casemates were eliminated. The two forecastle 6in guns were moved down to the main deck, under the single 6in currently on the upper deck, and placed in a double casemate. That would retain the twelve 6in but place a heavier gun at the bow. In B the upper deck casemates were retained, but the two forecastle 6in were simply eliminated.

DNC strongly objected to the 8in gun. When framing armament policy for the Naval Defence Act ships, the Board sought to reduce the number of separate calibres in service, and specifically decided to drop the 8in of the *Mersey* class. Many *Mersey* class commanding officers asked that their 8in guns be replaced by lighter 6in, to reduce weight towards the ends of the ship. Surely as these ships came in for refit, the possibility of replacing their 8in guns with 6in QF would be raised. The 8in now proposed was a new gun, and experience showed that new guns badly delayed programs. It was most unlikely that the Ordnance Committee would simply accept the Elswick gun as it stood. DNO stood his ground in hopes that the army would buy the gun (for coast defence). Ultimately DNO backed down because there would be little point in buying the gun if only a few ships would mount it.

Arrangement C was provisionally selected, with casemated 6in guns (one each side) adding to ahead fire, and two-storey casemates (instead of the single shielded guns initially proposed) firing aft alongside the 9.2in gun. Having reluctantly dropped his preferred Plan A, DNO also rejected C as he had never favoured arming these ships with 9.2in guns.

Arrangements D and E eliminated the 9.2in gun aft, leaving the all-6in armament White clearly preferred (as in the *Powerful*s). In D, the two bow chasers of C were replaced by a single forecastle 6in gun, but the forward casemate was two-storey, so ahead fire was five 6in guns. Similarly, there were five 6in stern chasers. Plan E had two 6in on the forecastle, for a total of six bow chasers. To compensate for the weight of the extra gun, the normal allowance per gun could be reduced from 200 to 150 rounds (the ship would still have space for over 2000 rounds in all). The ship might need some extra beam to retain her stability. White cautioned that the crews of the forecastle guns would probably be seriously affected when the casemate guns fired right ahead, particularly when elevated. DNO preferred D. He considered the extra gun in E no great advantage. Its crew would often be unable to fire in combination with the casemate guns, and the blast from the two guns (except when firing more than 25 degrees off the bow) would endanger those in the conning tower just abaft them.

When First Naval Lord Richards, Controller Fisher, DNO and DNC met to discuss the alternatives, a further arrangement (F) was prepared. The casemated main deck guns were moved together so that the two-storey bow casemate could be moved aft, the resulting conditions being similar to those on HMS *Royal Arthur*. Now the two forecastle 6in guns were more acceptable, though DNO still disliked the arrangement. He doubted that all four forward guns of *Royal Arthur* had ever been fired right ahead at one time. The cost was worse ammunition service, because instead of receiving ammunition directly up from the forward magazine and shell room, the casemate guns now had to be served from the lengthwise ammunition passages. A final Board meeting selected Scheme E. The forecastle guns might, moreover, be moved forward a few feet, and blast screens placed above the casemate guns (that was not done). The crews of the forecastle guns might be protected by stops placed on the casemate guns.

Scheme E had a total of fifteen 6in guns, a single gun replacing the 9.2in gun aft and the forward casemate being doubled up. Two shielded 6in stern chasers in the original design were replaced by two-storey casemates. There were two single 6in casemates on each side between the double ones. The Board approved this design on 13 July 1895. Later a second 6in gun was added on the quarterdeck, weight compensation including elimination of the military tops planned for the ships and a reduction from twelve to three 3pdrs. In the course of

Argonaut in 1907-9 with spotting tops and with a range drum visible on the fore side of her forward spotting top. In this position the range drum was used to show other ships in company the range at which this ship was firing, so that they could concentrate on the same target. This photograph also shows the new high topmasts for greater wireless range. The object atop the canvas protecting the compass platform (the roof of the charthouse) was probably a chart table. Upon completion *Argonaut* went to the China Fleet (1900-1904). She returned home to commission in reserve at Chatham (1904-5) and had a nucleus crew in 1906-9. She was part of the Portsmouth reserve force in 1909-11, and was a member of the 7th Cruiser Squadron of the Third (reserve) Fleet in 1912-14. In 1914-15 she was assigned to the 9th Cruiser Squadron operating in mid-Atlantic. She was hospital ship at Portsmouth in 1915-17, and accommodation ship for stokers in 1918.
(National Maritime Museum N20544)

Argonaut in 1910 with more developed spotting tops and two range drums, facing fore and aft, on her foretop. Ships usually carried their aft-facing range drum on their after spotting top, but in this (and many other) ships the after top was very low, hence not very visible.
(National Maritime Museum N01058)

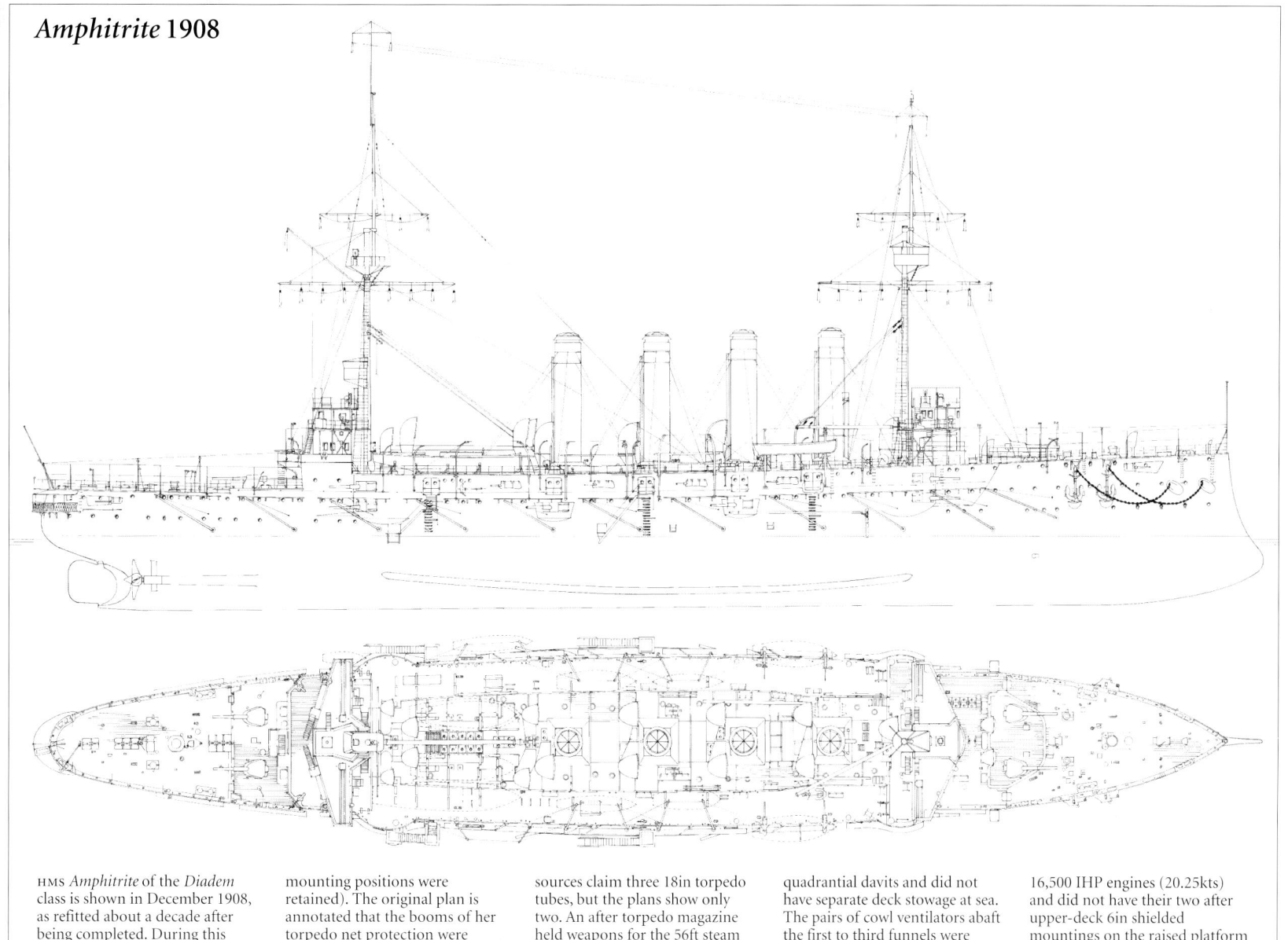

Amphitrite 1908

HMS *Amphitrite* of the *Diadem* class is shown in December 1908, as refitted about a decade after being completed. During this refit fire control tops were fitted and the number of 3pdr QF reduced from eight to two (four mounting positions were retained). The original plan is annotated that the booms of her torpedo net protection were removed in 1916 (i.e., by 2 May 1916), but others of the class had theirs removed by 1910. Many sources claim three 18in torpedo tubes, but the plans show only two. An after torpedo magazine held weapons for the 56ft steam vedette, which had dropping gear. Note that the two 32ft sailing cutters were carried in patent quadrantial davits and did not have separate deck stowage at sea. The pairs of cowl ventilators abaft the first to third funnels were slightly staggered, but their ventilation trunks were not. The four 1895 program ships had 16,500 IHP engines (20.25kts) and did not have their two after upper-deck 6in shielded mountings on the raised platform shown here. In 1917 *Amphitrite* was converted into a minelayer.

design, the ships kept growing.[20] As with the *Powerful*s, White felt compelled to defend his preferred protective deck/coal protection. He had to provide figures for an alternative version with a 4in belt.

Four ships were built under the 1895-96 Estimates (*Diadem*, *Andromeda*, *Europa*, and *Niobe*), one presumably replacing one of the two *Arrogant*s planned under the Spencer Program but not built. Four more were built under the 1896-7 Estimates: *Ariadne*, *Argonaut*, *Amphitrite*, and *Spartiate*. Again this was one more than had been planned a few years earlier. These *Ariadne*s were designed from the outset with sixteen 6in guns and with somewhat more powerful machinery (18,000 vs 16,500 HP under natural draught, for 20.75 rather than 20.5kts). Estimated machinery weight was 1550 rather than 1525 tons, the extra weight balanced by a reduction in equipment weight.

These were the last large protected cruisers built for the Royal Navy.[21]

7 THE FAST WING OF THE BATTLE FLEET

Cressy Class

DNC William H White conceived a new type of cruiser, which he sold to the Admiralty. He wrote in the spring of 1897 that for nearly the past two years, since completion of the *Diadem* design, he had been thinking through the implication of an ongoing armour revolution. In 1889-93 it took a plate 10½in thick to resist 6in (100lb) armour-piercing projectiles striking at about 2000ft/sec. In 1897 a 6in plate could do as well. Thickness, and therefore weight, had declined in a ratio of 100 to 57. There were actually two separate leaps, the Harvey process (1891-93) and then Krupp Cemented. Later it was estimated that 5¾in of Krupp Cemented (as in *Canopus* and *Drake*) was equivalent to 7½in of Harvey, to 12in of steel, and to 15in of wrought iron.[1] In these terms, the 6in of *Canopus* and *Drake* was equivalent to 7.8in of Harvey armour and to 12.5in of the compound armour used in the *Royal Sovereign* class battleships of 1889. White considered 6in of Krupp Cemented a reasonable bargain in his *Canopus* class battleships because it was light enough to cover a much larger area than in the *Royal Sovereigns*. This armour was light enough to be used in a big cruiser.

White visited France and Italy privately while recovering from illness (and again in 1896), and he also made official visits to Germany and Russia in 1896. In Italy in 1896 he was impressed by that country's new construction policy. The Royal Italian Navy could not afford conventional battleships. Instead it began building cruisers so well protected and armed that they could, if necessary, engage battleships. At about 7500 tons, the *Garibaldi* class mounted a 10in gun forward with two 8in aft and could make about 20kts, with 5in protection. This design was so impressive that ships laid down for the Royal Italian Navy were snapped up by foreign navies. Four were sold to Argentina, and Spain bought one in 1896 (purchase of a second was cancelled). Two more ordered by Argentina in 1901 were bought by Japan in 1904 during the run-up to the Russo-Japanese War. To White, only the new Italian cruisers, and a few other recent ones, were well enough protected to undertake close action with battleships.

The Royal Navy could not substitute cruisers for battleships. However, White considered it was time to build cruisers 'capable of taking part in fleet actions as adjuncts to battleships' because thanks to the new lightweight armour they could 'come to *close quarters* with the enemy without running undue risks'. They could and should work with battleships to form a fast wing of the battle fleet. This was a matter not only of armour but also of improved guns. Cruisers designed to work with battleships had to be of about the same length, so that they could manoeuvre together. They also should have similar endurance. White denied that his new idea reversed his earlier rejection of thin side armour, as in the French *Dupuy de Lôme*. He still held that British protected cruisers were capable of meeting, on more than equal terms, foreign cruisers with thin vertical side armour and weak protective decks.

White had just designed the *Canopus* class battleships with 6in side armour. He proposed a cruiser with similar protection (5in bulkheads and 5in casemates). Given side protection, the deck joining the lower edge of the belt could be considerably thinner (1½in) and less curved, the upper edges of the belt being joined to a thinner deck (1in). He rejected the foreign practice of limiting the vertical spread of the armour, arguing that for both battleships and fast cruisers it was best to extend it from the main deck down to the (lower) protective deck well below water. White later pointed out that it was not yet possible to apply the special ar-

Euryalus as completed. On completion she became flagship of the Australia station (1904-5). On her return she was reduced to reserve with a nucleus crew at Portsmouth (1905-6). In 1906-9 she was boys' training ship attached to the 4th Cruiser Squadron of the North America and West Indies station. On returning she joined the new Third (reserve) Fleet, first at Portsmouth (1909-13), then at Devonport (1911-13), and then at the Nore (1913-14). On the outbreak of war she joined the 7th Cruiser Squadron in the North Sea (she fought at Heligoland). Then she joined 12th Cruiser Squadron escorting Atlantic convoys in 1914-15. Then she was sent to the Mediterranean in 1915-16 (she was at the Dardanelles), becoming flagship of the East Indies station in 1916-17. She was selected for conversion to a minelayer (like *Amphitrite*) at Hong Kong, work beginning in November 1917. This project was abandoned incomplete at the end of the war in 1918, and she was discarded.
(Allan C Green, courtesy of State Library of Victoria)

Bacchante with early versions of standard pre-1914 modifications (spotting tops, wireless gaff on mainmast). By about 1911 ships had larger boxier tops and had range drums on the fore sides of their forward spotting tops. On completion *Bacchante* became flagship of the Mediterranean Fleet cruiser division (1902-4), after which she was reduced to reserve with a nucleus crew at Portsmouth (1905-6). She then went back to the Mediterranean, in the 3rd Cruiser Squadron (1906-8) and then in the 6th Cruiser Squadron (1909-12). She was reduced to reserve as part of the Third (reserve) Fleet in the Nore (1912-14: 6th Cruiser Squadron). On the outbreak of war she became flagship of the 7th Cruiser Squadron (North Sea), transferring to 12th Cruiser Squadron as an Atlantic convoy escort in 1914-15. She went to the Mediterranean in 1915-16 (she was at the Dardanelles), and then became flagship of 9th Cruiser Squadron based at Sierra Leone in 1917-19, being paid off in April 1919.

mour process to plates less than 6in thick, when the armour was bent into the special shapes needed for ships.

White laid his revolutionary idea before the Board on 3 May 1897. Enough was decided for him to create a sketch design, which he submitted on 10 June 1897, looking forward to the 1897-98 program. Protection amounted to 1800 tons, 50 per cent over the figure for the *Diadem*s and 20 per cent over that for the *Powerful*.[2] White showed that it was considerably superior to foreign ships, which might have the same thickness, but in a very narrow waterline belt.[3]

A cruiser intended as an adjunct to battleships should have guns powerful enough to damage enemy battleships. Without enough weight to provide battleship guns, White and the Board opted for next best, the new type of 9.2in gun then under consideration. It could wreck battleship secondary batteries. Compared to a *Diadem*, which was of about the same size, two 9.2in weighed considerably more than four upper deck 6in.[4] The Naval Lords left the number of 6in open, but White's sketch showed twelve in the two-storey casemates used in the *Diadem* and *Powerful*. Given the weight of the heavy guns, White offered either twelve guns with 100 rounds per gun (but capacity for 200) or ten 6in with the usual 200 rounds per gun. He preferred the twelve-gun armament for a ship operating with the fleet in the Channel or the Mediterranean, which could replenish her magazines fairly easily. If the same ship had to operate on a distant station, where she could not refill so easily, she could carry the extra rounds and sacrifice some speed. The Naval Lords agreed at an 18 June meeting. Because both the 9.2in *and* the 6in gun were new models, weight grew unex-

Hogue with standard modifications (from aft). Her wireless gaff is down, and she has a semaphore at the head of her mainmast. As completed she served with the Channel Fleet (1902-4), then with the China Fleet (1904-6) after refitting. She was boys' training ship for the North America and West Indies station (4th Cruiser Squadron) in 1906-8, relieving the cruiser *St George*. Then she was reduced to reserve, first as an individual unit (with nucleus crew) at Devonport (1908-9) and then as a unit of the new Third (reserve) Fleet at the Nore (1909-11). She was refitted at Chatham in 1912-13 and then returned to the Third Fleet detachment at the Nore. On the outbreak of war she joined the 7th Cruiser Squadron operating in the North Sea. With her sisters *Aboukir* and *Cressy* she was patrolling the Channel to shield a lane through which British troops and supplies were being sent to France when all three were sunk by *U-9* on 22 September 1914.

O'Higgins 1899

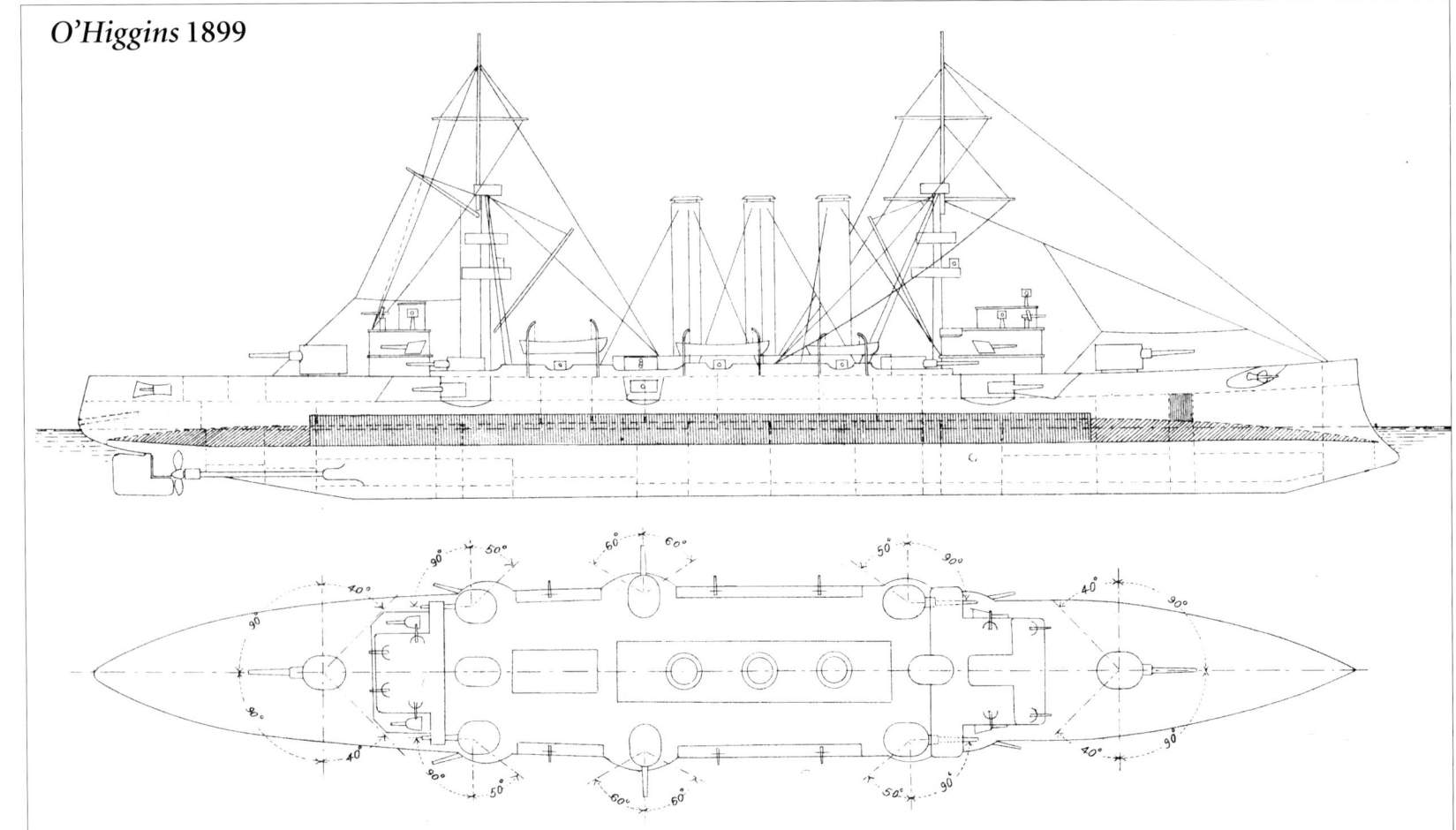

The Chilean armoured cruiser *O'Higgins*, in a drawing published to illustrate Philip Watts' 1899 article on Elswick cruisers. She well illustrates the virtues Armstrong promoted and the weaknesses Sir William White cited to explain why his own armoured cruisers were less impressive – on paper. For him the greatest weakness was the short narrow armour belt amidships, the weight of which precluded much of a protective deck. The belt was only 7ft wide (260ft long) and 7in thick over machinery (5in at ends), closed by 5in bulkheads. The deck below was only 1½in thick in way of the belt, 2in thick at the ends. What most struck contemporary observers was how much had been crammed into only 8476 tons (8234 on trials: 412ft pp×62ft×22ft). Work began with a September 1895 request for tenders for a fast 7300-ton cruiser armed with two 8in guns and ten 6in, with a 7in belt. Armstrong offered a 7500-tonner (400ft × 62ft × 22ft) with engines capable of producing 16,000 IHP under forced draught (21¾kts). The first two design proposals offered the desired two single 8in at the ends plus 6in and, in one case, 4.7in guns. However, a third proposal offered two more 8in in wing positions. Philip Watts presented these alternatives to the Chilean Naval Commission in Paris, apparently learning that they were intrigued by the additional two 8in guns. They wanted the two guns on not more than 8000 tons, but that proved impossible, and an entirely new 8300-ton design was quickly prepared. It retained the single 8in guns at the ends. The other two could be in main deck casemates in the citadel or in separate gunhouses with barbettes. The latter arrangement was chosen, and the ship was armed with four 8in/45, ten 6in/40, four 4.7in/45, ten 12pdr, ten 6pdr, four machine guns, and three torpedo tubes. Despite the fact that the ship was considerably larger than the original design, belt armour was not modified. The Japanese cruisers *Asama* and *Tokiwa* were conceived as modified versions of *O'Higgins*. This drawing is from the 1899 paper by Philip Watts in the *Transactions of the Institution of Naval Architects*.

---

pectedly; design displacement had to be increased from 11,850 tons to about 12,000.

The Naval Lords wanted a trial speed of 21 to 22kts. White proposed to use machinery similar to (but more powerful than) that of the *Diadem*s, with Belleville boilers, which he thought would suffice for 21½kts under natural draught on 8-hour contractor trials. The ships would maintain about 19¾kts in smooth water, compared to 19kts for the *Diadem*s.[5] This was not terribly sparkling compared to foreign cruisers whose stated speeds were higher; the French *Jeanne d'Arc* was credited with 23kts. White made his usual argument that foreign trial speeds were unrealistic and that sustained speed was what counted. Conversely, if the new cruiser were forced like the French, she too would make 23kts. The Naval Lords decided, against White's advice, that the ships should be sheathed, even though that would cost half a knot on trials. If White was right about continuous steaming, the sheathed ship (free of underwater growth) would win out.

The Naval Lords wanted battleship endurance. The new cruiser was about the size of a battleship, so she needed about as much coal: 1600 tons (as in *Canopus*). There was not enough space; the engines and boilers took up too much of the volume of the hull (that would not have been a problem in a *Diadem*, with 2000-ton capacity). With bunkers full, the cruiser should be able to steam for 30 days at 10kts (7200nm).

White retained the long high forecastle considered so desirable in the *Diadem*s, though slightly lower. This was the most that he could do without sacrificing stability, and he warned the Board against adding anything during the design process. The cost would inevitably rise, to an estimated £650,000, which was still £50,000 less than *Powerful*. White thought the French had paid £800,000 for their *Jeanne d'Arc*, the closest equivalent (though much less powerfully armed).

On 12 January 1898 White submitted his sheer draught and midship section for the Board Stamp, explaining that the design had been delayed largely by delays in fixing the characteristics of the new guns. To maintain the desired 21kts with the new displacement (i.e., with a hull of the same form), the ship had been lengthened 5ft over the *Diadem* class, and beam had been increased by 6 inches; extreme draught aft was 6in more. Displacement had increased 700 tons, of which 540 was due to sheathing, the rest due to the new guns and mountings. That would cost half a knot (to 21kts). The design received the Board Stamp on 20 January 1898. Controller Rear Admiral Wilson cautioned against trying to cut complement, because in action the ships would need both maximum speed (i.e., the maximum number of stokers) *and* maximum rate of fire (i.e., the largest possible ammunition parties to pass ammunition from magazines to guns).[6]

Six of these *Cressy* class cruisers were built under the 1897-98 program. They were the first British cruisers in a decade with side protection.

White had invented the battlecruiser. In effect he had reached the same conclusion the Germans did about a decade later, that a fast ship with battleship protection but somewhat lighter guns would be well worthwhile. The standard of protection adopted for the *Cressy*s – a battleship standard – was retained in later armoured cruisers and in the *Invincible* and *Indefatigable* class battlecruisers. In these terms the battlecruisers were armoured cruisers – or, conversely, they were all protected like pre-dreadnought battleships (*Dreadnought* had the 9in belt armour of the last pre-dreadnought class, the *King Edward VII*s). The important caveat is that after 1900 capped projectiles, which could penetrate 6in Krupp Cemented armour at useful battle ranges, were coming into service.

Drake Class

It seems that the Board did not find White's speed argument entirely convincing; it wanted a cruiser that really made 23kts *in British terms*. By April 1898 White was considering an unprecedented powerplant: 30,000 HP. By this time water-tube

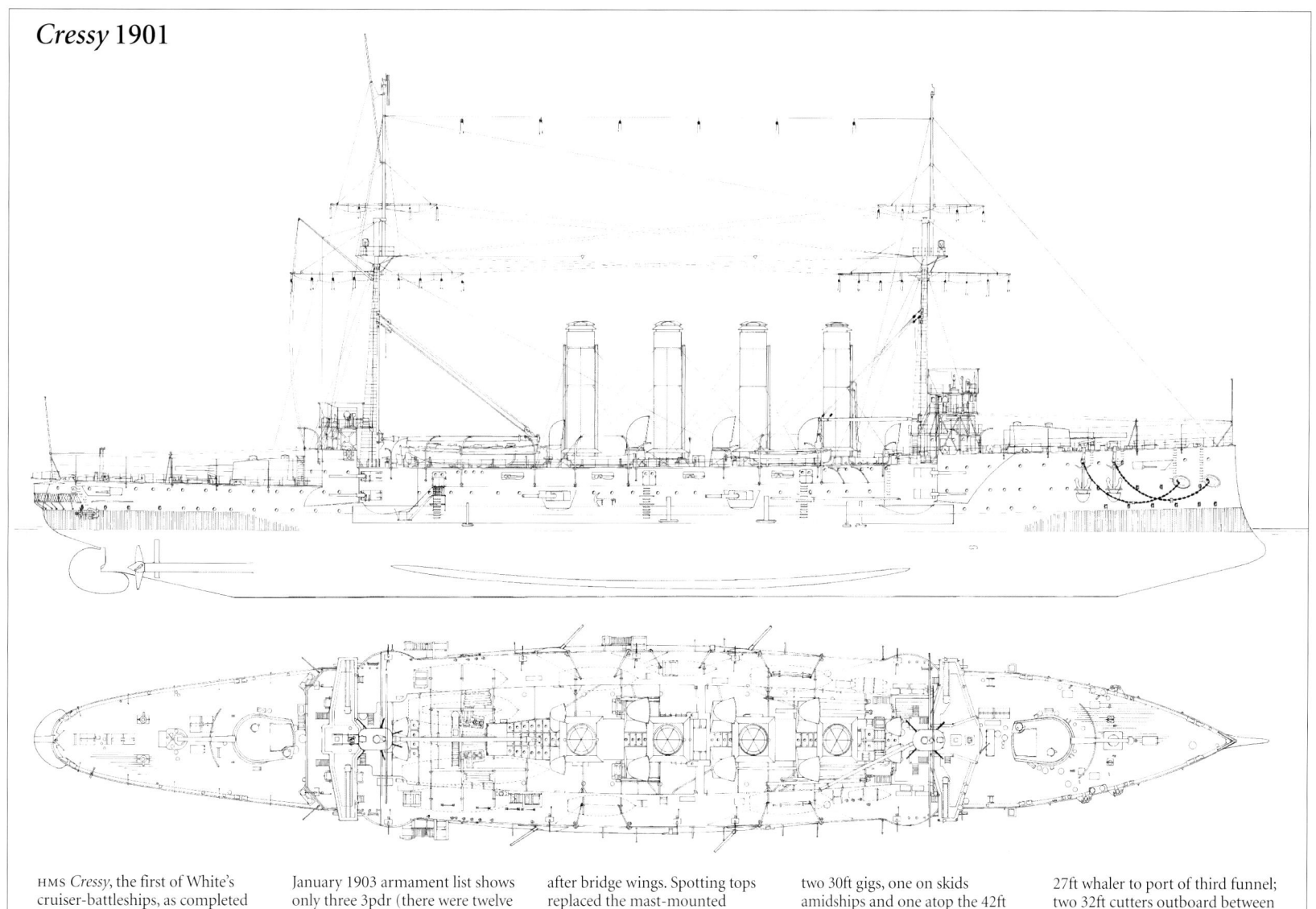

Cressy 1901

HMS *Cressy*, the first of White's cruiser-battleships, as completed in May 1901. Rigging has been omitted from the plan view for clarity. Plans show twelve mounting positions for 3pdr or 0.303in Maxim guns, but the January 1903 armament list shows only three 3pdr (there were twelve 12pdr 12cwt guns). That list does show eight 37mm (1pdr) machine guns, which were later crossed out. Field carriages for two 12pdrs were stowed on deck beneath the after bridge wings. Spotting tops replaced the mast-mounted searchlights about 1905-6. Boats carried as completed include, from aft forward and from port to starboard: one 36ft sailing pinnace; one 42ft sailing launch; two 30ft gigs, one on skids amidships and one atop the 42ft sailing launch when not slung out on davits; one 56ft steam pinnace; one 40ft steam pinnace; one 30ft cutter to port and one 26ft cutter to starboard of the after stack; one 27ft whaler to port of third funnel; two 32ft cutters outboard between second and third funnels; one 13ft balsa catamaran to port; and one 16ft dinghy to starboard abreast the fore funnel.

(A D Baker III)

Drake as completed. On commissioning she joined the Channel Fleet Cruiser Squadron (1903-4). She then joined the 2nd Cruiser Squadron of the new Atlantic Fleet (1905-8), and became flagship of 1st Cruiser Squadron Channel Fleet in 1908-10; then she was part of 5th Cruiser Squadron Atlantic Fleet in 1910-11. She was flagship of the Australia station in 1911-13. She returned home to join 6th Cruiser Squadron Second Fleet in 1913-14; it joined the Grand Fleet in 1914. She was refitted late in 1915, then transferred to the North America and West Indies station, on which she escorted Atlantic convoys (1916-17). She was torpedoed and sunk by *U-79* off Rathlin Island, north of Ireland, 2 October 1917.

boilers were controverial. White had to show that nothing else would provide what was needed. Cylindrical boilers sufficient for 28,000 HP over an 8-hour trial at natural draught would weigh 2000 tons. If they were moderately forced, and only required to maintain that power for 4 hours, the weight could be cut to 1680 tons. If highly forced, and limited to a 3-hour trial, that could be cut further to 1400 tons. That compared with 1250 tons for Bellevilles (with economizers) on an 8-hour natural draught trial. Moderately forced on a 4-hour trial, the same type of Bellevilles could be cut to 1080 tons. The small-tube type in the French *Jeanne d'Arc*, moderately forced on a 3- to 4-hour trial, could produce the required power on 1000 tons (an approximate figure, as the French had not published details). The French small-tube boilers did use much more water; the type initially planned for *Jeanne d'Arc* required three times as much water per horsepower as a Belleville.

To White, what really counted was continuous steaming at sea. Cylindrical boilers sufficient for 28,000 HP on trial would would make 17,000 HP continuously. Lighter-weight installations requiring more forcing on trial would do much worse on a sustained basis. Bellevilles capable of making 28,000 HP on the 8-hour natural draught trial could sustain 21,000, as could the small-tube boilers of the *Jeanne d'Arc* (based on a 60-hour trial by HMS *Pelorus*).

By mid-May 1898 the alternatives were Belleville and small-tube boilers. As in *Diadem*, Bellevilles could be forced to 28,000 HP, and could produce 16,000 HP continuously. Based on French performance, small tubes could produce 24,000 HP on trial (12,000 HP continuous). Engineer-in-Chief Durston wrote that such powers 'exceed anything so far as is known yet at-

Drake with standard modifications, photographed while flagship of the Australia station. Note the rangefinder atop her bridge and the absence of the usual (at this time) range drum on her fore spotting top. Rangefinders are visible on both her spotting tops. Note also her high topmasts, to gain wireless range.
(Allan C Green, courtesy of State Library of Victoria)

Asama and Tokiwa 1897

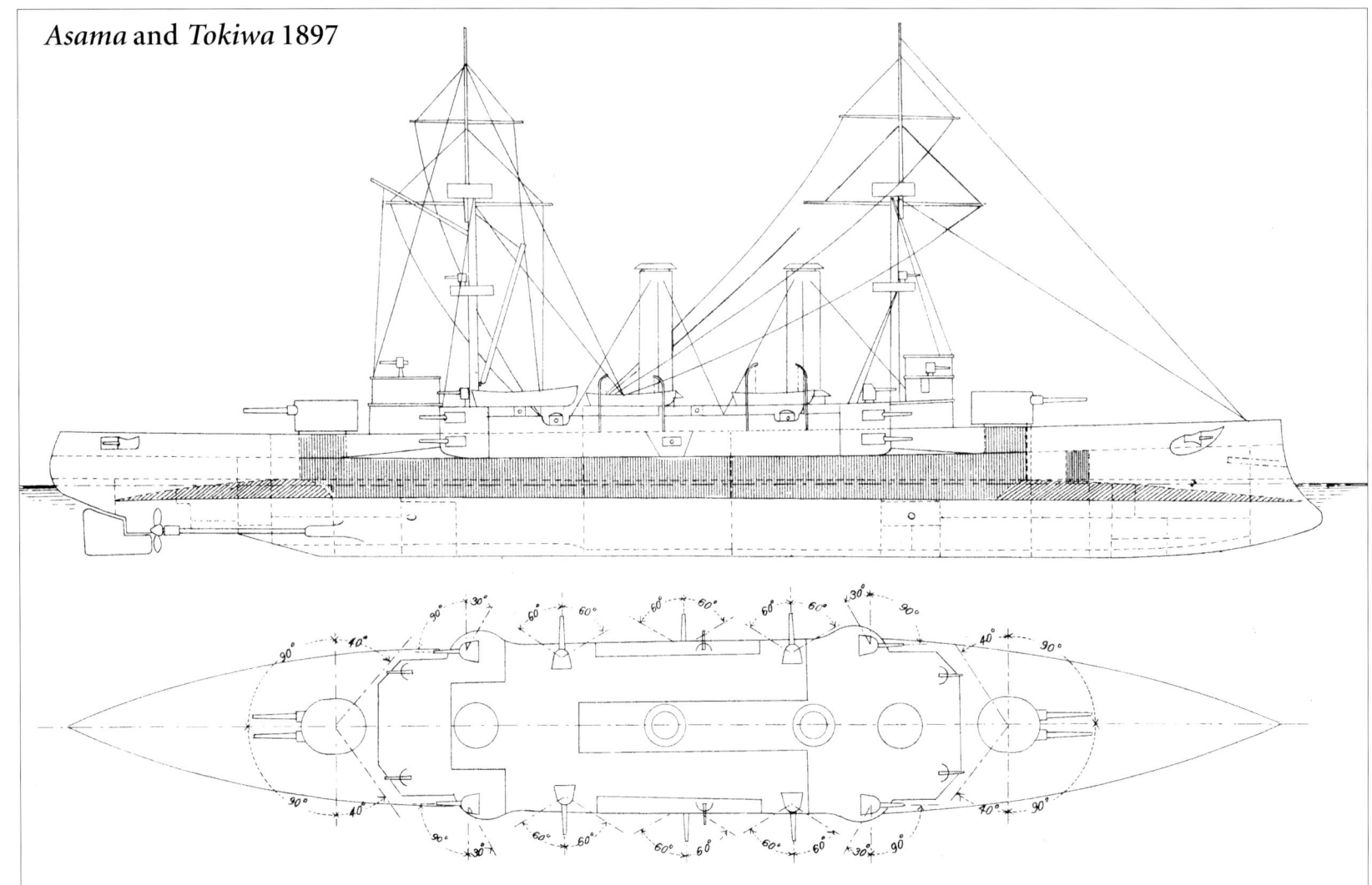

The Japanese armoured cruisers *Asama* and *Tokiwa* were conceived as modified versions of the Chilean *O'Higgins*, but grew into something much more impressive. In June 1896 Andrew Noble in Japan ordered two stock cruisers laid down, presumably because he thought the Japanese would buy them. More detailed instructions received by the yard in July specified a displacement of 9650 tons, an armament of four 8in and fourteen 6in, and a speed of 21.5kts. Japan bought both ships in June 1897. Clearly an informal agreement had been reached, but finances were not yet available when the ships were laid down. The initial proposal called for mounting the 8in guns in twin turrets. As with *O'Higgins*, the belt was only 7ft wide (5ft below to 2ft above the waterline) and it was the same thickness, but this time it was to be 375ft long out of a total length of 400ft (8500 tons, 400ft × 64ft × 22ft). The main belt would be supplemented by a 7in citadel, 208ft long on the side above the belt, with diagonal ends (to the barbettes) extending length to 250ft on the centreline. All of this weight had to be paid for, so even under forced draught the ship would make only 20kts (12,500 IHP). An alternative limited the main belt to the machinery spaces (146ft long), with 6in extensions (68ft forward, 58ft aft) and 3in extensions beyond that. The solution was to increase displacement to 9520 tons (in a July 1896 proposal which clearly was the successful one) so that forced draught power could be increased to 16,000 IHP (21kts), with enough power under natural draught (13,000 IHP) for 20kts. Note that these ships had William White's two-storey casemates fore and aft, with an additional main-deck casemate between them and four shielded 6in on the upper deck. This drawing is from the 1899 paper on Elswick cruisers by Philip Watts.

---

tempted anywhere'. As much as a third more power would have to be extracted from a given heating surface than in *Diadem*. Durston thought the French were grossly overstating the ratio of heating surface to power. For example, he suspected that on a continuous basis the big cruiser *Jeanne d'Arc* was getting something closer to 14,000 than the stated 21,000 HP. Durston pleaded for patience while the Royal Navy solved its water-tube boiler problems. Higher power and speed required faster-moving pistons; the British were already matching the highest piston speeds of foreign warships.

To support the cruiser project, in February 1898 the Director of Naval Intelligence asked all his sections to supply information on the protection of current foreign cruisers: the French *Jeanne d'Arc* (the ship against which the new cruisers were being built), the big Russian *Rossiya*, the German *Fürst Bismarck*, the US *Brooklyn*, and the Chilean (British-built) *O'Higgins*.[7] The French ship had a battleship-style belt, extending 2ft 4in above the waterline, 5.9in thick, with a strip of 5in armour above it. The Russians had an 8in belt (of Harvey steel) extending 4ft 6in above the waterline to 4ft below. *Brooklyn* had a Harvey steel belt only 3in thick, extending 3ft 6in above to 5ft below the waterline. *O'Higgins* had a 7in Harvey steel belt 7ft deep.

About this time White proposed a modified armour arrangement. The weight of the athwartship bulkhead closing the fore end of the belt in the *Cressy* and *Canopus* classes might be used instead to extend the belt to the bow (the after athwartship bulkhead would remain). The thinnest plating (2in) would be mainly up to the main deck, but for about 40ft towards the bow it would be carried up to 22ft above water, reducing the risk of flooding due to riddling by enemy fire, and also the risk of raking from enemy stern guns. Deck thicknesses would be reversed: 1½in on the main deck amidships and 1in on the lower deck. White pointed to the greater length, hence greater deck target, presented by the new ships. Presumably he was also thinking of longer ranges and plunging fire.

White still strongly believed in coal as protection, arguing that the *Resistance* experiment showed that coal placed against the side of a ship would deaden the force of a torpedo. He eliminated the triple sides of the ship abeam the boilers, bringing the coal down 8 or 10ft, but keeping it abreast the boiler spaces. It seemed better to increase the number of transverse bulkheads dividing up the bunkers, rather than retain the wing bulkheads. 'If the transverse bulkheads can be arranged between the backs of each set of boilers arranged athwartships the ship will be as torpedo proof as it is possible to make her.'

White considered two kinds of ship. One was a fast *Cressy*, which would need 28,000 to 30,000 IHP to make 23kts on trial under natural, not forced, draught. The alternative was a smaller ship armed only with 6in guns (one version had two shielded guns at the ends plus eight in casemates, presumably two two-storey ones on each side).

The largest big cruiser was *Powerful*-sized with *Cressy* armament, 500ft x 70ft x 26ft (13,800 tons). One step down was a 13,200-tonner (480ft x 70ft x 26ft). The ship could be shrunk by changing the rules, providing only enough power to make 23kts under forced draught. Not surpisingly, the result was about the size of a *Cressy*: 450ft x 69ft 6in x 25ft (12,000 tons), 21,000 IHP under natural draught (21.5kts) but 28,000 IHP under forced draught. The much smaller alternative (450ft x 6ft5 x 25ft, 10,000 tons) would also make 23kts only under forced draught (24,000 IHP). The design required small-tube boilers. This ship would be armed with two twin 6in turrets and ten casemated 6in. A larger all-6in ship would have had four 6in in turrets, eight in double casemates, and three on each side between the double casemates, a total of eighteen.

White took the 500ft of the *Powerful* as the upper limit on length, considering it the limit imposed by docks. Draught was ultimately restricted by the Suez Canal. Minimum freeboard

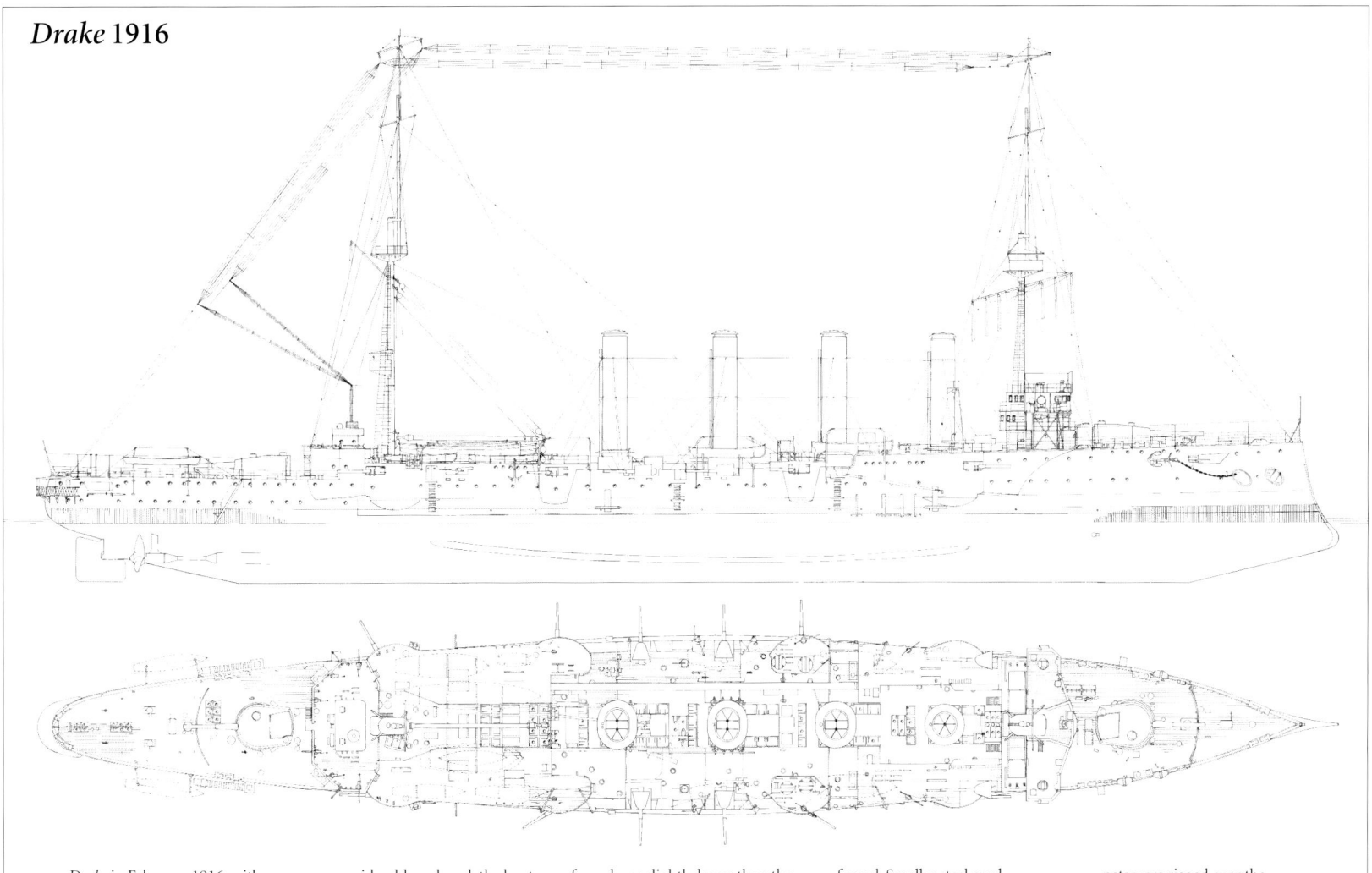

Drake 1916

HMS *Drake* in February 1916, with her lower-deck casemate 6in guns moved up to the upper deck to make them usable in rough weather. She had been refitted in 1915-16. Moving up the 6in guns cost her two 6in and several 12pdr. The original after superstructure was considerably reduced, the boat complement also significantly cut back, and the number of yards reduced. A second pair of embrasures for 12pdrs, placed directly below the pair of the bow, had been removed early in the ship's career. Note that the fore funnel was slightly lower than the other three. This class employed canvas windsails rather than metal structures to ventilate the engineering spaces. These were normally stowed in the four circular structures atop the 6in casemates abreast the second funnel. Smaller steel cowl ventilators are seen stowed forward of the fourth funnel. Note also that the forecastle was clear of anchor-handling gear, the anchor windlass being mounted on the upper deck below the visible line-handling capstan. Steel wire mesh splinter nets were rigged over the amidships deck area prior to going into battle. The fire control positions were added to the masts during a 1905 6 refit. Standing rigging is omitted from the plan view for clarity. Note the cage radio antennas shown in the elevation.

(to the upper deck) amidships had to be at least that of the *Cressy* class. Minimum depth of hold (as measured to the lower protective deck) was fixed by the height of the boilers set below the lower protective deck. Minimum depth between the lower protective deck and the main deck was set by the need for sufficient height to work the bunkers above the lower protective deck and the need for the main deck 6in guns to be high enough above water. White calculated that these factors added up to a minimum freeboard of 14ft, as in the *Cressy*, which had 15in less than *Diadem* and 3ft 6in less than *Powerful*. Minimum freeboard at the bow was set by the height needed to drive the ship at speed into a sea and also the risk involved in hits in the bow when chasing an enemy in a seaway. White recalled the value of a high bow in the *Royal Arthur* and *Crescent*. The 20 to 22-knot Atlantic liners typically had 30 to 33ft high bows. The *Powerful* had 34ft bows, the *Diadem*s 32ft, and the *Cressy*s 31ft; he proposed 30ft for the new ships.

To save weight, White planned to eliminate the boat decks that were a prominent feature of recent first-class cruisers and battleships. They were intended mainly to protect the crews of upper deck guns (12pdrs) from debris falling from above, e.g., from the destruction of the ship's boats. Below the boat decks the bulwarks amidships were built up, providing a shelter for the crew, and sleeping berths for hot climates. In bad weather these decks kept the ships much drier. All of this added considerable topweight. White proposed to transfer the 12pdrs to the main deck. He admitted that the guns would lose some of their command – which (he did not admit) was important for these anti-torpedo weapons.[8] Another way to reduce topweight was to revert to lower casings around the funnels and to minimize the weight of cowls and other ventilators.

Armament could be split into three components: bow chaser, stern chaser, and broadside. Bow fire was by far the most important: the new cruisers were intended specifically to deal with the French, as well as other fast cruisers. Stern fire might be less important right now, but in future other navies would have even faster cruisers, so the ships needed powerful stern chasers. The choice of a bow chaser was controversial; for example, Controller still liked the Elswick 8in. White favoured the 9.2in gun because the ship would face enemy armoured cruisers; no volume of 6in fire could smash them. The 8in gun was neither a QF weapon nor an armour penetrator like the 9.2 (on the basis of a very simple formula, White estimated the ratio of penetration as 40 to 26 in favour of the 9.2). White also brought up the likelihood of delay: the navy had never been happy with a gun bought off the shelf. He disliked the two shielded 6in of a *Diadem*, but they could be protected by an armoured screen with suitable ports, or placed in an armoured turret. Adopting the 6in turret would leave enough weight for an additional 6in gun and its casemate on the main deck amidships.

Controller circulated White's three alternative armament arrangements: (1) similar to *Cressy* but with 12pdrs on the main deck (common to all three); (2) four 6in instead of two 9.2in, the two foremost behind an armoured screen; (3) no armoured screen, six 6in instead of two 9.2in, four being in twin turrets and two in casemates.[9]

Both DNO and White disliked the armoured screen, which seems to have originated with the Board. Placed about 65ft abaft the bow, it would extend down to the main deck, and thus would provide some protection against the raking fire a cruiser would encounter during a long chase. However, during the same chase the enemy ship would be firing at high enough elevations that her shells would be plunging into the ship, many coming over the top of the screen. The French were interested in high-angle guns (Navy Minister Lockroy was a particular enthusiast). If they adopted such weapons any vertical screen would be ineffective. Controller Rear Admiral A K Wilson envisaged engagements opening at 6000yds, with sustained fire at 4000. DNO pointed out that at any range beyond 3000yds the height of the proposed bulkhead was insufficient to protect the deck astern of it against plunging fire; it would have to be raised nearly 22ft to protect the whole hull against fire descending at a 5-degree angle. To protect the ship against the standard heavy French cruiser gun (7.6in) at 4000yds would require a bulkhead 47ft above water, 13ft higher than proposed. To protect against the German 5.9in gun, it would have to extend 60ft above water.[10]

First Naval Lord Richards liked the 500-footer best, suggest-

Monmouth as completed. On commissioning she joined the 1st Cruiser Squadron (1903-6), after which she was on the China station (1906-13). On return from China she joined the Third (reserve) Fleet. On the outbreak of war she joined the 5th Cruiser Squadron (mid-Atlantic); she was later sent to the South Atlantic and sunk at Coronel, 1 November 1914.

Cornwall as refitted about 1907, with high topmasts for wireless (the spreader is visible on the foremast) and spotting tops. The foretop was an expansion of the earlier searchlight platform, the searchlight usually (but not here) being moved to below it. On completion she joined the 2nd Cruiser Squadron Atlantic Fleet (1904-6), and after a Devonport refit in 1907 she became cadet training ship attached to the North America and West Indies station (1908-14). On the outbreak of war she joined the 5th Cruiser Squadron (mid-Atlantic), and then went south to join the squadron hunting down von Spee's German squadron. With HMS *Glasgow* she sank the German cruiser *Leipzig* at the Falklands, 8 December 1914. She helped bottle up the German cruiser *Königsberg* in East Africa in 1915, and was at the Dardanelles that year. She was on the China station in 1915-17, and then on the North America and West Indies station (as a convoy escort) in 1917-19. In 1919 she became cadet training ship at Devonport, paying off that year.

ing only that another 6in gun be added on each side (given the ship's great length). His decision was dated 6 July 1898. Controller and others agreed. White was able to add two full double casemates between the end casemates, for a total of sixteen 6in guns, retaining the 9.2s at the ends, and fourteen 12pdrs, only four of which were on the main deck (First Naval Lord particularly wanted these anti-torpedo guns higher in the ship). It helped that there was a new lighter version of the 12pdr (twelve were the more powerful 12cwt version, two the shorter 8cwt on a shelter but dismountable as boat or field guns). White was also able to provide a total of 2400 rounds of 6in (the Legend showed 100 rounds per gun as a standard allowance). The line of casemates contributed to the side protection of the ship. They and other items (such as net defence) added about 400 tons,

Bedford in 1909, with wireless antenna spreaders barely visible near her fore topmast. Note the windsails (rather than cowls) on her ventilators. On completion she joined the 1st Cruiser Squadron Channel Fleet (1903-6), then was reduced to reserve with a nucleus crew at the Nore (1906-7). She then went to the China Fleet, and was wrecked at Quelport Island in the China Sea, 21 August 1910.

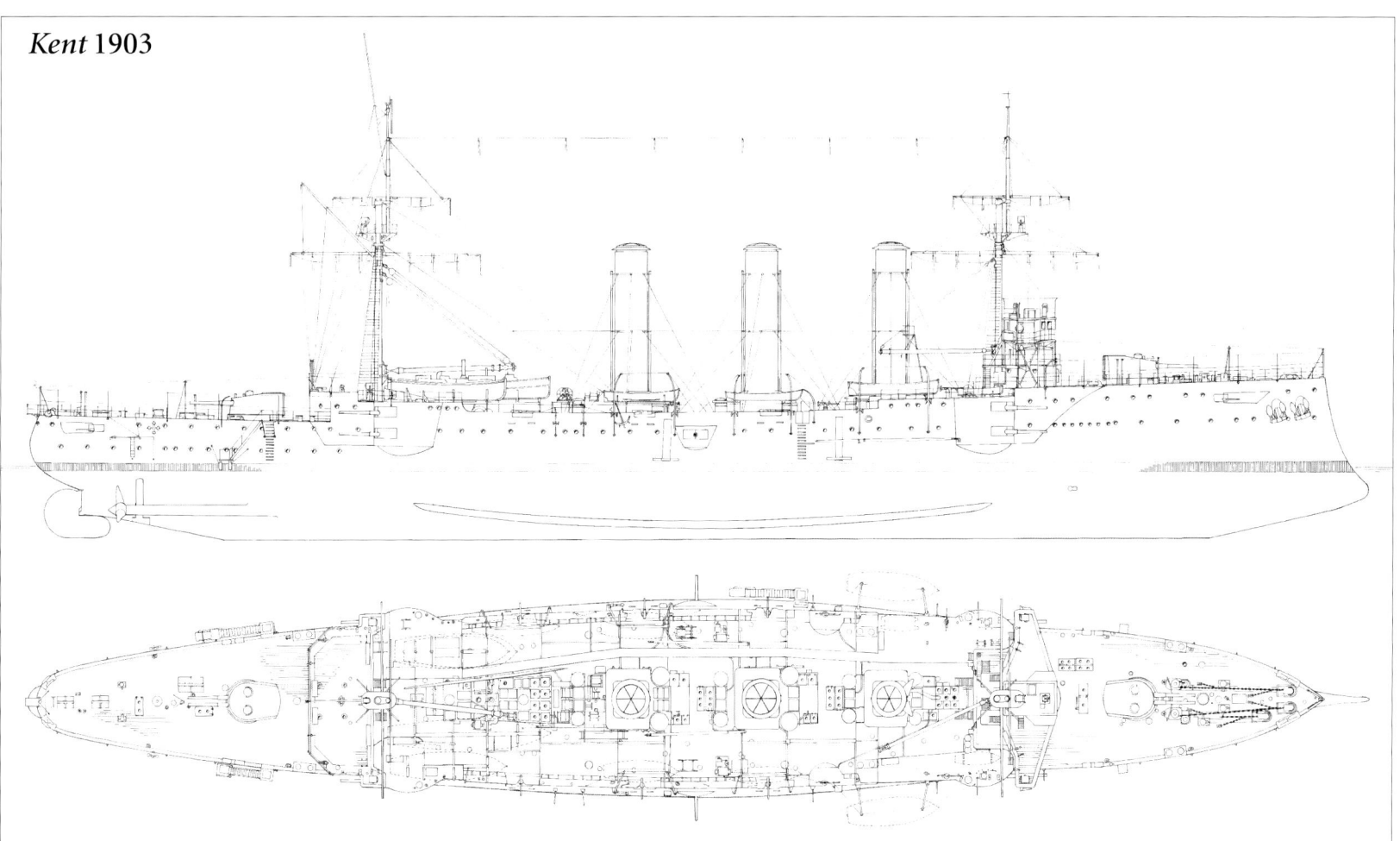

Kent 1903

HMS *Kent* is shown as completed, October 1903. Two 0.303in Maxim machine guns were mounted at the after end of the superstructure. There were six searchlights. When not in use, the searchlights on the bridge deck and after superstructure were stowed further inboard on the sets of four deck fittings shown. The ventilators for the boiler rooms are shown as circles in the plan view. When opened, they pivoted on their after edges through to the vertical. The double lines on the deck amidships represent rails for ash carts, which rolled to the four chutes seen on the sides of the deck. The need to deal with coal ash was a major limitation on warship operation, as boilers had to be shut down periodically (and often) so that ash could be cleaned out of the grates and dumped. Boats are shown in their inboard (stowed) positions, but the two 32ft rowing cutters abreast the foremast were always swung outboard and did not have on-deck stowage. The other boats shown, forward to aft and port to starboard, were: a 16ft skiff to starboard in chocks, a 27ft whaler to starboard of the second funnel, a 30ft gig in davits to port, and a 36ft sailing pinnace stowed within a 42ft sailing launch to port, with a 56ft steam pinnace inboard and a 40ft steam pinnace outboard to starboard. The latter four boats were handled by the boat derrick. Due to its complexity, the only rigging shown in the plan view is that for the boat davits.

(A D Baker III)

much of it high in the ship; White had to accept greater beam (71ft) and displacement (14,100 tons). He could still guarantee 23kts if he could have 30,000 HP. The changes would add about £20,000, so the ship would cost about £850,000 in all.

Controller Rear Admiral Wilson approved the design on 11 July 1898. Four ships of this *Drake* class were built under the 1898-99 program. A follow-on 'New *Drake*' class seems to have been planned, but the very different *Duke of Edinburgh* class was built.[11]

Monmouth Class

From the outset, White had envisaged an alternative design for a smaller 23-knot cruiser. By late 1897 he was asking his assistant to produce a design for a 9500-ton ship.[12] The project seems to have been suspended while the *Drake*s were being designed, but by late June 1898 Engineer-in-Chief was being asked detailed machinery questions. An undated Legend compared designs for 23-knot cruisers (with natural draught) armed with four 6in in turrets plus eight or ten in casemates, displacing 7700 to 9750 tons.[13] The 9750-ton design seems to have been favoured from the outset. The Cover shows virtually no design development. White submitted a sketch design on 27 September 1898 in connection with the Supplemental Programme for 1898-99 (due to the Fashoda crisis between Britain and France).[14]

The French threatened British trade, so the new cruisers were primarily counters to their new French 'corsair cruisers' *Chateaurenault* and *Guichen*, which had been modelled on the US cruisers *Columbia* and *Minneapolis*. Compared to the US ships the French used water-tube boilers for greatly increased power, hence speed. These 8000- to 8300-ton ships were armed with two 6.4in and six 5.5in QF guns and had large coal supplies (1400 to 1450 tons) for extreme range. *Chateaurenault* had a silhouette somewhat like that of an Atlantic liner, so that she could approach her victims without unduly alarming them. A smaller third ship, *Jurien de la Graviere*, was described as a station cruiser (i.e., for foreign operations), but according to White she was really designed to attack trade. She was more heavily armed (eight 6.5in), and her displacement had been reduced (to about 5600 tons) largely by cutting her coal supply (for which the design was criticized in France). All three were intended to achieve 23kts on trials, though that meant short-duration runs with a degree of forcing well beyond British practice. Based on boiler heating surface, White estimated that the two larger French ships could maintain about 20½kts on a sustained basis in smooth water. White also drew attention to new Japanese cruisers, which had about the same displacement as his new cruiser.[15]

White pointed to four 23kt cruisers of about 6000 tons recently ordered by the Russians (one in the United States, two in Germany, one in France, with a second rumoured in the United States) and two more were likely to be built.[16] White considered them modified versions of the Russian *Diana* class, which he felt was based on his own British *Talbot* class 'all the particulars of which were obtained by the Russian designers'. They were said to be able to maintain 23kts under natural draught for lengthy trials (12 to 24 hours); White's information suggested that the Russian boilers had the same proportion of heating surface to power as the British, so that they would sustain the same power for about as long. The Russian ships were said to be armed with twelve 6in (vs eleven in the comparable British cruisers), twelve 3in (12pdr) QF, six 3pdr, and six torpedo tubes (three submerged). White also pointed to a larger group of 21-knot cruisers, the three French *Kléber*s (armoured cruisers, about 7500 tons) and a similar Russian ship recently laid down at La Seyne.[17] The French ships were credited with ten 6.4in guns. White was unimpressed with their protection.

In addition to all these French and Russian cruisers ten others had reported speeds of 22½ to 23kts: two US, two Japanese, two Argentine, two Chilean, and two Chinese. All but the first two were of Elswick design, and only the Chilean *Esmeralda* had side armour. White believed that, despite their trial performance, all of these ships had sea speeds of 18 to 19kts, and less in some cases.

Taking all of these ships together, White summarized requirements for the new armoured trade protection cruiser. She had to be capable of 21kts in smooth water on a sustained basis, and of 23kts on 8-hour trial with natural draught. Armament should be superior to those of the new Russian and French cruisers (*Kléber* class), with suitable protection for her guns and their crews. Minimum armour thickness would be 4in, with thinner armour carried to the bow. Coal capacity would be about 1600 tons (half of which would be carried at normal draught). This was, unsurprisingly, the small-cruiser design White had prepared the previous year as part of the *Drake* design process. Its fourteen 6in guns were superior to any of the French or Russian armaments. The new 6in QF gun should penetrate all of the armour on a *Kléber*.[18] Protection followed that of the *Drake* class, but with reduced thickness. The most significant difference from the 1897 design was the powerplant: Belleville (not small-tube) boilers for 22,000 HP. Power for continuous steaming was 16,000 IHP, giving estimated natural draught trial speed and continuous sea speed of 23kts and 21kts, respectively.

White pointed out that, although the proposed cruiser could fight various French ships quite effectively, there were already ships with superior fighting qualities, achieved by sacrificing other qualities. The six new Japanese armoured cruisers were better protected and armed – but slower.[19]

The new ships would be built under contract. White estimated that they would cost £480,000 to £500,000 each, compared to £540,000 for a *Kléber*, in each case exclusive of armament. Given a sketch design, Controller Rear Admiral Wilson compared equal-cost fleets: 7 large cruisers (*Drake*s) or 10 smaller ones. The *Drake*s would have 14 × 9.2in guns and 112 × 6in guns in casemates; the smaller cruisers, 40 × 6in guns in turrets and 100 in casemates. Taking into account both the greater impact of each 9.2in hit, and the reduced rate of fire of 6in guns in twin turrets, White considered the overall firepower of the two groups about equal. The smaller ships needed more men, about 6850 compared to 6300 for the *Drake*s. They were not nearly as well protected, with 4in rather than 6in belts. For the same total of coal, the smaller ships would have about an eighth less radius of action.

White estimated that one large cruiser could engage two French *Montcalm*s with about the same chance of success as the small cruiser could engage one of them, but she need not fear meeting two of them. The large cruiser could meet many foreign battleships (if caught singly). To Wilson, the greatest advantage of the large cruiser was 'the certainty that an Admiral would have that whatever service he sent them on, they are sure not to fall in with any single cruiser superior to themselves in either speed or power, and that in most cases their superiority will be so overwhelming that they will be able to destroy their enemy with comparatively little injury to themselves'. Against this, the small cruiser (60ft shorter, and 18in less draught) could enter harbours the large cruiser could not, and the greater number of small cruisers would cover more ground. Wilson considered this last insignificant, given the large number of existing British cruisers. What mattered was the ability to catch and kill the fastest and most powerful of the enemy's cruisers – and that took a *Drake*. The existence of *Drake*s would force an enemy to concentrate his own cruisers, and that in turn 'would limit his sphere of action more than the reduction in numbers limits ours'.

The advantages of the large cruisers would, moreover, increase over time. It would be much more difficult for foreign navies to match the larger cruisers, not least because they lacked the necessary drydocks. Wilson wrote that 'it is not often that an opportunity occurs of gaining so marked an advantage over our rivals as we have now. The construction of these large cruisers is no leap in the dark, the long and ultimately successful trials of the *Powerful* and *Terrible* have made us familiar with all the difficulties of the problem and their construction will be even less dependent on untried appliances than is usually the case with a new design.'

Wilson pressed to make all four of the Supplemental ships *Drake*s. Since the *Drake* design already existed, they could be ordered at once. Since the small-cruiser design did not yet exist, the six that could be bought could not be laid down until March of the next year (1899). In addition to the six *Drake*s he envisaged (four plus the original pair), White proposed another two, their construction not to be settled until the Admiralty knew more about the progress of the French and Russian programs.

In addition to the large cruisers, Wilson proposed an improved faster third-class cruiser 'to act as the eyes of the fleet and as scouts for the large cruisers'. They materialized as the 'Gem' class described in an earlier chapter. Note that, unlike the large cruisers, they were not designed for 23kts, which would limit them in any role cooperating with the *Drake*s.

Junior Naval Lord Rear Admiral A W Moore liked the idea of six *Drake*s, but he also felt that the navy badly needed a group of smaller armoured cruisers. The question was whether to complete the *Drake* group before proceeding to the smaller ships. Second Naval Lord Admiral Frederick Bedford echoed Moore's views. A 22 October meeting of the Naval Lords, with First Lord Goschen present, decided that the four Supplemental cruisers should all be of the 9750-ton type.

In the end, the Supplemental was split between two repeat *Drake*s and two of the new small cruisers (*Kent* and *Essex*). Two more (*Bedford* and *Monmouth*) were included in the 1899-1900 program (for some reason the class was called *Monmouth*, not *Kent*). Another six were built under the 1900-1901 program.

White submitted the sheer draught and midships section on 21 February 1899. He had increased beam by 6in to secure sufficient stability, so displacement had increased to 9800 tons. Changes in the last group were very minor, such as enlarged evaporators and subdivision of the main condensers (machinery weight increased by 40 tons). In January 1900 the Board decided that one of the last pair should have Niclausse boilers.

The ships were always considered somewhat undergunned. In December 1911 Controller asked for a study to see whether the twin 6in turrets could be replaced by 7.5in or 9.2in guns. Removal of the twin 6in guns would save nearly 130 tons,

HMS *Carnarvon* shows enlarged spotting tops and range-repeating drums in this pre-1914 photograph. The after top was placed low to keep it below funnel smoke, just as HMS *Dreadnought* was given a very low after spotting top. Note that the after range drum was high (at the level of the tops) even though the spotting platform was low. The drums were installed after the spotting tops (some ships had the drums in 1909, but tops without drums in 1907; others lacked range drums as late as 1912 or 1913). Photographs of a few ships of this and earlier classes show a shrouded more or less circular shape alongside the forward spotting top; it may have been a flat dial like the later range dials. *Essex* apparently had a range drum only on her foremast. HMS *Antrim* may have been unique in having her forward range drum half way down her foremast, well below the spotting top (it displaced the forward searchlight). As with battleships, the range drums were removed by 1914. Armoured cruisers were not given range clocks during the First World War, although some light cruisers had them.
(Allan C Green, courtesy of the State Library of Victoria)

Devonshire as completed, with small fire control tops and a wireless gaff on her mainmast. On completion she joined 1st Cruiser Squadron Channel Fleet (1905-6); this squadron joined the Atlantic Fleet in 1906-7, and *Devonshire* was in 2nd Cruiser Squadron Atlantic Fleet in 1907-9. She was then reduced to reserve as part of the new Third (reserve) Fleet at Devonport (1909-11), then upgraded to 3rd Cruiser Squadron Second Fleet in 1913-14. On the outbreak of war the 3rd Cruiser Squadron joined the Grand Fleet (1914-16); *Devonshire* fought at Heligoland and at the Dogger Bank, but not at Jutland. She was at the Nore in 1916, and then in the 7th Cruiser Squadron Grand Fleet that year. She was on the North America and West Indies station in 1916-19.

THE FAST WING OF THE BATTLE FLEET

Devonshire as refitted, with high topmasts and wireless spreaders. The cage wireless antennas are not visible, but the spreaders which kept their separate wires apart are visible in the stern-on view.

Antrim 1905

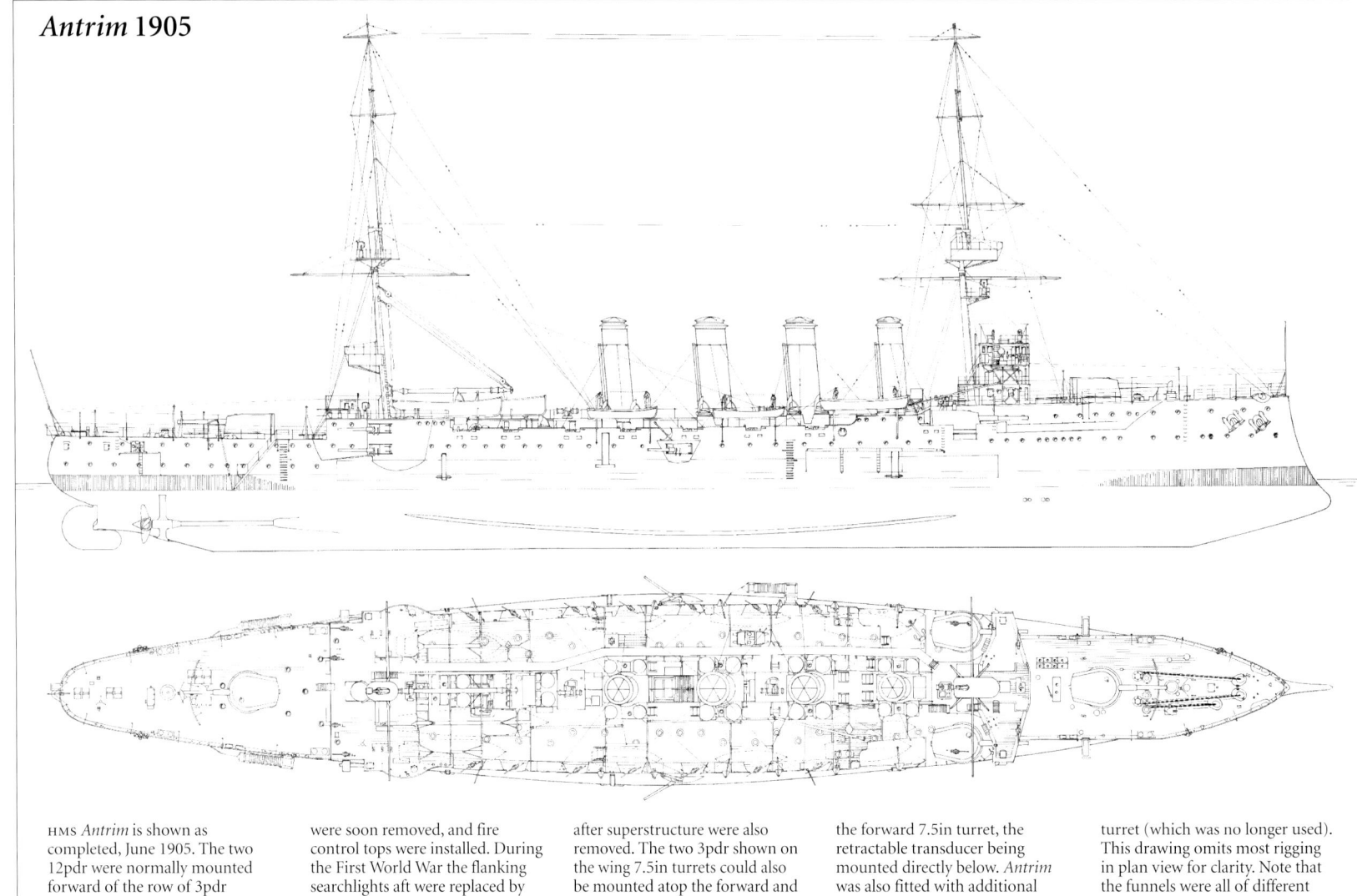

HMS *Antrim* is shown as completed, June 1905. The two 12pdr were normally mounted forward of the row of 3pdr amidships, but could be mounted on the two steam pinnaces or used as landing artillery. The torpedo magazine occupied two deck levels and could accommodate at least ten torpedoes. The two searchlights on the mast platform were soon removed, and fire control tops were installed. During the First World War the flanking searchlights aft were replaced by one on rails and one fixed to port near the centreline. The small deckhouse aft was removed. The lower 6in guns were moved to the upper deck amidships in 1916, four 3pdr being removed. The two bridge 3pdr and four more on the after superstructure were also removed. The two 3pdr shown on the wing 7.5in turrets could also be mounted atop the forward and after 7.5in turrets. Antrim was taken from reserve (into which she went in 1919) for Asdic trials (1920-21) and then used for cadet training in 1922. Asdic equipment was placed in a deckhouse between the bridge structure and the forward 7.5in turret, the retractable transducer being mounted directly below. *Antrim* was also fitted with additional radio equipment, including a direction-finding array and a new deckhouse for D/F equipment added between the first and second funnels. Some of the radio antenna wires interfered with training of the forward 7.5in turret (which was no longer used). This drawing omits most rigging in plan view for clarity. Note that the funnels were all of different diameter. As on the *Monmouth* class, the ventilators could be raised and lowered as well as rotated. The drawing shows all raised in the profile and closed in the plan view.

(A D Baker III)

and adding 9.2in guns would increase displacement about 200 tons and cost only about 0.1kt at full power. The proposed 9.2in shield would have been 6in thick in front and 3in on the side; it would not have been a full gunhouse as in larger cruisers. Weight would be saved if the twin 6in were replaced by a single 7.5in as in the *Devonshire* class (see below), but DNC (now Sir Philip Watts) preferred the 9.2in. Nothing was done.

Devonshire Class

Another six repeat *Monmouth*s were included in the 1901-2 program. The twin 6in were replaced by single 7.5in guns. In effect the 7.5in was the accepted equivalent to the abortive 8in gun. Boiler spaces were redesigned so that they could accept all the available water-tube boilers (Niclausse, Dürr, Babcock & Wilcox, or Yarrow) as well as the Bellevilles of the earlier ships.[20] That entailed 3ft more of boiler room length (and about 2ft more width). Engine rooms were lengthened by another 4ft, on the basis of experience gained in working out the machinery arrangement of the *Monmouth* class. When magazine and torpedo room arrangements were rethought, the total increase in length came to 10ft, and the beam had to be increased a foot. Machinery weight increased from 1795 to 1945 tons. New hull lines were worked out, involving a displacement of 10,200 tons. Machinery output (22,000 IHP) and speed did not change, the increased length and better hull form making up for the greater displacement. Although the new ships had many features in common with the *Monmouth*s, they were considered an entirely new design, and treated as such. DNC reported that every detail affecting accommodation and efficiency had been reconsidered, and many rearrangements and simplifications introduced.

The new design was submitted to the Board on 2 November 1901. While the ships were being built, additional single 7.5in guns were substituted for the forward two-storey casemates, for a total of four 7.5in. The after casemates and the single-level 6in mount between the casemates were retained.

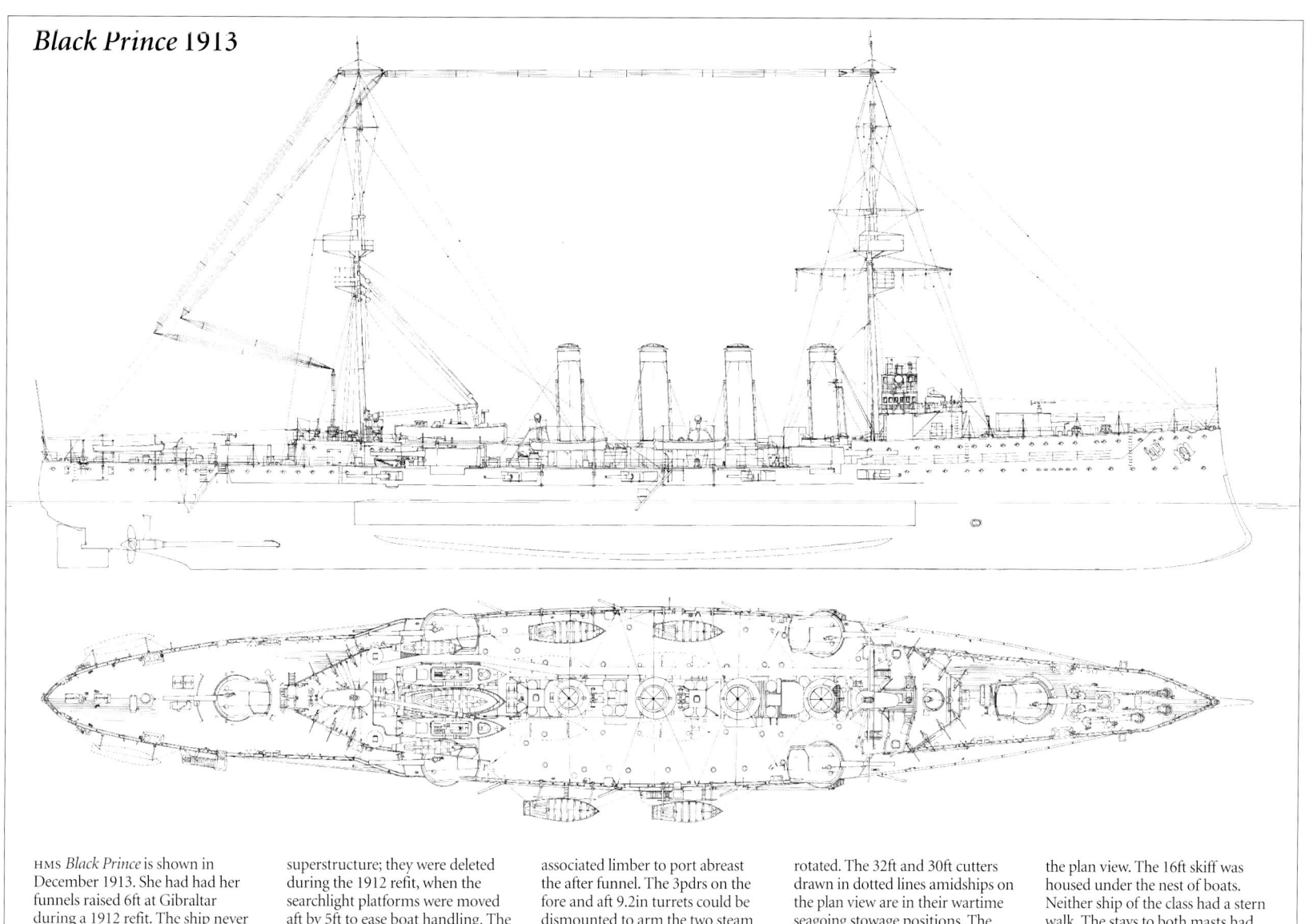

Black Prince 1913

HMS *Black Prince* is shown in December 1913. She had had her funnels raised 6ft at Gibraltar during a 1912 refit. The ship never had anti-torpedo nets. As completed she had two single 12pdr QF at the forward end of the row of QF guns on the after superstructure; they were deleted during the 1912 refit, when the searchlight platforms were moved aft by 5ft to ease boat handling. The two fixed 36in searchlights replaced rail-mounted 24in searchlights in 1913. The 12pdr field gun and its carriage were stowed with their associated limber to port abreast the after funnel. The 3pdrs on the fore and aft 9.2in turrets could be dismounted to arm the two steam pinnaces. Note the use of clamshell ventilators, which are shown closed in both views; they could be opened to about 45 degrees and rotated. The 32ft and 30ft cutters drawn in dotted lines amidships on the plan view are in their wartime seagoing stowage positions. The two 30ft gigs are shown in their harbour davits aft in the elevation, and in their stowed position outboard of the steam pinnaces in the plan view. The 16ft skiff was housed under the nest of boats. Neither ship of the class had a stern walk. The stays to both masts had ratlines, which are not shown here to avoid clutter.
(A D Baker III)

Black Prince and *Warrior* Classes

For the 1902-3 program the Royal Navy reverted to large armoured cruisers. Sir William White retired, to be succeeded by Sir Philip Watts, who had been traded to Elswick for him more than fifteen years earlier. The new cruisers were the first design he signed: HMS *Black Prince* and *Duke of Edinburgh*.

The new cruiser began under the designation 'New *Devonshire*'. On 18 March 1902 new DNC Watts asked about three possible alternative batteries for *Devonshire*: (1) the present two 7.5in and ten 6in; (2) four 7.5in in pairs, four 7.5in in single casemates, and eight 6in in single casemates; and (3) two 9.2in in end barbettes, four 9.2in in pairs in barbettes, and eight 6in in single barbettes. The step beyond (2) to the new design was to put all six 9.2in guns in single barbettes, two at the ends and two on each side.

An undated sketch, probably the beginning of the design, showed a flush-decked hull carrying six single 9.2in in turrets, with eight 6in in casemates below the weather deck. This sketch showed a 6in belt extending up to the main deck (the deck below the weather deck, on which the 6in guns were mounted), covered by a 1½in deck, with a ¾in armour deck below it (the *Drake* arrangement). Unlike *Drake*, this design showed a 1¼in deck covering the 6in battery, which was also protected by an upward extension of the 6in belt. The important differences from *Drake* protection were that side armour extended all the way aft (3in thick) and that the extension forward was much thicker (4in rather than 2in).[21]

This sketch seems to have been the basis of characteristics chosen at a 2 April 1902 conference between the Naval Lords and DNO. The conference adopted the armament and protection of the New *Devonshire* sketch (it also asked for the effect of increasing belt armour to 7in). The conference added a new requirement that the funnel casings (or their bases) would be protected (that proved impossible). As in the *Drake*s, speed should be 23kts (sustained ocean speed not to be less than 20kts). Legend coal weight would be 1000 tons (capacity 2000).

Natal just before the First World War, with funnel identification bands, high topmasts, and a range drum on her foremast. Note also the rangefinder forward of her bridge.
(Allan C Green, courtesy of State Library of Victoria)

THE FAST WING OF THE BATTLE FLEET

Natal with torpedo booms, newly completed

Natal as completed, as yet without either funnel identification bands or torpedo nets (but the shelf for the nets is in place). On completion she joined the 5th Cruiser Squadron Home Fleet (1907-9), then 2nd Cruiser Squadron Home Fleet (1909-14, Home Fleet becoming the Grand Fleet in 1914. She was destroyed by a powder explosion at Cromarty Firth, 30 December 1915.

Duke of Edinburgh in 1909. She had successfully tested the prototype below-decks (hence protected) transmitting station for fire control. It replaced earlier arrangements in which fire was controlled from aloft. On completion she joined the 2nd Cruiser Squadron (Atlantic Fleet: 1906-8), followed by 1st Cruiser Squadron (Channel Fleet 1908-9), 5th Cruiser Squadron (Atlantic Fleet 1909-13) and then 1st Cruiser Squadron Mediterranean Fleet 1913-14. She captured a German merchant ship in the Red Sea in August 1914. She was in the Persian Gulf in November 1914, then returned to the Grand Fleet (1st Cruiser Squadron December 1914-16). While part of the 1st Cruiser Squadron she fought at Jutland, where her sister *Black Prince* was destroyed. The only ship of her squadron to survive Jutland, after the battle she joined the 2nd Cruiser Squadron Grand Fleet. She left for a large refit in 1917. That was probably when she was fitted with a director and tripod legs for her foremast. After the refit she escorted Atlantic convoys, going to the North America and West Indies station in 1918. In contrast to the surviving 'Counties', she and the other large armoured cruisers were not at all wanted for the post-war fleet.

DNC produced four outline designs (A, B, C, D). A had a forecastle, six 9.2in and ten 6in guns, and 6in armour to the height of the upper deck. The additional 6in gun was worked in abaft the after wing 9.2in turret. B had no forecastle, but had an additional 9.2in gun (the forward turret was a twin). C had only eight 6in, all in twin gunhouses on the upper deck (between the wing 9.2in guns), with no armour above the main deck. D was similar to C, but had cylindrical boilers. The Naval Lords chose A. Boilers were still a problem: the Naval Lords wanted alternative versions with all-water-tube boilers, with one-fifth cylindrical boilers, and with all cylindrical boilers (A1, A2, A3). A3 was so much larger that it could easily accommodate another two 6in guns at a cost of perhaps 60 tons.[22] There was interest in saving weight by grouping the 9.2in guns at each end of the ship as closely as possible (in, say, an equilateral triangle), with common base protection instead of single barbettes. Other alternatives included revised numbers of rounds per gun (6in increased to 150, 9.2in decreased to 100 per gun) and increased power (30,000 rather than 25,000 HP).

By late May it seemed that A2, a mix of cylindrical and water-tube boilers, was the favourite: Controller Rear Admiral William H May assured DNC that he could go ahead with that design. Instead, on 30 May A1 was ordered, on the understanding that if the mixed boiler arrangement were chosen speed would be reduced to 22.6kts. A detailed analysis showed that the available space would accommodate 5000 HP of cylindrical boilers and 18,500 HP of water-tubes, for a total of 23,500 HP. This combination would weigh more than the all water-tube arrangement. By mid-June 1902 work was proceeding on the basis of A1 and a legend coal load of 1250 tons. Legend displacement was 13,550 tons. With all water-tube boilers the ship was expected to make 22¾kts (22⅓kts with one-fifth cylindrical boilers on the same total machinery weight). Early in July the Board decided to adopt A1 with mixed boilers (Babcock & Wilcox and cylindrical).

The Royal Navy was moving towards adopting oil fuel, so the hull specification was revised to make the whole of the double bottom under the boiler and engine rooms suitable for oil fuel. Piping would also be fitted. The oil would supplement, not replace, coal, although by 1902 there was interest in shifting to oil-firing. Engineer-in-Chief considered it most efficient to fit a proportion, say half, of the boilers to burn only oil and the rest for coal with oil spray for a spurt of higher power.[23]

There was still no definite decision as to whether the 6in guns would be in a box battery or in twin gunhouses, and whether the 9.2in mountings would be of the *Cressy* type (small central powder hoist, outer shell hoists and shell carrier) or of the 7.5in type in the *Devonshire* class (central hoist for powder and shell), or whether the 9.2in shields would be of *Cressy* type (6in front, 3in sides) or 6in all round. Controller chose the box battery, *Cressy* type mountings, and *Devonshire* type shields (5.5in sides, 4.5in rear, later increased). The box battery offered ahead and astern fire (the 6in gunhouses would have been blocked by the 9.2in wing turrets). In October 1902 it was decided that the ships would not have the new versions of the 9.2in and 6in guns under development, as adopting them would delay completion; they would therefore have 9.2in Mk X and 6in Mk VII guns.

Four more large cruisers, *Achilles*, *Cochrane*, *Natal*, and *Warrior*, were included in the 1903-4 program. Initially they were simply to have been repeats of the *Duke of Edinburgh* class, and in May 1903 tenders were invited on that basis.[24] The only significant difference was to have been substitution of Yarrow for Babcock & Wilcox boilers (they retained the cylindrical boilers of the earlier class). However, First Lord the Earl of Selbourne wrote late in the month that he was unhappy with the 6in guns, the ports of which would be even nearer the water than the lower 6in ports of the *Drake*s – which 'could hardly

HMS *Cochrane* in 1910.
(Paul Webb)

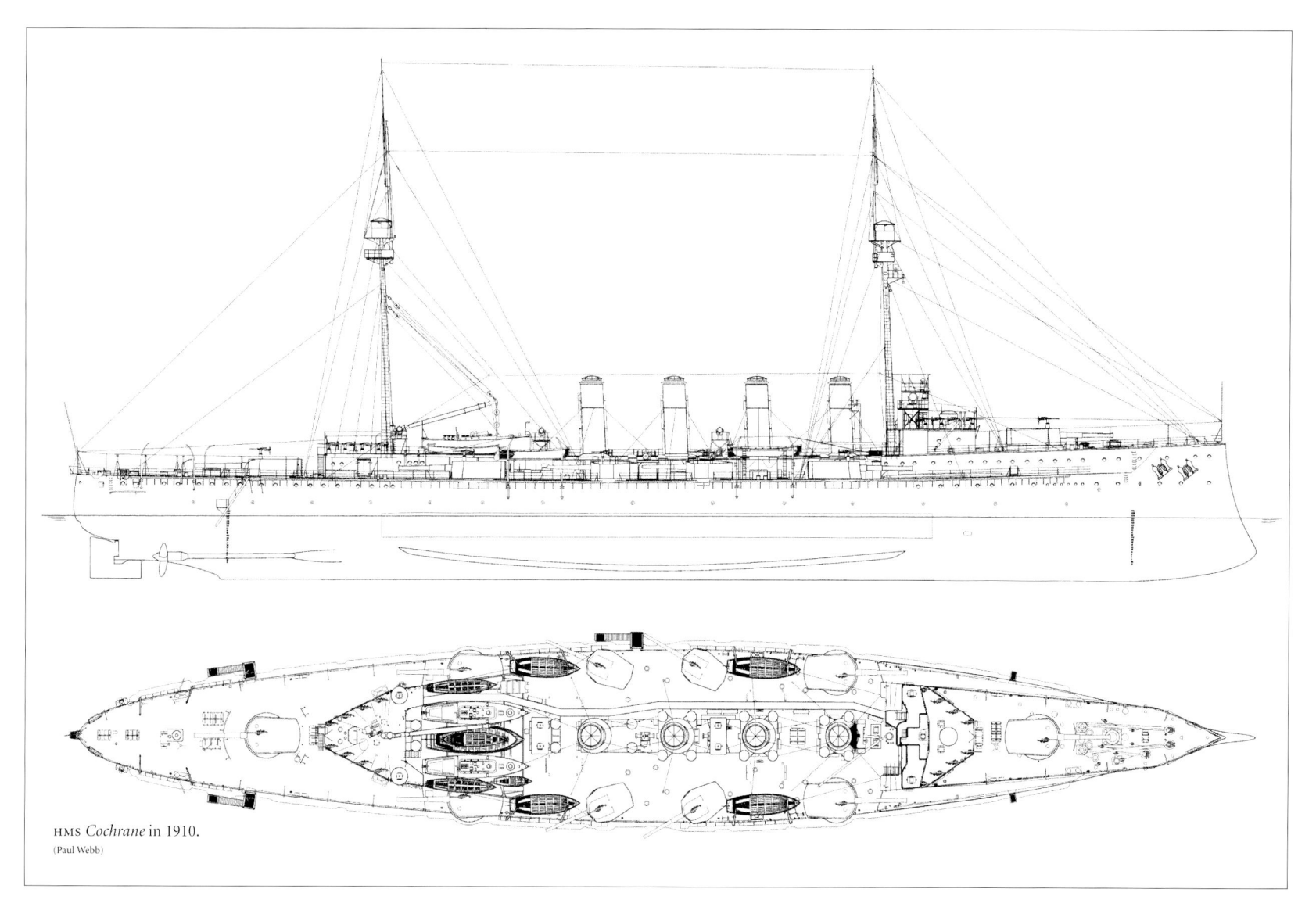

be fought at all except in a dead calm'. The first proposal was to revert to the earlier design C, with twin 6in gunhouses on the upper deck. Watts considered it essential to keep the heavy upper deck armament as low as possible. That did place the 6in guns a few inches lower than in the *Drake*s, but the guns were further aft, and the new ships were less likely to pitch (due to the different arrangement of weights); they would be better able to fight their forward 6in guns in moderate weather. First Lord and First Naval Lord decided not to change the design at all. Later it emerged that officers in the Mediterranean and in the Cruiser Squadron had pressed to have the guns raised.

In December 1903 a new idea was proposed: replace the 6in guns by single 7.5in guns on the upper deck. In effect this was design C with a single 7.5in instead of each twin 6in turret – as in the *Devonshire*s. Controller reported that the change would cost about 100 to 150 tons and about 3 inches in metacentric height, both of which were acceptable if the change was considered desirable and important. The arcs of the broadside 9.2in guns would be somewhat reduced, there would be some loss of upper deck space, and some armoured side and bulkheads between main and upper decks would be lost.

At the same time estimated weights of the *Duke of Edinburgh* were recalculated on the basis of actual weights of the *Monmouth*s. It seemed that their hulls would weigh 200 tons less than expected, and machinery might weigh 85 tons less. Late in February, DNC Watts pointed out that he now had enough weight in hand to provide the 7.5in guns and to retain the side armour which in the past had covered the 6in battery below the upper deck. Controller asked whether the change could be made not only in the repeat ships but also in the first two.

Unlike the 6in guns but like the 9.2s, the 7.5s would be in hydraulically-powered mountings. The pump planned for the ships might still suffice, provided that not all of the mountings were working at maximum power at the same time. Even so, it would be prudent to add a second hydraulic pump, and also to increase the diameter of the pressure pipes. Elswick, Vickers, and the yards all had to be told to stop work on the hydraulic system pending a decision (since the design was Elswick's, and it was incomplete, Vickers had not yet begun work).

The question was resolved at a 23 March 1904 Board meeting. The raised guns could clearly be fought better in a seaway. They could be controlled better, particularly at long range – an issue of increasing interest, as the Royal Navy was experimenting that year with longer-range fire control. Turrets would enable the 7.5in guns to be fired over a wider arc. Because they were isolated, a single hit could not wipe out the whole secondary battery. Fewer secondary guns would make fewer hits, but each hit would be more effective. At the Board meeting the estimated cost of altering the two *Duke of Edinburgh* class was set at £398,000, of which £200,000 would have to be found in the 1904-5 estimates. The total cost of altering the later four ships would be £250,000, of which only about £40,000 to £50,000 would have to be found in 1905-6. It was not difficult for the Board to decide that, given the advanced state of the *Duke of Edinburgh*s, they should not be altered. A decision as to the others was postponed to await the opinion of Admiral Fawkes and some of the captains of the Cruiser Squadron.

When the Board convened again on the 30th, the admiral and his captains unanimously favoured raising the guns, as main deck guns could not be fought in a moderate seaway if ships were making any speed; they also much preferred the 7.5s. The Board approved the heavier armament. At the same time, the six *Devonshire*s were modified with two more 7.5in guns in wing mountings, the additional cost being associated with that of the modification to the *Warrior*s. By this time, a further armoured cruiser (which became *Defence*) was also being designed, and the new 7.5in single mounting was expected to arm it as well.

Once the First World War began, the two *Duke of Edinburgh*s clearly began to find their 6in guns too wet, and there were calls that they be rearranged. By October 1915 *Black Prince* had shifted two guns on each side to her upper deck.

Minotaur Class
A fresh design was prepared for the 1904-5 program ('armoured cruiser 1904'). Controller Rear Admiral William H May formally began the process in August 1903.[25] All guns of the main and secondary armament should be in turrets 'with a good command so that they could be fought in a seaway' – as was then being argued for the earlier class. Alternative armaments should be (i) a combination of 9.2in and 7.5in guns, (ii) 9.2in and 6in guns; or (iii) all 7.5in. Protection should be at least as good as in *Duke of Edinburgh* with, if possible, 7 or 8 inches at the waterline. Continuous speed should be 23kts for 8 hours. Mean draught should be about that of the previous class. Cost

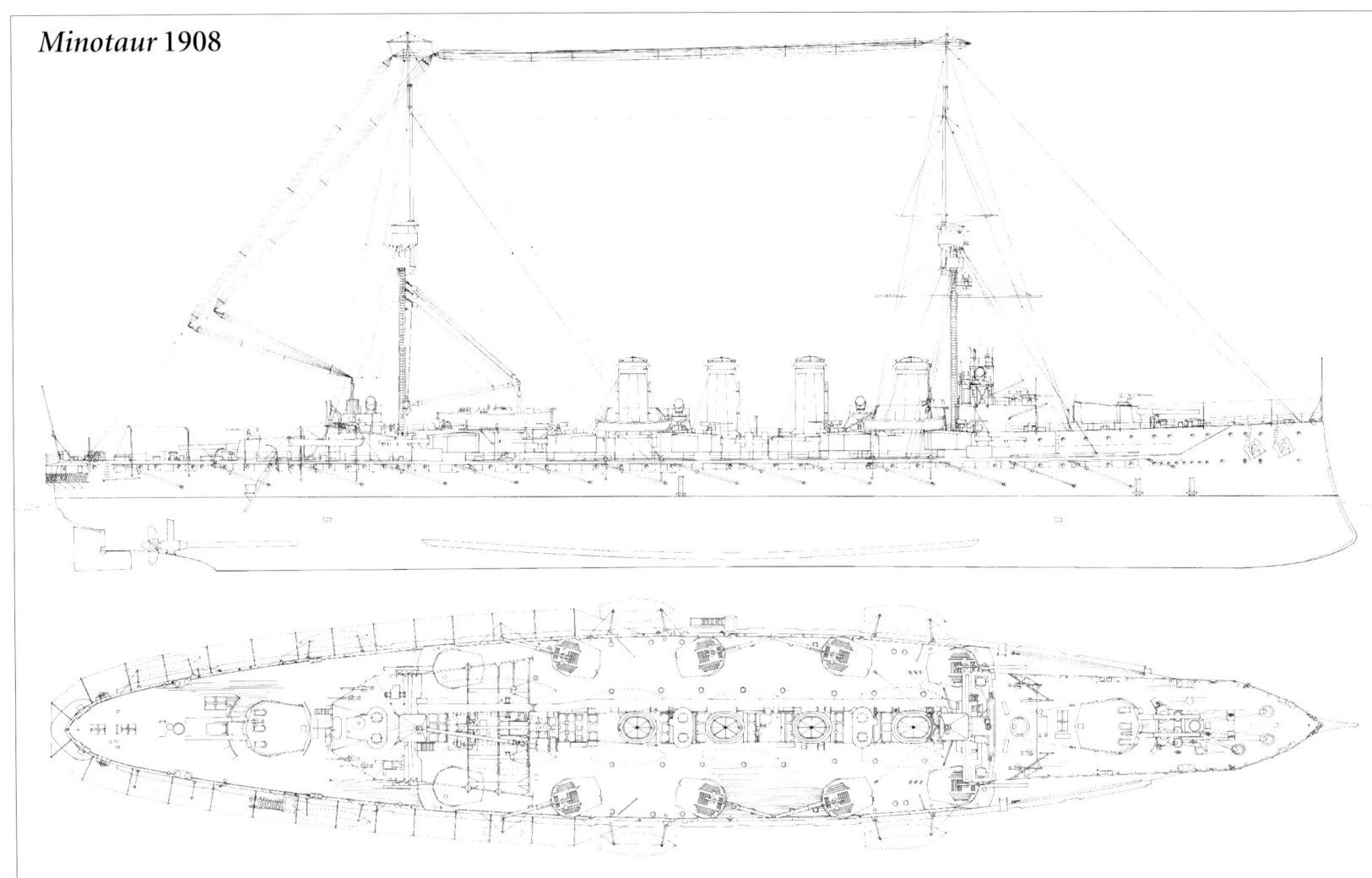

Minotaur 1908

HMS *Minotaur* is shown newly completed in April 1908. Her funnels were raised 15ft in 1909. The forward spotting platform, 73ft 9in above the upper deck, carried a 9ft rangefinder on athwartship rails. The after station was later removed. The small conning tower aft was intended as a secondary ship-control position. The 12pdrs atop the 9.2in turrets could be dismounted for use as field guns. Dotted lines on deck amidships show wartime (as imagined in 1908) deck stowage for cutters, whaleboat, and one 30ft gig, presumably in portable crutches (no fixed fittings appear in the as-fitted drawings). Booms shown aft in the plan view supported canvas awnings to shade officers' berthing and messing areas. The anti-torpedo net stowage shelves were gratings, not solid as shown.
(A D Baker III)

THE FAST WING OF THE BATTLE FLEET

Minotaur as completed, with short funnels. On completion she joined the 5th Cruiser Squadron Home Fleet (1908-9), then transferred to 1st Cruiser Squadron Home Fleet (1909-10). She was flagship of the China Fleet 1910-14, capturing a German merchant ship, bombarding the German wireless station on Yap, and escorting Australian troop convoys in November 1914. She was flagship of the Cape station in December 1914. She then returned home for a refit in 1915-16. She was flagship 2nd Cruiser Squadron Grand Fleet 1916-19, fighting at Jutland.

Defence with funnels raised. About 1912 *Cochrane*, and probably the others, was fitted with range drums on both masts. A 1916 photo showed her little modified except that both her tall topmasts had come down (the after one was eliminated altogether). *Minotaur* had range drums before her funnels were raised, but they seem to have been removed when that was done (about 1911). A photograph taken at that time shows two flaps down on the platform immediately below the spotting top, which was square rather than round in her case. She also shows a small platform atop her compass platform. It was added to *Defence* after her funnels were raised. *Shannon* had it and the range drums in a 1911 photograph, but not in another photograph dated 1911 – dates are inexact. The other photo does show range drums.
(Perkins via NHHC)

should not exceed that of *Duke of Edinburgh*, and if possible should be less. Sketch designs should be ready by 1 December. Watts offered eleven alternatives:

(1) two twin 9.2in and six twin 7.5in;
(2) two twin 9.2in and ten single 7.5in;
(3) two single 9.2in and six twin 7.5in;
(4) eight twin 7.5in;
(5) two single 9.2in and eight twin 7.5in;
(6) ten twin 7.5in;
(7) two single 9.2in and ten single 7.5in;
(8) twelve single 7.5in;
(9) six single 9.2in and six twin 6in (design C for the previous class with another pair of twin 6in);
(10) six single 9.2in and six single 7.5in (*Warrior* with an additional 7.5in on each side); and
(11) six twin and six single 7.5in (total 18).

The associated Legend showed less power than the previous class (typically 21,000 IHP). The difference was presumably due to adopting a longer hull (490ft, 508ft at the waterline). Protection matched that of the previous class; Watts estimated that an extra inch at the waterline would cost 110 tons. Excluding guns and stores, estimated cost varied from the £1,050,000 of (2) to £1,120,000 for (11). *Duke of Edinburgh* would cost £1,060,000 if she were armed with the same 9.2in/50 planned for the new ship.

The Royal Navy was in a severe financial bind, so Controller asked whether the cost could be cut by reducing armament. That did not help very much; the ships were costly because of their size and protection. The Naval Lords wanted more protection: the slopes of the lower deck should be thickened from ¾in to 2in (300 tons, £30,000).[26] They also wanted more torpedo tubes (four on the beam, requiring an additional submerged torpedo room) and one astern (50 tons, £9000). Controller proposed using only water-tube boilers to save about 110 tons – at the cost of another £10,000. Later Controller asked about the effect of reducing speed to 22kts.

DNO considered most of the designs too crowded; only (1), (3), and (4) seemed satisfactory. He did not want 6in guns at all. Given the fleet scouting role, he wanted 9.2in guns: 'they may very possibly be subjected to battleship fire in the *exigen-*

cies of action and would then find the want of more effective belt piercing ordnance.' That killed (4). He favoured (1), but preferred two pairs of 10in guns (a calibre then being considered) plus paired 7.5s, perhaps balancing the increased weight of the heavier gun by reducing the number of 7.5s. He thought the 9.2in had reached its limit. By the time the new ships were afloat it would be giving way to 10in guns 'to obtain greater penetrative power at long range'. DNO pointed to the US *Tennessee* class, of 14,500 tons, armed with two pairs of 10in guns (he omitted to point out that they did not have anything like the 7.5). The battleships *Swiftsure* and *Triumph*, with their 10in guns, 'probably foreshadow the greater development of the 10in gun for vessels of about the tonnage of the class proposed, with perhaps greater speed met by reduction of belt thickness, in other Navies, and I think we should be prepared for this.'

All of this was unpleasantly expensive, so DNC was asked for further designs whose secondary armament was mounted in casemates or a box battery, but at least 15ft above water, doing away with expensive secondary turrets. He submitted them early in February 1904. Nos 12 and 13 had two pairs of 9.2in guns, plus 6in (in, respectively, two pairs and fourteen single mounts, the latter between decks; or ten twin mounts). Nos 14 and 15 had six single 9.2in, as in the *Duke of Edinburgh* (but in the new 50-calibre version), and either ten single 7.5in between-deck mountings or twelve single 6in in between-deck mountings. Nos 14 and 15 were somewhat smaller ships, 480ft long. The 490ft ships were rated at 23kts (under forced draught; sustained sea speed was 21kts). The shorter ships were rated at 22kts under forced draught (20½kts on a sustained basis at sea). To meet the seakeeping objections, all the guns were raised about 4ft. To increase speed to 23kts, the ship would have to be lengthened by about 15ft, adding 550 tons.

A 10 February Naval Lords meeting decided that money 'ought not to stand in the way of having a good design of armoured cruiser'. It would be better to reduce numbers than to accept a poor design. Quality was particularly important because the ships would not be completed for three years; Controller wrote that 'vessels now designed should be with the object that they shall be up to date 10 years hence'. Speed should be at least 23kts, as in most of the designs, and coal at legend draught 1000 tons (capacity 2000). Having overcome the cost issue, the Naval Lords chose turreted guns over casemates. DNC was able to mount turret guns 20ft above water, compared to 15ft for casemates. Too, turrets were isolated, hence could not all be destroyed by a single hit, as a box battery could. Similarly, the Naval Lords unanimously demanded 9.2in guns, which should be mounted in the most commanding possible positions, on the centreline at the ends. They also preferred the 7.5in to the 6in secondary gun even though, roughly, two 6in could be had for one 7.5. The all-7.5in option was rejected once

Shannon from ONI 1908 with short funnels, as completed. On commissioning she joined the 5th Cruiser Squadron Home Fleet (1908-9), transferring to 2nd Cruiser Squadron Home Fleet (1909-12). She was flagship of 3rd Cruiser Squadron Home Fleet (1912-13), then in 2nd Cruiser Squadron Home Fleet from 1913 onwards (Home Fleet became the Grand Fleet in 1914). She escorted Atlantic convoys in 1917-18, having fought at Jutland.

more: 'in certain cases even cruisers with the 9.2in gun could take their place in line of battle.'

The only options left were Designs 1 and 2, the difference being that the secondary battery of Design 1 was six pairs of 7.5in guns, whereas No 2 had ten single 7.5s. Both had paired 9.2s at the ends. This pairing gave the same broadside as the earlier class with six 9.2in, albeit at a somewhat slower rate of fire (due to twin mountings). Ahead fire was reduced, but it could be argued that only rarely could all three forward 9.2s in the earlier design fire together. Although No 1 offered one more broadside 7.5in gun, and heavier ahead and astern fire, the Naval Lords much preferred single mountings, which would equal or probably exceed the rate of fire of the twins. A single hit would disable one rather than two 7.5s. First Lord, who had not been present at the conference, agreed: the new ship would be Design 2. To absorb its high cost, the 1904-5 program consisted of three rather than four armoured cruisers.

To save time, the ships used the same twin 9.2in mountings which had been designed for the *Lord Nelson* class battleships, despite increased weight: the battleships had thicker shields than had been envisaged for the cruisers. The 7.5in guns were a new 50-calibre type, requiring entirely new mountings.

The main open question was adoption of all water-tube boilers (either Babcock & Wilcox or Yarrow: 27,000 IHP, far more than in *Warrior*), which was made subject to the conclusions of the Boiler Committee.[27] As in the *Duke of Edinburgh* and *Warrior* classes, the double bottom was prepared for oil stowage.[28] The issue of full vs hollow hull lines was revived, and finally put to the test: HMS *Shannon* was built with full (straight) lines, and ran comparative trials against HMS *Minotaur*. They seemed to show decisively that the conventional hollow hull form was better, even in a seaway.

Iwate was one of four armoured cruisers built for Japan by Armstrong. She and her sister *Idzumo* were in effect water-tube boiler versions (using Bellevilles) of the *Asama* and *Tokiwa*. The ships were slightly shorter and beamier (9600 tons, 400ft × 68ft 6in × 23ft 9in). Bellevilles offered considerably more power than cylindrical boilers, but they could not be forced, so these ships were run only at natural draught. Rated power was 14,500 IHP for 20.75kts; on trials, *Iwate* made 22.3kts on 15,739 IHP. She is shown at Gatun Locks on the Panama Canal.

By the end of 1904, with the three ships under construction, it was time to develop a design for the 1905-6 program. At the end of December Controller Rear Admiral May sketched two alternatives. One was *Minotaur* rearmed with no fewer than sixteen 9.2in guns in eight twin turrets. She would retain her end turrets, and she would have three twin 9.2 on each beam. This was an 'all-big-gun' armoured cruiser, armed with the standard British armoured cruiser weapon. She would have no forecastle. May considered this design 'very urgent' as he was thinking not about the next year's ship but about changing the *Minotaur*s already being built.

The day after receiving May's request, Watts answered that the extra weight would increase draught by 6 inches, for a legend draught of 26½ft. The boiler room bulkheads would have to be adjusted slightly. The ship would retain sufficient stability. 'As the 7.5in mountings are ordered it is desirable that an early decision should be given if the change is to be made.' Watts produced the desired Legend, offering both a design with eight twin mounts and one with six twins and two singles (fourteen 9.2in). Both would have had the same dimensions as *Minotaur* and the same powerplant.

By this time Admiral Sir John Fisher was First Sea Lord. While commanding the Mediterranean Fleet, he had become interested in a new kind of all-big-gun ship armed with 10in guns, which were thought to be the most powerful which could be fired rapidly (by 1904 it was becoming clear that the 12in could be fired as quickly, to much greater effect). Fisher had William Gard, the constructor at his fleet dockyard, Malta, produce sketch designs. The one for his future armoured cruiser showed sixteen 10in guns. Gard seems generally to have been grossly over-optimistic in estimating what was possible, and May's sixteen-gun cruiser was probably a more realistic approach to Fisher's big-gun cruiser.

May's alternative was an entirely new ship, protected like *Minotaur*, but armed with eight 12in (i.e., battleship) guns in pairs, with a speed of 25½kts (with reciprocating engines). May's sketch showed two turrets side by side on the forecastle and two more superfiring aft on the centreline. The height of the centres of the forward guns was the same as in *Minotaur*, and freeboard forward not less than 30ft. Without much space aft, the officers would live amidships. Beam would be increased as required to give the necessary stability. Watts immediately began sketching such a ship.[29]

This second alternative led to the ship Fisher ended up choosing, the battlecruiser. It became Design A in a series of alternatives. A drawing showed the two side-by-side turrets sharing a common armoured box, as did the two superfiring turrets aft. An undated Legend showed the sort of hull required to support both the heavy guns and the machinery (41,000 HP) needed for the desired 25½kts.[30] An alternative Design B had the two after turrets side by side. The next Legend was for Designs D and E; they had a slightly larger hull and slightly more power.[31] This alternative had a more conventional armament arrangement in which one turret each was placed fore and aft, with two more side by side in the waist (sharing a common armour box). Like A and B, these designs showed four funnels. E differed from D in that the two waist 12in mounts were skewed somewhat, the after superstructure forming a distinct block with a single funnel (with three funnels on the forward superstructure).

All of these designs were designated 'new armoured cruiser'.

Design E became the *Invincible* class battlecruiser, clearly the direct successor to the *Minotaur*s and to similar armoured cruisers.[32] The new ships were much faster and more heavily armed, but both changes had been coming for some time. The key step had been taken in 1897, when Sir William White convinced the Board that it was possible to build a fast cruiser which could be both a cruiser and a semi-battleship. Again and again the Board chose heavier guns because it expected the big armoured cruisers to fight everything up to and including battleships. It was not, moreover, a matter of sacrificing armour for speed; the *Drake*s had what White considered battleship armour, and their successors had the same level of protection. What changed was speed and firepower, both of which demanded much larger and more expensive ships.

Looking at the big armoured cruisers as fast if lightly-armed (*not* lightly-armoured) battleships affects perceptions of First World War naval action. When Admiral Craddock steamed out to face von Spee, he left the old battleship *Canopus* behind. That seems a lot less risky given that his flagship *Good Hope* had much the same level of protection as the battleship. The battle which followed showed that the armour deck redistribution in the later big armoured cruisers was vital: even the German 8.2in armour-piercing shells penetrated 6in side armour. Without much lower-deck armour, *Good Hope*'s vitals were poorly protected, and she was destroyed. The two *Invincible*s which destroyed von Spee's squadron were not too much better protected than *Good Hope*. That adequately explains why they chose to fight at maximum range, even though they had to expend so much of their ammunition. That *Good Hope* suffered magazine explosion whereas the Germans did not should have been a wake-up call.

There was one further attempt to design an armoured cruiser with 9.2in guns. In November 1907 DNC sketched a 25-knot ship whose characteristics were discussed and generally approved at a 12 November Sea Lords conference. It was an alternative to Battlecruiser Design E for the 1908-9 program, an improved *Invincible* (in the event neither was built, *Indefatigable* being a less elaborate improvement on *Invincible*). In effect this was a smaller version of *Invincible* with 9.2in rather than 12in guns.[33] Nothing came of the design; HMS *Indefatigable* was bought instead. The project demonstrated that not too much would be saved by going back from 12in to 9.2in guns, as it was almost the displacement of an *Invincible*.

Invincible and her sisters were the ultimate armoured cruisers, with the same protection as their predecessors but with battleship-calibre guns.
(Abrams of Devonport via RNHB)

APPENDIX: Vickers Designs

The armoured cruiser *Rurik* (right) was built by Vickers to meet Russian specifications reflecting the lessons of the Russo-Japanese War. *Rurik* was armed with four 10in/50 and eight 8in/50 and twenty 4.7in, all of Vickers design, and displaced 15,190 tons (490ft pp x 75ft x 26ft); she made 21kts on three-quarters power (19,700 IHP). Probably the first approach to this design was Vickers' Design 179 'to requirements of Admiral Dubussof') armed with twelve 10in/45, twenty 12½pdr QF, and five submerged 18in tubes on 14,550 tons (480ft x 75ft x 25½ft), to make 21kts for 24 hrs on 19,700 IHP (note the coincidence of this latter figure with the sustained power figure for *Rurik*). This design featured a 6in belt. *Rurik* herself was Design 160C, Designs 160A and B being large armoured cruisers for 'Z.Z.', who may have been Vickers' salesman Basil Zaharoff. Design 160E was a turbine-powered *Rurik*, without a forward boiler room. Design 217 was a 23kt turbine *Rurik* (17,000 tons, 535ft x 78½ft x 25¾ft, 30,000 IHP) with the armament and protection of the earlier ship; an alternative reciprocating engine design was also prepared. Design 217A was much the same design prepared for 'Z.Z.' so that he could offer it to other navies. The price estimate was dated 18 May 1906. The Vickers design book includes a very similar ship (Design 459) 'for China' with the same armament (but sixteen rather than twenty 4.7in) and the same belt thickness on 14,750 tons (490ft x 75ft x 26½ft, 22.5kts, no HP given). An alternative Chinese Design 460 had six 8in guns and fourteen 4.7in on 14,600 tons (490ft x 75ft x 26½ft). However, Design 461 for China was armed with eight 10in and sixteen 4.7in on the same dimensions (15,000 tons, 22.5kts on 27,000 HP). Vickers offered Russia a 27-knot scout (Design 284) armed with four 12in and twelve 4.7in guns on 10,200 tons (535ft x 61ft, 36,000 IHP, presumably using turbines).

Vickers entered the warship-building business in 1897 when it bought Naval Construction & Armaments Ltd, which was essentially the warship yard at Barrow-in-Furness. Vickers already made armour and guns, so with this acquisition it became a fully-integrated warship builder. Armstrong was already well established, so Vickers found itself offering innovative hybrids in hopes of gaining sales. Its first major export success seems to have been the Chilean battleship *Libertad* (bought by the Royal Navy as *Triumph*), which it did not design (she was designed by Sir Edward Reed, a sister being built by Armstrong). To further complicate any understanding of the record, in at least one case the Vickers design book includes a modified version of an Elswick (Armstrong) design, in this case Elswick's No 463 for Chile with speed increased to 23kts (undated, but probably about 1907). Vickers and Armstrong joined together to offer design and construction services to Spain (in 1908) and to Turkey (1914); Vickers also set up its own subsidiary in Russia in 1912, specifically to support the Black Sea Fleet. In 1897 several navies, like those of Argentina, Brazil, Portugal, Spain, and Turkey, had old second-class ironclads. Replacing them with modern battleships would have been extremely expensive.

In its attempt to break into the warship market, Vickers offered what it called 'cruiser-battleships' as an alternative. In effect Ansaldo in Italy (which was associated with Vickers) was offering the same thing in the form of cruisers armed with 10in guns, some of which it sold to Argentina and Japan. The earliest was its Design 16, a 9800-tonner armed with four 8in QF guns in twin mounts, fourteen 6in QF in a 10in citadel, twelve 14pdr QF, and five 18in torpedo tubes (one above water). The ship would have a 9in belt. She would be of roughly *Monmouth* size: 420ft x 66ft x 23½ft, with similar power and speed (21,000 IHP, 22kts). Given the much less impressive protection of the Royal Navy cruiser, she probably had a much narrower belt (she had 6in armour to her upper deck). Vickers also characterized lightly armed battleships as cruiser-battleships. Design 20 (for which a cost estimate was dated 7 May 1901) was a smaller ship with something closer to the standard British armoured cruiser battery of two 9.2in and twelve 6in on 8600 tons (350ft x 68ft x 24ft) to make 21kts (16,000 IHP) with maximum belt thickness of 9in. A modified version (20D) had twin 8in instead of 9.2in singles. Design 26 (cost estimated dated 15 July 1899) offered two 9.2in and ten 6in QF on only 6700 tons (370ft x 60ft x 21½ft) with a 9in (i.e., battleship) belt and a speed of 20kts (12,000 IHP). Design 28A was somewhat larger at 9300

tons (420ft x 66ft x 23ft 2in) with thinner armour (7in belt) and single 8in rather than 9.2in guns, weight going into more powerful machinery (20,500 IHP for 22kts). An alternative 28B traded off more armament (twin 8in) for less power (19,000 IHP, 21kts). Another design of this period, closer to a small battleship, was No 34, with two twin 9.2in guns on 9300 tons (355ft x 68ft x 25ft, 13,500 IHP for 20kts). By about 1901 the 10in gun was being promoted as a superior capital ship weapon, much more powerful than the 9.2in (500lb rather than 380lb shell) but much faster-firing than the standard 12in battleship gun. It was the weapon Admiral Fisher initially wanted for his new-generation capital ships, and the Royal Navy developed a new 10in weapon. Vickers offered Design 42 (a 'first class battleship-cruiser'), with two such guns in single mounts plus fourteen 6in, on 11,250 tons (450ft x 68ft x 25ft, 19,500 IHP for 21kts) with a 7in belt. A corresponding and somewhat later armoured cruiser (Design 94) was similarly armed on 7750 tons (365ft 9in x 61ft 6in x 23ft 10in, 21kts on 15,500 IHP, 7in belt). Vickers also continued to offer 'cruiser-battleships' with lighter guns. Thus Design 43A had two twin and two single 8in QF plus ten 6in QF on 11,150 tons (420ft x 67ft x 24ft, 22,000 IHP for 22kts) with a 7in belt. Weight-savers included mounting ten of the 6in in a main deck citadel instead of in the individual casemates the Royal Navy favoured. An alternative had ten 7.5in (the new Royal Navy intermediate calibre, which dates the design to about 1902), of which four were in twin mounts with dwarf (rather than full-height) barbettes. A cost estimate was dated 19 November 1902, but the intended buyer was not named. Design 58 (cost estimate 20 November 1902) reflected the new trend towards more powerful secondary armament, which would culminate in single-calibre ships: two 9.2in and sixteen 7.5in (rather than 6in) on 10,650 tons (410ft x 70½ft x 24½ft, 15,000 IHP for 20kts, 6in belt 129ft long). A modified version had three 10in (one twin forward, one single aft) and twelve 7.5in; another had two twin 9.2in and sixteen 7.5in, and an 8in belt. In May 1904 Vickers proposed a single-calibre fast battleship to Chile (Design 127), armed with twelve 10in (changed to 9.2in) with nothing else larger than a 14pdr (3in) QF gun: two twin mounts (one at each end) and eight upper-deck casemates. This ship would have displaced only 11,800 tons (436ft × 71ft × 24ft 7in) and would have made 19kts (12,500 IHP), with a 7in belt. The Vickers design book shows the design quoted on 5 May 1904 and a revised quote dated 6 April 1906. The Chilean proposal may have paralleled successful Armstrong and Vickers proposals to Brazil for battleships and a cruiser armed with 10in guns, for the big Brazilian 1904 program (the surviving Armstrong book of reports by the Elswick yard records the Brazilian order for a 9300-ton armoured cruiser). Design 129 (cost estimate 5 May 1904) may have been a somewhat similar ship for Turkey, armed with twelve 9.2in guns in twin mounts (at the ends and on the quarters, in the arrangement used by the German *Nassau* class dreadnoughts): 14,800 tons (500ft × 74ft × 27ft, 23kts on 30,000 IHP), with a 7in belt. At the same time (5 May 1904) Vickers quoted prices for a first-class battleship (Design 132) armed with twelve 12in guns (twin mounts fore and aft, eight singles on the broadsides) displacing 18,000 tons (440ft × 79½ft × 27¼ft) to make 20kts on 22,000 IHP, with a 9in belt. These data correspond broadly with the particulars of the Japanese *Satsuma* class, their first dreadnoughts. The Vickers design notebook counts the battleship design as part of the 'first program' for an unnamed client. An associated cruiser-battleship (127A) had twelve 9.2in instead of 12in guns, plus fourteen 14pdr QF (the battleship had 22) and twelve 3pdr, with two 18in torpedo tubes, on 14,000 tons (470ft × 73ft × 27ft, 23kts on 27,000 IHP). The ship would have had a 7in belt. These seem to have been the last cruiser-battleships before about 1908, since the next such ship in the file is Design 426, a cruiser-battleship for Argentina. However, Design 151 ('second program') was an equivalent ship described as a first-class armoured cruiser (again, for 'Z.Z.') armed with twelve 9.2in in twin mounts plus twenty 14pdr QF and four submerged torpedo tubes on 14,750 tons (535ft × 70ft × 26½ft, 24kts on 30,000 IHP with water-tube boilers), with a 7in belt. An alternative first-class armoured cruiser of the same program (Design 153) was armed with two twin 9.2in and four twin 7.5in on 11,200 tons (440ft × 69ft × 24ft, 23.5kts on 22,000 IHP). She would have had a 6in belt. This program included a 2925-ton protected scout (25.5kts). Another first-class armoured cruiser for Z.Z. was Design 164 (twelve 8in, 11,900 tons, 22kts, 6in belt over the machinery, thinner elsewhere). Design 172 was an armoured cruiser offered to Brazil in 1904 (cost was revised in April 1906) armed with twelve 7.5in QF and ten 14pdr plus four 18in tubes on 9500 tons (420ft × 63½ft × 23½ft, 23kts) with an 8in belt – as much a cruiser-battleship as the others. As an indication of that, the revised Design 172A was armed with eight 10in guns (two twin, four single) and ten 14pdr plus the torpedo tubes on 9950 tons (425ft × 65ft × 23¾ft); she would have made 23kts. Only Design 172A (eight 10in guns) was submitted to Brazil. The Brazilians chose not to proceed with the armoured cruiser – for the moment. An Elswick annual report of about 1907 stated that the yard had secured a contract for a 9300-ton armoured cruiser for Brazil, but clearly no such ship was built. Design 243, a cruiser for Turkey, fit the cruiser-battleship category although she was not so classified: she was armed with two 12in/45 (single mountings) and ten 4in/50 plus two 18in submerged tubes on 6000 tons (350ft × 60ft × 20½ft, 20kts) and had a 7in belt. A cost estimate was dated 1 August 1906.

Vickers continued to offer heavy-gun cruisers: Design 433 was a scout for Turkey armed with four 10in/50 and eight 6in QF with a 6in belt over machinery and magazines on 9650 tons (515ft × 62ft × 20ft, 26kts, presumably using turbines, no SHP given). Design 448 was 'Cruiser X', which was probably the first stage in the *Kongo* design. Design 462 was a heavy-gun cruiser for Turkey: eight 9.2in and fourteen 4in QF on 11,950 tons (474ft × 68½ft × 25ft, 24kts) with a 7in belt. Design 470 was a Turkish battlecruiser: six 12in/50 and fourteen 4in on 12,550 tons (470ft × 70ft × 25¼ft, 23kts). In addition to these hybrids, Vickers offered a long series of designs it called armoured cruisers, the difference presumably being a matter of marketing. Its first was Design 7, armed with two 8in in one twin mounting plus fourteen 6in (9500 tons, 420ft × 66ft × 23½ft, 22kts on 21,000 IHP, 7in belt). It described a smaller ship (Design 9: 6000 ton, 400ft × 50ft × 21ft, 23kts on 17,000 IHP) as a belted cruiser (two single 8in, ten 6in QF, four 4.7in QF, eight 14pdr). The belted cruiser had a partial belt, 296ft long, rather than a complete belt, but Vickers did not specify how much of either belt was of maximum thickness. The company also offered protected cruisers of similar size and main armament. Its Design 12 (belted cruiser) was armed with an unusually powerful battery of six 8in (twins at ends, singles in main deck casemates on the broadside) and fourteen 6in QF plus twelve 14pdr QF (anti-torpedo guns) on 9700 tons (420ft × 66ft × 24½ft, 21kts on 16,500 IHP). Design 19A was, in effect, an armoured cruiser version, the difference being a complete belt (10,650 tons, 410ft × 68½ft × 25½ft, 20kts on 14,000 IHP), with two more 6in QF and a complete belt of maximum 7in thickness (Design 19, with 8in maximum thickness and speed correspondingly reduced to 19kts, was described as a cruiser battleship). As an indication of dates (most designs were undated), a cost quote to Argentina for the later Design 35A (8600-ton protected cruiser, 350ft × 65ft × 24ft, two twin 9.2in, twelve 7.5in, fourteen 14pdr QF, 20kts on 13,500 IHP) was dated 19 December 1900. Prices were given for the ship with either Belleville or cylindrical boilers. Design 78 (cost estimate dated 28 November 1902) showed how armour could be traded off for more armament. Maximum belt thickness was reduced to 4in (and that thickness extended over only 186ft, the rest of the belt being 3in forward, the main belt ending in an after bulkhead). Armament was two twin 9.2in and eight 8in or 7.5in QF plus eight 14pdr on 10,400 tons (440ft × 68¾ft × 23¾ft, 23kts on 22,000 IHP). This was not too far from a *Minotaur*, on a much lighter displacement – which of course meant lower export cost. A parallel Design 79 sacrificed two 9.2in to add 2 inches of belt armour (Design 79A had a single-calibre battery: twelve 7.5in or 8in, all in twin mountings, plus twenty 14pdr; the cost estimate was dated 28 November 1901). Another alternative single-calibre armoured cruiser (Design 85) was armed with sixteen single 7.5in, as in one of the alternatives advanced for the *Minotaur* class. In this case six were in upper-deck shields (not turrets) and ten were in a main deck casemate. This ship would have displaced 10,000 tons (410ft × 68½ft × 23½ft, 20kts, IHP not given, 7in belt). Mixed calibres were still more popular. Thus No 98 (cost estimate 28 November 1902, revised 5 April 1906) was armed with eight 7.5in QF (two twins and four singles), ten 6in QF, and twelve 14pdr QF on 9750 tons (412ft × 67½ft × 24¼ft, 22.5kts on 19,000 IHP).

Rurik 1909

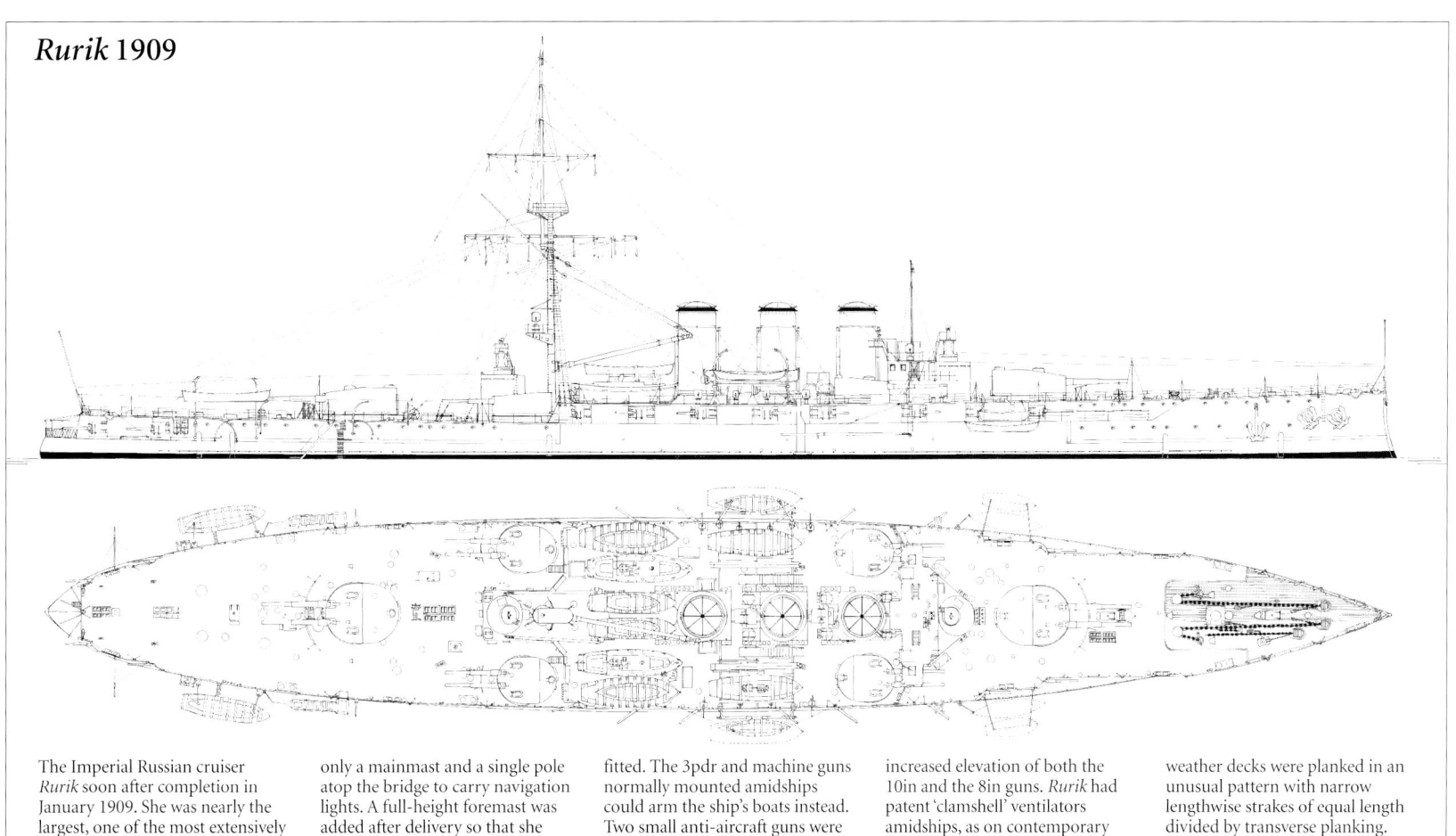

The Imperial Russian cruiser *Rurik* soon after completion in January 1909. She was nearly the largest, one of the most extensively armoured, and nearly the most heavily armed of armoured cruisers, though she did not match the battleship guns the Japanese adopted at this time. She was designed with two masts of equal height, but was completed with only a mainmast and a single pole atop the bridge to carry navigation lights. A full-height foremast was added after delivery so that she could fly signals on it (otherwise they could fly only from the distant mainmast). The new foremast was given tripod legs in 1917. Both fore and aft conning towers were topped by director towers. No rangefinders were fitted. The 3pdr and machine guns normally mounted amidships could arm the ship's boats instead. Two small anti-aircraft guns were added during the First World War. Although the ship is generally credited with two underwater torpedo tubes, they do not appear on the Vickers plans. An unusual feature was the small hinged plates on the turrets which permitted increased elevation of both the 10in and the 8in guns. *Rurik* had patent 'clamshell' ventilators amidships, as on contemporary Royal Navy armoured cruisers. The tops could be elevated or closed, and the ventilators rotated as needed. As delivered, the ship apparently had steel weather decks without wooden planking, except at the bow. At some point the weather decks were planked in an unusual pattern with narrow lengthwise strakes of equal length divided by transverse planking. The ship's boats were not of the usual Royal Navy pattern. They are shown in harbour position in the elevation and stowed for sea in the plan view (harbour positions are shown as dashed lines).
(A D Baker III)

Designs intended for specific foreign customers give some idea of what the navies involved were seeking.

Argentina. In March 1912 Vickers offered Design 586 to Argentina, a conventional fast (27-knot) cruiser: 6800 tons (475ft × 47½ft × 18ft) armed with five 6in and four 4in guns, with a 3in belt. This was broadly what the Royal Navy built during the First World War, but with less efficient (hence much heavier) machinery. An alternative Design 580 was larger (9000 tons, 560ft × 56ft × 28ft) with the same speed (55,000 SHP) and a heavier armament (eight 6in, ten 4in, four torpedo tubes). Design 588 was the same ship with ten 6in and six 4in. Argentina bought no new cruisers.

Brazil. This country bought mainly from Armstrong, but the Vickers design file includes a light armoured cruiser for Brazil (Design 673), probably offered in 1913: 4700 tons, 430ft × 46½ft × 15½ft, 28kts (37,000 SHP), armed with ten 6in/50, four 3pdr, and two submerged 21in tubes. Presumably these ships would have been part of the program including the abortive third Brazilian dreadnought *Riachuelo*. Much the same design was later offered to Greece as Design 681. One alternative was a *Dartmouth* type cruiser (Design 682). Another was a much smaller ship (Design 686: 3500 tons, 410ft × 39½ft × 13½ft, 28kts on 30,000 SHP, two 6in and six 4in). Greece actually bought an Armstrong design roughly comparable with a *Dartmouth*, which was taken over by the Royal Navy during the First World War as the *Chester* class.

Chile. Design 136 was a protected scout for Chile: 3500 tons (394ft × 42½ft × 14¼ft, 25kts) armed with two 7.5in QF guns and eight 14pdr QF plus two 18in deck torpedo tubes. Design 189 was a 6000-ton (350ft × 67ft × 20½ft) cruiser for Chile armed with six 7.5in/50, six 4.7in QF, eight 14pdr QF, and two submerged torpedo tubes, capable of 22kts under forced draught (14 express boilers). Protection included a 6in belt. About January 1906 Vickers offered Chile a 10,500-ton (430ft × 69ft × 24ft) armoured cruiser armed with four 10in (twin mounts), eight 7.5in (twins), and fourteen 14pdr plus two submerged torpedo tubes; it would make 22.5kts on trial. That the list of data noted reciprocating engines suggests that by this time turbines were considered a normal alternative. The modified Elswick Design 463A mentioned above was an 8200-tonner (400ft × 61ft × 22ft, 23kts on 21,500 IHP) armed with twelve 7.5in in twins, with a 6in belt. Design 410 (in Vickers' series) was a scout for Chile, probably offered in 1909: four 7.5in, eight

4in, and 2 submerged tubes on 5850 tons (444ft × 48ft × 18ft, speed not given). Chile bought no new cruisers.

China. Design 104 was for China, presumably offered to be part of the naval revival program after the Sino-Japanese War (no ships were ordered): two 7.5in, six 6in QF, and sixteen 14pdr (plus the usual pair of 18in torpedo tubes) on 4800 tons (408ft × 47½ft × 17ft). No speed was given; the deck covered only the machinery (1½in flat with 1¾in to 4½in slopes). Design 182 was an armoured cruiser for China (undated, but probably 1904, with cost revised in 1906) armed with four 10in in twin mounts plus eight 7.5in QF and twelve 14pdr QF plus four 18in submerged torpedo tubes, and protected by a 6in belt, displacing 9500 tons (412ft × 67½ft × 24ft, 22kts). Design 326 was a later armoured cruiser for China (probably 1907): 8000 tons (400ft × 63ft × 21ft 4in, 21kts on 14,000 IHP) armed with four 10in (twins) plus eighteen 6in (tween deck mounts), four 14pdr, and eight 6pdr. A companion protected cruiser (327C) was dated August 1907; she would have been armed with three 8in (one twin, one single) and fourteen 4.7in QF. She would have displaced only 4000 tons (394ft × 49ft × 15¼ft, 23kts on 14,500 IHP). Design 334, with much the same characteristics, was an alternative. An alternative 328 with the same displacement and machinery mounted two 8in, fourteen 4in (10 on upper deck mountings, 4 tween deck), and two submerged tubes. Yet another alternative was an armoured cruiser (329) armed with ten 9.2 in guns (two twins, six singles) plus twelve 4in QF (tween deck) and two submerged tubes; she would have displaced 8000 tons and had the same dimensions as Design 326. These designs were alternatives offered together. Shortly afterwards Vickers offered a much smaller protected cruiser (Design 360, undated: 4200 tons, 400ft × 47ft × 17¼ft, 24kts on 17,000 IHP, two 8in plus ten 4.7in and two 18in deck tubes). Another armoured cruiser was offered in August 1909: Design 416 (7500 tons, 395ft × 58ft × 36½ft, 22kts, four 8in, fourteen 6in, ten 12pdr). An alternative design (417) offered two 9.2 in and twelve 4.7in on 6000 tons (350ft × 56ft × 21ft, 20kts). There was also an alternative (418) with the same armament as 416, and 419 with the armament offered earlier in Design 360. The Chinese were also interested in a small cruiser for training. Design 446 was a 2750-tonner (320ft × 40ft × 13½ft, 23kts) armed with two 6in/50 and six 4.7in QF guns. An alternative Design 450 (price quoted 12 February 1910) was a 2400-tonner (330ft × 39ft × 13ft, 21kts, eight 4in QF and two submerged tubes). Negotiations with China ended with the Revolution in October 1910. By that time three training cruisers had been ordered, of which Vickers built *Ying Swei* and Armstrong built *Chao Ho* (the Vickers ship was presumably to Design 446). The third ship, *Fei Hung*, was awarded to the New York Shipbuilding Co, and was sold to Greece as *Helle*.

Ecuador. Vickers offered Ecuador a 3650-ton cruiser, Design 490 (400ft × 43ft × 14¼ft, 24½kts) armed with two 6in, eight 4in, eight 3pdr, and two submerged 18in torpedo tubes. This design was probably offered late in 1910 or early in 1911. Ecuador bought nothing.

Peru. Design 126 was a protected cruiser for Peru; it eventually became the *Almirante Grau* class. The initial Vickers design was a 1900-tonner (290ft × 37ft × 11½ft) armed with two 6in QF and four 14pdr (unusually, it had no torpedo tubes) rated at 19kts. Design 130 was a revised cruiser design for Peru, with three 4.7in guns. Vickers later offered Peru the more powerful Design 167 (two 7.5in QF, six 4.7in QF, ten 6pdr QF, two 18in tubes on 3250 tons, 330ft × 43½ft × 16ft, 20kts on 7000 IHP), followed by Design 170 (two 6in QF, eight 14pdr, two 18in submerged tubes, 3200 tons, 370ft × 40ft × 14ft, 24kts on 14,000 IHP). Armstrong designated the same design for Peru as its Design 331. Vickers built the ships, but the mention of Armstrong suggests that the two companies collaborated, which was apparently often the case. Vickers also offered this design to Turkey, as Design 242. Peru apparently continued to consider buying more ships, because Vickers prepared Design 371, a protected cruiser (4500 tons, 400ft × 47ft × 16½ft, 24kts on 17,000 IHP, two 7.5in and ten 4in guns, two submerged tubes). This design featured a belt over machinery and magazines 5ft deep. Peru bought second-hand French warships instead of new ones, including the old armoured cruiser *Dupuy de Lôme*.

Portugal. The country had an Armstrong-built cruiser dating from 1898. A new government taking over in 1910 was interested in rebuilding the fleet. Vickers offered Design 465 in April 1910, a fast 5000-tonner (436ft × 47ft × 15¼ft, 25¼kts, two 8in/50, eight 4in QF, and two submerged 21in tubes. Nothing came of this project. Some time in 1912 Vickers began and then stopped a further study for a 25-knot Portuguese cruiser (Design 613), but then developed a design (614) for what amounted to a 20-knot sloop (submitted January 1913): 2300 tons, 330ft × 40ft × 13ft, armed with two 15cm and six 10cm guns. This ship was unusual in that she would have had a mixed reciprocating (2800 IHP) and turbine (2200 IHP) powerplant, to gain high turbine speed without unduly sacrificing endurance. Design 614 was a shorter 2000-ton version. Portugal bought no cruisers, but post-war apparently revived interest in them.

Romania. In December 1912 Vickers offered Romania a 27-knot (23,500 SHP) protected scout (Design 634): 3100 tons, 400ft × 39¼ft × 13½ft, with six 6in/50, six 4in/50, and two 21in deck tubes. An alternative Design 635 was slower (24kts) and shorter (3200 tons, 370ft × 41½ft × 14½ft), but much more heavily armed, with two 7.5in and six 4in guns. The proposals were inspired by the Romanian 1912 program, which included 6 light cruisers and 12 large destroyers (it replaced an 1899 program calling for 6 light battleships). Romania bought no cruisers, but it did buy large destroyers (from Italy) which might be considered cruiser substitutes in the limited waters of the Black Sea.

Russia. In addition to powerful ships like *Rurik*, Vickers designed smaller cruisers for Russia. Design 580 was probably submitted in the spring of 1912. It may have had the first triple turrets to be offered for a cruiser, four of them for 6in/50s, backed by four 65mm guns and eight 3pdrs, plus six 18in submerged torpedo tubes. This would have been a large (11,000 tons, 600ft × 60ft × 18¾ft), fast (30kts on 60,000 SHP) ship. Design 581 was a 27-knot alternative with greater machinery weight, but otherwise similar. The design was probably rejected in favour of the *Svetlana/Admiral Nakhimov* class, with their fifteen single 130mm guns on 6750 or 7600 tons. In June 1912

Vickers offered a smaller cruiser (597) with two rather than four triple 6in turrets, and the same high speed (30kts on 50,000 SHP). She would have displaced 7200 tons (metric), 530ft x 52ft x 16½ft. Yet another alternative (Design 598) was armed with nine 6in/50 (the file does not indicate triple turrets), making 30kts on 50,000 SHP; she would have displaced 7550 tons (540ft x 52½ft x 16½ft.

Turkey. Design 120 was a protected cruiser for Turkey, which presumably lost out to Armstrong's bid for *Abdul Hamid* and Cramps for *Medjidieh*: eight 6in and eight 14pdr plus two 14in (rather than the usual 18in) above-water (rather than submerged) tubes on 3450 tons (310ft x 43½ft x 16½ft), credited with 20kts on 9200 IHP. This design was a revised version of an earlier Design 14A dating back at least to 1898: technology had more or less stabilized. About 1904 Vickers offered Turkey an armoured cruiser (Design 177) armed with two twin 8in QF and ten 6in QF plus fourteen 14pdr and two 18in submerged tubes, on 6000 tons (400ft x 51½ft x 19ft, 22kts on 14,500 IHP), with a 6in belt. About 1910 Vickers offered Turkey Design 454, a fast (25-knot) protected cruiser (3100 tons, 380ft x 40½ft x 14¼ft, armed with two 6in and six 4in and two broadside torpedo tubes). Design 456 was a smaller more lightly armed alternative (2800 tons, 376ft x 39½ft x 13ft, two 4in and six 14pdr plus the two tubes). About the spring of 1912 Vickers offered Turkey Design 523, a fast (27½-knot) minelaying cruiser (6850 tons, 500ft x 50ft 4in x 17½ft armed with six 6in/50, four 3pdr QF, and 100 mines). Brazil was offered a smaller (2900 tons) and much slower (20kts) minelayer (Design 529) armed with eight 4in and 120 mines (an even smaller Design 536 had four 4in guns). In June 1912 Vickers offered a protected scout (Design 603): 3100 tons (400ft x 39¼ft x 13½ft, 27kts on 23,500 SHP) armed with six 6in/50, ten 4in, and two 21in deck tubes. An alternative (Design 604) offered 28kts on 3500 tons. Another (605) offered 25kts on 17,500 SHP, but armament was increased to six 6in and eight 4in; this ship would have displaced 2900 tons (370ft x 40½ft x 14¼ft). Design 660 was the Brazilian scout cruiser *Bahia* (built by Armstrong) for Turkey. Design 665 was a repeat of HMS *Dartmouth* offered to Turkey, and Design 666 was a light armoured cruiser (3500 tons). On the outbreak of war Turkish scouts were about to be laid down in the United Kingdom, but they were never built, and the war ended further British construction for Turkey.

'Cruiser' could mean something more like a sloop, and Vickers produced designs for smaller ahips for lesser navies. Thus Design 62 (cost estimate dated 20 March 1901) was an 18-knot (5000 IHP under forced draught) 1450-tonner (220ft x 33ft x 13ft) armed with six 4.7in QF and six 6pdr plus the usual two submerged torpedo tubes.

Uruguay. Design 109 (cost estimate 20 April 1903) was a similar ship offered to Uruguay, armed with two 6in QF, four 4in QF, four 6pdr, and two 18in submerged torpedo tubes on 1350 tons (230ft x 34¾ft x 12ft); speed was not given. Uruguay was later offered the somewhat larger Design 269 (price estimated quoted on 17 January 1907): 2800 tons (370ft x 39ft x 13½ft, 20kts on trial, two 12pdr QF and ten 3pdr QF). Design 270 was somewhat smaller (2350 tons, 330ft x 40ft x 13½ft). In March 1907 Vickers offered something even smaller, the 1000-ton (240ft x 29¾ft x 9¾ft) Design 301, armed with one 6in QF, five 4in, and two 18in deck tubes, and capable of 18kts. This was a gunboat calling itself a cruiser. The companion design (302) was a 2000-tonner (305ft x 36½ft x 12½ft, 18kts) armed with two 6in, six 4in, and the two deck tubes. About December 1907 Vickers offered Uruguay a torpedo cruiser (Design 342, 1500 tons, 290ft x 35ft x 10½ft, 21kts on 6000 IHP), armed with two 4.7in QF, four 14pdr QF, and two 18in deck tubes; there was also a similar Design 344 – an enlarged version of the British torpedo gunboats of the 1880s and early 1890s. Uruguay eventually bought a ship (*Uruguay*) from Vulkan of Stettin.

Cuba. In October 1910 Vickers offered to Cuba Design 485, a 2000-tonner (285ft x 36½ft x 13ft, 18kts on 4700 IHP) armed with two 4in QF and four 6pdr QF. The alternative (486) was a 1000-tonner armed with four 6pdrs. Cuba bought a 2055-ton ship (*Cuba*) from Cramps in the United States. She was classed as a cruiser.

Mexico. Also in the market for sloop/cruisers, Mexico was offered Design 303 (quoted May 1907), a 2600-tonner (290ft x 43½ft x 13½ft, speed not given) armed with four 6in/50 in twin mounts and eight 4.7in QF in twin mounts, with a 4in belt. The alternative Design 304 was slightly longer (305ft x 39½ft x 14ft, 20kts on 7000 IHP), armed with twelve 4.7in/50 (two twins, eight singles), with a 4in belt. Yet another alternative was Design 308 (10 May 1907), protected like the ship built for Peru (Design 170): 3050 tons (370ft x 40½ft x 14¼ft, 22.5kts on 10,000 IHP, two 6in, ten 4.7in, sixteen 6pdr, two 18in deck tubes). Mexico bought the somewhat smaller cruiser-transport *General Guerrero* from Vickers in 1908. She was armed with six 4in guns.

Spain. The Vickers design file includes Design 447 (2150 tons, 300ft x 36½ft x 14ft, 20kts, two 4in QF and eight 76mm QF) and the similar Design 451, neither of them dated but both clearly produced about 1910, given the dates of designs with similar numbers. No such ships were built. However, the Armstrong-Vickers consortium built conventional cruisers in Spain. The first such design in the Vickers file is No 649 of 10 March 1913, a 3100-tonner (390ft x 36½ft x 12ft, 26kts on 20,000 SHP) armed with ten 4in and two 21in upper deck tubes. It was never built.

Design 113 (Design 64 modified) was a protected cruiser, probably offered to one of the Central American republics (this note has a question mark in the original): six 6in QF and ten 14pdr on 3600 tons (345ft x 45ft x 16¼ft, 20kts). The most unusual ship in the Vickers design file was No 128, a 'proposed swift ship for carrying submarines', in effect an updated version of the torpedo-boat carrier typified by Vulcan. At this time Vickers held a monopoly on Royal Navy submarine design and construction, and it was acting as agent for the US Electric Boat Company, which owned the Holland submarine patents. The proposed ship was a 16,000-tonner (510ft x 77ft x 27ft, 22.5kts on 30,000 IHP) armed with four 9.2 in (one twin forward, two singles aft), eight 7.5in QF in single upper deck mounts, twenty 14pdr QF, and twenty 3pdr QF – plus two 'large submarines' of the British A.1 type. The ship was credited with a 7in belt.

8 EPILOGUE: FISHER'S REVOLUTION

Headlong change is difficult to handle. The steel cruisers had very durable hulls, but they were obsolete long before they wore out. Yet, given the growth of foreign cruiser forces, the Royal Navy needed to maintain its numbers. In 1902, with few steel cruisers yet disposed of, the Royal Navy had 163 cruisers built, building, or authorized. Against that France had 65, Russia 32, and Germany 38. The Royal Navy needed the numbers to fill out the stations envisaged in the focal area strategy, and also to support its main fleets. By the turn of the twentieth century, small affordable cruisers no longer seemed adequate to face potential foreign commerce raiders. What could the Royal Navy do?

There were really only two possibilities. One was to make the most of the large fleet of existing hulls, modernizing to keep them viable. The other was some radical change in the strategy of trade protection.

Modernization could not work. The *Orlando*s were a case in point. When modernization was proposed in October 1902, it was hardly enough that they were perfectly good seaboats. They were 'a mass of wood work', with little steel under their wooden decks. Their 6in guns were close together on the upper deck, protected only by 1¼in shields. One shell bursting among them would put several out of action. A shell bursting on the deck underneath would cause greater damage to guns and crews. Nor were the ships well protected against torpedo attack, as their 6pdrs were mostly on the main deck, where control was nearly impossible. They were much too slow, good for only 16.5 to 16.8kts under natural draught on full-power trials, and 13.5 to 14kts on a sustained basis (3/5th power). This was aside from their notorious overweight, which submerged their belts and left them effectively unprotected.[1] First Naval Lord Admiral Walter Kerr decided to repair the *Orlando*s as they came in for refit, and to retain them for emergency service only.

Admiral Sir John Fisher adopted the second alternative. In October 1904 he was appointed First Sea Lord (a title he much preferred to First Naval Lord), with a specific mandate for radical change to cure the Royal Navy's persistent and worsening financial problem. That was why he spent so much of his time pressing for 'the scheme, the scheme, nothing but the scheme', by which he meant an integrated approach to modernization – and to cost control. Cost control included discarding the mass of cruisers which, like *Orlando*, were worthless as fighting ships. Three of the *Orlando*s were sold in 1905, one in 1906, and three in 1907. With them went the *Medea*s and many older cruisers. Others became depot ships.

Fisher initially accepted the focal area concept of trade pro-

Thames as a submarine depot ship.

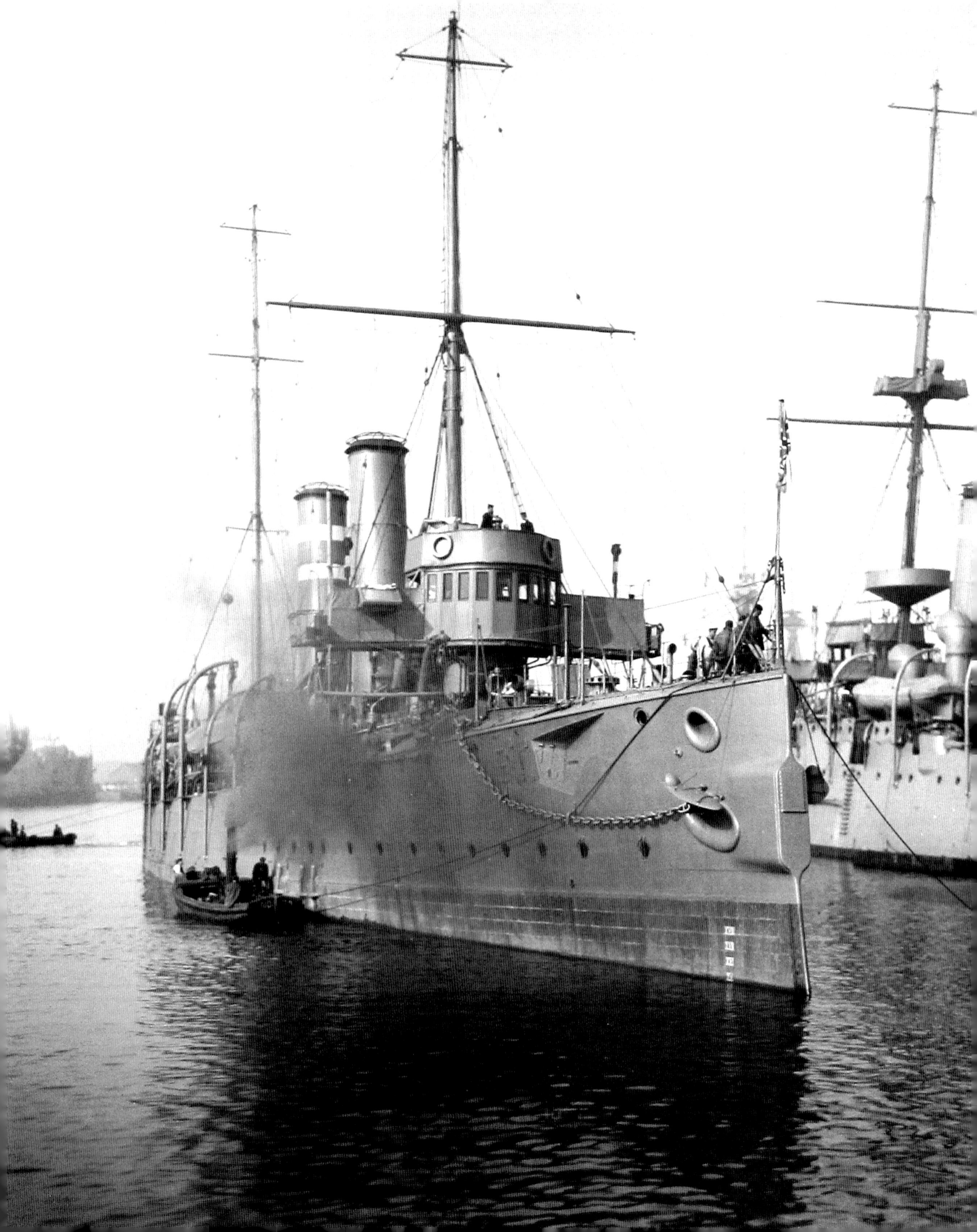

Intrepid as a minelayer, as converted at Chatham, 1909-10. On completion as a cruiser she was held in reserve at Portsmouth in 1892-96, then went to the North America and West Indies station (1896-99). On return she was assigned to Portsmouth in 1899-1902, then went to the Mediterranean (1902-4) and then into reserve at Portsmouth in 1904-9 until being converted to a minelayer. After conversion she was in reserve with a nucleus crew at the Nore in 1911, then joined the minelaying squadron of the Second Fleet in 1912-14. She was stationed at Dover in 1914-15, and was then depot ship for North Russia 1915-16 and in the White Sea (Archangel) in 1917. She then returned home and was converted into a blockship and expended at Zeebrugge, 23 April 1918.

tection, but he presumably knew that he would not long have the numbers it demanded. In the Mediterranean he had developed a new kind of naval warfare. There he faced the French and Russian fleets. He had to deal with them separately before they could unite. He could not maintain separate adequate fleets off both Toulon and the entrance to the Turkish straits. Without radio, cruisers at both places could not alert a British fleet more centrally located. Fisher realized that the telegraph line the French used to communicate with the Russian Black Sea Fleet passed through Malta. He arranged to intercept and decode the messages. He could predict the movements of the two fleets, and he could hope to intercept them at sea – not out of the usual blockading position – before they merged. Scouting was vital: Fisher's Mediterranean Fleet had to spot its quarry as early as possible. Among other things, Fisher's new concept of intelligence-based operations demanded the greatest possible fleet speed, because information was intermittent and of fleeting accuracy. Fisher was proud that he had led the engineers of his fleet to achieve a reliable 18kts, where most of the world's fleets, whatever their rated speeds, were only good for about 14kts.

Fisher took with him to the Admiralty the idea that intelli-

Latona enters Malta during the First World War. In January 1915 she, *Naiad*, *Apollo*, and *Iphigenia* laid the first British offensive minefield of the war, in the Heligoland Bight, but the operation highlighted their vulnerability and led to the conversion of fast cruisers and destroyers. *Latona* recommissioned for the Mediterranean in August 1915, the only ship of the class to continue as a minelayer. In April 1916 she laid fields off the Italian ports of Bari and Termoli to deter Austrian cruisers which had been shelling them. In May 1917 she was converted to accommodate SNO Salonika, and beginning in March 1918 was base ship at Corfu in connection with the Otranto (mine) Barrage. Mines that *Latona* laid in the autumn of 1917 sank the German cruiser *Breslau* and disabled the battlecruiser *Goeben* during their surprise sortie from the Turkish Straits in January 1918.

gence, properly handled, could become the basis for naval operations. That included dealing with raiders. To the extent the Admiralty kept track of merchant ship sailings and arrivals (for example through local British consuls), it could detect patterns of raider operation in merchant ship sinkings (non-arrivals). Merchant ships equipped with radio, which was just coming into service, could report they were under attack. Enemy raiders could be tracked, albeit only approximately. Instead of placing large cruisers everywhere a raider might go, fast cruisers in the right places could be directed towards the expected positions of the raiders. Fisher wrote about large fast cruisers directed centrally by the Admiralty, which would collect all the intelligence, hounding the enemy's cruisers to their deaths.

Of course there were other reasons to seek higher speed in large cruisers, and the idea that such ships could work with a battle fleet had not died at all. The big change that Fisher instituted was to abandon building anything *but* the largest possible cruisers, which became the battlecruisers. At the outset, in 1905-6, Fisher seems to have envisaged a merger of the battleship and the big armoured cruiser. He ordered three such ships – and only one new-type battleship, HMS *Dreadnought*. In 1905 the big armoured cruisers still seemed to have battleship protection. The Royal Navy was leading the world in what was then considered long-range fire control, and as ranges opened 6in Krupp Cemented armour still seemed adequate. The situation was changing, however. Improving capped shells raised the minimum standard of true battleship armour. Fisher was compelled to accept a program with many more battleships than big armoured cruisers.

Intelligence-based operation made possible the thin blockade the Royal Navy operated during the First World War, initially with large cruisers and then (using the 10th Cruiser Squadron) with converted liners. Intelligence as to which ships were carrying which cargo where translated into directing the cruisers to meet specific merchant ships far out to sea, mainly north of Scotland (where the liners' seakeeping and speed really mattered).

Fisher was responsible for great efforts to extend gun range through improved fire control. In 1904 the Channel and Mediterranean Fleets both experimented with improved techniques intended to increase effective range to 4000yds. Within a few years the fleet was doing much better; by about 1910 the expected battle range was 8000yds. About that time the armoured cruisers were given prominent fire control tops forward and aft, the forward top being higher than the after (which was generally well below the cross-trees). The *Black Prince*s and their successors were unusual in that their after fire control tops were as high as their forward ones. *Powerful* and *Terrible* and the *Diadem*s had similar tops. In at least some cases ships had range repeating drums on these tops (a photo shows one on *Bacchante*). They were removed about 1914.

The big cruisers envisaged as part of the battle fleet stayed in the fleet. They had the same armour as first-generation battlecruisers, and they were still faster than most battleships. They were still useful scouts. In August 1914 the Grand Fleet included one battlecruiser squadron and three cruiser squadrons, all of them consisting of 23-knot armoured cruisers. Two consisted of big cruisers with heavy belts, the other (3rd Cruiser Squadron) of 'Counties'. Each squadron consisted of four cruisers. The rest of the cruisers were dispersed around the world, including armoured cruiser squadrons in the Mediterranean and in China. In January 1916 the Grand Fleet included four squadrons of such ships (four in 1st CS, three each in 2nd, 3rd, and 7th. Again, that made sense, because these ships were as well protected as the early battlecruisers (though they had nothing like as much firepower). *Black Prince* and *Defence* were blown up at Jutland, but severe damage to *Warrior* left her flooding, not exploding (her captain thought that in calmer seas he could have made it home). After Jutland, although some big armoured cruisers were nominally part of the Grand Fleet, they were used only on detached duties.

The great wartime surprise was underwater warfare. All the tactical experience gained in exercises involved targets that could be seen. Any ship which could not be seen, apart from a small torpedo boat, could not see or attack. The pre-war Royal Navy found that poor visibility made it difficult or impossible to block the North Sea as completely as it might like, but radio intelligence soon reduced that problem. Submarines and mines were an entirely different proposition. That was demonstrated when *U 9* sank three armoured cruisers in a few minutes in the Channel: *Aboukir*, *Hogue*, and *Cressy*. They were patrolling to protect the 'steam bridge' which now brought British troops to France rather than the other way around. Among other things, their sinking demonstrated that, however well White's coal belt might protect against shellfire, it was irrelevant against torpedoes – which had been a recognized threat (albeit not from submarines) for many years.

That *Drake* did not sink immediately after having been torpedoed (2 October 1917) suggests that the problem was not simply survivability but the absence of survivable auxiliary power: if the boilers were put out of action, the ship could not maintain pumps (*Drake* hoisted a 'not under control' signal after being torpedoed). *King Alfred* managed to beach after being torpedoed or mined in Lough Swilly on 11 April 1918.

War experience showed that White's two-storey casemates had been a mistake; officers complaining that the lower guns

Amphitrite as a minelayer. Her gun armament was reduced to four 6in (all on the upper deck) and one 3in anti-aircraft gun. Upon completion as a cruiser she was retained for special service in 1901-2, then assigned to the China Fleet in 1902-5. On her return she was reduced to reserve at Chatham with a nucleus crew (1905-7) and then moved to Devonport (1908-9, carrying troops in 1908). She was then tender to HMS *Vivid* as stokers' training ship (1910-14), although in 1912-14 she was nominally attached to the 9th Cruiser Squadron of the Third (reserve) Fleet. On the outbreak of war the squadron was mobilized for service in mid-Atlantic (1914-15). She was then reduced to harbour service at Portsmouth in 1915-16. She was converted into a minelayer at Devonport in 1916-17. She was assigned to the Nore Command in 1917-19, replacing HMS *Ariadne* on the Dover Barrage; she was paid off in June 1919. Of this class, in 1918 *Europa* was reduced to ten 6in guns, her lower-deck casemate guns having been removed altogether. She also had ten upper deck 12pdr and two main deck 2pdr, and two 3pdr anti-aircraft guns.

Fisher tried to solve his financial problem by disposing of the ships that 'could neither fight nor run away'. HMS *Lapwing* was a *Redbreast* class composite gunboat, in effect a small slow cruiser. Her armament of six 4in QF and four machine guns was not too far from that of a cruiser, but she could make only 13kts, which by the time she was completed (1890) was no longer adequate for a cruiser. She was completely unprotected, and she displaced only 805 tons (165ft × 31ft × 11ft). Endurance was 2500nm at 10kts. *Lapwing* was discarded in 1910.

were too close to the water had been right. War operation required constant high-speed steaming and frequent alterations of course (for example to zig-zag), which poured water into the lower casemates in anything but the calmest weather.[2]

The eight main deck guns of the *Diadem* class were removed, two being mounted on each side of the upper deck in spray shields, the others being surrendered.

In the *Drake*s, the three forward main deck guns were moved to the upper deck in spray shields, the after pair remaining. Four 12pdrs were landed, leaving eight mounted on the shelter decks and the tops of the casemates.

All three lower deck casemate guns on each side in the *Monmouth*s were moved to the upper deck and fitted with spray shields, their lower-deck ports being plated up. They were mounted between the two double casemates. That displaced six 12pdrs, which were mounted on the forward casemates and the after shelter deck. According to the official history, the ships' seakeeping was much improved. The first ship refitted was HMS *Lancaster* (1915).

The *Devonshire*s had only two lower-deck guns on each side, which were mounted in spray shields on the upper deck abaft the 7.5in turret on each side. That displaced 3pdrs, which were landed. According to the official history, this 'greatly increased the utility of these cruisers in the work which they had to per-

EPILOGUE: FISHER'S REVOLUTION   281

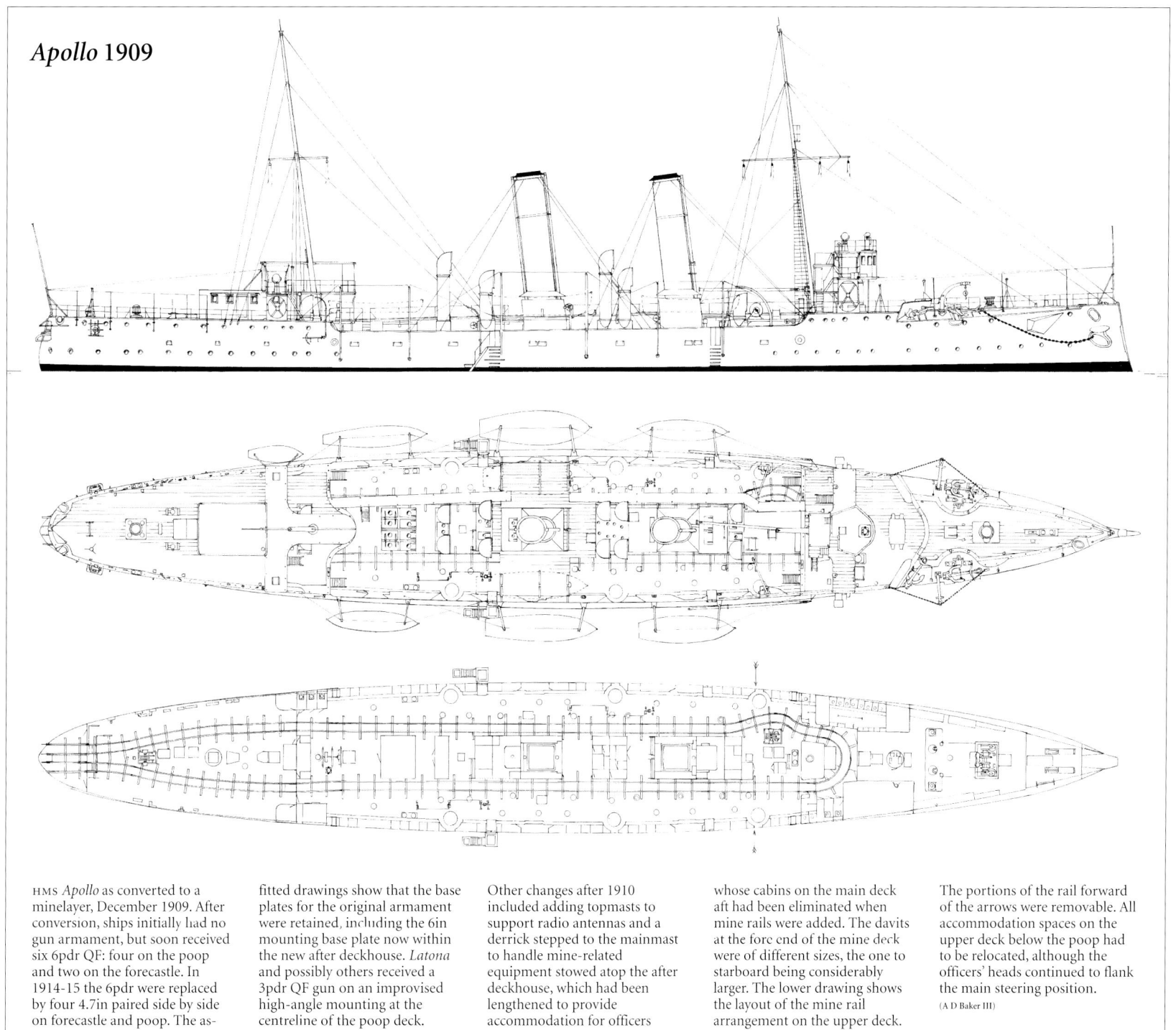

Apollo 1909

HMS *Apollo* as converted to a minelayer, December 1909. After conversion, ships initially had no gun armament, but soon received six 6pdr QF: four on the poop and two on the forecastle. In 1914-15 the 6pdr were replaced by four 4.7in paired side by side on forecastle and poop. The as-fitted drawings show that the base plates for the original armament were retained, including the 6in mounting base plate now within the new after deckhouse. *Latona* and possibly others received a 3pdr QF gun on an improvised high-angle mounting at the centreline of the poop deck. Other changes after 1910 included adding topmasts to support radio antennas and a derrick stepped to the mainmast to handle mine-related equipment stowed atop the after deckhouse, which had been lengthened to provide accommodation for officers whose cabins on the main deck aft had been eliminated when mine rails were added. The davits at the fore end of the mine deck were of different sizes, the one to starboard being considerably larger. The lower drawing shows the layout of the mine rail arrangement on the upper deck. The portions of the rail forward of the arrows were removable. All accommodation spaces on the upper deck below the poop had to be relocated, although the officers' heads continued to flank the main steering position. (A D Baker III)

form during the war', presumably meaning open-ocean patrol.

According to the post-war official history, it had always been recognized that the 6in guns of the *Black Prince* class armoured cruisers were 'quite useless in anything but the calmest weather'. These were the first ships to have their 6in guns moved. Three were mounted on each side of the upper deck between the 9.2in turrets, and one on each side of the forecastle; the other two were landed. Even in their new positions, the exposed 6in guns were considered of little value due to the ships' low freeboard.

Other wartime changes included rearrangement of searchlights (some were moved to the foremast under the fire control top) and reductions of topmasts – which had been raised to improve radio performance, but made ships visible at excessive ranges. After Jutland the surviving ships of the final armoured cruiser generation were given tripod foremasts supporting directors.

Minelaying

Although the mass of cruisers built during the previous decade were not discarded, they were clearly being reduced to secondary roles. Several *Apollo* class cruisers were modified for a new role, as cruiser minelayers. The success of offensive minelaying, by both sides, had been a major surprise of the Russo-Japanese War of 1904-5. It led the Royal Navy to resume work on offensive (contact) mines, which it was then in process of abandoning. These weapons would have to be delivered by fast ships capable of penetrating waters under enemy observation. Plans called for the capacity to lay 4000 mines, 500 per ship.

The *Apollo* class cruiser *Iphigenia* was the first converted. Her armament was landed and two mine rails laid along her decks. Seven others followed.[3] The ships were disarmed on the ground that they would not revert to their original cruiser role during their remaining service life, and that they would be protected by cruisers while laying mines. By May 1908 questions were being asked about their need for guns in the minelaying role. DNC offered to provide two 4.7in guns on the forecastle. Controller was unimpressed. He doubted that a pair of guns forward would do much good, particularly if the ships were fleeing enemy forces. There was no point in remounting the ships' former 6in battery, but he did think it might be wise to mount some light QF guns to defend against an enemy's inshore squadron of light torpedo boats, perhaps using 6pdrs removed from destroyers (which were then being rearmed with heavier guns).[4] He observed that there was no point in testing mines to see whether they would explode if hit by gunfire: if a minelayer were pursued before she could lay her mines, she should simply drop them in the path of the enemy ships. The last two ships were given the 6pdrs, but this armament was soon condemned as insufficient, Vice Admiral Home Fleet recommending four 4.7in or 4in. In 1911 the favoured armament was two 4in on the forecastle and two more on the poop, but on 7 March 1911 First Sea Lord decided against taking any action.

The issue did not die. DNO proposed one 4.7in on the forecastle (on the centreline, where the single 6in gun had been mounted) and two more on the poop. Controller liked the idea; later the ships were assigned four 4.7in each.

Some of the ships Fisher would have discarded proved extremely useful once war broke out in 1914. The RAN cruiser *Pioneer* is shown in East Africa about 1915, helping close the bases the Germans would have used to support surface raiders. *Pioneer* and *Encounter* shelled Dar-es-Salaam in Zanzibar in June 1915.

Natal shows early war modifications in 1915, including a false bow wave to mislead U-boat commanders.

King Alfred shows typical war modifications, including relocated guns (note the guns in shields on her upper deck), dazzle camouflage, and life rafts. In April 1918 she still had her 9.2in guns, plus ten upper deck and four main deck 6in. She had no anti-aircraft weapons. Soon after completion she went into reserve at Chatham with a nucleus crew. She then became flagship of the China Fleet (1906-10), returning to the Second Fleet (5th Cruiser Squadron 1912, 6th Cruiser Squadron 1913-14). On the outbreak of war 6th Cruiser Squadron joined the Grand Fleet. *King Alfred* was detached to 9th Cruiser Squadron (mid-Atlantic) 1915-17 and then to the North America and West Indies station for Atlantic convoys (1917-19).

Cochrane in New York harbour, 1917-18. Upon completion she joined 5th Cruiser Squadron Home Fleet (1907-9), after which she served in 2nd Cruiser Squadron Home Fleet (1909-14; Home Fleet became the Grand Fleet in 1914). She served with the Grand Fleet through the First World War, except for a large refit in September 1917-February 1918, when, presumably, she was fitted with a director and with tripod legs to her foremast. She fought at Jutland. *Cochrane* was wrecked in the Mersey estuary, 14 November 1918. *Shannon* shows standard wartime modification to the largest armoured cruisers. Her foremast was reinforced by tripod legs to carry a director for her 9.2in guns (the cylinder atop the new platform just below her spotting top). Her fore topmast was taken down to make it difficult to judge her course from a distance (her dazzle camouflage helped). All the armoured cruisers of this last generation which survived Jutland were given tripod legs to support a main battery director, but (see below) the director platform remained empty for some time. Director design was authorized in February 1915, and orders placed in April/August 1916, but production and installation were deferred in view of the higher priority of light cruiser installation. Thus the official British naval fire control history gives dates of completion of director installation as: *Minotaur* (August 1918), *Shannon* (October 1918), *Achilles* (October 1918), *Cochrane* (November 1918), *Duke of Edinburgh* (October 1918). Confusingly, according to the post-war Admiralty publication describing progress in gunnery 1914-18, two of the five big armoured cruisers received director control for their main batteries in 1916, one in 1917, and two in 1918 (the ships are not specified). By the end of the First World War, three armoured cruisers had secondary battery directors: two were fitted in 1916, and one in 1917. Presumably these were the programmed dates, not the actual ones, and presumably, too, they reflect dates of refits during which tripod legs were fitted to the foremast.

(National Maritime Museum L5406)

EPILOGUE: FISHER'S REVOLUTION 285

Minotaur shows wartime modifications as she is seen arriving in Portsmouth on 15 December 1918. She had just formed part of the escort for the High Seas Fleet as it surrendered on 21 November. Her bridgework has been extended and her searchlights regrouped. By April 1918 she, *Achilles*, *Cochrane*, and *Duke of Edinburgh* each had a single 3in anti-aircraft gun. She also had two 3pdrs on her shelter decks. *Shannon* had no 3in gun, but she did have two 6pdr AA guns on her shelter decks. *Monmouth* class cruisers (but not the *Devonshire*s) generally had two 3pdr AA guns on their upper decks (*Cornwall* had three, but *Berwick* had hers removed). The surviving *Drake*s had no such guns, but *Bacchante* and *Euryalus* each had two 3pdrs on their upper decks.
(National Maritime Museum N01221)

Shannon at sea during the winter of 1917-18. Note the anti-rangefinding baffles on her funnels and her tripod foremast. *Shannon* may have been the only large cruiser with these baffles. A 1917 photograph showed her with the baffles and the tripod but as yet without the director on the foremast. At that time she showed a single 3in anti-aircraft gun at the after end of her after superstructure.

In addition, *Amphitrite* and *Ariadne* were converted into minelayers in 1917. *Euryalus* began minelayer conversion at Hong Kong in November 1917 but was not completed.

Shore Bombardment
By April 1915 all the *Edgar* class cruisers had surrendered their 9.2in guns to *M 15* class monitors. Four were modified for bombardment duty: *Edgar*, *Endymion*, *Grafton*, and *Theseus*. Work began in December 1914, the first two being completed the next March (however, the April 1915 armament list shows only *Theseus* rearmed). They were given two single 6in at the ends where the 9.2in guns had been mounted, and they retained their earlier broadside battery of ten 6in (in April 1918 *Edgar* and *Grafton* each had only one centreline 6in). They were given monitor-style bulges (the only cruisers thus modified), timber stiffening, and prominent bow gallows for paravanes. They lost 4kts but seakeeping and handling were reportedly not changed. Thus modified, *Grafton* survived a torpedo on 11 June 1917, and *Edgar* survived an April 1918 hit. All four served in the Dardanelles and then in the Mediterranean.

Vindictive (the only one of her class to serve as a cruiser during the First World War) was an entirely different kind of assault ship, modified specially for the Zeebrugge raid (23 April 1918) and then scuttled at Ostend (10 May 1918). She was given a false upper deck, mortars, and other close-range weapons. She did not apparently retain her original 6in guns. Photos of her badly damaged after the Zeebrugge attack show a large fighting top added to her foremast, and her bridge was protected by splinter mattresses. Another tower was erected aft, the mainmast having been removed.

Argyll as modified in wartime. This undated photo was retouched (note the heavy work on the rigging of the foremast). It was probably taken in wartime; note the short topmasts. On completion *Argyll* joined the 1st Cruiser Squadron (Atlantic Fleet 1906-7, Channel Fleet 1907-9), and then 5th Cruiser Squadron (Atlantic Fleet: 1909-12). She was detached to escort King George V to India in 1911-12. She then joined 3rd Cruiser Squadron of Second Fleet in 1913; this squadron joined the Grand Fleet in 1914-15. She fought at Heligoland. She was wrecked on Bell Rock, on the east coast of Scotland, 28 October 1915, probably not long after this photographs was taken.

Donegal in wartime dazzle camouflage. Note that her forward lower 6in gun has *not* yet been removed. On completion she joined the 1st Cruiser Squadron Channel Fleet (1903-5), and then was commissioned to join the China Fleet. However, she ran aground on passage to China, and after repairs at Chatham she was reduced for a time to reserve with a nucleus crew before joining the new Home Fleet (1907-9). She then served in 4th Cruiser Squadron on the North America and West Indies station (1909-12), and then returned home to the Training Squadron (1912). She was reduced to reserve as part of the Third (reserve) Fleet (5th Cruiser Squadron). She was refitting at the outbreak of war. With 5th Cruiser Squadron she was then assigned to mid-Atlantic operations, based at Sierra Leone. In 1915 she was in 6th Cruiser Squadron of the Grand Fleet, then in 7th Cruiser Squadron Grand Fleet escorting convoys to Archangel. From March 1916 she was in 2nd Cruiser Squadron Grand Fleet. That September she was in 9th Cruiser Squadron in the mid-Atlantic, and in 1917 she joined 4th Cruiser Squadron on the North America and West Indies station; she was paid off into Devonport reserve in May 1918.
(Abrahams of Devonport via RNHB)

Roxburgh with wartime modifications, probably shown post-war; note her tall topmasts. On completion she joined the 1st Cruiser Squadron (Channel Fleet 1905-6, Atlantic Fleet 1906-7, then Channel Fleet 1907-9). She was reduced to Third (reserve) Fleet at Portsmouth (1909-11), then joined 5th Cruiser Squadron (2nd Fleet, 1912) and then 3rd Cruiser Squadron (2nd Fleet 1913-14, Grand Fleet 1914-15). Her bows were seriously damaged by a torpedo from *U-39* on 20 June 1915, repairs continuing to April 1916. That was probably when her lower casemate guns were moved to her upper deck. She rejoined the Grand Fleet after being repaired, but then went to the North America and West Indies station (1916-19). While there she rammed and sank *U-89* off northern Ireland on 12 February 1918. She was wireless training ship in 1919-20.

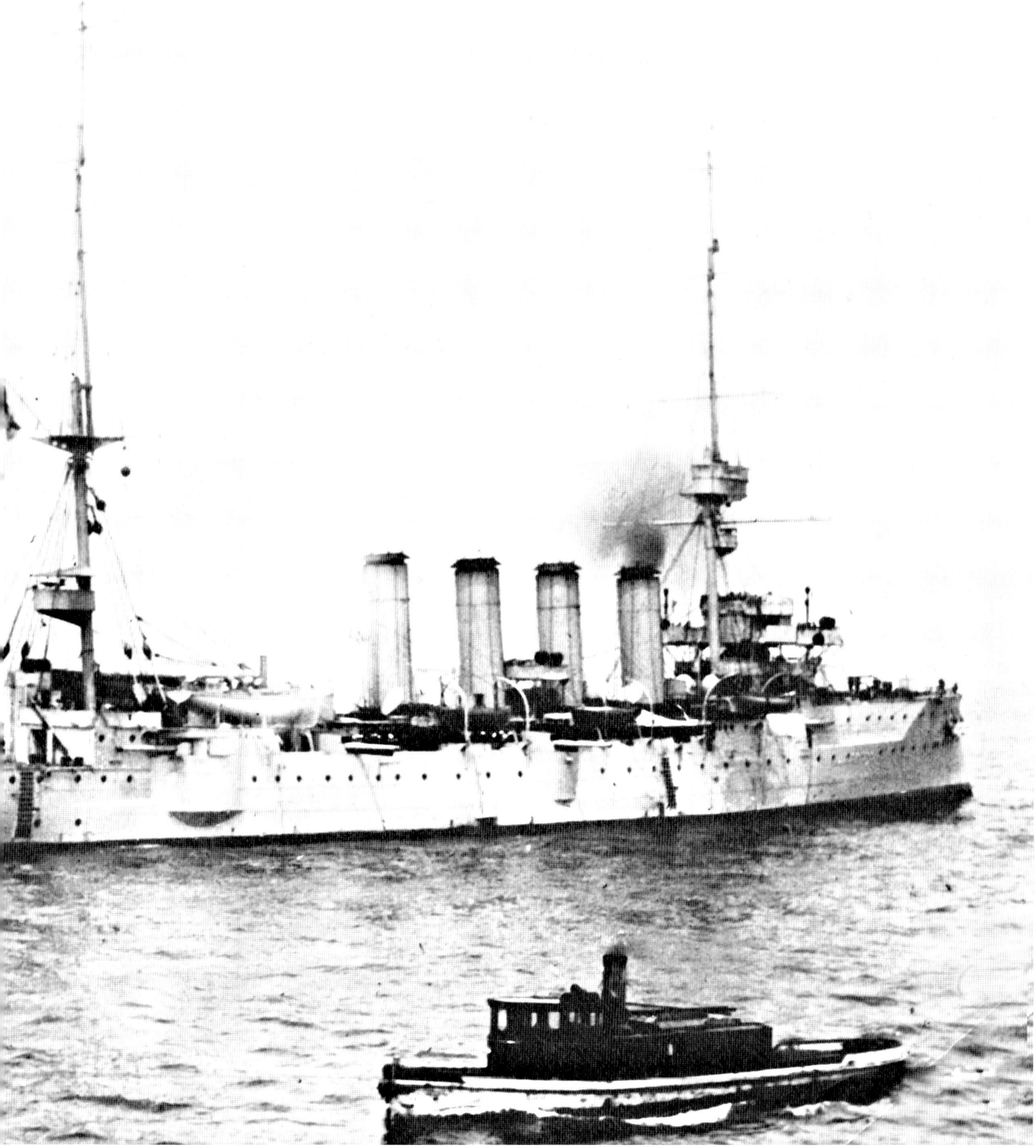

Theseus bulged as a special assault ship. In April 1918 she was armed with twelve 6in guns (2 upper deck, 6 main deck, 4 shelter deck), four 12pdr 12cwt (3in), four 6pdr anti-aircraft guns, and one 2pdr pompom. Other modified ships varied in their minor armament. Thus *Edgar* and *Endymion* had three 6pdr; *Theseus* had four (and four 12pdr). *Grafton* had one 12pdr and two 6pdr anti-aircraft guns, and no 12pdr 12cwt guns at all.

Edgar bulged, from aft.

Vindictive leaves for Zeebrugge. She was refitted specifically to moor alongside the Zeebrugge mole, her assault party climbing up over its parapet and onto the mole to destroy the German guns defending the harbour. The assault group comprised three companies of Royal Marines (580 men) and a Bluejacket Assault Party (200 men). *Vindictive* was to moor with her port side to the mole. To bring her troops up to the level of the parapet, a false deck extending from forecastle to quarterdeck was built on the skid beams on the port side. Three broad ramps led up to it, and eighteen ramps (which are visible here) could be deployed from it onto the mole. The false deck sheltered the troops en route to the objective. The explosive involved was guncotton, in wheeled Post Office wicker baskets which could go along the ramps. Each ramp was wide enough (27 inches) for one man. At high tide, which was considered the best time for the attack, the top of the false deck would be four to seven feet above the level of the the mole. Because the side of the mole sloped inwards, the side of the ship might be as much as thirty feet from the mole. The troops would be supported by fire from the ship. In addition to at least two of the original 6in guns, an 11in howitzer was mounted on the quarterdeck, with 7.5in howitzers on forecastle and false deck (the latter on the centreline, forward of the after bridge). A new foretop protected by mattresses carried three pompoms (2pdr) and six Lewis machine guns. Another ten Lewis guns were mounted on the false deck between the ramps. Batteries of Stokes mortars (four each) were mounted fore and aft of the series of ramps. Mattress-protected flamethrower houses were built fore and aft of the false deck on the port side. The conning tower was protected by sandbags. Masts were cut down. The mainmast was laid across the quarterdeck to act as a fender protecting the port propeller. When the attack was carried out, German fire destroyed all but two of the gangplanks before *Vindictive* could reach her attack position, and the wash and surge from her screws pushed her away from the mole; the ferry *Daffodil* jammed her into place.
(National Maritime Museum N01463)

Endymion bulged, from forward, giving some idea of the width of the bulges.

Bibliography

SHIPS' COVERS
Many have multiple volumes. Note that Covers for the Reed era are missing (numbers in parentheses): screw sloop *Vestal* (25), screw corvettes *Danae*, etc (26), screw frigate *Inconstant* (36), screw frigate *Raleigh* (1873), cruiser *Active* (40). Also missing are the Covers for the belted cruiser *Nelson* (42) and the corvette *Thetis* (48).

Covers consulted:
Shannon (41)
Wood Ships (51) (includes *Juno* and *Thalia*)
Corvettes (71) (includes *Active* and *Volage*)
Opal class (63)
Bacchante and *Highflyer* (67)
Comus class (73)
Iris and *Mercury* (77)
Leander class (83)
Heroine class (84)
Imperieuse and *Warspite* (88)
Calypso and *Calliope* (90)
New *Enchantress* (despatch vessel) (91)
Mersey class (95)
Surprise and *Alacrity* (96)
Scout and *Fearless* (97)
Curlew and *Landrail* (99)
Orlando class (101)
Barham and *Bellona* (112)
Archer class (113)
Barracouta class (114)
Medea class (115)
Pallas class colonial cruisers (116)
Blake and *Blenheim* (117)
Vulcan (118)
Edgar class (119)
Apollo class (122)
Astraea class (123)
Powerful and *Terrible* (135)
Talbot class (138)
Arrogant class (139)
Diadem class (140)
Juno and *Dido* (141)
Pelorus class (143 and 145A)
Ariadne class (149)
Pioneer and *Pandora* (153)
Cressy class (157)
Drake class (158)
Kent class (164)
Challenger and *Encounter* (167)
Suffolk class (173)
New *Drake* (not built) (175)
'Gem' class (179)
Devonshire class (181)
Duke of Edinburgh class (194; *Warrior* is 194A/B)
Minotaur class (199)
Invincible class (215)
Apollo minelayer conversions (218)

PRIMARY SOURCES NOT MENTIONED IN THE NOTES
Carnarvon Committee reports (*Reports of the Royal Commission approved to enquire into Defence of British Possessions and Commerce Abroad*: PRO CAB 7/2, 7/3, and 7/4; copies of Sir Henry T Holland, Bart, MP)
Committee on Boilers (third report, 1878, is PRO ADM 116/178; reports for 1892 and later are ADM 116/869, 870, 871, and 873 [872 repeats parts of other volumes])
Fire Control in HM Ships (Technical History series, TH 23, December 1919)
List of His (or *Her*) *Majesty's Ships, Showing Their Armaments* (confidential Admiralty publication, various years, 1872-1918)
Manual of Gunnery for Her Majesty's Fleet 1885 (PRO ADM 186/869)
Margin of weight to be allowed for contingencies in future designs of HM Ships (S.7257/1887: PRO ADM 1/6873)
Naval Staff Memoranda 1896 to 1912 (PRO ADM 116/866B: actually 1896 plus 1905-12, includes a detailed analysis of the requirements of the focal area strategy)
Navy List (for distribution of ships: 1880-1914)
Progress in Naval Gunnery 1914 to 1918 (July 1919: CB 902; PRO ADM 186/238)
Steam Ships of England (predecessor to CB 1815, gives data on ships, various editions in PRO, Admiralty Library, and Brass Foundry: years consulted were 1878-1918; early editions are lists without much data)
Subvention and Subsidies of Merchant Vessels 1875-1905 (PRO ADM 116/1224: collected papers)
Subvention of Merchant Ships for Employment as Armed Cruisers (PRO ADM 116/271: correspondence 1886-87)
Thurston notebook of Vickers warship designs (National Maritime Museum, copy courtesy Stephen McLaughlin)
Type and Armament of Ships Required for HM Navy (for 1880-1900) (PRO ADM 1/7254)

SECONDARY SOURCES
Admiral G A Ballard, 'The Unarmoured Branches of the British Navy of 1875', series in the *The Mariner's Mirror* (1935-1940)

Nathaniel Barnaby, *Naval Development in the Century* (Philadelphia: Linscott, 1904)

James Phinney Baxter, *The Introduction of the Ironclad Warship* (Cambridge: Harvard University Press, 1933)

John Beeler, *British Naval Policy in the Gladstone-Disraeli Era, 1866-1880* (Stanford University Press, 1997)

————, *Birth of the Battleship: British Capital Ship Design 1870-1881* (London: Chatham Publishing, 2001)

Peter Brook, *Warships for Export: Armstrong Warships 1867-1927* (Gravesend: World Ship Society, 1999)

D K Brown, *Before the Ironclad: Development of Ship Design, Propulsion, and Armament in the Royal Navy, 1815-1860* (London: Conway Maritime Press, 1990)

———, *Warrior to Dreadnought: Warship Development 1860-1905* (London: Chatham Publishing, 1997)

———, *The Grand Fleet: Warship Design and Development 1906-1922* (London: Chatham Publishing, 1999)

R A Burt, *British Cruisers in World War One* (London: Arms and Armour Press, 1987)

John Darwin, *The Empire Project: The Rise and Fall of the British World System 1830-1970* (Cambridge University Press, 2009)

P Dislere, *Les Croiseurs: La Guerre de Course* (Paris: Gauthier-Villars, 1875). Dislere was secretary of the Conseil des Travaux of the French Navy

F J Dittmar and J J College, *British Warships 1914-1919* (London: Ian Allan, 1972)

Mrs Fred Egerton, *Admiral of the Fleet Sir Geoffrey Phipps Hornby GCB: A Biography* (London: Blackwood, 1896)

Denis Griffiths, *Steam At Sea* (London: Conway Maritime Press, 1997)

C I Hamilton, *The Making of the Modern Admiralty: British Naval Policy-Making 1805-1927* (Cambridge University Press, 2011)

C J Hamilton, *Anglo-French Naval Rivalry 1840-1870* (Oxford University Press, 1993)

Engineer Rear Admiral Scott Hill, 'Battle of the Boilers', *Journal of Naval Engineering* (July 1955)

F W Hirst, *The Six Panics and Other Essays* (London, Methuen, 1913)

John Houghton, *The Navies of the World 1835-1840* (Melbourne: Minuteman Press, 2011)

J W King, *The War-Ships and Navies of the World, 1880* (Annapolis: Naval Institute Press, 1982 reprint of 1880 book)

Andrew Lambert, *Warrior: The World's First Ironclad, Then and Now* (London: Conway Maritime Press, 1997)

Nicholas Lambert, *Sir John Fisher's Naval Revolution* (Columbia: University of South Carolina Press, 1999)

David Lyon and Rif Winfield, *The Sail and Steam Navy List: All the Ships of the Royal Navy 1815-1889* (London: Chatham Publishing, 2004)

Ruddock F Mackay, *Fisher of Kilverstone* (Oxford: Clarendon Press, 1973)

R B Matzke, *Deterrence through Strength: British Naval Power and Foreign Policy under Pax Brittanica* (Lincoln: University of Nebraska Press, 2011)

Douglas Morris, *Cruisers of the Royal and Commonwealth Navies* (Liskeard: Maritime Books, 1987)

Oscar Parkes, *British Battleships: Warrior 1860 to Vanguard 1950* (London: Seeley, Service 1957)

Roger Parkinson, *The Late Victorian Navy: The Pre-Dreadnought Era and the Origins of the First World War* (Woodbridge: Boydell & Brewer, 2008)

Barrie Pitt, *Zeebrugge: Eleven VCs Before Breakfast* (London: Cassell, 2003 [reprint of 1958 edition])

N A M Rodger, 'The Design of the *Inconstant*', *The Mariner's Mirror* (February 1975)

———, 'The Dark Ages of the Admiralty', *The Mariner's Mirror* (November 1975, February 1976, and May 1976)

———, 'British Belted Cruisers', *The Mariner's Mirror* (February 1978)

———, 'The First Light Cruisers', *The Mariner's Mirror* (August 1978)

Theodore Ropp (ed Stephen S Roberts), *The Development of a Modern Navy: French Naval Policy 1871-1904* (Annapolis: Naval Institute Press, 1987)

Stephen S Roberts and Jack Bauer, *Register of Ships of the US Navy 1775-1990: Major Combatants* (New York: Greenwood, 1991)

Donald M Schurman, *Imperial Defence 1868–1887* (London: Frank Cass, 2000)

J D Scott, *Vickers: A History* (London: Weidenfeld and Nicholson, 1962)

Bernard Semmell, *Liberalism and Naval Strategy: Ideology, Interest, and Sea Power during the Pax Britannica* (Boston: Allen & Unwin, 1986)

Paul H Silverstone, *Civil War Navies 1855–1883* (Annapolis: Naval Institute Press, 2001)

Jon Tetsuro Sumida, *In Defence of Naval Supremacy: Finance, Technology, and British Naval Policy 1889-1914* (Boston: Unwin Hyman, 1989)

US Navy Office of Naval Intelligence, *Information from Abroad* (1894 edition)

C C Wright, 'British Naval Policy 1857-1878' (thesis, Harvard College, 1970)

Notes

INTRODUCTION

1 The Russians claimed they were protecting Christians in places like Bulgaria, then ruled by Turkey. Ottoman suppression of Christians was widely reported in Europe. In 1876-77 the Disraeli administration was caught between public opinion (and its own sympathy) for the Christians and the strengthening British strategic interest in keeping Turkey intact as a barrier against Russian expansion south.

2 John Darwin, *The Empire Project: The Rise and Fall of the British World System 1830-1970* (Cambridge University Press, 2009) shows just how indirect the connection between the increased importance of the Mediterranean sea route and British presence in Egypt was. Turkey and then Egypt defaulted on bonds in 1876. As the main creditors, Britain and France sought dual control of Egyptian finances. In an unpleasantly familiar way, they demanded austerity which Egyptian nationalists rejected. It would have included ending subsidies the Khedive ruling Egypt paid to keep the support of landowners and the army. Given his own debts, the Ottoman Sultan, in theory the ultimate overlord of Egypt, tried unsuccessfully to impose a new more pliable Khedive. By September 1881 Egypt was run by a senior army officer, Colonel Arabi, who had no interest in placating creditors. Britain and France considered the security of the Canal far more important than Egyptian independence. An Anglo-French fleet appeared at Alexandria in June 1882 to apply pressure. Egyptians massacred the European community. During the run-up to the 1880 election Prime Minister Gladstone firmly rejected colonialism, but the massacre convinced a majority of his Cabinet that Egypt was on the point of anarchy, and that the Canal itself was in danger. By this time the French had changed governments and were no longer interested in joining the British. Gladstone ordered his fleet to shell Alexandria, which only made Arabi more popular. A British army overthrew Arabi and began what was originally intended as a short presence while Egyptian finances were overhauled. The British remained in Egypt until 1952.

3 The Russians occupied Pendjieh on the Afghan frontier on 30 March 1885. Their advance had been considered a war warning. The British mobilized reserves on 26 March and occupied Port Hamilton on the Korean coast as an emergency base on 2 April. The Royal Navy was ordered to shadow Russian ships. Gladstone felt compelled to call for a total of £11 million in emergency funds, of which £6½ million was for naval and military preparations. The situation was all the more difficult because the government was already absorbed with the Egyptian-Sudanese crisis which culminated in the death of General Gordon. A larger intelligence and planning staff was needed; Hall's Foreign Intelligence Committee was turned into the Naval Intelligence Department (NID), which also had staff functions. Hall became its first director; his son was the famous Rear Admiral 'Blinker' Hall of First World War intelligence.

4 The growing Franco-Russian threat probably explains why, about 1900, the British Government sought an alliance with a third power. The Germans were rejected due to excessive demands. Instead Japan was chosen. Alliance with them dramatically reduced pressure in the Far East. Japan no longer posed a threat and it diluted the Russian threat there. The Germans were not perceived as a threat (alongside the French) until about 1902.

5 Professor Andrew Lambert, '"I will not have a war with France:" Deterrence, diplomacy, and mid Victorian politics', in A Baines, ed, *Warrior* (Portsmouth, 2011). This scare engendered the Parliamentary returns in ADM 116/1 and /2 cited below. The presumed threat to Canada was based both on recent border problems and on the US invasion of Canada in 1812.

6 Milne papers, NMM, courtesy of Professor John Beeler. MLN/144/31,2,6,7,8,9, 10, 11, 12, 13: 'Confidential Paper relative to Unarmoured Ships, and Proposal for an Establishment.'

7 Milne papers, NMM, courtesy of Professor John Beeler. MLN/144/3 3,4,5: 'Position of Cruising Ships for Protection of Trade,' December 1874. This paper is very similar to Milne's trade protection argument in a paper in the Trade Protection papers, NHB. The NHB Trade Protection file includes an April 1905 paper describing an Admiralty meeting on trade protection, with First Sea Lord Admiral Fisher in the chair. The other attendees were Captain C L Ottley, DNI (which at that time included a naval staff); Captain R H S Bacon, naval assistant to First Sea Lord; Captain E F Inglefield, assistant director of naval intelligence; Captain G A Ballard, assistant director of naval intelligence (and, it seems, Fisher's war planner); Commodore Wilfred Henderson; and W F Nicholson, Private Secretary to First Sea Lord. That paper opened with a history of earlier attempts to devise a method of protecting trade, beginning with Milne's 1874 paper and then passing to the 1885 paper which it described as an elaboration of Milne's idea.

8 Justifying French seizures of colonies around the Mediterranean, a French admiral wrote that without regular supplies of fuel warships would be little more than immobile floating flags. The quotation was prominently displayed in an exhibit on French nineteenth-century naval colonial warfare at the Museé de la Marine in 2004.

9 FIC No 73, 'The Protection of Commerce by Patrolling the Ocean Highway and by Convoy,' issued May 1885. No author is identified. Copy in Trade Protection file, NHB.

10 NID paper included as the Appendix to the 1905 paper cited above. In recent years the French had 'deliberately built a considerable number of vessels of this [armoured cruiser] class, largely intended for the *guerre de course*.' Only France had openly espoused commerce raiding as a preferred strategy. The French had only enough large cruisers for either battle fleet operations or trade attack.

NOTES TO PAGES 14-25

thought that their new kind of threat to harbours and fortresses had been decisive. In his August 1866 memo on types of ships the Royal Navy needed, Controller Rear Admiral Robert M Robertson pointed to low-freeboard turret ships specifically to destroy enemy fleets in their harbours (as summarized in the 1871 report of the Committee on Designs). Official British fleet armament lists categorize these ships explicitly as 'coast defence and attack' units.

13 Captain W H Hall RN, 'Remarks on a Naval Campaign', FIC No 51, 24 September 1884, in ADM 231/5.

14 In 1886 the Royal Navy listed British and foreign warships for Parliament. The French had no armoured cruisers, but they had twelve smaller (second-class) armour-clads, with a thirteenth (*Duguesclin*) building. Four of these *Cuirassés de Croisière* were to be stricken in 1887. The French had no protected cruisers, but three ships under construction had protective decks (*Sfax*, *Tage*, and *Cecile*). The French classed what the British considered sloops as third-class cruisers. ADM 1/6819, marked FIC.

15 The idea of taking up fast merchant ships from trade was not new. According to ADM 116/1224, a file on subvention of merchant ships, beginning in 1840 (with the Royal Mail Company) mail contracts included clauses (with subsidies) requiring contractors to maintain a sufficient number of ships of not less than 400 NHP, capable of carrying the largest guns in use by the Royal Navy for wartime use. A late 1852 Admiralty report evaluated arming P&O and Royal West India mail packets. Between them the two companies had 53 ships (23 of iron), of which 8 were fit for war purposes, but not as substitutes for conventional warships. Other fleets were later analysed. Subsidies were expensive, and in 1853 the Treasury decided to abandon them. The public mistakenly imagined that the postal steamers would be a useful wartime addition to the fleet. They would probably be used only to carry troops and despatches, their high speed protecting them from capture. At times after that the Admiralty did require that the owners be willing to charter them 'in cases of great public emergency'. When Barnaby revisited the issue in November 1875, there were no longer wooden mail steamers, and the iron-hulled ones lacked the subdivision required in warships. Fast mail steamers had both cylinder heads and parts of boilers above water, where they were vulnerable. In a March 1876 follow-up Barnaby proposed modifications to make fast merchant ships usable. Machinery could be shielded by solid screens of iron, coal, or stores between decks. Sufficient subdivision was essential in the face of the torpedo threat. That some merchant ships were already sufficiently subdivided suggested to Barnaby that the problem was not economics but rather the absence of any requirement. He produced sketches showing how existing ships could be modified. Barnaby proposed an Admiralty List of ships capable of steaming for at least 12 hours at no less than 12kts and sufficiently subdivided to survive on a smooth sea if holed in any one compartment. The first list of liners earmarked for

wartime conversion as armed merchant cruisers appears to have been issued in February 1888: eighteen ships of 15kts and over, sixteen of which had been surveyed for conversion. Eight ships, two of them under construction (White Star's *Majestic* and *Teutonic*) were then being subsidized. Eleven were being subsidized in July 1895.

16 *British Naval Manoeuvres* Vol I in NHB contains accounts of the 1885, 1887, 1888, and 1896 exercises.

17 ADM 231/11, NID 137 of November 1887.

18 Due to the clarity of the night, the torpedo boats could see their targets, but could not be seen beyond 1000yds. They attacked from ahead on one bow; if observed, they shifted to the other bow. Ships found it difficult to designate these targets due to their rapid approach and rapidly changing bearings. Crews found it impossible to see the fore sights of their guns except when the boats were illuminated by searchlights. Even in daylight it was difficult to hit such small objects at a relative speed of 27 to 30kts (sum of speeds of ship and torpedo boat). All of these factors affected the torpedo defences of cruisers.

19 The plans for the manoeuvre are in ADM 1/6924B. The full report is in ADM 231/14 (NID 179 of October 1888).

20 The Admiralty distributed operational intelligence through war signal stations connected to it by telegraph. The A fleet stationed a cruiser at each signal station to await information that the enemy had broken out. The cruisers had to be recalled to strengthen the blockading force, but torpedo boats remained. Before the exercise the A fleet commander heard a great deal about the information collected by Lloyd's signal stations and by HM Coastguard, but the mass of telegrams he received was mostly noise (e.g., reports of his own fleet's movements). The fleet commander never received the warning he wanted, partly due to sheer traffic volume: in one day: for example, *TB 42* received 908 telegrams at Scilly. A central intelligence-collating station in London was essential. This was the origin of the later Admiralty War Room.

21 ADM 1/6926A. Members were Admiral Sir William Dowell, Admiral Sir R V Hamilton, and Rear Admiral Sir Frederick Richards (a future First Naval Lord). Set up late in September, the committee first met on 16 October 1888. It dealt with the main issues mentioned in the manoeuvre instructions. The supplementary report on qualities of ships appears in the parliamentary version of the report, not in the Admiralty version.

22 Report in NID papers, ADM 231/27.

23 Report in NID papers, ADM 231/18.

24 Report in NID papers, ADM 231/30

25 Report in NID papers, ADM 231/35

26 These very short lightweight guns used small charges, making possible a large calibre (hence heavy projectile) for their weight. The first British 68pdrs were carronades. Small charges meant short maximum range: about 400yds for a 68pdr and 200 for a 12pdr. Introduced in 1779, they were the first real innovation in naval ordnance in centuries. They were named after the Carron foundry in Scotland, where they were first made.

27 The major developers were Woolwich (called Blomefield, after the supevisor there) and Dundas. Lyon and Winfield, 31, list six 32pdr guns. The smallest (25cwt) was an 18pdr bored out to 6.3in calibre, 6ft (11.4 calibres) long. Three 32pdrs were produced by Monk in 1839: (A) 50cwt, 6.375in, 9ft long; (B) 45cwt, 6.35in, 8ft 6in; and (C) 42cwt, 6.35in, 8ft long. Of these, (A) replaced the earlier 42pdr. A 56cwt gun (Blomefield) and a 58cwt gun (Dundas, 1855) fired 6.41in shot; both were 9ft 6in long. There were three 42pdrs, all of 6.97in calibre: 67cwt (Dundas 1853: 9ft 6in long) and 75cwt and 84cwt, both 10ft long (about 17.2 calibres long overall). Two 56pdrs (7.65in calibre) were produced in 1839 by Monk, weighing 98 and 87cwt, 11 and 10ft long, respectively.

28 The first 68pdrs (calibre 8.05in) were 60 and 50cwt (8ft and 6ft 8in long, respectively). In 1853 Dundas produced two heavier 68pdrs (95 and 88cwt, 10ft and 9ft 6in long, respectively). Later there was a 112cwt gun, 10ft 10in long. All of these guns had 8.12in bore. Shell guns corresponding to the 68pdr were designated by calibre rather than by shell weight, because the shell weight depended on the filling. In addition to the ones listed above, there were a 65cwt shell version for large ships and a 52cwt for corvettes.

29 Paixhans published his *Novelles force maritime* in 1821, citing numerous experiments and proposals by officers to bore out existing guns to larger calibre to fire heavy shells horizontally. Shells had been used sporadically, beginning in the eighteenth century. Paixhans guns were first tested at Brest in 1824, smashing the old liner *le Pacificateur*; the sixteenth shell was so damaging that it was concluded that a similar shell at the waterline would have sunk the ship. Similar ships had withstood sustained pounding by solid shot. Shell guns proved effective on board the steamer *Karteria* during the Greek War of Independence (1827). In 1829 the Admiralty ordered tests of 10in and 12in shell guns, and shell guns were adopted during the following decade. Paixhans and others argued as early as 1825 that only iron armour could resist shell guns. D K Brown, *Before the Ironclad* (London: Conway, 1990), 133-4, describes the trials which convinced the Royal Navy to adopt shell guns, against the old (1772) battleship *Prince George* in 1835. Of 80 time-fuzed shells fired, 38 did not explode. Two time-fuzed shells placed on board caused considerable damage but, to the surprise of those conducting the tests, failed to start a fire. A further test (against HMS *York* in May 1853) employed fuzes which exploded on striking, rather than being time-fuzed. Damage was limited.

30 The first version of the 10in gun weighed 84cwt and was 9ft 4in long; it was considered too heavy. The 65cwt gun (9ft long) was introduced in 1838. It fired a 96lb hollow shot, compared to 56lb for the 8in.

31 D K Brown argued that there was no operational proof: the old expedient of heating shot before firing was far more effective. Prior to the Crimean War the only case of damage by shellfire was the Battle of Eckenfjorde (5 April 1849), when Prussian shore batteries destroyed the Danish *Christian VIII*. According to Brown, *Before the Ironclad*, 143, she was destroyed by red-hot shot. At

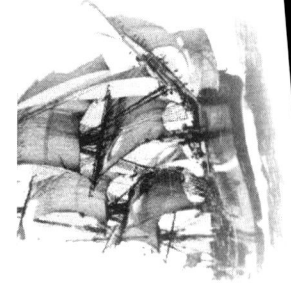

Sinope in November 1853 the Russians destroyed several Turkish ships with shells. At Sevastopol shells set HMS *Albion* on fire twice. She had to be towed out of action. Other ships were also damaged, but fires started by shells were contained. Brown, *Before the Ironclad*, 64, notes further that shellfire was about 25 per cent less accurate than solid shot because of the off-centre effect of the fuze and of powder moving about inside the shell. Tests with solid shot in 1847 in the calm water of Portsmouth Harbour showed 75 per cent hits on a battleship-size target at 1500yds, and 45 per cent at 2000, declining to as little as 8-9 per cent at 3000. The trials were carried out in connection with claims that a steamer could disable or even sink a battleship while manoeuvring to avoid being hit.

32 ADM 1/6012. Robinson saw a French 8in armour plate with a row of projectiles from a 14-ton (9.45in) gun sticking out of it, just as he had seen a British 8in plate (as in HMS *Hercules*) with a row of protruding projectiles from a 12½-ton (9in) gun, at that time the heaviest in British service. Chief French constructor Dupuy de Lôme personally arranged for Robinson to see two other French guns, the 5-ton (6.3in) equivalent to the British 64pdr, and the 8-ton (7.46in) equivalent to the British 6½-tonner, as well as naval gun mountings. The French showed and explained their interrupted-screw breech mechanisms (three-sector, so that it closed in one sixth of a turn), which incorporated an expanding cup to help seal against the escape of gas. Captain Hood personally tried the French breech mechanism, which 'was decidedly heavy work, and that with rolling motion the difficulty of placing the projectile in the guide plate, and forcing it home would certainly be much increased, the method of closing the breech is simple and strong and (as the gun cannot be fired until the breech is properly screwed up) it is quite safe, so long as the stop, which prevents the lever handle of breech plug from moving after the breech has been screwed up, is in proper order, but should this stop be broken or damaged to such an extent as to prevent its working properly (which is possible in action) then I believe there would be a great probability of the breech plug becoming unscrewed by the explosion, the effect of which would be most disastrous'. All the large French guns were cast iron, with steel bands hooped around their chambers. The French claimed that they could fire more than a thousand rounds from their guns without damage. Krupp showed its 14in 50-ton cast steel gun, not yet complete. The enclosed report, the ordnance section of which was probably written by Hood, claimed that the British type of muzzle-loading gun could be fired more rapidly, because the operations involved in opening and closing the breech slowed loading. The delay was worsened when deposits had to be cleared from the breech, or by 'the numerous delays inherent in a complicated mechanical operation'. The higher the elevation, the worse the delay.

Key argued that British crews were protected from rifle fire by the port, which was lowered when the gun was run back to be reloaded. He claimed the marked superiority for British guns, whose 'mode of construction is more certain, of greater strength and more durable than that of the French, while the muzzle loading system is from its simplicity and freedom from risk of damage also superior to the French system of breech loading.'

33 Admiral G A Ballard RN (ret), 'The Unarmoured Branches of the British Navy of 1875', *Mariner's Mirror* 21 No 3 (1935), 256.

34 This account is based heavily on Denis Griffiths, *Steam at Sea* (London: Conway Maritime Press, 1997).

35 Brown, *Before the Ironclad*, 171-2.

36 According to Griffiths, 43, a successful compound engine using a separate high-pressure cylinder was built in 1781. Griffiths dates the first marine compound engine to the re-engining of the steamer *James Watt* (renamed *Stad Keulan*) in 1829

37 Fire-tubes were tried in marine boilers as early as 1837; they were seen as a natural extension of the earlier flue-type boilers. Compared to a box boiler, a fire-tube boiler was more efficient and also more compact.

38 According to the 1892 report of the Boiler Committee (ADM 116/869), the large shipping companies found triple expansion engines operating at 150psi 20 per cent more efficient than double-expansion engines operating at 90 to 100psi, and about 25 per cent more efficient than the older double-expansion engines operating at 60psi.

39 Griffiths dates the earliest water-tube boilers to the Collins Line *Atlantic* class ships. They used vertical water-tubes, and they operated at 17psi. A similar boiler equipped the US Navy sloop *Hassalo* (1866).

40 'Marine Boilers', by Passed Asst Engr Robert S Griffin USN in *Information From Abroad 1894* (Washington: Government Printing Office) describes various water-tube boilers. The British were compelled to abandon cylindrical boilers because they were unable to generate one IHP from less than 1.5 square feet of heating surface. HMS *Vulcan* in particular could not generate her designed 12,000 IHP; the best she got on her initial trials was 8000. Any attempt to do better produced leaky tubes or priming or both. Lengthening the smoke pipes 20ft (to get better draught) did not help, nor did it help to remove tubes to improve circulation, or to shorten the grates, or other expedients. Finally the 'Admiralty ferrule', which had worked on board the battleship *Thunderer* was tried. The ship exceeded her designed forced draught power by 32 IHP. Placed in fire-tubes, the ferrule incorporated an air space which became red hot. Unfortunately it caused a problem called 'bird nesting', in which a ring of coal particles formed around the open hot mouth, gradually growing to close the tube altogether.

41 Fresh water was also desirable in cylindrical boilers, as was pointed out by the 1892 Boiler Committee (ADM 116/869): it prevented deposits on heating surfaces. Ships should not have to clean their boilers before going to sea. Fresh water would also reduce the labour of cleaning the internal parts of boilers, and would eliminate crippling salt deposits on surface condensers. These advantages were 'more than commensurate' with the extra expense of

providing a separate supply of reserve feed water. The required supply could be reduced by increasing ships' ability to make fresh water.

42 According to the 1902 report, no current water-tube boiler was as economical as the cylindrical; large battleships and cruisers should have cylindrical boilers sufficient for all auxiliaries and to drive the ship at 'ordinary' (cruising) speed.

43 Eng Rear Admiral Scott Hill, 'Battle of the Boilers', *Journal of Naval Engineering* (Royal Navy) July 1955. One of the protagonists, William Allan, MP for Gateshead, ensured that the technical battle spilled over into the popular press – which was reasonable given what was at stake.

44 This Boiler Committee succeeded earlier ones. An 1892 report headed off a proposal to reduce steam pressure and pressed for triple-expansion engines. Five volumes in the Admiralty Cases series (ADM 116/869 through ADM 116/873) cover the period December 1892 through 1904, summary reports being in the first two volumes.

45 The other principal officers were the Accountant-General, the Physician of the Navy (later called the Medical Director-General), the Comptroller of Victualling, and the Storekeeper-General. It appears to have responded both to the shift to peacetime concerns and to earlier administrative problems. Later it was sometimes regarded as the triumph of materiel over war-fighting, since it shifted the Board's focus from operations (e.g.. by Admiral Custance in 1907: C I Hamilton, *The Making of the Modern Admiralty* (Cambridge University Press, 2011, 69). Custance's characterization may have been part of an attack on Admiral Fisher and his demand for new materiel such as HMS *Dreadnought*.

46 C I Hamilton, 118. The Board took a longer more strategic view only in crises such as that caused by the French building program of 1858-59. In 1860 Lord Clarence Paget claimed that the Admiralty had never fully discussed warship form, size, armament, rig, stowage, coal, accommodation, crew, draught, and size and quality of engines.

47 C I Hamilton, 133, attributes the creation of the separate department to Symonds' ignorance of and contempt for steam.

48 D K Brown, *Before The Ironclad* (London: Conway, 1990), 38. The technically sophisticated Seppings was succeeded by the un-technical Symonds, who was contemptuous of the evolving science of ship design. Symonds' First Lord, Sir James Graham (took office 25 November 1830), closed the School of Naval Architecture established at Portsmouth. Grapham seems to have chosen Symonds based on his record of successful yacht designs, which had led previous First Lord Melville (Robert Dundas) to ask him to design an 18-gun sloop (*Columbine*), which performed well in 1828 sailing trials. Symonds then designed the successful brigantine *Pantaloon*, and he was invited to design the frigate *Vernon* in 1831. Symonds was interested mainly in hull form and sail plan (the powerplant of a sailing warship). Graham seems to have seen shipwrights as artisans rather than specialized technologists. According to Brown, Symonds survived after 1841 because he was backed by many serving officers. Symonds' troubles mounted, in Brown's view, because he was unable to make calculations involved in his designs, and also unwilling to consult those who could. His ships were fast in light winds but tended to roll too quickly: they were poor gun platforms and strained their hulls and rigging.

49 Walker brought in two graduates of the school of naval architecture at Portsmouth (closed by Graham in 1832) as senior shipwrights (naval architects) to design the ships he envisaged: Isaac Watts and Joseph Large. Later a DNC, Nathanial Barnaby, a graduate of the successor Central Mathematical School (opened in 1848), was one of six constructional draughtsmen.

50 Into the 1870s the Admiralty correspondence papers (ADM 1 series in PRO) called him the Surveyor.

51 Steam increased the cost of a ship by about 50 per cent, according to C I Hamilton, 144. In 1858-59 the Admiralty was provided for the first time with cost estimates for new ships.

52 The first Director of Naval Ordnance was Captain Astley Cooper Key, later First Naval Lord. He was appointed Acting Director-General of Naval Ordnance on 3 September 1866 to advise the Board in the dispute between Sir William Armstrong and the Royal Gun Factory (Woolwich). Decisions had been made by the army-oriented Ordnance Select Committee, the navy being represented only by the Controller and the Junior Naval Lord, neither of whom had technical backing. Cooper Key was chosen because as Captain of the gunnery training establishment HMS *Excellent* (1863-66) he was the navy's gunnery expert. Later he strongly advocated higher professional training for naval officers. In 1870 he was recalled from Malta to be President of the new War College at Greenwich (1870-75). He then became Commander of the North America and West Indies Station (December 1875 to May 1878). On his return he commanded the Reserve Squadron which was mobilized against Russia in the summer of 1878. Upon being offered the post of First Naval Lord he said that Phipps Hornby, then Commander in the Mediterranean, would be better, but he was senior and was chosen. According to Naval Staff Training and Staff Duties Division, *Naval Staff Monograph (Historical): The Naval Staff of the Admiralty, Its Work and Development* (September 1929), ADM 234/434, issued as CB 3013 and reclassified BR 1845, 15, about 1877 Admiral Phipps Hornby asked Cooper Key and the other likely candidate for First Naval Lord, Vice Admiral Sir Beauchamp Seymour, to join him in refusing appointment unless the Government was prepared to create a supporting staff; Cooper Key refused and got the job. As First Naval Lord, he presided over the beginnings of a British naval staff in the form of the Naval Intelligence Department.

53 Unfortunately no Covers for these ships have survived. The report is in Parliamentary Papers for 1872 (XIV).

54 Milne was Senior Naval Lord between 13 July 1866 and 18 December 1868 and between 27 November 1872 and 7 September 1876. He bridged the transition from

Gladstone's administration to Disraeli's, the new First Lord being G Ward Hunt (appointed 4 March 1874).

55 C I Hamilton mentions the embarrassments. The Naval Staff Monograph is more diplomatic: 'all who had to do with the Russian crisis could see clearly that the Admiralty system of collecting intelligence of foreign navies was gravely defective'. Admiral Cooper Key, who had experienced the embarrassments as commander of the Baltic squadron, did not favour a separate intelligence organization, but the First Lord, who had experienced the acute anxiety of the 1878 crisis, did. Nothing happened for the remainder of Disraeli's term, which ended with the May 1880 election. The new First Lord, Northbrook, revived the idea after Colonel (later General) Charles Gordon wrote him that 'it was through want of knowledge that we came to grief in many places ... [we had] a great inclination to drift along till the crisis came on us' (Naval Staff Monograph, 21). Gordon was too prominent to be ignored. Perhaps Cooper Key's most important point was that the purpose of collecting information was to make it possible for the Admiralty to be prepared with plans in the event of war. The intelligence operation should become a staff operation supporting the Admiralty. Plans for the new organization were being made when the Egyptian crisis revealed that far too little was known of the defences of Alexandria when the bombardment was being planned. In November 1882 a Foreign Intelligence Committee (FIC) was formed under Commander (soon Captain) W H Hall (Admiral Cooper Key was nominally chairman). The Committee received permanent Treasury sanction in March 1884.

56 'Naval Intelligence and Protection of Commerce', typescript in Trade Protection papers at NHB, lecture dated 13 May 1881.

57 Americans will see a parallel to the 'Revolt of the Admirals' of 1949 with two differences. The important difference is that this one succeeded. The other is that the US Chief of Naval Operations, roughly equivalent to First Naval Lord, publicly supported the navy's dissent from the governing Truman Administration, and thus had to resign. The US equivalent to Fisher was Captain Arleigh Burke who, like Fisher, survived to reach the ultimate naval office.

58 According to C I Hamilton, 194-5, Lord George Hamilton, who took office as First Lord when the Conservatives returned to power (1 July 1885) considered Barnaby's ships lacking in fighting power. White's export cruisers seemed much better. Barnaby offered to resign, saying that he was tired. He was probably also sick of his brother-in-law's sniping. Ironically, White was soon defending his own Royal Navy designs against apparently superior foreign ones.

59 ADM 1/7254. The 'Memorandum as to future Naval Expenditure' is unsigned, but a marking at the bottom of the page suggests that it was printed in July 1891. The context suggests the author and the intended recipient. According to the memo, over the past 22 years (since 1869), 312 ships above the size of torpedo gunboats were deleted from the navy list, and 200 added.

1. STEAM, SAIL, AND WOODEN HULLS

1 Revised rates were established by a 30 January 1856 Order in Council: First was ships with 110 guns and up, and with complements of 1000 and up; Second was ships carrying between 80 and 110 guns, and between 800 and 1000 men; Third (the smallest capital ships) carried between 60 and 80 guns and 600 to 800 men (there were also some special cases). Below came two frigates rates (based on numbers of men on board). Sixth Rate was corvettes: all other ships commanded by Captains and with complements of fewer than 300. All vessels commanded by Commanders were sloops. In March 1862 the list was modified: sloops were ships commanded by a Commander carrying their principal armament on one deck with broadside ports (lesser ships had pivot guns). Notes courtesy of Dr Stephen Roberts. The distinction between Captains' and Commanders' commands survived to distinguish cruisers from sloops into the late nineteenth century.

2 Ironically, during the Second World War the Royal Navy reversed the order of sloop and corvette. Corvettes were coastal (later small ocean-going) sloops. The term frigate was revived in 1943 as an intermediate category. Confusingly, the US Navy and the French navy both later reverted to the earlier connotations of these terms. Large post-war US destroyers were called frigates (DL); they were later redesignated destroyers or cruisers. The French referred to their large *Suffren* class destroyers as frigates, their smaller escorts as corvettes.

3 Brown, *Before the Ironclad*, 90, quotes his diary: 'I have been ordered to report on the monstrous iron screw steamers ... both were found wanting in displacement and volume and were three times mistaken.' Symonds also reported very adversely on the fouling of the iron ships, for which no acceptable antidote then existed.

4 ADM 92/11, Submission 88 of 1 February 1845, courtesy Dr Stephen Roberts.

5 *Nile* was built in London, launched 7 June 1834, and armed with two 10in shell guns (presumably chasers) and twenty lighter guns. Dimensions: 180ft x 33ft x 13ft (fwd)/14ft (aft), 1452 tons displacement, 240 NHP. Weights were: 540 tons hull, 200 tons machinery, 45 tons boiler water, 320 tons of coal. As of early 1840 the only other large steam warship in the world was the Russian steam frigate *Bogatyr* (186ft x 32ft, 240 NHP). The US Navy had built a much earlier double-hull steamer (actually a coastal battery), *Fulton*, but she burned, her engine already removed, in 1829. In March 1839 Congress authorized the first two large post-Fulton steam warships, the paddle frigates *Mississippi* and *Missouri* (1732 tons, 220ft x 39ft). The first large French steam warship, *Infernal* (320 NHP), was laid down in January 1840, with two more powerful ones (450 NHP: *Asmodée* and *Gomer*) to follow. John Houghton, *The Navies of the World 1835-1840* (Melbourne: Minuteman Press, 2011).

6 These were Symonds' designs. Work appears to have begun in January 1835, specifically to accommodate a new 110 NHP Boulton & Watt engine. Drawings were

approved on 29 April 1836, *Gorgon* being assigned to Pembroke on 16 May and *Cyclops* on 25 June. In fact, *Gorgon* was equipped with two 160 NHP engines; in September 1837 the Surveyor wrote that he considered the 110 NHP engines 'quite inadequate to make the *Gorgon* an effective steam vessel'. She should be kept in the covered dock until better engines were ready, the engines bought for the ship being assigned instead to a mail packet 'which it appears will soon be required', either between Pembroke and Waterford or between Holyhead and Dublin. Alternatively *Hydra*, ordered from Chatham, might be adapted to receive these engines 'for whatever service their Lordships may design her ...' *Hydra* was fitted with the 220 NHP engines. In June 1838, the engines of *Gorgon* just having been tested, the Surveyor pointed out that because they were much more powerful than those for which the ship had been designed (360 rather than 220 NHP) the ship would burn coal at a much higher rate, hence should be enlarged to carry more coal (as lengthened, she was expected to carry 400 tons of coal and 30 tons of water under her engines). Details of *Cyclops*: 190ft 3in (gun deck) x 37ft 6in x 23ft, 1190 55/94 tons burthen, displacement 1862 tons. Engines were rated at 320 NHP (1100 IHP, 9.5kts). She was designed for one 10in 98pdr 112cwt chaser at each of bow and stern plus sixteen main deck 32pdrs and four upper deck 48pdrs, but was completed with only the two chasers and four 8in (68pdr) 95cwt on the broadside. The 98pdrs were replaced by 84cwt guns in 1845, and the 68pdrs by 65cwt guns. In 1856 she was again rearmed, with two 68pdr chasers and four broadside 10in 84cwt. *Gorgon* was 178ft (gun deck) x 37½ft x 23ft, 1108 67/94 tons burthen, displacement 1610 tons, with 320 NHP engines (she made 9.5kts on 800 IHP). Armament was two 10in 84cwt chasers and two 68pdr 64cwt and two 42pdr 22cwt carronades on the broadside. The original design called for ten main deck and six upper 32pdrs. By 1856 she had a 68pdr as her forward chaser, and her broadside guns were 32pdr 42cwt. Both ships were modified to help lay an Atlantic cable in 1858.

7 Presumably under PW 1842, which began at the end of March. On 18 March the following steam vessels were ordered. First class, to duplicate *Cyclops*: *Beelzebub* (renamed *Firebrand*) and *Centaur* at Portsmouth, *Sampson* and *Gladiator* at Woolwich, and *Vulture* and *Janus* (renamed *Dragon*) at Pembroke. Second class, to duplicate *Driver*: *Thunderbolt* and *Scourge* at Portsmouth, *Sphinx* and *Infernal* (renamed *Eclair*) at Woolwich, and *Spiteful* and *Inflexible* at Pembroke. In June, the Surveyor asked that engines of the first-class ships be of at least 350 NHP, with a minimum of 400 to 500 tons of coal (16 to 20 days' steaming). As built, ships varied in NHP, the maximum being 560 NHP (total) in *Dragon*. She made 11.5kts under steam. Dimensions of *Vulture*: 190ft 0½in (gun deck) x 37ft 6in x 23ft, 1190 55/94 tons burthen, displacement 1960 tons. All guns were on her upper deck: two 68pdr 95cwt chasers, four 8in 95cwt.

8 *Cyclops* was originally to have been armed with sixteen 32pdrs on her main deck plus four upper deck 48pdrs and bow and stern 68pdrs. She was built without the main deck battery, but with 68pdrs instead of 48pdrs on her upper deck. The *Firebrand* group and *Sampson* had only upper deck guns: four 8in (65cwt) and two 68pdr chasers, bow and stern. The *Centaur*s had a more powerful upper deck battery. In addition to the chasers, *Centaur* had four 68pdr (65cwt) and two 32pdr carronades. *Dragon* had two 8in (112cwt), four 8in (65cwt), and two 24pdr carronades.

9 She had water-tube boilers and a rotary engine, but made only 6kts. Completed in 1846, she was converted three years later into a tug for Gibraltar and then refitted as a gun-vessel for the Crimean War. She was sold in 1856.

10 Initially *Retribution* had only one 8in/68pdr (112cwt) chaser and nine 8in/68pdr (65cwt) guns, all on the upper deck. Later twelve (and then eighteen) 32pdrs (50cwt) were added on her main deck.

11 Notes from ADM 92/11, courtesy of Dr Stephen Roberts. A table compared Fincham's design with a *Southampton* class sailing frigate and with the prototype screw sloop HMS *Rattler*. Fincham's ship had a 300 NHP engine, compared to 200 NHP for *Rattler* (as completed *Dauntless* had a 580 NHP engine). As designed she was 200ft (gun deck) x 44.4ft x 19.3ft (fwd)/20.3ft (aft); 1786 tons burthen, 2745 tons displacement. As built she was 210ft x 39¾ft x 26ft; 1497 tons burthen, 2242 tons displacement. The length given is length on the gun deck, *not* length between perpendiculars. Fincham wanted 600 tons more than *Southampton* to carry engines and coal. Surveyor Symonds retorted that the extra displacement would reduce performance under sail. Fincham expected over 8kts under steam (the ship made 10.3kts on her increased power, 1388 IHP). Symonds was dubious. *Rattler* was better formed for speed, and her 200 NHP engine drove her 890-ton hull at 8 to 10kts. It was difficult to imagine that a 2745-ton ship could be driven at over 8kts by a 300 NHP engine. Above all, Symonds considered the screw propulsion 'experiment is upon too large and extensive a scale to risk a failure; a ship so disproportionate would be nearly useless as a sailing vessel. I therefore recommend that it be first tried in a Corvette, in which case that one be built of iron for the purpose'.

12 Details of *Penelope*: 215ft 2in (gun deck) x 40ft 9in x 19ft 3in (fwd)/20ft 3in (aft), 1616 tons burthen, displacement 2766 tons. Her engines were rated at 650 NHP. Conversion entailed lengthening the ship by 63ft 4in, leaving sufficient space on each side for twelve gun ports. Not all of them were occupied; the ship was armed with eight 8in/68pdr (68cwt) guns on her main deck, and with two 42pdr (84cwt) chasers and ten 42pdr (23cwt) carronades on her upper deck. According to Brown, *Before the Ironclad*, 68, John Edye (responsible for the conversion) advocated the fastest possible transition to steam. Of 30 similar ships, 15 were in good enough condition to convert; 4 could be done each year. Less powerful machinery (500 NHP) would be more compact, reducing the length of the machinery space by 12ft 8in and reducing machinery weight by 245 tons, hence

draught by 14in (to 18ft 6in), giving greater freeboard at the gun ports. A load of 400 tons of coal would last 21 days.

13 *Terrible*: 226ft 2in (gun deck) × 42ft 6in × 27ft depth, 1847 7/94 tons burthen, displacement 3189 tons. Her engines were rated at 800 NHP (2059 IHP, 10.9kts). Armament was four 68pdr 95cwt, four 56pdr 98cwt, and three 12pdr on her main deck, plus four 68pdr 95cwt and four 56pdr 98cwt on her upper deck. She helped lay the transatlantic cable in 1865, and then helped tow the floating dock to Bermuda in 1869.

14 *Avenger* (Symonds design): 210ft (gun deck) × 39ft × 25⅔ft (depth), 1444 36/94 tons burthen, displacement not known. Two 8in 112cwt chasers, four 8in 65cwt on slides, four 32pdr 25cwt carronades; 650 NHP engines, IHP not known.
Odin (frigate, John Fincham design): 208ft (gun deck) × 37ft × 24⅙ft (depth), 1301 73/94 tons burthen, displacement not known. Ten 32pdr 56cwt on main deck, two 68pdr 112cwt and four 10in 84cwt on upper deck; 560 NHP engines, IHP not known.
Sidon: 210ft 8in (gun deck) × 37ft 0½in × 27ft (depth), 1315 63/94 tons burthen. Two 68pdr 88cwt chasers on main deck, with fourteen 8in 60cwt; four 8in 52cwt on quarterdeck, two 8in 52cwt on forecastle; 560 NHP engines, IHP not known. *Sidon* was refitted as a trooper in 1851.
Leopard: 218ft (gun deck) × 37½ft × 25⅙ft (depth), 1412 65/94 tons burthen. Twelve 32pdr 56cwt on main deck, four 10in 85cwt and two 68pdr 95cwt on upper deck. She was rearmed in 1862 with eight 32pdr 56cwt and four 40pdr 32cwt on the main deck and one 68pdr 95cwt plus five 100pdr 82cwt Armstrong breech-loaders on her upper deck. Engines 560 NHP, IHP not known. See below for *Dauntless* and *Conflict*, which were completed as screw sloops.

15 Plans for *Niger* were submitted on 20 February 1845. Details: 185ft × 32ft 8in × 21ft 6in depth, 911 tons burthen. She was lengthened in 1858 to 194ft 4in (gun deck) × 34ft 8in × 15½ft (mean), 1072 6/94 tons burthen, displacement 1454 tons. She was originally armed with one 56pdr 87cwt, one 10in 85cwt, four 8in (68pdr) 65cwt, and two 32pdr 25cwt. In 1850 she was rearmed with fourteen guns, probably all 32pdr 56cwt, and a 68pdr was added in 1856. Her engine was rated at 400 NHP (1002 IHP, 10.3kts). ADM 92 notes courtesy of Dr Stephen Roberts.

16 An Admiralty Minute dated 26 May 1847 stated that these ships would be of 1200 tons, which would bring them up to the class of frigates, with four 32pdr 46cwt guns on their main decks. Sloops were of 1055 and 1124 tons burthen. Surveyor's 18 June 1847 submission described them as enlarged *Sphinx*es with 12in more depth in their holds and with 240 tons greater displacement (139 tons greater than *Bulldog*). As described in August 1847, these ships had 400 NHP engines and 507 tons of coal, with 3 months of provisions for their 160 men. Dimensions: 198ft (waterline) × 37ft (extreme) × 14ft (fwd)/14ft 6in (aft), (1235 tons burthen, displacement 1961 tons 7cwt). Armament was four 32pdr 56cwt on the main deck plus one 68pdr 95cwt, one 10in 85cwt, and four 32pdr 42cwt on the upper deck.

17 Projected armament at this time included four 32pdr 56cwt guns on the main deck. In August 1847 *Magicienne* and *Valorous* were ordered lengthened to 210ft.
Magicienne: 210ft (gun deck) × 36ft × 24½ft, 1255 31/94 tons burthen, 2300 tons displacement; 400 NHP engines (1300 IHP, 9 to 10kts).
Tiger: 205ft (gun deck) × 35ft 11⅞in × 24ft 6in, 1221 49/94 tons burthen, displacement not known. 400 NHP engines (1300 IHP, 9 to 10kts).
Furious: 206ft × 37ft × 23¼ft, 1287 tons burthen, displacement not known. 400 NHP engines, IHP not known.
Magicienne and *Tiger* were John Edye designs; *Furious* was by John Fincham.

18 *Salamander*: 175ft 5in (gun deck) × 32ft 2in × 12½ft (fwd)/13½ft (aft), 818 tons burthen, displacement 1014 tons, with 220 NHP engines (506 IHP, 7.2kts).
Rhadamanthus: 164ft 7in (gun deck) × 32ft 10in × 11ft (fwd)/13ft (aft), 813 tons burthen, 1086 tons displacement, 220 NHP engines (385 IHP, 10kts).
Phoenix: 174ft 7in (gun deck) × 31ft 10in × 12ft (fwd)/12½ft (aft), 812 tons burthen, 1024 tons displacement, 220 NHP engines (IHP not known).
Medea: 179ft 4½in (gun deck) × 31ft 11in × 13ft 10in (fwd)/14½ft (aft), 835 tons burthen, 1142 tons displacement, 350 NHP engines (IHP not known).

19 Symonds specification, Edye design: 150ft (gun deck) × 32¾ft × 11½ft (fwd)/12ft (aft), 715 43/94 tons burthen, 1006 tons displacement. Engines 140 NHP. *Hermes* was lengthened in 1842 to 170ft, 827 88/94 tons burthen, displacement not known. She was re-engined in 1843 with 220 NHP machinery and made 8.5kts.

20 Symonds (i.e., Surveyor) design. Details: 165ft (gun deck) × 32ft 10in × 12ft 1in (fwd)/13ft (aft), 814 91/94 tons burthen, displacement 1096 tons. They had 220 or 240 NHP engines. Armament: two 8in 65cwt chasers and two 32pdr 50cwt.

21 They were designed by Symonds. Details: 180ft (gun deck) × 34⅓ft × 13ft (fwd)/13½ft (aft), 965 79/94 tons burthen, displacement 1283 tons. The engines were rated at 280 NHP. Armament: two 10in 84cwt chasers, two 68pdr 64cwt, two 42pdr 22cwt carronades. One 10in was replaced by a 68pdr 95cwt gun in 1856, and four 32pdr 42cwt replaced the smaller guns. A 110pdr Armstrong breech-loader replaced the 68pdr in 1862, at least in *Vesuvius*.

22 The 6ft additional length (and 11in more depth) and 183 tons greater displacement were to accommodate the heavier weights of engine, coal, and armament. Plans submitted in May 1847 showed 189ft (wl) × 35ft (ext) × 13ft 3in (fwd)/13ft 9in (aft) (depth 20ft 5in), 1048 40/94 tons burthen, displacement 1561 tons 19cwt. The ships were to have 300 NHP engines and to carry 389 tons of coal, with provisions for 3 months and 40 tons of water. Complement was 140. Planned armament was one 8in 65cwt, one 10in 85cwt, and four 32pdr 42cwt. *Alecto* as built: 164ft (gun deck) × 32ft 8in × 18ft 7in depth, 800

tons burthen, displacement 878 tons. She had 200 NHP (370 IHP) engines.

23 Dimensions of *Driver* class (including *Thunderbolt*): 180ft (gun deck) x 36ft x 21ft, 1055 62/94 tons burthen, displacement 1590 tons. Armament: two 10in 84cwt chasers, two 68pdr 64cwt and two 42pdr 22cwt carronades. In 1856 one of the chasers was replaced by a 68pdr 95cwt gun, and the four broadside guns were all made 32pdr 42cwt. Later a 110pdr breech-loader replaced the 68pdr chaser.

24 In February 1845, returning Fincham's design for a screw frigate to Their Lordships, the Surveyor stated that to test the merits of the screw propeller he would like a ship very similar to *Devastation*. The two ships should have similar engines producing the same power. The Surveyor referred to Board Minutes dated 12 December 1844 and 11 January 1845, which are all too late to refer to *Rattler*, but are appropriate for *Niger*. ADM 92/11 Submission 95 of 4 February 1845, courtesy of Dr Stephen Roberts. According to Brown, *Before the Ironclad*, 118, the Board decided to build *Basilisk* the year *after* having approved *Niger*; she was a paddle version of *Niger*, rather than the other way around. *Basilisk* details: 190ft (gun deck) x 34ft x 21½ft (depth), 1001 34/94 tons burthen, displacement 1710 tons. She was completed 5in beamier than designed (1031 tons burthen). Armament was one 68pdr 95cwt chaser, one 10in 84cwt chaser, and four broadside 32pdr 42cwt. Her engine was rated at 400 NHP (1033 IHP).

25 In October 1847 the Board tried to arbitrate an argument about the lines of *Resolute* and *Barracouta*, asking for improved lines of HMS *Sidon* adapted to new 400 NHP engines. The Committee was also to take into account the lines of the frigate *Leopard*, with a view to combining the good qualities of the *Odin* with those of the *Sidon*. *Resolute* could not be modified because she was so far advanced. *Barracouta* details: 190ft 2in (gun deck) x 35ft x 20ft 5in (depth), 1048 40/94 tons burthen, displacement 1076 tons. She had 300 NHP engines (881 IHP, 10.5kts). Armament: two 10in 84cwt chasers and four 32pdr 25cwt carronades; in 1856 one 10in was replaced by a 68pdr 95cwt gun and the 25cwt carronades replaced by 42cwt guns. In 1862 the 68pdr was replaced by an Armstrong 110pdr breech-loader mounted on a slide.

26 The crisis began with the Greek War of Independence (1827). Mehmet Ali lent his army and his fleet to the Pasha to help suppress the rebels. He was promised Crete and Syria as a reward, but when the Greeks succeeded he got neither. Ali's son seized Syria (modern Lebanon, Syria, and Israel) in 1832. During the 1832-33 crisis the British declined to help the Turks, but the Russians provided both troops and warships in the Bosporus. Their reward was a treaty which the British soon regretted. It could be seen as the first step in turning Turkey into a Russian satellite. The Turks needed foreign help partly because in 1827 they had lost their whole fleet at Navarino (to an allied – including Russian – fleet led by the British). It was never clear precisely how the battle had begun out of a marine standoff; the British had never wanted to destroy the Turkish fleet. The new Turkish fleet which defected to Mehmet Ali in July 1839 comprised 13 ships of the line (60 to 120 guns) and 7 frigates (44 and 50 guns). The Egyptians were rapidly expanding their own fleet after its destruction (with the Turkish fleet) at Navarino. They had 7 ships of the line, 10 frigates, and the steam frigate *Nile*.

27 Some in the Cabinet regarded the constitutional monarchy of France as a surer ally than despotic Russia. Representatives of British merchants in Egypt lobbied the Cabinet, sometimes in collusion with the French. R B Matzke, *Deterrence through Strength: British Naval Power and Foreign Policy under Pax Brittanica* (Lincoln: University of Nebraska Press, 2011), 169.

28 Matzke, 171, describes Palmerston's reasoning. Matzke, 174, points out that early in the crisis the French calculated that the British could not achieve sea control in the eastern Mediterranean, presumably based on the current strength of the Mediterranean Fleet and the considerable strength of the Egyptian fleet after the Turks defected to it. On a global basis the British had enough strength to blockade the Egyptians while isolating and attacking Syria, making that country untenable for the Egyptians. Manning was the only real problem. The Royal Marines were crucial in filling out ships' complements.

29 The 1847-48 panic was the first described by F W Hirst, *The Six Panics and Other Essays* (London: Methuen, 1913); the others were 1851-53, 1859-61, 1884, the *Dreadnought* panic, and the then-current Airship Panic. Matzke, 43, agrees with Hirst that the war scare was ignited mainly to increase naval and military investment.

30 A 9 June 1845 memorandum for First Lord Thomas Hamilton, Earl of Haddington listed 28 British ships abroad at any one time, by stations: East Indies and China (3), Pacific (2), River Plate (2), Cape of Good Hope (1), West Indies and North America (2), West Coast of Africa (6), and Mediterranean including packets (9), plus 3 in transit. The large presence on the coast of Africa was to help suppress the slave trade. The French had only 8: River Plate (2 small ships), East Indies (2 small ships), Pacific (1 large ship), and West Indies (1 ship), plus, presumably, 2 in transit. The large Pacific presence was presumably due to the recent annexation of Tahiti. ADM 1/5553, courtesy of Dr Stephen Roberts.

31 The British were well aware that steam could help the defence as much as the offence. Probably the most important consequence of adopting steam power was limited endurance under steam. A watching blockade of an enemy steam force in harbour was difficult at best. The endurance problem prompted interest in direct attack on ships in port. A later version of this endurance problem is evident in the 1888 Manoeuvres. According to Matzke, the real role of the new coaling base at Alderney was to support a steam blockade of Cherbourg.

32 Blockships were to have a speed of 5 to 6kts and three weeks' provisions and water. The ships were made self-propelled (rather than being assigned tugs) so that they could reliably move to their stations in any weather (e.g.,

a light breeze the French might choose for their invasion) and transit as required. Given the desired speed, liners were allocated 450 NHP engines and frigates 35 NHP. The planned total was four liners and four frigates. Conversion of the frigate blockships was delayed pending trials of the full frigate conversion *Amphion*. Brown, *Before the Ironclad*, 122, gives the initial planned allocation: 2 liners and 2 frigates off the Solent and the Isle of Wight to protect Portsmouth; 2 frigates off the Medway to protect Chatham; 2 liners and 2 frigates off Plymouth; and 2 liners off Pembroke. The frigates were the 44-gun *Eurotas*, *Horatio*, *Seahorse*, and *Forth*. During the Crimean War they were refitted as screw mortar frigates. Conversion was approved on 2 September 1845. *Horatio* was the only one fitted with an engine (of 250 NHP), the other three being re-registered as sailing frigates in December 1852); they were not fitted with engines (of 200 NHP) until their Crimean War conversions. The 350 NHP engine intended for *Horatio* was ordered installed instead on board the 50-gun frigate *Worcester* at Chatham, but this conversion was cancelled on 8 April 1848.

33 Naval Staff Monograph, 5. The letter was dated 9 January 1847.

34 In June 1845 First Naval Lord Admiral Cockburn wrote that the *Rattler* trials convinced him that the screw was efficient and that it would be adopted generally in future: 'we are now adapting ships] building for the screw.' The French still preferred paddles, and 'we are therefore taking the lead in getting rid of paddles'. He referred specifically to plans to place a 300 NHP engine on board the large frigate *Amphion* as an auxiliary powerplant. If that succeded, many more frigates and to two?] ships of the line would receive screws. Installation seemed inexpensive, with few problems. HMS *Penelope*, now on the coast of Africa, 'is reported to have answered so remarkably well that I have decided similarly to deal with another of our 42 gun ships but to be given screw vice paddle which would give her decided superiority over *Penelope* when under sail only'. This was partly to counter engine builder and naval architect Sir Charles Napier, who favoured paddles. ADM 1/5553 (courtesy Dr Stephen Roberts).

35 Successful bidders were Scott, Sinclair (*Pegasus*: 192ft × 35½ft × 21¼ft, 1144 tons burthen), Napier (*Simoom*: 230ft × 38ft × 22½ft, 1391 tons burthen), Fairbairn (*Megaera*: 196ft × 36ft × 20½ft, 1202 tons burthen), and Ditchburn (*Vulcan*: 215ft × 38½ft × 24ft, 1509 tons burthen). In June 1845 the Admiralty directed that *Megaera* and *Pegasus* carry bow and stern chasers on their main decks, to fire along the line of the keel, from stern and bridle ports. They were both to be classed as second-class frigates rather than as sloops. An offer to lengthen *Pegasus* 12ft (with greater engine power) was approved in August. *Megaera* was also lengthened.

36 Conversion involved much more than opening up the ship and inserting boilers and an engine. The ship was lengthened 16ft by the bow, and the bow altered so that a 32pdr 56cwt gun could be mounted to fire along the centreline: once a ship had steam power, she could manoeuvre into position for a raking shot. As completed, *Amphion* was armed with twenty main deck guns (six 8in 65cwt and fourteen 32pdr 56cwt) and sixteen upper deck guns (two 68pdr 95cwt chasers and fourteen 32pdr 42cwt). She was reduced to 30 guns in 1848, but had all 36 again by 1856. *Amphion* details: 177ft (gun deck) × 43ft 2in × 19ft 2½ in (mean), 1474 tons burthen, displacement 2049½ tons. She had a 300 NHP engine (592 IHP, 6.8kts).

37 John Fincham submitted a sketch of a 46-gun steam frigate with auxiliary power (300 NHP) about the beginning of August 1844, and the detailed design was sent to Portsmouth on 11 February 1845. In March she was listed alongside three iron ships (*Simoom*, *Vulcan*, and *Megaera*) as well as the wooden screw frigate *Watt* (ultimately named *Retribution*). *Arrogant* details: 200ft (gun deck) × 45ft 8¾ in × 20ft (mean), 1872 21/94 tons burthen, displacement 2690 tons. She had a 360 NHP engine (774 IHP, 8.6kts).

38 *Encounter* (John Fincham) as designed: 180ft (gun deck) × 33ft 2in × 20ft 10in depth, 894 40/94 tons burthen (no displacement known). As lengthened in 1848: 190ft (gun deck) × 33ft 2in × 13ft 11in (mean), 953 tons burthen, displacement 1482 tons. As conceived as a paddle sloop in December 1844, armament was two 85cwt, four 65cwt, and two 25cwt. The Surveyor was ordered to prepare lines for a screw sloop with the same armament, which became *Encounter* (named, as a screw sloop, 5 February 1845). Armament was one 56pdr 87cwt and one 10in 85cwt chasers plus four 8in 68pdr 65cwt and two 32pdr 17cwt carronades. Alternatively, she could mount two 56pdr 85cwt chasers and 32pdr 25cwt carronades instead of the 17cwt guns. In 1850 she was rearmed with 12 guns, increased to 14 in 1856; all were probably 32pdr. Her engine was rated at 360 NHP (673 IHP, 10.3kts).

39 *Phoenix* as converted to the Oliver Lang design: 174ft 7in (gun deck) × 31ft 10in × 12¼ft (mean), 809 tons burthen, displacement 1024 tons. Armament was one 10in 84cwt and one 8in 52cwt chasers plus eight broadside 32pdr 17cwt carronades. Her engine was rated at 260 NHP (489 IHP, 8.7kts).

40 Designed by Symonds (Surveyor), drawings submitted 3 May 1845: 185ft (gun deck) × 34ft 4in × 22ft 8½in (depth), 992 13/94 tons burthen. Like *Encounter*, they were lengthened on the slip in 1848 (by the stern): 192ft 6½in (gun deck) × 34ft 4in × 15¾ft (mean), 1038 69/94 tons burthen, displacement 1628 tons. They had 400 NHP engines (geared to the propeller in *Desperate*). *Conflict* made 772 IHP for 9.4kts. Armament: two 56pdr 85cwt chasers, eight 8in 65cwt, two 32pdr 25cwt carronades.

41 As of June 1847, the Surveyor expected these ships to be 3ft 6in longer with 12in greater beam, adding 198 tons to displacement to carry the additional weights of engine, coal, and armament compared to *Rattler*.
Miranda: 196ft 0½in (gun deck) × 34ft × 13½ft (mean), 1039 16/94 tons burthen, displacement 1523 tons; 250 NHP engine (613 IHP, 10.8kts).
Brisk: 193ft 7¼in (gun deck) × 35ft × 13¾ft (mean), 1074 81/94 tons burthen, displacement 1474 tons, 250 NHP

engine (505 IHP, 7.4kts).

Archer: 186ft 4in (gun deck) x 33ft 10in x 14¾ft (mean), 970 40/94 tons burthen, displacement 1337 tons.

42 The Board decided in November 1847 to have a steam sloop of the same type as *Tiger*, then being built at Chatham, built under contract at Moulmein, Burma, presumably to take advantage of the teak wood available there. The engine room was was sufficiently capacious (when empty) to carry enough teak to build a further ship in the United Kingdom. *Tiger* was 1221 tons burthen, armed with one 68pdr 95cwt gun, one 10in 85cwt, and eight 32pdr 56cwt, with a 400 NHP engine. The name *Malacca* was assigned in October 1848. Drawings were submitted for approval in December 1848. When the builder died and his estate found it difficult to go on, under the existing contract the British government completed the hull and sailed it to the United Kingdom for installation of its engine. ADM 92/13, courtesy of Dr Stephen Roberts. Details: 192ft (gun deck) x 34ft 4in x 22ft 8in (depth), 1034 28/94 tons burthen. She was armed with one 10in 85cwt chaser and eighteen 32pdr 32cwt. The alternative was one 8in 65cwt chaser and sixteen 32pdr 32cwt. As built she had a 200 NHP engine (692 IHP, 9.2kts). She was re-engined in 1862, producing 707 IHP for 9.5kts. She was sold in 1869 to the Imperial Japanese Navy, becoming their *Tsukuba*.

43 *Reynard*: 147ft (gun deck) x 27ft 10in x 11ft 6in (mean), 516 37/94 tons burthen, displacement 656 tons, 60 NHP engine (165 IHP for 8.2kts). Armament: two 32pdr 56cwt and six 32pdr 25cwt carronades.

Plumper: 140ft (gun deck) x 27ft 10in x 11ft 4½in (mean), 490 24/94 tons burthen, displacement 577 tons, 60 NHP engine (148 IHP, 7.4kts). Armament as *Reynard*.

44 A squadron under William Fanshawe Martin consisted of the blockship (screw capital ship) *Hogue*, two screw frigates, two sailing capital ships, two sailing frigates, and the 800 NHP paddle frigate *Terrible*. According to C J Hamilton, *Anglo-French Naval Rivalry 1840-1870* (Oxford: Clarendon Press, 1993), 52, the performance of the steam ships showed convincingly that the screw was superior to the paddle in steaming and in towing, and that a ship under canvas and steam could be manoeuvred by screw (it had been feared that the screw would somehow fail if the ship sailed too fast).

45 Referring to the 7 August 1848 order to build the 60-gun frigates *Emerald* and *Impérieuse* at Deptford and to successful screw experiments, the Surveyor proposed building *Impérieuse* as a 50-gun screw frigate powered by an engine similar to that on board the frigate *Arrogant*. In February 1851 Steam Department wrote that the machinery of the ship should be set because she would soon be ready for launching. By this time experience with *Arrogant* showed that direct drive was best for a frigate, not only for ships with auxiliary steam power but even for those with full power. Although *Impérieuse* was nearly 500 tons (presumably burthen) larger than *Arrogant*, Steam Department proposed to install engines of the same NHP, but with larger boilers, both to improve durability and also to provide more steam. Steam Department later stated that *Impérieuse* boilers would be nearly a third larger, the ship developing at least a third more power (IHP, not NHP). Machinery was now more compact than in *Arrogant*. *Impérieuse* was 212ft x 50ft x 21ft 2in (fwd)/22ft 3in (aft) (2258 tons burthen, 3260 tons displacement) compared to *Arrogant's* 200ft x 45⅔ft x 20ft (2589 tons displacement). Complements exclusive of engineers were 500 for *Impérieuse* with a projected reduced (50-gun) armament compared to 450 for *Arrogant* (46 guns). The Surveyor proposed to arm *Impérieuse* with thirty main deck guns (all 8in 65cwt) and twenty upper deck guns (two 68pdr 95cwt chasers and eighteen 32pdr 45cwt). ADM 92/14, courtesy of Dr Stephen Roberts. *Impérieuse* as built: 212ft (gun deck) x 50ft 2in x 16ft 9in, 2355 45/94 tons burthen, displacement 3345 tons. *Aurora* was lengthened 15ft from her design: 227ft (gun deck) x 50ft 2in x 16ft 9in, 2550 55/94 tons burthen, displacement 3498 tons. *Impérieuse* had a 360 NHP engines, the others 400 NHP; she made 1296 IHP for 9.9kts, which was typical. The fastest of the class was *Forte* (1539 IHP, 11.4kts).

46 As of September 1857 rated armament was thirty main deck guns (eight 8in 65cwt and twenty-two 32pdr 58.6cwt) and twenty-one upper deck guns (the 68pdr pivot gun plus two 8in 65cwt and eighteen 32pdr 45cwt). Data taken from a note in ADM 92 (Submission 1137) making *Newcastle* one of the *Euryalus* class rather than, as planned, one of the *Emerald* class. The battery listed was on board *Euryalus*. Plans to build four new screw frigates on the lines of *Impérieuse* were approved on 4 November 1853 (*Forte*, *Chesapeake*, *Aurora*, and *Topaze*).

47 *Tribune* details: 192ft (gun deck) x 43ft x 12ft 11in, 1569 24/94 tons burthen, displacement 2220 tons. Armament was twenty main deck 32pdr 56cwt (9ft 6in) plus one 10in 85cwt chaser and ten 32pdr 42cwt (8ft) on the upper deck.

48 The Surveyor submitted a design in September 1849. He had had to enlarge the ship to provide recoil space for her guns and sufficient hatchways for ventilation, the result being 192ft x 36ft (about 1150 tons burthen, 1650 tons displacement) with an armament of two 95 or 85cwt chasers and sixteen 32pdr 40cwt guns. A comparative table produced by the Surveyor at this time showed that only *Malacca* was of comparable size: 192ft x 34ft 4in (1034 tons burthen, 1650 tons displacement), with one 68pdr 95cwt and one 10in 85cwt chasers and the same broadside armament as the new ship. Drawings were forwarded on 29 November 1849; the selected engine was rated at 250 NHP. Dimensions given at that time were 192ft (pp) x 36ft 4in x 15ft 6in (fwd)/16ft (aft), 1153 39/94 tons burthen (displacement 1732 tons). Complement was 190 or 200, armament being two 10in 85cwt chasers and sixteen 32pdr 42cwt (8ft) broadside guns. Loads were 200 tons of coal (8 days at full power), 78 tons of water (3 months), and 40 tons of provisions (5 months). The builder, Mare, went bankrupt due to wage and price inflation affecting its gunboat orders during the Crimean War. The same problem destroyed Pitcher, which built two Russian sloops taken over by the Admiralty, and its

effect on Scott Russell caused serious problems with the steamship *Great Eastern*. Brown, *Before the Ironclad*, 149-50. The use of private yards became common again only with the Naval Defence Act of 1889.

49 *Pylades*: 192ft 9in (gun deck) × 38ft 4in × 19ft 7in, 1267 72/94 tons burthen, displacement 1956 tons, 350 NHP engine (1106 IHP, 10.1kts). Armament: twenty 8in 42cwt on broadside, one 10in 68pdr (95cwt) bow chaser. This is the version using the *Highflyer* lines but with 2ft more beam.

50 *Cruizer*: 160ft (gun deck) × 31ft 10in × 17ft 5in depth, 747 51/94 tons burthen, displacement 1045 tons; 60 NHP (100 in ships after *Cruizer*); *Cruizer* made 6.6kts on 132 IHP, but *Fawn* made 8.8kts on 434 IHP, which was the greatest power of any in the class. Armament: one 32pdr 56cwt chaser, sixteen 32pdr 32cwt.
Greyhound: 172ft 6in (gun deck) × 33ft 2in × 17ft 5in depth, 877 53/94 tons burthen, displacement 1260 tons; 200 NHP engine (743 IHP, 9.8kts). Armament: five 40pdr Armstrong breech-loaders, twelve 32pdr.
Cameleon: 185ft (gun deck) × 33ft 2in × 17ft 5in depth, 950 8/94 tons burthen, displacement 1365 tons; 200 NHP engine (*Cameleon*: 678 IHP, 10kts). Armament: as *Greyhound*.
As completed after having been suspended, *Reindeer* had one 110pdr chaser and five 64pdr.

51 Submission 850 of 31 October 1850 compared the new design to *Cruizer*: 147ft × 27ft 10in (extreme) × 11ft 3in (fwd)/12ft 6in (aft), 690 tons displacement compared to 160ft × 32ft × 12/14ft (951 tons). Burthen tonnage was, respectively, 516 vs 748 tons. The new ship would need 110 men to operate one 32pdr 56cwt bow chaser and ten 32pdr 17cwt carronades on the broadside, compared to 150 men and the same forward pivot gun but sixteen 32pdr 32cwt broadside guns in *Cruizer*. She would also have reduced endurance: 13 rather than 20 to 25 days' steaming, 3 rather than 4 months of provisions, and 3 months (in both) of water (but the smaller ship could distill fresh water at sea). Both classes had 60 NHP engines. ADM 92/14, courtesy of Dr Stephen Roberts.

52 *Liffey* class: 235ft (gun deck; 285ft overall) × 50ft 1½in × 18ft 4½in (depth), 2651 tons burthen (2667 as completed), displacement 3915 tons. These ships had 600 NHP engines and were designed for 11.8kts. Armament was thirty 8in 65cwt on the main deck and twenty 32pdr 56cwt on the upper deck, plus one 68pdr 95cwt chaser. *Newcastle* was ordered to this design on 31 March 1855, but was built to a modified design.

53 The conversion having been stopped, in February 1857 *San Fiorenzo* was the only sailing ship left on the stocks, ⅝th completed. Her slip could not be lengthened. The Surveyor recommended that she be launched and docked for conversion, but the Board decided instead that she should be broken up, her materials used to build a similarly-formed but lengthened steam frigate. Presumably as compensation, on 2 March 1857, near the end of the 1856-7 program year, the sailing frigate *Narcissus*, building at Devonport, was ordered launched, docked, lengthened, and converted to a 2635-ton screw frigate. That was soon rethought; on 23 March she was ordered broken up and the materials used to build a similarly formed but lengthened screw frigate. Details of *Narcissus*: 228ft (gun deck, 261ft overall) × 51ft 3in × 20ft (fwd)/23ft 9in (aft), 2664 57/94 tons burthen, displacement 3548 tons; 400 NHP (1731 IHP, 10.6kts). Armament: eight 8in 65cwt shell guns and twenty-two 32pdr 58cwt on her main deck, eight 32pdr 56cwt on her upper deck plus one 68pdr 95cwt chaser.

54 *Swallow*: 139ft (gun deck) × 27ft 10in × 13ft 5in depth, 484 68/94 tons burthen, displacement 625 tons, 60 NHP (182 IHP for 6.6kts). Armament: one 32pdr 56cwt chaser, eight broadside 32pdr 25cwt (length 5ft 4in, replaced 1854 by 6ft guns).

55 Dimensions: 151ft (gun deck) × 29ft 1in × 15ft 10in, 577 30/94 burthen, 861 tons displacement. The engine was rated at 150 NHP (*Gannet's* produced 617 IHP for 10.8kts). Planned armament was eleven 32pdr smooth-bores (bow chaser plus broadsides), but in practice it varied considerably. In August 1866 (ADM 1/5891) Controller proposed that *Gannet* be refitted with a heavy gun (100pdr of 6¼ tons) on a slide amidships and lighter guns (40pdr Armstrongs) on pivots at bow and stern. This was much the armament fitted to the gunboat *China* of the Anglo-Chinese fleet. The Board approved the change on 25 August.

56 *Pearl*: 200ft (gun deck, 225ft 3in overall) × 40ft 4in × 23ft 11in depth, 1462 22/94 tons burthen, displacement 2187 tons, 400 NHP engine (1324 IHP, 11.3kts). Armament: one 10in 68pdr 95cwt bow chaser, twenty 8in 42cwt on broadside.

57 C J Hamilton contrasts French steam ships with British ships designed for mixed power. In October 1853 the French capital ship *Napoleon* easily towed a French line of battle ship through the Turkish Straits. The British *Sans Pareil* could not get through while towing a collier. However, some British observers reported that the French ship had serious machinery problems, including leaks due to excessive vibration. According to Hamilton, 85, British steam capital ships built from 1855 on were full steam ships, at least comparable to the best French ships. Because so few true steamers participated in the war, the main lesson was the superiority of sail-steam ships over sailing warships.

58 *Diadem* and *Doris*: 240ft (gun deck) × 48ft × 16ft 7in depth, 2479 42/94 tons burthen, displacement 3714 tons, 800 NHP engine (*Doris*: 3087 IHP, 12.9kts). Armament: twenty 10in 85cwt shell guns on the main deck, ten 32pdr 56cwt plus two 68pdr chasers on the upper deck. Plans called for the chasers to have been 95cwt (10in) shell guns.

59 *Cossack* and *Tartar* were being built by W H Pitcher under the Russian names *Witjas* and *Wojn*. Details: 195ft (gun deck) × 38ft 6in × 17ft 7in (fwd)/17ft 8in (aft), 1322 60/94 tons burthen, displacement 1965 tons; 250 NHP engine (*Cossack*: 870 IHP, 9kts). Armament: twenty 8in 42cwt on broadsides.

60 *Emerald*: 237ft (gun deck) × 52ft × 16ft 8in depth, 2857 10/94 tons burthen as designed, 2913 86/94 as built,

displacement 3503 tons; 600 NHP (2323 IHP, 12kts). Thirty 8in 65cwt shell guns on main deck, twenty 32pdr 56cwt plus one 68pdr 95cwt chaser on upper deck.

61 *Bristol* class: 250ft (gun deck) × 52ft × 19ft 2in depth, 3027 40/94 tons burthen, designed for 3600 tons displacement and 4020 tons loaded. They had 600 NHP engines (*Newcastle*: 2354 IHP, 12.4kts). Armament matched that of the *Emerald* class. This design was approved 12 August 1858.

62 *Jason*: as originally designed, 225ft (gun deck) × 40ft 8in × 24ft 2in (depth); 1623 14/94 tons burthen (as built 1702 17/94 burthen tons, displacement 2431 tons); 400 NHP engine (1516 IHP, 12kts). Armament: twenty broadside 8in 68pdr 65cwt, one 7in 110pdr 82cwt Armstrong breech-loader chaser. Armstrong guns were removed in 1864 after accidents. These were 'troop frigates'. *North Star* was to have been of this class, but was modified by covering the battery (design approved 23 January 1860). Beam increased to 42ft 10in and depth to 24ft 1in; burthen tonnage was 1856 82/94. She was further modified in 1865, cut back to 200ft on her gun deck (1619 tons burthen). She may have been designed for 22 guns rather than the 21 of the *Jason*s.

63 Lyon and Winfield classify *Ister* as the first of a modified *Bristol* class, of which only *Endymion* survived the wave of cancellations: 240ft (gun deck) × 47ft 10in × 17ft 3in in depth, 2478 30/94 tons burthen, displacement 3197 tons; 500 NHP engine (*Endymion*: 1620 IHP, 11.3kts). Armament: eight 6.3in 64pdr, twenty-two 32pdr (but rated as 36-gun frigates).

64 Extract from ADM 92 dated 26 June 1856, courtesy of Dr Stephen Roberts. On 2 July 1856 the Board approved new plans for a 36-gun frigate with the heaviest guns and 1000 NHP engines, and a corvette with covered deck with 26 of the heaviest guns and 1000 HP. In each case the object was to obtain a steam vessel of the greatest speed carrying the heaviest armament. The frigates were to be *Orlando* and *Mersey* (see below) and the corvettes *Ariadne* and *Galatea*. Like the *Diadem*s, *Ariadne* was reclassified as a frigate (Fourth Rate) in 1856, together with *Galatea*. Two more *Ariadne*s were ordered in February 1861: *Acasta* (Deptford) and *Hyperion* (Woolwich). They were cancelled in December 1863.
Orlando and *Mersey* details: 300ft (gun deck) × 52ft × 19ft 10in depth, 3726 70/94 burthen tons, displacement 5385 tons; 1000 NIP engine (*Orlando*: 3617 IHP, 13kts, *Mersey* 3691 IHP, 12.6kts). Armament was twenty-eight 10in (85cwt) shell guns on the main deck and twelve 68pdr (95cwt) on the upper deck; the latter may have been on slides
Details of the corresponding design for *Ariadne* and *Galatea* were: 280ft (gun deck) × 50ft × 19ft 4in depth, 3201 78/94 tons burthen, displacement 4426 tons as designed. As built, *Ariadne* displaced 4583 tons and *Galatea* displaced 4686. Armament was twenty-four 95cwt (10in) shell guns on her broadside, with two 68pdr (62cwt) in pivots on her upper deck (soon replaced by two 110pdr Armstrong breech-loaders). Actual engine output was 3350 IHP, for 13.1kts. In 1858 *Ariadne* and *Galatea* were derated from 1000 to 800 NHP.

65 *Rosario*: 160ft (gun deck) × 30ft 4in × 15ft 10in, 668 76/94 tons burthen, displacement 913 tons, 150 NHP engine (436 IHP, 9.2kts). Armament: one 40pdr 58cwt Armstrong breech-loader (on slide), six 32pdr 30cwt (6ft 4in), four 20pdr Armstrong breech-loaders on pivots.

66 On 10 February 1858 Walker proposed building ships with his greater length and finer lines to test the idea. He submitted designs for two classes of sloops: *Jason*, *Orestes*, *Orpheus*, and *Barrosa*; and *Rinaldo*, *Pelican*, *Perseus*, *Cameleon*, and *Zebra*; designs for longer finer-lined liners and frigates were being developed. On 22 February he submitted a proposal to lengthen the frigate *Immortalite*, then building, at the bow. In March he submitted a proposal to lengthen the liner *Howe* by 15 feet. In July Walker submitted details of modifications of the 90-gun liner, the two 50-gun frigate classes then under construction, and the 10-gun sloops of the PW 1858 program.

67 Gladstone was then Chancellor of the Exchequer in a Liberal government led by Lord John Russell. F W Hirst's cynical description of the outbreak of the panic suggests that it may have soured Gladstone on later attempts to increase naval spending.

68 Andrew Lambert, '"I will not have a war with France"'. At this time the Admiralty Board was chosen politically. Derby brought in Sir John Pakington as First Lord, Admiral Sir Richard S Dundas as First Naval Lord, Admiral Sir William Fanshawe Martin as Second Naval Lord, Captain Alexander Milne as Junior Naval Lord, Captain James Drummond as Secretary, and Lord Lovaine as Civil Lord.

69 One measure was total NHP. According to the 1858 Cabinet report (ADM 116/1) in 1852 the Royal Navy had 44,482 NHP compared to 27,240 for the French; since that time the British had added 55,030 NHP and the French 54,804 (engines under construction were included). Of the British increase, 18,700 NHP had been for capital ships. Of the French, 26,640 had been devoted to ships of the line and 3600 to the iron-sided frigates, which were clearly really capital ships. Thus the French had added nearly 10,000 more NHP to their capital ships. The British had added 7793 NHP to the power of frigates and block-ships, the French 13,100 for frigates. The British had devoted far more effort to smaller warships, from corvettes down. The British had also built a much larger gunboat force during the Crimean War. Overall, in 1858, the British had 464 steam warships compared to 264 French. Most ships were out of commission in reserve. In November 1858 the Admiralty estimated that the French had 6 liners in commission and another 18 available for service in a short time. The British had 9 screw liners in commission in home waters, plus 4 in ready reserve (1st Division, with stores on board) and 11 in a 2nd division of ready reserve, a total of 24 to the French 24, plus 4 in commission in the Mediterranean. ADM 92/20 (courtesy of Dr Stephen Roberts) includes Walker's 27 July 1858 comparison of the British and French navies: 'although a few years ago we were far

ahead of them in respect of screw Line of Battle Ships, they are now for the first time equal to us and unless some extraordinary steps are at once taken to expedite the building of Screw Ships of the Line, the French at the close of next year will be actually superior to us as regards the most powerful class of Ships of War ... [we must] increase the rate of building Line of Battle Ships and convert such Sailing Ships of the Line as may be fit for the purpose, but it is clear from past experience that the present strength of the Dock Yards is inadequate ... This condition of things would not have occurred if the successive Programmes of the last few years could have been carried out but the exigencies of the late Crimean war so interfered with the building of Ships that it was found utterly impossible to do so. We are therefore deficient of a considerable number of new powerful ships which were intended to be added to our Navy while many of those which have been added, converted from Sailing Ships carrying only 80 guns are very inferior to the converted Ships of the French which as Sailing Ships carried 90 or 100 guns.' Walker also alluded to 'the heavy iron plated ships' which 'are too important to be lost sight of and if not met by corresponding Ships would still further increase their Superiority as regards the most formidable Class of Ships of War'. In November he added that in the event of war the British would be unable to match the French frigate force because so many British frigates were required 'to protect our extensive and valuable commerce both at home and abroad, and our distant possessions'. The French could unite their Channel and Mediterranean fleets to form a preponderant force unless the British maintained a large Home Fleet as they did during the Napoleonic Wars to maintain control of the Channel 'which if once lost would cost this Country an ocean of Blood and millions of money, to repair'. The French could transfer seamen quickly by rail from the Mediterranean to the Channel, making it possible to mobilize ships quickly in the Channel ports. The Russians might join the French (they signed a secret treaty with France in 1858). Russia would probably have upwards of 20 screw ships of the line by the end of 1860. Walker thought the British needed three fleets: North Sea (20 ships of the line), Channel (30), and Mediterranean (about 20), each with a proportionate number of frigates and smaller craft. At least 80 line of battle ships would be required afloat, in addition to those on the stocks and those refitting. He did not propose cruiser numbers, but he compared British and French steam cruiser forces. The British had 19 screw frigates to the French 19, and 16 paddle frigates to the French 19. They had 14 screw corvettes (and no paddle corvettes) vs 9 French screw corvettes and 9 French paddle corvettes. The British had 27 screw sloops and 49 paddle sloops (and 26 screw gun-vessels) to 83 French sloops and gun-vessels.

70 ADM 116/1 and ADM 116/2. The papers include extensive reports by the British agent in France, Lt-Colonel R Claremont, who drew particular attention to the new French ironclads and to the success of French experiments with armour. Figures for the French were based on consular reports and on Lt-Colonel Claremont's reports, the most recent received in October 1858.

71 Nothing was done with them (*Hercule* and *Jemappes*). The report stated that no French liners would be converted after *Dugesclin*, which had just been ordered.

72 British ships in commission were 5 ships of the line, 4 blockships (no French equivalent), 24 frigates (7 of which were later rerated as corvettes), 56 corvettes and sloops, and 66 gun-vessels and smaller ships. The equivalent French figures were 2 liners, 21 frigates, 28 corvettes and sloops, and 62 smaller ships.

73 Ships should be converted as docks became available. Thus on 3 January 1860 the Surveyor directed 'there being a dock vacant at Sheerness into which the *Leander* could be taken, she should be] docked for the purpose of being converted into a 51 gun screw frigate to receive a 400 HP engine ...' The low power indicates an auxiliary steam plant rather than a primary one. Surveyor expected her to make 10.89kts. Specified armament was thirty-four main deck guns (eight 8in 65cwt and twenty-six 32pdr 56cwt) and seventeen upper deck guns (one 68pdr 95cwt pivot gun, two 8in 65pdr, and fourteen 32pdr 45cwt). Dimensions were 240ft (between perpendiculars) × 50¾ft × 20¼ft (fwd)/22⅓ft (aft). The same day the Surveyor ordered the *Octavia*, *Arethusa*, and *Constance* conversions at, respectively, Portsmouth, Chatham, and Devonport to fulfill Their Lordships decision 'to test the merits of different modes of supplying superheated steam to marine engines with a view to economizing fuel'. Ships would be lengthened amidships and fined aft, and the powerplants would produce 500 NHP. This proposal was approved on 4 January. Documents from ADM 92, courtesy of Dr Stephen Roberts.

74 Lambert, "'I will not have a war with France'", points to shrinking timber supply as a crucial limit. It prevented Dundas from building both new battleships (armed with 68pdrs) and new heavy frigates. Timber was one reason the British and French were converting existing ships. The Surveyor pointed to the timber problem in June 1860.

75 Firms were asked for both second-class frigate and first-class sloop (i.e., corvette) designs. Planned armament varied, as all four ships were to different designs.

76 Professor Andrew Lambert, "'I will not have a war with France'". dates the wooden design to 1857. His *Warrior: The World's First Ironclad, Then and Now* (London: Conway, 1987), 13, 22, describes Walker's formal February 1858 proposal. In June 1858 Walker proposed building two iron-hulled ironclads under contract and two wooden-hulled ones in Royal Dockyards. The iron ships could not be sheathed, hence could not serve on foreign stations without being fouled (or docked, and docks were often not available). Only the two iron-hulled ships were ordered, as HMS *Warrior* and HMS *Black Prince*.

77 Opinion of the 'late Board' (i.e.the 1861-66 Board) quoted by Robinson in his summary of PW 1866 and 1867 in ADM 1/5981, paper dated 8 August 1866. Robinson noted that opinion varied as to the viability, in

war, of the paddlers.

78 ADM 1/5891, document dated 20 September 1864.

79 The first two ships of the class, *Ranger* and *Espoir*, were built by Deptford and Pembroke under PW 1857. They displaced 570 tons and were powered by an 80 NHP engine; they mounted one 68pdr, two 24pdr howitzers, and two 20pdr breech-loaders. *Steady* made 11kts on 360 IHP, a typical performance. Unlike frigates, corvettes, and sloops, gun-vessels were often built by private yards.

80 *Roebuck* was built by J Scott Russell and completed by Deptford; dimensions given by Lyon and Winfield, 220-21, are 200ft (gun deck) x 30¼ft x 14½ft (868 40/94 tons burthen). The ships were powered by a single-screw 350 NHP engine (*Roebuck*: 1099 IHP for 11.4kts, which was typical). Armament was one 68pdr 95cwt and four 32pdr 25cwt.

81 ADM 1/6020, dated 3 December 1867, describes both the rationale for the class and the proposed follow-on *Blanche* class.

82 Data from Lyon and Winfield: 187ft (gun deck) x 36ft x 15ft 5in, 1061 tons burthen (displacement 1574 tons as designed; *Amazon* 1525 tons, and others varied). The engine was rated at 300 NHP (*Amazon*: 1455 IHP, 12.3kts). Armament was two 7in on centreline rotating slides (on racers) and two 64pdr 64cwt on broadsides. The two heavy guns could be moved to fire on either broadside. As rearmed with a single-calibre armament *Dryad*, *Nymphe*, and *Vestal* each had nine truck-mounted 64pdrs, including a bow chaser. There was no stern chaser, but ports were cut in the poop. *Daphne* received the bow gun but was considered too worn to be worth full rearmament. *Amazon* and *Naiad* were both lost before rearmament. Ballard, *Mariner's Mirror* 24, No1 of (1938) identifies 187ft as the length between perpendiculars.

83 Admiral G A Ballard, 'British Corvettes of 1875: The Larger Wooden Ram-Bowed Type', *Mariner's Mirror* 24, 1, (1938). Ballard attributes this design feature to Reed. His successor Barnaby abandoned it, according to Ballard (*Mariner's Mirror* 25, 1 of 1939) at the request of some members of the Board.

84 Surveyor's draft PW 1865 program in ADM 1/5941 (18 January 1865) shows no new construction at Portsmouth, but only the ship at Chatham.

85 Robinson's August 1866 summary of the steam fleet listed six ships building: *Nymphe*, *Daphne*, *Danae*, *Dryad*, *Blanche*, and *Sappho*. Names Robinson proposed in 1866 were *Spartan*, *Tenedos*, *Sirius*, *Dido*, *Prosperine*, and *Diomede*. Of these, *Proserpine* and *Diomede* were dropped as the program was cut to four such ships. The other four were *Blanche*s. The list did not include the follow-on *Briton* class.

86 Ships were completed with two 7in chasers on traversing slides and four 6.3in 64pdrs on the broadside, but the six guns were soon increased to eight, and ships were rearmed with twelve 64pdrs and rated as 12-gun corvettes in 1876.

87 ADM 1/5981, document dated 23 August 1866, reprinted for the 1871 Committee on Designs but considered too confidential to be included in their published report. This document differs from comments Robinson made (in principle describing it) before the 1871 Committee (Report of Committee on Designs, 316).

88 The accompanying Legend of the *Blanche* class showed dimensions of 212ft (pp), 185⅔ft (on the keel, for tonnage) x 36ft x 13½ft (fwd)/16½ft (aft), with a displacement of 1698 tons (1268 8/94 burthen); in his account of these ships, Ballard (*Mariner's Mirror* 24, No2 of 1938) gives a displacement of 1706 tons. The engine was rated at 350 NHP (2100 IHP); no estimated speed was given. The ship would carry 240 tons of coal, 3 weeks' water and 12 weeks' stores (17 tons). Armament listed in the Legend was two 7in 6½-ton and four 64pdr 64cwt, not the number indicated by Robinson in the accompanying submission. The Legend gave the complement as 140. Calculated weights added up to 1709 tons 18cwt rather than to the 1698 listed above. Ballard notes that in these ships the two revolving 7in guns were placed close together between funnel and mainmast, unlike the positions at the ends in the modified version, the *Briton* class. These guns could be run to fire on either broadside, between the ports for the 64pdrs. The 64pdrs (on trucks) were at two ports in the forward end of the waist, and two at ports on the quarterdeck. For bow or stern fire the guns were run forward or aft to ports cut in the topgallant forecastle or the poop. Before their second commission, fore and aft fire was of greater interest, and another pair of 64pdrs was added as permanent chasers, forward and aft. Then the 7in guns were eliminated, leaving the chasers plus ten 64pdrs on the broadside. That made a total of twelve 64pdrs Mk III (wrought-iron type) on trucks. The original complement of 180 had to be increased to 200. *Eclipse*, *Blanche*, *Danae*, and *Dido* all had single-expansion engines, but *Sirius* and *Spartan* had four-cylinder double expansion 'Allen Patent' engines – which proved uneconomical. *Tenedos* had a two-cylinder compound engine, which consumed nearly a third less coal. *Spartan* was re-engined; *Sirius* had insufficient boiler pressure to make conversion practicable. Propellers were non-hoisting, so that the ships could fire from stern ports. Attached to the file on the *Blanche* design was a Legend for a lengthened *Blanche* which became the *Briton* class: 220ft (pp), 193ft 6¼in (keel) x 36ft x 13ft 6in/16ft 6in, 1852 tons (1922 tons burthen), with the same engines, but this time estimated speed was given as 13kts. This Legend gave Robinson's armament of two 7in and eight 64pdr. Complement was given as 175. Weights added up to 1813 tons, so the displacement available offered a 19-ton surplus, in effect a margin. The *Briton*s (lengthened *Blanche*s) were initially armed with two 7in guns on slides (fore and aft) plus eight 6.3in 64pdr 71cwt on the broadside, but *Thetis* was completed with fourteen 6.3in 64pdr Mk III (two on traversing slides, twelve on the broadside).

89 Program details from a table showing unarmoured ships ordered since 1866, Committee on Designs, 328. It is assumed here that all the ships of a year's program were ordered that year. According to Ballard, 'British Corvettes

of 1875: The Larger Wooden Ram-Bowed Type', these ships had parallel midbodies extending over a greater proportion of their 220ft length than the later *Amethyst*s, which were known for their bulky midparts and short but fine entries and runs. Ballard reports that the *Briton*s rolled more uneasily than their successors, and yawed more in a following sea, behaviour he attributed to perhaps too light construction. *Briton* class dimensions: 220ft (pp) x 36ft x 12¾ft (fwd)/16¼ft (aft), 1322 ton burthen, 1860 tons displacement (Ballard claims 1874 tons for *Briton*). Rated power was 350 NHP; *Briton* made 13.1kts on 2149 IHP. As designed, armament was two 7in 112pdr (7½-ton) as bow and stern chasers plus eight 6.3in 64pdr 71cwt on the broadside. After their first commission *Briton* and *Druid* had their heavy chasers replaced by 64pdrs, the weight saved increasing the broadside to six 64pdr 71cwt Mk III on revolving slides. *Thetis* was built with the new armament.

90 ADM 1/5943, proposal dated 9 September 1865, for a ship to be built at Deptford (*Plover*). This file contains proposed names for fifteen of them. The file does not include the usual Legend (to which it refers). Design displacement was 774 tons; as completed they displaced 805. Dimensions as built: 170ft (gun deck) x 29ft x 6⅓ft to 10½ft, 663 tons burthen, 160 NHP (*Plover* 977 IHP, 11.3kts). Armament was two 40pdr 35cwt Armstrong breech-loader chasers plus one 7in 6½-ton muzzle-loader amidships.

91 Most of Robinson's memorandum was devoted to ironclads, because only they could deal with two of Robinson's three naval threats: invasion and the seizure of valuable posts, possessions, and colonies (cruisers answered the threat to trade). Despite the breakneck construction of the past few years, it still seemed that the British were barely ahead of the French. In addition to listing cruisers for trade protection, Robinson proposed a second-class ironclad to replace old wooden screw frigates on foreign stations. It became the belted cruiser described in a later chapter.

92 Data from Lyon and Winfield: 200ft (pp) x 40ft 4in x 16ft 7in (1459 tons burthen, displacement 2216 tons); they were powered by 400 NHP engines (*Thalia*: 1597 IHP for 11.1kts). The low speed alone would qualify them as obsolescent war vessels, but it was acceptable for transports. Armament matched that of the *Amazon*s: two 7in, four 64pdr 71cwt, but in 1876 they were rearmed. In both 64pdrs replaced the 7in guns, and *Juno* was given two more 64pdr. The Cover on Wooden Ships has a section devoted to this class, the initial Legend of which ('Screw Vessel Adapted for Carrying Troops') is dated 8 February 1866 (it was superseded by a second Legend on 16 February). An attached letter from Reed's assistant describes the initial sketch as an enlarged (hull weight 1298 rather than 1190 tons) *Clio* (*Pearl* class) with 275 tons of coal (Controller wanted 300). Speed was deduced from that of *Clio* and *Pearl*, 11kts. Calculations began with *Clio* lengthened 10ft to provide troop capacity. The Legend (hand-written, without a special Legend form) dated 21 February gives the final dimensions, except for draughts of 16ft 6in forward and 17ft 6in aft, and an estimated speed of 10¾kts on 400 NHP; coal capacity is given as 230 tons (5½ days at full speed, 11 days at ordinary cruising] speed). 'When 300 troops with their Baggage are received on board the ship will be immersed about 6in more than the draught given above.' Armament was given as two 6½-ton revolving guns and four 64pdr guns on slides and carriages, a total of 43 tons. Weights added up to 2145 tons, the drawing allowing for 2155 tons of displacement, offering a surplus (in effect a building margin) of 10 tons. A later Legend (rejected) showed 210ft (pp) x 42ft 6in x 16ft 6in (fwd)/17ft 6in aft, 1770 56/94 tons burthen, and a displacement of 2300 tons. The Cover includes a Legend form dated 17 May 1867, with the names of both *Juno* and *Thalia* on it, presumably reflecting the final 200ft design; weights totalled 2129½ tons, and displacement based on the lines plan was given as 2155 tons, so the surplus tonnage increased. A later sheet, probably dated about 1878, shows the armament of *Thalia* as eight 64pdr 64cwt guns Mk III on Mk III carriages with iron slides, plus landing guns.

93 ADM 1/5981, document dated 19 September 1866.

2. IRON HULLS

1 The design requirement was to maintain 15kts for 24 hours, ships being provided with 750 tons of coal. *Ammonoosuc* (later renamed *Iowa*), *Chatanooga*, *Idaho*, *Madawaska* (renamed *Tennessee*), *Neshaminy* (renamed *Arizona* and then *Nevada*), *Pompanoosuc* (later renamed *Connecticut*), and *Wampanoag* (renamed *Florida*). Only *Florida* (ex-*Wampanoag*) and *Iowa* (ex-*Ammonoosuc*) were considered successful on trial. Official reports credited both with average speeds of about 16¾kts. Florida was credited with maintaining this speed for 37½ hours. Captain Ward, the Britsh attaché, was sceptical, as the speed of the ship's propeller was only 15.9kts (the ship's speed by log was 16.6). Admiralty analysts in the Constructor's Department pointed out that four-bladed propellers of the type used sometimes exhibited *negative slip* (their italics). The ship's speed seemed high in comparison with British ships tested on a measured mile. Probably the actual trial speed was about 16kts (her apparent superiority over HMS *Inconstant* 'could not be accounted for on any scientific basis'). As of 1872, *Iowa* was laid up at Boston 'and is said not to be worth repair unless urgently needed'. Captain Ward reported that on trials *Tennessee* was badly strained and nearly lost. *Idaho* was so unsuccessful on trials that she was rebuilt as a rigged (unpowered) storeship. *Chatanooga* was damaged by ice after having been laid up after trials. *Nevada* twisted her hull on the slip; she was never completed. *Connecticut* was never launched. According to the official British report on US ships, as revised in 1872 (ADM 1/6271), only *Florida* and *Tennessee* were in good condition. The original armament of the *Florida* (*Wampanoag*) was ten 9in smooth-bores, three 60pdr

(5.3in) rifled guns, two 24pdr howitzers, and two 12pdr howitzers, but later it was increased to 23 guns. The ships were exceptionally long in proportion to beam, with unusually fine entrances and runs, and unusually light scantlings. Coal and machinery accounted for 84 per cent of the carrying capacity of the ship. Machinery took up so much space that coal had to be stowed on the berth deck. That limited the crew, hence limited the sail power the ship needed for cruising. According to the US Board on Steam Machinery Afloat 'no wooden vessel of war, of [*Florida*'s] great length and small proportionate depth, however well put together, can probably endure rough seas without evincing sooner than common, and perhaps much sooner, a palpable want of longitudinal rigidity; and the effect of this upon long shafts and their bearings would at least prove a source of perplexity and a detriment to steaming, to say nothing of other ill-consequences'. The British authors of the 1872 report found this view consistent with Royal Navy experience of long steam frigates such as HMS *Orlando*. By this time the US Navy clearly no longer valued such fast but lightly-built ships. That the four-bladed propeller needed to absorb the ship's enormous power could not be hoisted when she was under sail further limited sailing qualities. Later writers considered it reactionary to demand much sail power, but at the time a cruiser needed sail in order to remain at sea for a protracted period. The total of engines, boilers, etc in *Florida* was given as 1260 tons (about 30 per cent of the ship's displacement): about 5cwt per IHP, compared to about 3cwt in contemporary British cruisers such as *Inconstant*. The two successful ships had machinery designed by Chief Engineer Isherwood, who claimed that it was deliberately made heavy in order to withstand the stress of sustained steaming at very high speed. His supporters considered the Board on Steam Machinery Afloat a reactionary attempt to retain sail even after it was completely outmoded.

2 Unfortunately, no Cover has survived for *Inconstant* and her near-sisters. Reed's 24 April 1866 design report is reproduced on page 291 of the report of the *Committee Appointed by the Lords Commissioners of the Admiralty to Examine The Designs Upon Which Ships of War Have Recently Been Constructed* (Parliamentary Papers for 1872, XIV). The Committee on Designs was appointed to clear up the controversy surrounding the sinking of HMS *Captain*. It reviewed all other major British warships then being built, or recently built, and so included considerable material on HMS *Inconstant* and on HMS *Blonde* (*Shah*). Members included Rear Admiral Phipps Hornby, William Froude, the hydrodynamics expert, George Rendel, the engineer for Armstrong, and the shipbuilder Peter Denny. Among those giving evidence was Nathaniel Barnaby, then Assistant Chief Constructor (in Reed's absence effectively Chief Constructor). Robinson's 25 April 1866 comments are in ADM 1/5980. The Board Stamp approving the sketch design was dated 27 April. Robinson made the connection to the US threat explicit: fast cruisers would 'capture privateers, sweep small war ships from the seas, and meet on more than equal terms the enormous, but frail, new Corvettes of the American Navy; and I most sincerely wish we had a few more *Inconstant*s in progress.' N A M Rogers, 'The Design of the *Inconstant*', in *Mariner's Mirror* 61, No 9 (1975), argues that *Inconstant* was a nearly forgotten parallel to *Warrior*, reacting to USS *Wampanoag* in much the same way that *Warrior* reacted to the French *Gloire*.

3 Robinson's remarks are from a hand-written 17 November 1867 note in ADM 1/5982. Reed's are from his 24 April 1866 submission to Robinson. At this stage the dimensions were 333ft x 50ft x 23ft (22ft forward and 24ft aft). As built *Inconstant* was slightly larger: 337ft x 50ft 4in x 22ft (20ft 8in forward, 24ft 7in aft). The design incorporated the full battery of ten 12½-ton guns on the gun deck and four 6½- ton revolving bow and stern chasers on the upper deck. Given the small battery, the officers and crew might be berthed on the main deck (gun deck). The lower deck could be fitted for trooping, with a capacity of 500. Reed thought the ship might well exceed 15kts if the engineers could get six times the NHP out of the engines, but he did not want to guarantee more than that. Reed also prepared a design for a twin-screw ship drawing no more than 18ft, but he was unwilling to submit it until after the trials of the ironclad HMS *Penelope*, the only British ship ever to have twin hoisting screws.

4 Committee on Designs, 292. Captain Waddilove, commanding *Inconstant*, gave endurance figures. *Inconstant* was faster than any existing ironclad under sail or steam, but at full power she would have only 2¼ days' worth of coal, which he considered a very great disadvantage (and there was no space for more coal). According to the ship's calculations (not actual experience), at 200 tons a day, she would make 15.7kts in moderate weather. At that rate she would steam 1222 miles. At 70 tons per day she would steam for nine days at 10kts (2160nm); at 7.5kts, 23½ days; at 5kts, 43 days (burning coal for galley fires and for airing boilers would amount to about 3 days of the 43). These figures were all based on burning 3lb of coal per IHP per hour, which could require the best coal and the best stoking. On the measured mile, the ship attained 7700 IHP, which Waddilove calculated would require 240 tons of coal per day. Waddilove considered the lines of his ship the best yet for speed. Because she carried her consumables very much forward, as she burned her coal she came down by the stern, which interfered with her steadiness under sail. That did not matter, because, in his view, if in the presence of an enemy she would certainly have steam up, and she would never try to fight without steam. That would also be the case if she were in a dangerous situation, for example off land. Staying or wearing would not make much difference while making a passage under sail. Ballast (180 tons) was added after *Inconstant* rolled too easily in service.

5 ADM 1/5981 includes lists of names for ships Robinson proposed for the 1866-67 through 1868-69 programs. Those for three *Inconstant*s were *Ramillies*, *Raleigh*, and

Granicus. Names previously proposed but dropped for the first and last were *Cleopatra* and *Calypso*.

6 As the ship was designed, her dimensions were reduced from the initial 280ft × 44ft × 22ft (21ft fwd, 23ft aft) with 800 NHP engines and 500 tons of coal to 270ft × 42ft × 21ft (20ft fwd, 22ft aft) with 650 NHP engines and 450 tons of coal. An undated list of weights associated with the 270ft design totalled 3357 tons. Actual displacement was 3078 tons. A Legend dated February 1870 gave a displacement of 3080 tons. Estimated complement was 400, but in July 1874 *Volage* had a complement of 325, including an engine room establishment of 35 (including 21 stokers). Much of the complement was needed to handle the sails. Reed found the ship considerably larger than might have been expected (burthen, not displacement, 2250 rather than 2000 tons) due to the fineness (hence length) required to achieve the proposed very high speed of 15kts.

7 During the 1870s policy changed to favour uniform batteries. Reportedly the two ships were rearmed in 1873 with eighteen 64pdr 64cwt guns instead of the former mixed battery. During an 1879 Portsmouth refit *Volage* (and presumably her sister) had her truck carriages replaced by modern slide carriages. She then had two revolving Mk II iron carriages and sixteen Mk III steel broadside carriages. By 1880 each ship also had two Gatling guns and two Nordenfelts, with limbers for field use (but presumably also available at sea). In 1902 the two ships were considered as reliefs for the depot ship HMS *Urgent* at Jamica. By this time *Volage* had been disarmed, but *Active* had ten 6in BL plus smaller weapons. All were obsolete. The proposed armament of the relief ship was two 6in QFC on VCP mountings plus two 0.45-calibre Maxims (machine guns).

8 Report of Committee on Designs, 315, memorandum submitted by Robinson with enclosure on the design of HMS *Raleigh*. Robinson's discussion of Childers' intervention was in connection with the problems of designing a sufficiently small turret ship, the abortive HMS *Fury*.

9 ADM 1/6177, Robinson note on 'Differences in the designs of the Frigates *Raleigh* and *Blonde* from those of the *Inconstant*, also differences between the Design of the *Fury* and that of the *Devastation* and *Thunderer*', 9 February 1870. This file includes a Legend for *Blonde* and *Raleigh*.

10 ADM 1/5982 Robinson paper, 'New Designs for Ships' No 20, 1866, dated 17 November 1866. Reed signed the description of the design. The ship is described as a 'New Iron Corvette of the *Inconstant* Class sheathed with 8in of wood and of 1000 [N]HP'. Reed commented that the great length and other features of *Inconstant* made for particularly good internal arrangements despite her numerous crew (600 men).

11 As described by Reed in February 1870, the new frigate was considerably smaller (298ft × 48ft × 21½ft, 3190 burthen tons, 800 NHP, with 550 tons of coal, vs 337ft 4in × 50ft 4in × 23ft, 4066 burthen tons, 1000 NHP, with 680 tons of coal).

12 The letter to Controller proposing the increased beam was sent by Barnaby on 22 October 1870 (Committee on Designs, 293). By that time Reed had left the Admiralty, and Barnaby was acting in his place. In the Atlantic without ballast *Inconstant* remained upright while some ships 'were showing the whole of their decks'. To his 'extreme regret' the squadron commander considered 'that wonderful steadiness, which had been secured with so much pains, had been obtained by too great a sacrifice of stability'. He accepted that the next ship should be much stiffer. *Blonde* already incorporated 90 tons of ballast in her structure, and her beam had been increased by 4 inches. Increasing to 52ft would give her a little more stiffness without ballast than *Inconstant* had with the 180 tons. The ship would be able to carry 100 tons more coal, and would have practically the same speed. The change was approved. The date of the new armament is not clear from the report.

13 Dissenting report dated 14 October 1871, by Admiral George Elliot and Rear Admiral A P Ryder recommending a 6000-ton *Blonde* and a larger and faster (18-knot) modified *Blonde*. Of sixteen members of the Committee, only six were naval officers. There were numerous dissents in the adopted report by, among others, Admiral Stewart and Captain Hood (later First Naval Lord).

14 Like the *Amazon*s, they had bow and stern chasers and broadside guns, but by the time these ships were being built armament was single-calibre. They had fourteen broadside guns, all 64pdr 64cwt, except that the last two had 71cwt guns. On their second commission all had their truck-mounted broadside guns replaced by slide-mounted 64pdr of a lighter type, and all had their ship rigs replaced by barque rigs (*Encounter* had been barque-rigged from the outset). Unfortunately, there is no Cover for this class, nor does there seem to be any reference in the Surveyor correspondence in ADM 1.

15 In the *Opal* class Cover.

16 Dimensions: 220ft (pp) × 40ft × 16½ft (fwd)/18ft (aft), 1864 tons burthen, 2120 tons displacement. Armament was twelve 64pdrs, of which two 64cwt were pivoted chasers and ten 71cwt were on the broadside. The engine was rated at 350 NHP (*Opal* made 2187 IHP for 12.5kts). The planned battery of fourteen 64pdr 64cwt guns was apparently too heavy (*Opal* floated too deep) and it was reduced to twelve. This class seems to have introduced slide mountings for the 64pdrs (previously they had been used only for heavier calibres). The earlier truck mountings were secured with guns out; with slides the guns were secured inboard. *Emerald*, *Tourmaline*, and *Garnet* were later rearmed with breech-loaders. The first two had four 6in on broadside sponsons plus eight 5in, all on Vavasseur pivot mounts; the bow and stern chasers were eliminated. *Garnet* had fourteen 5in, two being mounted in each of the bow and stern in embrasures so that they could fire right forward or right aft. This battery was simpler to install and it was also lighter. However, it strained the bow and stern, which were already carrying more weight than they could support. According to

Ballard, who served in *Tourmaline*, these were remarkably steady gun platforms.

17 The class was to have been named *Magicienne*. That was the name on the July 1873 design report, and it was still being used as late as the spring of 1874. The name ship was renamed *Opal*. On 12 February 1873 Barnaby wrote to his assistant Mr. Dunn that he thought it likely that future corvettes of the *Encounter* class would be built with iron frames and wood planking 'like *Fantome*' (composite screw sloop). That did not apply to the two ships to be built that year at Sheerness and Devonport, *Diamond* and *Sapphire*. This was the origin of the *Emerald* class. About the beginning of June 1873 Barnaby ordered the ship broadened to 40ft, compared to 37ft for the previous class. The ends were fined so that displacement did not exceed that of the previous class (*Modeste*). After a model was tank-tested, Barnaby ordered the rounding of the lines reduced as much as possible in the wake of the engines and boilers at the after end of the engine room, and the fore end of the boiler room. To do that while retaining the same displacement, he increased mean draught 6in, keeping the engines and boilers where they were in the water. Displacement would be removed from the fore part of the ship, fining the entry. The lines had to be made somewhat fuller to provide for the heavier (because beamier) hull. Keeping the same upper deck as in the previous class made for excessive overhang at the bow, so the foremast, gun, and other items were all brought 5ft aft and the upper deck made narrower at the bow. The two alternative after gun arrangements were (i) a 64pdr on a revolving (presumably slide) mounting with the side recessed and (ii) two 64pdrs on truck carriages with the deck filled out. Barnaby preferred (and Controller approved) (i). A Legend was dated July 1873, weights being those for the previous *Modeste*. Dimensions at this stage were 220ft (pp) x 40ft x 15½ft (fwd)/16¼ft (aft), for a displacement of 1864 tons. Rated power was 350 NHP (2100 IHP) for an estimated speed of 13kts, and 240 tons of coal were to be carried. Armament was two 64pdr 64cwt guns (71cwt crossed out) in revolving mountings at the ends and ten (twelve crossed out) 64pdr on slides on the broadside. Complement was 220. Unfortunately the Cover for the *Fantome* class, which would have explained Barnaby's initial interest in composite construction, has been lost.

18 Admiral G A Ballard, 'British Corvettes of 1875: The Six Composite Sisters', *Mariner's Mirror* 23, No 2 (1937) saw these ships as an experiment, given so unusual a hull form, but the Cover makes it clear that it was a logical result of the tank tests.

19 According to Ballard, after the Pacific squadron encountered a strong head gale the fleet commander said that *Opal* behaved better lying-to than any ship he had ever seen. The Commodore on the Cape considered *Tourmaline* remarkably free of yaw when scudding through a violent quartering sea. The only complaint was that they could not steam fast against a heavy sea, because they pitched their bows under and made no headway (presumably due to their excessively fine entry). They behaved better in a heavy sea under sail than under steam, but in ordinary weather they were equally handy under either, and Ballard credited them with the smallest turning circles of any ships of their tonnage. He was in *Tourmaline* when she beat into Hong Kong harbour through a crowd of merchant ships.

20 According to Admiral Ballard, 'The Unarmoured Branches of the British Navy of 1875', 263, this armament arrangement was controversial. The guns could be fired through ports in the bulwarks on either side of the ship. Critics objected that traversing from one side to the other would take too long. Advocates pointed to the action between the US steam sloop *Kearsage* and the Confederate *Alabama*, both of which fought to the finish without changing engaged sides. This type of mounting had been introduced in Crimean War gunboats. Given the traversing mountings, although a *Cormorant* had only six guns, four of them could be fired on either side, including a pair of 7in whose weight of metal was nearly twice that of any single gun on board a corvette (except for the five large ones). These ships had nearly the same broadside as ships double their size – 432lb vs 448lb for *Emerald*.

3. THE FIRST ARMOURED CRUISERS

1 Robinson described the ships in his evidence to the Committee on Designs.

2 This referred to HMS *Alexandra*, originally laid down as HMS *Superb* and renamed in March 1874. The ship later named *Superb* was bought from Turkey during the Russian war scare in 1878.

3 A table of calculated coal endurance was sent to First Lord on 21 April 1875:

	Ordinary (280 tons)	Increased (500 tons)
Full Speed	4½ days 1242nm	8 days 2208nm
10kts	7⅓ days 1760nm	13 days 3120nm
6kts	19½ days 2800nm	34¾ days 5004nm

4 According to Oscar Parkes, *British Battleships* (London: Seeley, Service, 1957), 237, *Shannon* was complete in July 1876, but was kept in the dockyard for a year while she was modified. Six 20pdr guns were mounted, she was fitted to fire torpedoes, conning tower armour was increased, a considerable deck structure was built up around the conning tower for boat stowage, armour glacis plates around the lower deck hatches were thickened, and some additional heavy fittings were added. Coal capacity was increased, according to Parkes, from 280 to 470 tons. Complement was increased from 330 to 450. Like many other ships of the time, she was overweight as completed, drawing a foot too much in 1876, and more when recommissioned in September 1877.

5 According to Parkes, *British Battleships*, 241, the ship was designed specially to attack in this way. Once the entire broadside had been fired by director, the ship would turn bows-on, reload, and approach again. Such tactics were suited only to duels – which is exactly what was expected

of a ship on a distant station, facing another second-class ironclad.

6 Unfortunately the Cover for this class is missing, so it is not clear exactly how and why the *Shannon* design was changed. This brief description is from Parkes, *British Battleships*, who reportedly had access to official material for ships built before 1905.

7 ADM 1/6012. Robinson was appointed commissioner for the exhibition, in charge of Admiralty exhibits. Robinson invited chief French constructor Dupuy de Lôme to see the models of British ships. De Lôme's was apparently very critical of an early version of HMS *Captain* (but was favourably impressed by a model of HMS *Inconstant* 'and he said much in her favour – and in favour of powerful and rapid unarmoured ships'. To Robinson, the most interesting part of the exhibition was the case of beautifully made models of French ironclads, which proved that data provided by attaché Captain Hore RN was complete and accurate. A model of the new battleship *Marengo* showed that the 14-ton breech-loader atop the barbette was completely exposed, with a platform at the breech end allowing the loaders to be sheltered by the gun itself. The rest of the gun crew was sheltered below by the armoured tower. That placed the gun unusually high, 23ft above water. Much of the rigging was carried through the lower part of the tower, the lower masts being unusually short and stout. Robinson saw the completed engines of the *Marengo*, which he considered needlessly heavy. Nor was he impressed with her armoured wooden hull. Because the hull could not be rigid enough at speed, two universal joints allowed her propeller shaft to flex while turning.

8 The decision to place heavier guns in barbettes may have been taken somewhat earlier. The Cover includes a 24 November 1880 request from Barnaby to White to calculate the power needed to get 16kts in a *Shannon*, and then to compare her with a similar ship armed with four 9in 18-ton BL in four barbettes (8in armour) and eight 6in on the main deck. A 24 November sketch in the Cover shows a ship with four barbettes, two each side by side, rather than the arrangement later adopted. There were two funnels. The Cover does not include any sketch of the final arrangement.

9 DNO decided that both of the after 6in guns should be fought only on the broadside, but that the single forward gun should have an alternative port, so that it could fire right ahead. Later DNO wanted to mount a gun at each port, which meant four on each side. Controller approved adding the guns if that were possible. The ships were completed with six 6in, but by 1892 they had ten.

10 As described in the Legend, the belt was 10in thick with 10in wood backing, closed at the ends by 9in bulkheads with 10in backing. The belt extended 5ft below and 3ft above the waterline. It was covered by a 1½in deck in two thicknesses, a slight retreat from *Nelson*, with the same 3in deck fore and aft, 5ft below the waterline. The barbettes were 8in thick, and the ship would have a 9in conning tower.

4. FAST STEEL CRUISERS

1 File on *Cormorant* class in the *Active* and *Mutine* Cover (71).

2 The first Legend in the Cover is dated 25 April 1876: 225ft (pp) x 44ft 6in x 17ft (fwd)/18ft 6in (aft), 2383 tons, with 2300 IHP and 280 tons of coal (capacity 380). Armament shown is the two 90cwt revolving guns at the ends and twelve 64pdrs on the broadside, in slides. No protective deck is indicated. A Legend dated May 1876 carries the names of the first group of six ships. In this one the ship is beamier (44ft 6in) and draws the same amount of water; displacement is 2394 tons. Armament is the same, and the deck is not indicated (the Legend form includes deck armour). A new Legend dated 1 February 1877 gave a displacement of 2383 tons and a normal coal capacity of 270 tons. It mentions the lifting screw in *Comus*, *Champion*, *Curacoa*, *Cleopatra*, and *Conquest*. The Cover includes a comparative Legend (USS *Trenton* vs HMS *Comus* and *Volage*) dated 16 June 1879. *Trenton* was credited with eleven 8in breech-loaders on two decks. In fact she had muzzle-loaders.

3 Unfortunately it has proven impossible to say for sure what the armament of these ships was when completed, due to the absence of key documents prior to 1887. The statement about *Comus* is based on a 10 December 1882 photo (in San Francisco) in the National Maritime Museum collection taken prior to 1886, clearly not showing any sponsons for 6in guns. The Cover includes details of an 1886 inclining experiment at Sheerness, conducted after she was refitted for service on the North America and West Indies station; she probably received her 6in guns at that time. The Cover is silent as to changes in armament, beyond arguments about the original muzzle-loading battery. The 1881 Legend showing the 6in battery for *Canada* and *Cordelia* compares them to *Constance*, which is shown with the earlier battery. Photos of *Cordelia* show two forward sponsons plus three ports in the side of the ship; it is not clear where the other two 6in were. The Cover includes an 1883 handbook for the 6in Vavasseur central pivot mounting in the two ships, which suggests but does not prove that they may have been the first of the class with 6in guns.

4 By 1895 both were in Category (D) dockyard reserve, and they were sold in 1899.

5 The *Cormorant* (*Osprey*) class was a very different 1130-tonner armed with two 70pdr chasers and four 64pdr. *Wild Swan* and *Pelican* of this class were rearmed with two 6in and six 5in breech-loaders. The fastest, *Pelican*, developed 1056 IHP on trials (12.24kts), and thus approached the performance of the *Satellite* class.

6 200ft x 38ft x 12¾ft (fwd)/15¾ft (aft), 1420 tons, with a 950 IHP engine for about 11kts. Armament was eight 6in and two Gatling guns.

7 The Cover is silent as to the reason for the change to 5in guns. The two 6in were in sponsons which provided fore and aft fire.

8 Data are taken from a Legend dated 4 November 1882,

9 The 15 April 1880 Legend actually showed 5000 IHP, the reduction from 7000 IHP corresponding to a reduction in machinery weight from 1032 to 800 tons. Some of the weight went into a stronger hull (1475 vice 1450 tons), and armament weight increased to 168 tons. Displacement therefore slightly increased, to 3748 vice 3735 tons.

10 Details of the competition are in the Cover for 'New Enchantress', Enchantress being the Admiralty yacht intended as a wartime despatch boat. Work was underway by December 1880. The Board killed the Admiralty yacht project about mid-February 1881 in favour of a conventional Despatch Vessel. By that time there was interest in providing a cruiser armament: 40pdr chasers bow and stern and four 64pdr on the broadside. Enchantress herself had only one 40pdr and one 9pdr, so this would have been a considerable change. A Legend for a 16-knot Despatch Vessel for General Service was dated April 1881: 300ft × 33ft × 12ft 9in/13ft 8ft (1675 tons), requiring 2500 IHP to make 16kts. The design seems to have been scaled up from the much slower gun-vessel *Lily*. A Legend dated 17 October 1882 gave details of the revived Admiralty design: 260ft × 32ft × 16ft (extreme), 1560 tons, with 2200 IHP engines for 15kts, and 300 tons of coal. Complement when unarmed would be 60, and when armed it would be 100. This ship was larger than the despatch vessel designed in 1883, but the two designs were probably related. The 30 May 1881 circular requesting bids called for a steel hull, twin screws, a trial speed of 16kts, and enough coal for six days at full speed. Armament was not to be included in the calculations, but ships would be armed with one or two light guns. Metacentric height was also specified. The letter went to twelve firms: Laird, Barrow, Elder*, A and J Inglis**, Denny, Saunders*, Napier**, Harland and Wolff**, J and G Thompson*, Thames Ironworks*, and Palmer*, of which the single-starred firms declined to tender and the tenders from the double-starred firms were not considered acceptable. A parallel Admiralty design may have fed into the later projects for torpedo cruisers.

11 A Legend dated 23 May 1882 in the *Mersey* Cover gives dimensions of 300ft × 44ft × 15ft 6in/19ft 6in and a displacement (weights added up) of 3150 tons. Power was given as 2800 IHP with natural draught and 3600 with forced draught, the ship making 16kts with forced draught. Freeboard would have been 14ft forward and 12ft 9in aft. Apparently the power estimate was grossly optimistic, because a new Legend dated 28 June showed 4500 IHP at forced draught for 16¾kts. In this version the ship's rig was reduced to a signal pole and a derrick. Machinery weight was increased from 550 tons (including engineers' stores) to 580 tons. Armament weight was about that of the original *Iris*, 112 tons.

12 The Legend gave dimensions of 276ft × 42ft × 18ft 6ft. Power was 3800 IHP at natural and 5500 IHP at forced draught. The deck was 1½in thick, with ¾in over the steering gear. On trials in 1885, *Bausan* actually made 17.4kts on 6470 IHP.

13 White's memo reporting these decisions was undated, but a copy was marked 8 July 1882. The decisions seem to have been to place the 6in guns of the torpedo ship in sponsons (or on the upper deck), and to place the 6in guns of the heavy-gun ship between the heavy guns, on the middle deck amidships. This was the arrangement Armstrong chose for *Bausan*. Although no follow-on *Calliope* would be built, the board envisaged a follow-on to the smaller corvette (at that time considered a sloop) *Satellite* with forced draught and larger engines. It and an improved *Wanderer* would be built by contract. The next sloop was actually the somewhat smaller *Nymphe* (1140 tons).

14 Rendel emphasized that cruiser shells would be hitting an ironclad at an oblique angle, considerably reducing the value of hits compared to theoretical figures.

15 Northbrook's list of six main priorities is, remarkably, buried in the series of precis of torpedo vessel papers in the Cover for the *Scout* and *Fearless* class torpedo cruisers. The other three priority projects were, in order: to properly equip and fit out the first-class torpedo boats; to conduct experiments to settle torpedo tube design; and to modernize the armaments of the *Raleigh* class and the other unarmoured ships. The conversion project for early long-hull ironclads seems to have involved re-engining them and double-screwing.

16 Hall's report included in the list of second-class armourclads then under construction not only *Imperieuse* and *Warspite*, which were later counted as armoured cruisers, but also *Conqueror*, always counted as a battleship. She was considerably smaller than the two armoured cruisers. Counting the two incomplete armoured cruisers, the seven *Orlando*s met Hall's requirement for nine such ships. The *Orlando* Ship's Cover does *not* mention Hall's analysis, but it is difficult not to notice the coincidence in numbers required.

17 A 15 June 1884 Legend compared New *Mersey* to *Mersey*. Dimensions of New *Mersey* were given as 350ft × 50ft × 19ft 6in (mean), with a complement of 350 rather than 300. Endurance would have been the same, 8000nm at 10kts or 12,000nm with full bunkers, both ships having the same 6000 IHP engines rated at 17kts. The deck would have weighed 715 tons (armour would have totalled 740), compared to 450 for *Mersey*. It included a 2in glacis around the cylinder heads.

18 Rendel wrote that a 6in belt would have been equivalent to the 3in slopes of the *Mersey*s, but it was considered insufficient. Armour weight including the conning tower rose from 450 to 880 tons. Having designed the world's most famous export protected cruisers, Rendel had particular insight into the change from deck to side protection. His *Esmeralda* had her entire deck underwater; the *Mersey* decks rose well above the water on the centreline. The underwater deck was almost impossible to hit from the side, but shot could rip up a ship's waterline unimpeded. To limit the effect of such

damage, *Esmeralda* used cork (to exclude water) and coal (as side protection). The deck in *Mersey* could be penetrated by a shot passing through the ship above water. Rendel refused to assign definite values to the two alternatives, preferring to say that the greater the resistance of the deck, the greater the safety of a ship protected like a *Mersey*, and that the new ship with her thick belt must be more secure against sinking or capsizing than *Esmeralda*. He proposed substituting it for New *Mersey* and buying an *Esmeralda* for trials.

19 Power was later considerably increased. A Legend dated 25 February 1885 showed 4500 IHP at natural draught but 8000 or 8500 IHP at forced draught, for a speed of 17½kts. Displacement was given as 5000 tons. On trial HMS *Orlando* made 19.1kts under forced draught, compared to a designed speed of 18kts. The constructor on board found her remarkably free of vibration. She also made remarkably little 'commotion' in the water.

20 Peter Brook, *Warships for Export: Armstrong Warships 1867-1927* (Gravesend: World Ship Society, 1999).

21 A first version was probably completed late in November (White called for modifications in a 26 November letter to his assistant Cotrell). The design was probably submitted in December 1885. Unfortunately S.10454/1885, the outline design for the new protected cruiser, page 36 of the *Medea* class Cover, is undated. The Cover is marked '20 knot protected cruiser', but the maximum trial speed referred to inside is 19kts.

22 When being prepared, the design was apparently criticized for its light armament compared to that of HMS *Comus*, which had four 6in BLR and eight 64pdr MLR. White replied that his ship's six 6in BLR were more powerful than the 64pdrs.

23 White was referring to the Japanese cruisers *Naniwa* and *Takachiho*, which were credited with 18.77kts on trial, and to the Austrian torpedo cruisers *Panther* and *Leopard*, rated at 18kts. He based his estimates of the steaming qualities of the new ship on the recent trials of the *Panther*. The Austrian ships failed to make the expected speed of 19kts, but Austrian navy constructor Siegfried Popper thought that they would have done so had better stokers been employed on trials. White's even faster Italian cruiser *Dogali* (rated at 19.5kts) had not yet been completed. White had also designed two fast (18-knot) cruisers for China, *Chih Yuan* and *Ching Yuan*, which made 18.5kts on trial under forced draught. In his late 1885 description of the new design, White added that 'a vessel of very similar character' was now well advanced at Elswick; he suggested simply buying it. He presumably had in mind the 2050-ton Italian cruiser *Dogali*, laid down as a stock ship, i.e., without any particular buyer in mind. The Greeks offered to buy her, and she was launched under the Greek name *Salaminia*, but they withdrew (hence she was available for purchase late in 1885). DNO (Captain J O Hopkins) also wanted the Admiralty to buy her. The Turks then made an offer, but they also withdrew. The ship ran trials as *Salaminia*, and was bought by Italy in January 1887, initially as *Angelo Eno*, but then as *Dogali*. She appears to have been the first stock cruiser built by Armstrong.

24 The original undated Legend showed dimensions of 250ft (267ft overall) x 37ft x 13ft (fwd)/16ft (aft), with a normal load of 200 tons of coal (capacity 486 tons). White's modifications are reflected in an 8 December 1885 Legend. Dimensions were 260ft (between perpendiculars) x 37ft x 13ft 6in /16ft 6in, for a displacement of 2280 tons (2248 tons by lines), compared to 2070 for the earlier version (weights totalled 2018 tons). Armament weight increased from 135 to 175 tons. In the revised drawing the edge of the protective deck at the waterline was 3½ft rather than 3ft below water, the deck being arched to rise well out above water amidships.

25 The first sketch showed four tubes in two torpedo rooms. White asked his assistant to add a third torpedo room forward of the boilers.

26 Comprising 1 Chief Engineer, 3 Engineers, 1 Chief ERA (Engine Room Artificer), 7 ERAs, 1 chief stoker, 10 leading stokers, and 48 stokers.

27 The January Legend called for a 265ft x 38ft x 13ft 9in/16ft 3in hull. The September version, presented as a faster alternative design, was 265ft x 39ft x 13ft 7in/16ft 3in, 2413 tons. Armament weight was cut from 175 to 170 tons; machinery weighed 630 rather than 600 tons. The hull was expected to weigh 970 rather than 950 tons. The figures given above are displacement from drawings; totals of estimated weights were 2411 tons for September and 2298 tons for January. A Legend dated 23 October 1886 showed a beamier hull: 265ft x 41ft x 15ft 2in/17ft 8in, 2780 tons, to make 19.5kts on 9000 IHP. Normal coal capacity was 400 tons.

28 White provided 200 rounds per 6in and 300 per 4.7in, the maximum he could fit in. The previous standard had been 85 rounds per gun. DNO (Captain Fisher) wanted the same number of rounds for each gun, considering that the end 6in guns would be chasers also capable of broadside fire.

29 It was dated 3 September 1888. Proposed dimensions were 285ft x 42ft x 15ft 6in/17ft 6in, displacement rising from 2800 to 3100 tons. In addition to the 6in and 4.7in guns, the ship would have eight 3pdr QF (anti-torpedo guns), two 0.45-calibre Nordenfelts, and four rather than six torpedo tubes (but the same 12 torpedoes). The longer hull required a longer, hence heavier, protective deck (245 rather than 220 tons), and the hull was somewhat heavier. As in *Medea*, there was 5in vertical armour around the cylinder heads, amounting to 100 tons. Calculated weights added up to 2982 tons, but this time White had to include a 4 per cent Board Margin (118 tons), giving a total of 3100. Further calculation showed that the ship had to be yet longer (290ft in a Legend dated 20 September), adding more armour (the deck was now 275 tons), and increasing displacement to 3200 tons (including a 123-ton margin).

30 A new Legend dated 18 December 1888 gave dimensions of 300ft x 43ft x 15ft 6in/17ft 6in and a displacement of 3420 tons, including 130 tons of Board Margin. Chatham figures, presumably reflecting the detailed design, showed 3610 tons (3470 plus 120-ton Board Margin). Power and

speed were still as in *Medea*, 9000 IHP for 20kts. The 200 extra tons in the Chatham figures were for wood and copper sheathing. In theory that would cost ⅙kt, but White was confident that the ship would still attain 20kts. At some point machinery weight increased 55 tons due to adoption of heavier boilers, for better steaming endurance.

31 The problem was insufficient space between gun and conning tower. Shell and powder were rammed separately in a BL gun, but as a single package in a QF gun. This long package had to be rammed from further back. At least 4ft was needed, but breech and conning tower were only 3ft 6in apart. The gun could not be loaded over a 20-degree arc to either side of dead ahead.

32 White referred to recent criticism of the wetness of *Medea* class due to their moderate freeboard and low bulwarks amidships. White claimed that he had proposed a completely flush-decked ship eight years ago (1882). Describing the *Astraea* class at the time the *Talbot* design was being offered, White emphasized the increased internal volume. For example, an *Apollo* might carry additional coal on deck, but she could not carry more than 550 tons internally. Nor could she carry anyone in addition to her normal complement. *Astraea* could carry 1000 tons of coal internally (giving her about twice the endurance) and she had much more capacious living quarters – so much so that some ships had been fitted as flagships for foreign stations.

33 Eight single-ended boilers instead of three double-ended and two single-ended.

34 A Legend dated 30 December 1889 showed dimensions of 320ft × 46ft 8 × 16ft 10in/18ft 10in and 4150 rather than 3600 tons. With the same powerplant, the ship would make 19½kts at forced draught, compared to 19¾kts for the *Apollo* as then planned. At natural draught she would make 18 to 18½kts compared to the 18½kts promised for an *Apollo*. Part of the protective deck was thickened to 2in on the flat and 3in on the slope; the weight of deck armour increased from 275 to 400 tons. By the time the design was complete, beam had been increased again, so that dimensions given in a Legend dated April 1890 were 320ft × 49ft 6in × 18ft/20ft (4360 tons). Deck armour now weighed 440 tons, and machinery weighed 740, compared to 630 for an *Apollo*. Weights added up to 4195 tons, plus a Board Margin of 165.

35 Captain Fitzgerald (Pembroke Dockyard) complained to Controller (Fisher) that the bow torpedo tube was '*downright poison* (and reduces the value of the ships for their legitimate duties by 25 per cent)'. It threw up so much water that the forepart of the ship was 'enveloped in hard-driving foam and spray [thrown up by the flat shutter of the bow tube], wet and very blinding'. It was impossible to work the forward 6in gun at all well. 'You will not find three captains on the active list who would go into action with a live torpedo in their bow tube, and not one that would fire it, if the ship was going more than five knots.' Fisher found no records of such complaints, but he also pointed out that the latest ships did not have bow tubes. Fitzgerald might be told that although nearly a hundred ships had bow tubes, its omission in later ships showed that the Admiralty was aware of the problem. If the two ships of the *Astraea* class found their bow tubes a nuisance in the upcoming manoeuvres, the issue would be revisited.

36 An undated Legend for New *Astraea* showed dimensions of 350ft × 52ft 6in × 19ft 3in/21ft 3in (5490 tons including 210 tons of Board Margin); *Astraea* was 320ft × 49ft 6in × 18ft 0in/20ft 0in (4360 tons). Complement was 330 compared to 299 for *Astraea* and 253 for *Apollo*, both figures up considerably since conception. Conning tower armour was increased from 3in to 6in, and the slopes of the protective deck from 2in to 3in (the 5in armour around the cylinders did not change). Deck armour now amounted to 500 tons, compared to 315 in *Astraea* and 275 in *Apollo*. A later but still undated Legend showed a foot more beam and a displacement of 5600 tons including Board Margin. Another Legend, apparently from January 1894, showed 350ft × 55ft × 19ft 6in/21ft 6in (5750 tons).

37 *Olympia* was the fastest of the lot, credited with 20kts under forced draught at 10,500 IHP. She was not sheathed or coppered. Had his new cruiser similarly not been burdened, she would have displaced 456 tons less, and would have gained half a knot. *Olympia* had very inferior (i.e., cramped) machinery spaces, and much less space for magazines and stores; she probably had fewer rounds per gun. She did have slightly heavier scantlings than *Talbot*, but the latter's sheathing would make up for that. She also had the only heavy guns in the group, four 8in (plus 5in guns which the British thought were quick-firers). The French ships were *Chasseloup-Laubat* and *Descartes*. White admitted that the French had saved considerable weight by adopting water-tube boilers, but he added that they had far less coal stowage. An attached sheet described an unnamed ship: 390ft (400 on the waterline) × 58ft × 23ft (7400 tons), producing 23,000 IHP at forced draught (23kts) or 20,000 at natural draught (21kts), with 750 tons of coal (2000 maximum). She had 8 double-ended and 2 single-ended boilers working at 160psi, which was high for the time. Three sets of engines drove three screws. The deck was 2½in on the flat and 4in on the slope. Armament was one 8in, two 6in, and lesser weapons. These data approximated the US Navy's *Columbia* and *Minneapolis*.

38 A Legend produced at about this time showed the same length as a *Talbot*, but 6 inches more beam (54ft rather than 53ft 6in), in both cases over sheathing, and draught of 19ft 6in fwd/21ft 6in aft rather than 17ft 10in forward/22ft aft. Freeboard was 9 inches less forward. Displacement was given as 5600 instead of 5420 tons. Complement was given as 470 rather than 436. Machinery weight was 870 rather than 940 tons, but armament weighed 465 rather than 365 tons. The new cruiser, unlike *Talbot*, had fighting tops on her masts. A later Legend (2 September 1896) compared the new ship to HMS *Juno*, which had the same wider beam (54ft) and displaced 5600 tons. She had a complement of 450.

39 A Legend produced at this time showed dimensions of

355ft 0in x 56ft 0in x 19ft 6in/21ft 6in (5950 tons). Machinery weight was given as 1100 tons. The hull form had not yet been tank-tested. Early in March 1900 alternative boiler arrangements were listed: two alternative Belleville 13,000 IHP arrangements, Belleville 12,500 IHP, B&W (Babcock & Wilcox) 11,850 IHP and B&W 13,000 IHP. Each arrangement showed three boiler rooms. The B&W designs all required greater length, e.g. the 13,000 IHP version had a 36ft forward boiler room and two 36ft 6in rooms. To get the same power Belleville needed three 33ft rooms. Controller favoured limiting power to 12,500 IHP rather than have an inconvenient arrangement of engine and boiler rooms. A Legend dated 9 April 1900 compared the new ship with both *Talbot* and the follow-on *Hermes* as completed. Dimensions were given as 355ft x 56ft x 19ft 3in/21ft 2in (5880 tons), the Board Margin being only 50 tons. Machinery of the Belleville and B&W alternatives was, respectively, 1060 and 1160 tons. The extra weight of the B&W plant was balanced by reducing the normal coal load from 600 to 500 tons. Complement was 490 rather than the 470 of *Hermes*.

40 Early in May DNO (Captain William May) argued for an extra gun forward to fire from right ahead to 30 degrees abaft the beam. If the quarterdeck guns were moved close enough together, the two after broadside guns could be given arcs extending to right astern. DNC offered twin mounts at both ends (such mountings would soon be incorporated in the 'County' class armoured cruisers). If the guns were concentrated on the centreline, the broadside guns might be placed in sponsons, giving them wider arcs. The change was feasible: the gun, additional ammunition, and additional crew would consume most of the remaining margin, and it would be necessary to sacrifice coal to provide a larger ammunition passage. Controller (Admiral A K Wilson, later First Sea Lord) decided in May to reject the extra gun forward on grounds not only of weight and extra crew, but also of the loss of coal to provide the necessary ammunition passage, but the episode probably planted the idea of twin 6in mounts in DNC's mind.

41 This change is *not* reflected in the Cover, but it is indicated in the official handbook *Steamships of England*.

5. THE TORPEDO AND SMALL CRUISERS

1 Not everyone was as enthusiastic. Controller (Captain Tryon) doubted that such a ship could get within torpedo range of a battleship armed with '2 to 4 monster guns, 8 to 10 auxiliary guns, and powerful machine guns'. She would not be so much more manoeuvreable than a battleship to be able to place herself in position to attack. He particularly doubted the value of a bow torpedo tube, which would slow a ship and might endanger her. Torpedo range was only 500yds, and at 15kts a ship would cover that in a minute. Advancing bow to bow against another ship, she might have less than 30 seconds to fire. It was also unlikely that she would be able to fire at a ship overtaking her from astern. Even so, a prototype would be worthwhile. First Lord Northbrook objected that any large torpedo vessel would herself be vulnerable to torpedoes, whereas shallow-draught torpedo boats were not. However, he too agreed that it would be worthwhile to build a prototype. Any new torpedo vessel should be usable as a peacetime cruiser: she should carry at least one gun and be capable of keeping the sea continuously in all weather. This seems to have been a reference to the proposed use of small corvettes like the *Calypso*s as torpedo vessels in wartime.

2 Page 11 of the Cover, marked 'Rendel,' shows data for the torpedo cruiser design dated 25 April 1883 alongside data for the Despatch Vessel design dated 25 July 1883. Both had the same length and beam, but the despatch vessel displaced 1320 rather than 1420 tons, and had 2200 rather than 2800 IHP engines, for a speed of 15 rather than 16kts. Both had a bunker capacity of 250 tons, and an ultimate capacity of 400 tons of coal using passages, but normal capacity (as reflected in displacement at which the ship ran trials) was 160 tons for the cruiser and 170 for the despatch vessel. With full capacity both ships were expected to steam 3500nm at 10kts, and with ultimate capacity 6000nm at 10kts. The main difference was in armament: 60 tons for the cruiser, 1 ton for the despatch vessel. As a consequence, the cruiser complement was 120, compared to 60 for the despatch vessel. Both had the same protection.

3 The first Legend in the Cover for the *Scout* and *Fearless* class torpedo cruisers shows dimensions of 220ft x 33ft x 12ft 6in/14ft 6in (1356 tons, with 1380 crossed out). Armament was two 5in guns (105 rounds each), 8 Nordenfelt and 2 Gardner machine guns, and 20 torpedoes (tubes were not specified). Expected speed was 16kts, like that of the new larger cruisers. A second legend for a 'Twin Screw Torpedo Cruiser' was dated 31 August 1883. The ship now had a foot more beam and 10 tons more displacement, and she was expected to need 3200 IHP to make her speed. She was now credited with only 12 torpedoes. She was expected to carry 300 tons of coal (later given as full capacity, with 170 tons as the normal load). This was the final design.

4 For example, the proof copy of the information for bidders was dated November 1883. The initial Legend in the Cover was dated July 1883. It showed virtually no armament (1 ton armament weight), the theory presumably being that at 16kts she could outrun heavy pursuers, beating off any fast light craft with her machine guns. On trials the despatch vessel *Surprise* made 17.65kts on 3027 IHP, compared to 17.38kts on 3441 IHP for the torpedo cruiser *Scout*.

5 When the ships were approved, tentative armament was two 5in and four torpedo tubes, two firing along the centreline and two on the broadside.

6 ADM 1/7254, 'Type and Armament of Ships Required for H.M. Navy (from 1880-1890).'

7 At this stage dimensions were 225ft x 36ft 9in x 13ft 6in (1630 tons); she was expected to make 16kts on 3500 IHP. Expected endurance was 7000nm at 10kts, as in *Scout*.

The final design (May 1886) showed slightly less beam (36ft) and displacement (1621 tons) and more powerful engines (4000 IHP) for higher speed (17.5kts).

8 An undated Legend compared the new design with those of *Swallow* and the torpedo cruiser *Scout*. At this stage the new ship had three 5in guns. The new ship was about the same length as *Swallow*, which was 195ft long. Dimensions were 195ft x 28ft x 11ft/12ft (735 tons); power was 850 IHP at natural and 1200 IHP at forced draught, something less than half of the output of the torpedo cruiser, and a bit less than that of HMS *Swallow* (1028 tons, 1000/1500 IHP). Estimated speed with forced draught was 14kts (12½kts with natural draught), which was half a knot faster (at forced draught) than that of the larger *Swallow* (which was credited with 11½ to 11¾kts at natural draught). *Swallow* had eight 5in guns (no 6in) and no torpedo tubes. Her armament totalled 73.5 tons, compared to 58 tons for the new ship, and her machinery weighed 200 rather than 135 tons, the new ship's machinery including steam steering. Displacement calculated from the sheer draught sent to Devonport was 817 tons. A Legend dated 22 August 1884 showed much the same dimensions, but a displacement of 790 tons (780 was crossed out).

9 *Curlew* class Cover, page marked 1 (but well into the Cover). No *Merseys* were built at Devonport, both 1884-85 ships being built at Pembroke. HMS *Thames* was laid down on 14 April 1884, but HMS *Severn* was not laid down until 1 December.

10 This seems to have been the protected gunboat design described in the opening pages of the *Buzzard* Cover. On 8 January 1885 Controller decided to begin next year (i.e., 1886-87 program) six general-service gunboats. DNC submitted some questions: should they have sail power, should they have copper bottoms, and, as they were Lieutenants' commands, should they be limited to £33,000 each? If they were not to have full sail power, they should have twin screws and a protective deck over their vitals; if they were not to be copper-bottomed, they should be built of steel. First Naval Lord wanted a 600-ton repeat *Mistletoe*, but slightly longer, with copper bottom and the same proportion of sail power, and with six 4in breech-loaders. Barnaby submitted a sketch design of a composite ship with a watertight (protective) deck over her vitals and with a speed of 12kts under forced draught, with very large coal stowage and with full sail power as in *Mistletoe*, but displacing 650 tons. Four guns would be in sponsons. This was not too far from a reduced-scale *Satellite*. His alternative was a steel ship with fore and aft sail as in *Mersey* and *Curlew*, with a steel underwater deck and large coal stowage, capable of 17kts using torpedo boat machinery, with four 4in (two on the centreline on poop and forecastle) plus five torpedo tubes (10 torpedoes). She would cost £40,000 rather than £33,000 and would require the sort of workmanship normally devoted to torpedo craft. If it were accepted by the Board, DNC expected to ask Thornycroft or Yarrow for tenders. DNO favoured the gun/torpedo ship, in effect a torpedo gunboat. Rendel liked New *Mistletoe*, but also wanted the gun/torpedo ship. Controller wanted four New *Mistletoes* and proposed building one gun/torpedo ship, as only seven of the planned ten *Scout* class torpedo cruisers had been ordered. First Naval Lord Cooper Key wanted at least six gunboats, but also considered the gun/torpedo ship very useful, and wanted one built. Civil Lord Brassey liked both types, and considered the gun/torpedo ship essential for war; half the ships should be of this type. The Board decided on four Improved *Mistletoes*. Drawings of the torpedo vessel were to be prepared in detail for submission. DNC submitted them in August 1885. Like the *Curlews*, this ship had an underwater protective deck. Barnaby saw it as both a gunboat *and* a seagoing torpedo vessel. Coal endurance would be 6000nm at 10kts. The position was reviewed in September 1885 by a new Board. There was already a design for a 19-knot torpedo boat catcher (430 tons). It was by no means clear that Barnaby's gun/torpedo ship would be nearly as efficient as a specially-built gunboat on a foreign station – which was what the Royal Navy needed on a day to day basis. New First Naval Lord Admiral Hood wanted a square-rigged composite gunboat of 700 to 750 tons with a speed of 15kts. There were already efficient torpedo and gun-vessels: the *Archers*, the *Curlews*, and the new 19kt torpedo vessel (which became the torpedo gunboat). Barnaby's assistants Wright and Morgan (Barnaby was gone) offered to meet the new requirement using lightweight (locomotive) boilers. They thought an existing gunboat (*Swallow*) was already close to what was wanted: 13½kts (14 in practice), a protective deck, and eight 5in guns, all on 1070 tons. The *Buzzard*, already on order, was an improved *Swallow* intended to make 15kts using improved machinery. To get any smaller would require a steel hull. Incoming DNC William H White agreed; it was not worthwhile to draw down to 750 tons. New *Mistletoe* became the *Rattler* class gunboat.

11 White wrote that his assistant should try 210ft x 30ft x 11½ft, with freeboard etc as in *Buzzard*. A somewhat later paper compared the new ship to *Buzzard* as completed. The new ship was 210ft x 32ft x 11ft/13ft (1250 tons); *Buzzard* was 195ft x 30ft x 11ft 2in/12ft 2in (1080 tons). Normal coal load was 125 tons compared to 100 for *Buzzard*, but *Buzzard* had a capacity of 15 tons. With normal coal, the new ship could steam 3000nm at 10kts, compared to 2100nm for *Buzzard*. *Buzzard* armament was given as eight 5in, 4 Nordenfelt and 4 Gardner machine guns. To these the new ship added a bow torpedo tube and four broadside tubes.

12 An armament list showing the 4.7in guns was attached to a September 1887 memo, but a Legend dated that October still showed the original 5in battery, with 85 rounds per gun. All lesser guns and torpedoes were the same in the 5in and 4.7in versions. At this stage dimensions were 210ft x 35 ftx 13ft/15ft (1500 tons), and power was given as 1900/3000 IHP for a speed at natural draught of 15kts and 16½kts under forced draught – less than spectacular results. Complement was 140, not far from where White started the much larger *Medea*. The 4.7in battery was approved late in October 1887.

13 Board instructions quoted by White in his January 1888 submission of the 'steel *Buzzard*' design were that the ships should resemble the wood-sheathed sloops whose design had already been approved in armament, protection, disposition of magazines, subdivision, accomodation and size. The steel bottom was to be unsheathed, and locomotive boilers could be used to attain at least 18kts. Coal supply and radius of action could be somewhat reduced, the wood-sheathed ships being intended for distant service.

14 Dimensions were now 220ft x 35ft x 13ft/15ft (1580 tons) and power was given as 2000/3000 IHP. There were no tubes at all in the Legend approved by the Board in November 1887.

15 The same 3 January 1888 Board decision called for two fixed submerged tubes in first-class cruisers, and two submerged and two above-water tubes in the torpedo depot ship *Vulcan*.

16 Oddly, their Cover numbers *preceded* those of the *Barracouta*s (112 vs 114).

17 An 18 January 1888 Legend compared the wood-sheathed sloop (*Barracouta*: 16½kts) with 18kt and 19½kt steel sloops and with the French *Forbin*, a 1935-ton protected cruiser credited with a speed of 20kts. The slower of the two steel sloops was rated at 18 to 18½kts; dimensions were 240ft x 35ft x 11¾ft/14¾ft (1600 tons). Dimensions of the faster sloop were 280ft x 35ft x 11½ft /14¼ft (1800 tons). The slow sloop required 4500 to 5000 IHP, the faster one 5500. All of the sloops had the same battery, including six 4.7in QF. *Forbin* was credited with two 5.5in guns, three 3pdr, four 37mm (1pdr), and 5 torpedoes; she was credited with 4000/6000 IHP engines and a speed of 19½kts. The sloops all carried 280 rounds per 4.7in gun, down from the 300 originally planned because it had been decided to stow shells and cartridges separately. By this time the *Barracouta* was credited with a complement of 160, but the new steel sloops were assigned 140.

18 New *Archer* was 240ft x 36ft x 13ft 6in, compared to 225ft x 36ft x 13ft 6in for *Archer*. The most important change was from horizontal compound to vertical triple expansion engines. In November dimensions were 240ft x 40ft x 14ft 3in/15ft 3in. DNC also produced a table comparing New *Archer* with the C class cruiser, presumably partly to show the impact of the new machinery technology. At economical speed a C class cruiser could steam for 16 days using her 470 tons of coal, but New *Archer* could steam for 20 days on 250 tons. Complement of the C class cruiser was 274, compared to 160 for New *Archer*. The C class cruiser had four 6in and eight 5in guns plus lesser weapons and 6 torpedoes, compared to six 6in and 12 torpedoes in the new ship (this undated table preceded the shift to QF guns in the new cruiser).

19 White attributed part of the increase to the introduction of the Board Margin.

20 This was apparently a sore point. White felt compelled to explain the increase in detail. He was arguing to limit the complement of the larger *Medea* in order to keep her from growing to the point where she could not possibly make the desired 20kts. To do that, he wanted some of the engine room complement to help with the guns. In this case, Engineer-in-Chief would probably want 61 men, of whom 12 would be available for guns. Outside the engine room, the proposed complement would be 14 more than for the *Barracouta*s (which had 9 engine room men available to help with the guns). White concluded that the complement he offered should not be exceeded in the completed ships.

21 Dimensions were 265ft x 41ft x 14ft 4in/16ft 6in (2535 tons), with 7200 IHP (forced draught) for a speed of 19kts. The ship would carry 300 tons of coal, for an endurance of 6000nm at 10kts. Complement was 190. By January 1895 it was 225, and there was sleeping space for 220 to 230 enlisted men in hammocks. The additional men were associated with the greater engine power and coal supply of the new ships.

22 Legend dated September 1888. As before, *Bellona* was 280 x 35ft (no draught given: 1830 tons), but rated power had been increased again, to 6000 IHP for 20kts. Armament was unchanged. Enlarged *Bellona* was 290 x 37ft (2150 tons) with 6500 IHP to maintain 20kts. The important difference was coal capacity: 300 rather than 140 tons, so the ship could steam for 5000 rather than 2600nm at 10kts. Complement increased from 160 to 170. The Colonial Cruiser (*Pearl* class) was 265ft x 41ft (2575 tons) with 7500 IHP to drive her less efficient hull at 19kts. Her 300 tons of coal would suffice for 6000nm at 10kts. Armament was eight 4.7in QF, eight 3pdr, and 12 torpedoes (one bow and two broadside tubes). Complement was 190.

23 The most comparable French class, *Linois*, was credited with four 5.5in and two 3.9in guns. Comparing the two designs, White listed the eight 4in guns of the British ship. However, it could be argued that, when attacking an unarmoured ship, the number of hits would probably count more than calibre. When the *Barham*s had been designed, there had been no 4in QF gun, so 4.7in was chosen. Another improvement was armour protection over parts of the two deck torpedo tubes (the French had more tubes, but entirely unarmoured). White pointed out in 1895 that his new cruiser was about 20ft shorter and 2ft beamier than the French ships, drawing considerably less. 'If the facts were fully known, it would be found that the French vessels in regard to their stability are not nearly in so satisfactory a condition as the *Barham* and *Bellona* or as the new vessels will be.' The pronounced tumble-home the French favoured greatly reduced deck area and accommodation, made boat-handling difficult, threw up large bow waves at speed, and let too much water onto the decks. White thought the French were trying to reduce topweight and also to get an easy rolling motion. *Barham* and *Bellona* behaved well in heavy weather without incurring the problems of the French ships.

24 The first was 280ft x 35ft x 12ft 3in/14ft 9in (1910 tons), compared to 1838 tons for *Barham*, which had similar length and beam. On those dimensions the ship could

produce the same 6000 IHP as *Barham*, for the same 19½kt speed. The larger alternative was 300ft × 36ft × 12ft 3in/14ft 9in (2080 tons), sufficient for 7000 IHP (20kts). Both alternatives had the same 250-ton coal capacity as *Barham*. Endurance at 10kts was given as 3000nm, or 3800nm with a maximum stowage of 350 tons in the larger ship. The shorter ship had the same 169-man crew; the larger had 185. Armament for both designs was eight 4in QF (300 rounds per gun), four 3pdr QF, two 0.45in Maxim machine guns, and two broadside torpedo tubes (total of twelve 14in torpedoes). Both alternatives had the same deck protection as *Barham*. Water-tube boilers were apparently heavier than locomotive boilers: *Barham* machinery weighed 275 tons, but the plant producing the same power in the new design was expected to weigh 291, and the 7000 IHP plant was expected to weigh 340 tons.

25 Maximum power was given as 7000 IHP, with 5000 IHP sustainable; corresponding speeds were 20 and 18½kts. Dimensions were 300ft × 36ft 6in × 12ft/15ft (2135 tons). Contemporary second-class cruisers like the *Talbot*s displaced more than twice as much, so a clear distinction could be drawn between second- and third-class cruisers.

26 Approved new dimensions were 305ft × 36ft 9ft (2200 tons), rather than the originally proposed 310ft × 37ft (2225 tons).

27 Reported dimensions were 394ft (waterline; about 380ft between perpendiculars) × 44½ft. The French press criticized the design as too expensive for its limited armament.

28 Bellevilles of a given output offered more power on a continuous basis, but they were considerably heavier, e.g. 630 vs 555 tons for the small-tube Normand, but the Belleville would produce 7000 IHP continuously, compared to 5250 for the Normand. Engineer-in-Chief calculated that Bellevilles would consume 2¼lbs of coal per IHP per hour at 10kts (1.9 at full speed), compared to 2.5 (2.3)lbs for small-tube boilers. Coal endurance was being calculated for 16½ rather than the usual 10kts, however. In June it was assumed that the ship would displace 3300 tons, and that she would make 21½kts on her 4-hour trial at 10,500 IHP.

29 Because they were super-destroyers or leaders, these ships are described in one of the author's previous books, *British Destroyers: From Earliest Days to the Second World War*.

30 As of 27 February, the lighter weapons were eight 3pdrs, three 0.303in Maxim machine guns, and two above-water torpedo tubes with 5 torpedoes. The 4in and 6in guns were all to have 200 rounds per gun, which compared to 300 in *Pelorus*. To save space, as of February it had been decided that 6in and 4in guns would share common magazines and shell rooms, with two hand-ups or hoists from each. The 3pdrs would be dealt with independently. Initially it seemed that armament weight would increase as much as 50 per cent over that of *Pelorus*. While the ship was being designed (August 1901) the captain of HMS *Excellent* objected that ammunition supply to the 4in guns in the waist would be too slow. Even though the new ship had the same ammunition arrangements as other unprotected cruisers, he wanted a ready-use magazine on each side for the 4in guns.

31 Particulars in the Cover, from the German magazine *Marine Rundschau*, were 328ft 1in × 38ft 9in (extreme) × 15ft 1in/16ft 4in (2558 tons), designed for 8000 IHP (twin screws, 170 RPM); on trial the ship made 21.594kts on 8631 IHP (166.4 RPM). A later paper (6 February 1901) described the endurance trial of the German *Nymphe*. White considered the claimed 19kts on 5600 HP a good performance (he thought an earlier report of a 72-hour trial of sister ship *Niobe*, 19.45kts on 4500 HP, overstated the speed by at least half a knot). The Germans were fairly open about naval data until just about this time.

32 The Cover includes June 1900 notes of a discussion between Charles Parsons (who was promoting turbines) and Controller Rear Admiral Wilson. Parsons proposed a 12,000 IHP plant for a 3000-ton cruiser. Unfortunately the turbines were connected directly to the propeller shafts. They had to spin at high (inefficient – for propellers) rates. A week later Parsons proposed installing turbines in *Pioneer* class cruisers. He thought he could offer considerably more than 10,000 IHP; speed might be as great as 23kts. As there was no accurate way to measure turbine power, these figures were all somewhat fanciful. Parsons renewed the turbine proposal in 1902, when the small fast cruiser project was revived.

33 The Legend, which compared the new ship to *Pelorus* as built, was submitted to the Board on 3 April. Dimensions: 330ft × 40ft × 13ft/16ft (2750 tons), 6500/9000 IHP for 19¾/21¼kts, and 300/600 coal (compared to 250/515 tons). Like *Pelorus*, this ship would have 14in torpedoes. Armament weight rose from 152 to 177 tons, and machinery from 386 to 494 tons (which was lower than initially estimated). This was all a rough estimate; hull weight had simply been scaled from that of *Pelorus*. Speed estimates were based on a propulsive coefficient of 0.45, slightly lower than that achieved in cruisers like *Barham*.

34 While the design was proceeding, in March 1901 Rear Admiral C C P Fitzgerald (ret) delivered a paper at the Institution of Naval Architects describing a much faster scout cruiser (3800 tons, 400ft × 44ft × 14ft, 16,000 HP for 25kts, but Fitzgerald had to assume much higher propulsive efficiency). The Cover includes the paper. White compared Fitzgerald's ship, his new third-class cruiser, and the design of a 4000-ton 25-knot ship submitted to DNC (internally) in May 1899. The 1899 design came close to Fitzgerald's in dimensions (400ft × 43ft × 16ft, 4000 tons), but needed more power (20,000 vs 17,500 IHP) to make its speed, and its continuous sea speed was less (21½kts on 50 per cent power, where Fizgerald used 75 per cent power for 23kts). In effect Fitzgerald made White's earlier point that high speed required a large ship, which could not carry much armament. His weights showed only 130 tons for armament, compared to 177 in the new third-class cruiser (of only 2750 tons) and 170 in the 1899 proposal. Protection was about the same in both designs (1in on the flat of the deck, 2in on the slopes, but Fitzgerald had a

4in conning tower compared to White's 3in). It is not clear to what extent, if any, Fitzgerald's ship influenced White's designs. It was armed with six 4in but no torpedo tubes (it would take another 200 tons to add the two 6in and the torpedoes of the new Admiralty design). For another 200 tons the ship could be armed entirely with 6in guns (eight of them).

35 Interest in installing turbines on board *Pandora* lapsed in 1901, when it was decided to use turbines in one of the new cruisers. Parsons dropped the objectionable reciprocating cruising engine of its previous proposal in favour of cruising turbines. As of November 1901 the firm guaranteed 9800 IHP. Engineer in Chief regretted that Parsons could no longer project higher speed for the turbine ship. It seemed inevitable that the turbine ship would burn more coal, however. Parsons had to stay within the same 550 ton limit as the other type of machinery. Engineer in Chief wanted the firm to state whether they would either provide the same boiler power, or provide a turbine capable of economically using all the steam produced on the given weight. White pointed out that the ship would make 22kts on 4550 EHP, and 22½ on 5200 HP, so a great deal depended not only on how much power the turbine could produce, but also on how efficient the propellers were at the much higher RPM involved.

36 The Cover contains a 3 May 1901 report on the German *Gazelle* class, which included *Nymphe*; the timing suggests that the report triggered the redesign. The ship was credited with dimensions of 328ft (pp) x 38.7ft x 15ft (fwd)/16.3ft (aft) draughts on trial, for a trial displacement of 2600 tons. *Gazelle* was credited with 6000 IHP and a sea speed of 20kts; later ships would have 8000 IHP. Later ships were expected to displace 200 or 300 tons more. It was natural to compare the new cruiser with the German ship, because its role was to beat off enemy cruisers shielding enemy destroyers from the British destroyers lurking off their bases. There were no comparable very fast small French cruisers (the French presumably lacked the money to build both big armoured cruisers and small fleet scouts). The Cover also includes an FO report (dated 28 June 1901) describing the Russian third-class cruiser *Boyarin*, launched on 8 June 1901 at Copenhagen, credited with a speed of 22kts on 11,500 IHP (345ft x 41.5ft x 16ft, 3200 tons, armed with six 4.7in QF guns and five torpedo tubes). She had a 1.5in deck (2in on slopes). It is not clear why the much faster small Russian cruisers, beginning with their German-built *Novik*, did not figure in the British discussion. According to a 7 July 1902 report of a German newspaper article quoted in the Cover, the new cruiser *Ersatz Zieten* (*Bremen*) would displace nearly 2950 tons and make 22kts with a radius of 5000nm at 10kts; the earlier smaller ships had insufficient coal.

37 Small-tube boilers would limit the volume, and particularly the height, of the boiler room. Engineer-in-Chief told DNC that in order to accommodate large-tube Babcock and Wilcox boilers the protective deck would have to be raised to about 3½ft above the normal waterline. It would have to be so steeply sloped as to lose much of its value.

38 According to a detailed summary of calculations dated October 1901, the 21¾kt rated speed was based on a propulsive coefficient of 44 per cent; if the actual figure was 46 or 47 per cent, speed would be 22kts on 9800 IHP. DNC stated that the ships would probably make 22kts, but that he preferred to guarantee 21¾kts.

39 Dimensions: 360ft (pp) x 40ft x 13ft (fwd)/16ft (aft) (*Pelorus* was 300ft long), 3000 (vs 2198) tons, with engines rated at 7000 (vs 5000) IHP at natural and 9800 (vs 7000) under forced draught, for a forced draught speed of 21¾kts. Complement would be approximately 317 rather than 224, and armament twelve (rather than eight) 4in QF guns (200 rather than 300 rounds per gun). Both ships had two 14in torpedo tubes (protected in *Pelorus*, unprotected in the new ship) with 5 torpedoes. In his design report DNC gave total complement as 313 compared to 224; of the additional 88 men, 44 were in the engine room, and 45 in the rest of the crew, presumably due to the increased number of QF guns. There was no space for any additional men.

40 White asked his assistant Mr Mundy what it would cost (in tonnage) to join poop and forecastle, with as much sheer as possible to keep weight down, and how much the ship would grow if draught and freeboard were both increased by 9 inches (total depth increased by 18in). The deeper ship would need a beam of 40 rather than 41ft, and probably 21 tons more hull and 6 tons more protective deck. For the same speed it would need 12 tons more of machinery. It would probably displace 3040 tons. Alternatively, extra weight could be used to reduce the maximum stress.

41 Armament weight increased from 191 to 200 tons, and machinery weight from 557 to 682 tons.

42 Dimensions were given as 360ft x 42ft 6in (40 crossed out) x 13ft 6in/16ft 6in (about 3400 tons), with 12,000 HP for 22kts and 350/800 tons of coal compared to 300/700 for a 'Gem' (a note in the Cover said that oil fuel should be considered). Complement was about 320, compared to 296 for the 'Gem'. Armament was ten 4in QF (200 rounds/gun, as in a 'Gem', but a new type), eight 3pdr (as in a 'Gem': 500 rounds/gun), 3 Maxim machine guns, and the same two 18in torpedo tubes (4 torpedoes). Armament weight increased from 191 to 205 tons, and machinery weight from 557 to 700 tons. The Legend gives no machinery details. The decision as to the main battery seems to have been taken about 5 February 1903.

43 The first Legend in the Cover, comparing New *Hecla* with *Hecla*, is dated 12 September 1887. Dimensions: 350ft x 58ft x 21ft 6in/24ft 6in (6365 tons, but lines gave a displacement of 6620). Two alternative gun armaments were given: four 6in, twelve 6pdr QF, and two 3pdr QF for the tops; or eight 36pdr (4.7in; they turned out to be 45pdrs) QF, eight 6pdr QF, and the two 3pdr. In each case there would be bow and stern torpedo tubes plus four broadside tubes above water and two below; she would have a total of 30 torpedoes. Protection was the usual deck armour: 2½in flat (3in on the sides), with 5in slopes

(3in at the lower edge, below water). At the ends, where the form was fine and the need for protection reduced, the deck was reduced to 2in. Cylinders protruding from the protective deck would be protected by a sloping 6in glacis, which White claimed (in the accompanying memo) was equivalent to 8½in vertical armour. The glacis was topped by a 2in deck. Forced draught power was given as 12,000 IHP for 20kts, and coal capacity as 1000 tons (sufficient for 12,000nm at 10kts). The ship was expected to make 18kts continuously (endurance 3000nm). Complement was 450. The cruiser would carry eight second-class torpedo boats (160 tons) in addition to her own twelve ship's boats (35 tons). The ship would also stow about 200 tons of mines and associated equipment, as in *Hecla*. In describing the ship White repeatedly referred to an alternative armament of four 70pdr QF guns, which he much disliked. They were presumably an abortive 5in design.

44 The idea is analogous to that adopted by the interwar Royal Navy, which well understood the value of aircraft, but could not carry nearly enough of them on board carriers, due to an unfortunate combination of treaty restrictions (in effect, on carrier numbers) and operating practices which drastically limited the number of aircraft per ship. The Royal Navy planned therefore to use its battleships and cruisers to launch additional strike aircraft, not the observation planes and scouts other navies assigned to surface combatants. That is why Swordfish were assigned to battleships; they could be catapulted carrying torpedoes. The concept proved badly flawed for many reasons.

45 Richards took office as First Naval Lord on 1 November 1893, having been Second Naval Lord since 25 August 1892. It is not clear when Richards first approached White. White's paper describing what he thought he should do was dated 7 November 1893. Fisher's list of requirements, which presumably reflected White's advice, was dated 11 November. DNO provided his own comments on 10 November. Richards wrote his list of requirements on 5 December, but by that time the project was well underway.

46 Dimensions were 320ft x 57ft (5700 tons). An August 1895 Legend compared the new cruiser with the *Juno* (*Talbot* class). Dimensions: 320ft pp/333ft wl/342ft loa x 57ft 6in x 20ft 0in/22ft 0in, 5800 tons (5750 crossed out). Power was given as 10,000 IHP for 18½ to 19kts. Estimated continuous sea speed was 17 to 17¼kts. On her full capacity of 1200 tons of coal (500 on trial) the ship could steam at 10kts for 34 days (*Juno* could steam for 31): 8160nm. Complement was 419. *Juno* had about the same displacement. The new ship had lighter armament (360 vs 406 tons), roughly as much machinery (900 tons), slightly more deck armour (545 vs 500 tons), and considerably more vertical armour (167 rather than 90 tons).

6. BIG CRUISERS TO PROTECT COMMERCE

1 White referred to the Minute in his instructions to his assistant Morgan, but the Minute has not survived in the relevant Cover.

2 Dimensions were to be 375ft x 63 or 64ft (extreme) x 24ft (25ft extreme). Armament would match that of *Orlando* except that the ship would mount ten 70pdr QF on her main deck instead of ten 6in on the upper deck, the QF guns on the main deck of *Orlando* being moved to the upper deck. The 70pdr QF gun did not materialize, so the ships had 6in. Torpedo armament would match that of *Orlando*. A Legend, marked First Class Protected Cruiser, was dated 12 October 1887. Dimensions were 375ft x 65ft x 24ft 9in/26ft 9in (8880 tons). Under forced draught the ship would develop 20,000 IHP to reach her 22kts. At this stage she was still credited with ten 70pdr QF. Complement was 550. A Legend of the approved design was dated 31 January 1888, giving the chosen names. On the same dimensions the ship was expected to displace 9000 tons, carrying 1500 tons of coal at load draught, sufficient for about 9 weeks at 10kts (15,120nm). Armament was given as two 9.2in, ten 70pdr QF (200 rounds per gun), eighteen 3pdr QF, and torpedo tubes.

3 Dimensions: 360ft x 60ft x 22ft/24ft (7000 tons), to make 20kts on 12,000 IHP (forced draught) or 18kts under natural draught (19½kts was pencilled in). The coal supply of 850 tons (at Legend displacement) was estimated to provide for 6 weeks of steaming at 10kts (10,080nm) or 6 days at full speed (18kts: 2592nm). Armament would match that of *Blake*, except that there would be twelve rather than eighteen 3pdrs.

4 Junior Naval Lord Rear Admiral Charles F Hotham considered 3pdrs 'only playthings'. He preferred four 6in or even 5in to the 9.2, which was too heavy for a fast cruiser. That judgement probably affected White when he sketched a design for the *Powerful* and *Terrible* a few years later. Hotham was Junior Naval Lord in 1888-89, and did not later return to the Board.

5 There must still have been sentiment favouring belt armour, because a few days after initial approval White asked his assistant how much weight would be needed to substitute a 225ft x 6½ft belt, as in *Orlando*, for the deck over the engines and boilers. On the same weight, he could have a 2½in belt, but to have an *Orlando* belt would cost 900 tons.

6 The *Powerful* class Cover begins with a comparison between *Rurik* and *Blake*. The reported coal supply was 1000 tons at Legend or trial displacement, with a capacity for 2000 tons. *Blake* was designed to carry 1500 tons. Reported Legend displacement was 10,930 tons (426ft waterline x 67ft x 26ft).

7 The two follow-on cruisers were reportedly of 11,700 tons, about 800 larger than *Rurik*; nothing more was known of them. In October 1891 the Naval Attaché at St Petersburg reported that the Russians planned ten such ships specifically to destroy enemy (i.e., British) commerce. In fact there were only two immediate follow-

ons, *Rossiya* and *Gromoboi*. *Rurik* had reportedly been designed to steam from the main Russian base at Kronstadt to Vladivostok without coaling.

8 In 1885 the Russians tried to take over neutral liners, so it was relevant that White's cruiser would match the sea speed of the liners *City of Paris* and *City of New York* (recently transferred to the American flag) and new vessels now building in the United States, and would outrun all or nearly all the German mail steamers. The Royal Navy had no cruisers capable of running down such ships.

9 According to White's history of the design dated 4 November 1897, initially nothing was done to counter the *Rurik* (laid down in 1890) because the Naval Defence Programme absorbed the full energy of the DNC department. White could only collect the available information 'and as occasion offered, I personally took into consideration the qualities which it would be necessary to secure in any new cruiser which should individually surpass the Russian ship'. He discussed the matter with Control Rear Admiral Sir John Hopkins in November 1891, his first step afterwards being to evaluate the *Rurik* design. White became convinced (correctly) that the Russian ship would be considerably overweight and therefore over-draught. It was probably also when he became convinced that she would be faster than stated. During 1892 White developed a sketch plan as the opportunity became available. He became convinced in particular that the key to the design would be lightweight water-tube boilers, as in the French navy. White and Engineer-in-Chief Durston chose the French Belleville. Early in 1893 White was in a position to submit a sketch design to the Board. Preliminaries were complete in June, and the detailed design was approved by the Board on 12 October 1893. White was proud that the ships were completed early: scheduled delivery was 6 January 1897, but they were delivered in June and July 1896, having been ordered on 6 January 1894.

10 Natural draught speed was about 2kts faster than in the *Blake*s, which would make about 20kts under similar conditions on the measured mile, and about 17½kts continuously at sea. Those ships had been designed for a degree of forcing no longer permissable except in an emergency: the recent (1892) Boiler Committee recommended limiting the margin between forced and natural draught power to 25 per cent. With about 60 per cent forcing, *Blenheim* exceeded 22kts. Under the new conditions the *Edgar*s were rated at 12,000 HP for 4 hours and 10,000 HP at natural draught.

11 White's sketch design was 500ft x 69 to 70ft x 27ft (with keel), 14,000 tons. She needed 23,500 to 24,000 HP to make the desired 22kts (natural draught). The same powerplant would give a speed of 22½ to 23kts in smooth water with moderate forcing. White envisaged six groups of boilers in separate compartments, paired two by two, groups of boilers arranged with their backs to a longitudinal bulkhead running down the centreline (as in battleships, to make it easier to feed the boilers). Each group would generate about 4000 HP under natural draught, so any two groups could drive the ship at 16kts. Two of the groups would be standard cylindrical boilers, the other four being water-tubes; the ship could cruise on her durable cylindrical boilers. To accelerate, she would rely on her water-tube boilers, which could raise steam much more quickly. Only about 8 per cent of natural draught power would be needed to maintain 10kts. White pointed out that twin screws made for a shorter machinery box than triple, and that they could absorb high power: the *Blake*s managed more than 20,000 HP with twin screws.

12 As with *Rurik*, White considered the narrow thin belt of the US ship a waste of armour weight. He doubted that a British twin 8in, if it could be developed in time (it could not) would be so much better than a 9.2in gun. White's reverse-engineering indicated to him that the Americans probably had no more than 50 rounds per gun, compared to the 120 rounds per 9.2in common in British ships, 150 to 200 per 6in, and 200 to 300 per 4.7in. He also pointed out that the difference between the US and British ships was really more like 4500 tons, if both were required have the same coal endurance.

13 There was no question of providing a battleship-style barbette extending all the way down to the magazine below the armoured deck. The guns were given a shallow barbette protecting the turntable and the lower parts of the mounting as well as the roller path. The gun was mounted in a closed revolving shield.

14 Dimensions: 500ft 0in x 70ft 6in (71ft 0in) x 26ft 9in (27ft 0in) mean, with revised figures in parentheses (14,000 tons including 200-ton Board Margin). Output was 25,000 IHP for 4 hours (22kts) and 18,000 IHP continuously (20kts). Complement was 960. Within two weeks 14,000 tons had been adopted as the design displacement, the Board Margin being in addition, so that rated displacement was 14,200 tons. The extra margin was justified by uncertainty as to the weight of the new Belleville water-tube boiler. Machinery came out slightly heavy (2260 vs 2200 tons in *Powerful*), as did armament (802 vs 790 tons) and hull (5803 vs 5720 tons). Deck armour was light (1360 vs 1450 tons). Weights for HMS *Powerful* added up to 13,785 tons, compared to the design total of 14,000 without the Board Margin. During construction, 120 tons of the 200-ton Board Margin was consumed by improvements such as lengthened masts, fighting tops, and increased sub-division of coal bunkers. Ships ran their trials at somewhat greater than design draught. In unfavourable weather at about 18,000 IHP *Powerful* maintained about 21kts for 30 hours. On her 4 hour maximum power trial (25,000 IHP) *Terrible* maintained 22.4kts (compared to the required 22). On this basis White considered both ships good for 23kts on the measured mile. There was no requirement for great manoeuvreability, since the ships were intended for independent service, and not as part of a battle fleet. Tactical diameter was about 1100yds (about 6½ lengths), which White considered quite good.

15 The Cover includes remarks by Controller (Rear Admiral A K Wilson) and White dated October 1898. DNO saw

no problem in passing a trunk for the second 6in gun through the main deck casemates to supply guns above them. In 1900, when the idea was raised again, Wilson remarked that it died the first time because the ships would not be available for refit for some time. White looked at three alternatives in 1898: upper deck mountings in shields; casemates in addition to the ones already in the ship; and a lighter and cheaper arrangement of side armour over the additional guns. Casemates were the most expensive alternative, and they would add the most weight.

16 In April 1894 Froude (at the model tank) was asked to suggest lines for a 400ft (vice 375ft in *Blenheim*) 10,000-ton cruiser capable of 21kts.

17 The alternatives are listed in the Cover. A was *Blenheim* with military tops and Belleville boilers, i.e., the minimum 'New *Blake*' (375ft x 65ft x 27ft). B was A with 6in casemates and a ready-use magazine for each (hence had to be slightly beamier, 67ft, 9625 tons). C added a forecastle and fore and aft bridges, and incorporated the new armament, variant C2 being lengthened to 400ft (10,355 tons). That was the starting point for estimates of the preferable hull form. D was a sheathed version of C2, trading off coal against the weight of sheathing. C and later versions had all twelve 6in in casemates. The later ships had somewhat shallower hulls. In E the hull was lengthened to 435ft. F added the desired protected ammunition passages and magazine lobbies, and had the coal bunkers subdivided longitudinally as in other White cruisers. F was 435ft x 68ft 8in x 24ft 3in/26ft 3in/25ft 3in (10,895 tons), slightly longer and beamier than the final design. The designers tried but failed to hold the ship to 10,000 tons.

18 As with the *Powerful*s, the question of triple screws was raised. Advocates pointed to greater subdivision (three rather than two engine rooms) and the possibility of using smaller lighter engines. However, each engine room would need about the same number of personnel. White also argued that with more engines confusion was more likely 'in trying circumstances'. As with the *Powerful*s, he pointed to the need for space aft for magazines and shell rooms. The ship would have two engine rooms abreast and a third abaft them. She would be 30ft longer and would displace about 10 per cent more (1100 tons), and cost would rise about as much (£50,000). She would need 10 per cent (nearly 200 tons) more coal, half the increase being included in the 1100 tons. The longer ship would be less manoeuvreable, and she might be more difficult to dock. By this time policy was to carry about half the ammunition at each end of the ship, so that the ship could continue to fight even if one end was seriously flooded. That took space which might otherwise go into a third engine room, not to mention the tunnel for the third shaft. White claimed that space outside the machinery was a less serious consideration in foreign cruisers, which carried smaller loads of stores and ammunition. An undated Legend compared *Diadem* as designed with twin screws and military masts, *Diadem* with triple screws and plain rig, and *Diadem* with triple screws and side armour (a 3½in belt on 2in backing, compensated for by reducing deck armour to 2in). The belt would have consumed 1000 tons. The belted *Diadem* would have displaced 12,900 tons, with a complement of 700 rather than the 650 of the *Diadem* design. The triple-screw ships were credited with sixteen rather than fifteen 6in guns. Triple-screw machinery would weigh 1750 tons, compared to 1525 (as then estimated) for *Diadem*.

19 Dimensions: 430ft x 68ft 0in x 24ft 6in/26ft 6in/25ft 6in compared to 375ft x 65ft x 24ft 9in/26ft 9in/25ft 9in for *Blake*, 10,500 compared to 9070 tons. Freeboard amidships would have been about the same as that of *Blake* (15ft 6in vs 15ft 0in) but less than that of *Powerful* (17ft 9in). The ships would have plain masts like that of the *Blake*s rather than military ones as in *Powerful*. The greatest change was much higher speed thanks to the water-tube boilers: 20½kts for 4 hours (15,500 IHP) and 19kts continuously (11,000 IHP) compared to 20kts under natural draught (13,000 IHP) for *Blake*. Coal capacity was 1100/2000 tons. In presenting the design, DNC said that the problem was much like that of the *Powerful*: a combination of high freeboard and heavy armament pushed up the centre of gravity in proportion to the depth of the ship, reducing the range of stability (to 60 to 65 deg) compared to less heavily-armed cruisers. Beam had to be increased, and to maintain speed the ship had to be made longer. The result was 55ft longer than *Blake* – but 70ft shorter than *Powerful*. The length of the beamier part of the hull was set by the combination of water-tube boilers and a torpedo room forward of the boiler rooms, and that in turn set overall length to make the ends fine enough for the ship to reach the desired speed. The boilers would probably be Bellevilles, but by the time the ships were built a British alternative might have been tested sufficiently to be chosen. The important point, which White made repeatedly in connection with other designs, was that water-tube boilers could maintain a higher fraction of their maximum power on a sustained basis, in this case 12,500 HP compared to 8000 for *Blake*. White estimated that, on the same weight of boilers and machinery, a ship with cylindrical boilers would develop about 15,000 (10 per cent less than with water-tube) on 4-hour forced draught trial, 12,500 HP under natural draught for 8 hours, and 7500 HP on a continuous basis, the corresponding natural draught speeds being 19 and 17.5kts. The cost estimate for the new ship was justified on the basis of the £413,000 paid for *Blake*.

20 A Legend dated 14 April 1895, but clearly revised afterwards, gave dimensions as 435ft (456ft waterline, 463ft overall) x 69ft x 24ft 3in/26ft 3in, 11,000 tons, with a complement of 650. Armament was sixteen 6in, fourteen 12pdr, twelve 3pdr, seven Maxim machine guns, and two submerged torpedo tubes (a stern torpedo tube was given up).

21 Within a few years the big protected cruiser seemed obsolete. In 1902 Vickers offered to armour the sides of the *Diadem*s to bring them up to the standard of protection of the similar-sized *Cressy*s by adding a 4in belt 310ft long with 2in to the bow and a 4in after

bulkhead. The 4in armour would extend from the main deck down to 5ft below the new waterline. Existing sheathing would be raised to the level of the main deck as backing. The company argued that side armour was needed to protect the ship's buoyancy and stability. Vickers estimated that this would weigh 900 tons (including 100 tons of backing, 40 of new framing, and 40 of bolts), which would sink the ship about 16 inches deeper into the water and would cost half a knot of speed; armour for eight ships would cost about £870,000. Vickers also proposed substituting one 7.5in gun at each end for the two upper-deck 6in QF. With open shields weight would be about the same (with closed shields draught would increase another 2 inches). The *Powerful*s could be similarly modified. Writing in April 1902, DNO was unenthusiastic. The additional draught would bring the sills of the lower 6in guns too close to the water. The proposed 4in belt 'would be mere patchwork' considering recent experiments and the calibre of guns on board enemy cruisers. As for armament, a single turreted 7.5in would be an improvement – but if the idea were entertained at all, it would be almost worthwhile to have twin 7.5s or single 9.2s. Controller considered the idea 'attractive at first sight' but not really feasible due to cost, loss of speed, and increased immersion. First Naval Lord Kerr agreed: 'they should remain as they are and not try to make them a match for cruisers of a later date.'

7. THE FAST WING OF THE BATTLE FLEET

1 D K Brown, *Warrior to Dreadnought* (London: Chatham, 1997), 150, citing the 1915 Admiralty gunnery handbook.
2 An undated (probably early 1898) Legend compared protection weights for *Cressy* and *Ariadne*, the last protected-cruiser design. *Cressy* had 900 tons of vertical armour: 720 on sides and bulkheads, 55 in backing, and 125 tons of nickel steel on her bow. *Ariadne* had none of these. *Cressy* had a 680-ton protective deck and a 300-ton main deck, the latter covering the belt from above. *Ariadne* had only the protective deck (1200 tons). *Ariadne* had thicker casemates (6in: 480 tons vs 5in: 445 tons), about the same conning tower armour (90 tons), thicker armour tubes (80 vs 25 tons, because they were not behind armour). *Cressy* had 80 tons protecting the bases of the 9.2in mountings. All of this added up to 2520 tons for *Cressy* against 1850 for *Ariadne* (and, as it happened, 2165 tons for *Powerful*).
3 White envisaged a belt 230ft long, extending from 5ft below the waterline to 6½ to 7¼ft above it (total depth would be about 12ft). The latest German armoured cruiser, *Ersatz Leipzig* (*Fürst Bismarck*) was to have a narrow if thicker (7¾in, tapered to 4in at bow and stern) belt rising only about 2½ft above water and extending about 5ft below; it was covered by a protective deck rather less than 2in thick. Above it the only protection of buoyancy and stability was a small cork-filled cofferdam, 'the value of which must be extremely small'. The Russian *Rossiya* had a narrow 10in belt stopping about 60ft from bow, with a 2½in steel deck above; 'such belts give little or no protection to buoyancy or stability due to their narrowness'. White claimed that the Russians were now imitating the arrangement of British battleships in their *Oslyaba* class. The newest French armoured cruiser *Jeanne d'Arc* was credited with a narrow 6in belt, with a thinner strake above. The American armoured cruisers had only very thin armour over very small areas. Only the Italian ships were any better, 'but their armour made at Terni is probably inferior to ours'.
4 The 9.2in guns would be protected like those in *Powerful*. The 6in battery would be protected like that in the battleship *Canopus*. Compared to *Diadem* the guns and ammunition would add 35 tons and their protection another 50, a total of 85 tons, over 6 per cent of total armament weight. White saw no contradiction with the *Diadem*s, which had been designed to deal with foreign cruisers on detached missions. There would be two submerged torpedo tubes in one room; there was no space for two rooms unless the ship was lengthened, at an unacceptable sacrifice of manoeuvreability.
5 About 21,000 rather than 18,000 HP.
6 To Wilson, with equal accuracy the advantage of faster fire was geometrical: every hit 'tends more or less to check the enemy's rate of fire, either by actual damage or moral effect. We ought not to grudge a single man who can be shown to have an appreciable effect in increasing the rapidity of fire. The French use mechanical appliances for the supply of ammunition more than we do, unwisely I think, and the cramped spaces in their turrets must limit the size of their guns' crews with probably a corresponding reduction in the rate of fire, but they are probably also much more limited by financial considerations in peace times than we are, and having compulsory service they are sure of getting full crews in war and more if they want them. With us it is certain that we shall never get more than our authorized crews, and in all probability we shall have in many cases to put up with considerably less. Large crews are also of immense importance for all the general work of war other than fighting, and since the greater part of them fight under cover the proportion of losses would not generally be much increased ... Unfortunately we know very little about the rate of ammunition supply in different ships because of the risk of injury to charges if they are handed up.' Wilson proposed experiments with dummy cartridges. He rejected a proposal by the President of Complement Committee to reduce the number in the 9.2in shell rooms by 16 on the ground that 32 shells are carried on the mounting, 'as this would imply we are to haul the flag down as soon as the 32 rounds have been fired. The intention is that the supply should be kept up on every opportunity and that it should be nearly as rapid as from the mounting itself. We do not know yet how many men are really required because the details of the mounting have been made solely with the view of increasing the rapidity of fire not of reducing the number of men. There is, however, one point which seems to have escaped the criticism of the complement committee and

that is the utility in action of stokers not required for steaming purposes.' This last echoed White's ideas in connection with the *Medea* design about a decade earlier. Machinery complement was calculated on a three-watch basis; Wilson pointed out that at most two watches were required in the engine room and stokeholds to maintain maximum speed (because a watch could not keep working in such conditions for very long). The third watch was considerably more than would be needed for fire brigade duties, leaving men available to help in supplying ammunition. There was even some question as to whether ammunition could be passed quickly enough to the 6in guns to exploit their QF capability. On the other hand, it seemed that those estimating requirements were unaware of just how far *Cressy* had gone towards full power operation of her 9.2in guns, a very different situation from earlier ones in, for example, the *Orlando*s. Ammunition was hoisted by power, brought up automatically inside the shield to a position adjacent to the loading tray. The gun was power-trained. The only manual tasks were elevating the gun and ramming the shell and cordite (and power elevation was being considered).

7 ADM 116/431, file on 'Design for New Cruisers of 23 Knots Speed/Board Approval'. The Cover includes a Legend, probably produced in October 1900, comparing the new cruiser (HMS *Drake*) with the new 13,400-ton US cruiser *California*, and with *California* with stores and ammunition as in *Drake*. The US ship had four 8in/45in twin turrets (later very similar ships had four 10in), compared to two 9.2in in *Drake*, and fourteen rather than sixteen 6in. She also had a lot less coal: 900/2000 rather than 1250/2500 tons (normal/capacity). Armour thicknesses were comparable. The US ship developed 23,000 HP under forced draught, compared to 30,000 under natural draught for *Drake*; corresponding speeds were 22 and 23kts – under very different conditions. US machinery weight was 2102 tons, compared to 2640 for *Drake*. The US figures were based on published data, but the US Navy divided up its weights on a somewhat different basis.

8 DNO made exactly this point. He did not like the fact that the guns were scattered, hence would be difficult to control; that they were in the part of the ship in which men normally slept, hence would interfere with living arrangements; and that they might well interfere with torpedo nets, if the latter were fitted.

9 Controller's 1 June 1898 memo in ADM 116/431.

10 Figures in ADM 116/431. DNO complained that the British ship was not superior to existing foreign ships in stern fire, and that if some of the foreign ships had guns of equal power to the British, they would be superior in stern fire.

11 The 'New *Drake*' Cover consists entirely of evaluations of foreign armoured cruisers, the implication being that an entirely new British design was wanted.

12 The memo in the Cover is undated, but it refers to Froude's memo of 12 December estimating that the ship would attain 23kts on 21,000 HP. Unusually, White specified waterline length (455ft) rather than length between perpendiculars. Waterline length was the relevant quantity for propulsion. He suggested using the same machinery weight as in the *Cressy*s. A later paper (28 June 1898) gives weights for machinery producing 24,000 HP at forced draught, using Belleville (1900 tons) or small-tube (1800 tons) boilers. White later asked for the maximum power he could get on 1600 tons. Normand or Belleville boilers could provide 21,000 HP. EinC Durstan pointed out that coal consumption with a large-tube boiler was less than 4/5th that of the small-tube type.

13 The largest ship, with ten guns in casemates, was 440ft (455ft on the waterline) x 65½ft x 25ft (9750 tons), with 22,000 HP engines. A 430ft (465ft) x 62ft x 22½ft (8850 ton) ship would make 23kts on 21,000 HP. The 7700-ton ship could make her speed only under forced draught (19,000 HP). All three designs had eight 12pdr 12cwt anti-torpedo guns and two 12pdr 8cwt dismountable guns, plus two submerged torpedo tubes. The two larger designs had 4in side armour and 3in bulkheads, with ¾in main decks and 1¼in lower decks. The 7700-ton ship had no belt armour, and was included only for comparison. As the design developed, it became clear that at least 22,000 HP would be needed.

14 The First Lord's statement referred to four additional cruisers. Second Naval Lord Admiral Bedford and Junior Naval Lord Rear Admiral Moore strongly pressed for an improved *Vulcan*. Moore considered the ship essential on the China station; 'if the *Vulcan* was sent to China, I expect the CinC in the Mediterranean would soon ask for another.' Controller Wilson was unenthusiastic; *Vulcan* was a poor combination of functions. Moore may have been more interested in the ship's ability to support destroyers than in her cruiser characteristics.

15 They were a disparate group: two *Asama*s and two *Idzumo*s built by Elswick, *Yakumo* by Vulkan, and *Adzuma* by A & Ch de la Loire of St Nazaire. They would have 7in and 5in side armour and would be armed with four 8in and fourteen 6in guns. The first two Elswick ships had cylindrical boilers which produced their rated power at high forced draught. The two *Idzumo*s had Bellevilles. The Japanese had sacrificed about 3 to 3½kts and some coal, hence were too slow to do the work of the new British cruisers. Similarly, the new Italian cruisers (which had inspired the *Cressy*s) sacrificed speed for protection and armament. The spectacular British-built Chilean *Esmeralda* and *O'Higgins* cut corners, in one case by relying on short-term forced draught and in the other by using too short an armour belt.

16 White did not name these ships. The German-built *Askold* and the US-built *Variag* both fit. The identities of the other two is unclear. White may have been mistaking the small but fast German-built *Novik* for a third. It is not clear what French ship he had in mind.

17 Presumably *Bayan*.

18 Armour details of the French ship had not been released, but it was said to be inadequate; if the *Pothuau* or *Charner* class were followed, it would probably not exceed

3½in. The French were, moreover, using nickel steel armour inferior to the Krupp armour the British used. In fact the *Kléber*s had belt armour 4in to 1in thick. White also argued that the French used an inferior form of casemate, the guns being carried on the upper deck atop an unarmoured structure 14 to 15ft deep. French critics already recognized this structure as a serious weakness.

19 This point came out in a discussion of whether the ships should have anti-torpedo net defence. Controller (Wilson) rejected net defence on the ground that so much had already been sacrificed for speed. Junior Naval Lord Moore argued instead that the ships would often operate on their own, protected only by speed which might be lost if the high-pressure machinery broke down. In that case only nets would protect them against torpedoes. Wilson won out: nets could be cut too easily by torpedoes, so they offered too little protection if a ship could not steam. If she could, they might foul her propellers. Better to rely on her speed and manoeuvreability to evade torpedo craft.

20 Each boiler choice increased machinery weight: 85 tons for Bellevilles, 85 for Yarrow (with forced draught), 110 for Dürr, 115 for Babcock & Wilcox, and 150 for Niclausse. The design had to accommodate the greatest possible increase, the 150 tons for Niclausse boilers. That plus enlarged dimensions increased displacement by 400 tons. Continuous steaming power depended on the boiler. The Bellevilles in the *Monmouth*s were rated at 16,500 HP (21½kts); Babcock & Wilcox, Niclausse, and Dürr were rated at 15,500 HP (20¾kts), and Yarrow at 14,500 HP (20¼kts).

21 The undated drawing showed dimensions of 480ft x 73½ft x 26¼ft (13,150 tons), with a freeboard forward of 21ft. An undated Legend shows versions A, B, and C of New *Devonshire*, corresponding to DNC alternatives A, B, and C as described after the 2 April meeting. This Legend did not include alternative D.

22 An undated Legend makes the cost of alternative boilers clear. A1 dimensions were 480ft x 70½ft x 26¼ft (13,100 tons). A2 was 490ft x 73½ft x 26¼ft (13,500 tons). A3 was 530ft x 73½ft x 26¼ft (14,600 tons). The additional length balanced the additional displacement, so that all could make 23kts on 25,000 HP (natural draught); A1 had a continuous rating of 17,500 IHP for about 21kts. It is not clear why ships about the same size as *Drake* were expected to reach the same speed on 5000 fewer HP. Controller later asked how much power he could get within the same space as A with all-cylindrical or one-fifth cylindrical boiler plants: 20,000 and 23,500, respectively. Corresponding speeds were 21.6 and 22.5kts. Increasing coal stowage to 1500 tons but keeping 25,000 HP would reduce speed to 22.6kts.

23 EinC estimated that oil fuel would impart about 30 per cent more energy than coal. With steam spray (of oil) that would be reduced to 17 per cent, and with compressed air spray it would be 25 per cent. A mixture of coal and oil would reduce the advantage over coal only to about 10 per cent, and when using coal and oil in equal proportions it would be about 5 per cent. On average, adopting oil fuel would reduce stokers by about 40 per cent, not to mention 'readier fuelling of ships in harbour and at sea'. These figures are from a 1902 paper in the *Warrior* Cover. Trials were being conducted on board the battleships *Hannibal* and *Mars*.

24 The Board wanted to use the repeat ships to test a widespread contention that ships should not have hollow bow lines, which reduced buoyancy at the bow. A ship with such lines might not rise properly to the sea and therefore would pitch badly. That pitching would reduce effective sea speed, whatever she could achieve in smooth water. Watts countered that the distinction might be illusory and that large cruisers were ill-suited to such a test. Froude reported that the ship with fuller bow lines would need more power, about 25,000 IHP, and would displace 400 or 500 tons more. Controller May found DNC's arguments unconvincing because tank tests at Haslar were really smooth-water speed tests. In 1903 there was no way to simulate a rough sea in a test tank. In February 1903 Controller asked whether the issue could be decided at sea by giving one of the *Duke of Edinburgh*s straight bow lines at a reasonable cost. DNC resisted: *Duke of Edinburgh* had so little hollowness that it did not affect pitching, and it would be far better to use other measures to reduce pitching. For example, merchant ships used horizontal wings, which resisted pitching, to support twin shafts. In July First Naval Lord Admiral Walter Kerr rejected tests. The governing factor was surely the length of the wave compared to the length of the ship, and waves varied enormously. Comparative trials would have to be greatly prolonged 'and after all the results would probably leave the question as much in doubt as ever'. He suspected that most officers were not really too concerned; that 'most officers would feel that if full lines do better steaming head to sea, hollow lines would score under other conditions'. The tangible fact was the expected cost of full lines, half a knot, 'and we hope, but we have no certainty, that under certain conditions [full lines] may be an advantage. It is all speculation.' However, Kerr did not want to force the issue. First Lord Selbourne thought the experiment worth trying, because even though hollow lines gained half a knot in a flat calm, 'how often is the sea as calm as a tank?' Alternative hollow and full lines were prepared for the new *Minotaur* class in May 1904. Large models were prepared. Pitching experiments showed that full lines offered no advantage in a seaway. That did not convince Controller May, who pointed out that bilge keels had proven effective even though theoretically they should have been useless. Kerr and Selbourne again disagreed, but this time the Board (5 August 1904) ordered one of the *Minotaur*s built with straight bow lines, with the same displacement and horsepower. *Shannon* was chosen. On trials she made about half a knot less than *Minotaur* with over 1000 HP more (22.49kts at 28,350 IHP vs 23.01kts at 27,050 IHP). These trials were conducted in rough weather (for speed trials), hence should have favoured the straight-line ship. That towing tank tests prejudiced designers to measures best suited to a flat calm was a

perennial problem, not limited to the Royal Navy. The contemporary US Navy prided itself on its scientific approach to design, based in large part on tank tests. US officers complained that the resulting ships were far too wet, the result being the total redesign of US battleships about 1914, in which clipper bows replaced rams and secondary guns

25 Watts had already asked his assistant for sketch designs. In a 23 July 1903 note he stated that the next year's cruiser the armament would probably be wholly on the upper deck, as in the new battleship (*Lord Nelson*), and in other respects they would probably largely resemble the *Duke of Edinburgh* class. He wanted sketches for (a) the present armament, (b) the same 9.2in guns, but 7.5in substituted for the 6in, (c) all 7.5in; all for 23kts.

26 In his final design report, DNC attributed the new armour arrangement to the development of armour piercing shells, which had already caused rearrangement of battleship deck armour. Instead of a main protective deck and a lower protective deck, the upper (main) deck armour was given up and moved down to the lower protective deck (the former upper armour deck was reduced to ½in, for structural purposes only). As in the battleships, the single protective deck was 1½in on the flat and 2in on the slopes, specifically to protect the vitals against shells penetrating the belt and bursting inside the ship. Moreover, the greater thickness of deck plating was of stronger material (KNC). A strake of 1¾in steel was laid on the upper deck to protect the uptakes from plunging fire. The gunhouses had battleship protection (8in face and rear, 7in sides; 6in sides for the 7.5s), and barbettes were 7in thick.

27 Adopting Babcock & Wilcox boilers might have made it possible to shrink the ships, but it was considered necessary to allow for either those boilers or Yarrows. *Minotaur* had Babcock & Wilcox boilers, the other two Yarrows. Total machinery weight was 6 or 7 per cent greater than in the *Drake*s, the increase being due to different boilers and other changes (despite a 10 per cent reduction in rated power).

28 To avoid delay, the scout cruisers of the previous year's program had not been modified to stow oil (they had no double bottoms). In May 1903 Controller Rear Admiral May requested proposals to enable all future ships to carry oil. As a first step, he asked the cost and extra weight involved in fitting bunkers and double bottoms to carry oil, and the amount of oil that could be carried. Destroyers would not have double bottoms. Provision was already being made to stow oil in the double bottoms of big armoured cruisers and battleships. *Duke of Edinburgh* could stow 800 tons of oil, which (counting its heat content) was comparable to its normal coal load. The associated cost was small (HMS *Bedford* had her forward boiler room fitted to burn oil for £7000). However, it would be difficult or impossible to make coal bunkers alternative oil stowage (it would be easier, though still difficult, to use bunkers to carry only oil, partly because the bulkheads would be subject to considerable pressure. In July 1903 Controller decided that the year's battleships and armoured cruisers would stow oil in their double bottoms. He also asked EinC 'how you would propose to stow all oil instead of coal below the waterline ...'

29 Watts' first sketches were dated 28 December 1904, the day *before* Controller's memorandum. They were for an armoured cruiser with eight 12in/50 guns with 80 rounds each (the ship actually had 45-calibre guns), 5 torpedo tubes, and about 20 smaller guns. His first cut was 520ft x 75ft x 26½ft, with an estimated 42,000 SHP using turbines. Protection would have matched *Minotaur*'s. Sketches of two alternatives with single turrets on the centreline and two in the waist, either side by side or splayed out en echelon, were dated 5 January 1905. In both sketches there was a conning tower amidships, between the two waist turrets, 'because blast of amidships guns firing fwd would put tower out of action'. Provision also had to be made for transfer of ammunition from one 12in station to another. Both of the sketches of the waist arrangements showed two funnels forward of the waist guns and two abaft them. A 7 January note from DNC called for his assistants to develop D and E further, making the forecastle only wide enough to house the foremost redoubt (barbette). The midships guns in E would be moved towards the centreline, keeping them as close together (fore and aft) as possible. Parallel designs were to be developed for turbines and for reciprocating engines, with four shafts for the turbine ship and two for reciprocating. A sheet dated 12 January showed further modifications of the designs: (1) E with the forward gun pushed as far back as possible; (2) a Modified A with E freeboard, and with the two side-by-side guns pushed aft, abaft the conning tower and the fore funnel, and with X turret pushed forward to forward of the mainmast; and (3) A with the forward turrets pushed aft but X and Y turrets in the original positions. The only departure from *Minotaur* protection, in a sheet apparently dated 2 January, was that the 12in guns have 8in shields and 8in barbettes. Later there was interest in trading off some side armour at the ends to provide 2½in (250 tons) of side armour over the magazines. For example, the 8in gunhouses of the 12in guns could be reduced to 7in on sides and rear, and the barbettes reduced from 8in to 7in.

30 The Legend is in the *Invincible* Cover, but it clearly refers to May's second alternative of December 1904. Dimensions were 540ft x 77ft x 26½ft (17,000 tons), with a freeboard of 30ft; power would be 41,000 HP for 25½kts. Nothing in the Legend indicates what type of engines were envisaged. The sketch shows four vertical funnels, as in a *Minotaur*. In addition to the 12in guns, the ship was armed with thirteen 4in guns and 5 submerged torpedo tubes (as in *Minotaur*).

31 Dimensions with reciprocating engines were 550ft x 79ft x 26½ft (17,750 tons), with 42,500 HP. With turbines they were 540ft x 79ft x 26ft (16,850 tons) with 37,000 IHP. These designs had an additional 4in gun. The sketch is marked 'given to DNC for Committee on Designs] Meeting 12 January 1905'. A slightly later Legend, dated 18 January, offered even greater savings

with turbines: 530ft x 79ft x 26ft (16,000 tons) for Design E. A later version (25 January) was 540ft x 79ft x 26ft (17,150 tons), requiring 42,000 SHP for 25½kts. Design C, for which no Legend survives, had the two forward turrets side by side and a single turret aft; it would have been 520ft x 76ft x 26ft (15,600 tons).

32 The *Invincible* Cover contains decisions taken by the Committee on Designs on 25 January 1905. Design E was preferred; 'the further aft the broadside guns can be kept the better so as if possible to keep the conning tower and forward mounting out of their blast.' An alternative design was to be worked out based on A, but with the forward guns kept much further aft, the two after guns on the upper deck on the centreline, one well aft, the other between the engine and boiler rooms if necessary. This Design F was soon dropped. On 13 January it was decided that E would be developed with turbine machinery, the officers to be accommodated forward.

33 ADM 1/24200. The twin 9.2in/50s were arranged much as in *Invincible*, except that the two en echelon gunhouses were further apart, giving the guns 60 deg rather than 35 deg arcs on the opposite sides. The foremost turret trained 10 deg less abaft the beam. Mountings were analogous to those in *Invincible*, with 100 rather than 80 rounds per gun. The anti-torpedo battery was sixteen 4in guns, but they were BL rather than QF. The ship had two rather than four submerged torpedo tubes, all aft. Weight of armament was 1690 rather than 2540 tons (*Invincible*). Dimensions were 525 x 74 x 25ft (15,750 tons). Power was 40,000 SHP. The ship would carry 1000 tons of coal at normal draught, as in *Invincible*, but maximum supply was 2500 rather than 3000 tons. Side armour was 6in with 4in above to the height of the main deck (*Invincible* had 6in). Forward of machinery spaces the ship had 4in side armour up to the main deck and the extreme fore end (forward of a bulkhead abaft the chain lockers) was 2½in thick. A 4in belt extended abaft the machinery space back to the far end of the after barbette, terminating in an athwartships bulkhead. Abaft that the side armour was 2½in thick. The protective deck matched that of *Invincible* but was 2in rather than 2½in aft and 1½in forward outside the citadel. Protection on the main deck forward was omitted. There was no underwater bulkhead to protect magazines against underwater explosions. Armour weight was 2985 tons, compared to 3460 in *Invincible*. Estimated cost was £1,454,000. Another docket described alternative A and B designs, with four and three twin 9.2in guns, respectively. B had all three gunhouses on her centreline. Length was reduced to 510ft and displacement to 13,000 tons. This ship would have cost £1,100,000. Both designs had 6in barbettes and 7in turrets. One sheet in the file refers also to designs C and D, but no details are given.

8. EPILOGUE: FISHER'S REVOLUTION

1 With 860 tons of coal and 78 tons of reserve feed water on board, the top of belt of HMS *Orlando* was 1ft 5½in below the waterline. That compared to the original design, in which the top of the belt was 3½ft *above* water with 900 tons of coal on board.

2 Technical History and Index No 34, 'Alteration in Armaments of HM Ships During the War' (Admiralty Technical History Section, May 1920), NHB.

3 *Thetis* followed as soon as *Iphigenia* had been proven at sea. Two more conversions were included in the 1907-8 program (but only *Latona* was converted). The 1908-9 program conversions were *Apollo* and *Andromache*, and the 1909-10 conversions were *Intrepid* and *Naiad*.

4 DNO proposed six 6pdrs: two on the forecastle, two in the waist, and two on the poop. This armament was approved in 1910 only for *Naiad* and *Intrepid*, but with two on the forecastle and four on the poop.

Data List

Prior to the 1870s there were no Ships' Covers, and almost no details of calculated weights have survived. For early cruisers, therefore, the data are given in notes to the main text rather than in tabular form. Data presented in the tables below are almost exclusively from Legends (design data) in Ships' Covers.

The figure for coal is first the rated capacity at normal draught and second full capacity. In some cases a distinction was drawn between coal above and below the protective deck, because the latter was to be burned first.

Weights in parentheses are the actual, as opposed to design, figures. The figure for general equipment includes complement, stores (including engineers' stores), masting, and torpedo defence netting. In some cases the weight of masting and rigging is given separately, but it is also included in the weight of general equipment. Machinery weight includes auxiliary machinery (e.g., for operating guns), but not engineers' stores, which are included in general equipment. British practice was not to separate out the weight of reserve feed water. In a few cases the weight of reserve feed water (RFW) was given (42 tons for *Highflyer*, 90 for *Ariadne*), and it was included in neither machinery weight nor in normal displacement. Remember that ships without water-tube boilers – the vast majority in this book – did not carry reserve feed water.

Figures in parentheses after numbers of guns are the number of rounds per gun. In a very few cases, figures in parentheses are actual versus planned numbers of guns. The numbers after torpedo tubes are the total number of torpedoes on board.

Length shown are bp (between perpendiculars), wl (waterline), oa (overall). Dimensions are in feet and inches (ft-in). Displacement (disp), coal and weights are in tons. Speed is in knots (ND = Normal Draught; FD = Forced Draught). Endurance is nautical miles/at speed in knots.

1. IRON FRIGATES AND CORVETTES

Class	Inconstant	Raleigh
Length bp	333-0	298-0
Beam	50-1	48-0
Hull Depth	17-5½	N/A
Freeboard		
Amids	10-3	10-6
Draught		
Fwd	22-0	20-0
Aft	24-0	23-0
Normal	5534	4505
Shafts	1	1
IHP	6000	6000
Speed (ND)	15	15
Coal	600	550
Complement	600	500
Weights:		
Hull	2855	2100
Machinery	1026	940
Armament	405	293
Equipment	1248	587
(Masts, Rigging)	(158)	(155)
Protection	None	None
Fuel	600	550
Margin	None	None
Normal	5534	4485
Armament:		
Guns		
12-ton (9in)	10	1
6½-ton (7in)	6	None
90cwt (7in)	None	None
70cwt (64pdr)	None	24

Note: *Inconstant* data are from a submission by Controller Rear Admiral Robinson for a slightly improved version. This ship was never built, but weights and other data are probably very nearly those of *Inconstant* as designed. A later paper by Robinson gives *Inconstant* dimensions as 337ft 4in bp × 50ft 3½in × 20ft 10in forward and 25ft 2in aft, with a coal capacity of 680 tons. Tonnage is given as 4066, but that is tons burthen. The *Inconstant* Cover has not survived. Data on *Raleigh* are from a Legend included in a 9 February 1870 paper produced by Controller Rear Admiral Robinson opposing that design (ADM1/6177). These were preliminary data, but no completed Cover has survived. Robinson's paper did not give comparable figures for *Inconstant*. It is not clear why the stated displacement of *Raleigh* differed from the total of loads, as the Legend does not indicate any surplus inherent in the ship's lines. *Volage* and *Boadicea* data are from Covers. Reference to a 70cwt gun is actually to the 64pdr 71cwt gun. Hull depths are depths in hold. Freeboard is to upper deck from load waterline. Note that Legends for *Inconstant* and *Raleigh* gave nominal, not indicated, horsepower, but that the expected ratio was clearly 6 to 1 (*Volage* did better, 4500 IHP for 600 NHP). Machinery weight seems to have been estimated on the basis of one ton per NHP. Overall length is not given because it included bowsprits. *Boadicea* and her two near-sisters had compound engines, whereas the earlier ships had single-expansion engines (*Rover* had compound engines, but she is not described in detail here). The Legend gives a single set of data for both *Bacchante* and *Euryalus*. A later list of weights for *Euryalus* shows a total armament weight of 253.5 tons and a complement of 382. Equipment weight, which included stores, was 436.5 tons. Machinery weight was given as 895 tons.

The *Boadicea* Cover includes material on the design of an abortive modified 15-knot frigate. On 24 January 1877 DNC gave instructions to begin the design, which was to have a protective deck. There were two alternative designs, one with a 1½in deck and one with a belt (as in *Nelson*) with a 1in deck on top and 1½in decks at the ends below water. Rig was to be light, armament subordinate, and the ship was to be long and fine (at the ends) as in French ships to achieve high speed. Vertical engines would be adopted if possible, the expected power requirement being 6000 IHP. The ship would be based on *Boadicea*, dimensions being expanded as necessary to accommodate the machinery. DNC expected the ship to need twin screws. The designs submitted were based mainly on *Shah* as to weight and centre of gravity. DNC decided to change armour thickness and to reduce the height of gun ports to 9ft, and made several other changes. On 17 March he was sent two sketches, which he forwarded to Controller with a report. A sketch of the belted ship (No 1 design, February 1877) showed 5½in sides and 5in bulkheads at the ends of the citadel, with a ¾in deck on top and 1½in underwater decks at the ends. The sketch showed that the combination of protection and speed was expensive: the ship was 330ft × 54ft × 21ft (fwd) 23ft (aft), 6180 tons, and would have required 6100 IHP. Armament was similar to that of *Boadicea*, and rig was light, as in *Iris* and *Mercury*. The corresponding protected cruiser (No 2 design) was not too much smaller: 320ft × 52ft × 20ft 6in/22ft 6in, 5670 tons, requiring 5800 IHP. No 2 would have cost about 10 per cent less than No 1. No 2 had a complete underwater deck with a cellular space (as in the *Comus* class) between it and the deck above (cells were 8ft wide and 24ft deep). Data on both designs (from a February 1877 Legend) is given. The February 1877 Legend compared them with *Shah* as built, and her data are reproduced here from that Legend. Each of the new designs had 50 per cent more coal capacity than the rated quantity, and *Shah* could carry 940 tons of coal. Armament was described simply as 'equivalent to *Boadicea*', without details. Protection weight in Design No 2 included 165 tons of bulkheads forming the cellular layer above the protective deck (which weighed 335 tons); in No 1, it included 265 tons of deck armour and 80 tons of backing. A pencilled list of weights alongside data for the two designs in a March 1877 Legend added up to 7200 tons, the increase due mainly to heavier protection (728 tons of side armour, 90 tons of backing, and 426 tons of deck armour). As finally submitted No 1 had 6in side armour and an underwater deck throughout.

DNO and Controller both preferred No 1, but the Board rejected both, preferring a *Boadicea* with sail power in the same proportion; sailing and steaming power as in *Boadicea* and *Raleigh*; a lifting screw; 540 tons of coal; a 1½in steel deck over engines and boilers (as in *Comus*); and an armament of two 9in guns as in *Raleigh* and twelve 90cwt guns as in *Boadicea*. Barnaby later wrote that on 11 April 1877 the Naval Lords had decided to combine the seagoing qualities of *Boadicea* with the protection of the *Comus* class. On 7 May DNC forwarded a Legend and mid-section for a 'new *Boadicea*': 300ft × 53ft × 23ft, 5565 tons, and 15kts. Given her complete rig, she had a large complement (500). This ship would cost somewhat less than No 2. Barnaby offered an alternative 'new *Volage*' without a double bottom but with the same 1½in deck over engines and boilers: 290ft×49ft×22½ft, 4450 tons, and about a sixth less expensive than 'new *Boadicea*'. On 15 August 1877 the Naval Lords approved the larger ship, which offered both deck protection and a double bottom. However, as late as December 1877 Barnaby was submitting alternative Legends of a 330ft ship with 6in and 5½in side armour (the old No 1) and a 300ft 5565-tonner (as submitted in April). Apparently the latter was necessary if the ship was to match *Boadicea*. When he asked Controller for authority to develop the design further, Barnaby was told that no decision had been taken.

By this time Controller (at the time not a member of the Board) and DNO had agreed with Barnaby to oppose the Naval Lords' ship. Barnaby pointed out that while the boilers and machinery were well protected, the men at the guns were more exposed than ever to the effects of shellfire. Shells which might pass through the *Boadicea* below her gun deck without exploding would burst in the cellular raft above the protective deck, blowing up the deck under the feet of the men at the guns. The *Comus* class did not suffer from this problem, because there was a deck space between the top of the cellular layer and the gun deck. Moreover, the gun crews in the *Comus* were in the open, hence less affected by explosions. In the proposed new ship 150 men would be between decks (in a length of 150ft) at the guns. Barnaby concluded that underwater deck protection was suited to only two classes of ship: (i) unarmoured ships with small gun crews and (ii) ships in which the combatants are protected against shellfire. He proposed a fast frigate with an underwater deck and with a heavily protected director to fire her guns remotely (as in his *Nelson*). She would be armed mainly with the ram and with torpedoes. This ship would not have men at the guns in a close engagement; they would prepare the guns and then take shelter as the ship swooped on her opponent and fired a whole broadside electrically. The naval Lords were unenthusiastic. Controller and DNO also thought that merchant ships could be taken up from trade to provide much the same fighting power. He asked whether *Highflyer* would be a *Boadicea* with a protective deck, as proposed by the naval Lords. His alternative was a fast ship with an underwater deck, ram, torpedoes, twin screws, large coal capacity, small sail power, and few guns.

By May 1878 Barnaby was referring to a 16-knot frigate whose speed would be reduced to 15¼kts if coal capacity was increased to 1000 tons, and to a requirement to lengthen the ship to 340ft (8100 tons) to retain 16kt speed with 1000 tons of coal. At this time the ship was a 330-footer (7450 tons). In November, Barnaby asked to forward the papers relating to the unarmoured ship planned for construction at Portsmouth (which was now free to work on the project). HMS *Highflyer* had been ordered from Portsmouth on 26 August 1878, and by November the yard was free to begin detailed design work. However, Barnaby had yet to receive formal orders to design the ship. Agreement apparently proved impossible: in 1879 *Highflyer* was cancelled in favour of the much smaller *Canada* and *Cordelia*. Barnaby's reflections on the *Highflyer* project, and particularly on the kind of ship which should have only a protective deck, seem to point ahead to the *Leander* design, a ship armed with relatively few of the new breech-loading guns rather than with a large gun-deck battery. Barnaby's rejected design for a protected-deck ram has not come to light.

Class	*Volage*	*Boadicea*	*Euryalus*
Length bp	270-0	280-0	280-0
Beam	42-0	45-0	45-6
Hull Depth	15-2	15-7	15-7
Freeboard			
Amids	9-0	13-10	14-2
Draught			
Fwd	16-6	20-8	20-4
Aft	21-6	23-2	22-10
Normal	3080	4027	3932
Shafts	1	1	1
IHP	4500	5250	5250
Speed	15	15	15
Coal	414	400	400
Complement	300	350	350
Weights:			
Hull	1485	2001	1906
Machinery	598	950	950
Armament	135.05	235	235
Equipment	447.95	425	425
(Masts, Rigging)	146.25	125	125
Protection	None	None	None
Fuel	414	400	400
Margin	None	None	None
Normal	3080	4027	3932
Armament:			
Guns			
12-ton (9 in)	None	None	None
6½-ton (7in)	6	None	None
90cwt (7in)	None	14	14
70cwt (64pdr)	2	2	2

Class	*No 1*	*No 2*	*Shah*
Length bp	330-0	320-0	334-8
Beam	54-0	52-0	52-0
Hull Depth	——	——	——
Freeboard			
Amids	14-8	14-8	——
Draught			
Fwd	21-0	20-6	24-4½
Aft	23-0	22-6	(Mean)
Normal			
Shafts	2	2	1
IHP	6100	5800	
Speed	15	15	16.4
Coal	540	520	600
Complement	400	400	600
Weights:			
Hull	3040	2905	3243.4
Machinery	1020	970	1198.5
Armament	245	245	462.1
Equipment			
(Masts, Rigging)	90	90	177.0
Protection	805	500	None
Fuel	540	520	600
Normal	6140	5630	6208
Armament:			
Guns			
12-ton (9in)	no data	no data	2
6½-ton (7in)			16
90cwt (7in)			None
70cwt (64pdr)			8

Class	April 1877	June 1877
Length bp	300-0	290-0
Beam	53-0	49-0
Hull Depth	——	——
Freeboard		
Amids	14-4	11-6
Draught		
Fwd	22-0	20-6
Aft	25-0	24-6
Normal	5565	4450
Shafts	1	1
IHP	6000	5700
Speed	15	15
Coal	540	400
Complement	500	350
Weights:		
Hull	2660	2100
Machinery	1040	965
Armament	290	200
Equipment	655	495
(Masts, Rigging)	183	145
Protection	300	240
Fuel	540	400
Normal	5485	4400
Armament:		
Guns		(no data given for this design)
12-ton (9in)	2 (bow + stern)	
6½-ton (7in)	None	
90cwt (7in)	12	
70cwt (64pdr)	None	
Maxim MG	None	
TT	Allowed for	

2. SLOW STEEL CRUISERS

Class	*Comus*	*Cordelia*	*Calliope*
Length bp	225-0	225-0	235-0
Beam	44-6	44-6	44-6
Hull Depth	N/A	N/A	N/A
Freeboard			
Amids	8-3	8-1	8-9
Draught			
Fwd	17-0	17-2	17-8
Aft	18-6	18-8	20-2
Normal	2377	2420	2835
Shafts	1	1	1
IHP	2300	2400	3000
			(4000 FD)
Speed	13	13	13¾
			(15 FD)
Coal	270	270	320
Complement	221	264	281
Weights:			
Hull	1146	1290	1446
Machinery	390	388	490
Armament	155	154	187
Equipment	291	318	392
(Masts, Rigging)	(77)	(82)	(92)
Protection	125	In Hull	In Hull
Fuel	270	270	320
Normal	2377	2420	2835

Armament:			
Guns			
6in BLR	None	10	4
5in BLR	None	None	12
90cwt (7in)	2	None	None
64pdr	12	None	None
MG			
Nordenfelt	None	2	4×4-barrel 2×2-barrel
Gardner	None	2×0.45in	2×5-barrel 2×2-barrel
Torpedoes	None	None	6×14in
Deck	————1½in flat only————		

3. SLOW WOODEN CRUISERS

Class	Juno	Amazon	Blanche
Length bp	200-0	187-0	212-0
Beam	40-4	36-0	36-0
Hull Depth	22-0	N/A	N/A
Freeboard			
Amids	N/A	N/A	N/A
Draught			
Fwd	16-6	15-5 Mean	16-4
Mean			
Aft	17-6		
Normal	2133	1574	1760
Shafts	1	1	1
IHP	400 NHP	300 NHP	350 NHP
Speed	10¾		
Coal	230	200	N/A
Complement	200		
Weights:			
Hull	1230		
Machinery	320		
Armament	82		
Equipment	271		
(Masts, Rigging)	(61)		
Fuel	230		
Normal	2133		
(2215)			
Armament:			
Guns			
6in BLR	None	None	None
90cwt (7in)	2	2	2
64pdr	4	2	4
MG	None	None	None
TT	None	None	None

Note: Instead of eight 6in BLR, *Royalist* had two 6in and ten 5in. *Pylades* and *Caroline* had fourteen 5in.

Class	Briton	Amethyst
Length bp	220-0	220-0
Beam	36-0	37-0
Freeboard		
Amids	N/A	N/A
Draught		
Fwd	12-9	14-11
Aft	16-3	17-7
Normal	1730	1978
Shafts	1	1
IHP	350 NHP	350 NHP
Speed	13	13
Coal	255	270
Complement	220	225
Weights:	No Weight Data	
Hull		
Machinery		
Armament		
Equipment		
(Masts, Rigging)		
Fuel		
Normal		
Armament:		
Guns		
6in BLR	None	None
90cwt (7in)	2	None
64pdr	8	14
Maxim MG	None	None
TT	None	None

Class	Opal (*Emerald* Class)	Heroine
Length bp	220-0	200-0
Beam	40-0	38-0
Freeboard		
Amids	7-3	6-0
Draught		
Fwd	16-8	12-9
Aft	18-10	15-9
Normal	2144	1420
Shafts	1	1
IHP	2100	950
Speed	13	11
Coal	260	140
Complement	221	150
Weights:		
Hull (inc steel deck)	1086	780
Machinery	381	190
Armament	123.5	116
Equipment	293.5	310
(Masts, Rigging)	(72.5)	(50.5)
Fuel	260	140
Normal	2144	1420
Armament:		
Guns		
6in BLR	None	8
90cwt (7in)	None	None
64pdr	14	None
Maxim MG	None	2 Gatling
TT	None	None

4. BELTED CRUISERS

Class	Shannon	Nelson
Length bp	260-0	280-0
Beam	54-0	60-0
Hull Depth	21-7¼	N/A
Freeboard		
Amids	12-0	N/A
Draught		
Fwd	20-0	23-9
Aft	22-6	25-9
Normal	5095	7473
Shafts	1	1
IHP (ND)	3500	6640
IHP (FD)	N/A	N/A
Speed ND	13	14
Speed FD	N/A	N/A
Coal	280	
Complement	350	
Weights:		
Hull	2133	2778
Machinery	645	1140
Armament	351	533
Equipment	479	670
(Masts, Rigging)	(120)	N/A
Protection	1207	1720
Fuel	280	540
Normal	5095	7381
(7470)		
Armament:		
Guns		
18-ton (10in)	2	4
12-ton (9in)	7	8
9.2in	None	None
6in	None	None
20pdr	None	6
9pdr	None	3
6pdr QF	None	None
3pdr QF	None	None
MG	6 Gatling	
TT	None	2×14in

Note: Orlando figures are *as designed*. A later return shows her designed to displace 5040 tons, but actually displacing 5535, with 750 rather than 440 tons of coal on board. Corresponding draught was 24ft forward and 22ft 6in aft, rather than the intended 20ft forward and 21 ft aft. The corresponding depth of armour below the load waterline was 5ft 6in rather than 4ft.

Class	Imperieuse	Orlando
Length bp	315-0	300-0
Beam	62-0	56-0
Hull Depth		
Freeboard		
Amids		
Draught		
Fwd	26-9½ Mean	17-6
Aft	14-3	
Normal	8400	5600
Shafts	2	2
IHP (ND)	8000	
IHP (FD)	10,000	8622
Speed ND		
Speed FD	16	19.1
Coal	750	
Complement	514	421
Weights:		
Hull	3680	2255
Machinery	1375	790
Armament	500	400
Equipment	440	425
Protection	1505	580
Fuel	900	750

Normal	8400	5600
Armament:		
Guns		
12-ton (9in)	None	None
9.2in	4 (120)	2 (120)
6in	6 (85)	10 (85)
20pdr	None	None
9pdr	None	None
6pdr QF	4	6 (500)
3pdr QF	4	10 (500)
MG	9	2 Nordenfelt 1in
		5 Nordenfelt 0.45in
TT	None	6 × 14in (20)

5. FAST STEEL CRUISERS

Class	*Iris*	*Leander*	*Mersey*
Length bp	300-0	300-0	300-0
Beam	46-0	46-0	46-0
Hull Depth	N/A	N/A	
Freeboard			
Amids	8-7½	8-7½	
Draught			
Fwd	17-6	17-6	16-3
Aft	22-0	20-6	20-2
Normal	3735	3748	3605
(figures for *Iris* and *Leander* are as 'per drawing', i.e., correspond to the underwater hull volume of the lines plan)			
IHP (ND)	7000	5000	6000
IHP (FD)	N/A	N/A	N/A
Speed ND	17½	16	17
Speed FD	N/A	N/A	N/A
Coal	700	725	500
Endurance	N/A	N/A	3500/10
(750 tons coal)			
Complement	257	257	350
Weights:			
Hull	1595 (1442)	1475	1490
Machinery	1064 (1032)	800	560
Armament	112 (124)	163	270
Equipment	333 (352)	365	285
Protection	None	200	500
Fuel	500	725	500
Margin	N/A	N/A	N/A
Normal	3624 (3477)	3728	3605
Armament:			
Guns			
64pdr	10	None	None
8in BLR	None	None	2
6in BLR	10		10
4.7in QF	None	None	None
12pdr QF	None	None	None
6pdr QF			
3pdr QF	None	None	None
MG			
TT	4 TC	4 TC	
Deck			
Flat	None	1½in	2in
Slope	(no slope)	3in	

Class	*Medea*	*Apollo* (Design)
Length bp	265-0	285-0
Beam	41-0	42-0
Hull Depth	N/A	N/A
Freeboard		
Amids	6-0	6-6
Draught		
Fwd	15-3	15-6
Aft	17-9	17-6
Normal	2800	3100
Shafts	2	2
IHP (ND)	N/A	N/A
IHP (FD)	9000	9000
Speed ND	N/A	N/A
Speed FD	20	20
Coal	400	400
Endurance	8000/10	8000/10
Complement	190	210
Weights:		
Hull	1020	1120
Machinery	648	648
Armament	180	215 (175)
Equipment	207	232
Protection	330	357
Fuel	400	400
Margin	None	118
Normal	2785	3100
Armament:		
Guns		
64pdr	None	None
8in BLR	None	None
6in BLR	6 (85)	2 (200)
4.7in QF	None	6 (300)
12pdr QF	None	None
6pdr QF	9	None
3pdr QF	None	8
MG		
TT	6 (12)	4 (12)
Deck		
Flat	1½in	1½in
Slope	2in	2in

Class	*Aeolus* (Sheathed)	*Astraea* (Sheathed)
Length bp	300-0	320-0
Beam	43-8	49-6
Hull Depth	N/A	N/A
Freeboard		
Amids	6-6	14-3
Draught		
Fwd	16-6	18-0
Aft	18-6	20-0
Normal	3600	4360
Shafts	2	2
IHP (ND)	7000	7000
IHP (FD)	9000	9000
Speed ND	18¼	18¼
Speed FD	19¾	19½
Coal	400	400
Endurance	N/A	N/A
Complement	252	264
Weights:		
Hull	1540	2025
Machinery	650	760
Armament	245	290
Equipment	238	283
Protection	397	437
Fuel	400	400
Margin	140	163
Normal	3610	4360
Armament:		
64pdr	None	None
8in BLR	None	None
6in BLR	2 (250)	2 (250)
4.7in QF	6 (250)	8 (250)
12pdr QF	None	None
6pdr QF	8	8
3pdr QF	None	None
MG	4 Nordenfelt	4 Nordenfelt
TT	4(12)	4 (12)
Deck		
Flat	1½in	1½in
Slope	2in	2in

Class	*Talbot*
Length bp	350-0
Beam	53-6
Hull Depth	34-6
Freeboard	
Amids	14-6
Draught	
Fwd	19-6
Aft	21-6
Normal	5600
Shafts	2
IHP (ND)	8000
IHP (FD)	9600
Speed ND	18½
Speed FD	19½
Coal	550
Endurance	N/A
Complement	380
Weights:	
Hull	2520 (2500)
Machinery	900 (940)
Armament	385 (365)
Equipment	415 (460)
Protection	620 (605)
Fuel	550
Margin	210
Normal	5600 (5420)
Armament	
64pdr	None
8in BLR	None
6in BLR	5 (200)
4.7in QF	6 (250)
12pdr QF	8 (300)
6pdr QF	None
3pdr QF	6 (500)
MG	1 Maxim (field mount)
TT	2 (12)
Deck	
Flat	1½in
Slope	3in

Class	Highflyer	Challenger
Length bp	350-0	355-0
Beam	54-0	56-0
Hull Depth	34-6	34-10
Freeboard		
Amids	14-7	14-6
Draught		
Fwd	19-6	19-3
Aft	21-6	21-3
Normal	5600 (5634)	5880
Shafts	2	2
IHP (ND)	10,000	12,500
IHP (FD)	N/A	N/A
Speed ND	20	20.75
Speed FD	N/A	N/A
Coal	600/1125	600/1150
Endurance	N/A	N/A
Complement	470	490
Weights:		
Hull	2600 (2715)	2665
Machinery	870 (850)	1060 (B&W boilers)
Armament	465 (446)	450
Equipment	495 (513)	499
Protection	520 (500)	556
Fuel	600	600
Margin	50	50
Normal	5600 (5634)	5880
Armament:		
64pdr	None	None
8in BLR	None	None
6in BLR	11 (200)	11 (200)
4.7in QF	None	None
12pdr QF	8 (300)	8 (300)
6pdr QF	None	None
3pdr QF	6 (10)	6
MG	6 Maxim	6 Maxim
TT	2 (10)	2 (7)
Deck		
Flat	1½in	1½in
Slope	3in	3in

6. FLEET RAM

Class	Arrogant
Length bp	320-0
Length wl	333-0 (333-6)
Length oa	342-0 (342-4)
Beam	57-0 (57-7)
Hull Depth	35-9 (35-11)
Freeboard	
Amids	14-3 (15-3)
Draught	
Fwd	20-0 (19-6½)
Aft	22-0 (20-9½)
Normal	5750 (5412)
Shafts	2
IHP (ND)	10,000 (10,290)
IHP (FD)	N/A
Speed ND	18½ to 19 (19)
Speed FD	N/A
Coal	500
Complement	384 (419)
Weights:	
Hull	
Machinery	900 (860)
Armament	360 (340)
Equipment	470 (467)
Protection	760 (653)
Fuel	500/1200
Margin	100 (10)
Normal	5750 (5410)
Armament:	
6in	4 (200)
4.7in	6 (200)
12pdr QF	8 (200)
3pdr QF	6 (3 as built)(500)
TT	2
Deck	
Flat	1½in
Slope	3in

7. TORPEDO CRUISERS

Class	Scout	Archer
Length bp	220-0	225-0
Beam	34-0	36-0
Freeboard		
Amids	5-9	4-10
Draught		
Fwd	12-6	13-5
Aft	4-6	15-5
Normal	1430 (as designed)	1630 (1771)
Shafts	2	2
IHP (ND)	N/A	N/A
IHP (FD)	3200	3500
Speed ND	N/A	N/A
Speed FD	16	17
Coal	250	250
Complement	120	140 (156)
Weights:		
Hull	750 (791 including 51 ballast)	798.7 (800 including 25 ballast)
Machinery	320 (373)	350
Armament	63 (73.5)	135 (149)
Equipment	131 (141.5)	161.5 (161.7)
Protection	(10)	—
Fuel	300 (250)	185 (250)
RFW	None	None
Margin	None	None
Normal	1564 (1596 as calculated, 1588 as inclined)	1630.2 (1771)
Armament:		
6in	None	6
5in	4	None
4.7in	None	None
3pdr QF	None	None
MG	8 × 1in Nordenfelt 2 × 0.45in	8 × 1in Nordenfelt 1 × 0.45in
TT	8 (originally 11) 20 torpedoes	8 (12)
Deck		
Flat	⅜in	⅜in
Slope	——	——

Class	Vulcan
Length bp	350-0
Beam	58-0
Freeboard	
Amids	14-3
Draught	
Fwd	22-0
Aft	24-0
Normal	6620
Shafts	2
IHP (ND)	N/A
IHP (FD)	12,000
Speed ND	N/A
Speed FD	20
Coal	1000
Complement	450
Weights:	
Hull	2355
Machinery	1000
Armament	380
Equipment	850
Protection	780
Fuel	1000
RFW	None
Margin	255
Normal	6620
Armament:	
6in	None
5in	None
4.7in	8 (300)
3pdr QF	12 (500)
MG	None
TT	8 (30)
Deck	
Flat	2½in
Slope	3in–5in

8. FIRST-CLASS CRUISERS

Class	Blake	Centaur
Length bp	375-0	360-0
Length wl	387-0	N/A
Length oa	400-0	N/A
Beam	65-0	60-8
Hull Depth	N/A	N/A
Freeboard		
Amids	15-0	N/A
Draught		
Fwd	24-9	24-1
Aft	26-9	25-7
Normal	9000	7700
Shafts	2	2
IHP (ND)	13,000	N/A
IHP (FD)	20,000	12,000
Speed ND	N/A	18
Speed FD	22	19½
Coal	1500	850
Endurance	15,000/10	N/A
Complement	500 (600)	520

DATA LIST

Weights:
Hull	3290	3100
Machinery	1540 (1605)	1000
Armament	580 (539)	605
Equipment	550 (545)	490
Protection	1190	
Fuel	1500	850
RFW	None	
Margin	350	296
Normal	9000 (9067)	7696

Armament:
9.2in	2 (120)	1
6in	10 (70)	12
12pdr QF	None	None
6pdr QF	None	12
3pdr QF	18	None
MG	None	
TT	4	4 (18)

Deck
Flat	5in	
Slope	6in	

Class	*Powerful*	*Ariadne*
Length bp	500-0	435-0
Length wl	521-0	456-0
Length oa	538-0	463-0
Beam	71-6	69-0
Hull Depth	44-6	40-0
Freeboard		
Amids	17-9	15-3
Draught		
Fwd	27-0	24-3
Aft	27-0	26-3
Normal	14,200	11,000
Shafts	2	2
IHP (ND)	18,000	18,000
	(continuous)	
IHP (FD)	25,000	N/A
Speed ND	20	20.75
Speed FD	22	19
Coal	1500/3000	1000/2000
Endurance	N/A	N/A
Complement	960	650

Weights:
Hull	6370 (6740)	4600 (plus 525 sheathing)
	(includes 620 protection for armament above protective deck)	
Machinery	2300 (2260)	1550
Armament	790 (800)	675
Equipment	930 (855)	650
Protection	2110 (1885)	1850
Fuel	1500	1000
RFW	N/A	
Margin	200	150
Normal	14,200 (14,040)	11,000

Armament:
9.2in	2 (105)	None
6in	12 (200)	16 (200)
12pdr	18 (300)	14 (300)
6pdr	None	None
3pdr	12 (500)	3 (500)
MG	9 Maxim	7 Maxim
TT	4	2

Deck
Flat	4in	4in
Slope	4in	4in

9. THIRD-CLASS CRUISERS

Class	*Barracouta*	*Barham*
Length bp	220-0	280-0
Beam	35-3	35-0
Freeboard		
Amids	5-3	5-0
Draught		
Fwd	12-0	11-9
Aft	15-0	14-9
Normal	1530	1830
Shafts	2	2
IHP (ND)	1960	N/A
IHP (FD)	3600	6000
Speed ND	15	N/A
Speed FD	16.5	20
Coal	190	140
Complement	152	160

Weights:
Hull	N/A	900
Machinery	266.21	281
Armament	132.73	115
Equipment	172.69	170
Protection	N/A	150
Fuel	190	140
Margin	None	70
Normal	1530	1830

Armament:
4.7in	6 (300)	6 (280)
4in QF	None	None
3pdr QF	4 (500)	4
MG	2 Nordenfelt	2 Nordenfelt
TT	4 (10)	2 (12)

Deck
Flat	1in	1in
Slope	2in	2in

Note: A Legend for *Barrosa* shows neither of her designed IHPs attained; actual figures were 2120 and 3110 IHP, for speeds of, respectively, 14.91 and 16.87kts. Weights are for *Blonde* as built. They did not include actual displacement or protection or hull weight. The Legend weights for the 'Gem' class were calculated based on 14in torpedoes, but the ships actually had 18in torpedoes.

Class	*Pearl*	*Pelorus*
Length bp	265-0	300-0
Beam	41-0	36-6
Freeboard		
Amids	6-0	7-9
Draught		
Fwd	14-4	12-0
Aft	16-6	15-0
Normal	2535	2135
Shafts	2	2
IHP (ND)	N/A	5000
IHP (FD)	7500	7000
Speed ND	N/A	18½
Speed FD	19	20
Coal	300	250/515
Complement	190	225

Weights:
Hull	1000	910
Machinery	540	360
Armament	165	145
Equipment	210	205
Protection	222	198
Fuel	300	250
Margin	98	67
Normal	2535	

Armament:
4.7in	8	None
4in QF	None	8 (300)
3pdr QF	8	8 (500)
MG	3 Nordenfelt	2 Maxim
TT	2 (12)	2×14in (5)

Deck
Flat	?	
Slope	?	

Class	'Gem' Class
Length bp	360-0
Beam	40-0
Freeboard	
Amids	7-4
Draught	
Fwd	13-0
Aft	16-0
Normal	3000
Shafts	2
IHP (ND)	7000
IHP (FD)	9800
Speed ND	20
Speed FD	21¾
Coal	300/700
Complement	313

Weights:
Hull	1400
Machinery	557
Armament	191
Equipment	269
Protection	253
Fuel	300
Margin	30
Normal	3000

Armament:
4.7in	None
4in QF	12 (200)
3pdr QF	8 (500)
MG	3 Maxim
TT	2 (5)

Deck
Flat	¾in
Slope	

10. ARMOURED CRUISERS

Class	*Cressy*	*Drake*
Length bp	440-0	500-0
Length wl	460-0	521-0
Length oa	472-6	

Beam	69-6	71-0
Hull Depth	39-9	N/A
Freeboard		
Amids	14-0	14-0
Draught		
Fwd	25-9	26-0
Aft	26-9	26-0
Normal	12,000	14,100
Shafts	2	2
IHP	21,000	30,000
IHP (continuous)	16,500	
Speed	21	23
Sea Speed	19.5	
Coal	800/1600	1250/2500
Complement	725	900
Weights:		
Hull	4800	5500
	(plus 540 sheathing)	
Machinery	1800	2550
Armament	770	870
Equipment	620	830
Protection	1880	3000
Fuel	800	1250
Margin	100	100
Normal	12,000	14,100
Armament:		
9.2in	2 (105)	2 (105)
7.5in	None	None
6in	12 (200)	16 (100)
12pdr	14 (300)	12 (300)
3pdr	3 (500)	3
MG	8 Maxim	9
TT	2 (7)	2
Belt	6in	6in
Deck		
Flat	1½in	1in
Slope	1½in (plus 1in on top of top belt)	1in (plus 1½in on of belt)

Note: Weights for *Hampshire* are Legend data for ships before the forward 6in casemates were replaced by 7.5in single mounts. This Legend includes 8 rather than 2 × 12pdr. Design displacement for the final design, with four 7.5in guns, was 10,700 tons.

Class	*Monmouth*	*Hampshire*
Length bp	440-0	450-0
Length wl	455-0	465-0
Length oa	467-6	473-6
Beam	68-0	68-7⅛
Hull Depth	38-9	38-4³⁄₁₆
Freeboard		
Amids	14-0	14-0
Draught		
Fwd	24-0	24-0
Aft	25-0	25-0
Normal	9800	10,700
Shafts	2	2
IHP	22,000	21,000
IHP (continuous)	16,000	15,500
Speed	23	23
Sea Speed	20	20¾
Coal	800	800/1033
Complement	678	610
Weights:		
Hull	4030	4200
Machinery	1795	1945
Armament	620	640
Equipment	590	585
Protection	1865	1930
Fuel	800	800
Margin	100	100
Normal	9800	10,200 (10,729)
Armament:		
9.2in	None	None
7.5in	None	4 (120)
6in	14 (100)	6 (100)
12pdr	8 (300)	2 (300)
3pdr	3 (500)	20 (500)
MG	8 Maxim	2 Maxim
TT	2 (7)	2
Belt	4in	4in
Deck		
Flat	1¼in	1¼in
Slope	——— flat on top of belt ———	

Class	*Duke of Edinburgh*	*Warrior*
Length bp	480-0	480-0
Length wl	498-3	498-3
Length oa	505-6	505-6
Beam	73-6	73-6
Hull Depth	40-3	40-3
Freeboard		
Amids	13-0	13-3
Draught		
Fwd	26-6	26-6
Aft	27-6	27-6
Normal	13,550	13,550
Shafts	2	2
IHP	23,500	23,500
IHP (continuous)	16,000	16,000
Speed	22⅓	22⅓
Sea Speed	20	20
Coal	1000/2000	1000/2000
Complement	769	770
Weights:		
Hull	5190	N/A
Machinery	2270	2185
Armament	1565	1810
Equipment	640	630
Protection	2845	N/A
Fuel	1000	1000
Margin	60	
Normal	13,550	
Armament:		
9.2in	6 (100)	6 (100)
7.5in	None	4 (100)
6in	10 (150)	None
12pdr	None	None
3pdr	20 (250)	28 (250)
MG	2 Maxim	2 Maxim (8000)
TT	2	4 (14)
Belt	6in	6in
Deck		
Flat	¾in	¾in
Slope	¾in (1in deck over belt)	¾in (1in deck over belt)

Class	*Minotaur*
Length bp	490-0
Length wl	508-0
Length oa	519-0
Beam	74-6
Hull Depth	40-0
Freeboard	
Amids	14-0
Draught	
Fwd	25-6
Aft	26-6
Normal	14,600
Shafts	2
IHP	27,000
IHP (continuous)	20,000 (approx)
Speed	23
Sea Speed	21 (approx)
Coal	1000
Complement	800 (approx)
Weights:	
Hull	5520
Machinery	2450
Armament	2065
Equipment	675
Protection	2790
Fuel	1000
Margin	100
Normal	14,600c
Armament:	
9.2in	4 (100)
7.5in	10 (100)
6in	None
12pdr	None
3pdr	28 (250)
MG	2 Maxim
TT	5
Belt	
Deck	
Flat	¾in
Slope	

List of Ships

In contrast to other books in this series, no attempt has been made to indicate when ships were decommissioned and recommissioned. For most of the period covered by this book, ships were commissioned for specific periods of service on various stations. On their return they might be decommissioned and placed in the Steam Reserve, or refitted for further active service. Ships were commissioned from the Steam Reserve for service on specific stations, or for particular (e.g., individual assignment) service or for short-term service, for example for the annual manoeuvres. See the individual ship histories in photo captions for examples of such careers.

The name of the yard is given under the name of each ship. The first of the two columns of dates gives date of laying down over the date of launch; the second column is date of completion, all in day-month-year format.

Abbreviations

Shipbuilders

Armstrong	Armstrong, Elswick
Barrow	Barrow Iron Shipbuilding Co (became Vickers Barrow yard)
Beardmore	Beardmore, Dalmuir
Brown	John Brown, Clydebank (previously J & G Thomson)
Chath	Chatham Royal Dockyard
Dept	Deptford Royal Dockard
Dev	Devonport Royal Dockyard
Ditch	Ditchburn & Mare, Blackwall
Doxford	William Doxford, Sunderland
Earle	Earle's Shipbuilding, Hull
Elder	John Elder & Co, Govan
Fairbairn	William Fairbairn & Co, Millwall
Hawthorn	Hawthorn Leslie, Hebburn-on-Tyne
L&G	London & Glasgow
Laird	John Laird and Sons, Birkenhead
Mare	C J Mare & Co, Blackwall
Moul	Moulmein, Burma
Napier	William Napier & Sons, Govan
Palmer	Palmer Shipbuilding & Iron Co, Jarrow
Pem	Pembroke Royal Dockyard
Pitcher	W & H Pitcher, Northfleet
Ply	Plymouth Royal Dockyard
Ports	Portsmouth Royal Dockyard
Raylton	Raylton Dixon & Co, Middlesbrough
Russell	J Scott Russell & Co, Millwall
Samuda	Samuda Brothers, Poplar
Scott	Scott, Sinclair & Co, Greenock
Sheer	Sheerness Royal Dockyard
Steph	Robert Stephenson, Hebburn
Thames	Thames Iron Works (or Shipbuilding Co), Blackwall
Thomson	J & G Thomson, Clydebank
Vickers	Vickers (originally Naval Construction and Armaments Co)
Wool	Woolwich Royal Dockyard
Young	Young, Magnay & Co, Limehouse

Fates

BU	Broken up
Coll	Collision
TS	Training Ship
W	Wrecked
WL	War Loss

PADDLE FRIGATES

Cyclops and later *Cyclops* Classes

Cyclops	8.38	4.2.40	BU 1864
Pem	10.7.39		
Vulture	9.41	7.6.45	Sold for BU 1866
Pem	21.9.43		
Firebrand	12.41	22.10.44	Sold for BU 1864
Ports	5.9.42		
Gladiator	2.42	25.4.46	BU 1879
Wool	15.10.44		

Sampson Class

Sampson	11.43	5.2.46	BU 1864
Wool	1.10.44		

Centaur/Dragon Class (Modified *Sampson*)

Centaur	12.44	3.2.49	BU 1864
Ports	6.10.45		
Dragon	1.44	7.47	BU 1864; ex-*Janus* 7.43
Pem	17.7.45		

Magicienne Class

Magicienne	9.47	20.2.53	BU 1866
Pem	7.3.49		
Valorous	3.49	7.7.53	BU 1891
Pem	30.4.51		

Furious Class

Furious	6.48	18.2.53	Coal hulk Portsmouth 1867, BU 1884
Ports	26.8.50		
Resolute			Ordered 25.4.47, shifted to Sheerness 8.1.49,
Ports			cancelled 23.3.50

CONVERSION OF SAILING FRIGATE

Penelope	—	7.43	Dates are of conversion; begun 11.6.42.
Chath		1.4.43	Had been launched as a sailing frigate 13.8.29, then completed 1.30 into reserve (in Ordinary), and not active until after paddle conversion

SINGLE-SHIP CLASSES

Gorgon	7.36	30.8.38	BU 1864
Pem	31.8.37		
Retribution	8.42	23.12.45	BU 1864; ex-*Watt* 4.44 ex-*Dragon* 8.42
Chath	2.7.44		
Terrible	11.43	25.3.46	BU 1879; ex-*Simoom* 12.42. Orig ordered from Woolwich. Largest British paddle warship
Dept	6.2.45		
Avenger	27.8.44	21.6.46	W 20.12.47
Dev	5.8.45		
Odin	2.45	12.8.47	BU 1865
Dept	24.7.46		
Sidon	26.5.45	26.11.46	BU 1864; enlarged *Odin*
Dept	26.5.46		
Leopard	8.46	3.53	Suspended 9.9.46 - 2.48; BU 1867
Dept	5.11.50		
Tiger	11.47	21.8.52	WL 12.5.54: grounded off Odessa, set on fire by Russian fire, blew up after bombardment by British ships. Russians salvaged engines, installed them in royal yacht *Tigr*
Chath	1.12.49		

Birkenhead	9.43	17.1.47	Troopship 1850-51, W 27.2.52; only iron paddle frigate
Laird	30.12.45		

PADDLE SLOOPS

Hermes Class

Hermes	4.34	25.11.35	Lengthened 1840-42, re-engined 1843, BU 1864
Ports	25.6.35		
Volcano	7.35	17.1.37	Workshop ship 1854, BU 1894
Ports	30.6.36		
Megaera	8.36	30.3.38	W 4.3.43
Sheer	30.6.36		
Acheron	10.37	8.1.39	Survey ship 1847, sold 1855
Sheer	23.8.38		

Hydra Class

Hydra	1.38	11.7.38	BU 1870
Chath	7.38		
Hecla	6.38	28.8.39	Re-engined 1848-49, sold commercial service (*Typhoon*) 6.63
Chath	14.1.39		
Hecate	6.38	7.12.39	Survey ship 1860, BU 1865
Chath	30.3.39		

Stromboli Class

Stromboli	9.38	6.9.40	BU 1867
Ports	27.8.39		
Vesuvius	9.38	20.4.40	Armstrong guns 1862, BU 1865
Sheer	11.7.39		

Alecto Class

Alecto	7.39	12.12.39	BU 1865
Chath	7.9.39		
Prometheus	7.39	20.2.40	BU 1863
Sheer	21.9.39		
Polyphemus	2.40	24.4.41	W 29.1.56
Chath	28.9.40		
Ardent	2.40	16.9.42	BU 1865
Chath	12.2.41		
Rattler			Re-ordered as screw sloop 24.2.42 (ordered 18.3.41); took part in the famous tug-of-war with *Alecto*. Was the first RN screw warship
Sheer			

Driver Class

Driver	6.40	5.11.51	W 3.8.61
Ports	24.12.40		
Styx	22.6.40	4.10.41	BU 1866
Sheer	26.1.41		
Vixen	6.40	28.12.41	BU 1862
Pem	4.2.41		
Devastation	27.7.40	30.11.41	BU 1866
Wool	3.7.41		
Geyser	8.40	8.3.42	BU 1866
Pem	6.4.41		
Growler	1.41	9.3.42	BU 1854
Chath	20.7.41		
Thunderbolt	4.41	8.2.43	W 3.2.47
Ports	13.1.42		
Cormorant	17.5.41	28.6.43	BU 1853
Sheer	29.3.42		
Spiteful	8.41	24.3.43	BU 1883
Pem	24.3.42		
Eclair	8.41	9.9.44	Floating factory (depot ship) 1863, BU 1865. Ex-*Infernal*, 26.8.44
Wool	31.5.43		
Virago	15.11.41	29.7.43	BU 1876
Chath	25.7.42		
Sphinx	5.44	3.11.46	BU 1881
Wool	17.2.46		

Bulldog Class (lengthened *Driver* Class)

Inflexible	1.44	9.8.46	BU 1864
Pem	22.5.45		
Scourge	2.44	13.5.46	BU 1865
Ports	9.11.44		
Bulldog	7.7.44	7.9.46	Armstrong guns 1861; WL 23.10.65
Chath	2.10.45		
Fury	6.45	6.7.47	BU 1864
Sheer	31.12.45		

Single-Ship Classes

Salamander	4.31	12.2.33	BU 1883
Sheer	14.5.32		
Phoenix	5.31	7.1.34	To screw sloop 4.44-2.45, BU 1864
Chath	25.9.32		
Rhadamanthus	9.31	2.11.32	Transport 1841, troopship 1851, BU 1864
Ply	16.4.32		
Medea	4.32	3.4.34	Sold 1867
Wool	2.9.33		
Janus	6.9.43	1.46	Tug at Gibraltar 1849, gun-vessel 1854, sold 1856
Chath	6.2.44		
Basilisk	11.46	7.52	BU 1882
Wool	22.8.48		
Buzzard	10.47	8.11.50	BU 1883
Pem	24.3.49		
Argus	6.48	2.5.53	BU 1881 (lengthened *Alecto*)
Ports	15.12.49		
Barracouta	5.49	30.7.53	BU 1881
Pem	31.3.51		

SCREW FRIGATES

Prototype Conversion

Amphion	15.4.40	13.5.47	Converted on the slip. BU 1863
Wool	14.1.46		

Prototypes

Arrogant	9.45	8.1.49	BU 1867
Ports	5.4.48		
Fervent			Intended as screw equivalent to paddle frigate *Terrible*; ordered, suspended 7.4.45, cancelled 22.5.49
Wool	20.2.45		

Single Conversion

Fox	9.55	3.62	Former sailing frigate launched 1829 but not completed; date of keel-laying is date conversion began. Work stopped 1856, completed as transport and storeship. BU 1882
Ports	18.3.56		

Single Conversion

Narcissus	11.49	23.2.61	BU 1883. Begun as sailing frigate, reordered and re-laid down 4.57 as steam frigate. Flagship of Detached (Flying) Squadron 1870
Dev	26.10.59		

Dauntless Class

Dauntless	9.45	16.10.50	BU 1885
Ports	5.1.47		

Vigilant Ports			Ordered 26.3.46, suspended 9.9.46, cancelled 22.5.49

Termagant Class

Termagant Dept	4.45 25.9.47	12.10.54	Re-engined 1854, BU 1867
Euphrates Dept			Ordered 26.3.46, suspended 9.9.46, cancelled 22.5.49

BLOCKSHIP CONVERSIONS OF OLD SAILING FRIGATES
(dates of laying down are dates conversion began)

Note: Horatio alone was completed as scheduled with engines and fitted as a screw mortar frigate during the Crimean War. The others did not receive engines until 1855; on 29.6.55 they were ordered lengthened and converted into screw mortar frigates with 200 NHP engines (originally all were to have had 250 NHP engines). These last three did receive engines (as indicated by dates of undocking) but apparently were not rearmed as planned due to the end of the Crimean War. Mortar armament was two 13in mortars plus two 68pdrs on the upper deck and eight 32pdrs on the lower deck. Screw blockship armament was four 10in shell guns on the upper deck and twelve 8in and eight 32pdrs on the lower deck (from 1853, eighteen 8in on the lower deck, and no 32pdr).

Horatio Chath	11.45 6.50,	12.49	Completed 12.49, engine fitted to screw mortar frigate Sheerness 1855, BU 1865
Eurotas Chath	12.45	4.51	Completed without engines 2.48, to screw mortar frigate Sheerness 7.55–10.4.56 (undocked 12.2.56), BU 1865
Seahorse Dev	11.45	7.47	Completed as screw mortar frigate at Devonport (undocked 3.56), to coal hulk, renamed *Lavinia* 1870, BU 1902
Forth Dev	10.45	7.47	Converted to screw mortar frigate at Devonport (undocked 21.1.56), to coal hulk, renamed *Jupiter* 12.69, BU 1883

Tribune Class

Tribune Sheer	4.51 21.1.53	3.8.53	BU 1866
Curacoa Pem	1.52 13.4.54	14.11.54	BU 1869

Forte/Imperieuse Class

Imperieuse Dept	11.50 15.9.52	30.3.53	BU 1867
Euryalus Chath	10.51 5.10.53	5.3.54	BU 1867
Aurora Pem	5.9.54 22.6.61	11.63	BU 1881
Forte Dept	5.5.54 29.5.58	7.4.60	Receiving ship 1880, coal hulk 1894, burned accidentally Sheerness 23.11.05
Chesapeake Chath	30.5.54 27.9.55	28.8.57	BU 1867

Liffey Class

Liffey Dev	12.7.54 6.5.56	11.1.59	Store hulk 1877, sold 1903
Shannon Ports	1.54 24.11.55	29.12.56	BU 1871
Topaze Dev	4.56 12.5.58	23.7.59	BU 1884
Bacchante Ports	.56 31.7.59	29.6.60	BU 1869
Liverpool Dev	14.11.59 30.10.60	11.12.60	BU 1875

Diadem Class

Diadem Pem	6.55 14.10.56	3.1.58	BU 1875
Doris Pem	6.56 25.3.57	30.3.59	BU 1885

Ariadne Class

Ariadne Dept	1.8.56 4.6.59	16.12.59	Part of *Vernon* 1880, cadet TS 1884, renamed *Actaeon* 6.6.05, sold 11.12.22
Galatea Wool	9.2.57 14.9.59	2.62	BU 6.1883
Acasta Dept	16.4.61	—	Cancelled 12.12.63
Hyperion Wool	—	—	Cancelled 12.12.63, not laid down

Emerald Class
(Converted on stocks, ordered 1854-56)

Emerald Dept	4.6.49 19.7.56	1.6.59	BU 1869. Conversion began 29.5.54
Melpomene Pem	9.49 8.8.57	18.6.59	BU 1875. Conversion began 30.6.56
Immortalite Pem	11.49 25.10.59	7.2.62	BU 1875. Conversion began 14.7.56

Mersey Class

Orlando Pem	11.56 12.6.58	13.11.60	BU 1871
Mersey Chath	26.12.56 13.8.58	21.4.59	BU 1875

Bristol Class

Newcastle Dept	6.12.58 16.10.60	21.9.74	Suspended, completed at Sheerness. Powder hulk 1889 Devonport, sold 1929
Glasgow Ports	12.9.59 28.3.61	24.5.71	Suspended, completed late. BU 1884
Tweed Pem	3.7.60	—	Cancelled 16.12.64
Bristol Wool	16.9.59 12.2.61	10.65	BU 1883
Undaunted Chath	28.5.59 1.1.61	16.7.61	Initially direct to reserve. BU 1882
Dryad Ports	2.1.60 —	—	Cancelled 16.12.64, all frames down 11.3.65
Belvidera Chath	30.4.60 —	—	Cancelled 16.12.64
Pomone Chath	10.9.60 —	—	Cancelled 12.12.63
Raleigh Ports			Never started; cancelled 12.12.63
Briton Ports			Never started; cancelled 12.12.63
Barham Ports			Never started; cancelled 12.12.63
Boadicea Chath			Never started; cancelled 12.12.63
Bucephalus Ports			Never started; cancelled 12.12.63
Dextrous Pem			Never started; cancelled 12.12.63

Ister Class

Ister Dev	8.11.60 —	—	Cancelled 16.12.64, all frames down by 29.4.65
Endymion Dept	26.10.60 18.11.65	9.66	Sold as hulk 1886, BU 1905; was suspended in 1862-63
Blonde Wool	10.9.60 —	—	Cancelled 12.12.63
Astraea Dev	21.10.61 —	—	Cancelled 12.12.63
Dartmouth Wool	6.11.60 —	—	Cancelled 16.12.64, all frames down by 28.2.65.

CONVERSIONS

Note: The First Lord, Pakington, announced in 1859 that he planned twelve or thirteen conversions to help match French frigate numbers, but only eight ships were converted, and there is no evidence of further orders. Yards are those at which ships were converted. Laying-down date is the date conversion began. Typically one section was launched so that the ship could be lengthened on the stocks. The launch date is that on which the completed ship was undocked.

Phaeton Sheer	15.4.59 12.12.59	1.11.61	BU 1875
Severn Chath	5.3.59 8.2.60	21.8.60	Completion is date machinery fitting was completed at Sheerness; ship went directly into reserve. First commissioned 19.7.62. BU 1876.
Sutlej Ports	N/A 26.3.60	18.9.62	Date is of first commission as screw frigate. BU 1869
Phoebe Dev	19.5.59 10.4.60	3.61	BU 1876
Octavia Ports	26.3.60 11.4.61	N/A	First commissioned as screw frigate 14.6.65. BU 1876
Leander Sheer	1.60 16.2.61	N/A	First commissioned as screw frigate 23.5.63. BU 1867
Arethusa Chath	23.4.60 9.8.61	N/A	First commissioned as screw frigate on 10 June 1865. Lent to Shaftesbury Homes as TS 1874 (engines removed), replaced 1931, sold for BU 1933
Constance Dev	5.5.60 15.4.62	N/A	First commission as steam frigate 10.6.65. BU 1875

IRON SCREW FRIGATES CONVERTED TO TROOPSHIPS

Greenock	3.9.45	1850	Originally *Pegasus*, sold to J Scott 30.4.49 Scott Russell 8.50 for Australian Royal Mail Co (*Esk* built in exchange). Renamed *Melbourne* 25.11.52, BU 1873
Vulcan Ditchburn	12.3.46 27.1.49	3.3.51	Sold for merchant use 2.67, converted to barque *Jorawur*
Megaera Fairbairn	8.45 22.5.49	29.12.51	W 16.6.71 due hull corrosion, a major Victorian scandal
Simoom Napier	10.45 24.5.49	30.3.55	BU 1887

SCREW CORVETTES

Highflyer Class

Highflyer Mare	1.50 13.8.51	10.4.52	BU 1871
Esk Russell	4.53 12.6.54	21.12.54	BU 1870

Cossack Class

(building for Russia, seized 5.4.54 on outbreak of Crimean War)

Cossack Pitcher	N/A 15.5.54	10.10.54	Ex-Russian *Witjas*. BU 1875. Completed for sea at Chatham
Tartar Pitcher	N/A 17.5.54	26.1.55	Ex-Russian *Wojn*. BU 1866 Completed for sea at Chatham

Pearl Class

Pearl Wool	1.54 13.2.55	25.1.56	BU 1884
Satellite Dev	8.7.54 26.9.55	23.12.56	BU 1879
Cadmus Chath	10.5.55 20.5.56	4.6.59	BU 1879
Scout Wool	10.54 31.12.56	9.7.59	BU 1877
Scylla Sheer	4.1.55 19.6.56	15.8.59	BU 1882
Charybdis Chath	29.3.56 1.6.59	19.11.60	Lent to Canadian Government 10.80, sold 1884
Pelorus Dev	25.3.56 5.2.57	10.9.57	BU 1869
Challenger Wool	3.10.55 13.2.58	28.5.61	Survey ship 1872, hulked as TS 1880, then receiving ship, accommodation ship Chatham 1910, BU 1921
Racoon Chath	21.4.56 25.4.57	8.2.58	BU 1877
Clio Sheer	25.6.56 26.8.58	18.9.59	TS 1876, BU 1919

Jason Class

Jason Dev	3.6.58 10.11.59	8.4.61	BU 1877
Barrosa Wool	2.8.58 10.3.60	18.2.61	BU 1877
Galatea Wool			Reordered 2.7.56 as screw frigate (see above)
Orpheus Chath	12.5.58 23.6.60	24.10.61	W 7.2.63
Orestes Sheer	26.87.58 18.8.60	2.9.61	BU 1866
Rattlesnake Chath	9.3.59 9.7.61	8.62	BU 1882
Wolverine Wool	10.4.59 29.8.63	4.64	Suspended 1862, resumed 1863. To NSW government as TS 18781, hulk 2.93, sold 1923

North Star Class

Note: Dido and later units might have been to a different design.

North Star Sheer	13.7.60		Cancelled 22.5.65, all frames down by 31.3.66
Favourite Dept	23.8.60		Reordered as ironclad corvette 1862
Ontario Wool	10.9.60		Suspended 5.2.62, cancelled 12.12.63
Weymouth Sheer	18.10.60		Cancelled 12.12.63
Alligator Wool	1.11.60		Suspended 5.2.62, cancelled 12.12.63
Menai Chath	5.1.61 19.8.65		Cancelled 16.12.64, all frames down by
Dido Dept	14.1.61		Cancelled 12.12.63

Falmouth		Cancelled 12.12.63, not begun	
Chath			
Nereide		Cancelled 12.12.63, not begun	
Wool			
Ganymede		Cancelled 12.12.63, not begun	
Chath			

SINGLE SHIPS

Pylades	9.5.53	29.3.55	BU 1875
Sheer	23.11.54		
Miranda	9.48	9.3.54	Improved *Rattler*, reclassed as corvette
Sheer	18.3.51		1862. BU 1869
Brisk	1.49	24.8.53	Sold for merchant service 1870.
Wool	2.6.51		Sloop reclassed as corvette 1862
Malacca	29.5.49	17.8.54	Completed with engine at Chatham.
Moul	9.4.53		Sloop reclassed as corvette 1862. Sold 4.69, resold to Japan as *Tsukuba*

SCREW SLOOPS

Prototypes

Rattler	4.42	30.1.45	BU 1856
Sheer	13.4.43		
Niger	5.45	16.8.50	Lengthened at Devonport before completion.
Wool	18.11.46		B 1869

Encounter Class

Encounter	6.45	12.10.49	BU 1866
Pem	5.9.46		
Harrier			Laid down 1846, but suspended 9.9.46 and
Pem			cancelled 4.4.51

Conflict Class

Conflict	7.45	20.11.49	Sold 1863
Pem	5.8.46		
Desperate	10.45	9.5.53	BU 1865
Pem	23.5.49		
Enchantress			Suspended 18.9.46, cancelled 4.4.51
Pem			
Falcon			Suspended 9.9.46, cancelled 4.4.51
Pem			

Archer Class

Archer	10.47	9.3.50	BU 1866
Dept	27.3.49		
Wasp	10.47 (?)	26.10.50	Sold 1869
Dept	28.5.50		

Cruizer Class

Cruizer	4.51	3.2.53	Later called *Cruiser*. Renamed *Lark* as TS
Dept	19.6.52		5.93, sold 1912
Hornet	6.51	14.7.54	BU 1868
Dept	13.4.54		
Harrier	11.51	3.11.54	BU 1866
Pem	13.5.54		
Fawn	4.5.54	26.11.59	Survey ship 1879, sold 1884
Dept	30.9.56		
Falcon	11.53	30.3.55	BU 1869
Pem	10.8.54		
Alert	1.55	24.1.58	Survey ship 1878, donated to American
Pem	20.5.56		Research Society 1884

Swallow Class

Ordered as gun-vessels, then classed as sloops

Curlew	19.10.52	18.10.54	BU 1865
Dept	31.5.54		
Swallow	30.9.53	23.10.54	Survey ship 1861, BU 1866.
Pem	12.6.54		
Ariel	11.53	12.4.55	BU 1865
Pem	11.7.54		
Lyra	8.7.54	11.12.57	BU 1876
Dept	26.3.57		

Racer Class (lengthened *Swallow*)

Cordelia	10.55	11.4.57	Completion is date of first commission.
Pem	3.7.56		BU 1870.
Racer	1.10.56	22.7.58	BU 1878
Dept	4.11.57		
Gannet	12.56	9.3.59	BU 1877
Pem	29.12.57		
Icarus	7.4.57	28.12.59	BU 1879
Dept	22.10.58		
Pantaloon	2.11.57	17.9.61	BU 1867
Dev	26.9.60		

Greyhound Class (*Cruizer* adapted to 200 NHP engine)

Greyhound	12.6	6.2.60	Harbour service 9.69, sold 1906
Pem	15.6.59		
Mutine	1.6.57	26.11.59	Sold for commercial use 2.70, renamed
Dept	30.7.59		*Chieftain*

Cameleon Class (lengthened *Cruizer*)

Cameleon	8.11.58	30.7.61	Sold 1883
Dept	23.2.60		
Pelican	16.6.59	25.9.61	Sold 1869, renamed *Hawk*, then to Portuguese
Pem	19.7.60		Navy as *Infanta Dom Henrique*
Rinaldo	1.3.58	8.6.61	Sold 1884
Ports	26.3.60		
Zebra	4.7.59	23.5.61	Into reserve on completion, but later active;
Dept	4.7.59		sold in Far East 8.73.
Perseus	20.7.60	9.62	TS Devonport 1886, renamed *Defiance II* 3.04,
Pem	21.8.61		sold 1931
Chanticleer	2.2.60	12.61	BU 1876
Ports	9.2.61		
Reindeer	1.5.60	10.66	Suspended 1862, resumed 5.63. BU 1876
Chath	29.3.66		
Harlequin	13.2.61	——	Cancelled 16.12.64, frames down by 2.2.65
Ports	——		
Tees	2.61	——	Cancelled 12.12.63
Chath	——		
Sappho			Cancelled 12.12.63, not begun.
Dept			
Trent	3.9.61	——	Completed as ironclad *Research*
Pemb	——		
Circassian	5.5.62	——	Completed as ironclad *Enterprise*
Dept	——		
Diligence			Cancelled 12.12.63, not begun
Chath			
Imogene			Cancelled 12.12.63, not begun
Ports			
Success			Cancelled 12.12.63, not begun
Pem			

Rosario Class

Rosario	13.6.59	7.62	To govt of South Australia 1874 as hulk for young criminals, BU 1884
Dept	17.10.60		
Peterel	5.12.59	3.62	Light vessel 12.77, coal hulk 12.85, sold 10.01
Dev	10.11.60		
Rapid	18.8.59	6.62	BU 1881
Dept	29.11.60		
Shearwater	2.4.60	12.62	BU 1877
Pem	17.10.61		
Royalist	20.10.60	10.63	BU 1875
Dev	14.12.61		
Columbine	16.5.60	5.63	BU 1875
Dept	2.4.62		
Africa	22.12.60	13.8.62	Sold to Chinese Imperial Customs as *China*, in Sherard Osborn's 'Vampire Fleet', resold to Egyptian Government 30.12.65
Dev	14.2.62	13.8.62	
Acheron	14.10.61	——	Cancelled 12.12.63
Dept	——		
Bittern	17.12.61	——	Cancelled 12.12.63, BU completed 11.2.65
Dev	——		
Fame	2.12.61	——	Suspended 5.2.63, cancelled 12.12.63
Dept	——		
Cynthia	2.12.61	——	Cancelled 12.12.63
Dev	——		
Sabrina	28.5.61	——	Cancelled 12.12.63
Pem	——		

Individual Ships

Plumper	10.47	17.12.48	Survey ship by 1860, BU 1865
Ports	5.4.48		
Reynard	8.47	1.8.48	W 31.5.51
Dept	21.3.48		
Victoria	1.55	22.11.55	For naval service of Victoria; first Australian steam warship. To Victorian customs dept 1880, sold for merchant use 1882, BU 1895
Young	30.6.55		

IRON CRUISERS (FRIGATES AND CORVETTES)

Individual Ships

Inconstant	27.11.66	8.69	Hulked 1898, TS 6.06 (renamed *Impregnable II*), renamed *Defiance IV* 1.22, then *Defiance II* 12.30. Sold 9.55 for BU
Pem	12.11.68		
Shah	7.3.70	12.75	Coal hulk C470 in 12.04, sold as coal hulk Bermuda 1919, wrecked there 1926
Ports	10.9.73		
Raleigh	8.2.71	6.74	BU 1905
Chath	1.3.73		
Volage	9.67	3.70	BU 1904
Thames	27.2.69		
Active	1867	3.71	BU 1906
Thames	13.3.69		
Rover	1872	21.9.75	BU 1893
Thames	12.8.74		

Bacchante Class

Boadicea	30.1.73	5.77	BU 1905
Ports	16.10.75		
Bacchante	15.3.73	7.79	BU 1897
Ports	19.10.76		
Euryalus	11.73	6.78	BU 1897
Chath	31.1.77		

BELTED CRUISERS

Shannon Class

Shannon	29.8.73	19.7.77	BU 1899
Pem	11.11.75		

Nelson Class

Nelson	2.11.74	26.7.81	Stokers' TS 1901, BU 1922
Elder	4.11.76		
Northampton	26.10.74	26.7.81	Hulked as boys' TS 6.94, BU 1905
Napier	18.11.76		

Imperieuse Class

Imperieuse	10.8.81	9.86	Hulked to destroyer depot ship Portland 1905 (*Sapphire II*), reverted to *Imperieuse* 6.09, BU 1913
Ports	18.12.83		
Warspite	25.10.81	6.88	BU 1905
Chath	29.1.84		

Orlando Class

Australia	21.4.85	11.12.88	BU 1905
Napier	25.11.86		
Galatea	21.4.85	3.89	BU 1905
Napier	10.3.87		
Orlando	23.4.85	6.88	BU 1905
Palmer	3.8.86		
Undaunted	23.4.85	7.89	BU 1907
Palmer	25.11.86		
Narcissus	27.4.85	7.89	BU 1906
Earle	15.12.86		
Immortalite	18.1.86	7.89	BU 1907
Chath	7.6.87		
Aurora	1.2.86	7.89	BU 1907
Pem	28.10.87		

ARMOURED CRUISERS

Cressy Class

Aboukir	9.11.98	3.4.02	WL 22.9.14 (torpedoed by *U 9*)
Fairfield	16.5.00		
Bacchante	15.2.99	25.11.02	Paid off 4.19, BU 1920
Brown	21.2.01		
Cressy	12.10.98	28.5.01	WL 22.9.14 (torpedoed by *U 9*)
Fairfield	4.12.99		
Euryalus	18.7.99	5.1.04	Minelayer refit (begun 11.17) stopped 1918, BU 1920
Vickers	20.5.01		
Hogue	14.7.98	19.11.02	WL 22.9.14 (torpedoed by *U 9*)
Vickers	13.8.00		
Sutlej	15.8.98	6.5.02	Overflow ship Rosyth 1917-18, BU 1921
Brown	18.11.99		

Drake Class

Drake	24.4.99	13.1.03	WL 2.10.17 (torpedoed by *U 79*)
Pem	5.3.01		
Good Hope	11.9.99	8.11.02	Ex-*Africa*. WL (Coronel) 1.11.14
Fairfield	21.2.01		
King Alfred	11.8.99	22.12.03	BU 1920
Vickers	28.10.01		
Leviathan	0.11.99	16.6.03	BU 1920
Brown	30.11.99		

Monmouth Class

Bedford	19.2.00	11.11.03	W 21.8.10

Fairfield	31.8.01		
Berwick	19.4.01	9.12.03	BU 1920
Beardmore	20.9.02		
Cornwall	11.3.01	1.12.04	Cadet TS *Devonport* 1919, paid off 1919,
Pem	29.10.02		BU 1920
Cumberland	19.2.01	1.12.04	Cadet TS 1919-21, BU 1921
L&G	16.12.02		
Donegal	14.2.01	5.11.03	Paid off 5.18, Devonport Reserve 1918-19,
Fairfield	4.9.02		BU 1920
Essex	1.1.00	22.3.04	Destroyer depot ship 1916 Devonport, paid off
Pem	29.8.01		1919-20, BU 1921
Kent	12.2.00	1.10.03	Paid off for disposal 1919, sold for Hong Kong
Ports	6.3.01		1920
Lancaster	4.3.01	5.4.04	Partly dismantled Birkenhead 1919, BU at
Armstrong	22.3.02		BU 1920
Monmouth	29.8.99	2.12.03	WL (Coronel) 1.11.14
L&G	13.11.01		
Suffolk	25.3.01	21.5.04	BU 1920
Ports	15.1.03		

Devonshire Class

Antrim	27.8.02	23.6.05	Nore Reserve 1919, Asdic trials ship 1920-21,
Brown	8.10.03		Cadet TS 1922, BU 1922
Argyll	1.9.02	12.05	W 28.10.15
Scott	3.3.04		
Carnarvon	1.10.02	29.5.05	Cadet TS 1919-21, BU 1921
Beardmore	7.10.03		
Devonshire	25.3.02	24.8.05	Paid off 1919-20, BU 1920
Chath	30.4.04		
Hampshire	1.9.02	15.7.05	WL (mined) 5.6.16
Armstrong	24.9.03		
Roxburgh	13.6.02	5.9.05	Wireless Training Ship 1919-20; sank *U 80*
L&G	19.1.04		12.2.18 (ramming). BU 1921.

Duke of Edinburgh Class

Black Prince	3.6.03	17.3.06	WL (Jutland) 31.5.16
Thames	8.11.04		
Duke of Edinburgh	11.2.03	20.1.06	BU 1921
Pem	14.6.04		

Warrior Class

Achilles	22.2.04	22.4.07	Reserve as stokers' TS *Chatham* 1918-19,
Armstrong	17.6.05		BU 1920
Cochrane	24.3.04	18.2.07	W 14.11.18
Fairfield	20.5.05		
Natal	6.1.04	5.3.07	Loss by internal explosion 31.12.15
Vickers	30.9.05		
Warrior	5.11.03	12.12.06	WL (Jutland) 1.6.16
Pem	25.11.05		

Minotaur Class

Defence	22.2.05	9.2.09	WL (Jutland) 31.5.16
Pem	24.4.07		
Minotaur	2.1.05	1.4.08	Reserve 1919-20, BU 1920
Dev	6.6.06		
Shannon	2.1.05	10.3.08	Paid off 1919 Sheerness to become
Chath	20.9.06		accommodation ship to *Actaeon* torpedo
			school until 1922; BU 1922.

FIRST-CLASS CRUISERS

Blake Class

Blake	7.88	2.2.92	Hulked as destroyer depot ship 8.07, BU 1922
Chath	23.11.89		
Blenheim	25.11.88	26.5.94	Hulked as destroyer depot ship 5.06, BU 1926
Thames	5.7.90		

Edgar Class

Edgar	3.6.89	2.3.91	BU 1921
Dev	24.11.90		
Hawke	17.6.89	16.5.93	WL 15.10.14 (torpedoed)
Chath	11.3.91		
Endymion	21.11.89	26.5.94	BU 1920
Earle	22.7.91		
Gibraltar	2.12.89	1.11.94	Disarmed 1915, depot ship for Northern Patrol
Napier	27.4.92		in Shetlands 1915-18; destroyer depot ship. A/S
			School Portland 1919-22, sold 1923
Grafton	1.1.90	18.10.94	Depot for British ships supporting White
Thames	30.1.92		Russians in Black Sea 1919, Nore reserve
			1919-20, BU 1920
St George	23.4.90	25.10.94	To submarine depot ship 1917, 1918-19,
Earle	23.6.92		BU 1920
Theseus	16.7.90	14.1.96	Depot ship for trawlers in Aegean and Black
Thames	8.9.92		Sea 1918-19, paid off Devonport 1919, BU 1921
Royal Arthur	20.1.90	2.3.93	Ex-*Centaur*. Guardship at Scapa Flow 1915,
Ports	26.2.91		then depot ship for 12th Submarine Flotilla
			(1st Submarine Flotilla in 1918). Rosyth
			1919-20, paid off 1920, BU 1921
Crescent	13.10.90	22.2.94	Guardship at Hoy 1915, Portsmouth 1915-17,
Ports	30.3.92		submarine depot ship at Scapa Flow 1917-18,
			Firth of Forth 1919, BU 1920

Powerful Class

Powerful	10.3.94	5.97	Training hulk 1913 at Devonport. Renamed
Vickers	24.7.95		*Impregnable II* in 1919, sold 1929 for BU
Terrible	21.2.94	5.97	Disarmed and trooping to Dardanelles 1915-
Thomson	27.5.95		16, then accommodation ship as part of Fisgard
			(renamed *Fisgard III*) 1916-31, BU 1932

Diadem Class

Amphitrite	8.12.96	17.9.01	Harbour service Portsmouth 1915-16,
Vickers	5.1.98		converted to minelayer Devonport 1916-17,
			replacing *Ariadne* in Dover Barrage; paid off
			6.19, and Portsmouth Reserve 1919-20; BU 1920
Andromeda	2.12.95	5.9.99	Boys' TS Devonport 1913-29; renamed
Pem	30.4.97		*Impregnable II* in 1919, became part of Torpedo
			School 1931 and renamed *Defiance*; BU 1956
Argonaut	23.11.96	19.4.00	Hospital ship at Portsmouth 1915-17,
Fairfield	24.1.98		accommodation ship for stokers 1918; BU 1920
Ariadne	29.10.96	5.6.02	WL 26.7.17 (torpedoed by *UC 65*). Had been
Thomson	22.4.98		converted to minelayer at Devonport 1916-17;
			Nore command 1917; laid 708 mines in Dover
			Barrage and Heligoland Bight
Diadem	23.1.96	19.7.98	Stokers' TS Portsmouth 1914-18 (but closed
Fairfield	21.10.96		10.15-1.18); BU 1921
Europa	10.1.96	23.11.99	Flagship at Mudros 1915-19, sold 1920 to
Thomson	20.3.97		become emigrant ship, but sank in gale off
			Corsica 1.21
Niobe	16.12.95	6.12.98	Paid off 10.15 and depot ship Halifax 1915-20;
Vickers	20.2.97		badly damaged by ammo explosion Halifax
			6.12.17, lost funnels, ventilators, masts. BU 1922
Spartiate	10.5.97	17.3.03	Stokers' TS *Portsmouth* from 1913; renamed
Pem	27.10.98		*Fisgard* 1915. BU 1932.

SECOND-CLASS CRUISERS

Iris and *Mercury*

Iris	11.10.75	4.79	BU 1905
Pem	12.4.77		
Mercury	16.3.76	9.79	Submarine depot ship 1905, hulk at Chatham 1914, BU 1919
Pem	17.4.78		

Leander Class

Leander	14.6.80	29.5.85	Depot ship 1904, BU 1920
Napier	28.10.82		
Arethusa	14.6.80	29.9.87	BU 1905
Napier	23.12.82		
Phaeton	14.6.80	20.4.86	TS Devonport 1909, to Bibby Line as TS *Indefatigable* 1913 (renamed 1.14), repurchased by RN as TS *Carrick II* in 1941. BU 1947
Napier	27.2.83		
Amphion	25.4.81	8.86	BU 1906
Pem	13.10.83		

Mersey Class

Mersey	9.7.83	6.87	BU 1905
Chath	31.3.85		
Severn	1.1.84	2.88	B 1905
Chath	29.9.85		
Thames	14.4.84	7.88	Depot ship 1903, sold to become South African TS *Gen Botha* at Cape 11.20, renamed *Thames* as accommodation ship 1942, out of service 1945, scuttled in Simons Bay 13.5.47
Pem	3.12.85		
Forth	1.12.85	7.89	Depot ship 1903, BU 1920
Pem	23.10.86		

Medea Class

Medea	25.4.87	5.89	B 1914
Chath	9.6.88		
Medusa	25.8.87	6.89	Hulked for harbour service 1910, calibrating ship *Bantry*, BU 1921
Chath	11.8.88		
Magicienne	10.8.87	11.2.89	BU 1905
Elder	12.5.88		
Marathon	10.8.87	7.89	BU 1905
Elder	23.8.88		
Melpomene	10.10.87	7.89	BU 1905
Ports	20.9.88		

Apollo Class

Andromache	29.4.89	12.91	Minelaying Squadron 1912-14 and then at Dover 1914-15; depot ship in Mediterranean 1915, accommodation ship Gibraltar 1916-19, then Devonport, paid off 1919, and BU 1920
Chath	14.8.90		
Apollo	27.5.89	4.92	Minelaying Squadron 1912-14 and then at Dover 1914-15; Sheerness 1915, Nore Command 1915-17, then depot ship Devonport 1917-20 (4th Destroyer Flotilla in 1918, destroyers in care and maintenance). BU 1920
Chath	10.2.91		
Latona	22.8.89	4.91	Minelaying Squadron Dover 1914-15, Mediterranean 1915-18, overflow ship Malta 1919-20, sold there 1920
Vickers	22.5.90		
Melampus	30.8.89	12.91	BU 1910
Vickers	2.8.90		
Naiad	3.10.89	1.92	Minelaying Squadron Dover 1914-15, then depot ship on Tyne 1917; BU 1922
Vickers	29.11.90		
Sappho	29.10.89	2.93	Tender to flagship, 1st Battle Squadron of Home/Grand Fleet 1912-15, subsidiary duties with Grand Fleet 1915-18, prepared as blockship but broke down en route to Ostend 5.18, BU 1921
Samuda	9.5.91		
Scylla	29.10.89	4.93	Paid off 1912, BU 1914
Samuda	17.10.91		
Sybille	11.10.89	5.94	W 16.1.01
Steph	27.12.90		
Terpsichore	27.8.89	4.92	Laid up 1907-13, disposal list 1913, BU 1914
Thomson	30.10.90		
Thetis	29.10.89	4.92	Minelaying Squadron Dover 1914-15, depot ship 1916-17. Blockship 23.4.18
Thomson	13.12.90		
Tribune	11.12.89	5.92	Laid up 1905, BU 1911
Thomson	24.2.91		
Aeolus	10.3.90	6.93	TS 1912-13, paid off 1913, BU 1914.
Dev	13.11.91		
Brilliant	24.3.90	4.93	Depot ship Tyne 1914-15, Lerwick 1915-18. Blockship 23.4.18
Sheer	24.6.91		
Indefatigable	6.9.89	4.92	Renamed *Melpomene* 1.10. Training Squadron 1912-13, BU 1913
L&G	12.3.91		
Intrepid	6.9.89	11.92	Minelaying Squadron 1912-14, then at Dover 1914-15; depot ship North Russia 1915-16, White Sea 1917. Blockship at Zeebrugge 23.4.18
L&G	20.6.91		
Iphigenia	17.3.90	5.93	Minelaying Squadron 1912-14 and then at Dover 1914-15, North Russia 1915-16, White Sea 1917. Blockship 23.4.18
L&G	19.11.91		
Pique	30.10.89	3.93	Laid up Sheerness and Blackwater 1904-11, BU 1911
Palmer	13.12.90		
Rainbow	30.12.89	1.93	Harbour service 1904-10, then to new RCN 1910; training cruiser on Pacific coast 1910-14, Pacific patrols once war broke out 1914-15, then depot ship 1915-20; sold 1920 as a freighter.
Palmer	25.3.91		
Retribution	31.1.90	5.93	Laid up in Firth of Forth 1904, BU 1911
Palmer	6.8.91		
Sirius	7.10.89	4.92	Blockship 23.4.18
Armstrong	27.10.90		
Spartan	16.12.89	7.92	Harbour service 1906, tender to *Defiance* at Devonport from 1907; renamed *Defiance II* in 1921; BU 1931
Armstrong	25.2.91		

Astraea Class

Astraea	14.8.90	4.94	Paid off 1919, BU 1920
Dev	17.3.93		
Bonaventure	9.12.90	1.94	Converted to submarine depot ship *Haulbowline* 1906-7, Home Fleet 1907-12 (escorted three China-bound submarines as far as Malta 1911), submarine depot ship Harwich 1912-14, Humber 1914, for 6th Submarine Flotilla on Tyne 1914-16, 2nd Submarine Flotilla on Tyne 1916-18, for disposal 1919, BU 1920
Dev	2.12.92		
Cambrian	1.4.91	9.94	Paid off 1914, Stokers' TS Devonport, renamed *Harlech* 1916, renamed *Vivid* 1921, BU 1923
Pem	30.1.93		
Forte	21.9.91	1.95	Laid up Medway 1913, BU 1914
Chath	9.12.93		
Charybdis	28.9.91	11.94	Badly damaged in collision 9.1.15 and laid up Bermuda 1915-18; leased as a cargo carrier 1918-20, sold 1922, BU 1923
Sheer	15.6.93		
Hermione	17.12.91	12.94	Depot ship for patrol vessels at Southampton from 1914, burnt out 1916 but remained in service. Sold for BU 1921 but resold to Marine Society 1922 to become TS *Warspite* on Thames; BU 1940
Dev	7.11.93		

Fox	11.1.92	1.95	BU 1920
Ports	15.6.93		
Flora	1.3.92	3.95	Sale list 1914, floating workshop Devonport, renamed *Indus II* in 1915; sold 1922
Pem	21.11.93		

Talbot Class

Diana	13.8.94	5.97	Paid off Queenstown 6.19, BU 1920
Fairfield	5.12.95		
Dido	30.8.94	6.97	Sub depot ship (6th S/M Flotilla) 1912-14, 3rd S/M Flotilla 1914, destroyer depot ship Harwich (3rd Destroyer Flotilla) 1914-15, 9th Destroyer Flotilla 1915-17, 10th Destroyer Flotilla 1918-19, depot ship for reserve destroyers at Portsmouth 1919-26, BU 1926
L&G	20.3.96		
Doris	29.8.94	6.97	Sold at Bombay 1919
Barrow	3.3.96		
Eclipse	11.12.93	11.96	Accommodation ship for submarine flotillas 1915-18, laid up 1918-19, BU 1921
Ports	19.7.94		
Isis	30.1.95	5.97	BU 1920
L&G	27.6.96		
Juno	22.6.94	5.97	BU 1920
Barrow	16.11.95		
Minerva	4.12.93	1.97	BU 1920
Chath	23.9.95		
Talbot	5.3.94	7.96	Laid up 1919, BU 1921
Dev	25.4.95		
Venus	28.6.94	3.97	BU 1921
Fairfield	5.9.95		

Highflyer Class

Hermes	30.4.97	5.10.99	WL 31.10.14 (torpedoed by *U 27*)
Fairfield	7.4.98		
Highflyer	7.6.97	7.12.99	Flagship of East Indies station 1919-21, sold at Bombay 1921
Fairfield	4.6.98		
Hyacinth	27.1.97	3.9.00	Paid off 1919, BU 1923
L&G	27.10.98		

Challenger Class

Challenger	1.12.00	3.5.04	Paid off Portsmouth 1919, BU 1920.
Chath	27.5.02		
Encounter	28.1.01	21.11.05	To RAN 1912, permanently transferred 1919, training ship at Sydney 1919-23, then submarine depot ship *Penguin* 1923, scuttled off Sydney Heads 14.9.32
Dev	18.6.02		

Arrogant Class

Arrogant	10.6.95	2.98	Submarine depot ship Portsmouth 1911-14 (replaced *Mercury*) and Dover 1914-18 (4th S/M Flotilla 1914-15, 5th S/M Flotilla 1915-18), base flagship of Dover Patrol 1915-18.For disposal 1919, but later accommodation ship for Submarine School Portsmouth. BU 1923
Dev	26.5.96		
Furious	10.6.95	7.98	Harbour service Portsmouth 1912. Had conducted wireless experiments in Mediterranean 1911. Laid up Motherbank 1913-15, renamed *Forte* 6.15 and hulk attached to *Vernon*. BU 1923
Dev	3.12.96		
Gladiator	27.1.96	6.99	Sunk collision 25.4.08, wreck raised and sold 1909
Ports	18.12.96		
Vindictive	27.1.96	10.98	Scuttled as blockship 10.5.18 at Ostend. Flagship at Zeebrugge
Chath	9.12.97		

THIRD-CLASS CRUISERS

Comus Class

Comus	17.8.76	23.10.79	BU 1904
Elder	3.4.78		
Curacoa	17.8.76	24.2.80	BU 1904
Elder	18.4.78		
Champion	17.8.76	7.12.80	Harbour service 1904, BU 1919
Elder	1.7.78		
Cleopatra	17.8.76	24.8.80	Harbour service 1905, renamed *Defiance III* in 1922, BU 1931
Elder	1.8.78		
Carysfort	17.8.76	15.9.80	BU 1899
Elder	26.9.78		
Conquest	17.8.76	18.4.85	BU 1899
Elder	28.10.78		
Constance	14.9.78	3.10.82	BU 1899
Chath	9.6.80		
Canada	7.7.79	1.5.83	BU 1897
Ports	26.8.81		
Cordelia	17.7.79	25.1.87	BU 1904
Ports	25.10.81		
Calypso	1.9.81	10.85	TS for Newfoundland Govt 9.02, renamed *Briton* 15.2.16, sold as store hulk 4.22 and still in use to store salt in 2004
Chath	7.6.83		
Calliope	1.10.81	25.1.87	RNVR drill ship 29.10.07, renamed *Helicon* 6.15, reverted to *Calliope* 10.31, BU 1951
Ports	24.7.84		

Barracouta Class

Blanche	1.5.88	2.91	BU 1905
Pem	6.9.89		
Blonde	1.5.88	7.91	BU 1905
Pem	22.10.89		
Barrosa	14.5.88	6.90	BU 1905
Ports	16.4.89		
Barracouta	2.7.88	3.91	BU 1905
Sheer	16.5.89		

Barham Class

Bellona	16.10.88	7.91	BU 1906
Hawthorn	29.8.90		
Barham	22.10.88	7.91	BU 1914
Ports	11.9.89		

Pearl Class

Katoomba	15.8.88	24.3.91	Ex-*Pandora*. BU 1906
Hawthorn	27.8.89		
Mildura	15.8.88	18.3.91	Ex-*Pelorus*. BU 1906
Armstrong	25.11.89		
Wallaroo	15.8.88	31.3.91	Ex-*Persan*. Hulked 1906, renamed *Wellington* 3.19, BU 1920
Armstrong	5.2.90		
Tauranga	20.8.88	6.91	Ex-*Phoenix*. BU 1906
Thomson	28.10.89		
Rinagarooma	20.8.88	3.2.91	Ex-*Psyche*. BU 1906
Thomson	10.12.89		
Pearl	1.4.89	10.92	BU 1906
Pem	28.7.90		
Phoebe	23.4.89	3.92	BU 1906
Dev	1.7.90		
Philomel	9.5.89	11.91	To New Zealand 1914, base ship at Wellington 3.21, sold as hulk 17.1.47, scuttled 6.8.49
Dev	28.8.90		
Pallas	1.7.89	7.91	Sold 1906
Ports	30.6.90		

Pelorus Class

Pandora	3.1.98	7.01	BU 1913
Ports	17.1.00		
Pelorus	21.5.95	2.97	Depot ship Suda Bay 1916-18, paid off 1919,
Sheer	15.12.96		BU 1920
Pegasus	16.5.96	12.98	WL (sunk by *Königsberg*)
Palmer	4.3.97	20.9.14	
Perseus	25.5.96	5.00	BU 1914
Earle	15.7.97		
Pactolus	4.5.96	12.98	Converted to submarine depot ship 1912, 9th
Armstrong	21.12.96		S/M Flotilla Ardrossan 1914-18, BU 1921
Pioneer	16.12.97	1.00	To RAN 12.12, paid off 1912-13, TS Sydney
Chath	28.6.99		1914-15, then East Africa then 1915-16 (bombarded Dar-es-Salaam with *Challenger* 13.6.15). Laid up Sydney 8.16, sold as hulk 1924, scuttled off Sydney Heads 2.31
Pomone	21.12.96	5.99	Harbour TS *Dartmouth* 1910-20, BU 1922
Sheer	25.11.97		
Prometheus	10.6.96	1.00	BU 1914
Earle	20.10.98		
Prosperpine	2.3.96	8.98	Sold at Alexandria 1919 and BU
Sheer	5.12.96		
Psyche	12.11.97	4.99	Loan to RAN 1915, TS for seamen and stokers
Dev	19.7.98		Sydney 1915-20, BU 1922
Pyramus	16.5.96	12.99	Depot ship at Mudros 1915-18, then
Palmer	15.5.97		Devonport, paid off 1919-20, BU 1920

'Gem' Class

Amethyst	7.1.03	17.3.05	BU 1920
Armstrong	5.11.03		
Diamond	24.3.03	1.05	Paid off 1919, BU 1921
Laird	6.1.04		
Sapphire	30.3.03	7.2.05	Paid off 1919, BU 1921
Palmer	17.3.04		
Topaze	14.8.02	11.04	Paid off 1919-20, BU 1920
Laird	23.7.03		

WOODEN CORVETTES POST 1865 (including sloops reclassified as corvettes)

Juno Class

Juno	1866	5.68	Sold 1887
Dept	28.11.67		
Thalia	1866	3.70	Troopship 10.86, powder hulk 1891, depot ship
Wool	14.7.69		2.15, BU 1920

Amazon Class

Amazon	1864	1866	Sunk in collision with collier *Osprey* in
Pem	23.5.65		Channel 10.7.66 due to confusion concerning rules of road by officer of the deck
Vestal	1864	1867	BU 1884
Pem	16.11.65		
Niobe	1864	1871	W 21.5.74
Dept	31.5.66		
Dryad	4.65	1867(?)	BU 1886
Dev	25.9.66		
Daphne	1865	1867	BU 1882
Pem	23.10.66		
Nymphe	1865	1867	BU 1884
Dept	24.11.66		

Eclipse Class

Danae	1865	11.67	War Dept hulk 1886, sold 1905
Ports	21.5.67		
Blanche	1865	1.68	BU 1886
Chath	17.8.67		
Eclipse	1866	6.68	War Dept mine hulk 1888-92, sold 1921
Sheer	14.11.67		
Sirius	1867	1869	BU 1885
Ports	24.4.68		
Spartan	N/A	8.71	BU 1882
Dept	14.11.68		
Dido	N/A	20.4.71	Hulked 1886, renamed *Actaeon II* in 1906,
Ports	23.10.69		BU 1922
Tenedos	11.11.67	7.72	BU 1887
Dev	13.5.70		

Briton Class

Druid	1868	2.72	BU 1886
Dept	13.3.69		
Briton	1868	11.71	Sold Bombay 1887
Sheer	6.11.69		
Thetis	29.8.70	1.2.73	BU 1887
Dev	26.10.71		

Amethyst Class

Encounter	19.6.71	7.73	Sold 1888
Sheer	1.1.73		
Amethyst	28.7.71	7.73	BU 1887
Dev	19.4.73		
Modeste	27.11.71	1.74	BU 1888
Dev	23.5.73		
Diamond	1873	7.75	Sold 1889
Sheer	26.8.74		
Sapphire	17.6.73	8.75	BU 1892
Dev	24.9.74		

Emerald Class

Opal	13.10.73	1.76	Sold 1892
Doxford	9.3.75		
Turquoise	8.7.74	13.9.77	BU 1892
Earle	22.4.76		
Ruby	8.7.74	14.6.77	Coal hulk *C.10* in 12.04, sold 1921
Earle	9.8.76		
Tourmaline	17.7.74	25.10.76	Coal hulk 1899, renamed *C.115* in 12.04, sold
Raylton	30.10.75		1920
Emerald	29.7.74	2.7.78	Powder hulk 1898, BU 1906
Pem	18.8.76		
Garnet	16.3.75	31.10.78	Sold 1904.
Chath	30.6.77		

Satellite Class

Satellite	4.10.80	24.7.83	RNVR drill ship 1904, BU 1947
Sheer	13.8.81		
Heroine	30.8.80	19.9.83	BU 1902
Dev	3.12.81		
Hyacinth	30.8.80	27.1.84	BU 1902
Dev	20.12.81		
Royalist	27.4.81	14.4.86	Hulk 2.00, renamed *Colleen* 12.13, to Irish Free
Dev	7.3.83		State Government 19.2.23
Rapid	21.4.81	9.9.84	Hulk 1906, coal hulk C.7 in 1912,
Dev	21.3.83		accommodation ship *Hart* 1916, sold at Gibraltar 1948
Caroline	24.10.81	27.1.86	Hulk 1897, training ship *Ganges* 4.08, renamed
Sheer	25.11.82		*Powerful III* in 9.13, *Impregnable IV* in 11.19. Sold 1929
Pylades	1.1.83	17.8.86	BU 1906
Sheer	5.11.84		

TORPEDO CRUISERS

Scout Class

Scout	8.1.84	10.86	BU 1904
Thomson	30.7.85		
Fearless	22.9.84	7.87	BU 1905
Barrow	20.3.86		

Archer Class

Archer	2.3.85	7.87	Commissioned 11.12.88. BU 1905
Thomson	23.12.85		
Mohawk	2.3.85	7.87	Commissioned 16.12.90. BU 1905
Thomson	6.2.86		
Brisk	2.3.85	20.3.88	BU 1906
Thomson	8.4.86		
Porpoise	2.3.85	12.2.88	BU 1905
Thomson	7.5.86		
Cossack	2.3.85	7.88	Commissioned 1.1.89. BU 1905
Thomson	3.6.86		
Tartar	2.3.85	7.88	Commissioned 30.6.91. BU 1906
Thomson	28.10.86		
Serpent	9.11.85	3.88	W 10.11.90
Dev	10.3.87		
Racoon	1.2.86	7.88	BU 1905
Dev	6.5.87		

TORPEDOBOAT CARRIER/CRUISER

Vulcan	18.6.88	7.91	Submarine depot ship 1914-18, hulked as TS, renamed *Defiance III* 2.31 as torpedo school ship Plymouth; sold for BU 2.55
Ports	13.6.89		

CRUISER/DESPATCH VESSELS

Surprise	14.2.84	8.86	BU 1919
Palmer	17.1.85		
Alacrity	14.2.84	8.86	Sold Hong Kong 1913
Palmer	28.2.85		

Abbreviations

See page 337 for abbreviations specific to the List of Ships

AP: armour piercing
ASW: anti-submarine warfare

BL: breech-loading (gun)
BLR: breech-loading rifle

CDC: Colonial Defence Committee
CinC: Commander-in-Chief
cm: centimetre = 0.3937in
CO: Commanding Officer
CS: Cruiser Squadron
CSS: Confederate States Ship
cwt: hundredweight (112lbs)

deg: degree
D/F: direction-finding
Disp: displacement
DNC: Director of Naval Construction
DNI: Director of Naval Intelligence
DNO: Director of Naval Ordnance

EHP: effective horsepower
EinC: Engineer-in-Chief
ERA: Engine Room Artificer

FD: forced draught
FIC: Foreign Intelligence Committee
FO: Foreign Office
ft: foot/feet = 0.30479m
ft/sec: feet per second
fwd: forward

HE: high explosive
HMAS: His/Her Majesty's Australian Ship
HMS: His/Her Majesty's Ship
HP: horsepower

IHP: indicated horsepower
in(s): inch(es) = 2.54cm

kt(s): knot(s) (a nautical mile per hour)
kg: kilogram = 1.204lbs
KNC: Krupp nickel cemented (armour)

lb(s): pound(s) = 0.4536kg
loa: length overall

m: metre = 3.2809ft or 1.093yds
mm: millimetre = 0.03937in
Mk: Mark
MLR: muzzle-loading rifle
MP: Member of Parliament

ND: normal draught
NHB: Naval Historical Branch, Portsmouth
NHP: nominal horsepower
NID: Naval Intelligence Department
nm: nautical miles (6080ft)
NMM: National Maritime Museum (since renamed Royal Museums Greenwich)

oa: overall (length)
ONI: Office of Naval Intelligence (US)

pdr: pounder
pp: between perpendiculars (length)
PRO: Public Record Office, Kew (now known as The National Archives)
psi: pounds per square inch
PW: Program of Works

QF: quick-firing (gun)
QFC: breech-loading guns converted to quick-firing
qr: quarter (32lbs)

RA (D): Rear Admiral (Destroyers)
RAN: Royal Australian Navy
RFW: reserve feed water
RN: Royal Navy
RNR: Royal Naval Reserve
rpm: revolutions per minute

SHP: shaft horsepower
SNO: Senior Naval Officer

TB: torpedo boat

USS: United States Ship

vs: versus

yd(s): yard(s) = 0.9144m

Index

Page numbers in *italics* refer to illustration captions. Ships are of the Royal Navy (HMS) unless otherwise stated.

25 de Mayo (Argentine cruiser) *151*

A

Abethell, Richard 54
Aboukir *241*, 279
Aboukir Bay, battle of (1798) 33
Abtao (Chilean screw corvette) *36*
Acasta 75, 76
Acheron 56, 68, 74, 76
Achilles 9, 260, *284*, *286*
Acre 57
Actif 44
Active 33, *49*, 85, *88-89*, 94, 124
Admiral Kornilov (Russian cruiser) 221
Admiralty in time of radical change 46-51
AE 1/AE 2 167
Aeolus 156
Afghanistan 14, 15
Africa 68, 74
Ajax 113
Alabama, CSS 13, 17, 18, 19, 20, *75*, 76
Alacrity 175, *175*
Albany, USS *151*, *208*
Albert, Prince 73
Alderney 33
Alecto 56
Alecto class 56
Alert 65, 68-69, 79
Ali, Mehmet 56, 57
Alligator 74, 76
Alma (French ironclad) *103*
Alma class (French ironclads) 102, *103*
Almirante Grau (Peruvian cruiser) 210
Amazon 75, 76-77
Amazon class *39*, 71, *75*, 76-78
Amazonas (Brazilian cruiser) 151
American Civil War (1861-65) 13, 17, 18, 19-20, 21, 23, 62, 76
Amethyst (1871) 97
Amethyst (1903) *192*, 211, *201*
Amethyst class *67*, 78, 97, *97*
Amethyst (or '*Gem*') class *192*, *193*, *194*, 195, 198-203, 205, 207, 209, 211, 253
Ammonoosuc, USS 82
Amphion (1840) 61, 64
Amphion (1881) 27, *135*, 136
Amphitrite 237, *237*, 279, 287
Andromeda 233, 237
Anglo-French crisis (1844-47) 59-60, 64
Anglo-Russian crisis (1877-78) 14, 18, 25, 49
Anglo-Russian crisis (1885) 15
Antrim 253, *256*
Apia (Samoa) hurricane (1889) 125, *130*
Apollo 157, *158*, 159, 216, *278*, *281*
Apollo class 51, 156-157, *158*, *159*, 196, 216, 281, 282
Archer 27, 61, *75*, *177*, 181
Archer class 31, 50, 175-177, *175*, *176*, *177*, *178*, 185, 189, 190
Archimedes (screw propeller demonstrator) 43
Ardent 56
Arethusa 31, *39*, 44, 53, 74, 78, *134*, 136
Argentine navy 148, 149, 151, 239
Argonaut *236*, 237
Argus 56, 79
Argyll 287
Ariadne (1856) 60, 69, 70, 78
Ariadne (1896) 237, 287
Ariadne class *60*, *75*, 76
Ariadne class (German cruisers) 118
Ariel 68

Armstrong 35, *36*, 41, 140, 146, 147, 209, 234, *242*, *266*
  cruisers 147, *148-149*, *150*, *151*, 154
  'flat-iron' Chinese gunboats 139-140, 146-147
Armstrong, Lord 41
Arrogant 61
Arrogant class 51, 166, 170, *201*, 213, *213*, 215-217, 229
Arturo Prat (Chilean gunboat) 147, *150*
Asama (Japanese cruiser) *242*, 246
Astraea 70, 74, 76, *201*, 216
Astraea class 51, 157, 158, *158*, *162*, *163*, 164
Auckland, Lord (First Lord of the Admiralty) 47
Audacious (or *Invincible*) class 102, *103*
Aurora *39*, 53, *58-59*, 64, 65, 66, 78, *143*
Aurora class 76
Australia 141
Austro-Hungarian navy 151
Avenger 55
Avon 28-29

B

Babcock & Wilcox boilers 46, 170, 171
Bacchante 46, 66, 67, 70, 90, *90*, 93, 95, *240*, 279, *286*
Bacchante class *67*, 95, *182*
Baird, Admiral 136, 144
Ballard, Admiral 28, *77*, *84*, 88, 89, 93, 94
Baltic Sea 14, 15
Baltimore, USS *36*
Barfleur 115
Barfleur class 115, *115*
Barham 46, 184, *189*, 196, *201*, 207
Barham (proposed *Bristol* class ship) 74, 76
Barham class 184-185, *184*, *189*, 211
Barnaby, Sir Nathaniel 14, 15, 25, 47, 48, 50, 88, 98, 102, 103, 105, 113, 114, 115, 116, 118, 122-123, 124, 125-126, 128, 129, 130, 131, 132, 135, 136, 139-140, 142, 144, 145, 146, 147, 174, 175, 177, 180, 181, 182, 213
Barracouta 54, 56, 79, *183*
Barracouta class 182-184, *183*, *186*, 189
Barrosa 70, 71, *71*, 78, *187*
Basilisk 55, 56, 79
Bayard class (French cruisers) 114
Beacon class 28-29
Bedford 251, 253
Bedford, Admiral Frederick (Second Naval Lord) 253
Belleville boilers 44-46, 166, 170, 202, 216, 245-246, *266*
Bellona 184, *184*, *189*, *190*
Bellona class 185, *190*, *190*, 196
Belvidera 74, 76
Belvidera class 76
Berehaven 25, 26, 29, 32, 33
Beresford, Lord Charles (Junior Naval Lord) 156
Berwick 286
Birkenhead (formerly *Vulcan*) 54, 55
Bittern 68, 74, 76
Black Prince 9, *257*, *260*, 262, 279
Black Prince class 257, 260-262, 279, 281
Blake 24, 46, 146, 218-221, *220*, 226, 228
Blanche *77*, 78, *188*
Blanche class *67*, *72*, 78, 79
Blanco Encalada (Chilean cruiser) 148, 149
Blenheim 24, 34, 46, 64, 146, 218-221, *218*, *219*, 220
Blonde 46, 70, 74, 76, *183*, *186*
Blonde (later *Shah*) 17, 20, 76, 83, *84*, 85, 87-88, 95, 104
Boadicea 75, 76, 90, *90*, *92*, *93*, 95, 122, 128
Boadicea class 18, 54
Boer War (1899-1902) 231
Boiler Committee 44, 45, 46, 266
Bonaventure 157, *165*
Bosporus 11, 14, 15
Boyarin (Russian cruiser) 211
Brandreath, Admiral 181
Brassey, Lord Thomas (Civil Lord of the Admiralty) 175, 181
Brazilian navy 151
Breslau (German cruiser) *159*, *278*
Brest 24, 32, 34
Brilliant 156, *160*, *161*

Brisk 54, 61, *75*, 78, 79
Bristol *39*, 70, 78
Bristol class *67*, 70, 71
Briton 74, 76, *77*, 78
Brooklyn, USS 233-234, 246
Bucephalus 75, 76
Buenos Aires (Argentine cruiser) *148*, 149
Bulldog 56
Bulldog class 56
Bulwark 46
Buzzard 79, *182*, *183*
Byzantium 11

B

Cadmus *39*, 65, 68, 69, 78-79
Cadmus class 26
Calliope 125, *130*, 131, *131*, 140
Calypso 27, *49*, 125
Cambrian 157, *165*
Cameleon 70, 79
Cameleon class 65
Canada 95, 124-125, 128
Canopus 238, 267
Canopus class 238-239, 246
Canton, CSS *36*
Captain 48, 83, 95
Carnarvon 253
Carnarvon Commission/Committee 17, 18, 19, 51
Caroline 129, *129*, 131
Carysfort 124, 128
Cecille (French cruiser) 221
Centaur (later *Royal Arthur*) 55, 158, *225*, 226, *227*, *228*, 235, 248
Chacabuco (Chilean corvette) *36*, 149
Challenger (1855) *39*, 60, 69, 70, 78, 79
Challenger (1900) 46, 171, *172*, *173*, 202
Challenger class 170-171, *172*, *173*, *201*
Champion 124, 125, 128
Chanticleer 72, 79
Charleston, USS 151
Charybdis 34, 69, 70, 71, 78
Chateaurenault (French cruiser) 252
Chatham 37, 55, 56, 64, 66, 68, 70, 77, 98, 124, 125, 143, 144, 156, 197, 198-199, 219
Chattanooga, USS 82
Cherbourg 17, 20, 23, 24, 32, 72, 73
Chesapeake 64, 66-67, 68
Chesapeake class 76
Childers, Hugh C E (First Lord of the Admiralty) 20, 48-49, 87
Chilean navy *36*, 147, *148*, 149, *150*, *242*, 246, 252
China 20, 24, *28*, 73, 79
Chinese navy 139-140, 146, 147, *150*, 149, 229, 231
  Peiyang Fleet 35
Ching Yuen (Chinese cruiser) 35
Chiyoda (Japanese cruiser) *36*
Circassian (formerly *Enterprise*) 68, 74, 75, 76
Cleopatra 124, *124*, 128
Clio 69, 70, 78, 79
Cochrane 261, *264*, *284*, *286*
Cochrane, Admiral Sir Thomas (Lord Dundonald) 54, 55
Codrington, Captain William (Junior Naval Lord) 147
Cold War (1947-91) 18
Coles, Captain Cowper 48
Collingwood 113
Colomb, Captain J C E 50
Colonial Cruisers 185, 189-191, 196
Colonial Defence Committee 49
Columbia, USS 252
Columbine 68, 79
Comus 124, *126*, 128, 135
Comus class *67*, 124-126, *126*, *127*, 128-129, 130, 131, 135, 147
Condor class 26
Condor class (French cruisers) 174
Confederate Navy (US) 13, 17, 18, 19, 20, *36*, 76, 80
Conflict 55, 61, 75

Conflict class 61
Conquest 25-26, 124, *124*, 128
Constance 39, 44, 53, 59, 74, 78, *94*, 124
Constitution, USS 16
Convoy Acts 17
Cooper Key, Admiral Sir Astley (First Naval Lord) 41, 50, 102, 112-113, 129, 130, 136, 139, 140, 142, 144, 174, 175, 176, 181
Cordelia (1855) 68, 70, 79, 95
Cordelia (1879) 124-125, *127*, 128
Cormorant 15, 25, 26, 56, 130
Corn Laws 10
Cornwall 250, *286*
Coronel, battle of (1914) 267
Corry, H T Lowry (First Lord of the Admiralty) 85, 87
corvettes, protected 124-126, 128-132
Cossack 29, 70, 78, 79
Cracker 64
Cracker class 64
Craddock, Admiral 267
Crescent 158, *225*, 226, 233, 248
Crescent class 201
Cressy 241, *243*, 279
Cressy class 238-240, 242-243, 246, 248, 260
Crimean War (1853-56) 13, 21, 37, 41, 47, 69
Cristoforo Colombo (Italian cruiser) 118
Croiseurs Estafette (French 'Despatch Cruisers') 199, 200, 201
cruiser, changing role of 21, 23
Cruizer (later *Cruiser*) 65, 70, 79
Cruizer class 65, 67, 68-69, 70
Curacoa (1852) 64, 66, 78
Curacoa (1876) *127*, 128
Curlew 27, 33, 68, 177, *180*, 181-182
Custance, Captain 202-203, 205
Cyclops 55
Cyclops class *57*
Cynthia 75, 76

D

Dacres, Sir Sydney (First Naval Lord) 87
Daffodil (ferry) 291
Danae 71, *72*, 77
Daphne 75, 76-77
Dartmouth 70, 74, 76
Dauntless 55, 60, 78
De Horsey, Rear Admiral 84
Deadman, Henry 196
Dee 54
Defence 9, 87, 262, *264*, 279
Deptford 37, 55, 64, 65, 68, 69, 70, 71, 76
Derby, Earl of 67, 72, 73
Designs, Committee on 44, 83, 95, 116
Desperate 55, 61, 75
Destructor (Spanish torpedo gunboat) 36
Devastation 55, 56, 79, 114
Devonport 37, 68, 70, 71, 76, 77, 78, 97, 129, 197, 198-199, 231
Devonshire 46, *254*, 255
Devonshire class 254, 255, 256, 260, 261, 262, 280-281
Dextrous 75, 76
Diadem (1855) 62, 69-70, 73
Diadem (1896) 237, 245, 246
Diadem class (1896) 51, *233*, 234-235, *234*, *236*, 237, *237*, 240, 242, 248, 279, 280
Diamond (1873) 97, *97*
Diamond (1903) *193*, *194*, 211
Diana 162, 166, *166*
Diana class (Russian cruisers) 252
Dido (1861) *72*, 74, 76, 77
Dido (1894) 162, 166, *166*
Diligence 75
Disraeli, Benjamin 13, 48, 49, 73
Dockyards, Royal 37, 55, 56, 64, 68-69, 70, 74, 77, 78, 97, 98, 124, 125, 128-129, 197, 198-199
Dogali (Italian cruiser) 147, *151*, 154
Dolphin 22

Domville, Admiral Sir Compton 46, 213, 216, 233
Donegal 288
Doris 53, 59, 67, 69-70, 76, 78, *166*
Doterel 16
Doterel class 19
Dover 59
Doxford 98
Dragon (later *Janus*) 54, 55
Drake 200, 238, *244*, *247*, 279
Drake class 243, 245-250, 252, 253, 257, 261-262, 267, 280, 286
Dreadnought 243, *253*, 278
Driver 56
Driver class 56
Druid *77*, 78
Druid class 67, *77*, 78
Dryad 71, *75*, 76-77
Dugesclin (French ironclad) 113
Duke of Edinburgh 260, 261, 264, 265, *284*, *286*
Duke of Edinburgh class 252, 262, 266
Dundas, First Naval Lord Admiral Sir Richard 16, 73
Dundas, Colonel 38
Dundonald, Lord (Admiral Sir Thomas Cochrane) 54, 55
Dupuy de Lôme 77, 158, 221, 229, 233, 239
Dürr boilers 46
Durston, Engineer-in-Chief 170, 197, 202, 224, 245-246

E

Earle's 98
Eclair 56
Eclipse (formerly *Sappho*) *72*, 77, *167*
Eclipse class 67
Eclipse (or *Talbot* class) 51, 157-159, 162, 166, *167*, *168*, 170, 216, 217, 252
Edgar 228, 287, *290*
Edgar class 51, 158, *201*, 221, *222*, *223*, 224-226, *225*, 287
Edye, John 54, 64
Egeria 14
Egypt 9, 13, 14, 55, 56
Egyptian navy 55
Elder, John 44, 124, 128
Elisabeta (Romanian cruiser) 150
Elk 29
Elliot, Admiral 125
Emerald (1849) 65, 70
Emerald (1874) 98, *98*, 99
Emerald class 65
Emerald (or *Opal*) class 67, 97, 98-99, *98*, *99*, 118, 125, 128
Enchantress 221
Encounter (1845) 61, 75, 96, 97-98
Encounter (1901) 171, *172*, *173*, 202, *282*
Endymion (1860) 39, 53, 67, 70, 74, 75, 78
Endymion (1889) *223*, *226*, 287, *290*, 291
Enterprise (later *Circassian*) 68, 74, 75, 76
Esk 54, 65, 78, 79
Esmeralda (Chilean gunboat) 147, *150*, 252
Espiegle 19, 46, 170
Essex 253, *253*
Etna (Italian cruiser) *150*
Ettore Fieramosca (Italian cruiser) 150
Europa 46, 237, *279*
Euryalus (1851) 64, 66, *90*, *93*, 95
Euryalus (1873) *239*, *286*, 287
Excellent (gunnery school) 27, 41, 48, 54, 102
Express 26

F

Falcon 65, 68-69, 79
Falklands, battle of the (1914) 250
Falmouth 27
Falmouth 74, 76
Fame 75, 76
Fantome 46
Fantome class 14, 98, 116
Favourite 74
Fawkes, Admiral 262

Fawn 65, 67, 79
Fearless 175, *175*, *176*, *178*
Fincham, John 54, 55, 64
Firebrand 55
Fisher, Admiral Sir John ('Jacky') (First Sea Lord) 14, 19, 20-21, 27, 41, 50, 51, 79, *139*, 156, 157, 191, 211, 215, 216-217, 233, 234, 235, 266, 275, 277-278, *280*, 282
Flandre class (French ironclads) 103
fleet, changing shape of 21, 23
Fleet, Channel 32, 278
Fleet, Grand 279
Fleet, Mediterranean 14, 32, 56, 57, 203, 277, 278
fleet manoeuvres and their lessons
 1885 25-27
 1887 27, 29
 1888 29-31, 32
 1889 33
 1890 33
 1892 33-34
 1894 34
 1896 34
 1897 34-35
 1898 35
 1901 35, 37
fleet operations: the 1884 Analysis 23-25
Flirt 29
Florida, CSS 76
Florida, USS (formerly *Wampanoag*) 80, *82*, 83
Forbin (French cruiser) 185
Forbin class (French cruisers) 185
Foreign Intelligence Committee 18
Forte 64, 66-67, 68, *163*
Forte (or *Impérieuse*) class 58, 64, 66-67, 68
Forth 136, 144
Forwood, Arthur 221
France 8, 9, 10, 14, 15-16, 19, 23, 24, 25, 50, 51, 56, 57, *64*, 72, 102 see also French navy
 British crisis with (1844-47) 59-60, 64
Franklin, USS 83
French navy 8, 20, 21, 23, 24, 32, 44, 45, 55, 59, *64*, 71, 73, 98, 102, 103, 112, 113, 114, 118, 158, 159, 174, 175, 185, 199, 202, 221, 229, 233, 239, 242, 245, 246, 249, 252, 274, 277
 Eastern Squadron 23
 Evolutionary Squadron 23
 Mediterranean fleet 32
Frolic 29
Froude, William 38
Furious 55, 56, *217*
Fürst Bismarck (German cruiser) 246
Fury 56

G

Galatea 60, 70, 78, *142*
Gannet 68, 70, 79
Ganymede 75, 76
Gard, William 266
Garibaldi class (Italian cruisers) 239
Garnet 99
'Gem' (or *Amethyst*) class *192*, *193*, *194*, *195*, 198-203, 205, 207, 209, 211, 253
German East Africa 16
German navy 16, 17, 18, 118, *170*, *173*, 209, 221, 243, 246, 250, 267, *278*, 274
Geyser 56
Gibraltar 9, 13
Gibraltar 222, *223*, *225*
Giovanni Bausan (Italian torpedo ram) 140, 142, 147, *150*
Gladiator 55, *57*, 78
Gladstone, William Ewart 13, 20, 48, 50, 51, 116, 174
Glasgow 67, 70, 78, *250*
Gloire (French ironclad) 71, 77
Goeben (German battlecruiser) *159*, *278*
Good Hope 267
Gorgon 54, 56, 57
Goschen, George (First Lord of the Admiralty) 48-49, 95, 102, 234, 253

Grafton 223, 287, *290*
Graham, Sir James (First Lord of the Admiralty) 56
Graham, Admiral William (Third Naval Lord) 154, 156
Grant, Captain 104-105
Grasshopper 29
Gravina (Spanish cruiser) *36*
Greenock (formerly *Pegasus*) 54, 61, 65
Grey, Admiral Sir Frederick (First Naval Lord) 48
Greyhound 65, 70, 79
Grinder (later *Miranda*) 61, 75, 78
Growler 56
Guichen (French cruiser) 252
guns 38, *39*, *40*, 41-42, *43*, *45*

H

Hall, Captain Robert 48
Hall, Captain W H 23-25, 145
Hamilton, Lord George (First Lord of the Admiralty) 50, 51, 146, 156, 211, 218
Harlequin 71, 74
Harrier 61, 65, 66
Harwich 59
Hastings 78
Hawke 223
Hawkins class *49*
Hay, Captain Lord John 54, 61
Hebe class 55
Hecate 56
Hecla (1837) 56
Hecla (1878) 25, 26, 33, 211
Hector 9
Hermes 46, 56, *171*
Hermes class 166, 170, *171*, *201*
Hermione 34, *162*, *163*, *164*
Heroine 129, *129*, 177
Highflyer (1850) 54, 61, 64-65
Highflyer (1897) 78-79, *170*
Highflyer class 166, *170*, 217
Hogue 241, 279
Hood, Admiral Sir Arthur (First Naval Lord) 41, 102, 103-104, 105, 116, 118, 147, 156, 191
Hopkins, Captain J O 181
Hornby, Admiral Sir Geoffrey Phipps 14, 15, 20, 25, 26, 27, 50, *101*
Hornet 29, 64, 65
Hotham, Admiral Charles F (Junior Naval Lord) 156, 225
Houston Stewart, Rear Admiral William 123, 130, 135, 136
Huascar (Peruvian ironclad) 20, *84*, 88
hulls 54
Hunt, G Ward (First Lord of the Admiralty) 48, 49
Hyacinth 129, *129*
Hydra 56, 79
Hyperion 75, 76

I

Icarus 68, 70, 79
Idaho, USS *82*
Idzumo (Japanese cruiser) *266*
Immortalite *39*, 65, *67*, 70, 71, *80*
Imogene 75
Imperatrice Eugenie class (French frigates) 64
Imperieuse (1850) *45*, 61, 64, 66, 67, 70
Imperieuse (1881) 24, 27, *108*, *109*, *110*, *111*, 113, 114
Imperieuse class (1881) 145
Imperieuse (or *Forte*) class 58, 64, 66-67, 68
Inconstant 17, 27, 33, 38, 54, 70, 76, 78, 80, *80-81*, 82-83, 85, *85*, 87-88, 95, 102, 116
Inconstant class 54, 79
Indefatigable 267
Indefatigable class 243
India 9, 14
Infernal (French steam warship) 55
Infernet (French corvette) 98
Infernet class (French cruisers) 118
Inflexible 56, 115
Institution of Naval Architects (later Royal) 37

Intrepid 161, 277
Invincible 267
Invincible class 243, 267, *267*
Invincible (or *Audacious*) class 102, *103*
Iphigenia 161, *278*, 282
Irene (German cruiser) 221
Iris 18, 95, 116, 118, *118*, *119*, *120*, *121*, 122-124, 132, 133, 135, 147
Isis 162, 166, *166*, 168
Isla de Cuba (Spanish cruiser) *150*
Isla de Luzon (Spanish cruiser) *150*
Ister 70, 76
Ister class *67*, 76
Italia class (Italian battleships) 113, 220
Italian Navy, Royal 113, 118, 140, 142, 147, *147*, 150, *151*, 154, 220, 239
Iwate (Japanese cruiser) *266*
Izumi (Japanese cruiser) *150*

J

Janus (formerly *Dragon*) 54, 55
Japanese Navy, Imperial *36*, 147, *148*, *149*, *150*, *151*, 229, 239, *242*, *246*, *266*, 281
Jason *39*, 70, 71, *71*, 78, 79, 216
Jason class 70, *71*
Jeanne d'Arc (French cruiser) 242, 245, 246
John Elder 44, 124, 128
Joinville, Prince de 57, 59, 60, 64
Juno (1866) 78, 79
Juno (1894) 162, 166, *166*, 167
Juno class (1866) 79
Jurien de la Graviere (French cruiser) 252
Jutland, battle of (1916) 260, *265*, 279

K

Kagoshima *40*
Kaiser Wilhelm der Grosse (German armed merchant cruiser) *170*
Kane, Captain 235
Katahdin, USS 213
Katoomba (formerly *Pandora*) 196
Kearsarge, USS 17
Kennedy, Rear Admiral 157
Kent 251, 253
Kerr, Admiral Lord Walter (First Naval Lord) 205, 211, 234, 275
Key, Cooper *see* Cooper Key (First Naval Lord)
King Alfred 279, 283
King Edward VII class 243
Kingstown 27
Kléber class (French cruisers) 252
Königsberg (German cruiser) *173*, *208*, 250
Krupp Cemented armour 238-239, 243, 278

L

Lamlash Bay 29, 31
Lancaster 280
Landrail 177, *180*, 181-182
Lang, Oliver 54
Lang, Oliver W 54
Laos (French mail steamer) 46
Lapwing 280
Latona 157, *159*, *278*
Leander (1860) 74
Leander (1880) 25, 113, 114, *133*, 136, 139
Leander class 24, 132-133, 135-136
Leipzig (German cruiser) *250*
Leipzig class (German cruisers) 118
Leopard 54, 55, 78
Liffey 66, 78
Liffey class *53*, 67, 68, 70
Lightning 44
Liverpool 27, 29, 32
Liverpool *39*, 70, 78
Lloyd, Engineer-in-Chief Thomas 43

Lockroy, French Naval Minister 249
London, City of 10, 20
Lorient 32
Lough Swilly 29, 32
Louis Philippe, King of France 60, 64, 67
Lowry Corry, H T *see* Corry, H T Lowry (First Lord of the Admiralty)
Lynx 29, 68, 70, 79

M

Madawaska, USS *82*
Magallanes (Chilean corvette) *36*
Magicienne 55, 56, 78, *152*, *153*
Magicienne class 116
Majestic (White Star liner) 233
Malacca 61, 64, 75, 78-79
Malmesbury, Lord 72, 73
Malta 24, 277
Mare (C J) & Co 65
Marengo (French battleship) 112
Mariner 19, 25-26, *27*
Mariner class 19
Martin, Admiral (Second Naval Lord) 16
May, Rear Admiral William H 209, 260, 261, 262, 264, 266
Medea (1832) 56
Medea (1887) 46, 147, *154*, 156, 185, 190, 189
Medea class 27, 147, 152, 154, *154*, 156, 158, 189-190, *191*, *201*, 213, 275
Medina 26
Medusa 46, *145*, 147, *154*, 156
Medway 26
Megaera 54, 56, 61
Mehmet Ali *see* Ali, Mehmet
Melpomene 65, 70
Menai 74, 76
Mercury 18, 25-26, *27*, 31, 95, 116, *116*, 118, *118*, *119*, 122-124, *122*, 132, 135, 147
Merrimack class 70
Mersey 31, *39*, *53*, *62*, 70, 76, 78, *139*, 143, 144
Mersey class 23, 24, *62*, 136, 139-140, 142-145, 146, 174, 235
Mersey, New, class 145
Mildura (formerly *Pelorus*) 196, 197, 198, 201, 202, 209, 245
Milford Haven 29
Miller (William C) & Sons 76
Milne, Admiral Sir Alexander (First Naval Lord) 17-18, 48, 49, *62*, 73, 95, 116, 122, 123
Mindello (Portuguese corvette) *36*
minelaying 281-282
Minerva 11, 166
Minneapolis, USS 233, 252
Minnesota, USS 64
Minotaur 262, *263*, 266, *284*, *286*
Minotaur class 262, 264-267
Miranda (formerly *Grinder*) 61, 75, 78
Modeste 97, *97*
Mohawk 27, 29, *186*
Monmouth 249, 253
Monmouth class 200, *249*, 252-253, 256, 261, 280, *286*
Montcalm class (French cruisers) 199, 252
Moore, Rear Admiral A W (Junior Naval Lord) 253
Morgan, Mr 130
Mutine 26, 65, 67, 79

N

Naiad 278
Naniwa (Japanese cruiser) *151*
Napier, Captain Sir Charles 54
Napoleon, Louis 67
Napoleon Bonaparte 8, 9, 19
Napoleonic Wars (1799-1815) 8, 9, 19, 21, 38, 57
Narcissus *39*, *40*, *53*, *67*, 68, 78, *142*, 144
Nasr-ed-din, Shah of Persia *84*
Natal 258, *259*, 260, *283*
Naval Constructors, Royal Corps of 37

Naval Defence Act (1889) 14, 32, 37, 50, 51, 156-157
Naval Defence Act (Spencer Program) (1893) 51, 196, 234-235, 237
naval presence 20-21
Navigation Acts 10
Nelson 43, *101*, *104*, 105-106, *106*, 113
Nelson, Admiral Horatio, Lord 33, 38
Nelson class 41
Nereide 75, 76
Neshaminy, USS *82*
New Caledonia 23
New Orleans, USS *151*, *208*
New York, USS 233
Newcastle *67*, 70, 78
Niagara, USS *64*, 70
Niclausse boilers 46
Niger 55, 56, 61, 75, 78, 79
Nile (Egyptian frigate) 55
Niobe 75, 76, 79, 207, 237
Noble, Sir Andrew 42, *246*
Noel, Admiral Gerard H (Junior Naval Lord) 196
North Star 71, 76
North Star class 76
Northampton 43, 105-106
Northbrook, Earl of (First Lord of the Admiralty) 50, 114, 144-145, 174
Northbrook Program 50, 51, 145, 175
Novik (Russian cruiser) 199-200, 211
Nueve de Julio (Argentine cruiser) *151*
Nymphe 75, 76-77
Nymphe class *25*, 132, 177
Nymphe class (German cruisers) 209, 211

O

Octavia 39, 44, *53*, 74, 78
Odin 46, 55
O'Higgins (Chilean corvette) *36*, *242*, 246, *246*
Olympia, USS *159*, 233
Olympic, SS *223*
Ontario 74, 76
Opal 98, *98*, 99, 126, 128
Opal (or *Emerald*) class *67*, 97, 98-99, *98*, *99*, 118, 125, 128
Ordnance Committee 42
Oregon 25, 26, 27
Orestes 70, 71, *71*, 78
Orlando (1856) *39*, *62*, 70, 76, 78
Orlando (1885) *141*, 146, 216, 219
Orlando class (1885) *9*, 24, 46, 50, *60*, 115, *142*, 145-146, 275
Orpheus 70, 71, *71*
Osprey 15, 76
Osprey class 15
Ottoman Empire 9-10, 56

P

Pactolus 197, 198
paddle warships 54-57, 59-60
Paixhans, Henri-Joseph 38
Pakington, Sir John (First Lord of the Admiralty) *68*, 73, 78, 102
Pall Mall Gazette 50
Pallas *94*, 196
Pallas class 51, 156, 185
Palmer 209
Palmerston, Lord 56-57, 59, 67
Pampero (Spanish screw corvette) *36*
Pandora *151*, 197, 198
Pandora (later *Katoomba*) 196
Pantaloon 68, 71, 79
Panther (Austro-Hungarian cruiser) *151*
Paris, Treaty of (1859) 13
Paris World's Fair (1867) 41, 102, 112
Parkes, Dr Oscar 51
Parramatta 222
Parsons turbines 209
Parthian (later *Wasp*) 61, 75, 79
Pearl (1854) 65, 68, *69*, 78, 79
Pearl (1888) *187*, *199*, 196
Pearl class (1854) 51, *60*, *69*, 70
Pearl class (1888) 185, *187*, 189-191, 196
Peel, Sir Robert 59
Pegasus 197, 198, *208*
Pegasus (later *Greenock*) 54, 61, 65
Pelican 15, 70, 79
Pelorus *69*, 70, 78, 79
Pelorus (later *Mildura*) 196, 197, 198, 201, 202, 209, 245
Pelorus class 51, 185, 196-198, *197*, 207, 209
Pembroke 29, 37, 55, 56, 61, 65, 66, 68-69, 70, 71, 76, 98, *123*
Pembroke 78
Penelope 55
Penguin 15
Peninsular campaign (1808-14) 21
Perseus (1860) 70, 71, 79
Perseus (1896) 197, 198, *203*
Persia, Nasr-ed-din, Shah of *84*
Persian (later *Wallaroo*) 196
Peruvian navy 20, *84*, *88*, *210*
Peterel 68, 71, 79
Petit Smith, Frank 42-43
Petropavlovsk 13
Phaeton (1858) 74
Phaeton (1880) 136
Philadelphia, USS *36*
Philomel 196, *201*
Philomel class 201
Phipps Hornby, Admiral Sir Geoffrey 14, 15, 20, 25, 26, 27, 50, *101*
Phoebe (1859) 74
Phoebe (1889) 196, *196*, *200*
Phoenix 56, 61, 75
Phoenix (later *Tauranga*) 196, *198*
Pike 26
Pioneer 197, *197*, 198, *282*
Pioneer class 201
Plover class *28*, 78, 79
Plumper 64
Plymouth 33, 56
Pollen, Arthur H *231*
Polyphemus 25, 26, 31, 56, 112, 135, 136, 139, 140, 143-144, 145, 146, 213, 215
Pomone (1860) 74, 76
Pomone (1896) 197, 198
Popoffkas (Russian armoured ships) 115
Porpoise 182
Portland 27, 33, 59
Portsmouth 37, 55, 56, 64, 70, 71, 77, 124, 125, 197, 198, 211, 231
  HMS *Excellent* (gunnery school) 27, 41, 48, 54, 102
Portuguese navy *36*
Powerful *9*, 44, 166, 226, 228-229, *230*, 231, *231*, 233-234, 235, 240, 242, 248, 253, 279
Powerful class 46, 51, 247
Prometheus (1839) 56
Prometheus (1896) 197-198, *197*, *206*
Proserpine 197, 198
Psyche (later *Ringarooma*) 196, 197, 198, *205*
Pylades (1853) 65, 78, 79
Pylades (1883) 129, *129*, 131-132
Pyramus 197-198, *209*

R

Racer 19, 25-26, 27, 68, 70, 79
Racoon 69, 70, 78, 79, 177
Rainha de Portugal (Portuguese corvette) *36*
Raleigh (1863) 74, 76
Raleigh (1871) 17, 23, 46, 83, *84*, 87, *87*, 90, 95, 104
Raleigh class 87
rams, fleet 213, 215-217, *217*
Randolph, Charles 44
Rapid *12*, 72, 79, *129*, 131
Rattler (1841) 56, 60, 61, 64
Rattler (1842) 72, 79
Rattlesnake 27, 29, 71, *71*, 78
Raven 106
Raylton Dixon 98
Redbreast class *30*, *280*
Reed, Sir Edward C *28*, 47, 48, 82, 83, 87, 88, *88*, 102, 114-115, 146
Reina Regente (Spanish cruiser) *36*
Reindeer 72, 75, 79
Rendel, George W (Civil Lord of the Admiralty) 140, 142, 145, 146, *150*, 175, 181-182
Renown 230
Repulse 9
Resistance *9*, 221, 229, 247
Resolute 55
Retribution 55
Reynard 64
Rhadamanthus 56
Richards, Admiral Sir Frederick William (First Naval Lord) 170, 213, 215, 216, 235, 249-250
Rifleman 29
Rinaldo 70, 71, 79
Ringarooma (formerly *Psyche*) 196, 197, 198, *205*
Ringdove 30
Roberts, Thomas 54, 56
Robinson, Vice Admiral Spencer (Second Naval Lord) *28*, 39, 41, 42, 47-48, 77, 78, 79, 82, 83, 85, 87, 102
Rochefort 23, 32
Rocket 29
Romanian navy *150*
Rosario 68, 71, 79
Rosario class 76
Rossiya 246
Rover 27, *94*, 95
Roxburgh 288
Royal Arthur (formerly *Centaur*) 55, 158, *225*, 226, *227*, *228*, 235, 248
Royal Sovereign class 238, 239
Royalist (1858) 68, 72, 79
Royalist (1881) 129, *129*, 131
Ruby 49, 54, 98
Rurik 226, 228, 229, *268*, *271*
Russell, J Scott 65
Russell, Lord John 60
Russia 9, 10-11, 13-14, 15-16, 17, 19, 47, 49, 50, 51, 69
  British crisis with (1877-78) 14, 18, 25, 49
  British crisis with (1885) 15
Russian Navy, Imperial 25, 115, 132, 199-200, 202, 211, 221, 226, 228, 229, 231, 246, 252, *271*, 274, 277
  Black Sea Fleet 277
  Volunteer Fleet 13
Russo-Japanese War (1904-5) 281
Russo-Turkish crisis (1875-77) 13-14
Ryder, Admiral 125

S

Sabrina 75, 76
St George 225
St Helena *84*
St Jean d'Acre fortress 57
Salamander 56, *59*, 79
Samoan hurricane (1889) 125, *130*
Sampson 55
San Fiorenzo 68
Sandfly 29
Sané class (French cruisers) 118
Sans Pareil 50
Sapphire (1873) *97*, *97*
Sapphire (1903) *194*, 211
Sappho (later *Eclipse*) 74, 77, *161*
Sappho class 201
Satellite (1854) *39*, 68, *69*, 78
Satellite (1880) 129, *129*
Satellite class 129-132, *129*, 177
Scott, Captain Percy *231*
Scott Russell, J *see* Russell, J Scott
Scourge 56
Scout (1854) *39*, *69*, 70, 78-79

Scout (1884) 175, *176*, 177, 182, 203
screw steamers 60-61, 64-79
Scylla 69, 70, 78-79
Seahorse 26
Seaton, Joseph 54, 56, *59*
Selbourne, Earl of (First Lord of the Admiralty) 260-261, 266
Seppings, Robert 56
Sevastopol 231
Severn 68, 74, *137*, 144
Seymour, Captain 123
Shah (formerly *Blonde*) 17, 20, 76, 83, *84*, 85, 87-88, 95, 104
Shannon (1854) 33, *43*, 66, *101*, 102-106, *103*, 112, 113
Shannon (1873) *264*, *265*, 266, *284*, *286*
Shannon class (1873) 41
Sharpshooter 44, 46, 166
Shearwater 68, 72, 79
Sheerness 37, 56, *59*, 64, 66, 70, 77, 78, 97, 129, 197
Sheldrake 46, 170
ship classification 52-54
shore bombardment 287
Sidon 54, 55
Simoom (later *Terrible*) 54, 55, 61
Sirius (1867) *72*, 77
Sirius (1889) 157, *161*
Smith, Frank Petit *see* Petit Smith, Frank
Smith, J A (Chief Inspector of Machinery) 46
Snap 26
Souvereine (French frigate) 64
Spanish navy 36, *150*
Spanker 44
Spartan 77
Spartiate *234*, 237
Spee, Admiral Graf von 267
Speedy 44, 185
Spencer Program 51, 196, 234-235, 237
Sphinx 56, 79
Sphinx class 55
Spider 29
Spiteful 56, 79
Spithead 27
    Queen's Jubilee Review (1887) 27, *116*
squadrons
    Channel 18, 24
    Cruiser 262
    Cruiser, 3rd 279
    Cruiser, 10th 278
    Cruiser, 11th *11*
    Detached 18
    First Reserve 24
    Flying *80-81*
    Particular Service 25
    Training 49
Stead, W T 50
Steady 76
steam power 42-46
Steamships of England 31, 131-132
Stewart, Rear Admiral William Houston 123, 130, 135, 136
Stopford, Admiral Sir Robert 57
Stromboli 56, 57
Stromboli (Italian cruiser) *150*
Styx 56
submarines 21 *see also* U-boats
Success 75
Suez Canal 13-14
Sultan 43
Surprise 175
Sutlej 74
Swallow 25, 68, 177
Swallow class 66, 70
Swiftsure 102, 103, 265
Symonds, Captain Sir William 47, 54, 55, 60
Syrian campaign (1839-40) 56-57

T

Tage (French cruiser) 221
Tahiti 24
Takachiho (Japanese cruiser) *151*
Takasago (Japanese cruiser) *149*
Talbot 166, *201*, 216
Talbot class 51, *67*, 157-159, 162, 166, *167*, *168*, 170, 216, 217, 252
Tangiers 59
Tartar 29, 70
Tauranga (formerly *Phoenix*) 196, *198*
TB 12: *119*
TB 39-50: 215
TB 80: 34
technology, changing 37-38
Tees 74
Temeraire 113
Tenedos 77
Tennessee class (US cruisers) 265
Termagent 60
Terrible 44-45, 46, 166, 226, 228-229, *230*, 231, *231*, 233-234, 253, 279
Terrible (formerly *Simoom*) 54, 55, 61, 78
Teutonic (White Star liner) 233
Thalia 70, 78, 79
Thames 31, 144, *275*
Thames Iron Works 36, 85, 95
Theseus 224, 287, *290*
Thetis 34, 77, 78, *161*
Thomson (Clydebank) of Glasgow 36
Thornycroft 175
    boilers 44, 198
Thunderbolt 56
Thunderer 40, 42, 114
Tiger 55, 56
Tokiwa (Japanese cruiser) *242*, 246
tonnage 46
Topaz 39, *53*, 67, *67*, 68, 70, *195*, 211
torpedo boats 215 *see also* TB entries
torpedo cruisers 174-177
Toulon 24, 34
Tourmaline 98, 99, *99*
trade protection 17-21
Trafalgar, battle of (1805) 21
Trent 74
Trent (British mail steamer) 62
Tribune 64, 66
Trident 56
Triumph 84, 102, 265
Tryon, Vice Admiral Sir George 31, 33
Tsingtao 16
Tsukushi (Japanese gunboat) 147, *150*
Turkey 13-14, 56 *see also* Ottoman Empire
Turquoise 98
Tweed 70, 76

U

U-9 *241*, 279
U-39 288
U-79 244
U-89 288
U-boats 17, 18 *see also* submarines
Undaunted 39, *67*, 70, 71, 78
United States 10, 13, 16-17, 21
United States Navy 16-17, 18, 36, 64, 70, 82, *82*, 83, *151*, 159, *208*, 213, 233-234, 246, 252, 265 *see also*
    Confederate Navy
    Annual Report 80

V

Valiant 9
Valorous 55, 56, 78
Vauban (French ironclad) 113
Vavasseur, Charles 41
Velasco (Spanish cruiser) 36

Venus 162, 166, *166*
Vestal 75, 79
Vesuvio (Italian cruiser) *150*
Vesuvius 56, 57
Vickers designs 268-273
Victor 76
Victoria 50
Victoria, Queen 73
Victory 38
Villeneuve, Admiral Pierre-Charles 8
Vindictive 213, 217, 287, *291*
Virago 56, 79
Vixen 56
Vladivostok 13, 19, 231
Volage 27, 46, *49*, 85, 87, 88, *88-89*, 90, *94*, 95, 123, 124
Volcano 56
Vulcan (1846) 61
Vulcan (1888) 27, 31, 139, *201*, 211, 213, *214*, *215*, 218, 219, 221
Vulcan (later *Birkenhead*) 54, 55
Vulture 55

W

Waddilove, Captain Charles 83, 95
Wake Walker, Rear Admiral Sir Baldwin 17, 47, 54, 65, 70, 71, 73-74
Wallaroo (formerly *Persian*) 196
Wampanoag, USS (later *Florida*) 80, *82*, 83
Wampanoag class (US cruisers) 78
Wanderer 22
Ward Hunt, G (First Lord of the Admiralty) 48, 49
Warrior (1861) 9, 54, 70, 74, 87, 115, 144-145
Warrior (1903) 260, 279
Warrior class (1903) 257, 260-262, 266
Warspite 24, 29, 31, *112*, 114
Wasp (formerly *Parthian*) 61, 75, 79
Watts, Isaac 47, 48, 73
Watts, Sir Philip 50, 146, *148*, *242*, 256, 257, 260, 261, 264-265, 266
Wellington, Duke of 59-60
Weymouth 74, 76
White, J S 216
White, Sir William H 23, 44, 48, 50-51, 113-114, 132, 135, 136, 140, 142-143, *145*, 146, 147, *151*, 152, *153*, 154, 156, 157, 158-159, 162, 170, 182-183, 184-185, 189, 190, 196, 198, 200, 201-202, 207, 209, 211, 213, 216, 218, 219, 220, 221, 225-226, 228-229, 231, 233-234, 235, 237, 238-240, *242*, 243, 245, 246, 247-248, 249, 250, 252, 253, 257, 267, 279
White Star Line 136, 139, 233
Whiting, William *201*, 207, 211
Wild Swan 15
William C Miller & Sons 76
Wilson, Rear Admiral A K 200-201, 202, 205, 213, 234, 243, 249, 252, 253
Wolverine 71, *71*, 75, 78
Woolwich 37, 55, 56, 64, 68, 70
Woolwich Arsenal 37, 41, 42
World War, First (1914-18) 13, 14, 16, 17, 18, *159*, *161*, 170, *173*, 267, 278, 279, 287
World War, Second (1939-45) 18

Y

Yalu, battle of the (1894) *149*, 229
Yang Wei (Chinese cruiser) *150*
Yarra 222
Yarrow 175
    boilers 46
Yoshino (Japanese cruiser) *148*, 149

Z

Zebra 70, 71
Zeebrugge Raid (1918) *161*, *291*
Zulu War (1879) 84